The Eastern Old Japanese
Corpus and Dictionary

By

Alexander Vovin
Sambi Ishisaki-Vovin

LEIDEN | BOSTON

Cover illustration: Mt. Fuji (EOJ Pu''zi* < pu 'fire' + nusi 'master'), Japan's highest mountain (3776 m) and the largest dormant volcano, on the border of Kapi and Suru''ga provinces.

The Library of Congress Cataloging-in-Publication Data is available online at https://catalog.loc.gov
LC record available at https://lccn.loc.gov/2021037637

Typeface for the Latin, Greek, and Cyrillic scripts: "Brill". See and download: brill.com/brill-typeface.

ISSN 0921-5239
ISBN 978-90-04-47119-1 (hardback)
ISBN 978-90-04-47166-5 (e-book)

Copyright 2022 by Alexander Vovin and Sambi Ishisaki-Vovin. Published by Koninklijke Brill NV, Leiden, The Netherlands.
Koninklijke Brill NV incorporates the imprints Brill, Brill Nijhoff, Brill Hotei, Brill Schöningh, Brill Fink, Brill mentis, Vandenhoeck & Ruprecht, Böhlau Verlag and V&R Unipress.
Koninklijke Brill NV reserves the right to protect this publication against unauthorized use. Requests for re-use and/or translations must be addressed to Koninklijke Brill NV via brill.com or copyright.com.

This book is printed on acid-free paper and produced in a sustainable manner.

Respectfully dedicated to Ishisaki Tetsuo and Ishisaki Fukiko

Sasha

...

両親へ感謝を込めて

賛美

Contents

Preface IX
Acknowledgments XI
Abbreviations XII
List of Charts XV

Introduction 1
1 *Hitachi Fudoki* 1
2 *Man'yōshū* Book Fourteen 2
3 Structure of Book Fourteen 3
4 Poems in Eastern Old Japanese and in Western Old Japanese 8
5 Can the Poems with an Unidentified Geographical Location Be Identified? 9
6 Determining the Geographical Locations of Unidentified Poems on the Basis of Their Linguistic Features 10
7 *Man'yōshū* Book Sixteen 12
8 *Man'yōshū* Book Twenty 13
9 Poems in Eastern Old Japanese and in Western Old Japanese 15
10 *Azuma asobi uta* 17
11 *Kokin wakashū* 17
12 *Man'yōgana* Script 17
13 A Brief Sketch of EOJ Phonology and Morphology 26
14 EOJ Specific Vocabulary 31
15 Ainu Loans in EOJ of Books Fourteen and Twenty 35
16 Opotəmə-nə Yakaməti Criteria for Not Including Certain *sakimori* Poems 38

PART 1
Eastern Old Japanese Corpus

1 常陸風土記歌謠・*Hitachi Fudoki* Poems 41

2 萬葉集卷第十四・*Man'yōshū* Book Fourteen 48
  1 東謌・Eastern Poems 48
  2 相聞・Relationship Poems 53
  3 譬喩歌・Allegorical Poems 127
  4 雜歌・Miscellaneous Poems 136
  5 相聞・Relationship Poems 146

3　萬葉集卷第十六・*Man'yōshū* Book Sixteen　261

4　萬葉集卷第二十・*Man'yōshū* Book Twenty　274

5　東遊び歌・*Azuma asobi uta*　422

6　古今和歌集・*Kokin wakashū*　426

PART 2
Dictionary of Eastern Old Japanese

Dictionary of Eastern Old Japanese　431
　　Some Preliminary Notes　431
　　　A　431
　　　E　434
　　　Ə　434
　　　ⁿG　434
　　　I　435
　　　K　438
　　　M　447
　　　N　452
　　　O　456
　　　P　458
　　　S　463
　　　T　469
　　　U　475
　　　W　476
　　　Y　478
　　　ⁿZ　482

Bibliography　483
Index　493

Preface

This book has no exact predecessors, although indexes found in Mizushima (1996 (1972), 1984a, 2003) come close. However, Mizushima's works, while being a wonderful example of Japanese philological approach, have their limitations, both in structural and scholarly sense. First of all, an index, even the best one, is not an equivalent of a dictionary, especially in the situation similar to Mizushima's research where one has to consult two different indexes that sometimes are not very conveniently organized. Second, Mizushima's work is limited to the *Man'yōshū* data. While the *Man'yōshū* Eastern Old Japanese data found in the books fourteen and twenty of this anthology occupy the lion's portion of the Eastern Old Japanese corpus, there are also other Eastern Old Japanese texts: Hitachi province (常陸國) poems from the *Fudoki* (風土記), *Azuma asobi uta* (東遊び歌), some poems from the *Man'yōshū* book sixteen, and one poem from the *Kokin wakashū* (古今和歌集), an anthology from the early Heian period. Thus, however minor texts they could be, the actual Eastern Old Japanese corpus is bigger than just books fourteen and twenty of the *Man'yōshū*. Without indexing the entire available corpus, the Mizushima's works cannot be considered complete. In addition, while the phonology and, to the lesser extent, grammar of Eastern Old Japanese received its proper attention from both Japanese and Western scholars (Fukuda 1965, Hōjō 1966, Mizushima 1984b, Kupchik 2011, to mention just the most fundamental ones), the vocabulary and the corpus itself did not. Consequently, we have been thinking about filling this gap for several years now. The present work is divided into a corpus, done by Alexander Vovin, and a dictionary, compiled by Sambi Ishisaki-Vovin on the basis of this corpus.

The presentation of the corpus itself follows the same model as Alexander Vovin's edition and translation of the *Man'yōshū*, but with the following peculiarities: Western Old Japanese poems from the *Man'yōshū* books fourteen and twenty are not included; the romanization system is based on the one adopted in Alexander Vovin's *A Descriptive and Comparative Grammar of Western Old Japanese* (vol. 1 and 2, 2nd edition, Brill 2020); the commentary to the Eastern Old Japanese in books fourteen and twenty is thoroughly revised as compared to their edition in Vovin (2012, 2013); the commentary to the Hitachi province poems, poems from the *Man'yōshū* book sixteen and a poem from the *Kokin wakashū* is much more detailed than in other translations to European languages; the translation of and the commentary to the *Azuma asobi uta* is done for the first time in the Western Japanology. There is another minor change: copulas *n-* and *tə* on one hand and a quotation verb *tə* on the other that were glossed before as DV (defective verb) are now glossed as COP (copula) or as QV (quotation verb). This change has not been implemented in Vovin 2020.1 and 2020.2, but will take place in this and all following publications.

The dictionary includes all words found in the Eastern Old Japanese poems, irrespective of the fact whether they are identical with their Western Old Japanese cognates or not. The simple motivation behind this approach is based on the fact that the Eastern Old Japanese texts are written in the Western Old Japanese orthography; therefore we are looking at the dim world of the Eastern Old Japanese phonology through the Western Old Japanese glass darkly, and an exclusion of similar looking words may result in throwing out a baby together with the tab water. We list all attestations of a given word in each of the texts constituting the Eastern Old Japanese corpus, but we do not provide any textual examples in the dictionary itself because these can be easily found in the corpus by using the information on attestations. We also provide etymological and/or comparative information in each dictionary entry with the main focus on Western Old Japanese and Ainu.

It is our hope that the present monograph will greatly facilitate the research not only on Eastern and Western Old Japanese in particular but also on the East Asian historical linguistics in general.

Alexander Vovin and Sambi Ishisaki-Vovin
Poligny, December 31, 2020

Acknowledgments

We are grateful to a number of colleagues who wittingly or unwittingly commented on certain aspects of this book while it was in the making: John Whitman, Bjarke Frellesvig, Takubo Yukinori, John Kupchik, Osada Toshiki, Juha Janhunen, José Andrés Alonso de la Fuente, and Aleksandra Jarosz. No less gratitude goes to the Brill's editorial team on both sides of the Atlantic ocean, who were our constant advisers and have overseen the publication of other books and articles by Alexander Vovin for many years: Uri Tadmor, Patricia Radder, Inge Klompmakers, Irene Jager, Kayla Griffin, and Elisa Perotti. The research work for this book was also partially supported by the European Research Council (EDJ 788812).

Our new friends in France: Irene Tamba, Augustin de Benoist, Sami Saleh, Christiane Babiak, as well as old ones from Japan, Russia, Turkey, Mongolia and the United States of America need to be equally mentioned here: Kawasaki Tamotsu, Vladimir Bokarius, Aleksei Egorov, Greg and Fan Brown, Ty Borders, Jim Baskind, Elena Perekhvalskaya, Mehmet Ölmez, Gürkan Doğan, Oyunch, Zayabaatar, and many others.

We also would like to express our gratitude to the European Research Committee (ERC), whose generous support (in the form of the grant #788812 for Alexander Vovin's advanced research project *An Etymological Dictionary of the Japonic Languages*) provided a partial funding for this book.

We would also like to thank the members of our family: our parents and parents-in-law Ishisaki Tetsuo and Ishisaki Fukiko, to whom this book is dedicated. And the last, but not the least, our children Jacob Tomotatsu Ishısakı-Vovın and Marie Alexandra Ishısakı-Vovın.

Alexander and Sambi Vovin
Poligny, Ile de France, December 30, 2021

Abbreviations

Languages

EMC	Early Middle Chinese
EOJ	Eastern Old Japanese
Lat.	Latin
MDJ	Modern Japanese
MJ	Middle Japanese
MK	Middle Korean
OJ	Old Japanese
OK	Old Korean
PA	proto-Ainu
PAN	proto-Austronesian
PJ	proto-Japonic
PJN	proto-Japanese
WOJ	Western Old Japanese

Texts and Sources

Japonic

AAU	Azuma asobi uta, 8–9th centuries
FK	Fudoki kayō, ca. 737 AD
IM	Ise monogatari, late 9th or early 10th century
KJK	Kojiki, 712 AD
KK	Kojiki kayō, 712 AD
MYS	Man'yōshū, ca. 771–785 AD
NK	Nihonshoki kayō, 720 AD
NR	Nihon ryōiki, early 9th century
NT	Norito, 7–9th centuries
OGJ	Okinawa go jiten
SSI	Shōsōin documents, 7–8th centuries
WMS	Wamyōshō, 931–938 AD

Korean

SKSK	Samkwuk saki, 1145 AD

Grammatical Terms

3pso	Third person singular indefinite object
ABS	Absolutive
ACC	Accusative
ADJ	Adjectivizer
ATTR	Attributive
BEN	Benefactive
CAUS	Causative
CL	Classifier
COM	Comitative
COMP	Comparative
CON	Conjunctive gerund
CONC	Concessive gerund
COND	Conditional gerund
CONJ	Conjunction
CONJC	Conjectural
CONV	Converb
COOP	Cooperative
COOR	Coordinative gerund
COP	Copula
DAT	Dative
DEB	Debitive
DES	Desiderative
DIR	Directive
DLF	Directive-locative focus
DP	Desiderative particle
DV	Defective verb
EMPH	Emphatic
EP	Emphatic particle
EV	Evidential
EXCL	Exclamative
FIN	Final verbal form
FP	Focus particle
GEN	Genitive
GER	Gerund
HON	Honorific
HUM	Humble
INTER	Interjection

IP	Interrogative particle
LOC	Locative
NEG	Negative
NML	Nominalizer
OBJ	Object marker
OSM	Oblique stem marker
PASS	Passive
PAST	Past tense
PERF	Perfective
PLUR	Plural
POSS	Possessive
POT	Potential
PREF	Prefix
PROG	Progressive
QV	Quotation verb
REC	Reciprocal
RETR	Retrospective
RP	Restrictive particle
SUB	Subordinative gerund
SUBJ	Subjunctive
SUP	Suppositional
TENT	Tentative
TENT2	Second tentative
TERM	Terminative
TOP	Topic

Charts

1 Poem variants in book fourteen   2
2 Mini-sequences in the identified section of book fourteen   6
3 Major and mini-sequences in the unidentified section of book fourteen   7
4 Sakimori poems by provinces with numbers and dates   15
5 Man'yōgana phonograms used in Eastern Old Japanese   18
6 Distribution of EOJ attributive verbal suffix -*o*   30
7 WOJ vs. EOJ differences in Eastern poems   38

Introduction

In the introduction we discuss our sources on Eastern Old Japanese as well as providing some other pertinent information.

1 *Hitachi Fudoki*

The *Hitachi Fudoki* (常陸風土記) is one of the four *Fudoki* (風土記) 'Gazetteers' that survived almost completely, the others being the *Harima Fudoki* (播磨風土記), the *Bungo Fudoki* (豊後風土記), and the *Hizen Fudoki* (肥前風土記). Only the *Izumo Fudoki* (出雲風土記) was preserved in its entirety. All other *Fudoki* survived only in small fragments, if at all: for example we do not have even a single fragment from the *Etchū Fudoki* (越中風土記). The Imperial order for the completion of the *Hitachi Fudoki* was issued in the sixth year of Wadō (和銅, 713 AD), and the text was compiled during the Yōrō years (養老, 717–724 AD).

Out of eleven districts that were included in the Hitati province, nine have complete descriptions, but the description of Kawati (河内) district survived only in fragments and the description of Shirakabe (白壁) district is lacking altogether. The main value of the *Hitachi Fudoki* is that it is a single gazetteer of a province in Eastern Japan that remains to this day almost in its entirety and not just in a few fragments. In addition, the *Hitachi Fudoki* is an authentic early Nara period text, while quite a number of fragments in other *Fudoki* are known only from later texts starting from the Heian period. Moreover, some of those fragments are preserved only in *kana* renditions and, therefore, do not keep the original orthography.

All this makes the *Hitachi Fudoki* an important source on both Eastern Old Japanese and the Ainu languages. The Ainu language is only of a peripheral value for the present work, as it is mainly dedicated to Eastern Old Japanese.

The *Hitachi Fudoki* contains nine poems, but only six of them are in Eastern Old Japanese (#2, 3, 5, 7, 8, 9), while the other three are written in an impeccable Western Old Japanese. Needless to say, only the poems in Eastern Old Japanese are handled in this publication. All poems in the Hitachi Fudoki are in the five-line *tanka* (短歌) form with a basic meter of the following numbers of syllables per line: 5-7-5-7-7. All poems are, strictly speaking, anonymous, although in four poems we have either direct or indirect indication of an author's gender.

2 *Man'yōshū* Book Fourteen

Book fourteen (14.3348–14.3577) includes 230 poems by the traditional count (all of them *tanka*), but the problem is that many poems have variants. The Japanese tradition normally counts only 'completely different' (Jpn. *zenkei iden*, 全形異伝) variants and this brings the number to 238 (Mizushima 1986: 2, 13). However, it is difficult to differentiate between 'completely different' variants and 'partially different', because, for example, the difference in just one line may be due to the application of the *honkadori* technique that results in the creation of a completely different text. This is especially true when the 'main' text is in Western Old Japanese, and the variant in Eastern Old Japanese, or vice versa, as in the case of poems 14.3358, 14.3482, 14.3493, 14.3537, and their variants. Therefore, we treat all the variant poems as separate poems, but in order not to break with tradition they are assigned the same number plus the following small letter *a* or *b*. None of the poems has more than two variants. In the chart below we present a list of all the poems that have variants.

CHART 1   Poem variants in book fourteen

Poems with variants in book fourteen	First variant	Second variant
3350 (WOJ)[1]	3350a (WOJ)	3350b (WOJ)
3358 (WOJ)	3358a (WOJ)	3358b (EOJ)
3359 (EOJ)	3359a (EOJ)	
3360 (WOJ)	3360a (WOJ)	
3362 (WOJ)	3362a (WOJ)	
3364 (WOJ)	3364a (WOJ)	
3376 (EOJ)	3376a (EOJ)	
3405 (EOJ)	3405a (EOJ)	
3438 (WOJ)	3438a (WOJ)	3438b (WOJ)
3440 (WOJ)	3440a (WOJ)	
3441 (WOJ)	3441a (WOJ)	
3476 (EOJ)	3476a (EOJ)	
3482 (WOJ)	3482a (EOJ)	
3493 (EOJ)	3493a (WOJ)	
3537 (WOJ)	3537a (EOJ)	
3538 (EOJ)	3538a (EOJ)	
Number of variants	16	3
Total number of variants: 19		

---

[1] The notation WOJ indicates Western Old Japanese and the notation EOJ Eastern Old Japanese.

This brings the total number of poems recorded in book fourteen to 249.

In contrast to books five and fifteen, all poems in book fourteen are anonymous, and none of them dated, with the possible exception of 14.3399 that can be dated either 702 or 713–714 AD. However, if one looks at the order of provinces in the identified section of book fourteen (see the section on the structure of book fourteen below), Muⁿzasi province appears as one of the provinces of the Tōkaidō region (東海道). Meanwhile, it is well known that Muⁿzasi was originally a province from the Tōsandō region (東山道), and was transferred into the Tōkaidō region only in 771 AD. This gives us the *non ante quem* date for the compilation of book fourteen: under these circumstances it could not have been put together earlier than 771 AD.

Four major *Man'yōshū* genres are present in book fourteen: miscellaneous poems (*zōka*, 雜歌), relationship poems (*sōmonka*, 相聞歌), allegorical poems (*hiyuka*, 比喩歌), and one elegy poem (*banka*, 挽歌), the last poem in the book. The spelling system in this volume is predominantly phonographic, although there are occasional semantograms used here and there.

3　Structure of Book Fourteen

The structure of book fourteen is very different from those of any other books in the *Man'yōshū*, as the main underlying principle of arranging its poems is geographical. First, the poems are divided into two major sections: poems from identified provinces (3348–3437) and poems from unidentified provinces (3438–3577). Each of these two groups is organized further by poetic genres in the following order: miscellaneous poems (*zōka,* 雜歌), relationship poems (*sōmonka*, 相聞歌), allegorical poems (*hiyuka*, 比喩歌), and one elegy poem (*banka*, 挽歌), found only in the unidentified section. Each genre in the identified section is further subdivided by Azuma provinces, with the provinces of the Tōkaidō region (東海道) placed first, and provinces from the Tōsandō region (東山道) next. Within each region the provinces closest to the capital are placed first, with the provinces farthest from the capital being the last. Not every Azuma province is present, and not every genre of poems is found for every province in the identified section. Thus, there are no poems from Iⁿga (伊賀), Ise (伊勢), Opari (尾張), Mikapa (三河), Kapï (甲斐), and Apa (安房) provinces among Tōkaidō region provinces and no poems from Apumi (近江), Mino (美濃) and Piⁿda (飛騨) among Tōsandō region provinces present in the collection. Therefore, the provinces represented in book fourteen are:

Tōkaidō region (東海道):
– Təpotuapumi (遠江)
– Suruⁿga (駿河)
– Iⁿdu (伊豆)

- Saŋgamu (相模)
- Muⁿzasi (武蔵)
- Kamitupusa (上総)
- Simotupusa (下総)
- Pitati (常陸)

Tōsandō region (東山道):
- Sinanu (信濃)
- Kamitukɛno (上野)
- Simotukɛno (下野)
- Mitinəku (陸奥)

Since the provinces are not known in the unidentified section, the poems are organized there exclusively by genres. The following list conveys the general structure of book fourteen:

Poems from identified provinces	3348–3437
Miscellaneous poems	3348–3352
Poems from Tōkaidō region	3348–3351
One poem from Kamitupusa province	3348
One poem from Simotupusa province	3349
Four poems[2] from Pitati province	3350–3351
Poems from Tōsandō region	3352
One poem from Sinanu province	3352
Relationship poems	3353–3428
Poems from Tōkaidō region	3353–3397
Two poems from Təpotuapumi province	3353–3354
Seven poems[3] from Suruŋga province	3355–3359a
Two poems from Iⁿdu province	3360–3360a
Fourteen poems[4] from Saŋgamu province	3361–3373
Ten poems[5] from Muⁿzasi province	3373–3381
Two poems from Kamitupusa province	3382–3383
Four poems from Simotupusa province	3384–3387
Ten poems from Pitati province	3388–3397

---

2 Including variants 3350a and 3350b.
3 Including variants 3358a and 3359a.
4 Including variants 3362a and 3364a.
5 Including variant 3376a.

Poems from Tōsandō region	3398–3428
Four poems from Sinanu province	3398–3401
Twenty-three[6] poems from Kamitukɛno province	3402–3423
Two poems from Simotukɛno province	3424–3425
Three poems from Mitinəku province	3426–3428
Allegorical poems	3429–3437
Poems from Tōkaidō region	3429–3433
One poem from Təpotuapumi province	3429
One poem from Suruŋga province	3430
Three poems from Saŋgamu province	3431–3433
Poems from Tōsandō region	3434–3437
Three poems from Kamitukɛno province	3433–3436
One poem from Mitinəku province	3437
Poems from unidentified provinces	3438–3577
Twenty-one[7] miscellaneous poems	3438–3454
One hundred seventeen[8] relationship poems	3455–3566
Five border guards' poems[9]	3567–3571
Five allegorical poems	3572–3576
One elegy poem	3577

Apart from the divisions into geographical regions and genres the structure of the identified section of book fourteen is rather vague. Several very loosely connected poetic mini-sequences, which should be called quasi-sequences, can be found in the identified section. The loose connection between the poems is usually based on referring to the same object, or a person, or in most cases the same place name. It must be kept in mind that with one notable exception (14.3348–14.3349) these mini-sequences are also found within the same geographical region, and there are no overlaps between two or more geographical regions. In addition, not every poem from the identified section can be assigned to a mini-sequence, as becomes clear from the chart below. Finally, in one case, there is a mini-sequence found within another mini-sequence, and in another case, one poem belongs simultaneously to two neighboring mini-sequences.

---

6 Including variant 3405a.
7 Including variants 3438a, 3438b, 3440a, and 3441a.
8 Including variants 3476a, 3482a, 3493a, 3537a, and 3538a.
9 Actually a subvariety of relationship poems. There is no 'border guard' genre in the *Man'yōshū*.

CHART 2   Mini-sequences in the identified section of book fourteen

Mini-sequences	Poems
Poems referring to boats	3348–3349
Poems referring to Mt. Tukupa and garments/cloth	3350–3351
Poems referring to Mt. Puⁿzi	3355–3358, 3358b
Poems referring to Asiⁿgara ~ Asiⁿgari mountains	3363–3364, 3369–3371
Poems referring to Kamakura region	3365–3366
Poems referring to Muⁿzasi province	3374–3379
Poems referring to Mt. Umaⁿguta	3382–3383
Poems referring to Kaⁿdusika area	3384–3387
Poems about the maiden from Kaⁿdusika	3384–3385
Poems referring to Mt. Tukupa	3388–3396
Poems referring to Kamitukɛno province	3404–3407, 3415–3418
Poems referring to Mt. Ikapo	3409–3410, 3414–3415, 3421–3423
Poems referring to Simotukɛno province	3424–3425

In the unidentified section of book fourteen the situation is somewhat different, because it is possible to trace longer sequences, although there is also a number of mini-sequences similar to those found in the identified section. Mizushima identifies two major sequences found in the unidentified section as 'poems narrating love feelings directly' (*seijutsu shinsho ka*, 正述心緒歌) and 'poems narrating love feelings by reference to things' (*kibutsu chinshin ka*, 寄物陳心歌) (1986: 3). These two sequences cover the poems 14.3455–14.3480 for the first sequence and poems 14.3481–14.3566 for the second. While there are no detectable sub-sequences in the first sequence, there are some sub-sequences in the second. Since most of these sub-sequences are considerably longer than mini-sequences found in the identified part, we prefer to use the term 'sub-sequence' rather than a 'mini-sequence' when referring to them. In addition, poems 14.3438–14.3454 also have three sub-sequences, two of which being similar in length to mini-sequences in the identified section, but in order to keep the unified terminology for the unidentified section of book fourteen, we have labeled them all as sub-sequences. Both the major sequences and sub-sequences of the unidentified section of book fourteen are listed in the chart below.

INTRODUCTION

CHART 3   Major and sub-sequences in the unidentified section of book fourteen

Major sequences	Sub-sequences	Poems
	Poems referring to sounds of bells	3438–3439
	Poems referring to flowers, plants, and their products	3443–3449, 3451–3452
Poems narrating love feelings directly		3455–3480
Poems narrating love feelings by reference to things		3481–3566
	Poems referring to garments and their parts	3481–3484
	Poems referring to weapons and utensils	3485–3490
	Poems referring to plants	3491–3509
	Poems referring to clouds	3510–3520
	Poems referring to birds and animals	3521–3542
	Poems referring to terrestrial phenomena	3543–3554
	Poems referring to boats and their parts	3555–3559
	Poems referring to metal	3560–3561
	Poems referring to seaweed	3562–3563
	Poems referring to heavenly phenomena and deities	3564–3566
Border guards poems		3567–3571
	Poems on lovers' separation	3567–3571
Allegorical poems and an elegy		3572–3577
	Poems referring to flowers and plants	3572–3577

The chart above only partially follows Mizushima's classification (1986: 3). We have borrowed his wisdom in approaching *Azuma uta* as a more coherent and not an absolutely chaotic collection, but not the exact execution of it, as his and our approaches are somewhat different, both in terms of assigning topics, as well as in actual subdivisions; e.g. Mizushima does not classify any poems beyond 14.3566 into any general topics. Contrary to Mizushima, we think that the remaining poems 14.3567–14.3577 can also be classified as the chart above shows. Two interesting results emerge from this point of view. First, all border guards poems are united by the topic of lovers' separation. This might be trivial enough, but the second alignment might be much more important, since both the allegorical poems and an elegy in the unidentified section of book fourteen share the same reference point – flowers and plants.

4 Poems in Eastern Old Japanese and in Western Old Japanese

In spite of its title, *Aⁿduma uta* (MdJ *Azuma uta*) 'Poems of Eastern Provinces', book fourteen is linguistically split between poems in Eastern Old Japanese (EOJ) and poems in Western Old Japanese (WOJ) like book twenty, but unlike any other book in the *Man'yōshū*, where all poems are in WOJ. Japanese *Man'yōshū* scholars rarely, if at all, take into consideration these linguistic differences, especially where book fourteen is concerned, although there is an implicit tendency to draw the line between WOJ and EOJ poems in the linguistically oriented research (Fukuda 1965; Hōjō 1966; Mizushima 1984b). Much more explicit differentiation between WOJ and EOJ poems is done in the recent study by Hino (2003). While some poems can be clearly classified as either EOJ or WOJ, there are also many cases where it is difficult to decide whether a given poem is really a WOJ or an EOJ one. Consequently, as yet, there is no complete agreement in the current Western scholarship regarding the EOJ or WOJ nature of poems. We present below, therefore, our own classification of poems in book fourteen as either EOJ or WOJ which does not necessarily coincide with Russell (2006) or Kupchik (2011) divisions. Since this classification deals only with poems in book fourteen, the prefix 14. is omitted below. Also, our classification includes variant poems as well, so the total count is 249 rather than 230 poems.

Poems in Eastern Old Japanese

3349, 3351, 3354, 3358b, 3359, 3359a, 3361, 3363, 3366, 3369, 3370, 3374, 3375, 3376, 3376a, 3377, 3378, 3379, 3382, 3383, 3384, 3385, 3387, 3388, 3389, 3392, 3394, 3395, 3397, 3398, 3399, 3400, 3401, 3402, 3404, 3405, 3405a, 3407, 3408, 3409, 3410, 3411, 3412, 3413, 3414, 3415, 3418, 3419, 3420, 3423, 3424, 3425, 3426, 3431, 3432, 3434, 3435, 3436, 3437, 3444, 3445, 3446, 3447, 3448, 3450, 3451, 3452, 3456, 3458, 3460, 3461, 3463, 3464, 3464, 3465, 3466, 3468, 3469, 3472, 3473, 3474, 3476, 3476a, 3478, 3480, 3481, 3482a, 3483, 3484, 3485, 3487, 3488, 3489, 3493, 3494, 3495, 3496, 3499, 3500, 3501, 3502, 3503, 3504, 3506, 3509, 3511, 3512, 3513, 3514, 3515, 3516, 3517, 3518,

3520, 3521, 3522, 3524, 3525, 3526, 3527, 3528, 3529, 3530, 3531, 3532, 3533, 3536, 3537, 3537a, 3538, 3538a, 3539, 3540, 3541, 3543, 3544, 3546, 3548, 3549, 3551, 3552, 3553, 3555, 3556, 3557, 3560, 3561, 3562, 3563, 3564, 3565, 3566, 3572, 3576.
Total: 154 poems.

Poems in Western Old Japanese

3348, 3350, 3350a, 3350b, 3352, 3353, 3355, 3356, 3357, 3358, 3358a, 3360, 3360a, 3362, 3362, 3362a, 3364, 3364a, 3365, 3367, 3371, 3372, 3373, 3380, 3381, 3386, 3390, 3391, 3393, 3396, 3403, 3406, 3416, 3417, 3421, 3422, 3427, 3428, 3429, 3430, 3433, 3438, 3438a, 3438b, 3439, 3440, 3440a, 3441, 3441a, 3442, 3443, 3449, 3453, 3454, 3455, 3457, 3459, 3462, 3467, 3470, 3471, 3475, 3477, 3479, 3482, 3486, 3490, 3491, 3492, 3493a, 3497, 3498, 3505, 3507, 3508, 3510, 3519, 3523, 3534, 3535, 3542, 3545, 3547, 3550, 3554, 3558, 3559, 3567, 3568, 3569, 3570, 3571, 3573, 3574, 3575, 3577.
Total: 95 poems.

5 Can the Poems with an Unidentified Geographical Location Be Identified?

A number of poems in the unidentified section include mention of certain place names that might allow us to tie them to specific provinces. However, given the fact that these poems were classified as 'unidentified' from at least the fourteenth century when the *Nishi Honganji-bon* was compiled, and also the fact that there is no ultimate certainty regarding the assignment of these placenames to specific Azuma provinces, we should be able to come up with at least a second independent piece of evidence that would demonstrate a link with a certain province. The following poems from the unidentified section that include specific placenames have been tentatively linked with the following provinces:
– Apa: 14.3501 (E)
– Kamitukɛno: 14.3473 (E), 14.3494 (E), 14.3560 (E)
– Kaŋga or Pïⁿda: 14.3509 (E)
– Kapï: 14.3543 (E)
– Mikapa: 14.3547 (W)
– Muⁿzasi: 14.3496 (E), 14.3525 (E)
– Pitati: 14.3444 (E), 14.3563 (E), 14.3572 (E)
– Saŋgamu: 14.3508 (W)
– Simotupusa: 14.3529 (E), 14.3449 (W), 14.3555 (E), 14.3558 (W)

– Sinanu: 14.3565 (E)
– Suruⁿga: 14.3448 (W), 14.3438 (W), 14.3442 (W), 14.3523 (W), 14.3447 (E)

The second independent piece of evidence can only come from a linguistics source at this point, namely, whether a given poem exhibits the same linguistic features that are attested in the same geographical variety of EOJ in other poems of books fourteen or twenty. In some cases we will be able to prove this point, but there are two obvious problems: (a) some poems from the list above are clearly written in WOJ, and (b) others are from the provinces like Apa, Pïⁿda (or Kaⁿga), or Kapï that are not otherwise attested in the extant identified EOJ corpus. We apply the same solution for these two cases: both the poems in WOJ and the poems in EOJ from the provinces that are not otherwise represented in the identified section of books fourteen or twenty are excluded from further consideration, because it is not possible to prove that poems in EOJ have the EOJ linguistic features coming from a certain province. Therefore, the list above can be reduced to the following list, excluding WOJ poems as well as EOJ poems that come from the provinces that have EOJ features that cannot be geographically identified:

– Kamitukɛno: 14.3473 (E), 14.3494 (E), 14.3560 (E)
– Muⁿzasi: 14.3496 (E), 14.3525 (E)
– Pitati: 14.3444 (E), 14.3563 (E), 14.3572 (E)
– Simotupusa: 14.3529 (E), 14.3555 (E)
– Sinanu: 14.3565 (E)
– Suruⁿga: 14.3447 (E)

The next step will be to determine whether these poems really share the linguistic features of their tentative provinces in Azuma.

6 Determining the Geographical Locations of Unidentified Poems on the Basis of Their Linguistic Features

Poem 14.3473 has two EOJ features: adjectival evidential suffix -*ka*-, and verbal attributive -*o*. Since the second feature is also attested in one identified poem from Kamitukɛno province (14.3423), this poem should be recognized as being from Kamitukɛno. Poem 14.3494 has verbal attributive -*o* and interrogative pronoun *aN*- 'what, why' that are also attested in other Kamitukɛno poems, so this poem should be recognized as being from Kamitukɛno. No such supporting linguistic evidence can be found for the poem 14.3560, so its Kamitukɛno origin remains much more problematic.

Poem 14.3496 has one EOJ feature: tentative suffix -*unam*-, corresponding to WOJ -*uram*-. Unfortunately, EOJ -*unam*- is not attested directly in other

Muⁿzasi poems. However, it is attested in one identified poem from Saⁿgamu province (14.3366) from Kamakura district that is right on the border with Muⁿzasi province. Although, this is not the same kind of evidence that we have seen for the poem 14.3494 above, it is somewhat compelling, because administrative divisions do not necessarily coincide with dialect boundaries. Therefore, we tentatively accept the possibility that the poem 14.3496 is indeed from Muⁿzasi province. Poem 14.3525 has EOJ specific order of morphemes -(*a*)*n-ap*- 'NEG-ITER' (vs. WOJ order -*ap-an*- 'ITER-NEG') also attested in another Muⁿzasi poem (14.3375), so this poem should be also classified as a poem from Muⁿzasi province.

Poem 14.3444 has the EOJ specific order of morphemes -(*a*)*n-ap*- 'NEG-ITER' (vs. WOJ order -*ap-an*- 'ITER-NEG') also attested in another Pitati poem (14.3394), so this poem should be classified as a poem from Pitati province. Poem 14.3563 has two EOJ features: tentative suffix -*unam*-, corresponding to WOJ -*uram*-, and verbal attributive -*o*. Neither of these features can be found in other identified poems from Pitati province, so we cannot be completely sure that this poem comes from Pitati province. Poem 14.3572 has one EOJ feature: EOJ progressive suffix -*ar*- (corresponding to WOJ -*er*-), that occurs in another identified poems from Pitati (14.3351), therefore this poem should be classified as a poem from Pitati province.

Poem 14.3529 has three EOJ features: EOJ progressive suffix -*ar*- (corresponding to WOJ -*er*-), EOJ iterative suffix -*ape*- (corresponding to WOJ -*apɛ*-), and usage of an converb in attributive function. Unfortunately, there are only five identified poems from Simotupusa province in book fourteen, among which only three poems are in EOJ. None of these three features is attested in these three poems, so the classification of 14.3529 as a poem from Simotupusa province remains problematic, but not impossible due to the paucity of identified Simotupusa poems in book fourteen. The same can be said about poem 14.3555, which has two EOJ features: EOJ iterative suffix -*ape*- (corresponding to WOJ -*apɛ*-), and usage of an converb in attributive function. Note that these two features are shared by both 14.3529 and 14.3555, so they might be poems from the same location. Unfortunately, there is no linguistic evidence that they are from Simotupusa province.

Poem 14.3565 has only one EOJ feature: EOJ *tuku* 'moon' (cf. WOJ *tukï*). Unfortunately, there are only five identified poems from Sinanu province in book fourteen, among which one poem is in WOJ. The EOJ nature of the remaining four poems is established solely on the basis of special EOJ vocabulary, which is not found in 14.3565, so its classification as a poem from Sinanu province remains problematic, but not impossible due to the paucity of identified Sinanu poems in book fourteen.

Poem 14.3447 has only one EOJ feature: EOJ locative case marker -*na* (corresponding to WOJ -*ni*). Unfortunately, there are only nine identified poems from Suruŋga province in book fourteen, among which only three poems are in EOJ. EOJ locative case marker -*na* is not attested in these three poems, so its classification as a poem from Suruŋga province remains problematic, but not impossible due to the paucity of identified Suruŋga poems written in EOJ in book fourteen.

Therefore, the final results of identifying the exact geographic locations of the EOJ unidentified poems in book fourteen on the basis of their linguistic features comes down to the following list:
– Kamitukɛno: 14.3473 (E), 14.3494 (E)
– Muⁿzasi: 14.3496 (E), 14.3525 (E)
– Pitati: 14.3444 (E), 14.3572 (E)

Consequently, only six poems among unidentified poems could have been assigned to certain provinces using both geographical and linguistic criteria. The result may seem rather dismal, but we believe that this is better than nothing.

7 *Man'yōshū* Book Sixteen

By the traditional count, book sixteen (16.3786–3889) comprises 104 poems (ninety-two *tanka*, seven *chōka*, three *sedōka*, one *bussokusekika*, and one bizarre poem (16.3878), which is usually defined as *sedōka*, but as a matter of fact has a very strange poetic meter not found anywhere else). The second longest *chōka* in the *Man'yōshū*, 16.3791 is found here as well. Book sixteen includes poems on occasion and miscellaneous poems (*yuen aru hei zōka* or *yoshi aru hei zōka*, 有由縁并雑歌), but there is no internal subdivision inside the book to *yuen aru* and *zōka*, unlike, e.g. book two that is subdivided into *sōmonka* 'relationship poems' and *banka* 'elegies'. None of the poems have dates, but some can be dated approximately. Probably none of the poems is earlier than the late seventh century. The contents of book sixteen is quite unusual because it includes a number of humorous poems. It also has many loanwords from Chinese. In addition, book sixteen has some vocabulary that does not occur elsewhere and certainly cannot be defined as 'poetic', e.g., *kuso* 'feces', 'stinky' (16.3828, 16.3832, 16.3855), *mar-* 'to defecate' (16.3832), *kapa kuma* 'privy', 'toilet' (lit. 'river bend') (16.3828), *siⁿgup-* 'to fuck' (16.3821), *tuno-nə pukure* 'penis' (?) (lit. 'horn's swelling') (16.3821), *tapusaki* 'loincloth' (16.3839), *waki kusa* 'armpits' hair' (lit. 'armpits' grass') (16.3842). The poems were composed by various authors, most of them anonymous. Another setback is that most of the authors whose names are known are otherwise completely obscure with their biographies unknown. Among the poems of authors with known biographies there are poems by Opotəmə-nə Yakamətimeans. The spelling system in book sixteen is mostly mixed logographic and phonographic, although there is a strong preference for logography.

There are three peculiarities of poems with Eastern Old Japanese features in book sixteen. First, there are only five of them, which makes their share much less than the respective share of Eastern Old Japanese poems in books fourteen and twenty. Second, one poem is from Hizen province (16.3865), three from Noto province (16.3878–3880), and one from an unidentified location (16.3885). Excluding the last poem with unknown whereabouts, none of the remaining four is, strictly speaking an *Eastern* Old Japanese poem, although, of course, we do not know how far west Eastern Old Japanese was spread: Noto peninsula might be still Eastern Old Japanese-speaking in antiquity in spite of the fact it is today a part of the greater Kansai linguistic area. But the first poem from Hizen province cannot possibly be an *Eastern* Old Japanese poem. Most likely it comes from a dialect in Kyūshū closely related to Eastern Old Japanese. The second independent piece of evidence for this point of view comes from a poem preserved in *Hizen Fudoki* (肥前風土記). We will address this issue in a separate publication. Third, Eastern Old Japanese features found in the poems from the book sixteen mostly involve grammatical morphemes, but not the vocabulary, with an exception of the poem 16.3878 and possibly one word in the poem 16.3879.

8   *Man'yōshū* Book Twenty

Book twenty (20.4293–4516) comprises 224 poems (218 *tanka*, six *chōka*) with unspecified genres. From the social point of view this book is the most varied one, as it includes poems from both the highest and potentially one of the lowest social classes. Namely, the variation in authors' social status extends from Empresses, Princes (one of them being future Emperor Junnin) down to the lowest border-guard soldiers. Needless to say, the various strata of the nobility are also richly represented in this book.

The structure of book twenty is very different from that of any other book in the *Man'yōshū*, although in certain respects it has similarities to book five, as there are many short mini-sequences, to book fifteen, as there are two (or rather three) major sections (linguistically defined: two sequences in WOJ at the beginning and the end of the book, and the sequence in EOJ in the middle, although it also has intervening poems in WOJ), and to book fourteen, because poems within the Eastern Japanese section are organized in geographical order, although this order is not very consistent. However, the main underlying principle of arranging its poems is chronological, and most of the poems in book twenty can be dated with a precision to a particular day.

First, the poems can be divided into two (or three) major sections: poems composed either by border-guards (OJ *sakimori*) themselves, or poems about border-guards' feelings or imitating border-guards' poems (4321–4436) and poems on different topics (4293–4320 and 4437–4516). The peculiarity of the *sakimori* section is that the poems composed by *sakimori* themselves (4321–4330, 4337–4359, 4363–4394, 4401–4407, 4413–4432, 4436) are intermingled with poems about *sakimori* and their feelings composed by non-*sakimori* authors, mostly by Opotəmə-nə Yakaməti (4331–4336, 4360–4362, 4395–4400, 4408–4412, 4433–4435). Furthermore, the poems composed by *sakimori* themselves include eighty-four poems collected by Opotəmə-nə Yakaməti between the sixth day and the twenty-ninth day of the second lunar month of the seventh year of Tenpyō Shōhō (March 23 to April 15, 755 AD) all of which have an identified author and an identified province or even district of origin (4321–4330, 4337–4359, 4363–4394, 4401–4407, 4413–4424) and nine old poems by *sakimori* or their wives that are all anonymous and are from unidentified provinces (4425–4432, 4436). The poems 4425–4432 were collected by Ipare-nə imiki Mərəkimi, and poem 4436 by Opopara-nə mapitə Imakï.

Most of the poems composed by *sakimori* themselves are in Eastern Old Japanese, although four poems are in Western Old Japanese: two (4326 and 4357) among the poems collected by Opotəmə-nə Yakaməti, and two among old *sakimori* poems (4425 and 4436). Poems collected by Opotəmə-nə Yakaməti are further subdivided by Azuma provinces, although the principle that we have seen in book fourteen with the provinces of the Tōkaidō region (東海道) placed first, and provinces from the Tōsandō region (東山道) next, and within each region the provinces closest to the capital placed first, with the provinces farthest from the capital being the last is not consistent in book twenty. Thus (see the list below), poems from Simotukɛno province that was one of Tōsandō provinces are found between the poems from Pitati province and Simotupusa province from Tōkaidō region. Also, Simotupusa province is closer to the capital than Pitati province, and Suruⁿga is closer than Saⁿgamu. Apparently, this geographical principle of arrangement was sacrificed for the chronological order in which poems were collected.

Not every Tōkaidō or Tōsandō province is present in book twenty. More specifically, there are no poems from Iⁿga (伊賀), Ise (伊勢), Opari (尾張), Mikapa (三河), Kapï (甲斐), and Apa (安房) provinces among Tōkaidō region provinces and no poems from Apumi (近江), Mino (美濃), Mitinəku (陸奥) and Pïⁿda (飛騨)

INTRODUCTION 15

among Tōsandō region provinces present in the collection.[10] This probably can be explained by the possibility that there were no *sakimori* sent as replacements from these provinces in this particular year. It is conspicuous, however, that the absent Tōkaidō provinces are the same provinces that are absent from book fourteen, and the Tōsandō provinces are also the same with the exception of Mitinəku. In contrast to book fourteen, Muⁿzasi province appears in book twenty as a part of the Tōsandō, and not Tōkaidō region. This is not surprising given the fact that in 755 AD Muⁿzasi province was still a part of Tōsandō. In Chart 4 below we present the *sakimori* poems recorded in book twenty accompanied by their poem numbers and date of collection or receipt by Opotəmə-nə Yakaməti:

CHART 4   Sakimori poems by provinces with numbers and dates

Region	Province	Poems	Date
Tōkaidō (東海道)	Təpotuapumi (遠江)	4321–4327	March 23, 755 AD
Tōkaidō (東海道)	Saⁿgamu (相模)	4328–4330	March 24, 755 AD
Tōkaidō (東海道)	Suruⁿga (駿河)	4337–4346	March 26, 755 AD
Tōkaidō (東海道)	Kamitupusa (上総)	4347–4359	March 26, 755 AD
Tōkaidō (東海道)	Pitati (常陸)	4363–4372	March 31, 755 AD
Tōsandō (東山道)	Simotukɛno (下野)	4373–4383	March 31, 755 AD
Tōkaidō (東海道)	Simotupusa (下総)	4384–4394	April 2, 755 AD
Tōsandō (東山道)	Sinanu (信濃)	4401–4403	April 8, 755 AD
Tōsandō (東山道)	Kamitukɛno (上野)	4404–4407	April 9, 755 AD
Tōsandō (東山道)	Muⁿzasi (武蔵)	4413–4424	April 15, 755 AD
unidentified	unidentified	4425–4432	April 18, 755 AD
unidentified	unidentified	4436	unknown

9   Poems in Eastern Old Japanese and in Western Old Japanese

Book twenty, like book fourteen, is linguistically split between poems in Eastern Old Japanese (EOJ) and poems in Western Old Japanese (WOJ), but is unlike any other book in the *Man'yōshū* (with the exception of book sixteen), where all poems are in WOJ. *Man'yōshū* scholars rarely, if at all, take into consideration these linguistic differences, especially where book fourteen is

---

10   Certainly, only Kapï, Apa, and Mitinəku provinces are proper Aⁿduma provinces.

concerned, although there is an implicit tendency to draw the line between WOJ and EOJ poems in the linguistically-oriented research (Fukuda 1965; Hōjō 1966; Mizushima 1984b). Much more explicit differentiation between WOJ and EOJ poems is done in the study by Hino (2003). While some poems can be clearly classified as either EOJ or WOJ, there are also many cases where it is difficult to decide whether a given poem is really a WOJ or an EOJ one. Consequently, as yet, there is no complete agreement in the current Western scholarship regarding the EOJ or WOJ nature of poems. We present below, therefore, our own classification of poems in book twenty as either EOJ or WOJ which does not necessarily coincide with Russell's (2006) or Kupchik's (2011) divisions. Since this classification here deals only with poems in book twenty, the prefix 20. is omitted below.[11]

Poems in Eastern Old Japanese
4321–4325, 4327–4330, 4337–4356, 4358–4359, 4363–4394, 4401–4407, 4413–4424, 4426–4432
Total: 89 poems.

Poems in Western Old Japanese
4293–4320, 4326, 4331–4336, 4357, 4360–4362, 4395–4400, 4408–4412, 4425, 4433–4516
Total: 135 poems.

With eighty-nine poems in EOJ vs. 135 poems in WOJ it is apparent that the WOJ poems in book twenty are dominant. The situation is opposite in book fourteen, which contains 154 poems in EOJ vs. ninety-five poems in WOJ.

The obvious advantages of poems in EOJ in book twenty is that the majority of them are dated with the place of origins of their authors, and are not anonymous, whereas all poems in book fourteen are anonymous, almost none have any dates, and the majority have unidentified place of origins. Also, from a literary view point, book twenty contains the only *chōka* in EOJ: 20.4372. All other EOJ poems, whether in book fourteen or book twenty, are *tanka*. There are, however, certain disadvantages of poems in EOJ in book twenty as compared to the same poems in book fourteen which we will discuss below in the section on Opotəmə-nə Yakaməti's principles of selection.

---

11   For the divisions between EOJ and WOJ poems in book fourteen see the introduction to book fourteen above.

INTRODUCTION

10   *Azuma asobi uta*

Azuma asobi (東遊) is a kind of song and dance performance that took place in the Imperial palace and various Shintō shrines starting from the Heian period (794–1192 AD). It was originally based on the folk performances in the Eastern provinces.

Each performance consisted of five acts. The first, the second, and the fifth did not include any dance, while the third and the fourth did. This order of acts was codified by the Imperial order on the tenth day of the eleventh lunar month of the twentieth year of Engi (延喜, December 22, 920 AD) (Konishi 1957: 274).

There are thirteen *Azuma asobi uta* known to us, but only two (#1 and #2) have Eastern Old Japanese features. They are written in the *man'yōgana* script, which is more or less accurate in spite of the fact that the text goes back to the early Heian period. The only confusion is that /kə/ is written as 古 /ko/.

11   *Kokin wakashū*

The *Kokin wakashū* (古今和歌集) 'A Collection of New and Old Japanese Poems' is the first poetic anthology in the *Hachidaishū* (八代集) 'Collections from the Eight Generations' stretching from early tenth to the early thirteenth century. It was compiled on Imperial order from Emperor Daigo (醍醐) by Ki-no Tsurayuki (紀貫之), Ki-no Tomonori (紀友則), Ōshikochi-no Mitsune (凡河内躬恒), and Mibu-no Tadamine (壬生忠岑). Three different years are given as the dates of the compilation: 905 AD, 914 AD, and 921 AD. Out of these, the last two seem to be more realistic, since the Imperial order was given in 905 AD, which makes it unrealistic to expect the compilation to be accomplished in the same year.

The *Kokin wakashū* consists of twenty books, which include altogether 1111 poems. The only poem of interest to us is located in book twenty under #1097, as one of two poems is from the Kapï province. This is the only source on Eastern Old Japanese that uses the *kana* and not the *man'yōgana* script.

12   *Man'yōgana* Script

The *man'yōgana* script in Eastern Old Japanese is considerably simpler than in Western Old Japanese. First, *ongana* signs clearly predominate, and there are much fewer *kungana* characters. Second, there are very few disyllabic signs.

Third, known to us the number of ongana signs is greatly reduced as compared with Western Old Japanese.

CHART 5 Man'yōgana phonograms used in Eastern Old Japanese

Transcription	***Man'yōgana*** **signs**
a あ	ongana: 阿 安 disyllabic kungana: 足 [asi]
i い	ongana: 伊 以 disyllabic ongana: 印 [ina] [ini]
u う	ongana: 宇 有[12]
e え$_1$	ongana: 衣[13]
o お	ongana: 於 意[14]
ka か	ongana: 加 可 賀 迦[15] 珂[16] 甲[17] 甘[18] kungana: 香[19] 所[20] disyllabic kungana: 葛 [ka^{n}du][21]
ki き$_1$	ongana: 伎 吉 岐[22] 枳[23]
kï き$_2$	ongana: 疑[24] 紀[25] 奇[26]
ku く	ongana: 久 区[27] 口[28] 苦[29] 君[30]
ke け$_1$	ongana: 祁[31] 家[32] 介[33]

12 Occurs twice only in book twenty in the postscript to MYS 20.4337 and in MYS 20.4392.
13 Attested only once in the whole EOJ corpus in AAU 2.
14 Attested only in the *Man'yōshū* book twenty.
15 Attested only once in MYS 20.4388.
16 Attested only once in a placename Naka (那珂) in the postscript to MYS 20.4413.
17 Occurs only in the name of Kapï (甲斐) province.
18 Occurs only in MYS 20.4404 in a person's name Usikapi (牛甘).
19 Occurs only in the *Man'yōshū* book fourteen.
20 Occurs only once in 16.3880.
21 Occurs only once in the placename Ka^{n}dusika (葛餝) in the postscript to MYS 20.4385.
22 Occurs only in FK and *Man'yōshū* book twenty.
23 Attested only in the *Man'yōshū* book twenty.
24 Attested only once in FK 9.
25 Attested only once in MYS 20.4349.
26 Attested only once in MYS 14.3375.
27 Attested only once in FK 3.
28 Attested only once in MYS 14.3533.
29 Attested only in the *Man'yōshū* book twenty.
30 Occurs only in the *Man'yōshū* book fourteen.
31 Attested only in the *Man'yōshū* book twenty.
32 Attested very frequently in the *Man'yōshū* book fourteen and only twice in book twenty.
33 Attested three times only in AAU 2.

INTRODUCTION

CHART 5   Man'yōgana phonograms used in Eastern Old Japanese (*cont.*)

Transcription	*Man'yōgana* signs
kɛ け₂	ongana: 氣
ko こ₁	ongana: 古 故
	kungana: 子 [34]
kə こ₂	ongana: 己 許 巨 [35] 去 [36]
	kungana: 木 [37]
ŋga が	ongana: 我 賀 [38] 河 [39] 何 [40]
ŋgi ぎ₁	ongana: 藝 [41] 岐 [42] 伎 [43] 枳 [44]
ŋgï ぎ₂	ongana: 疑 宜 [45] 義 [46]
ŋgu ぐ	ongana: 具 [47]
	disyllabic ongana: 群 [ŋguri] [48]
ŋge げ₁	ongana: 牙 [49]
ŋgɛ げ₂	ongana: 義 [50]
ŋgo ご₁	ongana: 胡 [51] 吾 [52] 故 [53] 兒 [54]

---

34 Occurs in personal names in the *Man'yōshū* book twenty.
35 Attested only once in MYS 14.3465.
36 Attested only in the *Man'yōshū* book twenty.
37 Occurs once in MYS 14.3548.
38 Attested in FK 2, and the *Man'yōshū* books fourteen and twenty.
39 Attested in the *Man'yōshū* books fourteen and twenty. In about one third of all examples it occurs in the placename Suruŋga (駿河).
40 Attested only three times in the Eastern Old Japanese corpus: in FK 8, MYS 16.3885, and MYS 20.4364.
41 Occurs mostly in the *Man'yōshū* book fourteen. There are also two examples in the *Man'yōshū* book twenty.
42 Occurs four times only in the *Man'yōshū* book twenty.
43 Attested three times in: MYS 14.3537a, MYS 20.4365, and MYS 20.4383.
44 Attested three times in the *Man'yōshū* book twenty in: MYS 20.4384, MYS 20.4386, and MYS 20.4390.
45 Attested in four examples only in the *Man'yōshū* book fourteen.
46 Attested only once in MYS 20.4349.
47 Attested in the MYS books fourteen and twenty.
48 Attested only once in MYS 16.3885 in the placename Peŋguri (平群).
49 Attested only once in MYS 14.3489.
50 Attested only once in MYS 16.3885.
51 Attested mostly in the *Man'yōshū* book fourteen, but also in 16.3880 and 20.4417.
52 Attested once in MYS 14.3564.
53 Attested once in MYS 14.3540.
54 Occurs only in the word TEŋgo 'maiden, beloved' < Ainu *tek* 'hand, arm' + *o* 'take in, embrace' in MYS book fourteen.

CHART 5 Man'yōgana phonograms used in Eastern Old Japanese (*cont.*)

Transcription	*Man'yōgana* signs
ⁿgə ご₂	ongana: 其[55] 己[56]
sa さ	ongana: 佐 左 沙[57] 作[58] 草[59] 散[60]
	kungana: 狭[61]
	disyllabic: 相 [saⁿga/sau][62]
si し	ongana: 志 之 思 斯[63] 師[64] 紫[65] 四[66] 詩[67] 指[68] 信[69] 悉[70]
	kungana: 爲[71]
	disyllabic ongana: 信 [sina][72]
	disyllabic kungana: 餝 [sika][73]
su す	ongana: 須 酒[74]
	kungana: 栖[75]
	disyllabic ongana: 駿 [suru][76]

[55] Attested in the *Man'yōshū* books fourteen and twenty.
[56] Attested only once in MYS 20.4325.
[57] Occurs only once in a personal name in the postscript to the poems 20.4347–4359 in book twenty of the *Man'yōshū*.
[58] Attested four times only in the *Man'yōshū* book twenty.
[59] Attested only once in MYS 14.3530.
[60] Attested only once in MYS 20.4366.
[61] Attested only once in the placename Naⁿgasa (長狭) in MYS 20.4354.
[62] Attested only in placenames Saⁿgamu (相模) and Sauma (相馬).
[63] Attested only in the *Man'yōshū* books fourteen and sixteen.
[64] Attested only twice in MYS 14.3408 and 14.3412.
[65] Attested only once in the placename Tukusi (筑紫) in the preface to the poems 20.4321–4424.
[66] Attested only once in MYS 14.3493.
[67] Attested only once in MYS 16.3885.
[68] Attested only once in MYS 14.3407.
[69] Attested only once in the placename Siⁿda (信太) in the postscript to the poems MYS 20.4365–4366.
[70] Attested only once in FK 7.
[71] Attested only once in MYS 16.3878.
[72] Attested only in the placename Sinanu (信濃).
[73] Occurs only once in the placename Kaⁿdusika (葛餝) in the postscript to MYS 20.4385.
[74] Occurs only in MYS 14.3487, 14.3506, 14.3564, and 14.3565. In all these cases 酒 is used to write the second syllable *su* in the sequence *susu* in order to avoid the repetition of the character 須 used to write the first syllable *su*.
[75] Occurs only once in the personal name Wokurosu (小黒栖) in the postscript to the poem 20.4377.
[76] Occurs in the placename Suruⁿga (駿河).

CHART 5   Man'yōgana phonograms used in Eastern Old Japanese (*cont.*)

Transcription	*Man'yōgana* signs
se せ	ongana: 世 勢[77] 西[78]
	kungana: 瀬[79]
so そ₁	ongana: 蘇 素[80] 宗[81] 祖[82]
sə そ₂	ongana: 曾
ⁿza ざ	ongana: 射
	disyllabic ongana: 蔵 [ⁿzasi][83]
ⁿzi じ	ongana: 自 慈[84]
ⁿzu ず	ongana: 受
ⁿze ぜ	ongana: 是
ⁿzo ぞ₁	–
ⁿzə ぞ₂	ongana: 叙[85]
ta た	ongana: 多 太[86] 他[87] 當[88]
	kungana: 田[89]
	disyllabic ongana: 丹 [taⁿdi]
	disyllabic kungana: 足 [tari]
ti ち	ongana: 知 智[90] 恥[91] 遅[92]
	kungana: 道[93]
	disyllabic ongana: 中 [tiⁿgu][94]

[77] Attested mostly in the *Man'yōshū* book fourteen and marginally in book twenty.
[78] Attested in FK 8, mostly in the *Man'yōshū* book fourteen and marginally in book twenty.
[79] Attested only once in MYS 14.3366.
[80] Attested only in the *Man'yōshū* book fourteen.
[81] Attested only twice in MYS 20.4324 and 20.4401.
[82] Attested only once in MYS 20.4389.
[83] Occurs only in the placename Muⁿzasi (武蔵).
[84] Attested only in the placename Kuⁿzi (久慈) in the postscript to the poem MYS 20.4368.
[85] Attested only twice in MYS 20.4337 and 20.4376.
[86] Attested only twice in AAU 1 and AAU 2.
[87] Attested only in the *Man'yōshū* book twenty.
[88] Attested only in the personal name Kurota (黑當) in the postscript to MYS 20.4325.
[89] Occurs mostly in proper nouns.
[90] Attested only once in MYS 16.3885.
[91] Attested only once in MYS 14.3458.
[92] Attested only once in MYS 20.4353.
[93] Attested only once in MYS 20.4341.
[94] Attested only once in MYS 14.3401, and possibly, but highly unlikely, also in MYS 14.3419.

CHART 5   Man'yōgana phonograms used in Eastern Old Japanese (cont.)

Transcription	Man'yōgana signs
tu つ	ongana: 都 豆[95] 追[96] 川|[97] 頭[98] 鬥|[99] kungana: 齋[100] disyllabic ongana: 筑 [tuki, tuku][101] 對 [tusi][102]
te て	ongana: 弖 天 提 氏[103]
to と₁	ongana: 刀 度[104] kungana: 戸[105] 門[106]
tə と₂	ongana: 等 止 登 得[107] kungana: 跡[108] disyllabic ongana: 徳 [təkə][109]
ⁿda だ	ongana: 太 kungana: 田[110]
ⁿdi ぢ	ongana: 治 道[111]
ⁿdu づ	ongana: 豆 頭[112] 川|[113] disyllabic ongana: 曇 [ⁿdumi][114]

---

95   Attested in MYS 14.3370 and 20.4327, 20.4340, 20.4342, and 20.4346.
96   The character 追 is always used to write the second syllable *tu* in the sequence *tutu* in order to avoid the repetition of the character 都 used to write the first syllable *tu*.
97   Attested twice in AAU 2.
98   Attested only once in MYS 16.3885.
99   Attested twice in FK 5.
100 Attested only once in MYS 14.3503.
101 Attested only in placenames.
102 Attested only in the placename Tusima (對馬) in MYS 14.3516.
103 Attested only once in MYS 20.4356.
104 Attested only once in MYS 14.3407.
105 Attested only twice in MYS 14.3460.
106 Attested only once in MYS 14.3530.
107 Attested only once in MYS 14.3415.
108 Occurs three times in MYS 16.3885.
109 Attested only once in a personal name in the postscript to MYS 20.4415.
110 Occurs mostly in proper nouns.
111 Attested only once in MYS 14.3399.
112 Attested only once in MYS 14.3432.
113 Attested only once in AAU 2.
114 Attested only once in a person's name Aⁿdumi (安曇) in the postscript to the poems MYS 20.4413–4424.

INTRODUCTION 23

CHART 5   Man'yōgana phonograms used in Eastern Old Japanese (*cont.*)

Transcription	*Man'yōgana* signs
ⁿde で	ongana: 提 侶 涅[115] 天[116] 代[117] 田[118] 泥[119]
ⁿdo ど₁	ongana: 度
ⁿdə ど₂	ongana: 杼[120] 騰
na な	ongana: 奈 那[121] 南[122]
	kungana: 中[123]
ni に	ongana: 尒 爾 仁[124]
nu ぬ	ongana: 奴 努[125] 濃[126]
	kungana: 宿[127]
ne ね	ongana: 祢 尼 禰[128] 年[129]
	kungana: 根[130] 宿
no の₁	ongana: 努 怒 奴
	kungana: 野
nə の₂	ongana: 乃 能
pa は	ongana: 波 播[131] 芳[132] 破[133] 伴[134] 泊[135]
	kungana: 者[136]

---

115   Attested five times only in the *Man'yōshū* book twenty.
116   Attested only once in AAU 2.
117   Attested only once in MYS 14.3414.
118   Attested only once in MYS 20.4330.
119   Attested only twice in MYS 20.4323 and 20.4359.
120   Attested only in book fourteen of the *Man'yōshū*.
121   Attested in the *Man'yōshū* books fourteen and twenty, but in the latter only in placenames.
122   Attested only once in MYS 14.3516.
123   Attested only once in MYS 14.3419 in the *Hirose-bon*.
124   Attested only three times in MYS 14.3452, 14.3537a, and 14.3576.
125   Attested only once in MYS 14.3518.
126   Attested mostly in the placename Sinanu (信濃).
127   Attested only once in MYS 14.3562.
128   Attested only twice in MYS 16.3878 and 16.3880.
129   Attested only once in MYS 14.3543.
130   Attested only once in MYS 14.3500.
131   Attested only once in MYS 14.3359.
132   Attested only in FK 9.
133   Attested only once in MYS 20.4372.
134   Attested only once in MYS 14.3529.
135   Attested six times in the *Man'yōshū* book fourteen in the word *kapa* 'river' written as *KApa* (河泊).
136   Attested only in the *Man'yōshū* book fourteen and sixteen and in the *Azuma asobi uta*.

CHART 5   Man'yōgana phonograms used in Eastern Old Japanese (cont.)

Transcription	Man'yōgana signs
pi ひ₁	ongana: 比 必[137]
	kungana: 日
pï ひ₂	ongana: 非 斐[138] 悲[139]
pu ふ	ongana: 布 不[140] 敷[141]
pe へ₁	ongana: 敝 平[142] 弊[143] 弁[144]
	kungana: 部
pɛ へ₂	ongana: 倍 閇
po ほ	ongana: 保 抱[145] 富[146]
ᵐba ば	ongana: 婆
ᵐbi び₁	ongana: 妣 婢
ᵐbï び₂	ongana: 非[147]
ᵐbu ぶ	ongana: 夫 父[148] 部
ᵐbe べ₁	ongana: 辨 便 別 弊[149] 部[150]
ᵐbɛ べ₂	ongana: 倍
ᵐbo ぼ	—
ma ま	ongana: 麻 万[151] 萬 馬 末[152]
	kungana: 眞[153] 真[154] 目[155]
	disyllabic kungana: 座 [masa]

137 Attested only twice in MYS 14.3537a and 14.3563.
138 Attested only in the name of the province Kapï (甲斐).
139 Attested only once in MYS 14.3503.
140 Attested five times in MYS 20.4345, 20.4372, and 4389.
141 Attested twice in MYS 14.3516 and 14.3572.
142 Attested only once in MYS 16.3885 in the placename Peŋguri (平群).
143 Attested six times in MYS 20.4388, 20.4389, 20.4393, and 4415.
144 Attested four times in MYS 20.4429, 20.4431, and 20.4432.
145 Attested only in the Man'yōshū book fourteen.
146 Attested three times in MYS 20.4368, 20.4373, and 20.4382.
147 Attested only once in MYS 20.4348.
148 Attested only once in the placename Titiᵐbu (秩父) in the postscript to MYS 20.4414.
149 Attested only once in MYS 20.4364.
150 Attested only in personal names.
151 Attested only twice in MYS 14.3561 and 29.4352.
152 Attested mostly in the Man'yōshū book fourteen, but it also occurs in the book twenty and in AAU 2.
153 Occurs mostly in personal names.
154 Attested only once in MYS 14.3461.
155 Attested three times in FK 9, 14.3502, and 16.3880.

INTRODUCTION   25

CHART 5   Man'yōgana phonograms used in Eastern Old Japanese (cont.)

Transcription	Man'yōgana signs
mi み₁	ongana: 美 彌 弥
	kungana: 三[156]
mï み₂	ongana: 未[157]
	kungana: 身[158]
mu む	ongana: 牟 武 無[159] 无[160] 模[161]
me め₁	ongana: 賣 馬
	kungana: 女[162]
mɛ め₂	ongana: 米
mo も₁	ongana: 毛
mə も₂	ongana: 母
mo も	ongana: 聞[163] 物[164]
ya や	ongana: 夜 也
	kungana: 屋[165] 矢[166]
yi い[167]	ongana: 伊
yu ゆ	ongana: 由 遊[168]
	kungana: 弓[169]
ye え₂	ongana: 延 要 叡[170] 曳[171]
	kungana: 江[172]
yo よ₁	ongana: 欲 用[173]

156 Attested only in proper nouns.
157 Except one example in *Man'yōshū* book twenty all other attestations are in book fourteen.
158 Attested only once in a personal name in MYS 20.4322.
159 Attested three times in MYS 14.3530, 20.4327, and 4413.
160 Attested only twice in AAU 1.
161 Attested only in the placename Saⁿgamu (相模).
162 Attested only in personal names.
163 Attested in MYS 14.3384 and MYS 14.3395.
164 Attested in MYS 14.3418, 14.3434, and 14.3511.
165 Attested only once in 14.3378.
166 Attested only in proper nouns.
167 On the *i* : *yi* contrast see Vovin (2020.1: 49–54).
168 Attested only once in 14.3423.
169 Attested only once in 16.3885.
170 Attested only twice in FK 9 and MYS 20.4428.
171 Attested only twice in MYS 20.4321 and 20.4322.
172 Attested in 20.4340, 20.4345, and 20.4372 (twice).
173 Attested three times in MYS 20.4390, 20 4394, and 20.4431.

CHART 5   Man'yōgana phonograms used in Eastern Old Japanese (*cont.*)

Transcription	Man'yōgana signs
yə よ	ongana: 余 与 餘[174]
	kungana: 代
ra ら	ongana: 良 羅[175] 浪[176]
ri り	ongana: 里 利 理
ru る	ongana: 流 留
re れ	ongana: 礼 例
ro ろ₁	ongana: 路 漏[177]
rə ろ₂	ongana: 呂 里 侶[178]
wa わ	ongana: 和
wi ゐ	ongana: 爲[179]
	kungana: 井[180]
we ゑ	ongana: 惠[181]
wo を	ongana: 平 遠[182] 袁[183]
	kungana: 小[184] 男[185] 雄[186]

13   A Brief Sketch of EOJ Phonology and Morphology

Since EOJ represents a dialect continuum, it is difficult to provide an exact description of its phonology and morphology. The matter is further complicated by the fact that the language essentially uses the WOJ system of writing. There are two basic monographs dealing almost entirely with EOJ phonology: Fukuda (1965), and Hōjō (1966), cf. also quite an innovative article by Hino

---

174   Attested only twice in MYS 20.4383 and 20.4405.
175   Attested only once in MYS 14.3409.
176   Attested only once in MYS 20.4390.
177   Attested only once in FK 9.
178   Attested only once in MYS 20.4331.
179   Attested three times in MYS 20.4355, 20.4372, and 20.4393.
180   Attested only once in MYS 14.3398.
181   Attested only twice in MYS 20.4363 and 20.4385.
182   Attested only twice in MYS 14.3484 and 14.3500.
183   Attested only once in the place name Miwori (美袁利) in MYS 20.434.
184   Attested only in personal names in the *Man'yōshū* book twenty.
185   Attested only twice in MYS 16.3885 and 20.4402.
186   Attested only once in the MYS 16.3865.

(2003). The most painstaking research that attempts to describe phonologies of individual EOJ dialects separately, and not as phonology of a single language has been done by Kupchik in his recent Ph.D. dissertation (2011). An interested reader should consult this excellent dissertation for details, as here we only offer some general notes.

As becomes apparent from the usage of WOJ *man'yōgana* script in EOJ, there is no EOJ dialect that has the same vocalism that WOJ has, and all EOJ dialects present somewhat reduced vocalic systems in comparison to WOJ. It would probably be unwise to speak about the 'collapse' of *kō-otsu* distinctions in EOJ, and to use the word 'misspelling' in reference to the confusion between WOJ *kō* and *otsu* vowels in EOJ texts. Although we used 'misspelling' several times when paying tribute to the tradition in my commentary, it should be taken with a big pinch of salt. The truth is that WOJ and various EOJ vocalic systems have taken different paths of development from proto-Japanese, and there is simply no one-to-one correspondence system that accounts for all vowel correspondences between WOJ and various EOJ dialects. However, the very fact that all EOJ dialects exhibit less complicated vowel systems than WOJ might be at least partially attributed to the influence of the Ainu substratum, since modern Ainu dialects all have only five-vowel systems, and proto-Ainu probably had no more than six vowels, *pace* Vovin (1993), where much richer proto-Ainu vocalism was proposed.

There are, however, several phonological and morphophonological phenomena that seem to be common to all or most EOJ dialects. They are briefly outlined below, and the examples cited are not necessarily exhaustive. Some examples, in fact, are cited from book twenty since they are not attested in book fourteen.

First, there is a mysterious correspondence of EOJ -*n*- to WOJ -*r*- in few forms: EOJ diminutive suffix -*na* (14.3384, 14.3385, 14.3402, 14.3436, 14.3444, 14.3446, 14.3483, 14.3544, 20.4358, 20.4416, 20.4422, 20.4424, 20.4426, 20.4428) vs. WOJ -*ra*, id., EOJ tentative -*unam*- (14.3366, 14.3476, 14.3496, 14.3526, 14.3552, 14.3563, 20.4390, 20.4391) vs. WOJ -*uram*-, id., EOJ *yun*- 'to sleep' (14.3476a) vs. late MJ *o-yor*- 'id.', and EOJ *noⁿgan-ape*- 'to flow constantly' (14.3476, 14.3476a) vs. WOJ *naⁿgar-apɛ*- 'id.'

Second, palatalization of *ti* > *si*, unknown in WOJ. Examples: EOJ *tas-i* 'rise and', 'depart-NML' (14.3395, 20.4372, 20.4383, 20.4423) vs. WOJ *tat-i* 'id.', *məs-i* 'hold and' (20.4415, 20.4420) vs. WOJ *mət-i* 'id.', EOJ *peⁿdas-i* 'separation' (14.3445) vs. WOJ *peⁿdat-i* 'id.', EOJ *iⁿdusi* 'where to' (14.3474) vs. WOJ *iⁿduti* 'id.', EOJ *tusi* 'earth' (20.4392, 20.4426) vs. WOJ *tuti* 'id.', EOJ *sisi* 'father' (20.4376) vs. WOJ *titi* 'id.', EOJ *tasi* 'long sword' (20.4413) vs. WOJ *tati* 'id.', EOJ *kasi* 'walking' (20.4417) vs. WOJ *kati* 'id.'

Third, following terminology proposed in Russell (2006), EOJ undergoes the process of contraction vs. the WOJ process of monophtongization. This can be best illustrated by their respective progressive and retrospective forms. While the PJN *i+a contracts to just -*a*- in EOJ at morphemic boundaries, it results in a new vowel -*e*- in WOJ. Examples: EOJ -*ar*-, progressive (14.3351 (twice), 14.3469, 14.3526, 20.4359, 20.4375, 20.4387, 20.4431) vs. WOJ -*er*-, id.; EOJ -*kar*-, retrospective (20.4388) vs. WOJ -*ker*-, id.

Fourth, EOJ consistently loses the final consonant *-y both in final position and before the next consonant, while WOJ undergoes the process of monophtongization, treating this final *-y as an element of a falling diphthong. Examples: EOJ *tuku* 'moon' (14.3395, 14.3476, 14.3476a, 14.3565, 20.4378, 20.4413) < PJN *tukuy vs. WOJ *tukï* 'id.', EOJ *pu* 'fire' (20.4419) < PJN *poy vs. WOJ *pï* 'id.', EOJ *kaⁿgə* 'reflection' (20.4322) < PJ *kankay vs. WOJ *kaⁿgɛ* 'id.', EOJ *koyə-* 'to cross' (20.4403) < PJN *koyay- vs. WOJ *koye-*, EOJ *sasaⁿgə-* (20.4325) 'to lift in one's hands' < PJ *sasaⁿgay- vs. WOJ *sasaⁿgɛ-* 'id.'

Fifth, while WOJ seems to preserve primary PJ vowels *e and *o in the last syllable of a nominal root according to Hayata's law (Hayata 1998), EOJ seems to behave quite erratically in this respect. On one hand, it seems to preserve quite well primary PJ vowels *e and *o in EOJ adjectival attributive -*ke* and verbal attributive -*o*, as well as possibly in some non-last syllables, but on the other hand it undergoes clear raising of *o > u and *e > i[187] in the final syllables of nominal roots, like EOJ *kumu* 'cloud' (20.4403) vs. WOJ *kumo* 'id.', EOJ *imu* 'younger sister, beloved' (20.4321) vs. WOJ *imo* 'id.' EOJ *yu* 'night' (20.4369) vs. WOJ *yo* 'id.', EOJ *kaⁿdu* 'gate' (20.4386) vs. WOJ *kaⁿdo* 'id.', EOJ *ipi* 'house' (20.4343) vs. WOJ *ipe* 'id.', EOJ *mi* 'wife' (20.4343) vs. WOJ *me* 'id.', EOJ *naⁿgati* 'length' (20.4341) vs. WOJ *naⁿgate* 'length'.

The brief sketch of EOJ morphology is not comprehensive either, and its sole purpose is to assist the reader who is only familiar with WOJ and/or MJ with the peculiarities of EOJ. A reader who is interested in more details should consult Kupchik (2011), and/or Vovin (2020.1, 2020.2). The references to the latter can be found throughout the commentary.

EOJ nouns do not show the alternation between compounding and free forms of nouns like WOJ. The attested forms in phonographic writing correspond to WOJ compounding forms, like EOJ *tuku* 'moon' (14.3395, 14.3476, 14.3476a, 14.3565, 20.4413) < PJN *tukuy vs. WOJ *tukï ~ tuku-* 'id.', EOJ *pu* 'fire' (20.4419) < PJN *poy vs. WOJ *pï ~ po-* 'id.', with an EOJ form always corresponding to WOJ compounding form. The explanation for this phenomenon was given above in the discussion on morphophonology.

---

187 Including cases of the secondary *e < *ia.

The case system of EOJ includes two case markers: locative -*na* (14.3408, 14.3447, 14.3461, 14.3487, 20.4407), not attested in WOJ, and comparative -*nəsu* (14.3413, 14.3424, 14.3514, 14.3525, 14.3541, 14.3552, 14.3561, 20.4415), that has only one dubious attestation in WOJ. Both case markers, therefore, should be recognized as EOJ specific.

EOJ diminutive suffix -*na* (14.3384, 14.3385, 14.3402, 14.3436, 14.3444, 14.3446, 14.3483, 14.3544, 20.4358, 20.4416, 20.4422, 20.4424, 20.4426, 20.4428) corresponding to WOJ -*ra*, id., was discussed above.

EOJ diminutive suffix -*rə* (14.3351, 14.3361, 14.3369, 14.3370, etc., multiple occurrences), seems to be a predominantly EOJ form, because among two WOJ examples of this suffix cited in Vovin (2005: 210), one comes from an EOJ text (FK 3), and the other one (NK 3) seems to invite different explanations. See the commentary to 14.3351 for more details.

A peculiar phonetic form of the first person pronoun *wanu* (14.3476, 14.3476a) or *wano* (20.4358) corresponding to WOJ *wa*[-] ~ *waN*- is attested in EOJ. There is also EOJ *warə* 'I' (20.4343) corresponding to WOJ *ware* 'id.'

EOJ adjectival attributive suffix -*ke* (14.3412, 14.3483, 14.3500, 14.3517, 14.3533, 14.3548, 14.3551, 14.3557, 14.3564, 14.3576, 20.4369), also spelled -*kɛ* (20.4376, 20.4382, 20.4394, 20.4414) corresponds to the WOJ adjectival attributive suffix -*ki*. EOJ form preserves PJN primary *e, while WOJ undergoes the process of raising *e > *i*.

EOJ adjectival evidential suffix -*ka*-[188] (14.3473, 14.3539, 20.4421) corresponds to WOJ -*ke*-, exhibiting the same vowel correspondence EOJ *a* : WOJ *e* as in EOJ progressive suffix -*ar*- vs. WOJ -*er*- and EOJ retrospective suffix -*kar*- vs. WOJ -*ker*-. Care must be taken not to confuse it with the EOJ -*k*-, a contracted form of the adjectival attributive suffix -*ke*-, found exclusively before the conditional gerund suffix -*a*ᵐ*ba* in the form -*k*-*a*ᵐ*ba* (14.3383, 14.3410).

EOJ has a peculiar form of a verbal negative suffix, -(*a*)*na*- (14.3407, 14.3436, 14.3461, 14.3487, 14.3557), corresponding to WOJ -(*a*)*n*-.

EOJ has a different order for the combination of iterative and negative suffixes: while in WOJ the iterative precedes the negative (-*ap-an*-), it is opposite in EOJ, where negative precedes the iterative: -(*a*)*n-ap*- (14.3375, 14.3426, 14.3444, 14.3482a, 14.3516, 14.3524, 20.4378).

EOJ has a special verbal attributive form in -*o* (14.3395, 14.3414, 14.3423, 13.3426, 14.3431, 14.3461, 14.3469 (twice), 14.3472, 14.3473, 14.3476 (twice), 14.3476a (twice), 14.3480, 14.3494, 14.3509, 14.3516, 14.3525, 14.3527 (twice), 14.3541, 14.3546, 14.3561, 14.3563, 16.3885, 20.4329, 20.4341, 20.4344, 20.4352, 20.4355, 20.4356, 20.4359, 20.4383, 20.4385, 20.4389, 20.4401, 20.4403, 20.4406,

---

188 Attested only with the following concessive gerund suffix -ⁿ*də*[*mə*].

20.4421, 20.4422, 20.4423), which sometimes is also spelled as -ə (14.3405, 14.3418, 14.3526, 14.3552, 20.4367, 20.4415, 20.4418). It is traditionally believed that EOJ verbal attributive suffix -o ~ -ə appears in many cases after consonantal verbs, r-irregular verbs, and progressive -ar- (Saeki 1959: 43). This formulation, however, is not completely accurate. We present below the chart where all the occurrences of the EOJ attributive suffix -o ~ -ə in the corpus are documented on the basis of their appearance after preceding morphemes.

CHART 6   Distribution of EOJ attributive verbal suffix -o

Preceding morphemes	Variant -o	Variant -ə
Consonantal verb root	14.3423, 14.3431, 14.3476, 14.3476a, 14.3525, 14.3527, 14.3541, 14.3561 (twice), 20.4352, 20.4385, 20.4389, 20.4421	
Tentative -(a)m-	14.3426, 14.3472, 14.3473, 14.3494, 14.3516, 20.4329, 20.4355, 20.4359, 20.4406, 20.4422, 20.4423	FK 7, 14.3405, 14.3418, 20.4367, 20.4415, 20.4418
Tentative -unam-	14.3476, 14.3476a, 14.3563	14.3526, 14.3552
Negative -an-	14.3469, 20.4341, 20.4344, 20.4356	
r-irregular verb root	14.3509	
Progressive -ar-	14.3469, 14.3546	
Vowel verb root arapare-	14.3414	
Perfective -n-	14.3395, 14.3461, 14.3486, 14.3527, 16.3885, 20.4401, 20.4403	

The chart above illustrates several important points. First, the only variation between variants -o and -ə occurs after the consonant /m/. But it is well known that the contrast between kō-rui syllable mo and otsu-rui syllable mə is lost in the Man'yōshū except statistically in book five (Bentley 1997). Given this as well as the fact that EOJ texts are written in WOJ orthography, we can safely conclude that there was no morphophonemic distinction between EOJ -o and -ə for the attributive form. In all likelihood, this form was just [o], although naturally we have no means of asserting the exact phonetic value.

Second, it becomes apparent that the EOJ verbal attributive suffix *-o* was much more widespread in its distribution as compared to its narrower distribution outlined in the traditional Japanese approach above. The evidence presented above strongly suggests that once this suffix could be found across the board in verbal paradigms, including vowel verbs. As a matter of fact, the WOJ vowel verb attributive suffix *-uru* can be an innovation, going back to a stative *-ur- + attributive *-u*, derived from *-o* by progressive assimilation (*-ur-o > *-uru*) as proposed in Russell (2006).[189]

There is also another EOJ attributive in *-a* that occurs much less frequently (14.3408, 14.3461, 14.3487, 14.3526, 14.3557, 20.4418, 20.4422, 20.4428).

The EOJ progressive *-ar-* and the retrospective *-kar-* have already been commented upon above in the discussion of EOJ morphophonology.

14   EOJ Specific Vocabulary

Below, we provide a list of all specific vocabulary items that occur in EOJ texts with the major exception of Ainu loanwords that are treated separately in the next section. Words that have differences with WOJ only in *kō-otsu* distinctions and placenames are excluded. WOJ or MJ cognates for EOJ words, if any, are also cited below.

– *a* 'foot, leg'. Cf. WOJ, *asi, a-* (in compounds only) 'id.' Attested in: 14.3387, 14.3533.
– *ama* 'mother'. Cf. WOJ *omə, amə* (attested only once) 'id.' Attested in: 20.4376, 20.4377, 20.4378, 20.4383.
– *aN-* 'what, why'. Cf. WOJ *nani* 'id.' Attested in: 14.3379, 14.3397, 14.3404, 14.3464, 14.3556, 14.3564.
– *aⁿze* 'why'. Cf. WOJ *naⁿzə* 'id.' Attested in: 14.3369, 14.3434, 14.3461, 14.3469, 14.3472, 14.3513, 14.3517, 14.3576.
– *atəri* 'brambling'. Cf. MJ *atori* 'id.' Attested in: 20.4339.
– *ikuⁿduk-* 'to catch one's breath, to breathe with difficulty'. Cf. WOJ *ikiⁿduk-* 'id.' Attested in: 14.3458.
– *ikiⁿdukusi* 'to be regrettable, to be lamentable'. Cf. WOJ *ikiⁿdukasi* 'id.' Attested in: 20.4421.
– *imɛ* 'beloved, wife'. Cf. WOJ *imo* 'id.' Attested in: 20.4345. See also *imu*.
– *imu* 'beloved, wife'. Cf. WOJ *imo* 'id.' Attested in: 20.4321, 20.4364. See also *imɛ*.

---

189   Another, even more attractive idea, recently proposed by Frellesvig and Whitman is that *-uru* at least in *nidan* conjugation may reflect the suffixed forms of OJ *e-* < **ay-* 'to get'.

- iⁿdusi 'where'. Cf. woj iⁿduti 'id.' Attested in: 14.3474.
- ipa 'house'. Cf. woj ipe 'id.' Attested in: 20.4375, 20.4406, 20.4416, 20.4419, 20.4423, 20.4427. See also ipi.
- ipi 'house'. Cf. woj ipe 'id.' Attested in: 20.4343. See also ipa.
- ituma 'free time'. Cf. woj itoma 'id.' Attested in: 20.4327.
- iyaⁿzeru 'excellent', 'well noticeable' (?). No woj cognates. Attested in: FK 7.
- kama 'wild duck'. Cf. woj kamo 'id.' Attested in: 20.4339. Cf. also EOJ kama 'id.'
- kamu, emphatic particle. Cf. woj kamə 'id.' Attested in: 20.4403.
- kaᵑgə 'reflection'. Cf. woj kaᵑgɛ 'id.' Attested in: 20.4322.
- kaⁿdunəkï 'paper mulberry tree'. Cf. woj kaⁿdi 'id.' Attested in: 14.3431, 14.3432.
- kaⁿdus- 'to abduct' (?). No woj cognates. Attested in: 14.3432.
- kapir- 'to return'. Cf. woj kaper- 'id.' Attested in: 20.4339.
- kaye 'generic name for reeds and grasses used to thatch roofs of houses'. Cf. woj kaya 'id.' Attested in: 20.4321.
- kayup- 'to go back and forth'. Cf. woj kayop- 'id.' Attested in 20.4324.
- ke- 'to come'. Cf. woj kə- 'id.' Attested in 20.4337.
- kekere 'heart'. cf. woj kəkərə 'id.' Attested in: KKWKS 1097.
- kɛ 'tree'. Cf. woj kï 'id.' Attested in: 20.4342, 20.4375.
- kɛmɛ 'mat made from wild rice straw'. Cf. woj kəmə 'id.' Attested in 20.4338.
- kɛri 'lapwing'. Cf. EMDJ keri 'id.' Attested in 20.4339.
- kɛtəᵐba 'word'. Cf. woj kətəᵐba 'id.' Attested in: 20.4346.
- kopusi 'be longing for, be missing (someone)'. Cf. woj koposi ~kopïsi 'id.' Attested in: 14.3476, 20.4419. See also kupusi.
- koyə- 'to cross'. Cf. woj koye- 'id.' Attested in: 20.4403.
- kəmo 'wild duck'. Cf. woj kamo 'id.' Attested in 20.4354. Cf. also EOJ kama 'id.'
- kəᵑgətə 'many'. Cf. woj kəkəⁿda 'id.' Attested in: 14.3502.
- kərəmu 'garment'. Cf. woj kərəmə 'id.' Attested in: 20.4401.
- kətu '[wooden] debris, trash'. Cf. woj kətumi 'id.' Attested in: 14.3548.
- kumu 'cloud'. Cf. woj kumo 'id.' Attested in: 20.4403.
- kupe 'fence'. No woj cognates. Attested in: 14.3537.
- kupusi 'be longing for, be missing (someone)'. Cf. woj koposi ~ kopïsi 'id.' Attested in: 20.4345. See also kopusi.
- kuye- 'to cross over'. Cf. woj koye- 'id.' Attested in: 20.4372 (twice).
- mama 'cliff'. No woj cognates. Cf. Hachijō mama 'id.' Attested in: 14.3349, 14.3369, 14.3384, 14.3385, 14.3387.
- mɛ, focus particle. Cf. woj mə 'id.' Attested in: FK 9, 20.4345.
- mɛt- 'to hold'. Cf. woj mət- 'id.' Attested in: 20.4343. See also məs-.
- mi 'wife'. Cf. woj me 'id.' Attested in: 20.4343.

- *miⁿdaye-* 'to be in disorder'. Cf. WOJ *miⁿdare-* 'id.' Attested in: 14.3563.
- *miⁿdo* 'water'. Cf. WOJ *miⁿdu* 'id.' Attested in: 14.3546.
- *mita* 'with'. Cf. WOJ *muta* 'id.' Attested in: 20.4394.
- *məs-* 'to hold'. Cf. WOJ *mət-* 'id.' Attested in: 20.4415, 20.4420. See also *mɛt-*.
- *muranapɛ-* 'to perform divination'. Cf. WOJ *uranap(ɛ)-* 'id.', MJ *uranape-* 'id.' Attested in: 14.3418. The correspondence EOJ *m-* : MJ *o-* is irregular; cf. *ura* 'multitude' for a reverse correspondence.
- *namï-* 'to lick, to taste'. Cf. WOJ *namɛ-* 'id.' Attested in: 14.3460.
- *naⁿgati* 'length'. Cf. WOJ *naⁿgate* 'id.' Attested in: 20.4341.
- *nayum-* 'to suffer'. Cf. WOJ *nayam-* 'id.' Attested in: 14.3533.
- *nino* 'cloth'. Cf. MJ *nuno* 'id.' Attested in: 14.3351, 14.3513.
- *nipasi* 'to be sudden'. Cf. WOJ *nipaka* 'sudden'. Attested in: 20.4389.
- *nipu* 'new'. Cf. WOJ *nipi* 'id.' Attested in: 14.3460. The vowel correspondence in the second syllable is puzzling, but it could potentially point to PJ *mipoy 'new' (initial *m- reconstructed on the basis of Ryūkyūan data).
- *noⁿgan-ape-* 'to flow constantly'. Cf. WOJ *naⁿgar-apɛ-* 'to flow constantly, to pass [of time]'. Attested in: 14.3476, 14.3476a.
- *noⁿzi* 'rainbow'. Cf. WOJ *niⁿzi* 'id.' Attested in: 14.3414.
- *nət-* 'to fill'. No apparent WOJ cognates (cf. WOJ *mit-* 'id.'[190]). Attested in: 14.3444.
- *ⁿze*, focus particle. Cf. WOJ *sə ~ ⁿzə* 'id.' Attested in: 20.4346.
- *omɛ* 'face'. Cf. WOJ *omə* 'id.' Attested in: 20.4342.
- *omɛp-* 'to think'. Cf. WOJ *oməp-* 'id.' Attested in: 20.4343.
- *opuse-* 'to speak (HON)'. Cf. WOJ *opose-* 'id.' Attested in: 20.4389.
- *osi* 'rock, rocky shore'. Cf. WOJ *isi* 'stone', *iso* 'rock, rocky shore'. Attested in: 14.3359.
- *osu* 'rock, rocky shore'. Cf. WOJ *iso* 'rock, rocky shore'. Attested in: 14.3385.
- *otap-* 'to sing'. Cf. WOJ *utap-* 'id.' Attested in: 14.3409, 14.3518.
- *panar-* 'to be separated'. Cf. WOJ *panare-*. Attested in: 20.4414.
- *panar-iso* 'rocks in the sea not connected to the shore'. Cf. WOJ *panare-so* 'id.' Attested in: 20.4338.
- *paru* 'needle'. Cf. WOJ *pari* 'id.' Attested in: 20.4420.
- *pe* 'leaf'. Cf. WOJ *pa* 'id.' Attested in: 14.3456.
- *peⁿdas-* 'to be separated'. Cf. WOJ *peⁿdat-* 'id.' Attested in: 14.3445.
- *pirəp-* 'to pick up'. Cf. WOJ *pirip-*. Attested in: 14.3400.
- *pita* 'one'. Cf. WOJ *pitə* 'id.' Attested in: 14.3435.
- *pu* 'fire'. Cf. WOJ *pï ~ po-* 'id.' Attested in: 20.4419.
- *pususa* 'many'. No WOJ cognates. Attested in: 14.3484.

---

190 Although the palatalization *m- > n-/_i* is possible, the vowel shift *i > ə* remains unexplained.

- *sake-ku* 'safely'. Cf. woj *saki-ku* 'id.' Attested in: 20.4372. Cf. also eoj *sa-ku*, *sakɛ-ku*.
- *sakɛ-ku* 'safely'. Cf. woj *saki-ku* 'id.' Attested in: 20.4368. Cf. also eoj *sa-ku*, *sake-ku*.
- *sakimuri* 'borderguard'. Cf. woj *sakimori (misspelled as *sakiməri*) 'id.' Attested in: 20.4364.
- *sa-ku* 'safely'. Cf. woj *saki-ku* 'id.' Attested in: 20.4346. Cf. also eoj *sakɛ-ku*, *sake-ku*.
- *sasaᵑgə-* 'to lift up high in one's hands'. Cf. woj *sasaᵑgɛ-* 'id.' Attested in: 20.4325.
- *sawe-sawe* 'hustle and bustle'. Cf. woj *sawi-sawi* 'id.' Attested in: 14.3481.
- *se* 'clear'. Cf. woj *si* 'id.' Attested in: 14.3546.
- *ser-* 'to bend'. Cf. mj *sor-* 'id.' Attested in: 14.3437.
- *si-* 'to do'. Cf. woj *se-* 'id.' Attested in: 14.3556.
- *siko* 'repugnant'. Cf. woj *sikə* 'id.' Attested in: fk 5.
- *sisi* 'father'. Cf. woj *titi* 'id.' Attested in: 20.4376, 20.4378. See also *təti*.
- *siru* 'behind'. Cf. woj *siri* 'id.' Attested in: 20.4385.
- *siru* 'white'. Cf. woj *siro* 'id.' Attested in: 20.4324.
- *səwape*, meaning unknown. No woj cognates. Attested in: 14.3566.
- *suᵑgos-* 'to pass'. Cf. woj *suᵑgus-* 'id.' Attested in: 14.3564.
- *tas-* 'to rise', 'to depart', 'to stand'. Cf. woj *tat-* 'id.' Attested in: 14.3395, 20.4372, 20.4383, 20.4423.
- *tasi* 'long sword'. Cf. woj *tati* 'id.' Attested in: 20.4413.
- *tayor-* ~ *tayur-* 'to cease'. Cf. woj *taye-* 'to break, to stop, to cease'. Attested in: 14.3368, 14.3392.
- *te*, quotation verb 'to say, to think'. Cf. woj *tə* 'id.' Attested in: 20.4344, 20.4346.
- *tor-* 'to shine'. Cf. woj *ter-* 'id.' Attested in: 14.3561.
- *tə*, focus particle. Cf. woj *sə* 'id.' Attested in: 14.3409, 14.3425, 14.3561, 20.4385, 20.4430.
- *təme* 'old woman'. Cf. woj *tome* 'id.' Attested in: fk 5.
- *tənəᵐbik-* 'to trail'. Cf. woj *tanaᵐbik-* 'id.' Attested in: 20.4403.
- *təti* 'father'. Cf. woj *titi* 'id.' Attested in: 20.4340. See also *sisi*.
- *təwerap-* 'to surge, to swell (of waves)'. Cf. woj *təworap-* 'to rock (of boats on the top of waves)'. Attested in: 20.4385.
- *tuᵑgi-* 'to report'. Cf. woj *tuᵑgɛ-* 'id.' Attested in 20.4365.
- *tuku* 'moon'. Cf. woj *tukï* 'id.' Attested in: 14.3395, 14.3476, 14.3476a, 14.3565, 20.4378, 20.4413.
- *tusi* 'earth'. Cf. woj *tuti* 'id.' Attested in: 20.4392, 20.4426.
- *ukera* 'ukera flower'. Cf. mj *wokera* 'id.' Attested in: 14.3376, 14.3376a, 14.3379, 14.3503.

- unəpara 'sea plain'. Cf. WOJ unapara 'id.' Attested in: 20.4328.
- ura 'multitude'. Cf. WOJ mura 'id.', but the correspondence EOJ o- : WOJ m- is irregular; cf. muranapɛ- 'to perform divination' for a reverse correspondence. Attested in: 14.3352.
- yaⁿde 'branch'. Cf. WOJ ye, yeⁿda 'id.' Attested in: 14.3493.
- ye, emphatic particle. Cf. WOJ yə 'id.' Attested in: 20.4340.
- ye- to be good'. Cf. WOJ yə- 'id.' Attested in: 14.3509, 14.3530.
- yese- 'to approach'. Cf. WOJ yəse- 'id.' Attested in: 20.4346.
- yəki 'snow'. Cf. WOJ yuki 'id.' Attested in: 14.3523.
- yəsar- 'to be attracted, to give one's heart'. Cf. WOJ yəsər- 'id.' Attested in: 14.3478.
- yuru 'lily'. Cf. WOJ yuri 'id.' Attested in: 20.4369.
- yun- 'to sleep'. Cf. late MJ o-yor- 'id.' Attested in: 14.3473, 14.3476a.
- wanu 'I'. Cf. WOJ wa[-] ~ waN- 'id.' Attested in: 14.3476, 14.3476a.
- wano 'I'. Cf. WOJ wa[-] ~ waN- 'id.' Attested in: 20.4358.
- warə 'I'. Cf. WOJ ware 'I, we'. Attested in: 20.4343.
- wosa^ŋgi 'hare'. Cf. WOJ usa^ŋgi 'id.' Attested in: 3529.

15   Ainu Loans in EOJ of Books Fourteen and Twenty

Here we present all Ainu loans that can be found in books fourteen and twenty, both in placenames and as independent words or suffixes. All cases of placenames of Ainu origin are indicated below as (p.n.). The absence of such a reference indicates that a loan is attested as an independent word or suffix, and not as a placename. The reader should be aware that due to the fact that Ainu is a polysynthetic language, many EOJ loanwords from Ainu are in fact compounds or complex morphological derivations in Ainu. Also, the reader is advised to look at the more detailed explanation of etymologies in the commentary to the first poem where a given Ainu loanword is attested.
- Akina (p.n.) < Ainu ay-kina 'arrow grass'. Attested in: 14.3431.
- aⁿzu 'crumbling cliff' < ? Ainu *-as- 'to split' + so 'rocky shore', 'hidden rocks in the sea'. Attested in: 14.3539, 14.3541.
- Aⁿdikama (p.n.) < Ainu: anci 'obsidian' + kama 'flat rock, rock'. Attested in: 14.3551, 14.3553.
- Asika^ŋga (p.n.) < Ainu askan(-ne) '(be) beautiful' + kat 'view, appearance'. Attested in: 20.4379.[191]

---

[191] It would be ironic if the family name of the Ashikaga shoguns might be also of Ainu provenance.

- Asiⁿgara ~ Asiⁿgari (p.n.) < Ainu *askar-i* 'clear place'. Attested in: 14.3361, 14.3363, 14.3368, 14.3369, 14. 3370, 14.3371, 14.3431, 14.3432.
- *atu-* 'sea' < Ainu *atuy* 'id.' Attested in: 14.3503.
- *i-*, nominal prefix 'thing-' < Ainu *i-* 'id.' Attested in: 20.4428.
- *i-*, indirect object prefix < Ainu *e-* 'id.' Attested in: 20.4430.
- *ka* 'top' < Ainu *ka* 'id.' Attested in: 14.3409, 14.3503, 14.3518.
- *ka* 'voice' < Ainu *háw* 'id.' Attested in: 20.4430.
- *kariᵐba* 'sakura' < Ainu *karinpa* 'sakura [bark]'. Attested in: 14.3399.
- Inasa (p.n.) < Ainu *inaw-san* 'the place where *inaw* [are offered]'. Attested in: 14.3429.
- *ka*, focus particle < Ainu *ka* 'id.' Attested in: 14.3361,[192] 14.4386.
- Kake (p.n.) < Ainu *ka-kes* 'upper end'. Attested in: 14.3553.
- Kanipa (p.n.) < Ainu *ka-ne-pa* 'upper bank' (lit. 'top-COP-bank'). Attested in 20.4456. This place name occurs in a WOJ poem.
- Kaⁿdusika (p.n.) < Ainu *ka-n-toska* < *ka-ne-toska top-COP-low.cliffs 'low cliffs that are above'. Attested in: 14.3349, 14.3350, 14.3384, 14.3385, 14.3386, 14.3387.
- Kiᵐbɛ (p.n.) < Ainu *kimpe* 'bear' (< *kim-pe* 'mountain thing'). Attested in: 14.3354.
- *kəⁿdək-* 'to bless with words' < Ainu *ko-itak* 'to speak to, to address words to' (normally contracted to *koytak*). Attested in: 14.3506.
- Kuⁿzi (p.n.) < Ainu *kus* 'to overflow'. Attested in: 20.4368.
- *mak-i* 'back-POSS' < Ainu *mak* 'back' + 3rd person possessive suffix *-i*. Attested in: 20.4413.
- *ma* 'wife' < Ainu *mat* 'woman, wife'. Attested in: 14.3502.
- *mato* 'girl' < Ainu *mat-po* 'girl' (< *mat* 'woman, wife', *po* 'child'). Attested in: 14.3407.
- Muⁿza (p.n.) < Ainu *mun* 'unedible grass' + *sa* 'shore, plain'. Attested in: 20.4355. See also Muⁿzasi.
- Muⁿzasi (p.n.) < Ainu *mun* 'unedible grass'[193] + *sa* 'shore, plain' + *-hi* third person singular possessive. i.e. 'grass plain' or 'grass shore'. Attested in: 14.3362a, 14.3374, 14.3375, 14.3376, 14.3376a, 14.3377, 14.3379. See also Muⁿza.
- *na* 'river' < Ainu *nay* 'id.' Attested in: 14.3401.
- Nipɛ (p.n.) < Ainu *nipet* 'wood river' (*ni* 'tree, wood' + *pet* 'river'). Attested in 20.4324.

---

192 Disregard the commentary to 14.3361 and refer to the commentary to 20.4430.
193 Ainu strictly differentiates between two types of grass: *kina* 'edible grass' and *mun* 'unedible grass'.

INTRODUCTION 37

- Nipu (p.n.) < Ainu placename Nipu 'storage in the forest on the river bank for storing frozen salmon' (< *ni* 'tree' + *pu* 'storage'). Attested in: 14.3560.
- *o-*, locative prefix < Ainu *o-* 'id.' Attested in 14.3473.
- *or-ə* 'its place' < Ainu *or-o* 'place-POSS'. Attested in: 20.4363.
- *pa* 'year' < Ainu *pa* 'id.' Attested in: 20.4378.
- *pa* 'to find' < Ainu *pa* 'id.' Attested in: 14.3499.
- *paka* 'rumor, gossip' < Ainu *páhaw* 'id.' Attested in: 14.3385.
- *pirə* 'oak' < Ainu *pero* or *pero-ni* 'id.' Attested in: 14.3538.
- *piⁿzi* 'sandbank' < Ainu *pis* 'shore', *pis-i* 'its shore'. Attested in: 14.3448.
- Pita (p.n.) < Ainu *pitar* 'stone field' < *pit-tar* 'pebbles-continue one after another'. Attested in: 14.3563.
- Puⁿzi (p.n.) < Ainu *pun-* 'to raise' + *sir* 'ground, place, mountain'. Attested in: 14.3355, 14.3356, 14.3357, 14.3358, 14.3358b.[194]
- Sinanu (p.n.) < Ainu *sinam* (< *sir-nam*) 'to be cold' + *nup* 'mountain field'. Attested in: 14.3352, 14.3399, 14.3400.
- *siⁿda* 'time, when' < Ainu *hi* 'time, occasion' + *ta*, locative case marker. Attested in: 14.3363, 14.3461, 14.3478, 14.3515, 14.3520, 14.3533, 20.4367, 20.4407.
- Sirupa (p.n.) < Ainu *sirpa* 'cape' (*sir* 'land' + *pa* 'head'). Attested in: 20.4324.
- *səmə* 'not' < Ainu *somo* 'id.' Attested in: 14.3382.
- *su* 'again' < Ainu *suy* 'id.' Attested in: 14.3363, 14.3487, 14.3564.
- *suⁿgu-* 'to grow old' < Ainu *sukup* 'id.' Attested in: 20.4378.
- *ta* 'here' < Ainu *ta* 'this, here'. Attested in: 20.4386.
- Tayupi (p.n.) < Ainu *tay-yúpe* 'dead shark' (*tay*[195] 'die' + *yúpe* 'shark'). Attested in: 14.3549.
- *teⁿgo* 'maiden, beloved' < Ainu *tek* 'hand, arm' + *o* 'take in, embrace'. Attested in: 14.3384, 14.3385, 14.3398, 14.3442, 14.3477, 14.3485, 14.3540.
- *tora* 'together' < Ainu *tura* 'id.' Attested in: 14.3409, 14.3561.
- Təya (p.n.) < Ainu *to-ya* 'lake shore' (*to* 'lake' + *ya* 'shore, dry land'). Attested in: 14.3529.
- Tukupa (p.n.) < Ainu *tuk* 'small mountain' + *pa* 'head, top'. Attested in: FK 2, FK 3, 14.3350, 14.3351, 14.3388, 14.3389, 14.3390, 14.3391, 14.3392, 14.3393, 14.3394, 14.3395, 14.3396, 20.4367, 20.4369, 20.4371.

---

[194] This etymology for Mt. Fuji (OJ *puⁿzi*) was provided in the introduction to book fourteen (Vovin 2012: 12). However, now I think that there is a better EOJ etymology: EOJ *pu* 'fire' (20.4419) + *-ⁿzi* < *-nusi* 'master', i.e. 'master of the fire'. The details of argumentation are published in Vovin (2018c).

[195] *tay* is a Sakhalin Ainu form corresponding to *ray* in Hokkaidō Ainu. Both reflect PA *δay.

- Tumu (p.n.) < Ainu *tum* 'middle (of water, land, or grassy area'). Attested in: 14.3438.
- *-y-*, indefinite direct object prefix < Ainu *i-* 'id.' Attested in: 14.3526, 20.4427.
- *ya* 'shore' < Ainu *ya* 'shore, dry land'. Attested in: 14.3562.
- Yupuma (p.n.) < Ainu *yup(u) 'strong' + *maw* 'wind', i.e., '[the mountain of] strong winds'. Attested in: 14.3475.

16 Opotəmə-nə Yakaməti Criteria for Not Including Certain *sakimori* Poems

It is quite apparent that in his collection of *sakimori* poems from different provinces, Opotəmə-nə Yakaməti was very selective in including poems in the *Man'yōshū*. Sometimes he left out more than 50% of poems from a given province, with quite a ubiquitous phrase noting: 但拙劣歌者不取載之 "However, [I] did not include [here] the poems of inferior [quality]". One can only wonder as to what he meant by 'inferior [quality]'. Differences between the EOJ poems in books fourteen and twenty can be summarized in the following chart:

CHART 7 WOJ vs. EOJ differences in Eastern poems

	Comprehension level with WOJ	EOJ	Ainu loans
MYS 14	+/–	many	many
MYS 20	+	average	very few

In short, in contrast to book fourteen, there are no poems in book twenty that are partially incomprehensible or poems with heavy dialect features. Consequently, it appears that Opotəmə-nə Yakaməti might have excluded all the poems that have strong EOJ features, or those poems that may not be comprehensible even to him. Thus, the poems from book twenty are likely to represent a more 'polished' form of EOJ that was more palatable to the speakers of WOJ, but far less authentic than the poems from book fourteen.

PART 1

Eastern Old Japanese Corpus

∵

CHAPTER 1

常陸風土記歌謡 • *Hitachi Fudoki* Poems

FK 2

本文 • *Original Text*
(1) 都久波尼爾 (2) 阿波牟等 (3) 伊比志古波 (4) 多賀己等岐氣波加 (5) 彌尼阿波須氣牟

仮名の書き下し • *Kana Transliteration*
(1) つくはねに (2) あはむと₂ (3) いひ₁しこ₁は (4) たがこ₂と₂き₁け₂ばか (5) み₁ねあはずけ₂む₂

Romanization
(1) Tukupa ne-ni (2) ap-am-u tə (3) ip-i-si ko pa (4) ta-ⁿga kətə kik-ɛ-ᵐba ka (5) mi-ne ap-aⁿz-u-kɛm-u

Glossing with Morphemic Analysis
(1) Tukupa peak-LOC (2) meet-TENT-FIN QV (3) say-CONV-PAST.ATTR girl TOP (4) who-POSS word listen-EV-CON IP (5) HON-peak/sleep meet-NEG-CONV-PAST.TENT-ATTR

Translation
(4) The girl who promised (2) to meet [me] (1) at Tukupa peak (5) probably did not meet [me] for a wonderful sleep [together]/at the peak (4) because [she] listened to someone's words.

Commentary
Mt. Tukupa, MdJ Tukuba (< Tukupa, with a secondary nasalization/voicing) is a mountain located in the South-West of present-day Ibaraki prefecture (Tukuba district) (Nakanishi 1985: 464). It is 876 m high, and has two peaks: male in the west and female in the east. In ancient times the higher Western male peak was considered sacred and was off-limits. The smaller Eastern female peak, on the other hand, is famous for being one of the renowned places for *utaⁿgaki* (EOJ *kaⁿgapi*)[1] orgies when the members of the opposite sex were allowed to indulge in unrestricted sexual interaction regardless of their marriage status.

---

1 Much more detailed information will be provided in the commentary to MYS 9.1759.

Tukupa cannot be interpreted as a Japanese placename, and its likely provenance is Ainu: Ainu *tuk* 'small mountain' + *pa* 'head, top', which is 'small mountain top' (Chiri 1956: 85, 134). At 876 m Tukupa is really a 'small mountain' by Japanese standards. The suggested Ainu form *Tukpa certainly contributed to the reflexes of both Ainu -*k*- and -*p*- as voiceless OJ -*k*- and -*p*-, rather than prenasalized -ⁿg- and -ᵐb-, normal OJ reflexes of Ainu intervocalic -*k*- [-G-] and -*p*- [-B-] (Vovin 2009b: 9–10).

Line two is hypometric (*ji tarazu*, 字足らず) and line four is hypermetric (*ji amari*, 字余り).

There is only one EOJ feature in this poem: past tentative auxiliary is spelled as -*kεm*-, cf. WOJ -*kem*-, suggesting that /e/ and /ε/ merged in Pitati EOJ as /e/.

FK 3

本文・*Original Text*
(1) 都区波尼爾 (2) 伊保利弖 (3) 都麻奈志爾 (4) 和我尼牟欲呂波 (5) 波夜母阿氣奴賀母

仮名の書き下し・*Kana Transliteration*
(1) つくはねに (2) いほりて (3) つまなしに (4) わがねむよ₁ろ₂は (5) はやも₂あけ₂ぬかも₂

Romanization
(1) Tukupa ne-ni (2) ipor-i-te (3) tuma na-si n-i (4) wa-ⁿga ne-m-u yo-rə pa (5) paya mə akε-n-u kamə

Glossing with Morphemic Analysis
(1) Tukupa peak-LOC (2) lodge-CONV-SUB (3) spouse not.exist-FIN COP-CONV (4) I-POSS sleep-TENT-ATTR night-DIM TOP (5) quick FP dawn(CONV)-PERF-ATTR EP

Translation
(2) Having lodged (1) at Tukupa peak (4/5) [I] wonder whether the night when I sleep (3) without [my] spouse (5) will be over quickly.

Commentary
On Mt. Tukupa see the commentary to FK 2.

Line two is hypometric (*ji tarazu*, 字足らず) and line five is hypermetric (*ji amari*, 字余り).

There are two EOJ features in this poem. First, a diminutive suffix *-rə*, which occurs in WOJ only once (in NK 3), but is widely used in Eastern Old Japanese. Second, since the emphatic particle *kamə* requires an attributive form before it, the WOJ form on line five would be *akɛ-n-uru kamə*. *Akɛ-n-u kamə* is an EOJ form, also attested in other EOJ texts.

FK 5

本文 · *Original Text*
(1) 多賀波麻乃 (2) 志多賀是差夜久 (3) 伊毛乎古比 (4) 鬥麻止伊波波夜 (5) 志古止賣志鬥毛

仮名の書き下し · *Kana Transliteration*
(1) たかはまの₂ (2) したかぜさやぐ (3) いもをこ₁ひ₁ (4) つまといはばや (5) しこ₁と₂め₁しつも₁

Romanization
(1) Takapama-nə (2) sita kaⁿze sayaⁿg-u (3) imo-wo kopi (4) tuma tə ip-aᵐba ya (5) siko təme situ mo

Glossing with Morphemic Analysis
(1) Takapama-GEN (2) bottom wind be.noisy-ATTR (3) beloved-ACC long. for(CONV) (4) spouse QV say-COND IP (5) repugnant old.woman lowly FP

Translation
(3) Longing for a beloved (2) who is noisy [as] a ground wind (1) at Takapama, (4) would [I] call you a spouse? (5) Repugnant old woman, [you are] also lowly!

Commentary
Takapama (MDJ Takahama, 高濱) is part of Ishioka city (Ishioka shi, 石岡市) in present-day Ibaraki prefecture. It is located inland in the center of the prefecture, not on the seashore as *hama* (濱) 'seashore' might suggest.

It is not quite clear what *sita kaⁿze* 'bottom wind' on line two is. Omodaka et al. speculate that this *hapax legomenon* may refer to a wind blowing along the ground, at the same time indicating that *sita kaⁿze* refers to a southern wind in the topolect of Uraga town (Uraga chō, 浦賀町) of Miura district (Miura gun, 三浦郡) in present-day Kanagawa prefecture (1967: 354). But Kanagawa is not even adjacent to Ibaraki, and also a single attestation in a modern topolect is unlikely to be inherited from EOJ.

The script is somewhat unusual in this poem. The character 差 used for the syllable /sa/ on line two and the character 鬥 for the syllable /tu/ on lines four and five are unique: as far as we can tell they do not occur in other Old Japanese texts.

There are three EOJ features in this poem: EOJ *kopi* vs. WOJ *kopï* 'long for and', EOJ *siko* vs. WOJ *sikə* 'repugnant', and EOJ *təme* vs. WOJ *tome* 'old woman'. They probably indicate the absence of contrasts /o/ : /ə/ and /ï/ : /i/ in the underlying topolect.

FK 7

本文・*Original Text*
(1) 伊夜是留乃 (2) 阿是乃古麻都爾 (3) 由布悉弖弖 (4) 和乎布利彌由母 (5) 阿是古志麻波母

仮名の書き下し・*Kana Transliteration*
(1) いやぜるの₂ (2) あぜのこまつに (3) ゆふしでて (4) わをふりみゆも (5) あぜこしまはも₁

Romanization
(1) iya{ⁿ}zeru n-ə (2) A{ⁿ}ze-nə ko-matu-ni (3) yupu si{ⁿ}de-te (4) wa-wo pur-i mi-y-umə (5) A{ⁿ}ze ko si map-am-ə

Glossing with Morphemic Analysis
(1) well.noticeable COP-ATTR (2) A{ⁿ}ze-GEN DIM-pine-LOC (3) white.bark.strip hang(CONV)-SUB (4) I-ACC wave-NML see-PASS-EXCL (5) A{ⁿ}ze girl EP dance-TENT-ATTR

Translation
(3) Hanging white bark strips (2) on a small pine in A{ⁿ}ze (1) that is well noticeable, (5) The girl from A{ⁿ}ze is going to dance. (4) Oh, [I] can see [her] waving at me!

Commentary
According to the preceding passage in the Hitachi Fudoki, the meeting between the author of the poem and the girl from A{ⁿ}ze took place during an *utagaki* sexual orgy in Kasima district (Kasima kəpori, 香島郡), which has the borders roughly coinciding with the administrative borders of Kashima city (Kashima shi, 鹿嶋市) in present-day Ibaraki prefecture.

EOJ *iya^nzeru* is a *hapax legomenon* with an unknown meaning, although sometimes it is assigned the meaning 'excellent', 'well noticeable' (Omodaka et al. 1967: 104).

A^nze was apparently located on the seashore in Kasima district. The etymology of this placename is obscure.

There are several EOJ features in this poem: the attributive *-ə*, the accusative *-wo* in *wa-wo* 'at me' instead of WOJ *wa-ni* 'to me' required by the verb *pur-* 'to wave', and *wa-wo pur-i mi-y-umə* '[I] see [her] waiving at me' with *pur-i* instead of WOJ *wa-ni pur-u mi-y-umə* with *pur-u*. It is not quite clear whether *-i* in *pur-i* is a nominalizer, or a special EOJ form of a final *-u*.

FK 8

本文・*Original Text*
(1) 宇志呆爾波 (2) 多多牟止伊閇止 (3) 奈西乃古何 (4) 夜蘇志麻加久理 (5) 和乎彌佐婆志理之

仮名の書き下し・*Kana Transliteration*
(1) うしほには (2) たたむと₂い〜₂ど₂ (3) なせの₂こ₁が (4) やそ₁しまかくり (5) わをみ₁さばしりし

Romanization
(1) usipo-ni pa (2) tat-am-u tə ip-ɛ-^ndə (3) na se n-ə ko-^nga (4) yaso sima kakur-i (5) wa-wo mi-s-a^mba sir-i-si

Glossing with Morphemic Analysis
(1) receding.tide-LOC TOP (2) stand-TENT-FIN QV say-EV-CONC (3) you beloved COP-ATTR lad-POSS (4) eighty island be.hidden-CONV (5) I-ACC look-HON-CON know-CONV-PAST.ATTR

Translation
(2) Although [you] said that [you] would stand (1) at [the brink of] the receding tide (3) you, [my] beloved lad (4) were hiding in the crowd, and (5) because [you] looked at me, [I] recognized [you].

Commentary
This poem is a response to the preceding FK 7.

OJ *usipo* is believed to have roughly the same meaning as *sipo* 'tide' (with the difference that *usipo* mostly means receding tide), but this does not explain initial *u*-, which might be an irregular contraction of OJ *umi* 'sea', but this is not very likely either phonetically or semantically. We wonder whether this *u*- can be same *u*- as in OJ *usirə* 'back' (cf. OJ *siri* 'back').

OJ *yaso* 'eighty' is often used in the meaning of 'many'.

Tsuchihashi believes that both the receding tide and eighty islands are metaphors for the crowd at the *utagaki* orgy (1957: 229). However, explaining them both along the same lines is going to bring contradiction to the syntactic structure of the poem: although you said that you would stand in the crowd, you were hiding in the crowd. Consequently, we adopt here only 'eighty islands' as a metaphor for the crowd.

Line five is hypermetric (*ji amari*, 字余り).

There is only one EOJ feature in this poem, but it is quite significant: EOJ *misa^{m}ba* 'because [you] looked' corresponding to WOJ *mise^{m}ba* 'because [you] let me see' with a typical correspondence of EOJ -*a*- to WOJ -*e*- (see the Introduction).

FK 9

本文・*Original Text*
(1) 志漏止利乃 (2) 芳我都都彌乎 (3) 都都牟止母 (4) 安良布麻目右疑 (5) 波古叡

仮名の書き下し・*Kana Transliteration*
(1) しろ₁と₂りの₂ (2) はがつつみ₁を (3) つつむと₂も₂ (4) あらふまめ₂うき₂ (5) はこ₁え₂

Romanization
(1) siro təri-nə (2) pa-ᵑga tutumi-wo (3) tutum-u təmo (4) arap-u ma mɛ ukï (5) pa koye

Glossing with Morphemic Analysis
(1) white bird-GEN (2) wing-POSS dam-ACC (3) wrap-FIN CONJ (4) wash-ATTR interval FP float(CONV) (5) wing cross.over(CONV)

Translation
(1/2/3) Even if the wings of a white bird wrap the dam (4) while [the sea waves] wash [it] (5) [they] cross over the wings.

Commentary

This is the only EOJ text where the character 芳 'fragrance' is used phonographically for the syllable /pa/ and the character 漏 is used phonographically for the syllable /ro/.

There is just one EOJ feature in this poem: focus particle *mɛ* corresponding to WOJ *mə*. The same phonetic shape mɛ of this particle is found in MYS 20.4345 and 4383.

Lines two and five are hypometric (*ji tarazu*, 字足らず).

CHAPTER 2

萬葉集巻第十四 • *Man'yōshū* Book Fourteen

1   東謌[1] • Eastern Poems

14.3349

本文 • *Original Text*
(1) 加豆思加乃 (2) 麻萬能宇良未乎 (3) 許具布祢能 (4) 布奈妣等佐和久 (5) 奈美多都良思母

仮名の書き下し • *Kana Transliteration*
(1) かづしかの₂ (2) ままの₂うらみ₂を (3) こ₂ぐふねの₂ (4) ふなび₁と₂さわく (5) なみ₁たつらしも₂

Romanization
(1) Kaⁿdusika-nə (2) mama-nə ura mï-wo (3) kəᵑg-u pune-nə (4) puna-ᵐ-bitə sawak-u (5) nami tat-urasi-mə

Glossing with Morphemic Analysis
(1) Kaⁿdusika-GEN (2) cliff-GEN bay turn.around(NML)-ACC (3) row-ATTR boat-GEN (4) boat-GEN-person make.noise-FIN (5) wave rise-SUP-EXCL

Translation
(4) Boatmen (3) from the boat that rows (2) along the circumference of the cliffs at the bay (1) in Kaⁿdusika (4) are making noise. (5) Waves seem to rise!

Commentary
This poem is from Simotupusa (下総) province. The poem does not have any typical phonological or morphological EOJ features, and what is even more interesting is that it faithfully preserves WOJ vocalism. However, it is possible to claim on lexical grounds that this poem is in EOJ, and not WOJ, because it has the EOJ word *mama* 'cliff', not attested in WOJ.

---

1 Among the early manuscripts (pre-Muromachi) the character 謌 for 'song, poem' in the *Nishi-Honganji bon* and the *Hosoi-bon*, while the character 歌 is found only in the *Kishū-bon*. In spite of the fact that the majority of the later manuscripts follow the *Kishū-bon* in that respect, I decided to rely on the evidence from the majority of the older manuscripts.

Kaⁿdusika (alternatively read as Katusika by some commentators) area is located in the vicinity of present-day Edogawa river on the border of Tokyo Metropolitan Area and Chiba prefecture (Itō et al. 1981: 310; Nakanishi 1985: 436). This placename is apparently meaningless in Japanese, as the logographic spellings like 勝鹿 'winning deer', 勝牡鹿 'winning male deer', 葛飾 'vine decoration' are nothing more than *ateji* (當て字). This placename appears five times in book fourteen of the *Man'yōshū* spelled phonographically as 加豆思加 / kaⁿdusika/ (three times) or 加都思加 /katusika/ (two times). However, since 都 /tu/ could be potentially (although seldom) used in the *man'yōgana* type A to write /ⁿdu/, the phonogram 豆 /ⁿdu/ is not used in the *Man'yōshū* to write /tu/ except in six cases out of 169 (5.807, 11.2353a, 17.3985, 20.4340, 20.4342, 20.4346). Among these six cases, the last three (20.4340, 20.4342, 20.4346) belong to EOJ, and the three cases belonging to WOJ are confined to the same word *wotutu/ututu* 'reality', which shows alternative spellings *ututu/wotutu/ woⁿdutu/wotuⁿdu*. Consequently, the reading Kaⁿdusika with /ⁿdu/ must be preferred.² Therefore, we think that Kaⁿdusika < *Kantusika has Ainu provenance: *ka-n-toska* < *ka-ne-toska *top-COP-low.cliffs* 'low cliffs that are above' (Chiri 1956: 42, 133), with expected raising of *o to *u*. Nakanishi indicates that the governor's office in Simotupusa province was located on the top of cliffs (1981: 241), and this lends further credibility to the interpretation of this placename (see the entry on *mama* below).

Mama is believed to be a word for 'cliff' (Omodaka et al. 1967: 689), and it is probably an EOJ word: it occurs in both EOJ and WOJ texts, but in both it almost always follows the EOJ placename Kaⁿdusika or is used in a poem where Kaⁿdusika is otherwise mentioned. This triggers a reasonable doubt as to whether *mama* is really a 'cliff' or simply a placename. Consequently, if this is the placename, lines one and two of the poem have to be translated as (2) along the circumference of the bay in Mama (1) at Kaⁿdusika. There are, however, two exceptions to the close connection of *mama* with Kaⁿdusika: first, it also appears in a different context in 10.2288, but this poem is otherwise written in logographic script and may have an alternative interpretation. Much more important is the evidence found in 14.3369, where *mama* occurs after the EOJ placename Asiⁿgari. Moreover, the existence of the word *mama* 'cliff' not only in modern dialects of Gunma, Niigata, Nagano, and Shizuoka prefectures (Omodaka et al. 1967: 690), but most importantly also in all Hachijō dialects

---

2   Cf. also discussion in Kupchik (2011: 130), who also added a WOJ case of 見豆良牟 *MI-ⁿd-uram-u* 'see-PERF-TENT2-ATTR', a misspelling for *mi-t-uram-u*. We express my gratitude to John Kupchik for directing our attention to this poem, as well as for his corrections of some of the previously incorrectly cited numbers in the draft of manuscript.

(Yamada 2010: 100–101) makes the placename interpretation much less realistic. In any case, it appears that either Mama or cliffs of Ka^ndusika were in the vicinity of Simotupusa's governor's office (Nakanishi 1981: 241).

There is a controversy about the reading and interpretation of 宇良未 *ura mï* 'circumference of the bay' on line two, due to the confusion of the *man'yōgana* signs 未 /mï/ and 末 /ma/ in different manuscripts of the *Man'yōshū*. We follow the reading *ura mï-wo* 'along the circumference of the bay', adopted by some scholars (Takagi et al. 1960: 408; Kojima et al. 1976: 445; Itō 1997.13/14: 272), although others prefer the reading *ura ma-wo* 'along the space of the bay' (Mizushima 1986: 22; Omodaka 1984.14: 10; Nakanishi 1981: 1053). Rowing from the bay straight into the offing would be dangerous. Thus, it was much safer to take the boat out, following its circumference. Therefore, the reading *ura mï-wo* 'along the circumference of the bay' makes more sense.

woj *puna-^m-bitə* may indicate either boatmen or passengers, but in this context it clearly refers to the boatmen, as passengers would not row the boat by themselves.

Postscript to the Poem 14.3349

本文 • *Original Text*
右一首下総國歌

Translation
The poem above is from Simotupusa province.

Commentary
Simotupusa (下総) province was located in the northern part of present-day Chiba prefecture. Simotupusa was one of the Great Provinces under the *Ritsuryō* code. According to the *Rituryō* code (*Ritsuryō sei*, 律令制),[3] all provinces of Yamatə were divided into four classes according to the size of their area and population: Great Provinces (Taikoku, 大國), Upper Provinces (Jōkoku, 上國), Middle Provinces (Chūgoku, 中國), and Lower Provinces (Gekoku, 下國). A rank of a governor was generally corresponding with the size of a province he ruled.

---

3 Promulgated in 701 AD.

14.3351

本文・Original Text
(1) 筑波祢尓 (2) 由伎可毛布良留 (3) 伊奈乎可母 (4) 加奈思吉兒呂我 (5) 尓努保佐流可母

仮名の書き下し・Kana Transliteration
(1) つくはねに (2) ゆき₁かも₁ふらる (3) いなをかも₂ (4) かなしき₁こ₁ろ₂が (5) にの₁ほさるかも₂

Romanization
(1) Tukupa ne-ni (2) yuki kamo pur-ar-u (3) ina wo kamə (4) kanasi-ki KO-rə-ŋga (5) nino pos-ar-u kamə

Glossing with Morphemic Analysis
(1) Tukupa summit-LOC (2) snow EP fall-PROG-ATTR (3) no yes EP (4) dear-ATTR girl-DIM-POSS (5) cloth dry-PROG-ATTR EP

Translation
(2) [I] wonder whether snow is falling (1) at Tukupa peak. (3) [I] wonder whether it is so or not. (4/5) [And I] wonder whether [my] dear girl is drying cloth.

Commentary
On Mt. Tukupa, see the commentary to FK 2.

This poem is clearly written in the EOJ dialect, since it has twice typical Eastern progressive forms in *-ar-*: *pur-ar-u* 'is falling' and *pos-ar-u* 'is drying'. The corresponding WOJ forms are *pur-er-u* and *pos-er-u*. Both sets of forms derive from the analytical construction *VERBAL.ROOT-i ar- 'VERBAL.ROOT-CONV exist-', but with different outcomes in EOJ and WOJ: while EOJ contracts the vowel cluster *ia into /a/, WOJ monophthongizes it into vowel /e/ (neutralized as /e/ after coronals). For more details see Vovin (2020.2: 792–803). Another piece of evidence for the EOJ nature of this poem involves the word *nino* 'cloth' (see below).

OJ *ina* 'no' and *wo* 'yes' seem to be functionally close to modern Japanese *iie* 'it is not so' and *hai* 'it is so', which are more likely to be the discourse markers of disagreement/agreement with a preceding statement rather than straightforward 'no' and 'yes'. This is further confirmed by the logographic spelling of *wo* with the Chinese character 諾 'agreement' (16.3796, 16.3798). Although there are several examples of *ina* 'no' attested in phonographic spelling in WOJ (Omodaka et al. 1967: 86–87) in addition to the only EOJ example in this poem, it appears that *wo* 'yes' is attested phonographically in WOJ also only once in 11.2539.

Diminutive suffix *-rə* occurs predominantly in EOJ, with only one example in WOJ: *mɛ-rə* 'mesh-DIM' (NK 3), apparently a *hapax legomenon*. It is sometimes believed that there is also another WOJ example, *yo-rə* 'night-DIM', but, as a matter of fact, it is attested in FK 3, which is a poem from Pitati province as well, and similarly to 14.3388 it has no other EOJ distinctive features other than the diminutive suffix *-rə*. In addition, *-rə* is not attested in WOJ after the word *se* 'elder brother, beloved'. For details see Vovin (2020.1: 208–210).

EOJ *nino* 'cloth' is considered to be an Eastern dialect form of WOJ *nuno* 'id.' The only slight problem here is that WOJ *nuno is not attested in the phonographic script, although the attestations of MJ *nuno* 'id.' are plenty (Miyajima 1971: 224; Miyajima 2014: 794–795; Saeki and Mabuchi 1969: 677). However, since only *kō-rui* /o/, and not *otsu-rui* /ə/ could be found in the same morpheme with /u/, the reconstruction of WOJ archetype as *nuno seems to be justified (Omodaka et al. 1967: 554). EOJ *nino* ~ WOJ *nuno was a rough quality cloth (as compared to a silk cloth) that was made from fibers of hemp, ramie, and other similar plants.

Postscript to the Poems 14.3350–3351

本文 • *Original Text*
右二首常陸國歌

Translation
Two poems above are from Pitati province.

Commentary
The territory of Pitati (常陸) province almost exactly corresponds to present-day Ibaraki prefecture (Nakanishi 1985: 478). Pitati was one of the Great Provinces under the *Ritsuryō* code. On the *Ritsuryō* code classification of Yamatə provinces see the commentary to the postscript to the poem 14.3349.

The variants 14.3350a and 14.3350b are apparently not counted as separate poems. Both are the poems in WOJ.

2   相聞・Relationship Poems

14.3354

本文・*Original Text*
(1) 伎倍比等乃 (2) 萬太良夫須麻尓 (3) 和多佐波太 (4) 伊利奈麻之母乃 (5) 伊毛我乎杼許尓

仮名の書き下し・*Kana Transliteration*
(1) き₁べ₂ひ₁と₂の₂ (2) まだらぶすまに (3) わたさはだ (4) いりなまし₂も₂の₂ (5) いも₁がをど₂こ₂に

Romanization
(1) Ki^{m}bɛ pitə-nə (2) ma^{n}dara-^{m}-busuma-ni (3) wata sapa^{n}da (4) ir-i-n-amasi mənə (5) imo-^{n}ga wo^n-dəkə-ni

Glossing with Morphemic Analysis
(1) Ki^{m}bɛ person-GEN (2) spotted-COP(ATTR)-cover-LOC (3) cotton many (4) enter-CONV-PERF-SUBJ CONJ (5) beloved-POSS DIM-bed-LOC

Translation
(4) Although [I] would [like to] enter (5) the bed of [my] beloved (3/4) [like] the cotton that is plentifully placed inside (2) the multicolor painted [bedding] covers (1) of people from Ki^{m}bɛ, (4) but ...

Commentary
This poem is from Təpotuapumi (遠江) province. This poem does not have any typical Eastern Old Japanese phonetic or morphological features, but the word *sapa^{n}da* 'many' is clearly EOJ, since its WOJ cognate is *sapa* 'id.' Therefore, we classify this poem as EOJ on a pure lexical basis. EOJ *sapa^{n}da* 'many' also occurs in 14.3395. On Təpotuapumi province see the commentary to the postscript to the poems 14.3353-3354.

Ki^{m}bɛ is a bothersome placename (cf. commentary on Ka^{n}dusika in 14.3349) that has no universal agreement on its reading: the majority of commentators, old and modern, prefer to read it as Kipɛ, while the minority insists on Ki^{m}bɛ (Mizushima 1984a: 37). In the Eastern Old Japanese part of book fourteen it appears once spelled as 伎倍 (this poem), which does not throw any light on its correct reading, since the *man'yōgana* sign 倍 can stand for either /pɛ/ or /^{m}bɛ/ (Omodaka et al. 1967: 900). Similar to the cases of Ka^{n}dusika and Sinanu mentioned above, Kipɛ or Kiᵐbɛ seems to be meaningless in Japanese. Not so in Ainu, where Kiᵐbɛ (but not Kipɛ) has a perfect explanation: Ainu *kimpe* 'bear' (< *kim-pe* 'mountain thing') (Kayano 1996: 209). Thus, *Kiᵐbɛ-nə payasi* is a 'bear forest' – the most unlikely place for the author to let his beloved stand alone! An alternative interpretation of Kiᵐbɛ in Ainu may be *kim* 'mountain' + *pet* 'river'. Early Ainu loans to Japanese normally lose final Ainu consonants. A good example is Sinanu that has Ainu origin: *sinam* (< *sir-nam*) 'to be cold' + *nup* 'mountain field'⁴ that is 'cold mountain fields'. The final consonant -*p* of *nup* 'field' and final consonant -*m* of *nam* 'to be cold' are lost. An alternative analysis might be *si-* 'true' + *nam* 'to be cold' + *nup* 'mountain field' 'truly cold mountain fields'. One problem with this analysis is that Ainu *nam* by itself means 'to be cold to the touch', like MDJ *tumetai*. However, Sakhalin Ainu *sinam* (< *sir-nam* 'weather-be.cold') means both 'to be cold to the touch' and 'to be cold' (Ōtsuka et al. 2008: 156), thus we prefer the first analysis. If this etymology is correct, then MJ Sinano in all probability represents a partial translation of the placename Sinanu, where *nu* 'field' < Ainu *nup* was replaced by MJ *no* 'field'. See also Vovin (2009b: 12).

OJ *pusuma* meant 'cover', 'bedding', so care must be taken not to confuse it with the meaning of MDJ (襖) *fusuma* 'sliding partition door'.

On *wata* 'cotton', although several *Man'yōshū* scholars insisted that unlike modern Japanese, the character 綿 does not mean 'cotton' here, but rather 'silk floss', because there is no evidence that cotton has already been transmitted to Japan at this period (Kojima et al. 1972: 115; Imura 1983: 242; Itō 1996: 251; Aso 2007: 251), this is incorrect. The existence of cotton in Japan is supported by the fact that it is mentioned in the *Wèi zhì wō rén zhuàn* (魏志倭人傳, ca. 290 AD); and then in 694 AD as a tax item sent from several provinces in Kyūshū (Kidder 2007: 15, 291).

The verb *ir-* 'to enter, to be placed inside' has a double meaning in this poem: it refers to both cotton being placed inside the bedding covers, as well as to the male protagonist going inside the bed of his female beloved.

The diminutive prefix *woN-* has the endearment function in this poem: it is the 'dear bed', and not the 'small bed'.

---

4 Chiri indicates that in Ainu placenames *nup* may mean both 'field' and 'mountain field' (1956: 69).

Postscript to the Poems 14.3353–3354

本文 • *Original Text*
右二首遠江國歌

Translation
Two poems above are from Təpotuapumi province.

Commentary
Təpotuapumi (遠江) province corresponds to the western part of present-day Shizuoka prefecture (to the West of Ōi river (大井川)) (Nakanishi 1985: 467). Təpotuapumi province was one of the Upper Provinces under *Ritsuryō* code. On the *Ritsuryō* code classification of Yamatə provinces see the commentary to the postscript to the poem 14.3349. The etymology of the placename Təpotuapumi is transparent: *təpo* 'distant' + *tu*, genitive-locative case marker + *ap(a)-umi* 'lake' (lit. 'fresh water sea').

14.3358b

本文 • *Original Text*
(1) 阿敝良久波 (2) 多麻能乎思家也 (3) 古布良久波 (4) 布自乃多可祢尓 (5) 布流由伎奈須毛

仮名の書き下し • *Kana Transliteration*
(1) あへ₁らくは (2) たまの₂をしけ₁や (3) こ₁ふらくは (4) ふじの₂たかねに (5) ふるゆき₁なすも₁

Romanization
(1) ap-er-aku pa (2) tama-nə wo sik-e ya (3) kop-ur-aku pa (4) Puⁿzi-nə taka ne-ni (5) pur-u yuki-nasu mo

Glossing with Morphemic Analysis
(1) meet-PROG-NML TOP (2) jewel-GEN cord reach-EV IP (3) long.for-ATTR-NML TOP (4) Puⁿzi-GEN high peak-LOC (5) fall-ATTR snow-COMP FP

Translation
(1/2) Will the meetings [with you ever] reach [the length of such a short thing as] the jewel cord? (3) [My] longing [for you] (4/5) is as [endless] as snow falling on the high peak of Puⁿzi!

Commentary

This poem should probably be classified as EOJ rather than WOJ, although the grounds for this classification are rather slim: the evidential form of the verb *sik-* 'to reach' in WOJ should be *sik-ɛ* with an *otsu-rui* /ɛ/, and not *sik-e* with a *kō-rui* /e/ that is an imperative form in WOJ. The imperative *sik-e* 'reach!' does not make any sense in this context. Therefore, we have to assume that the evidential form *sik-ɛ* was really meant in this case, and the merger of /e/ and /ɛ/ after velars is a feature typical for EOJ, and not WOJ. Still, this is the only EOJ feature found in this poem, which otherwise looks perfectly WOJ, and it could potentially be attributed to a scribal error made in the Heian period.

Mt. Puⁿzi (MDJ Fuji) is the highest mountain in Japan (3776 m) that straddles the border between present-day Shizuoka and Yamanashi prefectures. It has a perfect Old Japanese etymology: EOJ *pu* 'fire'[5] + ⁿ*zi* < *nusi* 'master'.[6]

14.3359

本文・*Original Text*
(1) 駿河能宇美 (2) 於思敝尒於布流 (3) 波麻都豆良 (4) 伊麻思乎多能美 (5) 波播尒多我比奴

仮名の書き下し・*Kana Transliteration*
(1) するがの₂うみ₁ (2) おしへ₁におふる (3) はまつづら (4) いましをたの₂み₁ (5) はははにたがひ₁ぬ

Romanization
(1) Suru^ŋga-nə umi (2) osi-pe-ni op-uru (3) pama tuⁿdura (4) imasi-wo tanəm-i (5) papa-ni ta^ŋgap-i-n-u

Glossing with Morphemic Analysis
(1) Suru^ŋga-GEN sea (2) rocky.shore-side-LOC grow-ATTR (3) shore vine (4) you-ACC trust-CONV (5) mother-DAT go.against-CONV-PERF-FIN

---

5 Cf. *pu* 'fire' in 20.4419.
6 Cf. *aroⁿzi* 'master', including EOJ-like adnominal *-o*: *ar-* 'to exist' + *-o* AND > MJ *aruzi*, replacing *aronzi* in early Heian. Cf. also OJ *toⁿzi* 'lady of the house' and *muraⁿzi* 'village master', 'village head'.

Translation

(5) [I] went against [my] mother, (4) trusting you (3) like shore vines (2) that grow at the rocky shore side (1) [of] Suruⁿga sea.

Commentary

Suruⁿga (駿河, MDJ Suruga) province corresponds to the central part of present-day Shizuoka prefecture (Nakanishi 1985: 456). Suruⁿga was one of the Upper Provinces under *Ritsuryō* code. On the *Ritsuryō* code classification of Yamatə provinces see the commentary to the postscript to the poem 14.3349.

The first line is hypermetric (*ji amari*, 字余り), but this is possibly just a graphic illusion, since *Suruⁿga-nə umi* was in all probability pronounced as [Suruⁿganumi] or [Suruⁿganəmi].

EOJ *osi* and *osu* (14.3385[7]) 'rocky shore' correspond to WOJ *iso* 'rock, rocky shore'. WOJ *iso* 'rock, rocky shore' is clearly etymologically connected to OJ *isi* 'stone', which further complicates the reconstruction of the archetype. We have surveyed this etymological conundrum in Vovin (2010: 126–127). The only other observation that we want to add at this point is that the PJ word for 'rock, rocky shore' was likely *eso and the PJ word for 'stone' was probably *esoy (Vovin 2011b: 224–225), although, as the EOJ form *osi* < *esoy appearing in this poem demonstrates, there also might be almost no difference between the meanings 'rock, rocky shore' and 'stone', especially in the light of the fact that 'rocky shore' appears to be a secondary development from 'rock'.

WOJ *pama tuⁿdura* 'shore vine' cannot be identified with certainty. Probably some vine, a creeper, or a climber growing on the seashore (Omodaka 1977.14: 31; Mizushima 1986: 54). OJ *tuⁿdura* is a general term for vines or creepers that grow in mountains or seashore. Their crawling branches that extend from a root creep on the ground and attach themselves to other objects, such as trees or rocks, by going around them. The word *tutⁿdura* is used in Old Japanese poetry as a metaphor for love connection (Nakanishi 1985: 321).

The first three lines are a poetic introduction (*jo*, 序) to the rest of the poem (Mizushima 1986: 54).

---

[7] The poem 14.3385 is from Simotupusa province.

14.3359a

本文 · *Original Text*
(1) 駿河能宇美 (2) 於思敝尓於布流 (3) 波麻都豆良 (4) 伊麻思乎多能美 (5) 於夜尓多我比奴

仮名の書き下し · *Kana Transliteration*
(1) するがの₂うみ₁ (2) おしへ₁におふる (3) はまつづら (4) いましをたの₂み₁ (5) おやにたがひ₁ぬ

Romanization
(1) Suruŋga-nə umi (2) osi-pe-ni op-uru (3) pama tuⁿdura (4) imasi-wo tanəm-i (5) oya-ni taŋgap-i-n-u

Glossing with Morphemic Analysis
(1) Suruŋga-GEN sea (2) rocky.shore-side-LOC grow-ATTR (3) shore vine (4) you-ACC trust-CONV (5) parent-DAT go.against-CONV-PERF-FIN

Translation
(5) [I] went against [my] parents, (4) trusting you (3) like shore vines (2) that grow at the rocky shore side (1) [of] Suruŋga sea.

Commentary
The only difference between 14.3359 and 14.3359a is found in line five, and it is completely lexical: *papa* 'mother' in 14.3359 vs. *oya* 'parent(s)' in 14.3359a. Everything else is identical, so the commentary to 14.3359 applies as well to 14.3359a.

Postscript to the Poems 14.3355–3359

本文 · *Original Text*
右五首駿河國歌

Translation
Five poems above are poems from Suruŋga province.

Commentary
Note that the variants of poems are not counted as separate poems, therefore the postscript mentions only five poems instead of eight.

On Suruŋga (駿河) province see the commentary to 14.3359.

萬葉集卷第十四・MAN'YŌSHŪ BOOK FOURTEEN　　　　　　　　　　59

14.3361

本文・Original Text
(1) 安思我良能 (2) 乎弖毛許乃母尓 (3) 佐須和奈乃 (4) 宇奈流麻之豆美 (5) 許呂安礼比毛等久

仮名の書き下し・Kana Transliteration
(1) あしがらの₂ (2) をても₁こ₂の₂も₂に (3) さすわなの₂ (4) うなるましづみ₁ (5) こ₂ろ₂あれひ₁も₁と₂く

Romanization
(1) Asiᵑgara-nə (2) wote mo kənə mə-ni (3) sas-u wana-nə (4) (h)unaru ma siⁿdum-i (5) kə-rə are pimo tək-u

Glossing with Morphemic Analysis
(1) Asiᵑgara-GEN (2) that side this side-LOC (3) set-ATTR trap-GEN (4) search interval become.quiet-CONV (5) beloved-DIM I cord untie-FIN

Translation
(4) The time for search (3) for the traps [they] set (2) on that side [and] this side (1) of the Asiᵑgara (4) is over. (5) [Therefore, my] beloved [and] I will untie our [garment] cords.

Commentary
We classify this poem as EOJ rather than WOJ on the basis of the presence of Ainu elements (see below) as well as on the basis of the misspelling of WOJ *ko* 'girl' as *kə* in line five.

Asiᵑgara or Asiᵑgari corresponds to Asigara Upper and Lower counties in Hakone mountains of present-day Kanagawa prefecture (Itō et al. 1981: 285; Nakanishi 1985: 415). Among these two variants Asiᵑgara is secondary, resulting from the progressive assimilation Asiᵑgari > Asiᵑgara. The place name Asiᵑgari is clearly of Ainu provenance: *Askar-i 'clear place'. For details see Vovin (2009b: 3–5).

The main problem of interpretation and translation of this poem is connected to line four. Exactly the same line occurs in 20.4430 (also an EOJ poem), but this second attestation offers little if any help at all for interpreting this poem. Mizushima cites thirteen different interpretations, which he groups into four major clusters, and ends up with presenting his own lengthy interpretation: "The game got caught in the trap, and was restless for a while, but finally it calmed down" (1986: 58–60). Certainly, there are too many words for one short line in his interpretation. Before we attempt to analyze this line, one point must be made clear from the beginning. While most early manuscripts of book fourteen clearly have 可奈流 /kanaru/ in the beginning of line four, the oldest of them, the *Genryaku kōhon* (the facsimile of the text is reproduced in Mizushima (1984a: 56))[8] has 宇奈流 in *kana* script. A *furigana* sign ル /ru/ written at the right side of the last letter, clearly disambiguates it as /ru/ and not /ro/, but the first *kana* letter does not enjoy this privilege and certainly looks more like う /u/ than か /ka/. We prefer to trust the *Genryaku kōhon* manuscript that predates most other old manuscripts by several centuries. Thus, we arrive at the point that the first three *kana* signs in line four are to be read as /unaru/, and not /kanaru/. Consequently, this annihilates all previous attempts by Japanese scholars to interpret this part of line four as if it were /kanaru/.

We believe that this poem, or more exactly its line four, might be a macaronic Ainu-Japanese line. The sequence /unaru/ certainly makes no sense in Old Japanese, but Ainu *hunar* 'to search' immediately comes to the mind. Neither EOJ nor WOJ has the phoneme /h/ in eighth century AD, and it was likely to be just ignored in Japanese transcriptions except in the position before /i/, where it was reflected as /s/ (see the commentary to 14.3363 below). Furthermore, Ainu final /-r/ is a phonemic transcription, but the phonetic representation always includes a vowel after final /-r/. This final phonetic vowel may be homorganic with the vowel of the previous syllable, but this is not a rule, cf. /par/ 'mouth' phonetically realized as [paro], and not *[para]. Consequently, *wana-nə (h)unaru ma siⁿdum-i* can be interpreted as 'the time when the search for the traps has quieted down'. Therefore, when the hustle and bustle for getting the prey from traps is over, lovers can enjoy some time together on the same mountain where the traps were laid.

In spite of the absence of the comitative case marker *-tə* between *kə-rə* 'beloved-DIM' and *are* 'I', the line five *kə-rə are pimo tək-u* should be interpreted as '[my] beloved [and] we will untie our [garment] cords', because it agrees better with the cultural practice of lovers untying the garment cords of each other at the long-awaited meeting of passion, rather than with a non-attested practice of a woman unilaterally untying a man's garment cords. There was a custom among lovers of tying and untying the cords of their garments. When lovers met, they untied the cords of each other's garments, in other words, a man untied a woman's garment cords, and the woman untied those of her lover's. When they parted, even for a little while, they would again tie each other's cords. These cords were not to be untied until the next meeting. It was believed

---

8 A facsimile of another manuscript of the *Genryaku kōhon* published by Benseisha in 1986 does not include MYS 14.3361.

that when a person would try to re-tie a cord that loosened naturally, it was proof that he or she was loved by his or her lover (Omodaka et al. 1967: 624).

EOJ *kə* 'girl' here corresponds to WOJ *ko*, and may demonstrate that there was no contrast between *ə* and *o* in the Sagamu dialect, see also 14.3669. However, it might be just a scribal error, cf. the same word in 14.3668 below spelled as *ko*.

On the diminutive suffix -*rə* see the commentary to 14.3351.

14.3363

本文 · *Original Text*
(1) 和我世古乎 (2) 夜麻登敝夜利弖 (3) 麻都之太須 (4) 安思我良夜麻乃 (5) 須疑乃木能末可

仮名の書き下し · *Kana Transliteration*
(1) わがせこ₁を (2) やまと₂へ₁やりて (3) まつしだす (4) あしがらやまの₂ (5) すぎ₂の₂こ₂の₂まか

Romanization
(1) wa-ⁿga se-ko-wo (2) Yamatə-pe yar-i-te (3) mat-u siⁿda su (4) Asiⁿgara yama-nə (5) suⁿgï-nə kə-nə ma ka

Glossing with Morphemic Analysis
(1) I-POSS beloved-DIM-ACC (2) Yamato-DIR send-CONV-SUB (3) wait-ATTR time again (4) Asiⁿgara mountain-GEN (5) cryptomeria-GEN tree-GEN interval IP

Translation
(1/2) Having sent my beloved to Yamato, (3/5) when [I] wait [for him], [I am thinking]: "Will [he come back] again through the cryptomeria trees (4) on Mt. Asiⁿgara?"

Commentary
In this poem in book fourteen we meet for the first time EOJ word *siⁿda* 'time'. There are two peculiarities concerning the usage of this word. First, it has a different morphosyntactic function as compared with EOJ *təki* 'time'. The EOJ word *təki* 'time' is a free noun that can be used in isolation or after another noun, and it does not appear after the attributive form of verbs signifying 'time, when an action X takes/took/will take place' except in one example (14.3572).

In contrast to EOJ *təki* 'time', EOJ *si^{n}da* 'time' is never used as a free noun and always introduces a temporal clause 'time, when ...' being used after the attributive form of a verb. This phenomenon is completely alien to WOJ texts, where *təki* 'time' is used in both functions. Second, *si^{n}da* 'time' is not attested in any pure WOJ text, in spite of the fact that Fukuda tried to argue that *si^{n}da* 'time' is a WOJ word since it is found once in FK 11 as well (1965: 426).[9] Since WOJ corpus is at least twenty times bigger than EOJ corpus, the lack of *si^{n}da* 'time' in WOJ is certainly hard to explain if this word had a common Japonic provenance. As a matter of fact, once again the borrowing explanation from the Ainu language seems to be the ultimate answer. Ainu temporal dependent clauses always involve *hita* [hida/hiDa] 'time, when ...' preceded by a verb. Unlike EOJ *si^{n}da* [si^{n}da] that is morphemically non-divisible, Ainu *hita* is clearly bi-morphemic: *hi* 'time, occasion' + *ta*, locative suffix. Therefore, the direction of loan can be only from Ainu to EOJ. A couple of comments on phonetic correspondences between Ainu *hi-ta* [hi-da] ~ [hi-Da] and EOJ *si^{n}da* [si^{n}da] are in order. First, neither EOJ nor WOJ had [h] in its phonemic or phonetic inventory: in the position before [i] we would expect it to be interpreted as [ç] pretty much in the same way as modern Japanese [h] is realized before [i]. The only possible approximation to [çi] that could be found in both EOJ and WOJ phonetic inventory was [si]. Thus, the realization of Ainu [hi] as EOJ [si] should not come as any surprise. Second, Ainu intervocalic voiceless stops are phonetically realized as voiced or half-voiced. Since neither EOJ nor WOJ had any plain voiced stops but only prenasalized voiced stops, Ainu intervocalic voiced were reflected in EOJ (and WOJ) as prenasalized voiced stops (Vovin 2009b: 9–10).

The word *su* following *si^{n}da* 'time' is defined as 'unknown' or identified as the final form *s-u* of the verb *se-* 'to do' (Nakanishi 1981: 246), or simply branded as 'difficult to explain' together with the preceding *matu si^{n}da* (Takagi et al. 1959: 412). There are even more incongruent explanations like Tsuchiya's that analyzes *mat-u si^{n}da su* 'wait-ATTR time ?' as *matu si ^{n}das-u* 'pine EP erect-FIN' (Tsuchiya 1977.7: 218–219). The lack of agreement here seems to indicate that none of these interpretations is correct. We believe that the word *su* in line three is another Ainu loan, namely Ainu *suy* 'again'. The phonetic shape *su* < *suy is in perfect compliance with EOJ reflexes of pre-OJ *-uy or *-oy, e.g. pre-OJ *tukuy 'moon, month' > EOJ *tuku*, and pre-OJ *poy 'fire' > EOJ *pu*. See also 14.3487 and 14.3564.

---

9   For the arguments that FK 11 is not written in WOJ see Vovin (2009b: 25–27).

On Asiⁿgara see the commentary to 14.3361.

OJ *suⁿgï* 'cryptomeria' is the tallest evergreen tree in Japan. *Suⁿgï* is endemic for Kyūshū, but it was planted all over Japan. The wood of cryptomeria is widely used for building, and given the straight nature of its trunk, it is very popular as a material for various kinds of poles and columns. The bark of *suⁿgï* was widely used for thatching roofs. Its needles are about 4–12 mm in length and are slightly bent. It blooms in March–April with male species having pale yellow oval flowers that cluster at the end of larger branches, while female species have globular green flowers that are attached to the end of small branches. The fruits have globular shape and are lignified. They ripen in October.

Although military service (that could include serving as a border guard (WOJ *sakimori*), palace guard, or any military unit) for the state was legally defined as one year by the *Ritsuryō* code, in practice it could be extended up to three years, and even beyond that (Mizushima 1986: 66).

14.3366

本文 · *Original Text*

(1) 麻可奈思美 (2) 佐祢尒和波由久 (3) 可麻久良能 (4) 美奈能瀬河泊尒 (5) 思保美都奈武賀

仮名の書き下し · *Kana Transliteration*

(1) まかなしみ₁ (2) さねにわはゆく (3) かまくらの₂ (4) み₁なの₂せがはに (5) しほみ₁つなむか

Romanization

(1) ma-kanasi-mi (2) sa-ne-ni wa pa yuk-u (3) Kamakura-nə (4) Minanəse-ŋ-GApa-ni (5) sipo mit-unam-u ka

Glossing with Morphemic Analysis

(1) INT-dear-GER (2) PREF-sleep(NML)-LOC I TOP go-FIN (3) Kamakura-GEN (4) Minanəse-GEN-river-LOC (5) [high] tide rise-TENT2-ATTR IP

Translation

(1) Because [she] is so dear [to me], (2) I will go to sleep [with her]. (5) [But] could the [high] tide filling (4) Minanəse river (3) in Kamakura [prevent me to go]?

Commentary

This poem is in Eastern Old Japanese, as demonstrated by the typical EOJ tentative marker *-unam-* that corresponds to WOJ *-uram-*.

There is also a disagreement between various commentaries whether the sequence 吾者 in line five should be read as *A pa* (Takagi et al. 1959: 415; Kojima et al. 1973: 455; Tsuchiya 1977.7: 282; Nakanishi 1981: 249; Mizushima 1986: 96; Itō 1997: 317; Satake et al. 2002: 319) or WA *pa* (Kubota 1967: 158; Omodaka 1977.14: 56). We follow here Kubota and Omodaka's opinion, because although *a pa* 'I TOP' occurs once in WOJ in phonographic spelling (KK 5), there are no examples of it in the *Man'yōshū*. Meanwhile, *wa pa* 'I TOP' occurs in the *Man'yōshū* alone in phonographic script ten times in EOJ corpus and once in WOJ corpus. The only phonographic WOJ example of *wa pa* is 20.4408, but this is a poem written by Yakaməti in imitation of a *sakimori* poem, so the usage there is likely to be influenced by EOJ. Therefore, we should treat the sequence *wa pa* 'I TOP' as an EOJ feature.

Kamakura district in Saŋgamu province corresponds to present-day Kamakura city in Kanagawa prefecture (Nakanishi 1985: 437).

Minanəse river is identified with present-day Inasegawa river (稲瀬川) in the city of Kamakura (Nakanishi 1985: 488). The place name Minanəse is quite transparent: OJ *mina* 'water'; *-nə*, genitive marker; and *se* 'rapids', thus 'water rapids'. Alexander Vovin have pointed out before that OJ *mina* should consist of *mi* 'water' and *-na*, obsolete plural suffix (1994: 253).[10] Now we think that this is a mistake and OJ *mina* 'water' in fact consists of *mi-*, honorific prefix, and *na* 'water', pretty much the same way as *mine* 'summit' and *miti* 'way' consist of honorific prefix *mi-* and *ne* 'summit' and *ti* 'road' respectively, for example: OJ *ti* is the original word for 'road' in Japanese. OJ and MJ *miti* apparently consists of the honorific prefix *mi-* and *ti* 'road'. OJ *ti* 'road' also occurs in compounds as such, cf. *ti-mata* 'road fork', *yama-ⁿ-di* 'mountain road', *umi-ⁿ-di* 'sea way', etc. OJ *na* 'water' is also attested in *naŋgï* 'water leek' (cf. *kï* 'leek'), *naⁿduk-* < *na-ni tuk-* 'soak in water', and in *namita* 'tear' (n.).

The image of the high tide filling the estuary of Minanəse river implies that this is a natural obstacle preventing the author from reaching his wife or beloved.

---

10   The traditional point of view is that *-na* represents a genitive case marker (Yamada 1954: 419–420; Tokieda 1989: 203). This cannot be true, because, as this example demonstrates, it is followed by another genitive *-nə*, and a sequence of two genitives is certainly impossible.

EOJ *mit-unam-u* 'probably fills' is in the attributive form, since the interrogative particle *ka* triggers the change of the final predicate into attributive regardless whether it precedes or follows it (Vovin 2020.2: 1127).

14.3368

本文 • *Original Text*
(1) 阿之我利能 (2) 刀比能可布知介 (3) 伊豆流湯能 (4) 余介母多欲良介 (5) 故呂河伊波奈久介

仮名の書き下し • *Kana Transliteration*
(1) あしがりの₂ (2) と₁ひ₁の₂かふちに (3) いづるゆの₂ (4) よ₂にも₂たよ₁らに (5) こ₁ろ₂がいはなくに

Romanization
(1) Asi^ŋgari-nə (2) Topi-nə kap-uti-ni (3) iⁿd-uru YU-nə (4) yə-ni mə tayor-an-i (5) ko-rə-^ŋga ip-an-aku n-i

Glossing with Morphemic Analysis
(1) Asi^ŋgari-GEN (2) Topi-GEN river-inside-LOC (3) go.out-ATTR hot.spring-COMP (4) life.time-LOC FP cease-NEG-CONV (5) girl-DIM-POSS say-NEG-NML COP-CONV

Translation
(5) Although [my] dear girl did not say [it], (4) [our love] will not cease for a life time (3) like the hot springs that go out (2) in the Topi river basin (5) in Asi^ŋgari.

Commentary
On Asi^ŋgari see the commentary to 14.3361.

Topi river corresponds to present-day Chitosegawa river (千歳川) in Lower Asigara county (足柄下郡) of Kanagawa prefecture (Nakanishi 1985: 467).

The main difficulty of this poem's interpretation is due to the word *tayorani*, also attested as *tayurani* in 14.3392. It is often understood as MDJ *yuragu* 'to sway' (Omodaka 1977.14: 46; Mizushima 1986: 77–78), but the approach is quite impressionistic and is not based on any kind of linguistic analysis. Unfortunately, the word form *tayorani* ~ *tayurani* appears only twice and only in EOJ corpus, but in both cases it is quite clear that it is used in reference to water that does not do something, as witnessed by the negative *-an-*.

Water does stop or break – and this metaphor is frequently used in OJ poetry. Therefore, we prefer a different interpretation that ties it to WOJ verb *taye-* 'to cease, to come to an end' (Takagi et al. 1959: 413–414; Nakanishi 1981: 247). The apparent difficulty here is to explain the phonetic shape of EOJ *tayor- ~ tayur-* vs. WOJ *taye-*, which is further aggravated by the fact that *taye-* also occurs in EOJ corpus. The morphological structure of EOJ *tayor- ~ tayur-* is also opaque: it may be a compound of *taye-* 'to break' and *ar-* 'to exist', but the phonological change of *e+a > o* appears to be irregular. This is likely to remain a puzzle, but it seems that the best solution is to assume the existence of a consonantal or a *r*-irregular verb *tayor-* 'to cease' in EOJ (*tayur-* being the variant with *o > u* raising).

Yə-ni mə in line four is sometimes understood as 'really, certainly' (Omodaka 1977.14: 46; Nakanishi 1981: 247), but this interpretation seems to be based on the *hapax legomenon* in 12.3084, where *yə-ni mo* (代二毛) is interpreted in this way, but it also can be much easier explained as 'life time-LOC FP', as it occurs exactly in the same meaning: 'in one's life time' and sometimes also followed by a verb in the negative form as in 12.3084, 14.3368, 14.3392, and in other poems of the *Man'yōshū*: 6.1053, 6.1055, 13.3234, 13.3329, 18.4058, and 20.4360.

On the diminutive suffix *-rə* see the commentary to 14.3351.

The fifth line is hypermetric (*ji amari*, 字余り).

14.3369

本文 • *Original Text*
(1) 阿之我利乃 (2) 麻萬能古須氣乃 (3) 須我麻久良 (4) 安是加麻可左武 (5) 許呂勢多麻久良

仮名の書き下し • *Kana Transliteration*
(1) あしがりの₂ (2) ままの₂こ₁すげ₂の₂ (3) すがまくら (4) あぜかまかさむ (5) こ₂ろ₂せたまくら

Romanization
(1) Asiⁿgari-nə (2) mama-nə ko-suⁿgɛ-nə (3) suⁿga-makura (4) aⁿze ka mak-as-am-u (5) kə-rə se ta-makura

Glossing with Morphemic Analysis
(1) Asiⁿgari-GEN (2) cliff-GEN DIM-sedge-GEN (3) sedge-headrest (4) why IP use.as.a.pillow-HON-TENT-ATTR (5) girl-DIM do(IMP) arm-headrest

Translation

(5) Girl, use [my] arms as [your] headrest. (4) Why would [you] use (3) a sedge pillow (2) [made of] small sedges from the cliffs (1) of Asiᵑgari?

Commentary

On Asiᵑgari see the commentary to 14.3361.

On *mama* 'cliff' see the commentary to 14.3349. In contrast to his commentary to 14.3349, Omodaka argues that in this poem *mama* is not a 'cliff', but a placename (1977.14: 47), but his argumentation is speculative.

OJ *suᵑge* 'sedge' in Nara period mostly referred to a specific type of sedge,[11] called *kasa suge* (笠菅) 'straw hat sedge' in MDJ, alternatively also called *mino suge* (蓑菅) 'straw raincoat sedge', because straw hats and raincoats were made of it. *Suᵑge* is a large perennial grass (reaching a height of up to one meter) that grows in the damp areas on land as well as in shallow ponds and marshes.[12] Its stalk has triangular shape, and leaves are very hard, so it is very easy to cut one's hands. It blooms in the summer, and is cut in the autumn, and after it dries, straw hats and raincoats are made from it. In the Nara period headrests for not so affluent people were also made of sedge as well as of straw.

EOJ *aⁿze* 'why' corresponds to WOJ *naⁿzə* 'id.' For details see Vovin (2005: 333–335).

On EOJ *kə* 'girl' see the commentary to 14.3361.

On the diminutive suffix *-rə* see the commentary to 14.3351.

14.3370

本文・Original Text

(1) 安思我里乃 (2) 波故祢能祢呂乃 (3) 尒古具佐能 (4) 波奈都豆麻奈礼也 (5) 比母登可受祢牟

仮名の書き下し・Kana Transliteration

(1) あしがりの₂ (2) はこ₁ねの₂ねろ₂の₂ (3) にこ₁ぐさの₂ (4) はなつつまなれや (5) ひ₁も₂と₂かずねむ

---

11 There are about 200 different types of sedges in Japan.
12 This might seem contradictory to the cliffs mentioned in the poem, but one should keep in mind that damp areas could be found around cliffs as well. Mizushima notes that in the modern Eastern dialects the word *mama* may mean not only 'cliff', but also 'slope' or 'depression near water' (1986: 79). In the meaning 'depression near water' *mama* is attested in Niigata, Nagano, and Shizuoka (Tōjō 1951: 775).

Romanization
(1) Asiⁿgari-nə (2) Pakone-nə ne-rə-nə (3) niko-ŋ-gusa-nə (4) pana t-u tuma nar-e ya (5) pimə tək-aⁿz-u ne-m-u

Glossing with Morphemic Analysis
(1) Asiⁿgari-GEN (2) Pakone-GEN peak-DIM-GEN (3) soft-COP(ATTR)-grass-COMP (4) flower COP-ATTR spouse be-EV IP (5) cord untie-NEG-CONV sleep-TENT-ATTR

Translation
(4) Are [you] a newly-wed bride (3) that is like a soft grass (2) at the Pakone peaks (1) in Asiⁿgari? [– Certainly not!] (5) [Why] would [I] sleep [with you] without untying the cords [of my garment]?

Commentary
On Asiⁿgari see the commentary to 14.3361.

Mt. Pakone is present-day Mt. Hakone (箱根) on the border of Kanagawa and Shizuoka prefectures. It is an active volcano with several craters, the highest peak being Kami-yama (神山) at 1,438 m. The characters 箱根 'box root' are likely to be *ateji*. The etymology of this placename is obscure, although *-ne* in Pakone may be OJ *ne* 'summit, peak'. The remainder *Pako-* is unlikely to mean 'box', as it would be a strange name for a mountain. At this point, we cannot think of an appropriate Ainu etymology either.

On the diminutive suffix *-rə* see the commentary to 14.3351.

Note that the second *tu* on line four is written with the *man'yōgana* sign 豆, which is usually used for the syllable /ⁿdu/ with a prenasalized voiced initial /ⁿd/, but there are also cases when it is used for the syllable /tu/ with a voiceless initial /t/ (Omodaka et al. 1967: 896).

The fifth line is hypermetric (*ji amari*, 字余り).

This poem is difficult to interpret exactly, due to two obscure expressions: *niko-ŋ-gusa* and *pana t-u tuma*: there are almost as many explanations as the *Man'yōshū* scholars, especially in the latter case. The various proposals for identification of *niko-ŋ-gusa* are listed in detail by Yamada and Nakajima (1995: 416–417), and hypotheses concerning interpretation of *pana t-u tuma* are meticulously provided by Mizushima (1986: 81–82).

As far as *niko-ŋ-gusa* is concerned, it seems that there are two leading interpretations, one claiming that it is simply 'soft grass', without any specification of the species, and another insisting that it refers to a specific plant *Hakone sida* 'Hakone fern' (Omodaka et al. 1967: 544). We prefer the first solution, because there are other cases of OJ *niko* 'soft, gentle' in compounds followed by the compressed form -N- of the copula attributive form *n-ə*, e.g. *niko-ⁿ-de* 'soft hands'. On the other hand, if we take *niko* in *niko-ŋ-gusa* to be a name of a specific plant, we will face the situation when, while all other OJ plant names that include *-kusa* as the second element of a compound are etymologically transparent, *niko* certainly is not. Since ferns are anything but soft, the possibility of *niko* 'soft' underlying the name of a plant should also be discarded.

Among many interpretations of *pana t-u tuma*, ranging from a 'promiscuous woman' to 'inaccessible woman', we prefer the interpretation of 'a newly-wed bride', who is shy to sleep with [her] husband, which goes back to Kamochi Masazumi (Mizushima 1986: 81).

Sleeping with untied cords of one's garment is a metaphor for sexual abstinence.

On the symbolism of tying and untying the cords see the commentary to 14.3361.

It seems that the spelling of the word *pimo* 'cord' as *pimə* 比母 rather than *pimo* 比毛 in this poem is an innovation. Since *pimo* 'cord' does not occur in the *Kojiki*, Omodaka et al. treat this word as *pimo* (1967: 624) with an unknown quality of the final vowel. However, it is more than likely that the final vowel was *kō-rui* /o/: the vocalic sequence *i-ə* in the structure [C]*iCə* is quite rare (for example, *irə* 'color', *sikə* 'disgusting'), and *Cimə, as far as we know, does not exist. On the other hand, [C]*imo* and [C]*iCo* occur frequently, e.g.: *imo* 'beloved' (< *imo), *iso* 'rock, rocky shore', *kimo* 'liver', *simo* 'frost, etc.

14.3374

本文 · *Original Text*
(1) 武蔵野尒 (2) 宇良敝可多也伎 (3) 麻左弖尒毛 (4) 乃良奴伎美我名 (5) 宇良尒侶尒家里

仮名の書き下し · *Kana Transliteration*
(1) むざしの₁に (2) うらへ₁かたやき₁ (3) まさでにも₁ (4) の₂らぬき₁み₁がな (5) うらにでにけ₁り

Romanization
(1) Muⁿzasi NO-ni (2) ura-pe kata yak-i (3) masaⁿde n-i mo (4) nər-an-u kimi-ⁿga NA (5) ura-ni [i]ⁿde-n-i-ker-i

Glossing with Morphemic Analysis
(1) Mu^{n}zasi field-LOC (2) divination-clan.member shoulder[blade] burn-CONV (3) clear COP-CONV FP (4) say-NEG-ATTR lord-POSS name (5) divination-LOC go.out(CONV)-PERF-CONV-RETR-FIN

Translation
(4) The name of [my beloved] lord which [I] did not tell [to anyone] (3/5) became clearly known through divination (2) when a diviner burnt [deer] shoulder [blade] (1) at the Mu^{n}zasi plain.

Commentary
This poem superficially looks like a perfect WOJ text, but the EOJ adverb *masa^{n}de n-i* 'clearly, surely, really' vs. WOJ *masa n-i* 'id.' betrays its EOJ origin.

Mu^{n}zasi is a place name of Ainu origin, derived from Ainu *mun* 'grass' + *sa* 'shore, plain' + *-hi* third person singular possessive. i.e. 'grass plain' or 'grass shore' (reflected in EOJ as *si*, cf. also Ainu *hita* 'time, when' > EOJ *si^{n}da* 'id.' in 14.3363). For more details see Vovin (2009b: 2). Mu^{n}zasi (武蔵) was one of the Great Provinces (Taikoku, 大國) under the *Ritsuryō* code. On the *Ritsuryō* code classification of Yamatə provinces see the commentary to the postscript to the poem 14.3349.

The practice of divination based on judging the cracks on a tortoise carapace (with a previously written text on it) that resulted from heating on fire has long roots in China that go back to the Shāng (商) dynasty (1766–1122 BC). This practice was adopted in Japan's Asuka and Nara periods as well, but besides tortoise carapaces deer shoulder blades were also used. See the commentary on the Chinese essay found after MYS 5.896 (Vovin 2011a: 147).

14.3375

本文 • *Original Text*
(1) 武蔵野乃 (2) 乎具奇我吉藝志 (3) 多知和可礼 (4) 伊尓之与比欲利 (5) 世呂尓安波奈布与

仮名の書き下し • *Kana Transliteration*
(1) むざしの₁の₂ (2) をぐき₂がき₁ぎ₁し (3) たちわかれ (4) いにし与₂ひ₁より (5) せろ₂にあはなふよ₂

Romanization
(1) Muⁿzasi NO-nə (2) wo^ŋ-gukï-^ŋga ki^ŋgisi (3) tat-i wakare (4) in-i-si yəpi-yori (5) se-rə-ni ap-an-ap-u yə

Glossing with Morphemic Analysis
(1) Muⁿzasi field-GEN (2) DIM-stalk-POSS pheasant (3) rise-CONV part(CONV) (4) go.away-CONV-PAST.ATTR night-ABL (5) beloved-DIM-DAT meet-NEG-ITER-FIN EP

Translation
(4) From the night when [he] went away, (3) rising up and parting with [me] (2) like a pheasant [flying up] from small stalks [of the bush] (1) in the Muⁿzasi plain (5) [I] have never met [my] beloved!

Commentary
On Muⁿzasi province see the commentary to 14.3374.

EOJ *kukï* is considered to be a *hapax legomenon*. Some scholars remain non-committed (Kojima et al. 1973: 454; Itō 1997: 317) regarding its interpretation, but there is also tendency to interpret it as 'promontory, cape' (Tsuchiya 1977.7: 230; Mizushima 1986: 91; Satake et al. 2002: 318) or 'cave' (Takagi et al. 1959: 415; Omodaka 1977.14: 54). Regarding the last interpretation Mizushima correctly indicates that the word for 'cave' is *kuki*, not *kukï* (1986: 91), and there is no evidence for the confusion of the *kō-rui* /ki/ with the *otsu-rui* /kï/ in the Muⁿzasi dialect (Kupchik 2011: 197). Pheasants normally nest among medium height grass or bushes. Consequently, there is nothing to prevent us from interpreting EOJ *kukï* in this poem as the same WOJ word for 'stem, stalk'.

On the diminutive suffix *-rə* see the commentary to 14.3351.

The verbal form *ap-an-ap-* 'to continue not to meet', with the iterative *-ap-* following negative, also demonstrates typical EOJ order of morphemes, since in WOJ the order is reverse, with negative following the iterative. For more details see Vovin (2009a: 820–828).

14.3376

本文・Original Text
(1) 古非思家波 (2) 素弓毛布良武乎 (3) 牟射志野乃 (4) 宇家良我波奈乃 (5) 伊呂尒豆奈由米

仮名の書き下し・Kana Transliteration
(1) こ₁ひ₂しけ₁ば (2) そ₁でも₁ふらむを (3) むざしの₁の₂ (4) うけ₁らがはなの₂ (5) いろ₂にづなゆめ₂

Romanization
(1) kopïsi-ke^mba (2) so^nde mo pur-am-u-wo (3) Mu^nzasi NO-nə (4) ukera-ŋga pana-nə (5) irə-ni [i]^nd-una yumɛ

Glossing with Morphemic Analysis
(1) miss-ATTR/COND (2) sleeve FP wave-TENT-ATTR-ACC (3) Mu^nzasi field-GEN (4) ukera-POSS flower-COMP (5) color-LOC go.out-NEG.IMP at.all

Translation
(1) If [you] miss [me], (2) [I] will wave [my] sleeves, but (5) in your [facial] color do not show at all [your love for me] (4) like *ukera* flower (3) from the plain of Mu^nzasi!

Commentary
On Mu^nzasi province see the commentary to 14.3374.

Ukera is probably an EOJ word. Unfortunately, the corresponding WOJ word is not attested phonographically, except in late *katakana* gloss as ヲケラ [wokera] (NS XXIX: 379), which is also supported by MJ *wokera* found in several sources, as well as by MDJ *okera*. EOJ *ukera* ~ MJ *wokera* ~ MDJ *okera* (Lat. *Atractylodes japonica*) is a perennial grass from the chrysanthemum family that grows in the wild. It reaches the height of approximately 60 cm (2 ft). It blooms in September–October with flowers ranging from white to a pale red color. Its metaphorical usage for revealing one's feelings in facial color probably comes from the pale red color. *Okera*'s young sprouts are edible, and roots are used as a stomach medicine.

On the sleeve-waving ritual by women see the commentary to 14.3389.

Postscript to the Poem 14.3376

本文・Original Text
或本歌曰

Translation
In a certain book the poem says:

Commentary

We do not know what the book is. This poem apparently is the variant of 14.3376 that will be presented below as 14.3376a.

14.3376a

本文・*Original Text*
(1) 伊可尓思弖 (2) 古非波可伊毛尓 (3) 武蔵野乃 (4) 宇家良我波奈乃 (5) 伊呂尓侣受安良牟

仮名の書き下し・*Kana Transliteration*
(1) いかにして (2) こひ₂ばかいも₁に (3) むざしの₁の₂ (4) うけ₁らがはなの₂ (5) いろ₂にでずあらむ

Romanization
(1) ika n-i s-i-te (2) kopï-ᵐba ka imo-ni (3) Muⁿzasi NO-nə (4) ukera-ᵑga pana-nə (5) irə-ni [i]ⁿde-ⁿz-u ar-am-u

Glossing with Morphemic Analysis
(1) how COP-CONV do-CONV-SUB (2) long.for-COND IP beloved-DAT (3) Muⁿzasi field-GEN (4) ukera-POSS flower-COMP (5) color-LOC go.out-NEG-CONV exist-TENT-ATTR

Translation
(2) If [I] long for [my] beloved, (5) would not [my feelings] show in [my facial] color (1) anyway (4) like *ukera* flower (3) from the plain of Muⁿzasi?

Commentary
On Muⁿzasi province see the commentary to 14.3374.

On EOJ *ukera* see the commentary to 14.3376.

The poem 14.3376a actually looks not like a variant of 14.3376, but as a reply to it, composed by a man.

Mizushima suggested that the metaphor involving *ukera* flower in this poem is to be understood in the sense that *ukera* is an inconspicuous white flower, so he interprets lines four and five as 'will not show in my face like *ukera* flower' (1986: 95). This interpretation, however, does not agree well with the usage of the same metaphor in 14.3376 above, and also ignores the fact that the whole sentence is interrogative, not affirmative, since there is an interrogative particle *ka* in the second line.

14.3377

本文 • *Original Text*
(1) 武蔵野乃 (2) 久佐波母呂武吉 (3) 可毛可久母 (4) 伎美我麻尒末尒 (5) 吾者余利尒思乎

仮名の書き下し • *Kana Transliteration*
(1) む₁ざしの₁の₂ (2) くさはも₂ろ₂むき₁ (3) かも₁かくも₂ (4) き₁み₁がまにまに (5) わは よ₂りにしを

Romanization
(1) Muⁿzasi NO-nə (2) kusa pa mərə muk-i (3) ka mo ka-ku mə (4) kimi-ⁿga manima n-i (5) WA pa yər-i-n-i-si-wo

Glossing with Morphemic Analysis
(1) Muⁿzasi field-GEN (2) grass TOP all face-CONV (3) thus FP be.thus-CONV FP (4) lord-POSS according COP-CONV (5) I TOP approach-CONV-PERF-CONV-PAST.ATTR-ACC

Translation
(1/2) The grass on the Muⁿzasi plain faces all [directions] (3) in this way and in that way. (5) I, [on the other hand], followed [only] my lord's will, but ...

Commentary
On Muⁿzasi province see the commentary to 14.3374.

Two topic particles *pa* in this poem are clearly contrastive.

There is a considerable disagreement between scholars whether 久佐波 in line two should be interpreted as *kusa pa* 'grass TOP' (Takagi et al. 1959: 415; Kubota 1967: 158; Kojima et al. 1973: 455; Tsuchiya 1977.7: 282; Nakanishi 1981: 249; Mizushima 1986: 96; Satake et al. 2002: 319), or *kusa^mba* 'grass leaves' (Omodaka 1977.14: 56; Itō 1997: 317). We believe that the second interpretation is untenable because there are no other examples of *kusa^mba* 'grass leaves' in OJ.

There is also a disagreement between various commentaries whether the sequence 吾者 in line five should be read as *A pa* (Takagi et al. 1959: 415; Kojima et al. 1973: 455; Tsuchiya 1977.7: 282; Nakanishi 1981: 249; Mizushima 1986: 96; Itō 1997: 317; Satake et al. 2002: 319) or *WA pa* (Kubota 1967: 158; Omodaka 1977.14: 56). We follow here Kubota and Omodaka's opinion, because although *a pa* 'I TOP' occurs once in WOJ in phonographic spelling (KK 5), there are no examples of it in the *Man'yōshū*. Meanwhile, *wa pa* 'I TOP' occurs in the *Man'yōshū* alone in phonographic script ten times in EOJ corpus and once in WOJ corpus. The only phonographic WOJ example of *wa pa* is 20.4408, but this is a poem written by Yakaməti in imitation of a *sakimori* poem, so the usage there is likely to be influenced by EOJ. Therefore, we should treat the sequence *wa pa* 'I TOP' as an EOJ feature.

The concessive usage of the accusative case marker -*wo* in the fifth line after the attributive form of verb indicates that the author regrets her action of trusting her lover, but does not put her complaint into words.

14.3378

本文 • *Original Text*
(1) 伊利麻治能 (2) 於保屋我波良能 (3) 伊波爲都良 (4) 比可婆奴流々々 (5) 和尓奈多要曾祢

仮名の書き下し • *Kana Transliteration*
(1) いりまぢの₂ (2) おほやがはらの₂ (3) いはゐつら (4) ひ₁かばぬるぬる (5) わにな たえ₂そ₂ね

Romanization
(1) Irima-ⁿ-di-nə (2) Opoya-ᵑga para-nə (3) ipawi-tura (4) pik-ᵐba nuru-nuru (5) wa-ni na-taye-sə-n-e

Glossing with Morphemic Analysis
(1) Irima-GEN-road-GEN (2) Opoya-POSS field-GEN (3) rock(?)-vine (4) pull/invite-COND slippery (5) I-DAT NEG-break.up(CONV)-do-DES-IMP

Translation
(3/4) If [I] ask [you] out, [come] smoothly [to me, like] a rock vine (2) from Opoya field (1) at the road to Irima (4) that smoothly [comes] if one pulls [it]. (5) Do not break up with me, please!

Commentary
Irima (入間) is the name of one of districts in Muⁿzasi province, it corresponds to present-day Iruma county (入間郡) in Saitama prefecture (Mizushima 1986: 97; Nakanishi 1985: 428).

The exact location of Opoya field is unknown. There are four competing explanations of the placename Opoya. One takes it as Ōyazawa (大谷澤) in Hidaka town (日高町) of Iruma county (入間郡) in Saitama prefecture, another one as Ōya (大谷) in Ogose town (越生町) of the same county, third as Ōwi town (大井町) of the same county, and the fourth as Sakado city (坂戸市, old Ōyake village (大家村) in Iruma county) (Nakanishi 1985: 433).

It is not clear what kind of vine *ipawi-tura* is, although there are several hypotheses concerning its identification with modern plants (Mizushima 1986: 98). *Ipawi-tura* is also attested in 14.3416, but does not appear in WOJ texts. The first element of this compound in all probability can be analyzed as *ipa* 'rock' and *wi-* 'to sit, to dwell'. Thus, *ipawi-tura* is a 'rock vine', or literally 'a vine that dwells on rocks'.

The EOJ language of the poem can be also argued on the basis by *wa-ni* 'I-DAT', which does not occur in WOJ corpus.

This poem involves a play on words: OJ *pik-* besides its usual meaning 'to pull, to drag' also means 'to ask out', 'to invite for a date' (of a man to a woman). Thus, we know that the author of this poem is a man.

There are two other similar poems, both in language and content, in book fourteen: 14.3416 and 14.3501.

14.3379

本文・*Original Text*

(1) 和我世故乎 (2) 安杼可母伊波武 (3) 牟射志野乃 (4) 宇家良我波奈乃 (5) 登吉奈伎母能乎

仮名の書き下し・*Kana Transliteration*

(1) わがせこ₁を (2) あど₂かも₂いはむ (3) むざしの₁の₂ (4) うけ₁らがはなの₂ (5) と₂き₁なき₁も₂の₂を

Romanization

(1) wa-ŋga se-ko-wo (2) aⁿ-də ka mə ip-am-u (3) Muⁿzasi NO-nə (4) ukera-ŋga pana-nə (5) təki na-ki mənəwo

Glossing with Morphemic Analysis

(1) I-POSS beloved-DIM-ACC (2) what-QV IP FP say-TENT-ATTR (3) Muⁿzasi field-GEN (4) ukera-POSS flower-COMP (5) time exist.not-ATTR CONJ

Translation

(1/2) What shall [I] say about my beloved, I wonder? (4) Like *ukera* flower (3) on the Muⁿzasi plain, (5) [my longing for him] is timeless, but ...

Commentary

On Muⁿzasi province see the commentary to 14.3374.

On EOJ *ukera* see the commentary to 14.3376.

This poem is unmistakably in Eastern Old Japanese since it has EOJ interrogative pronoun *aⁿ-* 'what, why' vs. WOJ *nani* 'id.' For details see Vovin (2020.1: 295–297).

The oldest manuscripts, *Genryaku kōhon* and *Ruijū koshū*, both have 杼 instead of 抒 /ⁿdə/ in line two, and the character 杼 is also found in some later manuscripts, like *Kishū-bon* and *Hosoi-bon*. However, in this case we prefer to use 抒 used in the *Nishi Honganji-bon* as an archetype for two reasons: first, the usage of 抒 as a *man'yōgana* sign in this poem is unique: it does not occur in any other OJ texts; second, while 杼 has a stop initial (EMC *dʳjwo*), 抒 has an affricate one (EMC *dzjwo*). In addition, it is very easy to confuse radicals 扌 and 木 especially in a cursive or a semi-cursive script.

Besides its direct meaning 'there is no time', *təki na-* is also used in the meaning 'timeless, usual, perpetual'. *Ukera* flowers are not timeless, of course, but they are typical for Muⁿzasi plain, where they usually bloom, hence the metaphoric comparison.

Since the author uses the word *se* 'elder brother, male beloved', she is surely a woman.

14.3382

本文 • *Original Text*
(1) 宇麻具多能 (2) 祢呂乃佐左葉能 (3) 都由思母能 (4) 奴礼弖和伎奈婆 (5) 汝者故布婆曾母

仮名の書き下し • *Kana Transliteration*
(1) うまぐたの₂ (2) ね₂ろ₂の₂ささばの₂ (3) つゆしも₂の₂ (4) ぬれてわき₁なば (5) なはこ₁ふばそ₂も₂

Romanization
(1) Umaⁿguta-nə (2) ne-rə-nə sasa-ᵐ-BA-nə (3) tuyu simə-nə (4) nure-te wa k-i-n-aᵐba (5) NA pa kopu-ᵐba səmə

Glossing with Morphemic Analysis
(1) Umaⁿguta-GEN (2) summit-DIM-GEN bamboo.grass-GEN-leaf-GEN (3) dew frost-GEN (4) get.drenched(CONV)-SUB I come-CONV-PERF-COND (5) you TOP long.for-COND not

Translation
(5) Whether you long for [me or] not, (4) if I come [back] drenched (3) by dew and frost (2) from the leaves of bamboo grass at the peak (1) of Umaⁿguta ...

Commentary
According to Nakanishi, Umaⁿguta peak was located in Umaⁿguta (馬來田) (or alternatively Maⁿguta (望陀)) district of Simotupusa province, but it is not clear to which mountain there it could refer (1985: 430). Itō et al. further comment that the old Umaⁿguta district is now in Kimitsu county (君津郡) of Chiba prefecture (1991: 302). Umaⁿguta can be specifically further defined as Umakuta village, presently known as Fukuta town (富來田町) (Takagi et al. 1959: 416). Both Omodaka and Mizushima suggest a slightly different location in near-by Kisarazu city (木更津市), where Mōda town (望陀町) is also found. They both further cite, in support of their point of view, the fact that in the list of counties found in the *Wamyōshō* there is 望陀 county transcribed in the *man'yōgana* as 末宇太 /mauda/ (Omodaka 1977.14: 62; Mizushima 1986: 106). While -*k*- before *u* certainly could easily drop in the Heian period language, the loss of -*g*- < OJ -*ŋg*- before *u* would be very unusual, so we are inclined to accept the point of view of Nakanishi, Itō et al., and Takagi et al., placing Umaⁿguta into modern Kimitsu county.

On the diminutive suffix -*rə* see the commentary to 14.3351.

The biggest problem in the interpretation of this poem is presented by lines four and especially five. In line four the problem is caused by *wa kinaᵐba* 'if I come', which is viewed by some scholars as a corruption of *wa yukinaᵐba* 'if I go'. However, Omodaka demonstrated quite convincingly that there is no need to look for a 'corruption' here (1977.14: 63). Much greater problem concerns *kopuᵐba* in line five. Traditionally, there are two ways to explain this form, but the methodology is basically the same, with *kopuᵐba* declared to be a 'corruption' (訛り) of either WOJ *kopureᵐba* 'because [you] long for [me]' (Omodaka 1977.14: 63) or *kopïmu* '[you] will long for [me]' (Mizushima 1986: 107). Needless to say, this approach is methodologically unacceptable, because EOJ is not a 'corruption' of WOJ, but a related language, which can have different paths of change as compared to WOJ. Moreover, there is not a single other example in the whole EOJ corpus, where EOJ -*uᵐba* would correspond to WOJ -*ureᵐba*, or to WOJ -*ïmu*. Thus, although substitution of EOJ *kopuᵐba* to WOJ *kopureᵐba* or *kopïmu* would make sense as far as the flow of the text is concerned, this will amount to the *ad hoc* rewriting of the text, which is not acceptable. Alexander Vovin has attempted before to explain ᵐ*ba səmə* through the prism of Ainu (2009b: 46), but in retrospect we believe that this attempt was far-fetched. We now think that the correct analysis of EOJ *kopuᵐba* on its own terms was offered by Kupchik in his recent Ph.D. dissertation. Kupchik suggested that EOJ *kopu-ᵐba* corresponds to the WOJ conditional gerund *kopï-ᵐba* 'if [you] long for [me]' (2011: 431). This makes sense from the point of view of historical linguistics: WOJ *kopï-* and EOJ *kopu-* are both derived from PJ **kopoy-* (cf. early WOJ *koposi* 'be longing for' (KK 110), later WOJ *kopïsi* 'id.', amply attested, EOJ *kopusi* 'id.' (14.3476, 20.4419)), with two different paths of development:

1. PJ **kopoy-* > WOJ *kopï-* (**oy* contracts to *ï*)
2. PJ **kopoy-* > pre-EOJ **kopuy-* > EOJ *kopu-* (**o* raises to *u*, and then **-uy* loses final **-y*)

This solution, however, leaves us with two conditional phrases in the poem: 'if I come' and 'if you long for me', leaving the text hanging in the air without the final phrase showing the realization of these two conditions. Japanese scholars have different views in analyzing the final *səmə* as a 'focus particle' *sə* + 'emphatic particle' *mə* (Kojima et al. 1973: 456; Nakanishi 1981: 250; Omodaka 1977.14: 63), 'emphatic statement' (Takagi et al. 1959: 416), 'emphatic particle' *ⁿzəmə* (Kubota 1967: 161; Tsuchiya 1977.7: 288; Mizushima 1986: 107; Itō 1997: 327). Emphatic particle *ⁿzəmə* does not exist either in WOJ or in EOJ, and there is no indication that the consonant in *sə* was prenasalized *ⁿz-*, as *sə* is spelled with 曾 /sə/. If we follow the point of view of Kojima et al., Nakanishi, and Omodaka, we run into one problem: while emphatic particle *mə* can follow focus particle *sə* (Vovin 2020.2: 1162), focus particle *sə* is not found in OJ after conditional *-(a)ᵐba* (Vovin 2020.2: 1095).[13] Tentatively, we suppose that this *səmə* may reflect the Ainu negative *somo* 'not', therefore line five can be interpreted as 'whether you long for me or not'.

14.3383

本文・*Original Text*

(1) 宇麻具多能 (2) 祢呂尓可久里爲 (3) 可久太尓毛 (4) 久尓乃登保可婆 (5) 奈我目保里勢牟

仮名の書き下し・*Kana Transliteration*

(1) うまぐたの₂ (2) ねろ₂にかくりゐ (3) かくだにも₁ (4) くにの₂と₂ほかば (5) ながめ₂ほりせむ

Romanization

(1) Umaⁿguta-nə (2) ne-rə-ni kakur-i-wi (3) ka-ku ⁿdani mo (4) kuni-nə təpo-k-aᵐba (5) na-ⁿga mɛ por-i se-m-u

---

13   There is a possible exception of *kə-ᵐba sə* in 11.2640, but it is open to interpretation.

Glossing with Morphemic Analysis
(1) Uma^ŋguta-GEN (2) summit-DIM-LOC hide-CONV-dwell(CONV) (3) thus-CONV RP FP (4) province-GEN far-ATTR-COND (5) you-POSS eye want-NML do-TENT-FIN

Translation
(2) [I] dwell in hiding at the peak (1) of Uma^ŋguta, and (3/4) when the [home] province is just so far, (5) [I] want [to see] your eyes.

Commentary
On Uma^ŋguta see the commentary to 14.3382.

On the diminutive suffix *-rə* see the commentary to 14.3351.

EOJ *təpo-k-aᵐba* 'when [it] is far' corresponds to WOJ *təpo-ke-ᵐba* 'id.' with expected outcome of PJ *ea > *ia > WOJ *e* and EOJ *a*. See also 14.3410 below. The conditional verbal gerund *-aᵐba* normally introduces either the irrealis or realis conditional clause in Western Old Japanese, but when used in conjunction with tentative verbal forms in *-(a)m-* or *-(u)ram-*, or negative tentative *-aⁿzi*, it may also introduce a temporal connection clause meaning 'when'. For the details see Vovin (2020.2: 660–661).

Postscript to the Poems 14.3382–3383

本文・*Original Text*
右二首上総國歌

Translation
The two poems above are from Kamitupusa province.

Commentary
Kamitupusa (上総) province was located in the central part of present-day Chiba prefecture. Kamitupusa was one of the Great Provinces under the *Ritsuryō* code. On the *Ritsuryō* code classification of Yamatə provinces see the commentary to the postscript to the poem 14.3349.

14.3384

本文・*Original Text*
(1) 可都思加能 (2) 麻末能手兒奈乎 (3) 麻許登可聞 (4) 和礼尓余須等布 (5) 麻末乃弖胡奈乎

仮名の書き下し・*Kana Transliteration*

(1) かづしかの₂ (2) ままの₂てご₁なを (3) まこ₂と₂かも (4) われによ₂すと₂ふ (5) ままの₂てご₁なを

Romanization

(1) Kaⁿdusika-nə (2) mama-nə TEⁿgo-na-wo (3) ma kətə kamo (4) ware-ni yəs-u tə [i]p-u (5) mama-nə teⁿgo-na-wo

Glossing with Morphemic Analysis

(1) Kaⁿdusika-GEN (2) cliff-GEN maiden-DIM-ACC (3) true matter EP (4) I-DAT make.approach-FIN QV say-ATTR (5) cliff-GEN maiden-DIM-ACC

Translation

(3) [Is it] true, I wonder (4) that [they] say that I am intimate (2) with the maiden from the cliffs (1) of Kaⁿdusika, (5) the maiden from the cliffs?

Commentary

On Kaⁿdusika see the commentary to 14.3349.

On *mama* 'cliff' see the commentary to 14.3349.

Teⁿgo 'maiden' is clearly an EOJ word (-*na* in *teⁿgo-na* is EOJ diminutive suffix -*na* corresponding to WOJ -*ra* (Vovin 2005: 208–209)), because even when it appears in WOJ texts, it is clearly associated with Kaⁿdusika (3.431–433, 9.1807–1808). Possibly Kaⁿdusika-nə *mama-nə* TEⁿgo-na 'maiden from Kaⁿdusika cliffs' was some legendary beauty, although it should not be taken as a personal name, because *teⁿgo* 'maiden' also appears in other EOJ texts not associated with Kaⁿdusika: one poem from Sinanu province (14.3398) and in four poems from unidentified provinces (14.3442, 14.3477, 14.3485, and 14.3540). Nevertheless, it is also found as a part of female name Teⁿgome (手古賣) in the census of Mino province of 702 AD (Omodaka et al. 1967: 483). We have suggested elsewhere that *teⁿgo* is probably from Ainu *ték-o* [tego] 'take in one's arms, embrace (lit.: *arm-take in*)', with Ainu -*k*- [-g-] regularly corresponding to OJ -ⁿg-, for more details see Vovin (2009b: 33–42).[14]

---

14 Cf. Frellesvig's alternative etymology that *teⁿgo* is EOJ pre-raised form of WOJ *tiⁿgo* 'baby' < *ti-nə ko 'milk/breast baby' (Frellesvig, p.c.). The problem here is that *tiⁿgo 'baby' is not attested in Western Old Japanese. The earliest attestation we are aware of is in WMS 2.8a (*tigo*, 知子), which gives us the date 931–938 AD as *non ante quem*. In the Heian period prose texts, MJ *tigo* appears for the first time only in the *Makura-no sōshi* (枕草子) (Miyajima 2014: 662–663), almost a century after WMS.

14.3385

本文 · *Original Text*
(1) 可豆思賀能 (2) 麻萬能手兒奈我 (3) 安里之波可 (4) 麻末乃於須比尓 (5) 奈美毛登杼呂尓

仮名の書き下し · *Kana Transliteration*
(1) かづしかの₂ (2) ままの₂てご₁なが (3) ありしはか (4) ままの₂おすひ₁に (5) なみ₁も₁と₂ど₂ろ₂に

Romanization
(1) Kaⁿdusika-nə (2) mama-nə tEⁿgo-na-ŋga (3) ar-i-si paka (4) mama-nə osu-pi-ni (5) nami mo təⁿdərə n-i

Glossing with Morphemic Analysis
(1) Kaⁿdusika-GEN (2) cliff-GEN maiden-DIM-POSS (3) exist-CONV-PAST.ATTR rumor (4) cliff-GEN rocky.shore-side-LOC (5) wave FP roaring COP-CONV

Translation
(1/2/3) [Due to] a rumor that the maiden from the cliffs of Kaⁿdusika was [there], (5) the waves were roaring, too (4) at the rocky shore of the cliffs.

Commentary
On Kaⁿdusika see the commentary to 14.3349.

On *mama* 'cliff' see the commentary to 14.3349.

On EOJ *teŋgo ~ teŋgo-na* 'maiden' see the commentary to 14.3384.

Line three represents a puzzle. The oldest surviving manuscripts where this poem is extant, the *Genryaku kōhon* and the *Ruijū koshū* both have 波可 *paka*, while the *Nishi honganji-bon*, the *Kishū-bon*, the *Ōya-bon*, and the *Kyōto daigaku-bon* have 婆可 ᵐ*baka*. Only the *Hosoi-bon*, the *Katsuji fukun-bon*, the *Katsuji mukun-bon*, and the *Kan'ei-bon* have 可婆 *ka*ᵐ*ba*. Thus, there is no evidence for 可婆 *ka*ᵐ*ba* until Edo period copies of the *Man'yōshū*. Moreover, the *Hosoi-bon*, the *Katsuji fukun-bon*, the *Katsuji mukun-bon*, and the *Kan'ei-bon* all represent the same line of manuscript development. On the other hand, the oldest Heian period manuscripts *Genryaku kōhon* and *Ruijū koshū* that represent two independent lines of manuscripts both have 波可 *paka*. Thus, identical corruption of the text in the same line of textual development is much more likely than independent preservation of an archaic form. *Paka* is further supported by Sengaku's commentary, *Man'yōshū chūshaku*. Nevertheless, most *Man'yōshū* scholars prefer to follow 可婆 *ka^mba* in Edo copies, because they argue that the reading *arisi^mbaka* or *arisipaka* does not make sense in the poem (Takagi et al. 1959: 417; Kojima et al. 1973: 457; Tsuchiya 1977.7: 240; Mizushima 1986: 111; Itō 1997: 332; Satake et al. 2002: 322). Nakanishi chooses *arisi^mbaka* and explains it as a 'corruption' of *ar-i-s-e^mba ka* 'is it because that [maiden] existed?' (1981: 250). This is difficult to accept, because non-final PJ *ia normally becomes *-a-* in Simotupusa EOJ, but *-e-* in WOJ, cf. PJ *-ki ar-i > WOJ *-ker-i*, but Simotupusa EOJ *-kar-i* (20.4388). Kubota chooses *arisipaka*, but notes that *arisika^mba* would be easier to explain. He further proposes that *ka* in *arisipaka* is an interrogative particle *ka*, but does not provide any explanation for *pa* (1967: 163). Omodaka also chooses *arisipaka* and thinks that *paka* was a noun meaning 'time' (1977.14: 66). However, there is no word *paka* 'time' in either WOJ or EOJ. We think that *paka* can actually be an Ainu loan: *páhaw* 'rumor, gossip', attested in Southwestern Hokkaidō dialects (Hattori 1964: 58). Note that there is a clear textual connection with the preceding poem, which also involves a gossip situation.

EOJ *osu-pi* 'rocky shore side': cf. EOJ *osi-pe* 'id.' in 14.3359 (a poem from Suruⁿga province). See also the commentary to 14.3359.

14.3387

本文・*Original Text*
(1) 安能於登世受 (2) 由可牟古馬母我 (3) 可都思加乃 (4) 麻末乃都藝波思 (5) 夜麻受可欲波牟

仮名の書き下し・*Kana Transliteration*
(1) あの₂おと₂せず (2) ゆかむこ₁まも₂が (3) かづしかの₂ (4) ままの₂つぎ₁はし (5) やまずかよ₁はむ

Romanization
(1) a-nə otə se-ⁿz-u (2) yuk-am-u koma məⁿga (3) Kaⁿdusika-nə (4) mama-nə tuⁿg-i-pasi (5) yam-aⁿz-u kayop-am-u

Glossing with Morphemic Analysis
(1) foot-GEN sound do-NEG-CONV (2) go-TENT-ATTR stallion DP (3) Kaⁿdusika-GEN (4) cliff-GEN join-NML-bridge (5) stop-NEG-CONV visit-TENT-FIN

Translation

(2) [I] want a stallion, which would go (1) without making any noise with its hoofs. (5) [I] would [then] visit [my beloved's place] without stopping (4) at the wooden plank bridge over the cliffs (3) of Kaⁿdusika.

Commentary

Line one is hypermetric (*ji amari*, 字余り), but this probably was not the case in pronunciation, as *a-nə otə* was likely to be pronounced [anətə].

EOJ *a* is the original OJ word for 'foot, leg'. WOJ free form *asi* 'id.' presents some opaque suffix *-si*, and WOJ bound form *a-* occurs only in compounds, e.g. *aᵐbumi* 'stirrups' (< *a-nə pum-i 'foot-GEN step-NML'), *ayupi* 'leg cords' (< *a-yup-i* 'leg-tie-NML').

In spite of the etymologically present diminutive prefix *ko-* in *koma* < *ko-uma, this word does not mean 'small horse', but 'stallion'.

On Kaⁿdusika see the commentary to 14.3349.

On *mama* 'cliff', see the commentary to 14.3349.

OJ *tuⁿg-i-pasi* is bridge made from co-joined wooden boards, so presumably crossing such a bridge on horseback would be very loud, and consequently the amorous visit could not be done in secret. Hence the author's wish for a stallion with hoofs which make no noise.

Postscript to the Poems 14.3384–3387

本文・Original Text

右四首下総國歌

Translation

Four poems above are from Simotupusa province.

Commentary

On Simotupusa province see the commentary to 14.3349.

14.3388

本文・Original Text

(1) 筑波祢乃 (2) 祢呂尒可須美爲 (3) 須宜可提尒 (4) 伊伎豆久伎美乎 (5) 爲祢弖夜良佐祢

仮名の書き下し・*Kana Transliteration*
(1) つくはねの₂ (2) ねろ₂にかすみ₁ゐ (3) すぎ₂かてに (4) いき₁づき₁み₁を (5) ゐねてやらさね

Romanization
(1) Tukupa ne-nə (2) ne-rə-ni kasumi wi (3) suŋgï-kate-n-i (4) ikinduk-u kimi-wo (5) wi ne-te yar-as-an-e

Glossing with Morphemic Analysis
(1) Tukupa peak-GEN (2) peak-DIM-LOC mist sit(CONV) (3) pass(CONV)-POT-NEG-CONV (4) sigh-ATTR lord-ACC (5) bring(CONV)-sleep(CONV)-SUB send-HON-DES-IMP

Translation
(2) The mist sits on the smaller peak (1) of Mt. Tukupa (3) and cannot move away. (4/5) [I] wish [you] would bring [your] sighing lord [here], sleep [with him], and send [him] back.

Commentary
It is difficult to say for sure whether this poem is in EOJ or in WOJ. The only possible EOJ form it has is the diminutive suffix -rə in ne-rə 'small peak' that is predominantly EOJ. On the diminutive suffix -rə see the commentary to 14.3351. We are inclined to treat this text as an EOJ one, but with some reservations.

On Mt. Tukupa see the commentary to FK 2.

The *Genryaku kōhon* in line five has *i ne-* (伊祢), while all other manuscripts have *wi ne-* (爲祢). Like other *Man'yōshū* scholars, we go along with the majority of manuscripts here. There are two reasons to believe that in spite of it being the oldest surviving manuscript, the *Genryaku kōhon* has a mistake here. First, by the end of the Heian period initial *i-* and *wi-* already have merged as /i-/. Second, to the best of my knowledge, *i-ne- with the prefix *i-* is not attested either in EOJ or WOJ. The phrase *i ne-* 'to sleep a sleep' will not fit into the context of this poem, either.

Both Omodaka (1977.14: 70) and Mizushima (1986: 116) treat *wi ne-* as 'to sleep together'. Doubtlessly, this compound has such a meaning, but it also means 'to bring someone somewhere and sleep together' (Omodaka et al. 1967: 825). We prefer this second meaning in our translation and interpretation, because the location in question is the smaller (female) peak of Mt. Tukupa, the famous site of *utaŋgaki ~ kaŋgapi* ritual orgies.

14.3389

本文・*Original Text*
(1) 伊毛我可度 (2) 伊夜等保曾吉奴 (3) 都久波夜麻 (4) 可久礼奴保刀尓 (5) 蘇提波布利弓奈

仮名の書き下し・*Kana Transliteration*
(1) いも₁がかど₁ (2) いやと₂ほそ₂き₁ぬ (3) つくはやま (4) かくれぬほと₁に (5) そ₁ではふりてな

Romanization
(1) imo-ⁿga kaⁿdo (2) iya təpo sək-i-n-u (3) Tukupa yama (4) kakure-n-u poto-ni (5) soⁿde pa pur-i-te-na

Glossing with Morphemic Analysis
(1) beloved-POSS gate (2) more.and.more distant become.distant-CONV-PERF-FIN (3) Tukupa mountain (4) hide-NEG-ATTR time-LOC (5) sleeve TOP wave-CONV-PERF-DES

Translation
(1) The gate of my beloved['s house] (2) became more and more distant. (4) While [I] am not hidden by (3) Mt. Tukupa, (5) I wish you would wave [your] sleeve [at me].

Commentary
It is difficult to say for sure whether this poem is in EOJ or in WOJ. The only evidence for the EOJ nature of this poem is the misspelling of *potə* 'time' as *poto*, which would be unlikely in WOJ. We are inclined to treat this text as an EOJ one, but with some reservations.

On Mt. Tukupa see the commentary to FK 2.

The act of a woman waving her sleeve to a man who departs on a journey represented not just saying 'good-bye', but a magical performance directed at sending one's own soul to protect the traveler, and at the same time taking his soul back to herself for protection (Mizushima 1986: 118–119).

14.3392

本文・*Original Text*
(1) 筑波祢乃 (2) 伊波毛等杼呂尓 (3) 於都流美豆 (4) 代尓毛多由良尓 (5) 和我於毛波奈久尓

仮名の書き下し・*Kana Transliteration*
(1) つくはねの₂ (2) いはも₁と₂ど₂ろ₂に (3) おつるみ₁づ (4) よ₂にも₁たゆらに (5) わがおも₁はなくに

Romanization
(1) Tukupa ne-nə (2) ipa mo təndərə n-i (3) ot-uru miⁿdu (4) yə-ni mo tayur-an-i (5) wa-ŋga omop-an-aku n-i

Glossing with Morphemic Analysis
(1) Tukupa peak-GEN (2) rock FP rumbling COP-CONV (3) fall-ATTR water (4) life.time-LOC FP cease-NEG-CONV (5) I-POSS think-NEG-NML COP-CONV

Translation
(5) Although [I] did not think [about it], (4) [my love for you] will not cease for a life time (3) like falling water (2) or rumbling rocks (1) at Tukupa peak.

Commentary
On Mt. Tukupa see the commentary to FK 2.

On *yə-ni mo* 'in one's life time' and *tayur-an-i* 'cease-NEG-CONV' in line four see the commentary to 14.3368.

In the description of Tukupa district in Fudoki there is a mention of steep rocks around the eastern peak of Tukupa and a spring that runs both in summer and winter (Akimoto 1958: 40). Mizushima notes that this might be Minanogawa river (男女川) that runs between male and female peaks of Tukupa, but the identification is not necessarily correct (1986: 123).

Line five is hypermetric (*ji amari*, 字余り), but it is probably a graphic illusion, since in all likelihood *wa-ŋga omop-an-aku n-i* was pronounced as [waŋgamopanakuni].

14.3394

本文・*Original Text*
(1) 左其呂毛能 (2) 乎豆久波祢呂能 (3) 夜麻乃佐吉 (4) 和須良許婆古曾 (5) 那乎可家奈波賣

仮名の書き下し・*Kana Transliteration*
(1) さご₂ろ₂も₁の₂ (2) をづくはねろ₂の₂ (3) やまの₂さき₁ (4) わすらこ₂ばこ₁そ₂ (5) なをかけ₁なはめ₁

Romanization
(1) sa-ŋ-gərəmo-nə (2) woⁿ-Dukupa ne-rə-nə (3) yama-nə saki (4) wasura-kə-ᵐba kosə (5) na-wo kake-n-ap-am-e

Glossing with Morphemic Analysis
(1) fifth[.lunar.month]-GEN-garment-GEN (2) DIM-Tukupa peak-DIM-GEN (3) mountain-GEN protrusion (4) forget(CONV)-come-COND FP (5) name-ACC call-NEG-ITER-TENT-EV

Translation
(4) Only when [I] forget (3) the mountain protrusion (2) of the smaller Tukupa peak (1) that is [dressed] in the fifth lunar month garment, (5) I will not repeatedly call [your] name.

Commentary
This poem contains several distinctive EOJ features, such as the negative suffix -(a)n- preceding iterative suffix -ap- in a verb (the order is opposite in WOJ), and EOJ specific converb form *wasura-* (cf. WOJ *wasure-*).

Sa-ŋ-gərəmo-nə[15] is traditionally considered to be a permanent epithet (*makura-kotoba*, 枕詞) to *wo* 'cord' and *wo(ⁿ)-*, diminutive prefix (Omodaka 1977.14: 75). However, since *utaŋgaki ~ kaŋgapi* ritual orgies were conducted in spring and fall, we believe that it is transparent here and could be translated literally as '[dressed] in the fifth lunar month garments'. Cf. also WOJ *sa-ᵐ-papɛ* 'fifth [lunar month] flies' (五月蠅): this is an interesting case from the spelling point of view. Although *sa-ᵐ-papɛ* 'fifth [lunar month] flies' as a word is attested in phonographic spelling in the *Nihonshoki kayō* along with the logographic gloss 五月蠅 that confirms its meaning, the name for the fifth lunar month is *sa-tukï*, and not just *sa-*. Possibly we deal here with a conventional way of contraction of *sa-tukï* to *sa*.

On Mt. Tukupa, MDJ Tukuba (< Tukupa, with a secondary nasalization/voicing) see the commentary to the poem FK 2.

On the diminutive suffix *-rə* see the commentary to 14.3351.

Yama-nə saki is a protruding part of a foot of a mountain. It probably refers here to the place where the lovers met for the first time.

The conditional verbal gerund *-aᵐba* normally introduces either the irrealis or realis conditional clause in Western Old Japanese, but when used in conjunction with tentative verbal forms in *-(a)m-*, *(u)ram-*, or negative tentative

---

15   Misspelled as *sa-ŋ-kərəmo-nə* in this poem.

-a^{n}zi it may also introduce a temporal connection clause meaning 'when'. For details see Vovin (2020.2: 660–661).

On the specific EOJ order of morphemes -(a)n-ap- 'NEG-ITER' see the commentary to 14.3375.

There is significant disagreement between Japanese scholars regarding the interpretation of the last line. Some of them analyze *na-wo kakɛ-* as 'to think of you in my heart' (Kojima et al. 1973: 459; Kubota 1967: 169; Omodaka 1977.14: 75; Satake et al. 2002: 324). The position of others is ambiguous: they interpret *na* from *na-wo kakɛ-* in their *kana-kanji* transliteration as 'you', but in the modern Japanese translation render the whole phrase as 'to call your name' (Takagi et al. 1959: 419; Nakanishi 1981: 252; Itō 1997: 341–42), or 'to call you' (Tsuchiya 1977.7: 248). The main issue is then whether *na* is 'you' or 'name' and whether *kakɛ-*[16] is 'think' or 'call'. Mizushima believes that this phrase should mean 'to call your name', because it is supported by *kimi-ŋga na kakɛ-te* 'I called my lord's name' in a variant poem 14.3362a, with this line exactly corresponding to *imo-ŋga na yo^{m}b-i-te* 'I called my beloved's name' in 14.3362 (1986: 126). We follow Mizushima's lead here, and we also would like to add that we are unaware of any other OJ examples when *na* in *na[-wo] kakɛ-* would mean 'you'.

There was a taboo on incantation of one's beloved name (Mizushima 1986: 126), which was lifted, however, once a certain distance was reached, since there was a belief that calling the name of a person could cause his/her soul to be separated from the body (Takagi et al. 1962: 97; Nakanishi 1981: 333; Yoshii 1988: 289). Once, for example, a mountain pass was reached, the incantation of the name could be done safely.

14.3395

本文 • *Original Text*
(1) 乎豆久波乃 (2) 祢呂尓都久多思 (3) 安比太欲波 (4) 佐波太奈利怒乎 (5) 萬多祢天武可聞

仮名の書き下し • *Kana Transliteration*
(1) をづくはの₂ (2) ねろ₂につくたし (3) あひ₁だよ₁は (4) さはだなりの₁を (5) またねてむかも

---

16   Misspelled as *kake-* in this poem.

Romanization
(1) woⁿ-Dukupa-nə (2) ne-rə-ni tuku tas-i (3) apiⁿda yo pa (4) sapaⁿda nar-i-n-o-wo (5) mata ne-te-m-u kamo

Glossing with Morphemic Analysis
(1) DIM-Tukupa-GEN (2) peak-DIM-LOC moon rise-CONV (3) interval night TOP (4) many become-CONV-PERF-ATTR-ACC (5) again sleep(CONV)-PERF-TENT-ATTR EP

Translation
(2) The moon rises at the peak (1) of the smaller Mt. Tukupa. (3/4) Because the nights between [the nights when we sleep together] became many (5) I wonder whether [we] would sleep together again?

Commentary
This poem is clearly written in EOJ.
  On Mt. Tukupa see the commentary to FK 2.
  On the diminutive suffix -rə see the commentary to 14.3351.
  EOJ *tuku* 'moon' (cf. WOJ *tuki*) represents a different path of development from PJ *tukuy: it is derived from the latter by dropping the final *-y, while PJ *-uy contracts into -*ï* in WOJ.
  EOJ palatalization *ti* > *si* in *tas-i* 'rises and' is not typical for WOJ (cf. WOJ *tat-i*).
  EOJ has perfective attributive -*n-o* (cf. WOJ -*n-uru*). It is clearly an attributive and not a final form here, since it is followed by an accusative case marker -*wo*. Although the character 怒 can be used for both syllables /nu/ and /no/, we take it as /no/, since EOJ has the attributive form -*o* in other cases as well. For perfective attributive -*n-o* see also 14.3461.
  EOJ *sapaⁿda* 'many' corresponds to WOJ *sapa* 'id.' See also 14.3354 and the commentary to 14.3354.
  Most commentators are unanimous in their opinion that moon mentioned here refers to a new moon indicating the beginning of a new month (Kubota 1967: 169; Kojima et al. 1973: 459; Tsuchiya 1977.7: 248; Nakanishi 1981: 252; Mizushima 1986: 127; Omodaka 1977.14: 77; Itō 1997: 343), although some others are non-committal (Takagi et al. 1959: 419; Satake et al. 2002: 325). We side with the non-committal group, and would go even further saying that although the new moon can technically rise, it certainly cannot be seen in the sky. Furthermore, there is an opinion that the moon here also refers to the beginning of the menstruation of the female author of the poem (Mizushima 1986: 127; Itō 1997: 343). Given the fact that the WOJ expression *tukï tat-* 'moon

rises' refers to beginning of menstruation and is attested at least twice (KK 27, 28), the play on words (*kakekotoba*, 掛詞) between 'moon' and 'menses' here is quite likely. See also 14.3476.

Apiⁿda yo is literally 'nights between' indicating the nights between the nights that the lovers slept together.

14.3397

本文 • *Original Text*
(1) 比多知奈流 (2) 奈左可能宇美乃 (3) 多麻毛許曾 (4) 比氣波多延須礼 (5) 阿杼可多延世武

仮名の書き下し • *Kana Transliteration*
(1) ひ₁たちなる (2) なさかの₂うみ₁の₂ (3) たまも₁こ₂そ₂ (4) ひ₁け₂ばたえ₂すれ (5) あど₂かたえ₂せむ

Romanization
(1) Pitati-n-ar-u (2) Nasaka-nə umi-nə (3) tama mo kəsə (4) pik-ɛ-ᵐba taye s-ure (5) aⁿ-də ka taye se-m-u

Glossing with Morphemic Analysis
(1) Pitati-LOC-exist-ATTR (2) Nasaka-GEN sea-GEN (3) jewel seaweed FP (4) pull-EV-CON break(NML) do-EV (5) why-QV IP break(NML) do-TENT-ATTR

Translation
(4) When [one] pulls (3) the jewel seaweeds (2) in the Nasaka sea (1) that is in Pitati, (4) [they] break, (5) [but] why should [we] break up?

Commentary
On Pitati province see the commentary to 14.3351.

Both EOJ and WOJ have three confusing verbs that have very similar forms but actually are completely different. They are *nar-* 'to become' (consonantal), *nar-* 'to be' (equational, *r*-irregular), a contraction of the copula converb *n-i* and *ar-* 'to exist', and *nar-* 'to be located at, to exist at' (existential, *r*-irregular), a contraction of the locative case marker *-ni* and *ar-* 'to exist'. In this poem we have the last, existential type of *nar-*.

Nasaka (浪逆) sea corresponds to the southern part of present-day inland Kitaura bay (北浦) located between Kasima (鹿島郡) and Namekata (行方郡) counties in Ibaraki prefecture (Nakanishi 1985: 470). This is the only poem in the *Man'yōshū* where the placename Nasaka appears. Sengaku's commentary mentions that the placename Nasaka is derived from the fact that in the old times during high tide the waves in the bay started to move in the opposite direction (Satake 1981: 378). if so, then *na-* is 'water' and *-saka* is 'opposite'. Since *saka* 'opposite' is an uninflected adjective, we have here *na saka* 'water opposite' showing a word order where a modifier follows the modified head noun, which is not the usual word order in Japonic.

On the EOJ interrogative pronoun a^n- 'what', 'why' see the commentary to 14.3379.

Postscript to the Poems 14.3388–3397

本文 • *Original Text*
右十首常陸國歌

Translation
The ten poems above are from Pitati province.

Commentary
On Pitati province see the commentary to 14.3351.

The first nine poems of this sequence, 14.3388–14.3396 are clearly connected to Mt. Tukupa, and all of them being love poems, have likely some connection with *utaᵑgaki ~ kaᵑgapi* rituals. On *utaᵑgaki ~ kaᵑgapi* ritual see the brief commentary to 14.3350. Much more detailed information will be provided in the commentary to the forthcoming edition and the translation of the *Man'yōshū* book nine, and more specifically to the poem MYS 9.1759, a *chōka* that provides substantial data on the *utaᵑgaki ~ kaᵑgapi* ritual.

14.3398

本文 • *Original Text*
(1) 比等未奈乃 (2) 許等波多由登毛 (3) 波尒思奈能 (4) 伊思井乃手兒我 (5) 許登奈多延曾祢

仮名の書き下し • *Kana Transliteration*
(1) ひ₁と₂み₂な乃₂ (2) こ₂と₂はたゆと₂も₁ (3) はにしなの₂ (4) いしゐの₂てご₁が (5) こ₂と₂なたえ₂そ₂ね

萬葉集卷第十四・MAN'YŌSHŪ BOOK FOURTEEN   93

Romanization
(1) pitə mïna-nə (2) kətə pa tay-u təmo (3) Panisina-nə (4) Isiwi-nə TEⁿgo-ⁿga (5) kətə na-taye-sə-n-e

Glossing with Morphemic Analysis
(1) person all-GEN (2) word TOP break.off-FIN CONJ (3) Panisina-GEN (4) Isiwi-GEN maiden-POSS (5) word NEG-break.off-do-DES-IMP

Translation
(1/2) Even if all the people stop talking [to me], (5) [I] wish that (4) the maiden from Isiwi (3) in Panisina (5) would not stop talking [to me].

Commentary
The EOJ linguistic nature of this poem can be established only lexically on the basis of one EOJ word *teⁿgo* 'maiden', on which see the commentary to 14.3384.

The word *kətə* here means 'word, speech'. The expression *kətə taye-* indicates 'to stop talking to someone', 'to break off the communication'.

Panisina district (埴科郡) corresponds to present-day Hanishina county (埴科郡) and Kōshoku city (更埴市) in Nagano prefecture (Nakanishi 1985: 476; Mizushima 1986: 132).

Isiwi (石井) is probably a name of a village in Panisina district, but its exact location is unknown (Nakanishi 1985: 476; Mizushima 1986: 132). It is attested only in this poem in the *Man'yōshū*.

14.3399

本文・*Original Text*
(1) 信濃道者 (2) 伊麻能波里美知 (3) 可里婆祢介 (4) 安思布麻之牟奈 (5) 久都波氣和我世

仮名の書き下し・*Kana Transliteration*
(1) しなぬぢは (2) いまの₂はりみ₁ち (3) かりばねに (4) あしふましむな (5) くつは け₂わがせ

Romanization
(1) Sinanu-ⁿ-di pa (2) ima-nə par-i-miti (3) kariᵐba ne-ni (4) asi pum-asim-una (5) kutu pak-ɛ wa-ⁿga se

Glossing with Morphemic Analysis
(1) Sinanu-GEN-way TOP (2) now-GEN clear-NML-road (3) sakura root-LOC (4) foot step-CAUS-NEG/IMP (5) shoes TOP put.on-IMP I-POSS beloved

Translation
(4) Do not let [your] [bare]feet step (3) on roots of sakura (2) at the road cleared now (1) on the way to Sinanu. (5) Put on your shoes, my beloved.

Commentary
The EOJ linguistic nature of this poem can be established on the basis of EOJ *kari*ᵐ*ba* 'sakura [bark]' (cf. WOJ *kani*ᵐ*ba* 'sakura bark') and the imperative form *pak-ɛ* 'put on!' instead of WOJ *pak-e*. Mizushima argues that this is an imperative form *pakɛ* of the vowel verb *pakɛ-* 'to make/let put on' (1986: 136), but 'make shoes to be put on' or 'let shoes to be put on' sounds too strained and artificial in the given context.

Sinanu (信濃) province corresponds to present-day Nagano prefecture (Nakanishi 1985: 452). Sinanu was one of the Upper Provinces under *Ritsuryō* code. On the *Ritsuryō* code classification of Yamatə provinces see the commentary to the postscript to the poem 14.3349. The majority of the *Man'yōshū* scholars read the name of this province as Sinano (Takagi et al. 1959: 409; Kubota 1967: 139; Omodaka 1977.14: 15; Nakanishi 1981: 242; Mizushima 1986: 29; Itō 1997: 278; and Satake et al. 2002: 309). The dissenting voices are those of Kojima et al. (1973: 446), Tsuchiya (1977.7: 203), and Kinoshita (2001). In spite of the fact that the placename Sinano is amply attested from the Heian period onward, we agree with the minority point of view here, because the character 濃 was used in OJ to write only the syllable /nu/, and never the syllable /no/ (Omodaka et al. 1967: 898). The fact that some *Man'yōshū* manuscripts gloss the last syllable with the *kana* sign for *no* is irrelevant, because they come at the earliest from the late Heian period (such as *Ruijū koshū*) or from the Kamakura period (such as *Nishi Honganji-bon*), and starting from the Heian period *kana* sign corresponding to 耐 < 濃 is used for the syllable /no/, and not /nu/. The place name Sinanu can be explained in OJ only as *sin-an-u* die-NEG-ATTR 'one who does not die', which is an unlikely explanation for a placename. We believe that Sinanu has Ainu origin: *sinam* (< *sir-nam*) 'to be cold' + *nup* 'mountain field'[17] that is 'cold mountain fields'. The final consonant *-p* of *nup* 'field' is expected to be lost in early loans into Japanese. An alternative analysis

---

17 Chiri indicates that in Ainu placenames *nup* may mean both 'field' and 'mountain field' (1956: 69).

might be *si-* 'true' + *nam* 'to be cold' + *nup* 'mountain field' 'truly cold mountain fields'. One problem with this analysis is that Ainu *nam* by itself means 'to be cold to the touch', like MDJ *tumetai*. However, Sakhalin Ainu *sinam* (< *sir-nam* 'wheather-be.cold') means both 'to be cold to the touch' and 'to be cold' (Ōtsuka et al. 2008: 156), thus we prefer the Ainu analysis. If this etymology is correct, then MJ Sinano in all probability represents a partial translation of the placename Sinanu, where *nu* 'field' < Ainu *nup* was replaced by MJ *no* 'field'.

The poems in book fourteen have no dates, but as Mizushima notes this poem might be the only one which can be traced to several possible dates, because according to *Shoku Nihongi*, two roads to Sinanu were built in 702, and 713–714 AD (1986: 134–136). It remains unclear, however, which road is meant here.

Kari^mba ne-ni in line three is universally explained by all commentators of the *Man'yōshū* as *kar-i-^m-bane-ni* 'cut-NML-COP(ATTR) stump-LOC' (Takagi et al. 1959: 420; Kubota 1964: 171; Kojima et al. 1973: 460; Tsuchiya 1977.7: 252; Omodaka 1977.14: 80; Nakanishi 1981: 253; Mizushima 1986: 134; Itō 1997: 347; Satake et al. 2002: 326). However, Kojima et al. accept this interpretation only with a question mark, and Satake et al. mention that *kar-i-^m-bane* is not attested anywhere else (2002: 326). Mizushima further points out that the verb *kar-* 'to cut' is a WOJ word, not attested in EOJ (1986: 134), but this might not be the case, as *kar-* is attested in 14.3445, which is a poem in EOJ. More importantly, *pane* 'stump' is a *hapax legomenon*, not attested anywhere else either in EOJ or in WOJ. Finally, leaving stumps in the middle of the newly constructed road seems as unreasonable as walking on them even if they are left: stumps should be very visible unless one walks at night. These facts are quite sufficient to cause a reasonable doubt in the traditional analysis and interpretation of this line. We believe that *ne* in *kari^mba ne-ni* is probably *ne* 'root'. It is much easier to imagine tree roots to be left in the road than tree stumps, especially if the road was designated mostly for walking and horseback riding rather than for wheeled transport. See 15.3590 (Vovin 2009: 46–47) and 18.4116 (Vovin 2016: 128–130) for stepping on rocks and roots while walking on the road. We are unaware of the existence of any *Man'yōshū* poem that describes stepping on tree stumps. We believe that remaining EOJ *kari^mba* is a loanword from Ainu *karínpa* 'sakura, sakura bark'. In most modern Ainu dialects *karínpa* means 'sakura bark', while 'sakura' itself is *karínpa ni* 'sakura bark tree' (Chiri 1976: 118), but in Yakumo dialect in the south of Hokkaidō, *karínpa* may mean both 'sakura' and 'sakura bark' (Hattori 1964: 201). The Yakumo evidence may point to the fact that Ainu *karínpa ni* 'sakura bark tree' is a back formation, and that originally *karínpa* meant just 'sakura'. One possible contrary piece of evidence that the primary meaning of

Ainu *karínpa* is just 'sakura bark' is WOJ *kani^mba* 'sakura bark' < Ainu *karinpa* by regressive nasal assimilation. In any case, whether EOJ *kari^mba ne* indicates just 'sakura roots' or 'roots [covered with] sakura bark', *sakura* bark is very rough and walking on it barefooted would not be a pleasant experience. See 14.3486 on one of the usages of the *sakura* bark.

Pum-asim-una (布麻之牟奈) 'do not let step' in line four appears in all old manuscripts except the *Genryaku kōhon*, which has *pum-as-i-n-am-u* (布麻之奈牟) 'you will step on' (Mizushima 1984a: 127–128). Takagi et al. (1959: 420), Kubota (1964: 171–172), Nakanishi (1981: 253), Mizushima (1986: 134) and Omodaka (1977.14: 80–81) follow the *Genryaku kōhon*. While Takagi et al., Kubota, Nakanishi, and Mizushima do not provide any justification for their position, Omodaka argues for *pum-as-i-n-am-u* on the basis of the fact that all known examples of the similar usage involve the form *asi pum-as-una* 'do not [let] your feet step' with a honorific suffix *-as-* (1977.14: 81). However, besides the fact that *asi pum-as-una is actually not attested in the *Man'yōshū*, the causative negative imperative form *-as-una* is perfectly attested in OJ alongside with honorific negative imperative *-as-una* (Vovin 2020.2: 595–596). Furthermore, the evidence from different manuscripts is more important than that from only one, even though this manuscript turns out to be the earliest one, like the *Genryaku kōhon*. We think that the explanation by Kojima et al. that the characters 牟 *mu* and 奈 *na* were transposed in the *Genryaku kōhon* (1973: 460) is correct. The same position regarding the priority of multiple manuscripts is supported by Tsuchiya (1977.7: 252–253), and Itō (1997: 348). Thus, we choose *pum-asim-una* in our edition and translation as the correct form.

14.3400

本文 · *Original Text*
(1) 信濃奈流 (2) 知具麻能河泊能 (3) 左射礼思母 (4) 伎弥之布美弓婆 (5) 多麻等比呂波牟

仮名の書き下し · *Kana Transliteration*
(1) しなぬなる (2) ちぐまの₂かはの₂ (3) さざれしも₂ (4) き₁み₁しふみ₁てば (5) たまと₂ひ₁ろ₂はむ

Romanization
(1) Sinanu-n-ar-u (2) Ti^nguma-nə ᴋᴀpa-nə (3) sa^nzaresi mə (4) kimi si pum-i-te-^mba (5) tama tə pirəp-am-u

Glossing with Morphemic Analysis
(1) Sinanu-LOC-exist-ATTR (2) Tiⁿguma-GEN river-GEN (3) pebble FP (4) lord EP step-CONV-PERF-COND (5) jewel COP pick.up-TENT-FIN

Translation
(4) If [my] lord would have stepped (3) on pebbles (2) in Tiⁿguma river (1) in Sinanu, (5) [I] would pick [them] up as jewels.

Commentary
On Sinanu province see the commentary to 14.3399.

Tiⁿguma river is present-day Tikuma river (千曲川) in the north-eastern part of Nagano prefecture. It originates at Mt. Kobusigatake (甲武信ヶ岳), flows through Ueda plain (上田盆地) and Nagano plain (長野盆地), and joins together with Sai river (犀川) in Nagano city. Then it flows north to Niigata prefecture, where it becomes Sinano river (信濃川) (Nakanishi 1985: 462). Its length is 214 km. Tiⁿguma river is mentioned in the *Man'yōshū* only in 14.3400 and 14.3401.

The word *saⁿzaresi* 'pebble' is a contracted form of *saⁿzare.isi*. The former is attested phonographically only in this poem, and the latter in WOJ, but it would seem to be a stretch to claim that this poem is in EOJ just on the basis of this fact, but see below on *pirəp-* 'to pick up'.

In this poem conditional -(*a*) ᵐ*ba* introduces a conditional clause, and not a temporal one in spite of the fact that the main verb contains the tentative suffix -*am-*.

All manuscripts have *pirəp-am-u* (比呂波牟) except *Ruijū koshū* that has *pirip-am-u* (比里波牟) (Mizushima 1984a: 129–31). We consider that *Ruijū koshū*'s form is a mistake, probably influenced by the fact that the WOJ form is *pirip-*. WOJ *pirip-* is a clear innovation caused by progressive vowel assimilation, therefore, contrary to Mizushima (1986: 139), the change is ə > *i*, and not vice versa. Consequently, *pirəp-* should be recognized as an EOJ form, which represents a common retention together with Heian period MJ *firof-* 'to pick up'.

14.3401

本文・Original Text
(1) 中麻奈尓 (2) 宇伎乎流布祢能 (3) 許藝弓奈婆 (4) 安布許等可多思 (5) 家布尓思安良受波

仮名の書き下し・ Kana Transliteration
(1) ちぐまなに (2) うき₁をるふねの₂ (3) こ₂ぎ₁でなば (4) あふこ₂と₂かたし (5) け₁ふにしあらずは

Romanization
(1) Tiⁿguma-na-ni (2) uk-i-wor-u pune-nə (3) kəŋg-i-[i]ⁿde-n-amba (4) ap-u kətə kata-si (5) kepu n-i si ar-aⁿz-u pa

Glossing with Morphemic Analysis
(1) Tiⁿguma-river-LOC (2) float-CONV-exist-ATTR boat-GEN (3) row-CONV-exit(CONV)-PERF-COND (4) meet-ATTR matter difficult-FIN (5) today COP-CONV EP exist-NEG-CONV TOP

Translation
(3) If (2) the boat that is floating (1) in Tiⁿguma river (3) would row out, (4) it will be difficult to meet, (5) if [it] is not today.

Commentary
The main problem in this poem is presented by *Tiⁿguma-na* 中麻奈 in the first line. There are numerous theories that both Omodaka (1977.14: 83–84) and Mizushima (1986: 140) discuss, but all of them except one cannot be considered valid. Omodaka presents the theory of Tsuzuku Tsuneo (都竹通年雄), who proposed that the character 中 is used according to its Nara and Heian period Sino-Japanese reading *tiŋ*, which could be used to represent phonographically the sequence *tiⁿgu* in the same way as 相 *saŋ* phonographically represents *saⁿga*. Consequently, 中麻 stands for the placename Tiⁿguma. The remaining *na* is nothing but the expected reflex of Ainu *náy* 'river', with the loss of final -*y* in EOJ in a final or a preconsonantal position. Thus, *Tiⁿguma-na* is 'Tiⁿguma river' (Omodaka 1977.14: 84–86). There are no other EOJ distinctive features in this poem, but the presence of this Ainu loanword probably makes it to be in EOJ, and not in WOJ, as the word *na* 'river' is not otherwise attested in WOJ.

On Tiⁿguma river see the commentary to 14.3400.

Line five is hypermetric (*ji amari*, 字余り), but this is probably just a graphic illusion, since *si araⁿzu* was in all probability pronounced as [saraⁿzu].

Postscript to the Poems 14.3398–3401

本文・*Original Text*
右四首信濃國歌

Translation
The four poems above are from Sinanu province.

Commentary
On Sinanu province see the commentary to 14.3399.

14.3402

本文・*Original Text*
(1) 比能具礼尓 (2) 宇須比乃夜麻乎 (3) 古由流日波 (4) 勢奈能我素侶母 (5) 佐夜尓布良思都

仮名の書き下し・*Kana Transliteration*
(1) ひ₁の₂ぐれに (2) うすひ₁の₂やまを (3) こ₁ゆるひ₁は (4) せなの₂がそ₁でも₂ (5) さやにふらしつ

Romanization
(1) pi-nə ⁿgure-ni (2) Usupi-nə yama-wo (3) koy-uru PI pa (4) se-na-nə-ⁿga soⁿde mə (5) saya n-i pur-as-i-t-u

Glossing with Morphemic Analysis
(1) SUN-GEN sunset-LOC (2) Usupi-GEN mountain-ACC (3) cross-ATTR day TOP (4) beloved-DIM-DIM-POSS sleeve FP (5) clear COP-CONV wave-HON-CONV-PERF-FIN

Translation
(3) On the day when [he] crossed (2) Mt. Usupi (1) at the sunset, (4/5) [my] dear beloved has clearly waved [his] sleeves [at me].

Commentary
The first line *pi-nə ⁿgure-ni* is traditionally considered to be a permanent epithet (*makura-kotoba*, 枕詞) to Usupi understood as *usu* 'thin' + *pi* 'day' (Omodaka 1977.14: 86; Mizushima 1986: 141). However, this alleged *makura-kotoba* occurs

in the whole *Man'yōshū* only once – in this poem. Therefore, we believe that it simply means 'at the sunset', in spite of the rather vehement (and unsubstantiated by evidence) objection by Tsuchiya, who calls this interpretation "blind" (1977.7: 256).

Mt. Usupi probably corresponds not to the mountains at present-day Usui mountain pass (碓氷峠), although such an equation exists (Nakanishi 1986: 428), but to Iriyama mountain pass (入山峠) that is located 2–3 km south from Usui mountain pass in Usui county (碓氷郡) of Gunma prefecture. Iriyama mountain pass is also known as 'old Usui mountain pass'. At the height of 1,035 m, Usupi mountain pass in Tōsandō (東山道) region was known alongside Asiŋgara mountain pass in Tōkaidō (東海道) region as the two most difficult places to pass through (Mizushima 1986: 141–142).

The form *se-na-nə* 'beloved-DIM-DIM' in line four is practically unique, and while *-na* is a typical EOJ diminutive suffix (Vovin 2005: 212–213), it also contains a diminutive suffix *-nə* that is attested besides this poem only in 14.3528. Cf., however, *imo-na-rə* 'beloved-DIM-DIM' in 14.3446 and *se-na-na* 'beloved-DIM-DIM' in 14.3544 that contain two EOJ diminutive suffixes in a row. Possibly *-na-nə* in *se-na-nə* is derived by nasal assimilation from *-na-rə*.

On the sleeve-waving ritual by women see the commentary to 14.3389. Presumably, the sleeve-waving ritual by men had the same or similar function.

14.3404

本文・*Original Text*
(1) 可美都氣努 (2) 安蘇能麻素武良 (3) 可伎武太伎 (4) 奴礼杼安加奴乎 (5) 安杼加安我世牟

仮名の書き下し・*Kana Transliteration*
(1) かみ₁つけ₂の₁ (2) あそ₁の₂まそ₁むら (3) かき₁むだき₁ (4) ぬれど₂あかぬを (5) あど₂かあがせむ

Romanization
(1) Kamitukɛno (2) Aso-nə ma-so mura (3) kaki-muⁿdak-i (4) n-ure-ⁿdə ak-an-u-wo (5) aⁿ-də ka a-ŋga se-m-u

Glossing with Morphemic Analysis
(1) Kamitukɛno (2) Aso-GEN INT-hemp bundle (3) PREF-embrace-CONV (4) sleep-EV-CONC satisfy-NEG-ATTR-ACC (5) what-QV IP I-POSS do-TENT-ATTR

Translation

(4) Although [I] slept [with her] (4) embracing [her], (2) like a bundle of precious hemp from Aso (1) [in] Kamitukɛno, (4) since it was not enough [for me], (5) what should I do?

Commentary

Kamitukɛno (上野) was one of the Great Provinces under the *Ritsuryō* code. It corresponds to present Gunma prefecture. On the *Ritsuryō* code classification of Yamatə provinces see the commentary to the postscript to the poem 14.3349.

Aso district (Aso kəpori, 阿蘇郡) corresponds to present-day Aso county (Aso-gun, 阿蘇郡) and Sano city (Sano-shi, 佐野市) of Tochigi prefecture (Nakanishi 1985: 417). It was in Simotukɛno province and not in Kamitukɛno province, but at some point in time it is believed to have belonged to the latter or to exist in both provinces (Mizushima 1986: 146). Omodaka further notes that from a geographical viewpoint it is more natural for Aso district to have been included in Kamitukɛno rather than in Simotukɛno (1977.14: 90).

OJ *mu^{n}dak-* 'to embrace' is probably an earlier form of WOJ *u^{n}dak-* and MJ *i^{n}dak-* 'id.' On the contrast between PJ **mu$^m/_n$-*, **u$^m/_n$-*, and **o$^m/_n$-* that all merged in WOJ as *u$^m/_n$-* see Vovin (2020.1: 67–69).

On EOJ interrogative pronoun *a^n-* 'what, why' see the commentary to 14.3379.

The first two lines are traditionally defined as a poetic introduction (*jo*, 序) to the rest of the poem (Omodaka 1977.14: 90; Mizushima 1986: 146).

The comparison of one's beloved with a bundle of hemp might seem shocking to modern readers, but one should not forget that first-class hemp was a precious commodity in Ancient Japan.

14.3405

本文・*Original Text*

(1) 可美都氣努 (2) 乎度能多杼里我 (3) 可波治尒毛 (4) 兒良波安波奈毛 (5) 比等理能未思弖

仮名の書き下し・*Kana Transliteration*

(1) かみ₁つけ₂の₁ (2) をど₁の₂たど₂りが (3) かはぢにも₁ (4) こ₁らはあはなも₁ (5) ひ₁と₂りの₂み₂して

Romanization
(1) Kamitukɛno (2) Woⁿdo-nə Taⁿdəri-ŋga (3) kapa-ⁿ-di-ni mo (4) ко-ra pa ap-an-am-o (5) pitə-ri nəmï s-i-te

Glossing with Morphemic Analysis
(1) Kamitukɛno (2) Woⁿdo-GEN Taⁿdəri-POSS (3) river-GEN-road-LOC FP (4) girl-DIM TOP meet-DES-TENT-ATTR (5) one-CL RP do-CONV-SUB

Translation
(4) [I] want [my] dear girl to meet [me] (5) when [she] is all by herself (3) at the road along the river (2) in Taⁿdəri at Woⁿdo (1) in Kamitukɛno.

Commentary
On Kamitukɛno province see the commentary to 14.3404.

Woⁿdo and Taⁿdəri are believed to be unidentified placenames in Kamitukɛno (Omodaka 1977.14: 91; Nakanishi 1985: 460, 500; Mizushima 1986: 148).

On the EOJ verbal attributive -*o* see the commentary to 14.3395 and a brief description of EOJ special grammar in the Introduction.

There is some disagreement between modern commentators whether the author himself wants to meet his girl (Omodaka 1977.14: 91), or he wants his girl to meet him (Mizushima 1986: 148). Although in WOJ the desiderative suffix -*ana*- can express either the desire to perform an action by oneself, or the desire of the speaker for the addressee to perform an action (Vovin 2009a: 665; Vovin 2020.2: 599), it seems that with the exception of usage found in 9.1781, the primary function of combination -*an-am*- consisting of desiderative -*ana*- with tentative -*am*- in both WOJ and EOJ is to express the desire of the speaker for the addressee to perform an action. Thus, we think that it is quite undeniably the second situation: the author wants his girl to meet him.

Postscript to the Poem 14.3405

本文 • *Original Text*
或本歌曰

Translation
A poem in a certain book says:

Commentary

We do not know what the book is. This poem is apparently a variant of 14.3405 that will be presented below as 14.3405a.

14.3405a

本文・*Original Text*
(1) 可美都氣努 (2) 乎野乃多杼里我 (3) 安波治尓母 (4) 世奈波安波奈母 (5) 美流比登奈思尓

仮名の書き下し・*Kana Transliteration*
(1) かみ₁つけ₂の₁ (2) をの₁の₂たど₂りが (3) あはぢにも₂ (4) せなはあはなも₂ (5) み₁るひ₁と₂なしに

Romanization
(1) Kamitukɛno (2) Wono-nə Taⁿdəri-ⁿga (3) apa-ⁿ-di-ni mə (4) se-na pa ap-an-am-ə (5) mi-ru pitə na-si-ni

Glossing with Morphemic Analysis
(1) Kamitukɛno (2) Wono-GEN Taⁿdəri-POSS (3) millet-GEN-road-LOC FP (4) beloved-DIM TOP meet-DES-TENT-ATTR (5) see-ATTR person exist.not-FIN-LOC

Translation
(4) [I] want [my] dear beloved to meet [me] (5) when there is no one who [can] see [us] (3) at the road along the millet [field] (2) in Taⁿdəri at Wono (1) in Kamitukɛno.

Commentary

On Kamitukɛno province see the commentary to 14.3404.

The exact location of Wono in present-day Gunma prefecture is not known (Nakanishi 1985: 500). There were three placenames Wono (spelled as 小野 or 乎乃 in *Wamyōshō*) in three different districts of Kamitukɛno province (Omodaka 1977.14: 91; Mizushima 1986: 149).

On placename Taⁿdəri see the commentary to 14.3405.

Japanese scholars believe that *apa* in line three is the result of the elision of the initial consonant *k-* in the word *kapa* 'river' appearing in the same context in 14.3405, (Omodaka 1977.14: 91; Tsuchiya 1977.7: 260; Mizushima 1986: 149).

Others take it to be a placename, but still suggest *k- > Ø-* (Takagi et al. 1959: 421; Kojima et al. 1973: 462). To the best of my knowledge, the shift *k- > Ø-* is not otherwise attested in the Kamitukɛno dialect of EOJ, see also Shirafuji (1987: 236). Nakanishi treats *apa* as *ap-a*, an attributive form of *ap-* 'to meet' (Nakanishi 1981: 254). Although there is another example of EOJ attributive in *-a* in a poem from the Kamitukɛno dialect (14.3408), it is strange to have *-ⁿ-di* 'GEN-road' after the attributive that can modify a following noun directly, thus *ap-a ti 'meet-ATTR road' would be expected. We think that the solution actually lies on the surface: after all, this is a variant poem, and it should not contain all the same words as 14.3405, and indeed it does not as is demonstrated by line five that is totally different from line five in 14.3405. *Apa* in all probability means what it means: 'millet', and just as *kapa-ⁿ-di* is a 'road along a river', *apa-ⁿ-di* is a 'road along a millet [field]'.

On EOJ diminutive suffix *-na* see the commentary to 14.3384.

On the EOJ verbal attributive *-o* (misspelled as *-ə* in this poem) see the commentary to 14.3395 and a brief description of EOJ special grammar in the introduction.

14.3407

本文 · *Original Text*
(1) 可美都氣努 (2) 麻具波思麻度尒 (3) 安佐日左指 (4) 麻伎良波之母奈 (5) 安利都追見礼婆

仮名の書き下し · *Kana Transliteration*
(1) かみ₁つけ₂の₁ (2) まぐはしまと₁に (3) あさひ₁さし (4) まき₁らはしも₂な (5) ありつつみ₁れば

Romanization
(1) Kamitukɛno (2) ma-ⁿgupasi mato-ni (3) asa PI sas-i (4) makirapasi-mə na (5) ar-i-tutu MI-re-ᵐba

Glossing with Morphemic Analysis
(1) Kamitukɛno (2) INT-beautiful girl-LOC (3) morning sun point-CONV (4) be.blinding-EXCL EP (5) exist-CONV-COOR see-EV-CON

Translation
(3) Morning sun shines (2) at the truly beautiful girl (1) [of] Kamitukɛno. (4) How blinding [your beauty] is, (5) when [I] continuously look [at you]!

Commentary

On Kamitukeno province see the commentary to 14.3404.

The main problem in interpreting this poem is in line two. Premodern scholars, such as Sengaku and Keichū believed that line two should be read as *maᵑgupasi mato-ni* 'at the beautiful window' (Omodaka 1977.14: 93; Mizushima 1986: 151–152). Most modern commentators of the *Man'yōshū* analyze it as *Maᵑgupa sima to-ni* 'at the straights of Maᵑgupa island' (Takagi et al. 1959: 422; Omodaka 1977.14: 93; Mizushima 1986: 151–152; Itō 1997: 364), or take an agnostic position (Kojima et al. 1973: 463; Satake et al. 2002: 329). Two scholars have different opinions: Nakanishi believes that line two should be analyzed as *maᵑgupasi mato-ni* 'at the beautiful circle' (1981: 255), and Tsuchiya thinks that this line should be read either as *maᵑgupasi ma-to-ni* 'at the beautiful person' or *maᵑgupasi ma-ko-ni* 'at the beautiful girl' with 麻度 /mato/ being either *ma-to* 'good/real person' or misspelling for *ma-ko* 'good/real girl' (1977.7: 263). The premodern interpretation has one problem: although we do not know exactly what 'windows' looked like in Ancient Japan, presumably there were just slits used for ventilation or illumination by sunlight (Omodaka et al. 1967: 684). It is highly unlikely that they were any ornate structures. Therefore it is not quite clear why a window would be described as 'beautiful'. The predominant modern explanation treating line two as *Maᵑgupa sima to-ni* 'at the straights of Maᵑgupa island' suffers from a setback that the location of either Maᵑgupa island, or its straits is unknown, although there is a theory placing it on Tonegawa river (利根川) in the second ward of Chiyoda town (千代田町) in Maebashi city (前橋市) in present-day Gunma prefecture (Nakanishi 1985: 484). Nakanishi's theory cannot stand scrutiny, because while there is an OJ uninflected adjective *mato* 'round', it is never used as a noun 'circle'. The same is true for both explanations by Tsuchiya. The misspelling for *ma-ko* 'good/real girl' must be rejected, because one cannot rewrite texts at one's whim. OJ *ma-to* 'good/real person' is otherwise not attested in the texts (it is actually *ma-pitə* as in 14.3552), and it also violates OJ phonology, since *pitə* 'person' has *otsu-rui* vowel /ə/, and not *kō-rui* vowel /o/.[18] We believe that the word *mato* is a loanword from Ainu: PA **mat-poo* 'girl, daughter',[19] with expected loss of C_2 in C_1C_2 cluster, thus *-tp-* > *-t-*. Thus, we interpret *maᵑgupasi mato* as 'beautiful girl'. The

---

18   EOJ *pitə* 'person' is attested multiple times in books fourteen and twenty without any single case of misspelling as **pito*.

19   This word is clearly a compound *mat* 'woman' + *po* 'child'. It is attested only in Sakhalin Ainu dialects: Taraika *matpo*, Ochiho, Shiraura, Shiranusi, Tarantomari, Maoka *mahpo*, Raichiska *mahpoo* (Hattori 1964: 40; Chiri 1975: 496; Ōtsuka et al. 2008: 100–101). The corresponding form in Hokkaidō dialects is *mat-ne-po* 'woman-COP-child' (Hattori 1964: 40; Chiri 1975: 496).

presence of such a basic Ainu loanword certainly makes this poem belong to the EOJ part of the corpus. EOJ *ma-ŋgupasi* 'beautiful' also appears in 14.3424 in the phrase *ma-ŋgupasi* KO-rə *'beautiful girl-*DIM*'*, which lends further support to my interpretation of *mato* as 'girl', especially that there are no other attestations of *ma-ŋgupasi* 'beautiful' in EOJ.

EOJ *makirapasi* 'to be blinding' is a *hapax legomenon* appearing only in this poem. It probably consists etymologically of *ma-* eye', *kir-* 'to cut', iterative suffix *-ap-*, and adjectivizing suffix *-asi*.

14.3408

本文 • *Original Text*
(1) 尒比多夜麻 (2) 祢尒波都可奈那 (3) 和尒余曾利 (4) 波之奈流兒良師 (5) 安夜尒可奈思母

仮名の書き下し • *Kana Transliteration*
(1) にひ₁たやま (2) ねにはつかなな (3) わによ₂そ₂り (4) はしなるこ₁らし (5) あやにかなしも₂

Romanization
(1) Nipita yama (2) ne-ni pa tuk-an-a-na (3) wa-ni yəsər-i (4) pasi-n-ar-u KO-ra si (5) aya n-i kanasi-mə

Glossing with Morphemic Analysis
(1) Nipita mountain (2) peak/sleep(NML)-LOC reach-NEG-ATTR-LOC (3) I-DAT approach-CONV (4) middle-LOC-exist-ATTR girl-DIM EP (5) strange COP-CONV dear-EXCL

Translation
(3/4) [My] dear girl who was becoming intimate with me, but stopped half way (2) as [she] did not sleep [with me], (1) [like] Mt. Nipita (2) that does not join [other] peaks, (5) is strangely dear [to me]!

Commentary
Mt. Nipita corresponds to Mt. Kanayama (223 m, 金山) in the north side of Kanayama town (金山町) in Ōta city (太田市) in present-day Gunma prefecture (Nakanishi 1985: 473).

There is a play on words in this poem: *ne* 'peak' and *ne-* 'to sleep'.

The EOJ form in *V-(a)n-a-na* functionally corresponds to WOJ *V-(a)n-u-ni* 'because/when not doing V'. It is likely to consist etymologically of the negative suffix *-an-*, EOJ-specific attributive *-a-* and EOJ-specific dative-locative case marker *-na*. Since verbal and nominal morphology do not mix in OJ, EOJ locative *-na* cannot follow the negative *-(a)na- directly, and there must be some intermediate nominalizing morpheme. We believe that this morpheme is EOJ-specific and a rare attributive in *-a*, on which see the commentary to 14.3526.

EOJ *wa-ni* 'I-DAT' is not attested in WOJ (Vovin 2020.1: 219).

OJ *pasi* is 'interval, between'. See also 14.3490.

14.3409

本文 · *Original Text*
(1) 伊香保呂尓 (2) 安麻久母伊都藝 (3) 可奴麻豆久 (4) 比等登於多波布 (5) 伊射祢志米刀羅

仮名の書き下し · *Kana Transliteration*
(1) いかほろ₂に (2) あまくも₂いつぎ₁ (3) かぬまづく (4) ひ₁と₂と₂おたはふ (5) いざねしめ₂と₁ら

Romanization
(1) Ikapo-rə-ni (2) ama-kumə i-tuⁿg-i (3) ka-numa-ⁿ-duk-u (4) pitə tə otap-ap-u (5) iⁿza ne-simɛ tora

Glossing with Morphemic Analysis
(1) Ikapo-DIM-LOC (2) heaven-cloud DLF-follow-CONV (3) top-marsh-LOC-arrive-FIN (4) person FP sing-ITER-FIN (5) INTER sleep-CAUS(IMPER) together

Translation
(2) Heavenly clouds follow [one another] (1) at the small Ikapo mountain (3) and go down to [its] upper marsh. (4) People are singing all the time. (5) Hey, let [me] sleep together [with you]!

Commentary
This is one of the most challenging poems in the whole *Man'yōshū*. Only lines one and two, as well as most of line five are transparent. The final element *tora* in line five and lines three and four are opaque. Consequently, it is no wonder

that there are as many interpretations of these opaque parts as commentators of the *Man'yōshū*. There are three possible solutions: these parts may consist of *hapax legomena* in EOJ, or they can be foreign elements. It is also possible that there is a mixture of OJ with another language here. We believe that it is probably the third possibility, and rather than discuss in detail all the conflicting proposals by Japanese scholars, we will present below the justification for our own interpretation.

Ikapo corresponds to mountainous area in the southwest of Ikaho town (Ikaho machi, 伊香保町)[20] in Gunma county (Gunma-gun, 群馬郡) of present-day Gunma prefecture. It also includes Misato town (Misato machi, 箕郷町)[21] and Haruna town (Haruna machi, 榛名町)[22] (Nakanishi 1985: 421). Mizushima also notes that Ikapo-rə mountain (-rə is a diminutive) probably refers to Haruna volcano (Haruna-san, 榛名山, 1391 m)[23] that has a lake in its caldera (1986: 154).

On the diminutive suffix -rə see the commentary to 14.3351.

Prefix *i-* is a marker of a directive-locative focus. For details see Vovin (2009a: 505–512).[24]

Ka-numa in line three may be a place name 'deer marsh' (鹿沼), as Kamochi Masazumi proposed (Kamochi 1912: 51). However, since this placename is not attested otherwise, we would like to entertain a different possibility. While OJ *numa* is certainly 'marsh', the preceding element *ka*, we believe, is a borrowing from Ainu *ka* 'top (not detached)'. Therefore, *ka-numa* is 'upper marsh'.

Practically all scholars see *tə* in *pitə tə* in line four as EOJ form of the focus particle *sə* (cf. *pitə sə*, which appears in 14.3518 in the almost identical line) (Omodaka 1977.14: 97; Mizushima 1986: 156), etc. There are four other cases that support the identification of EOJ *tə* as a cognate of WOJ *sə*: 14.3425 (a poem from Simotupusa), 14.3561 (an unidentified poem), 20.4385 (a poem from Simotupusa), and 20.4430.

The mysterious word *otapapu* in line four has conflicting interpretations as either 'be noisy' or 'be quiet' (Omodaka 1977.14: 97; Mizushima 1986: 156). None will work here unless some significant 'corruption' explanations are involved. We suppose that the initial *o* may be an EOJ old unraised vowel,

---

[20] Incorporated into Shibukawa city (Shibukawa-shi, 渋川市) in 2006.
[21] Incorporated into Takasaki city (Takasaki-shi, 高崎市) in 2006.
[22] Incorporated into Takasaki city (Takasaki-shi, 高崎市) in 2006.
[23] Haruna-san is currently classified as a dormant volcano.
[24] I have somehow missed the example of the usage of the directive-locative prefix *i-* in this poem in my grammar (Vovin 2020.2: 512).

which is otherwise found in WOJ as *u*. Consequently, the WOJ corresponding form with a raised vowel is *utapapu*, which easily recognizable as an iterative form *utap-ap-u* 'to sing continuously' of the verb *utap-* 'to sing'. Incidentally, Proto-Ryūkyūan reconstructions are *Uta 'song' and *Utawi- 'to sing' (Thorpe 1983: 328), with the capital *U demonstrating that the PJ form might have either initial *o- or *u-. What is important, however, is that Proto-Ryūkyūan forms cannot be traced back to PJ *u with certainty. If my proposal is right, then EOJ offers evidence for PJ *ota 'song', and not for *uta.

The beginning of line five is transparent: *iⁿza ne-simε* 'hey, let [me] sleep [with you]' with *-simε* being the causative imperative form. The word *tora*, also appearing in the same context in 14.3518, is opaque. We think that it is a borrowing of Ainu *tura* 'together'. The only weak point of this explanation is that Ainu has *u*, and not *o*, but it might be just a minor irregularity.

The interpretation we propose allows us to view this poem as an *utaᵑgaki ~ kaᵑgapi* ritual poem, where singing exchange was followed by sexual intercourse. On *utaᵑgaki ~ kaᵑgapi* ritual see the brief commentary to 14.3350. Much more detailed information will be provided in the commentary to the forthcoming edition and the translation of the *Man'yōshū* book nine, and more specifically to the poem MYS 9.1759, a *chōka* that provides substantial data on the *utaᵑgaki ~ kaᵑgapi* ritual.

14.3410

本文 · *Original Text*
(1) 伊香保呂能 (2) 蘇比乃波里波良 (3) 祢毛己呂尒 (4) 於久乎奈加祢曾 (5) 麻左可思余加婆

仮名の書き下し · *Kana Transliteration*
(1) いかほろ₂の₂ (2) そ₁ひ₁の₂はりはら (3) ねも₁こ₂ろ₂に (4) おくをなかねそ₂ (5) まさかしよ₂かば

Romanization
(1) Ikapo-rə-nə (2) sop-i-nə pari para (3) nemokərə n-i (4) oku-wo na-kane-sə (5) masaka si yə-k-aᵐba

Glossing with Morphemic Analysis
(1) Ikapo-DIM-GEN (2) go.along-NML-GEN alder field (3) cordial COP-CONV (4) future-ACC NEG-worry-do (5) now EP good-ATTR-COND

Translation

(5) If the present is good, (4) do not worry about the future (3) [so] intensely, (2) [like] the fields of alders that line up (1) the little Ikapo [mountain].

Commentary

On Ikapo mountain see the commentary to 14.3409.

On the diminutive suffix -*rə* see the commentary to 14.3351.

OJ *pari* 'alder' (MDJ *hannoki* (ハンノキ), *Alnus Japonica*) is a tall deciduous tree (15–20 m high, approximately 60 cm in diameter) that grows everywhere in Japan. It has long oval pointy leaves that have tomentum on their down side. It has male flowers on the tip of branches and female flowers on the downside of branches that bloom in February–March. Brown oval-shaped fruits ripen in October–November. Both fruits and bark of alder were used to produce dyes and tannin.

First three lines constitute a poetic introduction (*jo*, 序) to the rest of the poem.

OJ *kane-* means 'to think about future', 'to worry about future'.

OJ *masaka* 'now' is a rare word, attested three times in WOJ and three times in EOJ. Its etymology is obscure. There is a difference in usage between *masaka* 'now' and *ima* 'id.' The former is always used adverbially, while the latter can be used both adverbially and as a modifier of a following noun (with the genitive case marker -*nə* attached to *ima*).

On EOJ conditional adjectival form -*k-a*ᵐ*ba* see the commentary to 14.3383.

14.3411

本文・Original Text

(1) 多胡能祢尓 (2) 与西都奈波倍弖 (3) 与須礼騰毛 (4) 阿尓久夜斯豆久 (5) 曾能可抱与吉尓

仮名の書き下し・Kana Transliteration

(1) たго₁の₂ねに (2) よ₂せづなはへ₂て (3) よ₂すれど₂も₁ (4) あにくやしづく (5) そ₂の₂かほよ₂き₁に

Romanization

(1) Taᵑgo-nə ne-ni (2) yəse(NML)-ⁿ-duna papɛ-te (3) yəs-ure-ⁿdəmo (4) ani k-u ya siⁿduk-u (5) sənə kapo yə-ki-ni

Glossing with Morphemic Analysis
(1) Taŋgo-GEN peak-LOC (2) draw.up(NML)-GEN-rope stretch(CONV)-SUB (3) draw.up-EV-CONC (4) INTERJ come-FIN IP submerge-ATTR (5) that face good-ATTR-LOC

Translation
(1/2/3) Though [I try] to draw [him] near, stretching draw-up rope [to him], (1) [like] to Taŋgo peak (4) will [he] come – oh, no! (4/5) because his hidden face is beautiful ...

Commentary
Taŋgo area corresponds to present-day Yoshii town (Yoshii machi, 吉井町)[25] in Tano county (Tano-gun, 多野郡) of Gunma prefecture (Nakanishi 1985: 459). Mizushima adds that Taŋgo was the name of district in Kamitukɛno province. Taŋgo peak is either Ushibuseyama mountain (Ushibuse yama, 牛伏山, 491 m) or Jōyama mountain (城山, 415 m[26]) in the southern part of present-day Yoshii town (吉井町).

The first three lines describe a *kunibiki* (國引き) ritual, which has the purpose to augment the lands by dragging the pieces of other lands towards one's own land. It is described in the *Izumo Fudoki* and in the *Norito* (Omodaka 1977.14: 99). Here it is used as a metaphor for dragging one's lover or husband home.

OJ *yəse-ⁿ-duna* is a rope for pulling over other lands used in the *kunibiki* ritual.

Only the *Genryaku kōhon* has 斯豆久 *sinduku*, and all other manuscripts have 斯豆之・斯豆志 *sindusi*. Since *sindusi* makes no sense, we follow the *Genryaku kōhon*. OJ *sinduk-* means 'to submerge', in the sense 'to be hidden' (Omodaka 1977.14: 99).

There is a problem in line five. *Ruijū koshū* has 可波 *kapa*, also glossed in *kana* as *kapa*. *Koyō ryaku ruijū shō* has *kapa* in *kana* and no *man'yōgana*. Both the *Nishi honganji-bon* and the *Kishū-bon* have 可把 *kapa*, but gloss it in *kana* as *kapo*. Japanese scholars believe that *Genryaku kōhon* has 可於 *kao*, but the *kana* gloss is *kapa*. Only a quite late *Ōya-bon* has 可抱. The Japanese scholarly tradition starting from Sengaku follows the reading *kapo* that is interpreted as 'face'. While it is difficult to decide, because most of the oldest manuscripts agree on *kapa*, 可於 *kao* found in *Genryaku kōhon* can only be a misspelling of *kapo*, not

---
25 Incorporated into Takasaki city (Takasaki-shi, 高崎市) in 2009.
26 361 m according to some other sources. It is not clear how or why this discrepancy originated.

kapa. This is a decisive argument in favor of *kapo*. Another argument in favor of *kapo* is a paleographic one: 抱 as a phonogram for *po* occurs only in book fourteen, and out of twelve attestations two are in Kamitukɛno poems (14.3411 and 14.3423), two in poems from Mitinəku province (14.3426 and 14.3427), and the rest are in unidentified section (14.3450, 14.3453, 14.3473, 14.3478, 14.3520, 14.3525, 14.3539, 14.3552).

Japanese scholars reverse the gender roles here (Omodaka 1977: 99; Mizushima 1986: 160), but we follow the traditional interpretation by Sengaku, who maintains that it is a woman who tries to draw a man near her (Satake 1981: 384). This makes more sense, since in Ancient Japan men visited women, but not vice versa.

14.3412

本文・*Original Text*

(1) 賀美都家野 (2) 久路保乃祢呂乃 (3) 久受葉我多 (4) 可奈師家兒良尒 (5) 伊夜射可里久母

仮名の書き下し・*Kana Transliteration*

(1) かみ₁つけ₁の₁ (2) くろ₁ほの₂ねろ₂の₂ (3) くずはがた (4) かなしけ₁こ₁らに (5) いやざかりくも₂

Romanization

(1) KamitukɛNO (2) Kuropo-nə ne-rə-nə (3) ku^{n}zu PA-^{ŋ}-gata (4) kanasi-ke KO-ra-ni (5) iya-^{n}-zakar-i k-umə

Glossing with Morphemic Analysis

(1) Kamitukeno (2) Kuropo-GEN peak-DIM-GEN (3) *kudzu* leaf-GEN-vine (4) dear-ATTR girl-DIM-DAT (5) more.and.more-COP(CONV)-become.distant-CONV come-EXCL

Translation

(5) Oh, [I] came [here] growing more and more distant (4) from [my] dear girl, (3) [like] vines of *kudzu* leaves [that crawl away] (2) at Kuropo peak (1) [in] Kamitukɛno!

Commentary

On Kamitukɛno (here spelled as Kamitukeno) province see the commentary to 14.3404.

First three lines constitute a poetic introduction (*jo*, 序) to the rest of the poem.

Kuropo corresponds to Akajōyama (赤城山) mountainous area in Seta county (勢多郡) of present-day Gunma prefecture. The highest peak in this range is Kurobidake (黒檜岳, 1,828 m). At its southern foot there is Kurohone village (Kurohone mura, 黒保根村), and on its northern foot is Tone county (Tone-gun, 利根郡) where we find Kuroho village (Kuroho mura, 黒保村) (currently called Shōwa village (Shōwa mura, 昭和村)). These two villages' names still reflect the old placename of Kuropo (Nakanishi 1985: 444).

On the diminutive suffix *-rə* see the commentary to 14.3351.

OJ *ku^nzu* 'kudzu', 'arrowroot' (*Puetaria thunbergiana*) is an abbreviation of *ku^nzu ka^ndura* 'kudzu vine' which is a type of vine that has a peculiar complex leaf consisting of three leaves. During the hot sunny days *kudzu* raises these leaves as a protection from the sunlight.

Opinions differ regarding the analysis of 我多 *ŋgata* in line three. The opinion of Edo period commentators that took the whole line three as a placename should be discarded, as well as the opinion that *ŋgata* is a 'corruption' of *ŋgatə* 'like' (Mizushima 1986: 161–162). The majority of scholars analyze *kata* in *ŋ-gata* as 'vine' (Takagi et al. 1959: 423; Kubota 1967: 180; Kojima et al. 1973: 464; Omodaka 1977.14: 99; Tsuchiya 1977.7: 269; Nakanishi 1981: 256; Itō 1997: 369; Satake et al. 2002: 330). Mizushima disagrees with this analysis, believing that *-kata* means 'shape', 'form' (1986: 161–162). However, if one interprets line three as *ku^nzu PA-ŋ-gata* '[like] the shape of *kudzu* leaves', it is not clear how it could fit into the context of the poem: 'I came far away like the shape' does not make any sense. Therefore, we follow the majority's opinion and interpret *-kata* as 'vine'.

OJ *kata* is a type of *ka^ndura* 'vine' (Omodaka et al. 1967: 190). It is not exactly clear what particular type it is. It is probably also attested in MYS 10.1928, 10.1929 and 13.3323 as *Sano kata* 'vine of Sano'. There is also possibility that it appears in MYS 1.19.

EOJ *-ke* in *kanasi-ke* is an adjectival attributive suffix retaining PJ unraised vowel *e. It corresponds to WOJ *-ki*.

14.3413

本文・*Original Text*

(1) 刀祢河泊乃 (2) 可波世毛思良受 (3) 多太和多里 (4) 奈美尓安布能須 (5) 安敝流伎美可母

仮名の書き下し・*Kana Transliteration*
(1) と₁ねがはの₂ (2) かはせも₁しらず (3) ただわたり (4) なみ₁にあふの₂す (5) あへ₁るき₁み₁かも₂

Romanization
(1) Tone-ŋ-GApa-nə (2) kapa se mo sir-aⁿz-u (3) taⁿda watar-i (4) nami-ni ap-u-nəsu (5) ap-er-u kimi kamə

Glossing with Morphemic Analysis
(1) Tone-GEN-river-GEN (2) river rapids FP know-NEG-CONV (3) directly cross-CONV (4) wave-LOC meet-ATTR-COMP (5) meet-PROG-ATTR lord EP

Translation
(5) [I] have [suddenly] met [my] lord (4) like [one] meets the waves (3) when [trying] to ford directly (2) without knowing even the river rapids (1) in Toneⁿgapa river!

Commentary
Toneⁿgapa river corresponds to present-day Tonegawa river (Tonegawa, 利根川) that originates near Tangoyama mountain (Tango yama, 丹後山, 1,809 m) on the border between Gunma and Niigata prefectures, then flows through the central Kantō region along the borders between Gunma, Saitama, and Ibaraki prefectures and flows into the Pacific Ocean in Chōsi city (Chōshi-shi, 銚子市). It is the second longest river (322 km) in Japan after Shinano river, but Tonegawa's basin is the largest in Japan, occupying an area of 16,640 km² (Mizushima 1986: 163).

EOJ *-nəsu* is a comparative case marker corresponding to WOJ *-nasu*. For details see Vovin (2020.1: 200–207).

14.3414

本文・*Original Text*
(1) 伊香保呂能 (2) 夜左可能為提尓 (3) 多都努自能 (4) 安良波路萬代母 (5) 佐祢乎佐祢弖婆

仮名の書き下し・*Kana Transliteration*
(1) いかほろ₂の₂ (2) やさかの₂ゐでに (3) たつの₁じの₂ (4) あらはろ₁までも₂ (5) さねをさねてば

Romanization
(1) Ikapo-rə-nə (2) ya-saka-nə wiⁿde-ni (3) tat-u noⁿzi-nə (4) arapar-o-maⁿde mə (5) sa-ne-wo sa-ne-te-^mba

Glossing with Morphemic Analysis
(1) Ikapo-DIM-GEN (2) eight-CL-GEN dam-LOC (3) rise-ATTR rainbow-GEN (4) appear-ATTR-TERM FP (5) PREF-sleep(NML)-ACC PREF-sleep (CONV)-PERF-COND

Translation
(5) If [we could] have slept there [together] (3/4) until the rising rainbow appears (2) at the dam eight *shaku* [high] (1) at little Ikapo [mountain].

Commentary
On Ikapo mountain see the commentary to 14.3409.

On the diminutive suffix *-rə* see the commentary to 14.3351.

OJ *saka* (尺, MDJ *shaku*) is a measure of length. There were two types of *saka* in the Nara period. One was big *saka* (大尺, 35.4+ cm, also called Korean *saka* (Koryō saka, 高麗尺)) used in land measurements and surveys, and another was small *saka* (*ko saka*, 小尺, 29.6+ cm) used for all other purposes. The height of a dam would be measured in small *saka*, therefore we can calculate that it was approximately 2 m 37 cm high.

OJ *wiⁿde* 'dam' has a transparent etymology: *wi* 'well' + -*ⁿ*- < -*nə*, genitive case marker' + *te* 'place, replacement', that is 'substitute of a well'. The motivation is quite clear, because both wells and dams serve as reservoirs to preserve water.

EOJ *noⁿzi* 'rainbow' is a cognate to WOJ *niⁿzi* 'id.' On the basis of system of beliefs in Ancient China, Nakanishi suggested that a rainbow may be used as a symbol for obscene lustful behavior (1981: 256). But it is more likely that rainbow just symbolizes daytime when lovers could not sleep together and must part. In any case it is difficult to decide because this is the only time when a rainbow is mentioned in the *Man'yōshū*.

There are two possibilities to analyze EOJ *arapar-o* 'appear-ATTR'. First, one might claim that it is a consonantal verb corresponding to WOJ *arapare-* 'id.', which is a vowel verb. Second, given the fact that the EOJ verbal attributive -*o* appears not only after consonantal and *r*-irregular verbs, but also after the perfective auxiliary -*n*-, which is an *n*-irregular verb with a mixed consonantal-vowel paradigm (and in all likelihood probably an original vowel verb), it is possible that EOJ *arapar-o* can be explained as a vowel verb *arapare-* followed by the attributive -*o*: *arapare-* + -*o* > *arapar-o* (cf. the similar process in WOJ when vowel verbs lose their final root vowel before attributive -*uru*). Unfortunately, EOJ *arapar-* or *arapare-* is *hapax legomenon*, so we do not have a second independent piece of evidence to confirm either the first or second analysis. We normally hate to rely on intuition alone, but there is no way around it this time, and it tells us that the second analysis is correct.

On the EOJ verbal attributive -*o* see the commentary to 14.3395 and a brief description of EOJ special grammar in the introduction.

OJ *sa-* is a prefix on verbs or on nominal phrases indicating that a certain location is involved. There is also an opinion that it marked intransitive verbs (Yanagida and Whitman 2009).

Japanese scholars take the first three lines as a poetic introduction (*jo*, 序) to the rest of the poem (Takagi et al. 1959: 423; Omodaka 1977.14: 101; Nakanishi 1981: 256; Mizushima 1986: 165), consequently treating -*nə* in *noⁿzi-nə* as a comparative case marker. We feel that this analysis disrupts the flow of the poem and leaves the alleged poetic introduction just to hang in the mid-air without any logical connection to the rest of the poem. Consequently, we treat -*nə* in *noⁿzi-nə* as a genitive case marker, marking the subject of the verb *arapare-* 'to appear'.

14.3415

本文・*Original Text*

(1) 可美都氣努 (2) 伊可保乃奴麻尓 (3) 宇恵古奈宜 (4) 可久古非牟等夜 (5) 多祢物得米家武

仮名の書き下し・*Kana Transliteration*

(1) かみ₁つけ₂の₁ (2) いかほの₂ぬまに (3) うゑこ₁なぎ₂ (4) かく₁こ₁ひ₂むと₂や (5) たねもと₂め₂け₁む

Romanization

(1) Kamitukɛno (2) Ikapo-nə numa-ni (3) uwe ko-naⁿgï (4) ka-ku kopï-m-u tə ya (5) tane motəmɛ-kem-u

Glossing with Morphemic Analysis

(1) Kamitukɛno (2) Ikapo-GEN marsh-LOC (3) plant(CONV) DIM-water.leek (4) thus-CONV long.for-TENT-FIN QV IP (5) seed look.for-PAST/TENT-ATTR

Translation

(4) Do [you] think that [I] would long so [much] for (3) a small water leek planted (2) in the Ikapo marsh (1) [in] Kamitukɛno, (5) that [I] would have looked for [its] seeds? [– Certainly not!]

Commentary

On Kamitukɛno province see the commentary to 14.3404.

On Ikapo mountain and area see the commentary to 14.3409.

OJ *naᵑgï* 'water leek' has a transparent etymology: *na* 'water+ -ⁿ- < *nə*, genitive case marker + *kï* 'leek'. On OJ *na* 'water' see the commentary to MYS 14.3366. Water leek is a flat and smooth glabrous annual grass that grows naturally in the shallow stagnant water of marshes, rice fields etc. It has dark green leaves about 2–5 cm long which end in an oval-shaped tip and bluish purple six-petal flowers that bloom from summer to early autumn. Leaves are edible and flowers are used for dyeing clothes. In this poem water leek is used as a metaphor for a female lover.

The adnominal function for converb is not attested in WOJ, but here *uwe* 'plant(CONV)' is clearly an converb form that modifies the following noun.

This poem was most likely composed by a man who got involved with a woman, and started to regret his suffering in this love affair (Kubota 1967: 182; Mizushima 1986: 168).

14.3418

本文 · *Original Text*

(1) 可美都氣努 (2) 佐野田能奈倍能 (3) 武良奈倍尓 (4) 許登波佐太米都 (5) 伊麻波伊可尓世母

仮名の書き下し · *Kana Transliteration*

(1) かみ₁つけ₂の₁ (2) さの₁だの₂なへ₂の₂ (3) むらなへ₂に (4) こ₂と₂はさだめ₂つ (5) いまはいかにせも₂

Romanization

(1) Kamitukɛno (2) SaNO-ⁿ-DA-nə napɛ-nə (3) muranapɛ n-i (4) kətə pa saⁿdamɛ-t-u (5) ima pa ika n-i se-m-ə

Glossing with Morphemic Analysis
(1) Kamitukɛno (2) Sano-GEN-paddy-GEN seedling-GEN (3) perform. divination(NML) COP-CONV (4) matter TOP decide(CONV)-PERF-FIN (5) now TOP how COP-CONV do-TENT-ATTR

Translation
(4) [They] decided the matter [of my marriage] (3) by divination (2) on the seedlings from Sano paddies (1) in Kamitukɛno. (5) What should [I] do now?

Commentary
On Kamitukɛno province see the commentary to 14.3404.

Sano corresponds to an area along Karasu river (烏川) in southeastern part of present-day Takasaki city (高崎市) in Gunma prefecture (Mizushima 1986: 150; Nakanishi 1985: 449).

There is a disagreement on how to explain *muranapɛ* in line three. Some Japanese scholars take it as 'group seedlings' (Kojima et al. 1973: 465; Kubota 1967: 184; Itō 1997: 373, 376), but others prefer 'divination seedlings' (Takagi et al. 1959: 424; Omodaka 1977.14: 104; Mizushima 1986: 172). The best explanation, we believe, was provided by Tsuchiya, who analyzes *muranapɛ* on line three as a verb (1977.7: 275). MJ verb *uranap-* 'to perform divination' is consonantal, and the verb is not attested phonographically in WOJ, but the conditional form attested in 11.2507 is traditionally glossed as *uranapɛ-ᵐba*, betraying the vowel verb. The verb *(m)uranapɛ-* to perform divination' is probably derived from noun *(m)uranapɛ* 'divination seedlings' by conversion. Nevertheless, the verbal nature of *muranapɛ* in line three should settle the issue, as there is no verb *muranapɛ 'to put seedlings in a bundle'. In addition, although the exact process of divination on rice seedlings remains unknown, this explanation certainly makes much more sense than 'group seedlings', as it remains unclear how one can decide anything on the basis of a group of seedlings. As for the initial *m-*, it is likely to be an EOJ archaism. See also the commentary to 14.3404 of reflexes of PJ *muᵐ/ⁿ- in EOJ and WOJ.

OJ *katə* 'matter' refers to marriage arrangement here. Apparently, the marriage for a girl who is the author of this poem was an arranged one, and not to her liking.

EOJ *se-m-ə* is the tentative attributive form of the verb *se-* 'to do'. The attributive *-ə* is a misspelling for *-o*, but this is to be expected in the *Man'yōshū* besides book five. On the EOJ verbal attributive *-o* see the commentary to 14.3395 and a brief description of EOJ special grammar in the introduction.

14.3419

本文・*Original Text*

(1) 伊可保世欲 (2) 奈可中吹下 (3) 於毛比度路 (4) 久麻許曾之都等 (5) 和須礼西奈布母

仮名の書き下し・*Kana Transliteration*

(1) いかほせよ₁ (2) なかちぐ・なかなかふき₁げ₁ (3) おも₁ひ₁ど₁ろ₁・おも₁ひ₁と₁ろ₁ (4) くま₂こ₂そ₂しつと₂ (5) わすれせなふも₂

Romanization

(1) Ikapo se-yo (2) nakatiⁿgu/nakanaka pukiⁿge (3) omop-i-[i]ⁿd-oro/omop-i-tor-o (4) kumakəsəsitutə (5) wasure se-n-ap-umə

Glossing with Morphemic Analysis

(1) Ikapo rapids(?)/beloved(?)-ABL (2) ? (3) think-CONV-exit-ATTR (?)/think-CONV-take-ATTR (?) (4) ? (5) forget(NML) do-NEG-ITER-EXCL

Translation

(1) From Ikapo rapids/From [my] beloved in Ikapo (5) [I] will not forget! (2/3/4) Not possible to analyze and/or translate at the present stage of our knowledge.

Commentary

This poem is practically impossible to analyze and translate, as only line five is clear. It is conspicuous that the *Genryaku kōhon* does not even have *kana* glosses for this poem. This probably means that the poem was impossible to understand at the end of twelfth century. Among the modern commentators Omodaka left this poem without a translation (Omodaka 1977.14: 105).

On Ikapo mountain and area see the commentary to 14.3409.

OJ *se* in line one can be either 'rapids' or 'beloved', 'husband'. Since the remaining context is opaque, the choice between these two is impossible.

Both the *Genryaku kōhon* and the *Ruijū koshū* have the character 吹 in line two, more recent manuscripts have 次 instead. We have followed the oldest manuscripts. It is possible to offer two tentative readings of this line, but we still cannot interpret either of them.

EOJ *omopiⁿdoro* in line three is analyzed either as *omop-i-[i]ⁿd-oro* 'think-CONV-exit-ATTR', or *omop-i-tor-o* 'think-CONV-take-ATTR'. In the first case, *-oro* will be the only case of attributive form containing unraised vowels that corresponds to both EOJ and WOJ -*uru*. In the second case, to the best of my knowledge, the compound *omǝp-i-tº/ǝr-* is not otherwise attested in OJ.

Line four can be read, but its analysis and meaning are completely unclear.

On specific EOJ order of morphemes -(*a*)*n-ap-* 'NEG-ITER' see the commentary to 14.3375.

The above analysis reflects both strengths and weaknesses of the traditional philological approach. However, this poem might be partially analyzable if we look at its text as it appears in the *Hirose-bon* (廣瀬本), which in spite of being a mid-Edo period manuscript, is believed to be the only surviving copy of the *Man'yōshū* that goes back to the no longer extant *Teika-bon* (定家本), copied by Fujiwara-no Teika (藤原定家), who alongside Motoori Norinaga is one of the two greatest Japanese philologists who has ever walked the Earth. The *Hirose-bon* text goes as follows (Hirose et al. 1994: 116):

本文・*Original Text*
(1) 伊可保世欲 (2) 奈可中吹乍 (3) 於毛比度路 (4) 久麻許曾之都等 (5) 和須礼西奈布母

仮名の書き下し・*Kana Transliteration*
(1) いかほせよ₁ (2) なかなふき₁つつ (3) おも₁ひ₁ど₁ろ₁ (4) くまこ₂そ₂しつと₂ (5) わすれせなふも₂

Romanization
(1) Ikapo se yo (2) naka-NA PUK-I-tutu (3) omop-i-[i]ⁿd-oro (4) kumakǝsǝsitutǝ (5) wasure se-n-ap-umǝ

Glossing with Morphemic Analysis
(1) Ikapo wind night (2) middle-LOC blow-CONV-COOR (3) think-CONV-exit-ATTR (4) ? (5) forget(NML) do-NEG-ITER-EXCL

Translation
(1) The wind [from] Ikapo [mountain] (2) continues to blow at (1) night. (5) [I] will never forget (4) ? (3) whom [I] recollect.

Commentary
The character 乍 instead of 下 in line two mostly disambiguates this line: 吹乍 should be taken as *puk-i-tutu* 'blow-CONV-COOR'. This semantographic way of writing is highly unusual for book fourteen.

I trust that 中 probably renders -*na*, EOJ locative case marker. The OJ word *naka* 'inside' etymologically consists of *na* 'inside' + *ka* 'place', and there are two cases in the *Nihonshoki* when 中 is used to write *na* (Omodaka 1967: 512). Thus, 奈可中 probably renders *naka-na* 'inside-LOC'.

The last character 欲 in line one then can be taken as standing for OJ *yo* 'night', constituting together with the following *naka-na* in line two *yo-naka-na* 'in the night'. The line break between the two parts of the compound *yo-naka* is, of course, unusual. *Yo-naka* occurs seven times in the *Man'yōshū*, and is always found within a line.

Puk-i-tutu 'continues to blow' requires the word for 'wind'. Could *se* in line one be an archaic form (with an unraised vowel *e) of OJ -*si* 'wind' found only in compounds like *pimukasi* 'East' < *pi* 'sun' + *muka* 'opposite' + *si* 'wind' and *nisi* 'West'[27] < *ni* (meaning unknown) + *si* 'wind'?

Line four, unfortunately, still remains completely opaque.

14.3420

本文 • *Original Text*
(1) 可美都氣努 (2) 佐野乃布奈波之 (3) 登里波奈之 (4) 於也波左久礼騰 (5) 和波左可流賀倍

仮名の書き下し • *Kana Transliteration*
(1) かみ₁つけ₂の₁ (2) さのの₂ふなはし (3) と₂りはなし (4) おやはさくれど₂ (5) わはさかるがへ₂

Romanization
(1) Kamitukɛno (2) SaNO-nə puna-pasi (3) tər-i-panas-i (4) oya pa sak-urɛ-ⁿdə (5) wa pa sakar-u ⁿgapɛ

Glossing with Morphemic Analysis
(1) Kamitukɛno (2) Sano-GEN boat-bridge (3) take-CONV-separate-CONV (4) parent TOP separate-EV-CONC (5) I TOP be.separated-FIN IP

Translation
(4) Although [my] parents [are going to] separate [us], (3) like taking apart (2) the boat bridge at Sano (1) [in] Kamitukɛno, (5) will [I] separate [myself from you]? [– Certainly not!]

---

27   Cf. Ryūkyūan *nisi* 'North'.

Commentary

On Kamitukɛno province see the commentary to 14.3404.

Sano corresponds to an area along Karasu river (烏川) in southeastern part of present-day Takasaki city (高崎市) in Gunma prefecture (Mizushima 1986: 150; Nakanishi 1985: 449).

EOJ *puna-pasi* 'boat bridge' is a bridge where planks are placed on the top of connected boats that are used as a foundation of a bridge instead of pillars (Omodaka 1977.14: 108).

On EOJ *wa pa* 'I TOP' see the commentary to 14.3377.

OJ *sakɛ-* is a transitive verb 'to split, to separate', while OJ *sakar-* is its intransitive counterpart 'to be split, to be separated'.

EOJ *ŋgapɛ* is an interrogative particle introducing irony, i.e. an affirmative or a negative question to which the opposite answer is expected.

14.3423

本文・*Original Text*

(1) 可美都氣努 (2) 伊可抱乃祢呂尓 (3) 布路与伎能 (4) 遊吉須宜可提奴 (5) 伊毛賀伊敝乃安多里

仮名の書き下し・*Kana Transliteration*

(1) かみ₁つけ₂の₁ (2) いかほの₂ねろ₂に (3) ふろ₁よ₂き₂の₂ (4) ゆき₁すぎ₂かてぬ (5) いも₁がいへ₁の₂あたり

Romanization

(1) Kamitukɛno (2) Ikapo-nə ne-rə-ni (3) pur-o yəki-nə (4) yuk-i-suŋgï-kate-n-u (5) imo-ŋga ipe-nə atari

Glossing with Morphemic Analysis

(1) Kamitukɛno (2) Ikapo-GEN peak-DIM-LOC (3) fall-ATTR snow-COMP (4) go-CONV-pass(CONV)-POT-NEG-ATTR (5) beloved-POSS house-GEN vicinity

Translation

(3) Like the snow falling (2) at the Ikapo peak (1) [in] Kamitukɛno, (4) [I] cannot pass (5) the vicinity of my beloved's house.

Commentary

On Kamitukɛno province see the commentary to 14.3404.

On Ikapo mountain and area see the commentary to 14.3409. Ikapo peak is present-day Haruna volcano (Haruna-san, 榛名山, 1391 m)[28] that has a lake in its caldera (Mizushima 1986: 154; Nakanishi 1985: 421).

On the EOJ verbal attributive -*o* see the commentary to 14.3395 and a brief description of the EOJ special grammar in the Introduction.

EOJ *yəki* 'snow' (apparent misspelling of *yoki) is a form with unraised primary PJ *o that corresponds to WOJ *yuki* 'id.' Cf. also Old Okinawan variant (and probably archaic) spellings *yoki, yoti* 'snow, hail' (Hokama et al. 1995: 699). EOJ and Ryūkyūan forms demonstrate that the PJ form was *yoki, not *yuki. Consequently, it shows that PJ *yoki 'snow' has no etymological connection to OJ *yuk-* 'to go' < *PJ *yik-* (in spite of the fact that both *yuki* 'snow' and *yuk-* ~ *ik-* 'to go') belong to the high register (Martin 1987: 579, 788)), which is sometimes suggested as an etymology for the WOJ and MJ word *yuki* 'snow' (> MDJ *yuki*).

Postscript to the Poems 14.3402–3423

本文・*Original Text*
右廿二首上野國歌

Translation
Twenty-two poems above are from Kamitukɛno province.

Commentary
On Kamitukɛno (上野) province see the commentary to 14.3404.

14.3424

本文・*Original Text*
(1) 之母都家野 (2) 美可母乃夜麻能 (3) 許奈良能須 (4) 麻具波思兒呂波 (5) 多賀家可母多牟

仮名の書き下し・*Kana Transliteration*
(1) し も₂ つけ₁ の₁ (2) み₁ か も₂ の₂ やまの₂ (3) こ₂ ならの₂ す (4) まぐはしこ₁ろ₂は (5) たがけ₁かも₂たむ

---

[28] Haruna-san is currently classified as a dormant volcano.

Romanization
(1) SimətukɛNO (2) Mikamə-nə yama-nə (3) kə-nara-nəsu (4) ma-ŋgupasi KO-rə pa (5) ta-ŋga ke ka mət-am-u

Glossing with Morphemic Analysis
(1) Simotukɛno (2) Mikamə-GEN mountain-GEN (3) DIM-oak-COMP (4) INT-beautiful girl-DIM TOP (5) who-POSS food.container IP hold-TENT-ATTR

Translation
(4) A girl truly beautiful (3) like a small oak (2) from Mikamə mountain (1) in Simotukɛno, (5) whose food container will [she] hold?

Commentary
Simotukɛno[29] (下野) province corresponds to present-day Tochigi prefecture. It was one of the Upper Provinces under the *Ritsuryō* code. On the *Ritsuryō* code classification of Yamatə provinces see the commentary to the postscript to the poem 14.3349.

The WOJ diminutive prefix is *ko-*, therefore EOJ *kə-* might be a spelling due to a lack of contrast between /o/ and /ə/ in the Simotukɛno dialect. However, Kupchik believes that there was no loss of contrast between /o/ and /ə/ in Simotukɛno (2011: 341). Thus, most likely it is a misspelling. There is also an alternative explanation that *kə-* in *kə-nara* here is not a diminutive prefix, but a bound stem *kə-* of the word *kï* 'tree' (Omodaka et al. 1967: 303).

Mikamə mountain (三毳山) is present-day Mikamo mountain (三鴨山, 225 m) located to the east of Sano city (Sano-shi, 佐野市) in Tochigi prefecture (Nakanishi 1985: 486).

The OJ *nara* 'oak' (*Quercus serrata*, MDJ *konara*) is a tall deciduous tree with height about 15 m. Both male and female flowers bloom on the same tree in the spring. Male flowers have long shape with brownish yellow stripes. Female flowers produce oval shaped hard fruits, which have round shaped shells. Its wood is used for making wooden utensils, firewood, and charcoal, and its bark is used for producing a dye.

On the EOJ comparative case marker *-nəsu* see the commentary to 14.3413.

---

29   Misspelled as Simətukeno here and in the following 14.3425. We know that the etymological spelling must have been Simotukɛno, because it was a lower (*simo*) province, as opposed to Kamitukɛno, an upper (*kami*) province. The element -*kɛ*- is likely to represent OJ *kɛ* (毛) 'hair', if Kojiki's logographic spelling 下毛野 is to be trusted (KJK II: 21b), therefore -*ke*- might also be a misspelling.

WOJ has *kɛ* 'container', therefore EOJ *ke* is likely to be a misspelling due to the loss of contrast between /ɛ/ and /e/ in the Simotukɛno dialect. Cf. also the same misspelling in the name of the province: Simətukeno instead of Simotukɛno.

Holding someone's food container is a metaphor for marriage (Mizushima 1986: 82).

14.3425

本文 · Original Text
(1) 志母都家努 (2) 安素乃河泊良欲 (3) 伊之布麻受 (4) 蘇良由登伎奴与 (5) 奈我己許呂能礼

仮名の書き下し · Kana Transliteration
(1) しも₂つけ₁の₁ (2) あそ₁の₂かはらよ₁ (3) いしふまず (4) そ₁らゆと₂き₁ぬよ₂ (5) ながこ₂こ₂ろ₂の₂れ

Romanization
(1) Simətukeno (2) Aso-nə ᴋᴀpara-yo (3) isi pum-aⁿz-u (4) sora-yu tə k-i-n-u yə (5) na-ⁿga kəkərə nər-e

Glossing with Morphemic Analysis
(1) Simotukɛno (2) Aso-GEN river.bed-ABL (3) stone tread-NEG-CONV (4) sky-ABL FP come-CONV-PERF-FIN EP (5) you-POSS heart tell-IMP

Translation
(4) [I] came (2) from the river-bed of Aso (1) [in] Simotukɛno, (4) as from the sky, (3) without treading on stones! (5) Reveal [to me] your heart!

Commentary
On Simotukɛno province see the commentary to 14.3424.

On Aso district see the commentary to 14.3404.

On the EOJ focus particle *tə* corresponding to WOJ *sə* see the commentary to 14.3409.

Postscript to the Poems 14.3424–3425

本文 · Original Text
右二首下野國歌

Translation

The two poems above are from Simotukɛno province.

Commentary

On Simotukɛno (下野) province see the commentary to 14.3424.

14.3426

本文・Original Text

(1) 安比豆祢能 (2) 久尒平佐杼抱美 (3) 安波奈波婆 (4) 斯努比尒勢毛等 (5) 比毛牟須婆佐祢

仮名の書き下し・Kana Transliteration

(1) あひ₁づねの₂ (2) くにをさど₂ほみ₁ (3) あはなはば (4) しの₁ひ₁にせも₁と₂ (5) ひ₁も₁むすばさね

Romanization

(1) Apindu ne-nə (2) kuni-wo san-dəpo-mi (3) ap-an-ap-amba (4) sinop-i-n-i se-m-o tə (5) pimo musumb-as-an-e

Glossing with Morphemic Analysis

(1) Apindu peak-GEN (2) land-ABS PREF-far-GER (3) meet-NEG-ITER-COND (4) long.for-CONV-PERF-NML do-TENT-ATTR COP (5) cord tie-HON-DES-IMP

Translation

(3) If [we] continue not to meet, (1/2) because the land of Apindu peak is far, (5) [I] want [you] to tie [your garment] cords, (4) as if [you] have been longing for [me]

Commentary

Apindu peak is a mountain in Aizu region (会津地方) of present-day Fukushima prefecture. The exact identification with any present-day mountain is not possible, but it is thought that it may be Bandai mountain (磐梯山, 1,819 m) in Yama county (耶麻郡) to the northeast of Aizuwakamatsu city (会津若松市) (Nakanishi 1985: 419).

Apindu ne-nə kuni-wo san-dəpo-mi 'because the land of Apindune peak is far': in Old Japanese the subject of the non-active predicate (in this instance an inflected adjective *təpo-* 'to be far') could be marked by the absolutive case marker (formally identical to the accusative case marker -*wo*). For details, see Vovin (2020.1: 172–175).

On specific EOJ order of morphemes -(*a*)*n-ap*- 'NEG-ITER' see the commentary to 14.3375.

On the EOJ verbal attributive -*o* see the commentary to 14.3395 and a brief description of EOJ special grammar in the introduction.

On a custom among lovers of tying and untying the cords see the commentary to 14.3361.

Postscript to the Poems 14.3426–3428

本文・*Original Text*
右三首陸奥國歌

Translation
Three poems above are from Mitinəku province.

Commentary
Mitinəku (陸奥) province included present-day Fukushima, Miyagi, Iwate, Akita, Yamagata, and Aomori prefectures (Nakanishi 1985: 487), although there are strong grounds to believe that at least the territory of present-day Aomori prefecture, as well as possibly northern parts of Akita and Iwate, may not have been under Yamatə control in the eighth century (Itō 1997: 388). Mitinəku was one of the Great Provinces under the *Ritsuryō* code. On the *Ritsuryō* code classification of Yamatə provinces see the commentary to the postscript to the poem 14.3349.

譬喩歌・Allegorical Poems

14.3431

本文・*Original Text*
(1) 阿之我里乃 (2) 安伎奈乃夜麻尒 (3) 比古布祢乃 (4) 斯利比可志母與 (5) 許己波故賀多尒

仮名の書き下し・*Kana Transliteration*
(1) あしがりの₂ (2) あき₁なの₂やまに (3) ひこ₁ふねの₂ (4) しりひ₁かしも₂よ₂ (5) こ₂こ₂ばこ₁がたに

Romanization

(1) Asiⁿgari-nə (2) Akina-nə yama-ni (3) pik-o pune-nə (4) siri pik-asi-mə yə (5) kəkəᵐba ko-ⁿ-gata n-i

Glossing with Morphemic Analysis

(1) Asiⁿgari-GEN (2) Akina-GEN mountain-LOC (3) drag-ATTR boat-COMP (4) ass drag-ADJ-EXCL EP (5) extremely come-GEN-be.hard COP-CONV

Translation

(4) [His] ass is dragged [by me], (3) like a boat that [they] drag [up] (2) to Akina mountain (1) in Asiⁿgari, (5) [but] it is extremely difficult [for him to come here]!

Commentary

On Asiⁿgari see the commentary to 14.3361.

The exact location of Akina mountain is unknown, but it is likely to be one of the mountains in the Hakone mountain range, although there is also an opinion that it might be Aⁿgina mountain (英那山) in Ayukawa district (愛甲郡) of Saⁿgamu province mentioned in the *Wamyōshō* (Nakanishi 1985: 414; Mizushima 1986: 193). The placename Akina does not seem to be Japonic and might be reflecting the Ainu *ay-kina* 'arrow grass', although such a compound is not attested in known Ainu sources.

On the EOJ verbal attributive -*o* see the commentary to 14.3395 and a brief description of EOJ special grammar in the introduction.

On OJ adjectivizer -*asi* see Vovin (2020.1: 432–434).

OJ exclamative form -*umə* ~ -*mə* is an Old Japanese verbal form not attested in Classical (Middle) Japanese or any other later forms of Japanese. The Japanese linguistic tradition treats this suffix as a combination of final predication form -*u* plus a final particle (終助詞, *shūjoshi*) *mə*, but this analysis is untenable for several reasons. See Vovin (2020.2: 626–630) for details.

OJ *kəkəᵐba* 'extremely', 'so much' is attested more frequently in EOJ than in WOJ. For details see Vovin (2020.2: 1002–1003).

In line five we would expect *kə-ⁿ-gata* 'difficult to come' with the *otsu-rui* vowel *ə* rather than *ko-ⁿ-gata* with the *kō-rui* vowel *o*, but this might be due to the loss of distinction between these two vowels in the Saⁿgamu dialect of EOJ. However, Kupchik believes that there was no loss of contrast between /o/ and /ə/ in Saⁿgamu (2011: 285). Thus, most likely it is a misspelling.

This poem apparently represents a complaint by a woman whose lover or husband fails to visit her.

14.3432

本文 • *Original Text*
(1) 阿之賀利乃 (2) 和乎可鶏夜麻能 (3) 可頭乃木能 (4) 和乎可豆佐祢母 (5) 可豆佐可受等母

仮名の書き下し • *Kana Transliteration*
(1) あしがりの₂ (2) わをかけ₁やまの₂ (3) かづの₂き₂の₂ (4) わをかづさねも₂ (5) かづさかずと₂も₂

Romanization
(1) Asiⁿgari-nə (2) wa-wo Kake yama-nə (3) kaⁿdu-nə Kï-nə (4) wa-wo kaⁿdus-an-e-mə (5) kaⁿdus-ak-aⁿz-u təmə

Glossing with Morphemic Analysis
(1) Asiⁿgari-GEN (2) I-ACC Kake mountain-GEN (3) paper.mulberry-GEN tree-COMP (4) I-ACC abduct-DES-IMP-EXCL (5) abduct(CONV)-be.open-NEG-FIN CONJ

Translation
(5) No matter how [you] abduct [me], (4) please abduct me (3) like a paper mulberry tree (2) from Mt. Kake (1) in Asiⁿgari!

Commentary
On Asiⁿgari see the commentary to 14.3361.

Mt. Kake is one of the mountains in Asiⁿgari range. It possibly corresponds to present-day Yagura peak (870 m, 矢倉岳) (Nakanishi 1985: 433) in Kanagawa prefecture. Mizushima thinks that *wawokake* in the second line represents the mountain name and not *wa-wo* 'I-ACC' plus the name of the mountain, or that at least a word play (*kakekotoba*, 掛詞) may be involved here (1986: 195).

Kaⁿdu in EOJ *kaⁿdu-nə kï* probably corresponds to WOJ *kaⁿdi* 'paper mulberry tree' (MDJ *kazinoki, Broussonetia kazinoki*) (Nakanishi 1985: 310). It is a tall deciduous tree, approximately 10 m high. It has big leaves that are split in three. In early summer *kazinoki* blooms with light green flowers and produces red fruits. Male and female species are represented by different trees. It is a sacred tree in Shintō, and for this reason it is frequently planted in the precincts of Shintō shrines as well as used for offerings. The bark of young branches is used for the production of Japanese paper. This is believed to be the same tree as the OJ *taku* 'mulberry tree'. OJ *taku* (栲) 'mulberry tree' is an old word for MDJ *kōzo* (楮). The cloth made from the bark of *taku* was called *tapɛ*. The resemblance to the Eastern Polynesian *tapa* (Tahitian *tapa*, Hawaiian *kapa*, etc.) 'cloth made from the bark of the mulberry tree' is striking, but may be coincidental, since the word is not attested in other Austronesian languages, and the direct contact between speakers of Old Japanese and Eastern Polynesians is unlikely. If, however, a borrowing took place it could have been only from Old Japanese to Eastern Polynesian, since the Old Japanese comes from pre-Old Japanese *tapay. Note that there are no final consonants in Polynesian. Of course, one may imagine that some Japanese were blown off their course all the way to Polynesia. The existence of doublets for the name of the same tree is interesting, as one of the doublets is likely to be a loan. This is the case, we believe, with the OJ *taku* 'mulberry tree', which is attested in EOJ only once in the *makura-kotoba* (permanent epithet, 枕詞) *taku-ᵐ-busuma* 'covers from the mulberry tree [bark cloth]' (14.3509). The etymology of OJ *taku* 'mulberry tree' is quite transparent: it must have been borrowed from OK predecessor of MK *tàk* 'mulberry tree'.

The first three lines constitute a poetic introduction (*jo*, 序) to the rest of the poem.

This poem is difficult to interpret due to the presence of two *hapax legomenoi* in lines four and five: *kaⁿdusanemə* and *kaⁿdusakaⁿzu*. Omodaka believes that both reflect the verb *kaⁿdus-* 'to abduct' (1977.14: 122–124). Kubota agrees with Omodaka's analysis (1967: 164). Both Tsuchiya and Mizushima agree with Omodaka on the first *hapax legomenon*, but treat the second one as *kaⁿdu sak-* 'to peal the bark/paper mulberry tree' (Kubota 1977.7: 288–289; Mizushima 1986: 195), but this is hard to believe, because there is no word *kaⁿdu* 'bark' in OJ. The interpretation of *kaⁿdu* as 'paper mulberry tree' is possible, but is impeded by the fact that it is called *kaⁿdunəkï* in the same poem. *Kaⁿdunəkï* is certainly transparent: *kaⁿdu* 'paper mulberry tree' + *n-ə*, attributive form of the copula *n-* + *kï* 'tree'. But there is no evidence that *kaⁿdu* could be used by itself in EOJ like *kaⁿdi* in WOJ. In addition, OJ *sak-* does not mean 'to peel', but 'to split, to divide in two'. Mizushima's point of view is also shared by Takagi et al. and Nakanishi, although they treat *kaⁿdus-* as 'to invite' (Takagi et al. 1959: 427; Nakanishi 1981: 260). Kojima et al. take a more cautious position taking both *hapax legomena* as opaque. They also point out that there are no other examples of exclamative suffix *-(u)mə* attested after desiderative imperative *-(a)n-e* (1973: 469). The same position is taken by Satake et al. (2002: 337). Itō interprets *kaⁿdu sak-* as 'to open the gate' (1997: 398), but OJ *sak-* does not mean 'to open', but 'to split'. The apparent difficulty with Omodaka's proposal is that we face two different roots or stems, if we treat *kaⁿdus-* and *kaⁿdusak-* as the same word. The analogy that Omodaka draws between these two on the one hand, and MDJ *kadowas-* ~ *kadowakas-* 'to abduct, to kidnap', *hiyas-* 'to cool'~ *hiyakas-* 'to make fun of' on the other hand, in spite of demonstrating the same verbal suffix *-ak-*, is not complete, as we would expect the second form to be *kaⁿdusakas-, and not *kaⁿdusak-*. Still, Omodaka's interpretation makes the most sense for the text interpretation, so we follow him in our interpretation and translation. Nevertheless, the translation must be viewed as a provisional one.

Postscript to the Poems 14.3431–3433

本文 · Original Text
右三首相模國歌

Translation
Three poems above are from Saⁿgamu province.

Commentary
Saⁿgamu (相模) province included most of present-day Kanagawa prefecture (Nakanishi 1985: 447). Saⁿgamu was one of the Upper Provinces under *Ritsuryō* code. On the *Ritsuryō* code classification of Yamatə provinces see the commentary to the postscript to the poem 14.3349. Saⁿgamu peak might be Mt. Ōyama (大山, also known as Aburi-san (雨降山), 1,246 m), which is located in the vicinity of the present-day cities of Isehara (Isehara-shi, 伊勢原市), Hadano (Hadano-shi, 秦野市), and Atsugi (Atsugi-shi, 厚木市) in Kanagawa prefecture.

14.3434

本文 · Original Text
(1) 可美都家野 (2) 安蘇夜麻都豆良 (3) 野乎比呂美 (4) 波比尓思物能乎 (5) 安是加多延世武

仮名の書き下し · Kana Transliteration
(1) かみ₁つけ₁の₁ (2) あそ₁やまつづら (3) の₁をひ₁ろ₂み₁ (4) はひ¶にしも₂の₂を (5) あぜかたえ₂せむ

Romanization
(1) Kamitukeno (2) Aso yama tuⁿdura (3) NO-wo pirə-mi (4) pap-i-n-i-si mənəwo (5) aⁿze ka taye se-m-u

Glossing with Morphemic Analysis
(1) Kamitukeno (2) Aso mountain vine (3) field-ABS be.wide-GER (4) crawl-CONV-PERF-CONV-PAST.ATTR CONJ (5) why IP break(NML) do-TENT-ATTR

Translation
(2/4) Although [my heart] crept [to you like] the vine from Aso mountain (1) [in] Kamitukɛno (3) because the field is wide, (5) why should [it/we] break?

Commentary
On Kamitukɛno province see the commentary to 14.3404.

On Aso district see the commentary to 14.3404. The exact location of Aso mountain is unknown. It could be either a mountainous region in the north of Aso district, or, according to another hypothesis, a mountain at the southeastern slope of Mt. Haruna (Haruna-san, 榛名山) in the vicinity of Misato town (Misato machi, 箕郷町) in Gunma county (Gunma-gun, 群馬郡) in present-day Gunma prefecture (Nakanishi 1985: 417).

On *tuⁿdura* 'vine' see the commentary 14.3359.

On the absolutive case marker *-wo* see the commentary to 14.3426. For details, see Vovin (2020.1: 172–175).

On EOJ *aⁿze* 'why' see the commentary to 14.3369.

Tuⁿdura 'vine' is a metaphor referring to a love relationship. The implied meaning of this poem is: 'it goes well, so why should it break?'

14.3435

本文 • Original Text
(1) 伊可保呂乃 (2) 蘇比乃波里波良 (3) 和我吉奴尓 (4) 都伎与良之母与 (5) 比多敝登於毛敝婆

仮名の書き下し • Kana Transliteration
(1) い か ほ ろ₂ の₂ (2) そ₁ ひ₁ の₂ は り は ら (3) わ が き₁ ぬ に (4) つ き₁ よ₂ ら し も₂ よ₂ (5) ひ₁ た へ₁ と₂ お も₁ へ₁ ば

Romanization
(1) Ikapo-rə-nə (2) sop-i-nə pari para (3) wa-ⁿga kinu-ni (4) tuk-i-yər-asi-mə yə (5) pita-pe tə omop-e-ᵐba

Glossing with Morphemic Analysis
(1) Ikapo-DIM-GEN (2) go.along-NML-GEN alder field (3) I-POSS garment-LOC (4) attach-CONV-approach-ADJ-EXCL EP (5) one-CL QV think-EV-CON

Translation
(2) [The fruits from] the fields of alders that line up (1) the little Ikapo [mountain] (3/4) have really dyed my garment (5) because, as [I] think, [it] has only one layer!

Commentary
On Ikapo mountain see the commentary to 14.3409.

On the diminutive suffix -rə see the commentary to 14.3351.

On OJ *pari* 'alder' see the commentary to 14.3410.

EOJ *pita* 'one' is hapax legomenon corresponding to WOJ and EOJ *pitə* 'id.' Possibly EOJ *pita* 'one' was triggered by analogy with *puta* 'two'.

EOJ evidential *-e-* is a misspelling for WOJ *-ɛ-* indicating in all probability the loss of distinction between /e/ and /ɛ/ in the Kamitukɛno dialect.

Line five is hypermetric (*ji amari*, 字余り), but this is likely to be a graphic illusion, since *tə omope*ᵐ*ba* in all probability was pronounced as [təmopeᵐba].

The metaphor in this poem implies that the feelings of one's lover (fruits of the alder that dyed the author's garment) match perfectly with that of the author, who has no secret thoughts (second layer of the garment that does not exist here).

14.3436

本文 • Original Text
(1) 志良登保布 (2) 乎尓比多夜麻乃 (3) 毛流夜麻乃 (4) 宇良賀礼勢奈那 (5) 登許波尓毛我母

仮名の書き下し • Kana Transliteration
(1) しらと₂ほふ (2) を尓ひ₁たやまの₂ (3) も₁るやまの₂ (4) うらがれせなな (5) と₂こ₂はにも₁がも₂

Romanization
(1) siratəpopu (2) wo-Nipita yama-nə (3) mor-u yama-nə (4) ura-ⁿ-gare se-n-a-na (5) təkə pa n-i moⁿgamə

Glossing with Morphemic Analysis
(1) (*makura-kotoba*) (2) DIM-Nipita mountain-GEN (3) guard-ATTR mountain-GEN (4) top.branch-GEN-wither(NML) do-NEG-ATTR-LOC (5) eternal leaf COP-CONV DP

Translation
(5) I wish that (4) top branches [of the trees] (2) on Mt. Nipita, (3) on [this] mountain that [they guard] (4) would not wither and (5) have eternal leaves.

Commentary
EOJ *siratəpopu* is probably a permanent epithet (*makura-kotoba*, 枕詞) to Mt. Nipita. Its structure and meaning are unknown. In the *Man'yōshū* it is a *hapax legomenon* attested only in this poem.

On Mt. Nipita see the commentary to 14.3408.

The notion of a guarded mountain is not completely clear, but potentially it could be due to the presence of an important shrine.

On EOJ form in *V-(a)n-a-na* see the commentary to 14.3408.

Although not noted in commentaries, *se-n-a-na* 'without doing' may also represent a play on words with *se-na-na* 'beloved-DIM-DIM' (14.3544).

This poem probably represents a metaphor of good wishes for one's lover's well-being and health (Omodaka 1977.14: 127).

Postscript to the Poems 14.3434–3436

本文・*Original Text*
右三首上野國歌

Translation
Three poems above are from Kamitukɛno province.

Commentary
On Kamitukɛno province see the commentary to 14.3404.

14.3437

本文・*Original Text*
(1) 美知乃久能 (2) 安太多良末由美 (3) 波自伎於伎弓 (4) 西良思馬伎那婆 (5) 都良波可馬可毛

仮名の書き下し・*Kana Transliteration*

(1) み₁ちの₂くの₂ (2) あだたらまゆみ₁ (3) はじき₁おき₁て (4) せらしめ₁き₁なば
(5) つらはかめ₁かも₁

Romanization

(1) Mitinəku-nə (2) Aⁿdatara ma-yumi (3) paⁿzik-i-ok-i-te (4) ser-asime-k-i-n-aᵐba (5) tura pak-am-e kamo

Glossing with Morphemic Analysis

(1) Mitinəku-GEN (2) Aⁿdatara INT-bow (3) take.off-CONV-put-CONV-SUB (4) bend-CAUS(CONV)-come-CONV-PERF-COND (5) bow.string insert-TENT-EV EP

Translation

(4) If (3) [you] take off the [bow string from] (2) the real Aⁿdatara bow (1) of Mitinəku (4) and make [the bow] bend, (5) I wonder whether [you] would [be able to] put the bow string back.

Commentary

On Mitinəku province see the commentary to postscript to the poems 14.3426–3428.

On Aⁿdatara peak corresponds to present-day Mt. Adatara (安達太良山, 1,700 m) in Ada county (安達郡) of Fukushima prefecture. It also appears in 7.1329 and 14.3437 (Nakanishi 1985: 417).

Throughout the history, Japanese bows were simple, long bows in sharp contrast to the more powerful shorter bows used by Inner Asian nomads, Koreans, and Chinese which could shoot arrows long distances. The lack of a composite structure dictated the longer length of the Japanese bow so that it could shoot arrows still shorter but somewhat comparable distances.

The second and third lines are hypermetric (*ji amari*, 字余り). In the case of the third line, it is probably just a graphic illusion as *paⁿzik-i-ok-i-te* was in all probability pronounced as [paⁿzikokite].

EOJ *ser-* 'to bend' corresponds to MJ *sor-* 'id.' (not attested in WOJ).

On the basis of WOJ grammar one would expect the attributive form in front of the particle *kamə*, not evidential as in this poem. This is likely to be an EOJ feature.

There are two 'misspellings' of ɛ as e (in *-asime-* and *-am-e-*), probably indicating that the contrast between them was non-existent in Mitinəku.

This poem is a metaphor for two lovers who may not go back to the same relationship because they did not meet for some time (Omodaka 1977.14: 128).

Omodaka believes that this poem was misclassified (probably by Opətəmə-nə Yakaməti) as a poem from Mitinəku due to the mention of the Aⁿdatara bow (1977.14: 129). Needless to say, there is zero evidence to the contrary.

Postscript to the Poem 14.3437

本文 · *Original Text*
右一首陸奥國歌

Translation
The poem above is from Mitinəku province.

Commentary
On Mitinəku province see the commentary to the postscript to the poems 14.3426–3428.

4 雜歌 · Miscellaneous Poems

14.3444

本文 · *Original Text*
(1) 伎波都久乃 (2) 乎加能久君美良 (3) 和礼都賣杼 (4) 故尓毛乃多奈布 (5) 西奈等都麻佐祢

仮名の書き下し · *Kana Transliteration*
(1) き₁はつくの₂ (2) をかの₂くくみ₁ら (3) われつめ₁ど₂ (4) こ₁にも₁の₂たなふ (5) せなと₂つまさね

Romanization
(1) Kipatuku-nə (2) woka-nə kuku-mira (3) ware tum-e-ⁿdə (4) ko-ni mo nət-an-ap-u (5) se-na-tə tum-as-an-e

Glossing with Morphemic Analysis
(1) Kipatuku-GEN (2) hill-GEN stalk-leek (3) I gather-EV-CONC (4) basket-LOC FP fill-NEG-ITER-FIN (5) beloved-DIM-COM gather-HON-DES-IMP

Translation

(3) Although I gather (2) stalk leeks at the hill (1) in Kipatuku (4) [I] still have not filled [my] basket. (5) [I] wish [you] gather [them] together with [your] beloved!

Commentary

It might look like this poem is from Pitati province, because it has the EOJ specific order of morphemes -(a)n-ap- 'NEG-ITER' (vs. WOJ order -ap-an- 'ITER-NEG') also attested in another Pitati poem (14.3394).

The exact location of Kipatuku hill is unknown. It could have been located in Maka ᵐbe district (真壁郡) of Pitati province (present-day Ibaraki prefecture) (Omodaka 1977.14: 138; Nakanishi 1985: 442; Mizushima 1986: 212).

OJ *kuku-* 'stalk' is a bound form of WOJ *kukï* 'stalk'. Cf. OJ *kukutati* that are seedlings of either a turnip (MDJ *kabura*), or greens (MDJ *aona*) (Omodaka 1977.14: 92; Mizushima 1986: 150), or a rape plant (MDJ *aburana*) (Omodaka et al. 1967: 253–254). In the *Wamyōshō* the word *kukutati* is defined as 蔓青苗 'seedlings of greens' (WMS 16.18b). For example, 蔓青 used to spell OJ *awona* 'greens' see MYS 16.3825. The etymology of *kukutati* is transparent: *kuku-*, the bound form of WOJ *kukï* 'stalk' + *tat-i*, nominalized form of verb *tat-* 'to stand'.

OJ *mira* 'leek' corresponds to MDJ *nira* 'id.', which is a perennial grass with leaves about 2–30 cm high. It has strong odor. Its spring leaves are delicious, and it blooms in summer with white flowers that have purple stripes. It was brought to Japan from China.

In spite of the fact that all manuscripts have 乃多奈布 *nət-an-ap-u* 'fill-NEG-ITER-FIN, many editions of the *Man'yōshū* 'correct' it to more palatable and more WOJ-looking 美多奈布 *mit-an-ap-u* 'id.' (Mizushima 1984a: 216–17). The shift *m-* > *n-* /_*i* can be easily explained as palatalization, and then the shift *i* > *ə* can be taken as vowel reduction. However, there is no other evidence for the shift *i* > *ə* [ə] in EOJ. Like Omodaka (1977.14: 138) and Mizushima (1986: 212), we follow here the manuscript tradition rather than later commentators' interpretations. Possibly we are dealing here with a unique EOJ verb *nət-* 'to fill'.

The evidential *-ɛ-* is misspelled as *-e-* probably due to the lack of contrast between *ɛ* and *e* in the EOJ dialect underlying this poem.

On the specific EOJ order of morphemes -(a)n-ap- 'NEG-ITER' see the commentary to 14.3375. This poem has EOJ specific order of morphemes -(a)n-ap- 'NEG-ITER' (vs. WOJ order -ap-an- 'ITER-NEG') also attested in other Pitati poems (14.3394), so this poem should be classified as a poem from Pitati province.

This poem looks like a collective production, composed by two authors: lines one to four belonging to one, and line five to another (Nakanishi 1981: 263).

We wonder whether this poem has any allusion to the following lines from the poem #3 in the Book of Songs (*Shījīng*, 詩經):

采采卷耳
不盈頃筐
嗟我懷人

I gather the *küan-er* plant,
But it does not fill my slanted basket,
I am sighing for my beloved one.[30]

14.3445

本文 • *Original Text*
(1) 美奈刀能 (2) 安之我奈可那流 (3) 多麻古須氣 (4) 可利己和我西古 (5) 等許乃敝太思尒

仮名の書き下し • *Kana Transliteration*
(1) み₁なと₁の₂ (2) あしがなかなる (3) たまこ₁すげ₂ (4) かりこ₂わがせこ₁ (5) と₂こ₂の₂へ₁だしに

Romanization
(1) minato-nə (2) asi-ŋga naka-n-ar-u (3) tama ko-suŋgɛ (4) kar-i-kə wa-ŋga se-ko (5) təkə-nə peⁿdas-i-ni

Glossing with Morphemic Analysis
(1) harbor-GEN (2) reed-POSS middle-LOC-exist-ATTR (3) jewel DIM sedge (4) cut-CONV-come(IMP) I-POSS beloved-DIM (5) bed-GEN be.separated-NML-LOC

Translation
(5) In order to get [our] bed separated [from the eyes of others], (4) my dear beloved, come to cut (4) beautiful little sedges (2) in the middle of the reeds (1) in the harbor.

---

30 Translation by Karlgren (1950: 3).

Commentary

The first line is hypometric (*ji tarazu*, 字足らず).

OJ *minato* 'harbor' etymologically goes back to *mi-*, honorific prefix, *na* 'water', and *to* 'door'. On OJ *na* 'water' see the commentaries to 5.902 and 14.3366.

OJ *asi* 'reed' is a perennial grass about 2 m high. It grows at the waterfronts and has long flat roots in the ground. Its stalks are hollow and have joints. Its leaves have the same shape as bamboo grass (*sasa*, 笹). In autumn it develops ears from multiple small striped purple flowers. Its stalks are used for making blinds (*sudare*, 簾).

On OJ *suᵑgɛ* 'sedge' see the commentary to 14.3369.

Little privacy was afforded to couples in the houses of commoners in the Nara period. Therefore, this poem should be taken as an invitation to have sexual intercourse outside the house, where there would not be too many prying eyes (Mizushima 1986: 214).

On the EOJ palatalization *t* > *s* before *i* appearing in *peⁿdas-i* < *peⁿdat-i* see the commentary to 14.3395.

14.3446

本文・Original Text
(1) 伊毛奈呂我 (2) 都可布河泊豆乃 (3) 佐左良乎疑 (4) 安志等比登其等 (5) 加多理与良斯母

仮名の書き下し・Kana Transliteration
(1) いも₁なろ₂が (2) つかふかはづの₂ (3) ささらをぎ₂ (4) あし₂ひ₁と₂ご₂と₂ (5) かたりよ₂らしも₂

Romanization
(1) imo-na-rə-ᵑga (2) tuk-ap-u ᴋᴀpa-ⁿ-du-nə (3) sasara woᵑgï (4) asi tə pitə-ᵑ-gətə (5) katar-i-yər-asi-mə

Glossing with Morphemic Analysis
(1) beloved-DIM-DIM-POSS (2) be.soaked-ITER-ATTR river-GEN-harbor-GEN (3) small reed (4) reed/bad QV person-GEN-word (5) talk-CONV-approach-SUP-EXCL

Translation

(4/5) It looks like the rumors reached [me] that (3) a small reed (1/2) in the river harbor, where [my] dear beloved soaks herself [in water], (4) is bad / [is] a reed!

Commentary

See the commentary to 14.3402 for the string of two diminutive suffixes.

Most commentators tend to see *tukap-* as 'to use [for washing]' (Omodaka 1977.14: 141; Mizushima 1986: 215), but we believe it can be better analyzed as *tuk-* 'be soaked in' + *-ap-*, iterative.

EOJ *sasara* 'small' is probably the same word as *sa ⁿzare* 'id.' in *sa ⁿzare-[i]si* 'pebble' in 14.3400.

OJ *woⁿgï* 'common reed' (荻, *Miscanthus sacchariflorus*) is a perennial grass 1.5 m high growing at the waterfronts. It has thin hollow stalks and joints. It looks like *susuki* 'Japanese pampas grass',[31] but its ears are bigger. The stalks of *woⁿgï* 'common reed' were traditionally used for thatching roofs. *Woⁿgï* 'common reed' is different from *asi* 'reed', on which see the commentary to 14.3445.

This poem includes a play on words *asi* 'reed' and 'bad', so it is difficult to interpret it exactly and translate. There are practically as many ways of interpretation as there are commentators of the *Man'yōshū*. We follow Mizushima that views this poem as a man's reproach of his wife or lover for adultery (1986: 216). *Woⁿgï* 'common reed' is probably a symbol for a rival. Note that it is smaller than a regular reed *asi*, which represents the author himself. Consequently, the rumor is that *woⁿgï* is called *asi*, in other words, it/he is trying to replace the husband (or a previous lover), and this is bad.

14.3447

本文 • Original Text

(1) 久佐可氣乃 (2) 安努奈由可武等 (3) 波里之美知 (4) 阿努波由加受弖 (5) 阿良久佐太知奴

---

[31] *Susuki* 'Japanese pampas grass' is a tall (1~2 m, 3ft 4in~6ft 8in) perennial grass which grows in the wild on river banks and mountains. In the autumn it develops long sword-like yellowish or purplish spikes. It is one of the 秋の七草 'seven autumnal plants', and is associated with autumn in Japanese traditional poetry.

仮名の書き下し・Kana Transliteration

(1) くさかげ₂の₂ (2) あの₁なゆかむと₂ (3) はりしみ₁ち (4) あの₁はゆかずて (5) あらくさだちぬ

Romanization

(1) kusa kaᵑgɛ-nə (2) Ano-na yuk-am-u tə (3) par-i-si miti (4) Ano pa yuk-aⁿz-u-te (5) ara kusa-ⁿ-dat-i-n-u

Glossing with Morphemic Analysis

(1) grass shadow-GEN (2) Ano-LOC go-TENT-FIN QV (3) clear-CONV-PAST.ATTR road (4) Ano TOP go-NEG-CONV-SUB (5) rough grass-GEN-stand-CONV-PERF-FIN

Translation

(3) The road that [they] cleared (2) with intention to go to Ano (1) that is in grass shadow (5) has been overgrown with rough grass (4) because [no one] goes to Ano.

Commentary

Kusa kaᵑgɛ-nə is supposed to be a permanent epithet (*makura-kotoba*, 枕詞) to Ano (Omodaka 1977.14: 144; Mizushima 1986: 217), but this may not be necessarily so for two reasons: (a) placename Ano occurs only in this poem in the *Man'yōshū*, and (b) *kusa kaᵑgɛ-nə* is also attested just one more time before the placename Arawi in 12.3192. Even if it is a permanent epithet, it can be translated, because it is absolutely transparent.

The exact location of Ano is not known. There are two main hypotheses: one identifies it with Ano manor (Ano shō, 阿野荘) in Suruᵑga province (corresponding to Ide (井出) in Numazu city (沼津市) in present-day Shizuoka prefecture), and another with Anō village (安濃村) in Age county (安芸郡) in present-day Mie prefecture (Nakanishi 1985: 418; Mizushima 1986: 217). However, as Mizushima notes, it is unlikely that a placename in Mie prefecture would appear in an Eastern poem (1986: 217).

EOJ *-na* is a locative case marker. See also 14.3408 and 14.3461.

14.3448

本文・Original Text

(1) 波奈治良布 (2) 己能牟可都乎乃 (3) 乎那能乎能 (4) 比自尓都久麻提 (5) 伎美我与母賀母

仮名の書き下し・*Kana Transliteration*
(1) はなぢらふ (2) こ₂の₂むかつをの₂ (3) をなの₂をの₂ (4) ひ₁じにつくまで (5) き₁み₁がよ₂も₂がも₂

Romanization
(1) pana-ⁿ-dir-ap-u (2) kənə muka-tu wo n-ə (3) Wona-nə wo-nə (4) piⁿzi-ni tuk-u-maⁿde (5) kimi-ŋga yə məŋgamə

Glossing with Morphemic Analysis
(1) flower-GEN-fall-ITER-ATTR (2) this opposite.side-GEN/LOC peak COP-ATTR (3) Wona-GEN peak-GEN (4) sandbank-LOC reach-ATTR-TERM (5) lord-POSS age DP

Translation
(5) [I] wish [my] lord would live (4) until (3) the peak of Wona, (2) which is the peak on the opposite side, (1) where flowers are falling, (4) will reach the sandbanks [in the sea].

Commentary
There are no distinctive EOJ features in this poem except the EOJ word *piⁿzi* 'sandbank, sandbar'.

The exact location of the peak of Wona is not known. It probably was located in Kamiona (上尾那) or Simoona (下尾那) areas of Inasa county (引佐郡) in present-day Shizuoka prefecture (Nakanishi 1985: 500; Mizushima 1986: 219).

EOJ *piⁿzi* 'sandbank, sandbar' is an interesting word. Besides this poem it is attested only in a fragment from Ōsumi Fudoki (大隅風土記) as a Hayato word *pisi* (必志) 'sandbank' (Akimoto 1958: 526). Cf. also Okinawan *hwisi* 'rocks and sandbanks that become visible during low tide'. Since there is some evidence from South Ryūkyūan[32] for the same word: Tarama, Hirara and Irabu *pɛi*, *shigaki pi:* (Jarosz and Majewicz 2013: 532), Japanese and Ryūkyūan words are possibly loans from Ainu *pís* 'shore', which might have entered Ryūkyūan prior to the proto-Ryūkyūan migration to the Ryūkyūan islands. The prenasalized voiced in EOJ *piⁿzi* is probably due to the fact that the word was borrowed into EOJ in its Ainu possessive form *pis-i* [pizi] or [piZi] 'its shore'.

---

32 I express my gratitude to Aleksandra Jarosz for pointing my attestation to the South Ryūkyūan cognates.

14.3450

本文 • Original Text
(1) 乎久佐乎等 (2) 乎具佐受家乎等 (3) 斯抱布祢乃 (4) 那良敝弖美礼婆 (5) 乎具佐可知馬利

仮名の書き下し • Kana Transliteration
(1) をくさをと₂ (2) をぐさずけ₁をと₂ (3) しほふねの₂ (4) ならべ₁てみ₁れば (5) をぐさかちめ₁り

Romanization
(1) Wokusa-wo-tə (2) Woŋgusa-ⁿ-zuke-wo-tə (3) sipo-pune-nə (4) naraᵐbe-te mi-re-ᵐba (5) Woŋgusa kat-i-mer-i

Glossing with Morphemic Analysis
(1) Wokusa-man-COM (2) Woŋgusa-GEN-assistant-man-COM (3) tide-boat-COMP (4) stand.side.by.side(CONV)-SUB see-EV-CON (5) Woŋgusa win-CONV-CONJC-FIN

Translation
(4) When [I] see (1) a man from Wokusa and (2) an assistant man from Woŋgusa (4) standing side by side (3) like sea boats, (5) it seems [to me] that Woŋgusa['s side] wins.

Commentary
Both Wokusa and Woŋgusa are placenames with unknown location. Nakanishi suggests the possibility that both may be the same placename (1985: 499), but we follow here the point of view that considers them to be different (Omodaka 1977.14: 147; Mizushima 1986: 221).

Since *sukɛ* 'assistant' is a nominalization of the verb *sukɛ-* 'to help', EOJ *suke* 'assistant' in this poem is a 'misspelling', which probably indicates that the contrast between *e* and *ɛ* was non-existent in this particular EOJ dialect.

Sipo-pune 'tide-boat' is a 'sea boat' that is a boat used for sailing in the sea, not a river or a lake.

EOJ *naraᵐbe-* is misspelled with *e* (cf. WOJ *naraᵐbɛ-*), which probably indicates that the contrast between *e* and *ɛ* was non-existent in this particular EOJ dialect. See also the same phenomenon in *suke* 'assistant' above.

Conjectural auxiliary *-mer-* has a unique attestation in this poem in the whole Old Japanese corpus. It must be taken as an EOJ feature, not only because it is not attested in WOJ, but also because it is clearly an auxiliary in

EOJ that is attached to the converb. While in MJ the conjectural suffix -*umer*- is quite frequent, it is not an auxiliary on the synchronic level, and although it is historically derived from an auxiliary, it shows a different way of agglutination as compared to -*mer*- in EOJ.

14.3451

本文・*Original Text*
(1) 左奈都良能 (2) 乎可尓安波麻伎 (3) 可奈之伎我 (4) 古麻波多具等毛 (5) 和波素登毛波自

仮名の書き下し・*Kana Transliteration*
(1) さなつらの₂ (2) をかにあはまき₁ (3) かなしき₁が (4) こ₁まはたぐと₂も₁ (5) わはそ₁と₂も₁はじ

Romanization
(1) Sanatura-nə (2) woka-ni apa mak-i (3) kanasi-ki-ŋga (4) koma pa taŋg-u təmo (5) wa pa so tə [o]mop-aⁿzi

Glossing with Morphemic Analysis
(1) Sanatura-GEN (2) hill-LOC millet sow-CONV (3) dear-ATTR-POSS (4) stallion TOP eat-FIN CONJ (5) I TOP 'Shoo!' QV think-NEG/TENT

Translation
(2) [I] have sown millet at the hill (1) in Sanatura, (3/4) and even if the stallion of my darling eats [it], (5) I would not think to shoo it away.

Commentary
The exact location of Sanatura hill is unknown. It could possibly be located in the vicinity of Sakatura Isozaki shrine (酒列磯崎神社) in Nakaminato city (那珂湊市) in present-day Ibaraki prefecture. There is also a hypothesis suggesting a location in Chiba prefecture (Nakanishi 1985: 449).

OJ *apa* 'foxtail millet' is an annual crop that is planted around June in dry fields, and it ripens in the fall. It has yellow grain and is included in 'Five cereals', four others being rice (*kəmɛ*, 米), wheat/barley (*muⁿgi*, 麦), beans (*mamɛ*, 豆), and millet (*kⁱᵐbi*,[33] 黍).

---

33 No OJ phonographic spelling is attested.

On *koma* 'stallion' see the commentary to 14.3387.

OJ *taⁿgɛ-* 'eat', 'drink' is a rare verb.

OJ *so* 'shoo' is a word used to chase away horses.

The only EOJ feature of this poem is first person pronoun *wa* 'I' found before topic marker *pa*.³⁴ There are no phonographic WOJ examples of *wa pa* except 20.4408, but this is a poem written by Yakaməti as an imitation of a *sakimori* poem, so the usage there is likely to be influenced by EOJ.

14.3452

本文 • Original Text
(1) 於毛思路伎 (2) 野乎婆奈夜吉曾 (3) 布流久佐尒 (4) 仁比久佐麻自利 (5) 於非波於布流我尒

仮名の書き下し • Kana Transliteration
(1) おも₁しろ₁き₁ (2) の₁をばなやき₁そ₂ (3) ふるくさに (4) にひ₁くさまじり (5) おひ₂ばおふるがに

Romanization
(1) omosiro-ki (2) NO-wo*ᵐ*ba na-yak-i-sə (3) puru kusa-ni (4) nipi kusa ma*ⁿ*zir-i (5) opï-*ᵐ*ba op-uru *ŋ*gani

Glossing with Morphemic Analysis
(1) charming-ATTR (2) field-ACC(EMPH) NEG-burn-CONV-do (3) old grass-LOC (4) new grass get.mixed-CONV (5) grow-COND grow-ATTR CONJ

Translation
(1/2) Do not burn the charming field (4/5) so that the new grass, if [it] grows, is mixed (3) with the old grass.

Commentary
OJ *oməsiro-* 'charming, attractive' etymologically consists of *omə* 'face' and *siro* 'white'.

OJ *puru* 'old' and *nipi* 'new' are uninflected adjectives. On uninflected adjectives see Vovin (2020.1: 377–389).

---

34 WOJ has *ware pa* in this case. For details see Vovin (2005: 219–229).

The only EOJ feature in this poem is conjunction *ŋgani* 'so that', which corresponds to WOJ *ŋgane* 'id.' This is the only example of this particle in EOJ. EOJ *ŋgani* ~ WOJ *ŋgane* 'so that' always follows the attributive forms of verbs and is not to be confused with both WOJ and EOJ conjunction *ŋgani* 'like', which follows the final form of verbs. For details see Vovin (2020.2: 1053–1056).

A partially similar poem is found in the *Ise monogatari* (伊勢物語) and its variant in the *Kokin wakashū* (古今和歌集):

むさしのはけふはなやきそわかくさのつまもこもれりわれもこもれり

Muzasi no fa kefu fa na-yak-i-so waka kusa-no tuma mo komor-er-i ware mo komor-er-i

Muzasi field TOP today TOP NEG-burn-CONV-do young grass-COMP spouse FP hide-PROG-FIN I FP hide-PROG-FIN

Do not burn field of Muzasi today! Both my husband and me are hiding [there]

(IM 12)

かすかのはけふはなやきそわか草のつまもこもれり我もこもれり

Kasuga no fa kefu fa na-yak-i-so waka kusa-no tuma mo komor-er-i ware mo komor-er-i

Kasuga field TOP today TOP NEG-burn-CONV-do young grass-COMP spouse FP hide-PROG-FIN I FP hide-PROG-FIN

Do not burn field of Kasuga today! Both my husband and me are hiding [there]

(KKWKS 1.17)

5   相聞・Relationship Poems

14.3456

本文・*Original Text*

(1) 宇都世美能 (2) 夜蘇許登乃敝波 (3) 思氣久等母 (4) 安良蘇比可祢弖 (5) 安乎許登奈須那

仮名の書き下し・*Kana Transliteration*

(1) うつせみ₁の₂ (2) やそ₁こ₂と₂の₂へ₁は (3) しげ₂くと₂も₂ (4) あらそ₁ひ₁かねて (5) あをこ₂と₂なすな

Romanization
(1) utu semi-nə (2) yaso kətə-nə pe pa (3) siⁿgɛ-ku təmə (4) arasop-i-kane-te (5) a-wo kətə nas-una

Glossing with Morphemic Analysis
(1) ephemeral cicada-GEN (2) eighty word-GEN leaf TOP (3) be.thick-CONV CONJ (4) resist-CONV-NEG.POT(CONV)-SUB (5) I-ACC word make(HON)-NEG/IMP

Translation
(2/3) Although many rumors are growing thick (1) in [this] ephemeral world, (5) do not talk about me, (4) failing to resist.

Commentary
As for WOJ *semi* 'cicada', Omodaka notes that in the *Man'yōshū* this insect singing in the summer is usually called *piⁿgurasi* 'evening cicada'. WOJ 比具良之 /piⁿgurasi/ (MDJ *higurasi*) is a kind of cicada with a high-pitched voice that sings at dawn and in the evening. It appears from summer to autumn, is approximately 5 cm long, has a dark reddish-brown color, frequently with green and black spots. The belly of the male species is big and slightly transparent and serves as a singing instrument. Symbolically the singing of the *piⁿgurasi* 'evening cicada' is probably meant to indicate the increasing sorrow felt in one's heart (1984.15: 46). Nevertheless, the word *semi* is also attested as *utu semi* 'ephemeral cicada' and just as *semi* 'cicada' in 8.1479 (Omodaka 1984.15: 46). The last attestation is in the logographic spelling as well as the attestations in 2.150 and 8.1568 that Omodaka does not mention. Therefore, the word *semi* certainly can be reconstructed on the Proto-Japanese level. Here it is used in the meaning of 'ephemeral world' (Mizushima 1986: 231).

OJ *yaso* 'eighty' < *ya* 'eight' + *-so*, bound morpheme 'ten' in decades. OJ *yaso* 'eighty' can be used metaphorically in the meaning 'many', cf., for example, one of the ancient names for Japan, *yaso sima-nə kuni* 'land of many (lit. 'eighty') islands'. The word *-so* 'ten' is probably a loan from otherwise unattested OK form, but cf. its later MK cognates *-zʌn* < *-sʌn*, *-hʌn*, etc., found in the MK words for decades (Yi 1961/1997: 229).

EOJ *pe* 'leaf' (vs. WOJ *pa* 'id.') is the only witness to this poem's EOJ nature. Omodaka argued that *pe* must be a 'layer', and not a 'leaf', because the OJ uncontracted form *kətə-nə pa* 'leaves of words' is not attested in OJ texts, where only contracted WOJ *kətə^mba* or EOJ *ketə^mba* appear (1977.14: 231). This objection, of course, is quite lame linguistically, as we cannot expect that the OJ corpus would necessarily contain both contracted and uncontracted forms in all cases. Thus, for example, only the contracted form *ap-umi* 'lake' (lit. 'fresh water sea') is attested, but the uncontracted for *apa umi is not. In addition, the expression *kətə-nə pe* 'layers of words' is not attested at all. Therefore, in spite of the fact that EOJ *pe* 'leaf' is a *hapax legomenon*, it serves as a better explanation for the text than *pe* 'layer'.

14.3458

本文 · *Original Text*
(1) 奈勢能古夜 (2) 等里乃乎加恥志 (3) 奈可太乎礼 (4) 安乎祢思奈久与 (5) 伊久豆君麻弖尓

仮名の書き下し · *Kana Transliteration*
(1) なせの₂こ₁や (2) と₂りの₂をかちし (3) なかだをれ (4) あをねしなくよ₂ (5) いくづくまでに

Romanization
(1) na se n-ə kwo ya (2) Təri-nə woka ti si (3) naka-ⁿ-dawore (4) a-wo ne si nak-u yə (5) ikuⁿduk-u-maⁿde-ni

Glossing with Morphemic Analysis
(1) I beloved COP-ATTR child EP (2) Təri-GEN hill road EP (3) inside-COP(ATTR)-saddle (4) I-ACC sound EP make.cry-FIN EP (5) catch.one's.breath-ATTR-TERM-LOC

Translation
(1) Oh, my beloved, (3) the saddle on (2) the hilly road to Təri [which you crossed going away] (4) makes me cry so loudly, (5) that [I need to] catch my breath.

Commentary
We follow the point of view of Takagi et al. who take *na* in the first line as the first person singular pronoun 'I' (1959: 432), and not as second person singular pronoun 'you', the point of view adopted by the majority of modern commentators (Kubota 1967: 209; Kojima et al. 1973: 476; Tsuchiya 1977.7: 315; Omodaka 1977.14: 157; Nakanishi 1981: 266; Mizushima 1986: 233; Itō 1997: 433; Satake et al. 2002: 345). *Na* 'you' hardly makes any sense here, and *na* 'I' is a pronoun borrowed from Korean: for details see Vovin (2020.1: 237–238).

The exact location of Təri hill is unknown. Nakanishi suggests that it might be in the vicinity of Taiyō village (大洋村) in Kashima county (鹿島郡) of present-day Ibaraki prefecture (1985: 468). Whether the name of the hill is connected etymologically with the word *təri* 'bird' is unclear, but may be likely.

OJ *ti* is the original word for 'road', 'way' in Japanese. OJ *miti* and MJ *miti* apparently consists of the honorific prefix *mi* and *ti* 'road'. OJ *ti* 'road' also occurs in compounds as such, cf. *ti-mata* 'road fork', *yama-ⁿ-di* 'mountain road', *umi-ⁿ-di* 'sea way' etc.

EOJ *tawore* has many different explanations. We follow here Omodaka's analysis of this word as corresponding to WOJ *tawori* 'mountain saddle', which in its turn goes back to the explanation found in the *Man'yōshū Ryakuge*[35] (1977.14: 158). The EOJ form *tawore* is probably archaic, reflecting original PJ *-e that raised to -*i* in WOJ in most cases.

EOJ *ikuⁿduk-* 'to catch one's breath, to breathe with difficulty' corresponds to WOJ *ikiⁿduk-* 'id.'

---

[35] The *Man'yōshū Ryakuge* (萬葉集略解, 1796 AD) 'An Abbreviated Commentary on the *Man'yōshū*' by Tachibana Chikage (橘千蔭, 1735–1808 AD), also known as Katō Chikage (加藤千蔭) is the chronologically fourth complete premodern commentary to the *Man'yōshū*. Tachibana was the student of Kamo Mabuchi (賀茂真淵, 1697–1770 AD). Kamo Mabuchi wrote the commentary only for books one, two, eleven, twelve, thirteen, and fourteen, which he considered to be the oldest in the anthology. The rest of the commentaries represent the conspectus of his explanations compiled by his students. The *Man'yōshū Ryakuge* is comparable in quality to Kamo Mabuchi's commentary, but overall is inferior to the *Man'yōshū Kogi* by Kamochi Masazumi (鹿持雅澄, 1791–1858 AD). Although ultimately a descendant of the Fujiwara (藤原) clan, Kamochi spent his life in the utmost poverty, and never left his native Tosa (土佐) province, acquiring all his knowledge of scholarship from books that he mostly borrowed from his friends, as he could not afford to buy them. His gigantic work in forty seven books (*Man'yōshū* books one, two, three, ten, eleven, twelve, fifteen, nineteen, and twenty have three books of commentaries each, and books four, five, six, seven, nine, thirteen, fourteen, sixteen, seventeen, and eighteen have two books of commentaries each) is not only the largest and most detailed among the premodern commentaries, it is also the most authoritative. It took about thirty years to complete, as Kamochi prepared the first draft in 1823, but it was not finished until after 1854. In a sense, all modern commentaries are ultimately based on Kamochi Masazumi's work. Of course, modern scholars brought in much other additional information, and the present reading or readings of the *Man'yōshū* is/are not identical to that of Kamochi, but the latter could be called the grandfather of all modern *Man'yōshū* studies.

14.3460

本文・*Original Text*
(1) 多礼曾許能 (2) 屋能戸於曾夫流 (3) 尒布奈未尒 (4) 和我世乎夜里弖 (5) 伊波布許能戸乎

仮名の書き下し・*Kana Transliteration*
(1) たれそ₂こ₂の₂ (2) やの₂と₁おそ₂ぶる (3) にふなみ₂に (4) わがせをやりて (5) いはふこ₂の₂と₁を

Romanization
(1) tare sə kənə (2) YA-nə TO osəᵐbur-u (3) nipu namï-ni (4) wa-ŋga se-wo yar-i-te (5) ipap-u kənə TO-wo

Glossing with Morphemic Analysis
(1) who FP this (2) house-GEN door push.and.shake-ATTR (3) new taste(NML)-LOC (4) I-POSS husband-ACC send.away-CONV-SUB (5) purify.oneself-ATTR this door-ACC

Translation
(1/2) Who pushes and shakes the door of this house? (5) This door [behind which I] purify myself (4) after sending my husband away (3) at the new [rice] tasting [festival].

Commentary
EOJ *nipu* 'new' corresponds to WOJ *nipi* 'id.' The latter also occurs in EOJ (see 14.3452).

EOJ *namï-* 'to lick, to taste' corresponds to WOJ *namɛ-* 'id.'; however, for the name of the new rice tasting festival *nipi napɛ* with the verb *napɛ-* 'to lick, to taste' was used in WOJ.

For WOJ *osəᵐbur-* 'to push and shake' cf. *wotəme-nə n-as-u ita to-wo osəmbur-ap-i* 'continuously pushing and shaking wooden door [behind which] the maiden deigns to sleep' (KK 2) and *wotəme-ra-ŋga sa-n-as-u ita to-wo os-i pirak-i* 'pushing and opening wooden doors [behind which] maidens design to sleep' (MYS 5: 804). Therefore, it seems to be a formulaic expression.

This poem presents the situation when during the food offering of the new rice to deities there was a taboo for men to enter the house. Here this taboo is preserved, but cf. 14.3386, where it is clearly violated. In this poem the woman apparently sends away an unwanted suitor who wanted to sneak in on her during her husband's absence.

14.3461

本文・*Original Text*

(1) 安是登伊敝可 (2) 佐宿尓安波奈久尓 (3) 真日久礼弖 (4) 与比奈波許奈尓 (5) 安家奴思太久流

仮名の書き下し・*Kana Transliteration*

(1) あぜと₂いへ₁か (2) さねにあはなくに (3) まひ₁くれて (4) よ₂ひ₁なはこ₂なに (5) あけ₁の₁しだくる

Romanization

(1) aⁿze tə ip-e ka (2) sa-NE-ni ap-an-aku n-i (3) MA-PI kure-te (4) yəpi-na pa kə-n-a-ni (5) ake-n-o siⁿda k-uru

Glossing with Morphemic Analysis

(1) why QV say-EV IP (2) PREF-sleep(NML)-LOC meet-NEG-NML COP-CONV (3) INT-day grow.dark(CONV)-SUB (4) night-LOC TOP come-NEG-ATTR-LOC (5) dawn(CONV)-PERF-ATTR time come-ATTR

Translation

(1) Why is it so? (2) [We] do not meet to sleep here [together], because (4) [you] do not come at night (3) after the bright day grows dark, and (5) [only] come when it dawns.

Commentary

Lines one and two are hypermetric (*ji amari*, 字余り), but this is probably just a graphic illusion, since *tə ipe* and *ni apanaku* was in all probability pronounced as [tipe] ~ [təpe] and [napanaku] respectively.

Evidential form *ip-e* of the verb *ip-* 'to say' has the vowel *e* instead of WOJ *ɛ* (WOJ *ip-ɛ*). Thus, the contrast between *e* and *ɛ* was probably non-existent in the EOJ dialect that underlies this poem.

EOJ *kə-n-a-ni* 'without coming', 'because [one] does not come' functionally corresponds to WOJ *kə-n-u-ni*. Cf. very similar formation *-an-a-na*, with an EOJ-specific locative *-na* in 14.3408.

EOJ *-na* is a locative case marker. See also 14.3408 and 14.3447. It is interesting that in this poem both locatives *-na* and *-ni* are found.

On EOJ perfective attributive *-n-o* see the commentary to 14.3395.

On EOJ *siⁿda* 'time' see the commentary to 14.3363.

14.3463

本文・Original Text
(1) 麻等保久能 (2) 野尓毛安波奈牟 (3) 己許呂奈久 (4) 佐刀乃美奈可尓 (5) 安敝流世奈可母

仮名の書き下し・Kana Transliteration
(1) まと₂ほくの₂ (2) の₁にも₁あはなむ (3) こ₂こ₂ろ₂なく (4) さと₁の₂み₂なかに (5) あへ₁るせなかも₂

Romanization
(1) ma-təpo-ku n-ə (2) NO-ni mo ap-an-am-u (3) kəkərə na-ku (4) sato-nə mi-naka-ni (5) ap-er-u se-na kamə

Glossing with Morphemic Analysis
(1) INT-distant-CONV COP-ATTR (2) field-LOC FP meet-DES-TENT-FIN (3) heart exist.not-CONV (4) village-GEN HON(?)-middle-LOC (5) meet-PROG-ATTR beloved-DIM EP

Translation
(1/2) [I] would like to meet [you] even in a distant field (5) oh, [my] beloved whom [I] was meeting (3) thoughtlessly (4) in the middle of the village!

Commentary
EOJ *-na* is a diminutive suffix corresponding to WOJ *-ra*.

In this poem a woman expresses desire to meet with her lover in a distant field away from the prying eyes in the village. For similar poems see 14.3405 and 14.3405a.

14.3464

本文・Original Text
(1) 比登其登乃 (2) 之氣吉尓余里弖 (3) 麻乎其母能 (4) 於夜自麻久良波 (5) 和波麻可自夜毛

仮名の書き下し・Kana Transliteration
(1) ひ₁と₂ご₂と₂の₂ (2) しげ₂き₁によ₁りて (3) まをご₂も₂の₂ (4) おやじまくらは (5) わはまかじやも₁

萬葉集卷第十四・MAN'YŌSHŪ BOOK FOURTEEN 153

Romanization
(1) pitə-ŋ-gətə-nə (2) siŋgɛ-ki-ni yər-i-te (3) ma-woŋ-gəmə-nə (4) oyaⁿzi makura pa (5) wa pa mak-aⁿzi ya mo

Glossing with Morphemic Analysis
(1) person-GEN-word-GEN (2) be.dense-ATTR-LOC be.based-CONV-SUB (3) INT-DIM-wild.rice-GEN (4) same pillow TOP (5) I TOP use.as.a.pillow-NEG/TENT IP EP

Translation
(1/2) [Just] because the rumors [about us] are frequent, (5) would not I use (4) the same pillow (3) [made] of [the stalks of] the wild rice? [– Certainly I would!]

Commentary
The only EOJ feature of this poem is the topic focus particle *pa* following *wa* 'I'. For details see the commentary to 14.3377 and 14.3451.

OJ *kəmə* 'wild rice' is a perennial plant that grows in clusters in marshes and ponds. It has quite broad long leaves and thick column-shaped round stalks growing upright. In the fall it blooms with pale purple flowers. The leaves and stalks of *kəmə* are used for making mats, headrests, etc. (Nakanishi 1985: 314; Mizushima 1986: 242–243). By conversion, OJ *kəmə* also means 'mat made from wild rice'.

OJ *oyaⁿzi* 'same' is apparently related to OJ *onaⁿzi* 'id.', with only the latter surviving into the modern Japanese language. The correspondence -*y*- to -*n*- is unique to this pair, and so far has no satisfactory explanation.

The 'same pillow' indicates the pillow used when sleeping together. In the Nara period pillows (actually headrests) were long and just one was used by a couple sleeping together (Mizushima 1986: 243).

14.3465

本文・Original Text
(1) 巨麻尓思吉 (2) 比毛登伎佐氣弖 (3) 奴流我倍尓 (4) 安杼世呂登可母 (5) 安夜尓可奈之伎

仮名の書き下し・Kana Transliteration
(1) こ₂まにしき₁ (2) ひ₁も₁と₂き₁さけ₂て (3) ぬるがへ₂に (4) あど₂せろ₂と₂かも₂ (5) あやにかなしき₁

Romanization
(1) Kəma nisiki (2) pimo tək-i-sakɛ-te (3) n-uru-ŋga [u]pɛ-ni (4) aⁿ-də se-rə tə kamə (5) aya n-i kanasi-ki

Glossing with Morphemic Analysis
(1) Koguryo brocade (2) cord untie-CONV-separate(CONV)-SUB (3) sleep-ATTR-POSS top-LOC (4) what-QV do-IMP QV EP (5) extreme COP-CONV be.dear-ATTR

Translation
(3) Besides (2) untying [her garment's] cords (1) [made of] Koguryo brocade and (3) sleeping [with her], I wonder what [else should I] do? (5) [She] is extremely dear [to me].

Commentary
Kəma is the Old Japanese name for the northern Korean kingdom of Koguryŏ (mid-fourth century–668 AD, 高句麗), one of the three kingdoms during the Three Kingdoms period (三國時代). At the height of its power Koguryŏ ruled the territory on the Korean peninsula from the Hankang basin in the south and up to the present North Korean–Chinese border, as well as all of South Manchuria and parts of Central Manchuria and possibly the southern part of the present-day Russian Maritime province.

Mizushima expresses some reservations that such a high price commodity as the Koguryŏ brocade that was imported would be affordable to peasants in the Eastern provinces of Yamatə. Nevertheless, he also notes that in 716 AD 1,799 immigrants from Koguryŏ were moved to seven provinces to the east of Suruga province, so there is a possibility that the Koguryŏ brocade was produced locally by Koguryŏ immigrant craftsmen (Mizushima 1986: 244). There is, however, another possibility as well. Nothing in this poem indicates that the author of this poem and his lover are members of the peasant class. They could be as well members of the local warrior or bureaucracy classes who could well be able to afford expensive goods. The most likely solution would be a combination of Mizushima's proposal and the present one for two reasons. First, it is unlikely that peasants would be able to afford even locally produced brocade. Second, Koguryŏ fell in 668 AD to the united armies of Silla (OJ Siraⁿgï, 新羅) and Tang China, and it is unlikely that this poem would go back to as early as the first half of the seventh century. Consequently, the Koguryŏ brocade was not transported from Koguryŏ in the eighth century. The relationship between

United Silla and Yamatə was never cordial, and the trade was limited. As a matter of fact, most of Yamatə trade in the Nara and Heian periods was done with Parhae (Jpn. Bokkai, 渤海), the successor state of Koguryŏ.

EOJ -*rə* is an imperative suffix, corresponding to WOJ -*yə*.

On EOJ interrogative pronoun *a*ⁿ- 'what, why' see the commentary to 14.3379.

14.3466

本文 • *Original Text*
(1) 麻可奈思美 (2) 奴礼婆許登尒豆 (3) 佐祢奈敝波 (4) 己許呂乃緒呂尒 (5) 能里弖可奈思母

仮名の書き下し • *Kana Transliteration*
(1) まかなしみ₁ (2) ぬればこ₂と₂にづ (3) さねなへ₁ば (4) こ₂こ₂ろ₂の₂をろ₂に (5) の₂りてかなしも₂

Romanization
(1) ma-kanasi-mi (2) n-ure-ᵐba kətə-ni [i]ⁿd-u (3) sa-ne-n-ap-e-ᵐba (4) kəkərə-nə wo-rə-ni (5) nər-i-te kanasi-mə

Glossing with Morphemic Analysis
(1) INT-be.dear-GER (2) sleep-EV-CON word-LOC go.out-FIN (3) PREF-sleep-NEG-ITER-EV-CON (4) heart-GEN cord-DIM-LOC (5) ride-CONV-SUB be.dear-EXCL

Translation
(1/2) When [I] sleep with her, because [she] is really dear [to me], there are rumors. (3) When [I] continue not to sleep [with her], (4/5) [she] is riding on [my] heart's little cord, as [she] is dear [to me]!

Commentary
On specific EOJ order of morphemes -(*a*)*n-ap-* 'NEG-ITER' see the commentary to 14.3375.

The evidential form is spelled as -*e*- (cf. WOJ -*ɛ*-) that probably indicates that the contrast between *e* and *ɛ* was non-existent in the dialect of this poem.

Heart's cord is a metaphor for a long-lasting feeling. Therefore, more fiction-like translation might be something like 'she is always in my heart'.

14.3468

本文 · *Original Text*
(1) 夜麻杼里乃 (2) 乎呂能波都乎尓 (3) 可賀美可家 (4) 刀奈布倍美許曾 (5) 奈尓与曾利鶏米

仮名の書き下し · *Kana Transliteration*
(1) やまど₂りの₂ (2) をろ₂の₂はつをに (3) かがみ₁かけ₁ (4) と₁なふべ₂み₁こ₂そ₂ (5) なによ₂そ₂りけ₁め₂

Romanization
(1) yama-ⁿ-dəri-nə (2) wo-rə-nə patu wo-ni (3) kaŋgami kake (4) tonap-uᵐbɛ-mi kəsə (5) na-ni yəsər-i-kem-ɛ

Glossing with Morphemic Analysis
(1) mountain-GEN-bird-GEN (2) tail-DIM-COMP first hemp-LOC (3) mirror hang(CONV) (4) recite-DEB-GER FP (5) you-DAT give.one's.heart-CONV-PAST/TENT-EV

Translation
(3) [I] hung the mirror (2) on the first [harvest's] hemp that is like the tail (1) of a mountain bird, (4) and as [I] had to recite [the incantation], (5) [I] gave my heart to you.

Commentary
This poem is notoriously difficult to interpret and understand. There are multiple theories, but none of them is completely accepted. The reason for this, we believe, is that we are dealing here with a description of a ritual. This ritual was clearly connected with the first harvest of hemp, and it was probably conducted by women, as magic incantations were done by women. Other details, such as the exact role of the mirror, and why is it hung on the hemp, remain unclear. We follow rather closely in our interpretation and translation the analysis and interpretation by Mizushima (1986: 249–250). Compare, for example, Omodaka's interpretation according to which the mirror is hung opposite the mountain bird's tail, and that it is the bird which sings, and not the woman (1977.14: 167–169).

OJ *yama-ⁿ-dəri* 'mountain bird' refers to a bird that looks like a pheasant, but is bigger. Its body has yellowish black color with reddish black spots. Two feathers in the tail are unusually long (Omodaka et al. 1967: 772).

On the EOJ diminutive suffix -rə see the commentary to 14.3351.

The converb form *kake* 'hang and' is spelled with *e* (cf. WOJ *kakɛ-*) that probably indicates that the contrast between *e* and *ɛ* was non-existent in the dialect of this poem.

There was a belief in ancient Japan that the reflection of a person who looked into a mirror would be preserved there, and, consequently, could be seen by another person who looks into the same mirror. Thus, *kaⁿgami* 'mirror' would fulfill a role similar to that of a photograph in the present day. Mirrors also functioned as amulets that have the ability to chase away evil spirits. It is suggested that a mirror presented as a keepsake has to be kept away from the eyes of others, since they could also then see the reflection of the giver, which was not desirable and potentially even harmful. This poem probably involves a play on words (*kakekotoba*, 掛詞): OJ *kake-* means both 'to hang' and 'to have someone in one's heart'. WOJ *ma-so kaⁿgami* 'really clear mirror' is a permanent epithet (*makura-kotoba*, 枕詞) to the verb *kakɛ-*.

14.3469

本文・*Original Text*

(1) 由布氣尓毛 (2) 許余比登乃良路 (3) 和賀西奈波 (4) 阿是曾母許与比 (5) 与斯呂伎麻左奴

仮名の書き下し・*Kana Transliteration*

(1) ゆふけ₂にも₁ (2) こ₂よ₂ひ₁と₂の₂ら₂ろ₁ (3) わがせなは (4) あぜそ₂も₂こ₂よ₂ひ₁ (5) よ₂しろ₂き₁まさの

Romanization

(1) yupu kɛ-ni mo (2) kə yəpi tə nər-ar-o (3) wa-ⁿga se-na pa (4) aⁿze sə mə kə yəpi (5) yəsir-ə-k-i-[i]mas-an-o

Glossing with Morphemic Analysis

(1) evening divination-LOC FP (2) this night QV say-PASS-ATTR (3) I-POSS beloved-DIM TOP (4) why FP EP this night (5) approach-CONV-come-CONV-HON-NEG-ATTR

Translation

(1) In the evening divination (2) it was revealed: 'Tonight [he will come]'. (4) Why then tonight (3) my dear beloved (5) does not come close?

Commentary

OJ *kɛ* 'divination' occurs only with preceding *yupu* 'evening'. Mizushima comments that this kind of divination was performed by going to the crossroads and figuring out future fortune or misfortune by listening to the words of passers-by (1986: 251).

On the EOJ verbal attributive -*o* see the commentary to 14.3395 and a brief description of EOJ special grammar in the introduction.

EOJ *yəsirə*- is a *hapax legomenon*. We can figure out from the context that it should somehow correspond to *yəsar-i* 'approach-CONV', but the main problem is that there are no other examples of converb -*ə* in the EOJ corpus. However, *yəsirə*- probably can be explained as a sporadic metathesis of *yəsər-i*.

14.3472

本文・*Original Text*
(1) 比登豆麻等 (2) 安是可曾乎伊波牟 (3) 志可良婆加 (4) 刀奈里乃伎奴乎 (5) 可里弖伎奈波毛

仮名の書き下し・*Kana Transliteration*
(1) ひ₁と₂づまと₂ (2) あぜかそ₂をいはむ (3) しからばか (4) と₁なりの₂き₁ぬを (5) かりてき₁なはも₁

Romanization
(1) pitə-ⁿ-duma tə (2) aⁿze ka sə-wo ip-am-u (3) sika-[a]r-amba ka (4) tonari-nə kinu-wo (5) kar-i-te ki-n-ap-am-o

Glossing with Morphemic Analysis
(1) person-GEN-wife QV (2) why IP she-ACC say-TENT-ATTR (3) so-exist-COND IP (4) neighbor-GEN garment-ACC (5) borrow-CONV-SUB wear-NEG-ITER-TENT-ATTR

Translation
(2) Why should [they] call her (1) the wife of [another] man? (3) If it were so, (5) [one] would not be borrowing (4) a garment from a neighbor, right?

Commentary
Married women were certainly a taboo for courting by other men, but not every man, like the author of this poem, agreed with this social rule. In this poem an attempt is made to ridicule this rule by putting on the same level

borrowing a garment from a neighbor with borrowing someone else's wife. Another poem demonstrating a similar attitude is 4.517.

The second line is hypermetric (*ji amari*, 字余り).

On EOJ *aⁿze* 'why' see the commentary to 14.3369.

On specific EOJ order of morphemes *-(a)n-ap-* 'NEG-ITER' see the commentary to 14.3375.

On the EOJ verbal attributive *-o* see the commentary to 14.3395 and a brief description of EOJ special grammar in the introduction.

14.3473

本文・*Original Text*
(1) 左努夜麻尒 (2) 宇都也乎能登乃 (3) 等抱可騰母 (4) 祢毛等可兒呂賀 (5) 於由尒美要都留

仮名の書き下し・*Kana Transliteration*
(1) さの₁やまに (2) うつやをの₂と₂の₂ (3) と₂ほかど₂も₂ (4) ねも₁と₂かこ₁ろ₂が (5) おゆにみえ₂つる

Romanization
(1) Sano yama-ni (2) ut-u ya wonə [o]tə-nə (3) təpo-ka-ⁿdəmə (4) ne-m-o tə ka KO-rə-ⁿga (5) o-yun-i mi-ye-t-uru

Glossing with Morphemic Analysis
(1) Sano mountain-LOC (2) hit-ATTR EP ax sound-COMP (3) be.far-EV-CONC (4) sleep-TENT-ATTR IP QV girl-DIM-POSS (5) PREF-sleep-NML see-PASS (CONV)-PERF-ATTR

Translation
(3) Although [she] is far away, (2) like the sound of the ax that hits [the trees] (1) on Mt. Sano, (4/5) [my] dear girl appeared in [my] dream saying: 'Shall [we] sleep together?'

Commentary
This poem has a philological problem: all manuscripts without exception have the 於由 in line five (Mizushima 1984a: 260), but most commentators rewrite it as 於母 (Takagi et al. 1959: 435; Kubota 1967: 217; Kojima et al. 1973: 480; Nakanishi 1981: 268–269; Mizushima 1986: 256–257; Itō 1997: 457, 460; Satake et al. 2002: 350), following the proposal made by Kamo Mabuchi (賀茂真淵) in

his *Man'yō kō* (萬葉考) 'The commentary on the *Man'yōshū*' that the character 由 is a misspelling of 母.[36] Tsuchiya is the only scholar who tries to interpret the text as it is with 於由, but he speculates that the word *oyu* means 'omen', 'sign', that he segments out of WOJ *oyə^{n}dure* 'tempting/confusing word(?)' (Omodaka et al. 1967: 168), basically on the basis of its character spelling 妖言 and then goes on to argue that 妖 is not necessarily a bad omen (1977.7: 328). Omodaka preserves the original text and considers the matter far from being settled, but ends up translating this problematic word as *omokage* 'visage, looks' (1977.14: 172–173). The motivation for the majority's opinion is quite clear: there is no noun *oyu attested in OJ, and substituting it with *omə* 'face, surface' makes at least a little bit of sense. However, besides the obvious contradiction to the text, as it is unlikely that all lines of manuscripts would have the same spelling error, there are other serious problems with Kamo Mabuchi's solution. First, the chance of confusing the characters 由 and 母 is almost nil, as they look very different not only in the standard *kaisho*, but also in the cursive *sōsho* and semi-cursive *gyōsho* script: 由 and 母. In addition, the assumption of misspelling largely rests on the idea that the *Man'yōshū*'s *Ur-text* was written in the cursive script, but this assumption can be easily challenged on the basis of the fact that the oldest manuscripts of the *Man'yōshū*:[37] *Katsura-bon* (桂本), *Ranshi-bon* (藍紙本), *Genryaku kōhon* (元暦校本), *Kanazawa-bon* (金沢本), *Amagasaki-bon* (尼崎本), and *Ruijū koshū* (類聚古集) all use the semi-cursive *gyōsho* script (行書), and that the recently excavated *mokkan* (木簡) fragments of the *Man'yōshū* from the Nara period have the standard *kaisho* script (楷書). Second, while OMƏKA^{N}GƐ-*ni* MI-YE- is attested once in the *Man'yōshū* (8.1630), **omə-ni mi-ye-* is not. This is very significant, as *omǝkaŋgɛ* 'visage, looks, appearance' is not the same as *omə* 'face, surface'. Note that all the commentators who opt for the *omə* option interpret it as *omǝkaŋgɛ*, and this certainly cannot be right. While we have no definite answer to this enigma, we have at least a tentative solution that might work. It is based on the observation that most attestations of -*ni mi-ye-* in the *Man'yōshū* occur with the preceding word *imɛ* 'dream', and the actual form -*ni mi-ye-t-uru* appearing in this poem, always occurs with the preceding *imɛ* 'dream' (MYS 2.150, 4.581, 12.3117, 15.3639) except in this poem. Since the *Man'yōshū* poetry is very formulaic, the combination analysis should lead us to the conclusion that the mysterious word

---

36 On *Man'yō kō* see the Introduction to the *Man'yōshū*, book fifteen, p. 14.
37 Currently I have no access to a facsimile of the *Tenji-bon* (天治本), the fifth oldest manuscript of the *Man'yōshū*.

oyu means 'dream'. Needless to say, such a word is not attested in either EOJ or WOJ. However, OJ *imɛ* 'dream' is believed to be derived from OJ *i* 'sleep' and *mɛ* 'eye'. We should not also forget that the MJ (and MDJ) word for dream is *yume*, which is a later form that is a result of *i*-breaking. Since we deal with EOJ here, there is a distinct possibility that *i*-breaking could occur in some of its dialects like it did in MJ. It must be further noted that 'sleep' and 'dream' are not differentiated in some languages, as, for example, in Russian where сон /son/ means both. This helps us to identify *yu* of *oyu* as 'sleep' and possibly 'dream', but it leaves *o-* of *oyu* as an unidentified segment, which is not good. One tentative solution for this problem is to assume that this *o-* is actually *wo[ⁿ]-*, a diminutive prefix as can be surmised from *Koyō ryaku ruijū shō* (古葉略類聚抄) 'An abridged selection of old leaves [of words] organized by categories' transcription, but since this manuscript is from the mid-Kamakura period and contains no actual *man'yōgana*, this solution is doubtful: the initial *o-* and *wo-* merged as *wo-* only in the Heian period. An alternative solution would be to see *oyu* as an Ainu-EOJ hybrid consisting of Ainu *o-*, a locative prefix and a tentative EOJ **yu* 'sleep, dream'. However, Ainu locative prefix *o-* can be attached only to verbal stems, but not to nominal stems.[38] Thus, the tentative EOJ **yu* 'sleep, dream' is better to be abandoned, and we prefer to interpret 於由尓 in line five as *o-yun-i* PREF-sleep-NML 'in the sleep/dream'. Note also that EOJ *yun-* 'to sleep' is also attested in 14.3476a below.

The first three lines constitute a poetic introduction (*jo*, 序) to the rest of the poem.

Sano corresponds to an area along Karasu river (烏川) in southeastern part of present-day Takasaki city (高崎市) in Gunma prefecture (Mizushima 1986: 150; Nakanishi 1985: 449). This placename actually may indicate that this poem is from Kamitukɛno province in spite of the fact that it is placed together with unidentified Aⁿduma poems in book fourteen. This identification can be further strengthened by the fact that poem 14.3473 has EOJ verbal attributive *-o*. which is also attested in one identified poem from Kamitukɛno province (14.3423).

The particle *ya* in the second line is the emphatic particle *ya*, not the interrogative particle *ya*.

EOJ inflected adjectival evidential marker *-ka-* corresponds to WOJ *-ke-*. The same vowel correspondence is observed with EOJ retrospective *-kar-* and WOJ *-ker-*. See also the commentary to 14.3385.

---

38   Many thanks to my former student Thomas Dougherty who pointed out this fact to me.

On the EOJ verbal attributive -o see the commentary to 14.3395 and a brief description of EOJ special grammar in the introduction.

On the diminutive suffix -rə see the commentary to 14.3351.

14.3474

本文 • *Original Text*
(1) 宇惠太氣能 (2) 毛登左倍登与美 (3) 伊侶弓伊奈婆 (4) 伊豆思牟伎弓可 (5) 伊毛我奈氣可牟

仮名の書き下し • *Kana Transliteration*
(1) うゑだけ₂の₂ (2) も₁と₂さへ₂と₂よ₂み₁ (3) いでていなば (4) いづしむき₁てか (5) いも₁がなげ₂かむ

Romanization
(1) uwe-ⁿ-dakɛ-nə (2) motə sapɛ təyəm-i (3) iⁿde-te in-aᵐba (4) iⁿdusi muk-i-te ka (5) imo-ŋga naŋgɛk-am-u

Glossing with Morphemic Analysis
(1) plant(NML)-GEN-bamboo-GEN (2) root RP sound-CONV (3) go.out(CONV)-SUB go.away-COND (4) where.to face-CONV-SUB IP (5) beloved-POSS lament-TENT-ATTR

Translation
(1/2) Even the roots of the bamboo that [I] planted are crying (3) when [I] go away from home – (4) facing what direction, (5) would [my] beloved lament?

Commentary
OJ restrictive particle *sapɛ* indicates maximum representation: 'even as much as ...' or 'even in addition to ...'. In the given context of this poem it implies that not only the stalks and leaves of bamboo are crying, but even its roots are. For the details on OJ particle *sapɛ* see Vovin (2020.2: 1188–1192).

The third line is hypermetric (*ji amari*, 字余り), but this is probably just a graphic illusion, since *iⁿdete inaᵐba* was in all probability pronounced as [iⁿdetenaᵐba].

EOJ *iⁿdusi* 'where to' is a *hapax legomenon*, which corresponds to WOJ *iⁿduti* 'id.' WOJ *iⁿduti* 'where to' is also attested twice in book fourteen, but both times in the poems without any distinctive EOJ features (14.3357, 14.3577). On the EOJ palatalization *t > s /_i* see commentaries to 14.3395 and 14.3445. On the odd nature of palatalization in this particular word see Vovin (2005: 322–323).

14.3476

本文 • *Original Text*

(1) 宇倍兒奈波 (2) 和奴尓故布奈毛 (3) 多刀都久能 (4) 努賀奈敝由家婆 (5) 故布思可流奈母

仮名の書き下し • *Kana Transliteration*

(1) うべ₂こ₁なは (2) わの₁にこ₁ふなも₁ (3) たと₁つくの₂ (4) の₁がなへ₁ゆけ₁ば (5) こ₁ふしかるなも₂

Romanization

(1) uᵐbɛ ko-na pa (2) wano-ni kop-unam-o (3) tat-o tuku-nə (4) noⁿgan-ape-yuk-e-ᵐba (5) kopusi-k-ar-unam-ə

Glossing with Morphemic Analysis

(1) indeed girl-DIM TOP (2) I-DAT long.for-TENT2-ATTR (3) rise-ATTR moon-GEN (4) pass/flow-ITER(CONV)-go-EV-CON (5) be.longing.for-CONV-exist-TENT₂-ATTR

Translation

(1) Indeed, [my] dear girl (2) will probably long for me. (3) As a month after month/As [her] menstrual periods (4) continue to pass/flow away, (5) [she] will be probably longing [for me].

Commentary

This poem has the most non-standard and non-WOJ outlook in book fourteen (except the poems that are problematic for understanding), as it contains many EOJ distinctive features.

On EOJ diminutive suffix *-na* see the commentary to 14.3384.

EOJ *wano* is first person pronoun 'I', possibly the oblique stem of *wa* 'I' (Vovin 2005: 226–27).

On EOJ tentative suffix *-unam-* see the commentary to 14.3366.

On the EOJ verbal attributive *-o* see the commentary to 14.3395 and a brief description of EOJ special grammar in the introduction. It is misspelled in *kopusi-k-ar-unam-ə* as *-ə*, which should come as no surprise after *m*, since the contrast of *o* vs. *ə* after *m* was lost in all books of the *Man'yōshū* except book five, where the contrast is still preserved, at least statistically (Bentley 2002).

On EOJ *tuku* 'moon, month' see the commentary to 14.3395.

EOJ *tat-o tuku* 'rising moon' is believed to indicate the beginning of a new month (Mizushima 1986: 260), but it also may be a play on words indicating the menstrual periods of a woman. See the commentary to 14.3395. The word *noⁿgane-* 'to flow' may represent further evidence in support of this point of view.

EOJ *noⁿgan-ape-* 'to flow constantly' is considered to be a cognate of WOJ *naⁿgar-apɛ-* 'to flow constantly, to pass [of time]'. Both verbs are derivations of EOJ *noⁿgane-* and WOJ *naⁿgare-* 'to flow' including iterative suffix *-apɛ-*, which tends to be used after vowel verbs roots instead of *-ap-* (Vovin 2020.2: 738). Given the vocalism of EOJ form *noⁿgane-*, it seems to be more archaic than WOJ *naⁿgare-*, the latter resulting from regressive vowel assimilation. A correspondence of EOJ *-n-* to WOJ *-r-* is rare, but it is confirmed by two other examples EOJ *-na* ~ WOJ *-ra*, diminutive suffix, EOJ *-unam-* ~ WOJ *-uram-*, tentative suffix, both found in this poem.

EOJ *kopusi* 'be longing for, be missing (someone)' corresponds to WOJ *kopïsi* 'id.' Both reflect PJ *kopoy-si, for details see the commentary to 14.3382 and Vovin (2011b).

Postscript to the Poem 14.3476

本文・*Original Text*
或本歌末句曰奴我奈敝由家杼和奴由賀乃敝波

Translation
This poem in a certain book has *noⁿgan-ape-yuk-e-ⁿdə wanu yuk-an-əp-e-ᵐba* as its last stanza.

Commentary
This postscript introduces a variant of 14.3476 that has different lines four and five and is presented below as 14.3476a.

14.3476a

本文・*Original Text*
(1) 宇倍兒奈波 (2) 和奴尒故布奈毛 (3) 多刀都久能 (4) 奴我奈敝由家杼 (5) 和奴賀由乃敝波

仮名の書き下し・*Kana Transliteration*
(1) うべ₂こ₁なは (2) わの₁にこ₁ふなも₁ (3) たと₁つくの₂ (4) の₁がなへ₁ゆけ₁ど₂ (5) わの₁がゆの₂へ₁ば

Romanization
(1) u^mbɛ ko-na pa (2) wano-ni kop-unam-o (3) tat-o tuku-nə (4) no^ŋgan-ape-yuk-e-^ndə (5) wano-^ŋga yun-əp-e-^mba

Glossing with Morphemic Analysis
(1) indeed girl-DIM TOP (2) I-DAT long.for-TENT2-ATTR (3) rise-ATTR moon-GEN (4) pass/flow-ITER(CONV)-go-EV-CONC (5) I-POSS sleep-ITER-EV-CON

Translation
(1) Indeed, [my] dear girl (2) will probably long for me. (3/4) Although a month after month/Although [her] menstrual periods continue to pass/flow away, (5) when [I] continue to sleep [with her] ...

Commentary
There is a philological problem concerning line five. All manuscripts have 賀由 instead of 由賀 (Mizushima 1984a: 265), which was introduced by Motoori Norinaga who suggested that characters 由 and 賀 were reversed (Mizushima 1986: 261). This point of view has been accepted by most modern commentators (Takagi et al. 1959: 436; Kojima et al. 1973: 481; Omodaka 1977.14: 175),[39] (Nakanishi 1981: 269; Mizushima 1986: 260–261; Itō 1997: 463, 465). Others preserve the original text, but do not offer any analysis of it (Kubota 1967: 219; Satake et al. 2002: 351). Tsuchiya preserves the original text, but offers quite a fantastic analysis of *yunəpe* as 'does not avoid' (忌まない) (1977.7: 331). This problem is similar to the problem discussed in the commentary to 14.3473 above, although in contrast to 14.3473 that involves alleged character misspelling, the problem in 14.3476a is connected to a possible character order reversion. The major problem is, however, the same: it is highly unlikely that all manuscript lines would contain exactly the same error. In addition, there are other problems. First, as was mentioned in the commentary to 14.3476 above, *wano* 'I' is likely to be an oblique form. Thus, one would expect it to be followed by a case marker, and not to be used in isolation. 和奴賀 *wano-ŋga* with *wano-* being followed by possessive case marker -*ŋga* perfectly satisfies this requirement. This leaves us, however, with 由乃敝波 *yunəpe^mba* being apparently unexplained. However, we believe there is a possibility to explain it. There is a EOJ verb *yun-* 'to sleep' that is also attested in 14.3473 above. There also might be a connection with the honorific verb *o-yor-* 'to sleep' that is attested for the first time in the *Kokon chomonjū* (古今著聞集, 1254 AD) that consists of the

---
39 Omodaka accepts this analysis with reservation.

honorific prefix o- (< MJ ofo- < OJ opo-) + yor- 'to sleep' that should be derived by conversion from MJ yoru < WOJ yoru 'night[time]'. WOJ yoru is clearly bimorphemic consisting of WOJ yo 'night' + -ru, an obsolete suffix that appears also in WOJ piru 'day[time]'. EOJ yu 'night' corresponding to WOJ yo 'id.' is attested in 20.4369. Given the correspondence of EOJ -n- to WOJ -r-, which was discussed above in the commentary to 14.3476, we can surmise that EOJ yun- 'to sleep' in yunəpe^mba might correspond to late MJ yor- in o-yor- 'to sleep'. Consequently, yunəpe^mba can be analyzed as yun-əp-e-^mba 'when [I] continue to sleep [with her]'. Therefore, if my analysis of the fifth line is correct, this line should imply unspoken 'her menstrual periods will stop', meaning that she will become pregnant, of course. This interpretation provides yet another support for the second meaning of tat-o tuku 'rising moon', which as noticed above in the commentaries to 14.3395 and 14.3476 may refer not only to the new moon, but also (and most certainly) to the onset of a menstrual period.

Japanese scholars normally read EOJ 和奴 'I' on lines two and five as wanu (ditto for 和奴 on line two of the preceding poem 14.3476). However, cf. noⁿgan-ape- 'to flow continuously' that is spelled 奴我奈敝, with the first character 奴 traditionally read as no. Although the character 奴 can stand for both no and nu, it is not very likely that it would be read in two different ways within the same poem. Furthermore, in the poem 20.4358 from Kamitupusa province we clearly have no, not nu in 和努 wano 'I', which further supports the reading wano in all three cases. Doing otherwise will unnecessary multiply the entities in direct violation of the Occham's razor.

On the rest, see the commentary to 14.3476.

14.3478

本文・*Original Text*
(1) 等保斯等布 (2) 故奈乃思良祢尓 (3) 阿抱思太毛 (4) 安波乃敝思太毛 (5) 奈尓己曾与佐礼

仮名の書き下し・*Kana Transliteration*
(1) と₂ほしと₂ふ (2) こ₁なの₂しらねに (3) あほしだも₁ (4) あはの₂へ₁しだも₁ (5) なにこ₂そ₂よ₂され

Romanization
(1) təpo-si tə [i]p-u (2) Kona-nə Sira ne-ni (3) ap-o siⁿda mo (4) ap-an-əpe siⁿda mo (5) na-ni kəsə yəsar-e

Glossing with Morphemic Analysis
(1) be.far-FIN QV say-ATTR (2) Kona-GEN White peak-LOC (3) meet-ATTR time FP (4) meet-NEG-ITER(CONV) time FP (5) you-DAT FP be.attracted-EV

Translation
(3) When [we] meet (4) and when [we] do not meet (2) at White peak in Kona, (1) which [they] say is far, (5) [I] am attracted to you.

Commentary
The exact location of White peak (*Sira ne*) of Kona is unknown. There are hypotheses equating it with Mt. Sirane (白根) in Azuma county (Azuma-gun, 吾妻郡) of present-day Gunma prefecture, with Mt. Sirayama (白山) in present-day Ishikawa prefecture (Nakanishi 1985: 446), or even with Tateyama mountain range (立山) in present-day Toyama prefecture (Mizushima 1986: 264).

On EOJ *si^{n}da* 'time' see the commentary to 14.3363.

On specific EOJ order of morphemes -(*a*)*n-ap-* 'NEG-ITER' see the commentary to 14.3375. Here we have -*an-əpe*- corresponding to -*an-apɛ*-.

On the adnominal function of the converb form in EOJ see the commentary to 14.3415.

EOJ *yəsar-* 'to be attracted, to give one's heart' is a *hapax legomenon*. It is believed to correspond to OJ *yəsər-*.

14.3480

本文・*Original Text*
(1) 於保伎美乃 (2) 美己等可思古美 (3) 可奈之伊毛我 (4) 多麻久良波奈礼 (5) 欲太知伎努可母

仮名の書き下し・*Kana Transliteration*
(1) おほき₁み₁の₂ (2) み₁こ₂と₂かしこ₁み₁ (3) かなしいも₁が (4) たまくらはなれ (5) よ₁だちき₁の₁かも₂

Romanization
(1) opo kimi-nə (2) mi-kətə kasiko-mi (3) kanasi imo-^{n}ga (4) ta-makura panare (5) yo-^{n}-dat-i k-i-n-o kamə

Glossing with Morphemic Analysis
(1) great lord-GEN (2) HON-word awesome-GER (3) dear beloved-POSS (4) arm-pillow separate(CONV) (5) night-LOC-depart-CONV come-CONV-PERF-ATTR EP

Translation
(1/2) Because the imperial command is awesome, (3/4) [I] went away from the arms of my dear beloved [that I used as] a pillow, and (5) departing at night, came [here]!

Commentary
On *opo kimi* 'great lord' normally refers to the presently ruling emperor (Omodaka et al. 1967: 394).

OJ *mi-kətə* 'honorable word' refers to an imperial command or edict. WOJ *mi-kətə-nəri* has the same meaning, but in contrast to OJ *mi-kətə* it seems to be always dealing with serious matters concerning the state, while OJ *mi-kətə* may be issued regarding more trivial cases.

The third line is hypermetric (*ji amari*, 字余り), but this is probably just a graphic illusion, since *kanasi imo* was in all probability pronounced as [kanasimo].

On the EOJ verbal attributive *-o* see the commentary to 14.3395 and a brief description of EOJ special grammar in the introduction.

On EOJ perfective attributive *-n-o* see the commentary to 14.3395.

Judging by the content of this poem it is probably a poem composed by a border guard (OJ *sakimori*). Mizushima notes that 'departing at night' must be a poetic hyperbola, since departures were normally done in the morning (1986: 269).

14.3481

本文 • Original Text
(1) 安利伎奴乃 (2) 佐惠佐惠之豆美 (3) 伊敝能伊母尓 (4) 毛乃伊波受伎尓弖 (5) 於毛比具流之母

仮名の書き下し • Kana Transliteration
(1) あり₁ぬの₂ (2) さゑさゑしづみ₁ (3) い へ₁の₂いも₂に (4) も₁の₂いはずき₁にて (5) おも₁ひ₁ぐるしも₂

Romanization

(1) arikinu-nə (2) sawe-sawe si ⁿdum-i (3) ipe-nə imə-ni (4) monə ip-aⁿz-u k-i-n-i-te (5) omop-i-ŋ-gurusi-mə

Glossing with Morphemic Analysis

(1) (*makura-kotoba*) (2) hustle and bustle become.quiet-CONV (3) home-GEN beloved-DAT (4) thing say-NEG-CONV come-CONV-PERF-CONV-SUB (5) think-NML-GEN-hard-EXCL

Translation

(2) [When] the hustle and bustle [of my departure] calmed down (1) like (*makura-kotoba*; 5) it is painful to think that (4) [I] came [here] without saying a word (3) to my beloved wife!

Commentary

OJ *arikinu-nə* is considered to be a permanent epithet (*makura-kotoba*, 枕詞) that is attached to *mi-pe* 'three layers', *takara* 'treasure', onomatopoeia *sawe-sawe* 'make noise while shaking', and to the verb *ar-* 'to exist' (Omodaka et al. 1967: 58). The structure and meaning of *arikinu* is obscure, although there are multiple different hypotheses, explaining it as 'new garment', 'silk[worm] garment',[40] 'existing garment', or simply as a repetition of the phonetic sequence *ari* when it precedes the verb *ar-* 'to exist'. We think that none of these explanations can be accepted, therefore we left *arikinu* untranslated.

EOJ *sawe-sawe* 'hustle and bustle of one's departure' is a *hapax legomenon* that corresponds to WOJ *sawi-sawi*, another *hapax legomenon* with the same meaning. Quite likely the syllable *we* in *sawe-sawe* preserves unraised PJ primary vowel *e, which underwent raising *e > i in WOJ. There are no other distinctive EOJ features in this poem, so we classify it as Eastern only tentatively.

This poem is probably an allusive variation (*honkadori*, 本歌取り) of the poem 4.503 that is a poem by Kakinəmətə-nə asəmi Pitəmarə.

Postscript to the Poem 14.3481

本文 · *Original Text*

柿本朝臣人麻呂歌集中出見上已記也

---

40   Via *ari* 'ant', although ants are not silkworms. Both are insects, but ...

Translation
[This poem] appears in Kakinəmətə-nə asəmi Pitəmarə's poetic collection. See above, as it has been already recorded.

Commentary
Kakinəmətə-nə asəmi Pitəmarə's collection is not preserved *per se*, but scattered in books two, three, seven, nine, ten, eleven, twelve, thirteen, and fourteen of the *Man'yōshū*. It includes two *chōka*, three *sedōka*, and between 327 and 349 *tanka* (depending on each commentator's count) (Mizushima 1986: 209).[41]

There is a discrepancy regarding the last but one character in different manuscripts. The *Genryaku kōhon* has 記, the *Ruijū koshū* and the *Nishi Honganji-bon* have 説, and the *Hosoi-bon* has 訖 (Mizushima 1984a: 274–275). Given the fact that in the *Nishi Honganji-bon* a smaller character 記 is written on the right side of 説, we are inclined to follow the *Genryaku kōhon* variant 記.

Omodaka believes that this postscript demonstrates that a compiler of book fourteen thought that this poem is the same as the poem 4.503 from Pitəmarə's poetic collection (1977.14: 181). Mizushima, however, points out that the compiler of book fourteen treated only the poem 4.503 as a poem from Pitəmarə's poetic collection (1986: 270). Omodaka's point of view seems to me to be a better explanation.

14.3482a

本文・*Original Text*
(1) 可良己呂母 (2) 須素能宇知可比 (3) 阿波奈敝婆 (4) 祢奈敝乃可良尒 (5) 許等多可利都母

仮名の書き下し・*Kana Transliteration*
(1) からこ₂ろ₂も₂ (2) すそ₁の₂うちかひ₁ (3) あはなへ₁ば (4) ねなへ₁の₂からに (5) こ₂と₂たかりつも₂

Romanization
(1) Kara kərəmə (2) suso-nə uti-kap-i (3) ap-an-ap-e-ᵐba (4) ne-n-ape-nə karani (5) kətə [i]ta-k-ar-i-t-umə

---
41 This count is quite strange, because there are nine *chōka* by Pitəmarə in the *Man'yōshū* book two alone.

Glossing with Morphemic Analysis
(1) Korea garment (2) hem-GEN PREF-cross.over-CONV (3) meet-NEG-ITER-EV-CON (4) sleep-NEG-ITER(NML)-GEN CONJ (5) word be.painful-CONV-exist-CONV-PERF-EXCL

Translation
(4) Just because we continue not to sleep [together] (3) when [we] do not meet (1/2) like the hems [of] a Korean garment, that cross over [each other without meeting], (5) rumors have been painful!

Commentary
The placename Kara 'Korea' here almost certainly means United Silla. Originally Kara referred to the state (or tribal union?) of Karak (WOJ *Mimana* 任那), which was sandwiched between Paekche and Silla. It was conquered by Silla in 562 AD. Later on the name Kara was applied to China as well, so there are texts where it is difficult to determine which country it refers to.

Mizushima maintains that *uti-kap-* 'to cross over' is an WOJ verb, corresponding to EOJ *uti-kapɛ-* (1986: 272), but the presence of *uti-kap-* in 14.3482a, which is clearly an EOJ poem strongly speaks against it.

Since Korean garments consisted of several robes of decreasing length from the inner one to an outer one, the previous hem was always longer than the following one, and consequently their edges did not meet. The imagery, therefore, is quite clear. The first two lines constitute metaphoric poetic introduction (*hiyu no jo*, 比喩の序) to the *apane*ⁿ*dəmə* 'although [we] do not meet' (Omodaka 1977.14: 181; Mizushima 1986: 272).

On specific EOJ order of morphemes *-(a)n-ap-* 'NEG-ITER' see the commentary to 14.3375.

EOJ evidential *-e* and nominalized iterative form *-ape*, corresponding to WOJ *-ɛ* and *-apɛ*, probably indicate that the contrast between *ɛ* and *e* did not exist in the EOJ dialect underlying this poem.

On the conjunction *karani* 'just because', 'as soon as' see Vovin (2020.2: 1057–1059).

On the OJ exclamative form *-umə ~ -mə* see the commentary to 14.3431.

14.3483

本文・Original Text
(1) 比流等家波 (2) 等家奈敝比毛乃 (3) 和賀西奈介 (4) 阿比与流等可毛 (5) 欲流等家也須家

仮名の書き下し・*Kana Transliteration*
(1) ひ₁ると₂け₁ば (2) と₂け₁なへ₁ひ₁も₁の₂ (3) わがせなに (4) あひ₁よ₂ると₂かも₁ (5) よ₁ると₂け₁やすけ₁

Romanization
(1) piru tək-e-ᵐba (2) tək-e-n-ape pimo-nə (3) wa-ŋga se-na-ni (4) ap-i-yər-u tə kamo (5) yoru tək-e-yasu-ke

Glossing with Morphemic Analysis
(1) day.time untie-EV-CONC (2) get.untied-NEG-ITER(CONV) cord-GEN (3) I-POSS beloved-DIM-DAT (4) meet-CONV-approach-FIN QV EP (5) night untie(CONV)-easy-ATTR

Translation
(2) [The garment] cords that do not get untied (1) when [I try to] untie [them] in the day time, (4) I wonder whether (5) [they] are easier to get untied at night (4) [because I] think that [I] will meet (3) with my dear beloved?

Commentary
On the custom of tying and untying the cords see the commentary to 14.3361.

EOJ *e* corresponding to WOJ *ɛ* probably indicates that the contrast between *ɛ* and *e* did not exist in the EOJ dialect underlying this poem.

On specific EOJ order of morphemes *-(a)n-ap-* 'NEG-ITER' see the commentary to 14.3375.

On adnominal function of the converb form in EOJ see the commentary to 14.3415.

On EOJ attributive *-ke* in *yasu-ke* see the commentary to 14.3412.

14.3484

本文・*Original Text*
(1) 安左乎良乎 (2) 遠家尒布須左尒 (3) 宇麻受登毛 (4) 安須伎西佐米也 (5) 伊射西乎騰許尒

仮名の書き下し・*Kana Transliteration*
(1) あさをらを (2) をけ₁にふすさに (3) うますと₂も₁ (4) あすき₁せさめ₂や (5) いざせをど₂こ₂に

Romanization

(1) asa-wo-ra-wo (2) wo-ke-ni pususa n-i (3) um-as-u təmo (4) asu ki se-sas-am-ɛ ya (5) iⁿza se woⁿ-dəkə-ni

Glossing with Morphemic Analysis

(1) hemp-hemp.thread-PLUR-ACC (2) hemp-container-LOC many COP-CONV (3) spin-HON-FIN CONJ (4) tomorrow wear(NML) do-HON-TENT-EV IP (5) INTERJ do(IMP) DIM-bed-LOC

Translation

(3) Even if [you] spin (1/2) many hemp threads into a hemp container, (4) would [you] wear [them] tomorrow [as a garment]? [– Certainly, you would not!] (5) Hey, let us go to bed!

Commentary

The spelling of EOJ *wo-ke* 'hemp container' corresponding to WOJ *wo-kɛ* 'id.' indicates that the EOJ dialect underlying this poem had no distinction between *e* and *ɛ*.

EOJ *pususa* 'many' has no cognate in WOJ.

The character 受 is mostly used for rendering a syllable /ⁿzu/ in the *Man'yōshū*, but it is also used to render non-prenasalized /su/ as well, see, e.g. see MYS 5.886. The negative *-aⁿz-* would hardly make any sense in this poem, so we trust that we are dealing with the mild honorific *-as-* here.

EOJ honorific *-sas-* is a unique EOJ honorific from, not attested in WOJ.

Diminutive prefix *woⁿ-* in line five conveys the meaning of endearment: something like 'our dear bed', that is difficult to translate to English exactly without creating a misunderstanding. Literally line five *iⁿza se woⁿ-dəkə-ni* means 'hey, let [us] make [to] our dear bed!' Consequently, this poem has to be understood as an address of an annoyed husband or lover to his wife or beloved, urging her to quit her work and to come to bed with him (Omodaka 1977.14: 184; Mizushima 1986: 275).

14.3485

本文・Original Text

(1) 都流伎多知 (2) 身尓素布伊母乎 (3) 等里見我祢 (4) 哭乎曾奈伎都流 (5) 手兒尓安良奈久尓

仮名の書き下し・*Kana Transliteration*
(1) つるき₁たち (2) み₂にそ₁ふいも₂を (3) と₂りみ₁がね (4) ねをそ₂なき₁つる (5) てご₁にあらなくに

Romanization
(1) turuki tati (2) MÏ-ni sop-u imə-wo (3) tər-i-MI-[ŋ]gane (4) NE-wo sə nak-i-t-uru (5) TEŋGO n-i ar-an-aku n-i

Glossing with Morphemic Analysis
(1) double.edge.sword long.sword (2) body-LOC be.close-ATTR beloved-ACC (3) take-CONV-look(CONV)-NEG.POT(CONV) (4) sound-ACC FP cry-CONV-PERF-ATTR (5) maiden COP-CONV exist-NEG-NML COP-CONV

Translation
(3) Failing to take care (2) of my beloved who is [as] close to me (1) [as my] double-edge sword [and my] long sword, (4) [I] sobbed loudly, (5) although [I] am not a girl.

Commentary
OJ *turuki~ turuŋgi* (劍、都留伎、都流藝) is a sword with a straight blade, as opposed to *katana* (刀、小刀、加太奈), which has a curved blade. *Katana* is of late provenance, being excavated no earlier than from the seventh century. Most of the *turuki* swords were double-edge swords. The etymology of WOJ *turuki* is obscure.

OJ *tati* '[long] sword' was predominantly a long sword used to fight on horseback, although some early comparatively short samples are also known. All *tati* swords from Asuka and Nara periods are with a straight blade. There are two basic types of *tati* 'long sword': *kabututi no tati* (頭椎大刀) and *kantō tati* (環頭大刀). *Kantō tati* is also called *Koma turuki* (高麗劍、狛劍) 'Koguryǒ sword'. *Kabututi no tati* was essentially a single-edge sword, while *Kantō tati* was a double-edge sword. It is possible that the first line *turuki tati* just means '[my] long sword [that is] a double edge sword', but there is no grammatical evidence for such an analysis, and the textual evidence from other Old Japanese texts, such as, for example MYS 5.804 goes against it.

On EOJ *teŋgo ~ teŋgo-na* 'maiden' see the commentary to 14.3384. Except for this word, the poem looks like WOJ. However, in addition to this EOJ word, there is also a specific Eastern cultural attitude towards swords (see below), not really attested in WOJ texts.

On the prenasalization of the negative potential auxiliary -kane- > -ⁿgane- in EOJ see also 14.3538.

The fifth line is hypermetric (*ji amari*, 字余り), but this is probably just a graphic illusion, since *n-i ar-an-aku n-i* was in all probability pronounced as [naranakuni].

The poem is apparently composed by a local Eastern warrior who treasures his swords as much as his wife or beloved. For the period we are concerned with, this should be taken in a positive, and not a negative sense, as it would be today in a Western society. There is a dissenting opinion of Tsuchiya, who believes that the author of this poem is a woman (1977.7: 338), but it seems that no one else among old or modern commentators shares his unusual point of view.

14.3487

本文・*Original Text*
(1) 安豆左由美 (2) 須惠尒多麻末吉 (3) 可久須酒曾 (4) 宿莫奈那里尒思 (5) 於久乎可奴加奴

仮名の書き下し・*Kana Transliteration*
(1) あづさゆみ₁ (2) すゑにたままき₁ (3) かくすすそ₂ (4) ねなななりにし (5) おくをかぬかぬ

Romanization
(1) aⁿdusa yumi (2) suwe-ni tama mak-i (3) ka-ku su su sə (4) NE-N-A-na nar-i-n-i-si (5) oku-wo kan-u kan-u

Glossing with Morphemic Analysis
(1) catalpa bow (2) end-LOC jewel·wrap-CONV (3) be.thus-CONV again again FP (4) sleep-NEG-ATTR-LOC become-CONV-PERF-CONV-ATTR (5) future-ACC worry-FIN worry-FIN

Translation
(2) Wrapping jewels at the end [of] (1) a catalpa bow, (3/5) [I] so worry and ponder again and again about the future, (4) [because] it became so that [we] do not sleep [together].

Commentary

OJ *aⁿdusa* 'catalpa tree' (梓) is a tall deciduous tree (up to 20 m or 63 ft). In Ancient Japan the provinces of Shinano and Kai were famous as the areas where catalpa grew. The wood of catalpa is heavy and hard, and consequently it is used for making agricultural tools, furniture, and the inside decorum of buildings. In Ancient Japan it was also used for making bows (*aⁿdusa yumi* 'catalpa bow'). There are various hypotheses, what is exactly the tree that corresponds to OJ *aⁿdusa*, but most likely that it is MDJ *mizume*, alternatively called *yoguso minebari* (夜糞峰榛), which grows in the wild in the mountains and has grey bark, and a very distinctive stinking smell. It has broad egg-shaped leaves. In the spring, it blooms with greenish yellow ear-shaped flowers. The fruits are shaped like pine cones, and are somewhat sticky.

Tying jewels (in this case, probably jade) to the end of a catalpa bow symbolizes commitment to one's beloved (Mizushima 1986: 279).

On EOJ *su* 'again' < Ainu *suy* 'id.' see the commentary to 14.3363. Needless to say, this interpretation disagrees completely with the tradition, as all the commentators treat this *su su* in this poem as OJ *s-u s-u* 'do-FIN do-FIN'. See also 14.3564. Ainu also uses the reduplicated form *suy suy* 'again and again, once again' (Kayano 1996: 280).

On EOJ form in *V-(a)n-a-na* 'V-NEG-ATTR-LOC' see the commentary to 14.3408.

EOJ *-na* is a special EOJ locative case marker. See also 14.3408, 14.3447, and 14.3461.

Kan-u is a final form of OJ vowel verb *kane-* 'to think about the future, to worry about the future'.

Although other modern commentators are non-committal, Mizushima believes that this is a poem by a man who has lost the relationship with his beloved (1986: 279). This is a possible interpretation if one understands line four in the sense that sleeping together stopped for good. But then worrying and thinking about the future would have probably been completely useless. What if the hapless man simply goes on a long journey, or is conscripted to military service as a border guard? Then only the temporal stopping of the sexual activity takes place, and if it is so, then the wrapping jewels at the end of his bow as a sign of devotion to his beloved as well as thinking about the future would make much more sense than in the case if the man was really dumped by his beloved. Itō goes as far as to suggest that the woman in question went over to another man (1997: 478–479). This is, of course, a pure speculation that has no textual evidence to rely upon.

萬葉集卷第十四・MAN'YŌSHŪ BOOK FOURTEEN 177

14.3488

本文・Original Text
(1) 於布之毛等 (2) 許乃母登夜麻乃 (3) 麻之波尓毛 (4) 能良奴伊毛我名 (5) 可多尓伊弖牟可母

仮名の書き下し・Kana Transliteration
(1) おふしも₁と₂ (2) こ₂の₂も₂と₂やまの₂ (3) ましばにも₁ (4) の₂らぬいも₁がな (5) かたにいでむかも₂

Romanization
(1) op-u simətə (2) kənə mətə yama-nə (3) ma-siᵐba-ni/n-i mo (4) nər-an-u imo-ŋga NA (5) kata-ni iⁿde-m-u kamə

Glossing with Morphemic Analysis
(1) grow-ATTR small.branch (2) this base mountain-GEN (3) INT-brushwood-LOC/frequently COP-CONV FP (4) say-NEG-ATTR beloved-POSS name (5) shoulder[blade]-LOC go.out-TENT-ATTR EP

Translation
(4/5) [I] wonder whether the name of [my] beloved that [I] did not pronounce (1/3) really frequently even in the brushwood with growing small branches (2) of this low mountain, (5) will appear at the [divination deer] shoulder [blade]?

Commentary
EOJ *op-* 'to grow' in line one is clearly a consonantal verb, as can be seen from *op-u simətə* 'growing small branches' in line one. See also EOJ consonantal verb *op-* 'to grow' in 14.3501 below. The corresponding verb in WOJ is a vowel verb *opï-*, and we would expect in WOJ *op-uru simətə* 'growing small branches'.

OJ *simətə ~ simotə* (籬) are small branches of low trees that grow densely together. The etymology of this word is obscure. One of the main usages of *simətə* was that it was used as a whip. From this usage the secondary meaning 'whip' has developed. See for example, the usage of *simətə* in the meaning 'whip' in MYS 5.892.

Mətə yama can either be a placename, or a reference to a low mountain, or to a foot of the mountain (Omodaka 1977.14: 189; Mizushima 1986: 280). We adopt here the point of view that it refers to a low mountain.

Siᵐba in line three represents a play on words, as it can both mean 'brushwood' and 'frequently'. We have tried to incorporate both into our translation.

The fifth line is hypermetric (*ji amari*, 字余り), but this is probably just a graphic illusion, since *kata-ni iⁿdemu* was in all probability pronounced as [kataniⁿdemu].

The practice of divination based on judging the cracks on a tortoise carapace or on a deer shoulder blade bone (with a previously written text on it) that resulted from heating on fire has long roots in China that go back to the Shāng (商) dynasty (1766–1122 BC). This practice was adopted in Japan's Asuka and Nara periods as well. Cf. also 14.3374, where the similar divination ritual is described.

14.3489

本文・*Original Text*
(1) 安豆左由美 (2) 欲良能夜麻邊能 (3) 之牙可久尓 (4) 伊毛呂乎多弖天 (5) 左祢度波良布母

仮名の書き下し・*Kana Transliteration*
(1) あづさゆみ₁ (2) よ₁ら₂やまべ₁の₂ (3) しげ₁かくに (4) いも₁ろ₂をたてて (5) さね ど₁はらふも₂

Romanization
(1) aⁿdusa yumi (2) Yora-nə yama-ᵐ-BE-nə (3) siⁿge-k-aku n-i (4) imo-rə-wo tate-te (5) sa-ne-ⁿ-do parap-umə

Glossing with Morphemic Analysis
(1) catalpa bow (2) Yora-GEN mountain-GEN-side-GEN (3) be.overgrown-ATTR-NML COP-CONV (4) beloved-DIM-ACC make.stand(CONV)-SUB (5) PREF-sleep (NML)-GEN-place clear-EXCL

Translation
(1) Catalpa bow (*makura-kotoba*) (2/3) As the side of Mt. Yora is overgrown [with bush], (4) [I] let my beloved stand, as (5) [I] am clearing a place [for us] to sleep!

Commentary
On OJ *aⁿdusa* 'catalpa' and *aⁿdusa yumi* 'catalpa bow' see the commentary to 14.3487. Here *aⁿdusa yumi* 'catalpa bow' is used as a permanent epithet (*makura-kotoba*, 枕詞), although it is not clear to what word in the following text of the poem it is connected. It is believed that it may be attached to Yora or syllable

/yo/ in Yora due to the 'common usage' (rather, diachronic alternation – A.V. and S.I-V.) of *kō-rui yo* in the placename Yora and *yu* in *yumi* 'bow' (Takagi et al. 1959: 439). It is, unlikely, however, that speakers of EOJ were aware of any of these diachronic alternations. Another opinion that it is attached to *yo* in Yora, because when one pulls the bow, its ends approach (*yər-*) oneself (Mizushima 1986: 281) ultimately goes back to Keichū's *Daishōki* (Omodaka 1977.14: 189), is nonsensical, because the only thing it demonstrates is the ignorance of the vowel distinction *o : ə* in *ko-rui* /yo/ and *otsu-rui* /yə/. Thus, the connection of the *aⁿdusa yumi* 'catalpa bow' to the rest of the poem remains unclear.

The exact location of Mt. Yora is unknown. Possibly it is located in Yora town (与良町) of Komoro city (小諸市) in present-day Nagano prefecture (Nakanishi 1985: 497; Mizushima 1986: 281).

EOJ *siⁿge-* 'be overgrown' corresponds to WOJ *siⁿgɛ-* 'id.' The EOJ 'misspelling' probably indicates that the contrast between /e/ and /ɛ/ did not exist in the EOJ dialect underlying this poem.

EOJ adjectival nominalized form *-k-aku* 'ATTR-NML' corresponds to WOJ *-keku* 'ATTR/NML'. For details see Vovin (2009a: 473–476).

On OJ *to* 'place' and its relationship to OJ *təkərə* 'id.' see Vovin (2010: 117).

On OJ exclamative form *-umə ~ -mə* see the commentary to 14.3431.

On clearing a place for lovers to sleep together see also 14.3479.

14.3493

本文・*Original Text*
(1) 於曾波夜母 (2) 奈乎許曾麻多賣 (3) 牟可都乎能 (4) 四比乃故夜提能 (5) 安比波多我波自

仮名の書き下し・*Kana Transliteration*
(1) おそ₂はやも₂ (2) なを こ₂そ₂またま₁ (3) むかつをの₂ (4) しひ₁の₂こ₁やでの₂ (5) あひ₁はたがはじ

Romanization
(1) osə paya mə (2) na-wo kəsə mat-am-e (3) muka-tu wo-nə (4) sipi-nə kwo-yaⁿde-nə (5) ap-i pa taⁿgap-aⁿzi

Glossing with Morphemic Analysis
(1) late early FP (2) you-ACC FP wait-TENT-EV (3) opposite.side-GEN/LOC ridge-GEN (4) chinquapin-GEN DIM-branch-GEN (5) meet-NML TOP differ-NEG/TENT

Translation

(1) Whether [you come] early or late, (2) [I] will certainly wait for you. (5) [Our] meeting would not be different from [the meeting] (4) of small branches of chinquapin trees (3) at the ridge on the opposite side.

Commentary

All manuscripts exhibit 多家波自 *takepaⁿzi* with 家 in line five, with the exception of the *Genryaku kōhon* and the *Ruijū koshū* that have 多我波自 *taⁿgapaⁿzi* with 我 (Mizushima 1984a: 294). Because both the *Genryaku kōhon* and the *Ruijū koshū* are the oldest manuscripts from two different lines, and because 多家波自 *takepaⁿzi* with 家 does not make any sense in OJ, like most modern commentators, we followed the *Genryaku kōhon* and the *Ruijū koshū*'s text and chose 多我波自 *taⁿgapaⁿzi*.

OJ *osə* 'late' and *paya* 'early' are uninflected adjectives. See Vovin (2020.1: 377–389) on uninflected adjectives in OJ.

EOJ *mat-am-e* '[I] will certainly wait for [you]' has an evidential suffix -*e* (cf. WOJ *mat-am-ɛ*) spelled as if it were an imperative suffix -*e*. This probably demonstrates that there was no contrast between /e/ and /ɛ/ in the EOJ dialect that underlies this poem.

OJ *sipi* 'chinquapin' is known in two MDJ varieties: *tsubura-jii* (*Castanopsis cuspidata*) and *suda-jii* (*Castanopsis Sieboldii*). It is an evergreen tree, growing in warm areas, especially close to seashores. Chinquapin is a luxuriant tall tree (with height up to 25m), with smooth bark and oval-shaped leathery leaves that are brownish on the underside. In May–June chinquapin starts to bloom with fragrant small male and female flowers that are ear-shaped and are found on the same tree. Chinquapin acorns are egg-shaped with a sharp point and are edible. Acorns of *tsubura-jii* are especially tasty. The chinquapin wood is used for building and making utensils, and its bark for dyeing. OJ *sipi* 'chinquapin' is used in poetry as the seasonal word for the summer.

OJ *wo* means not only 'peak', 'hill', but also 'mountain ridge' as opposed to a valley (Omodaka et al. 1967: 828; Mizushima 1986: 287).

EOJ *yaⁿde* 'branch' corresponds to WOJ *ye ~ yeⁿda* 'id.' EOJ *yaⁿde* 'branch' in this poem is a *hapax legomenon*.

The metaphor of meeting like branches of a chinquapin tree is probably based on the fact that chinquapins are luxuriant trees with their branches growing very closely together and frequently overlapping (Omodaka 1977. 14: 193).

Mizushima believes that in this poem a man is waiting for a woman, because OJ personal pronoun *na* 'you' 'is used in many cases by a man in reference to a woman' (1986: 287). There is certainly no gender bias in the usage of OJ *na* 'you', as there are OJ texts, where *na* is used by a woman in reference to a man, see, e.g. KK 3, KK 5, MYS 14.3546, etc. Quite to the contrary, as the variant 14.3493a[42] demonstrates, it is quite clear that a woman is waiting for a man in this poem.

14.3494

本文 · *Original Text*
(1) 兒毛知夜麻 (2) 和可加敝流弖能 (3) 毛美都麻弖 (4) 宿毛等和波毛布 (5) 汝波安杼可毛布

仮名の書き下し · *Kana Transliteration*
(1) こ₁も₁ちやま (2) わかかへ₁るての₂ (3) も₁み₁つまで (4) ねも₁と₂わはも₁ふ (5) なはあど₂かも₁ふ

Romanization
(1) Komoti yama (2) waka kaperute-nə (3) momit-u-maⁿde (4) NE-m-o tə wa pa [o]mop-u (5) NA pa aⁿ-də ka [o]mop-u

Glossing with Morphemic Analysis
(1) Komoti mountain (2) young maple-GEN (3) leaves.turn.red/yellow-ATTR-TERM (4) sleep-TENT-ATTR QV I TOP think-FIN (5) you TOP what-QV IP think-ATTR

Translation
(4) I think that [we] should sleep [together] (2/3) until the young maple becomes red (1) on Mt. Komoti. (5) What do you think?

Commentary
Mt. Komoti (< *ko-mət-i* 'child holding', also supported by logographic spelling of *ko* 'child' as 兒) is in all probability identical to present-day Komoti-yama (子持山, 1192 m), which straddles Kita-Gunma county (Kita Gunma-gun, 北群馬郡), Azuma county (Azuma-gun, 吾妻郡), and Numata city (Numata-shi, 沼田市) in Gumma prefecture (Nakanishi 1985: 447). This mountain is known as a site for sexual rituals in antiquity, so the context of the poem makes this identification almost perfect. Mizushima, however, brings up another possibility

---

42   Not included here, because the poem 14.3493a is in WOJ. But this poem has *kimi* 'lord' instead of *na* 'you'. *Kimi* 'lord' could only be used by a woman in reference to her male lover, but not *vice versa*.

as well: Komoti-yama (子持山, 1110 m) in Matsuida town (Matsuida machi, 松井田町)[43] of Usui county (Usui-gun, 碓氷郡) in Gunma prefecture. He further notes that there is a Komoti jinja 'Child-holding shrine' (子持神社) constructed between 938–946 AD at the mid-slope of the same mountain at the height of 520 m, and that this mountain was close to Nakasendō tract (中山道) (Mizushima 1986: 289). We fail to see how a proximity to the Nakasendō tract or a construction of a shrine in the Heian period makes this choice more justifiable than the previous one, which has obvious connection to sexual rituals. Thus, we side with Nakanishi's identification cited above. Omodaka cites several more hypotheses, but remains non-committal (1977.14: 194). In any case, since both mountains are located in Gunma prefecture, one can identify this poem as being from Kamitukɛno province, especially given the fact that the presence of the EOJ verbal attributive -o and the EOJ interrogative pronoun a^n- 'what, why' that are also attested in other identified Kamitukɛno poems further support the likely attribution of this poem to Kamitukɛno province.

OJ *waka* 'young' is an uninflected adjective. See Vovin (2020.1: 377–389) on uninflected adjectives in OJ.

OJ *momit-* is a verb meaning 'to turn red and/or yellow (of autumn leaves)'. Only its nominalized form *momiji* (with a secondary voicing) survived in the modern Japanese language with the specialized meaning 'red maple leaves'.

EOJ *kaperute* 'maple' (there are no WOJ phonographic attestations) has a transparent etymology: *kaperu* 'frog' + *te* 'hand'.

EOJ *ne-m-o* '[we] should sleep' is the attributive tentative form of the verb *ne-* 'to sleep'. On the EOJ verbal attributive -o see the commentary to 14.3395 and a brief description of EOJ special grammar in the introduction.

On the EOJ interrogative pronoun a^n- 'what, why' see the commentary to 14.3379.

14.3495

本文 · *Original Text*
(1) 伊波保呂乃 (2) 蘇比能和可麻都 (3) 可藝里登也 (4) 伎美我伎麻左奴 (5) 宇良毛等奈久文

仮名の書き下し · *Kana Transliteration*
(1) いはほろ₂の₂ (2) そ₁ひ₁の₂わかまつ (3) かぎ₁りと₂や (4) き₁み₁がき₁まさぬ (5) うらも₁と₂なくも

---

43 Matsuida town was incorporated into Annaka city (Annaka-shi, 安中市) in 2006.

Romanization
(1) ipapo-rə-nə (2) sop-i-nə waka matu/mat-u (3) kaᵑgir-i tə ya (4) kimi-ᵑga k-i-[i]mas-an-u (5) ura motə na-ku mo

Glossing with Morphemic Analysis
(1) rock-DIM-GEN (2) go.along-NML-GEN young pine/wait-FIN (3) limit-NML QV IP (4) lord-POSS come-CONV-HON-NEG-ATTR (5) heart base exist.not-CONV FP

Translation
(2) Young pines along (1) the rocks... (5) [I] am restless (4) as [my] lord did not come, (2) [and I] am waiting [for him] (3) thinking: '[Is] it the end?'

Commentary
OJ *ipapo* 'rock' consists of *ipa* 'rock' and an obsolete suffix *-po*, the meaning of which is difficult to determine, although sometimes it is believed to be a grammaticalization of *po* 'ear (of the grain)' (Omodaka et al. 1967: 94). If this is true, then *ipapo* is probably something like 'rocky outcrops'.

On EOJ diminutive suffix *-rə* see the commentary to 14.3351.

On OJ *waka* 'young' see the commentary to 14.3494.

The first two lines represent a poetic introduction (*jo*, 序), quite loosely connected to the rest of the poem. There is also a play on words (*kakekotoba*, 掛詞) between *matu* 'pine' and *mat-u* 'wait-FIN' on line two.

OJ *ura* 'inside', 'back' is used here metaphorically for heart as an internal organ. See also 14.3443 and 14.3500 for the same usage.

14.3496

本文 • Original Text
(1) 多知婆奈乃 (2) 古婆乃波奈里我 (3) 於毛布奈牟 (4) 己許呂宇都久思 (5) 伊弖安礼波伊可奈

仮名の書き下し • Kana Transliteration
(1) たちばなの₂ (2) こ₁ばの₂はなりが (3) おも₁ふなむ (4) こ₂こ₂ろ₂うつくし (5) いであれはいかな

Romanization
(1) Tatiᵐbana-nə (2) Koᵐba-nə panari-ᵑga (3) omop-unam-u (4) kəkərə utu-kusi (5) iⁿde are pa yik-ana

Glossing with Morphemic Analysis
(1) Tatiᵐbana-GEN (2) Koᵐba-GEN maiden-POSS (3) love-TENT2-ATTR (4) heart adorable(FIN) (5) EXCL I TOP go-DES

Translation
(4) The heart (2) of the maiden from Koᵐba (1) in Tatiᵐbana [district] (3) which seems to love [me] (4) is adorable. (5) Oh, I want to go [to her]!

Commentary
Tatiᵐbana district (橘樹郡) was located in the area corresponding to the territory of Minato Kita-ku (港北区) of Yokohama city and the northern part of Kawasaki city in present-day Kanagawa prefecture (Nakanishi 1985: 460). Therefore, one can identify with certainty this poem as being from Muⁿzasi province. Since this poem is found inside the poetic sequence with reference to plants, the place name Tatiᵐbana here may be meaningful or intentional (OJ *tatiᵐbana* 'mandarin orange').

OJ *tatiᵐbana* 'mandarin orange' is a low evergreen tree (3~4 m, 9 ft 9 in~13 ft 4 in) that grows in the wild. It blooms in early summer with five-petal white flowers, and bears yellow fruit from autumn to winter. The fruit is not edible, as it is extremely sour.

The WOJ sequence *pana tatiᵐbana*⁴⁴ 'flowers of mandarin orange' contradicts the SOV word order which requires a modifier to precede a head noun: one would expect *tatiᵐbana -nə pana*, which is also attested in the *Man'yōshū* (five times), but is much less frequent than *pana tatiᵐbana* (thirty-three times). This unusual word order may indicate that originally Japonic had SVO word order.⁴⁵

The location of Koᵐba [village?] within the Tatiᵐbana district is unknown (Nakanishi 1985: 460).

OJ *panari* 'maiden' has also the original meaning 'divided hair' that refers to the hairstyle worn by girls and unmarried women. A girl's hair ends were cut when she was around two or three years old, and as the hair grew, it was divided at the top of head into two strands, right and left, that were left to hang down to the shoulders, where the hair was trimmed again. This hairstyle was maintained until a girl turned eight years old. From this time and until

---
44 Not attested in EOJ.
45 There are exceptions, though: Tibetan has SOV word-order, but a modifier follows the modified, e.g. རྒྱལ་པོ་ཆེན་པོ་ rgyal-po chen-po 'great king', lit: king (རྒྱལ་པོ་ rgyal-po) great (ཆེན་པོ་ chen-po).

fifteen-sixteen years old (that was presumably the marrying age) the hair was left uncut. This hairstyle was called *panari* 'divided hair' (a nominalization *panar-i* of the verb *panar-* 'to divide, to separate'), and consequently the term for the hairstyle was metonymically transferred to those who had their hair arranged in this manner. Married women were supposed to raise their hair in a coiffure, but this was not always strictly followed (Omodaka et al. 1967: 587).

On EOJ tentative suffix *-unam-* see the commentary to 14.3366. Although EOJ tentative *-unam-* is not attested directly in other Muⁿzasi poems, it is attested in one poem from Sa^ŋgamu province (14.3366) from Kamakura district that is right on the border with Muⁿzasi province. Although this is not the same kind of evidence that we have seen for the poem 14.3494 above, it is somewhat compelling, because administrative divisions do not necessarily coincide with dialect boundaries. Therefore, we tentatively accept the possibility that the poem 14.3496 is indeed from Muⁿzasi province.

OJ *utukusi* means 'adorable', 'dear', but not 'beautiful' as modern Japanese *utsukushii*.

The fifth line is hypermetric (*ji amari*, 字余り).

OJ verb *yik-* 'to go' is an extremely rare verb as compared to *yuk-* 'id.', since *yik-* occurs in OJ corpus only seven times (all of them in the *Man'yōshū*). It is always found in hypermetric lines, but otherwise there is no obvious difference in usage between *yik-* and *yuk-* (Omodaka et al. 1967: 69).

14.3499

本文・*Original Text*

(1) 乎可尓与西 (2) 和我可流加夜能 (3) 佐祢加夜能 (4) 麻許等奈其夜波 (5) 祢呂等敝奈香母

仮名の書き下し・*Kana Transliteration*

(1) をかによ₂せ (2) わがかるかやの₂ (3) さねかやの₂ (4) まこ₂と₂なご₂やは (5) ねろ₂と₂へ₁なかも₂

Romanization

(1) woka-ni yəse (2) wa-ⁿga kar-u kaya-nə (3) sa-ne-kaya-nə (4) ma-kətə naⁿgəya pa (5) ne-rə tə [i]p-ena kamə

Glossing with Morphemic Analysis

(1) hill-LOC make.approach(CONV) (2) I-POSS cut-ATTR *kaya*-GEN (3) PREF-sleep(CONV)-*kaya*-GEN (4) INT-matter soft find (5) sleep-IMP QV say-DES EP

Translation

(1) [I] bring [her] to the hill, and (4) [she] finds that (2) the *kaya* grass that I cut, (3) the *kaya* grass for sleeping together (4) [is] really soft. (5) [I] wonder whether [she] wants to say: 'Let us sleep [together]!'

Commentary

On OJ *kaya* 'kaya grass' is a cover term for various grasses like *susuki* 'Japanese pampas grass', *suᵑgɛ* 'sedge', *ti ~ tiᵑgaya* 'cogon grass', etc. that are used to thatch roofs. As it becomes clear from the poem 14.3499, it was also used to make a bed for lovers sleeping together.

EOJ *naᵑgəya* 'soft' corresponds to WOJ *naᵑgoya*. This probably indicates that the phonemic contrast between the *kō-rui* vowel /o/ and the *otsu-rui* vowel /ə/ did not exist in the EOJ dialect that underlies this poem.

The word *pa* in line four cannot possibly be an OJ topic marker, because it makes no grammatical sense in this position. We believe that it is actually a loan of Ainu *pa* 'to find', and this verb not only makes sense in this position in this poem, it makes a great improvement towards the understanding of this poem and its smooth reading, something which is lacking in modern commentaries that do not agree with each other (Omodaka 1977.14: 198–199; Mizushima 1986: 297).

EOJ *ne-rə* 'sleep-IMP' corresponds to WOJ *ne-yə* 'id.' EOJ [*i*]*pena* cannot be a negative form (Mizushima 1986: 297), because negative suffix cannot conclude a verbal form. Neither can it be an EOJ locative case marker *-na* (Omodaka 1977.14: 199), because locatives are not found in front of *kamə*. Although the vowel /e/ instead of /a/ might represent a problem, it is not inconceivable that in some EOJ dialects desiderative *-ana* could be an auxiliary rather than a suffix, therefore *-i-ana* 'CONV-DES' would likely contract to *-ena*. Certainly, EOJ overall demonstrates the tendency for PJ *ia to contract as EOJ *a* vs. WOJ *e*, but given the fact that this poem is from an unidentified section of EOJ, we cannot rule out the fact that in some EOJ dialects there was a process similar to WOJ rule *ia > *e*.

14.3500

本文 • Original Text

(1) 牟良佐伎波 (2) 根乎可母乎布流 (3) 比等乃兒能 (4) 宇良我奈之家乎 (5) 祢乎遠敝奈久尓

仮名の書き下し・*Kana Transliteration*

(1) むらさき₁は (2) ねをかも₂をふる (3) ひ₁と₂の₂こ₁の₂ (4) うらがなしけ₁を (5) ねををへ₁なくに

Romanization

(1) murasaki pa (2) NE-wo kamə wop-uru (3) pitə-nə KO-nə (4) ura-ŋ-ganasi-ke-wo (5) ne-wo wope-n-aku n-i

Glossing with Morphemic Analysis

(1) gromwell TOP (2) root/sleep-ACC EP finish-ATTR (3) person-GEN child-GEN (4) heart-LOC-be.lovely-ATTR-ACC (5) sleep(NML)-ACC finish-NEG-NML COP-CONV

Translation

(1/2) Does the gromwell's root have an end, I wonder? (3/4) Although [that] person's daughter is lovely, (5) [I] have not yet slept with [her] (lit.: the fact is that [I] did not finish the act of sleeping).

Commentary

OJ *murasaki* 'gromwell' (紫草, *Lithospermum erythrorhizon*) is a perennial grass that grows in the wild in the mountains and in the meadows. Its stalk ranges from 30 cm (1 ft) to 60 cm (2 ft). It blooms in summer time with small five-petal white flowers. It just has alternate leaves, and no leafstalks. Its root has purple color, hence the name of the plant. The root is thick and grows deep into the ground. The purple liquid extracted from the root is used for dyeing in combination with the lye extracted from the camellia tree as a color fixative. Other usage of the root is medicinal, and being regarded as an important plant, it was also cultivated. The gromwell from the Muⁿzasi province was especially famous (Mizushima 1986: 298).

The first two lines represent a poetic introduction (*jo*, 序), loosely connected to the rest of the poem. We encounter again here the play on words *ne* 'root' and *ne-* 'to sleep'. The second line asking about the end of a root hints at the anticipation of the situation outlined in the fifth line: I have not yet slept with her, but will there be an end to this situation when I am able to finish the act of sleeping with her?

OJ *pitə-nə ko* 'person's child' or 'person's girl' does not necessarily mean 'other person's wife/lover' (Omodaka 1977.11: 31), it may simply indicate 'a young girl still under parental supervision' (Mizushima 1986: 299).

OJ *ura-ŋ-ganasi-* 'to be dear/lovely', lit. 'to be dear/lovely to [one's] heart' consists of *ura* 'heart', *-ŋ-*, a contracted form of the locative case marker *-ni*, and *kanasi-* 'to be dear, to be lovely'. Cf. *ura-ŋ-ganasi-* in MYS 15.3584 'to be sad in [one's] heart' that exhibits another meaning of *kanasi-* (the one that survived into MDJ). See also 14.3443 and 14.3495 for OJ *ura* 'inside', 'back' that is used here metaphorically for heart as an internal organ.

On EOJ attributive *-ke* in *ura-ŋ-ganasi-ke* see the commentary to 14.3412.

EOJ *wope-* 'to finish' corresponds to WOJ *wopɛ-* 'id.' This probably demonstrates that there was no contrast between /e/ and /ɛ/ in the EOJ dialect that underlies this poem.

14.3501

本文・*Original Text*
(1) 安波乎呂能 (2) 乎呂田尒於波流 (3) 多波美豆良 (4) 比可婆奴流奴留 (5) 安乎許等奈多延

仮名の書き下し・*Kana Transliteration*
(1) あはを²ろ²の² (2) を²ろ²たにおはる (3) たはみ₁づら (4) ひ₁かばぬるぬる (5) あをこ²と²なたえ₂

Romanization
(1) Apa wo-rə-nə (2) wo-rə TA-ni op-ar-u (3) tapam-i-ⁿ-dura (4) pik-aᵐba nuru-nuru (5) a-wo kətə na-taye

Glossing with Morphemic Analysis
(1) Apa hill-DIM-GEN (2) hill-DIM paddy-LOC grow-PROG-ATTR (3) bend-NML-COP(ATTR)-vine (4) pull/invite-COND slippery (5) I-ACC word NEG-break(CONV)

Translation
(4) If [I] ask [you] out, [come] smoothly [to me], (3) [like] a water vine (2) that is growing in mountain paddies (1) in the hills of Apa (4) that smoothly [comes] if one pulls [it]. (5) Do not break up with me, please!

Commentary
Apa province (安房國) was located in the extremity of Bōsō peninsula (Bōsō hantō, 房総半島) in present-day Chiba prefecture. It was one of the Middle

Provinces under *Ritsuryō* code. On the *Ritsuryō* code classification of Yamatə provinces see the commentary to the postscript to the poem 14.3349.

The fact that Apa province is mentioned in this poem, means one can probably identify this poem with certainty as being from this province. Mizushima has some reservations about this identification, since placename Apa also occurs in Pitati (1986: 299–300). Nakanishi is more inclined to see this placename as corresponding to Apa province, but he also leaves the identification with a question mark (1985: 419).

On EOJ diminutive suffix *-rə* see the commentary to 14.3351.

EOJ *op-ar-* 'grow-PROG' corresponds to WOJ *op-er-* 'id.' On the EOJ progressive suffix *-ar-* corresponding to WOJ *-er-* see the commentary to 14.3351.

On EOJ *op-* 'to grow' as a consonantal verb see the commentary to 14.3488.

EOJ *tapami^{n}dura* (lit. 'bending vine') is a *hapax legomenon* indicating some kind of vine. It is variously identified as *mikuri-gusa* 'bur reed' (三稜草, *Sparganium erectum*), *junsai* 'water shield' (ジュンサイ, *Brasenia schreberi*), or *hirumushiro* '?' (ヒルムシロ, *Potamogeton distinctus*) (Omodaka et al. 1967: 436). We adopt a neutral translation 'water vine'.

On double meaning of OJ *pik-* 'to pull, to invite' see the commentary to 14.3378. This double meaning dictated the necessity to translate line four twice.

For poems with a similar content see 14.3378 and 14.3416.

14.3502

本文 · *Original Text*
(1) 和我目豆麻 (2) 比等波左久礼杼 (3) 安佐我保能 (4) 等思佐倍己其登 (5) 和波佐可流我倍

仮名の書き下し · *Kana Transliteration*
(1) わがめ₂づま (2) ひ₁と₂はさくれど₂ (3) あさがほの₂ (4) と₂しさへ₂こ₂ご₂と₂ (5) わはさかるがへ₂

Romanization
(1) wa-ŋga mɛⁿd-u ma (2) pitə pa sak-ure-ⁿdə (3) asaŋgapo-nə (4) təsi sapɛ kəŋgətə (5) wa pa sakar-u ŋgapɛ

Glossing with Morphemic Analysis
(1) I-POSS love-ATTR wife (2) person TOP make.separate-EV-CONC (3) morning.glory-COMP (4) year RP many (5) I TOP be.separated-FIN IP

Translation

(2) Although others [try to] separate (1) my beloved wife [from me], (3) who is [beautiful] like a morning glory, (5) Will I be separated [from her] (4) even if [her] years [are] many? [– Certainly not!]

Commentary

The traditional interpretation of 目豆麻 *mɛⁿduma* as a haplology of *mɛⁿd-u [tu]ma* 'beloved wife' (Omodaka 1977.14: 202; Mizushima 1986: 302) in line one is problematic. The first problem is that *mɛⁿde-* 'to love' is a vowel verb, at least in WOJ (there is another EOJ attestation 目豆兒 MƐⁿD-U KO 'beloved child' in 16.3880, besides this one, but it is written in the logographic script), so we would expect attributive *mɛⁿd-uru*, not *mɛⁿd-u*, but the poetic meter indicates the adnominal form to be *mɛⁿd-u*, not *mɛⁿd-uru*. On the other hand, the EOJ verb could be consonantal, and not the vowel, cf. EOJ *op-* 'to grow' vs. WOJ *opï-* attested in 14.3488 and 14.3501 above. The second problem is more serious: we would expect a haplology to happen only in the case of two identical syllables, in other words *mɛⁿduma* can only be derived from **mɛⁿduⁿduma*, but not from **mɛⁿdutuma*, since /ⁿdu/ and /tu/ are not identical syllables. **mɛⁿduⁿduma* < **mɛⁿd-u-nə tuma* 'love-FIN-GEN spouse' certainly will be ungrammatical for the Nara period language. All this prompts us to come up with a different solution: *-ma* in *mɛⁿduma* has nothing to do with OJ *tuma* 'spouse', but represents a loan of Ainu *mat* 'wife', with the expected loss of the syllable final *-t* in EOJ. This solution eliminates the problem presented by the traditional haplology explanation, and also explains much better the social background of the poem, namely, why other people try to separate the author from his wife. The reason appears to be purely ethnic – she happens to be an Ainu.

OJ *asaⁿgapo* 'morning glory' (朝顔, *Ipomoea nil*) < **asa-nə kapo* 'morning face' is an annual plant that originated in the tropics of Asia and was imported to Japan from China. It has sinistrorse stalk and blooms with big trumpet-shaped flowers in summer. Flowers can be purple, red, indigo, or striped. Seeds can be black, brown, or white. The dried seeds of morning glory are used in Chinese medicine as a laxative or a diuretic known as *kengosi* (牽牛子). Morning glory is a season word for autumn.

EOJ *kaⁿgətə* is a *hapax legomenon* that is believed to mean 'many', although as with any *hapax legomenon*, this remains only a working hypothesis.

On EOJ interrogative particle *ⁿgapɛ* that introduces an irony question see the commentary to 14.3420.

14.3503

本文・*Original Text*

(1) 安齋可我多 (2) 志保悲乃由多尓 (3) 於毛敝良婆 (4) 宇家良我波奈乃 (5) 伊呂尓弖米也母

仮名の書き下し・*Kana Transliteration*

(1) あつかがた (2) しほひ₂の₂ゆたに (3) おも₁へ₁らば (4) うけ₁らがはなの₂ (5) いろ₂にでめ₂やも₂

Romanization

(1) atu-ka-ŋ-gata (2) sipo pï-nə yuta n-i (3) omop-er-amba (4) ukera-ŋga pana-nə (5) irə-ni [i]nde-m-ɛ ya mə

Glossing with Morphemic Analysis

(1) sea-top-GEN-tideland (2) tide dry(NML)-COMP carefree COP-CONV (3) think-PROG-COND (4) ukera-POSS flower-COMP (5) color-LOC go.out-TENT-EV IP EP

Translation

(3) If I would be thinking [about you], (2) as carefree as an ebbing tide is (1) on the sea tideland, (5) would [my love] show in [my facial] color (4) like an *ukera* flower? [– Certainly not!]

Commentary

The main controversy in this poem is related to the second character in line one. Most modern commentators take it to be the character 齊 'to put in order', which they read ⁿze (Takagi et al. 1959: 443; Omodaka 1977.14: 204; Mizushima 1986: 303; Nakanishi 1981: 274), or se (Kubota 1967: 236; Kojima et al. 1973: 488; Tsuchiya 1977.7: 355; Itō 1997: 497; Satake et al. 2002: 359), or very rarely sa (Takeda 1966 [1955]: 382), creating the placename here to be 安齊可 aⁿzeka ~ aseka ~ asaka. There are two problems here. First, the character 齊 is not used in the *Man'yōshū* as a phonographic *man'yōgana* sign except in this poem. The only OJ text where it is used as a phonogram is the *Nihonshoki*, where it appears six times (Ōno 1953: 248–249, 298; Mori 1991: 228). But the *Nihonshoki* employs a different kind of *man'yōgana* from the *Man'yōshū*: *man'yōgana* B (Vovin 2020.1: 28–30). Second, although most manuscripts have the character 齊, the two oldest ones, the *Genryaku kōhon* and the *Ruijū koshū* have different characters (Mizushima 1984a: 311). The *Ruijū koshū* has the *sōsho* character that probably reflects 父 on the top of the bottom part of 齊, but to the best of my knowledge such a character does not exist. The *sōsho* form found in the *Genryaku kōhon* is much more interesting, as it reflects the character 齋 'holy', and not 齊 'to put in order'. Although most manuscripts present 齊 and not 齋, the direction of a scribal mistake is most likely to be 齋 > 齊, and not 齊 > 齋, because the former includes omission, and the latter addition. Addition is unlikely as a source of a scribal mistake. Both 齋 and 齊 would be used as the same *ongana*, but given the fact that 齋 does not appear as an *ongana* sign at all in the OJ corpus, the only possible solution is that it might be used as a *kungana* sign. The *kun* readings of 齋 are *itu* 'holy' and *ituk-* 'to serve to deities'. Given the fact that we need just one syllable, and the fact that *a* rendered by 安 and /i/ of *itu* or *ituk-* cannot be found next to each other due to the rules of OJ phonotactics (vowel clusters are not allowed), the character 齋 most likely stands for the syllable *tu*. Since *kungana* in contrast to *ongana* tends to be less precise, the possibility seems even more reliable. Consequently, we can read 安齋可 as *atuka*. We believe that *atuka* is a loanword from Ainu *atuy-ka* 'on the sea' (*atuy* 'sea', *ka* 'top'). Note that Ainu *-y* > EOJ *-Ø*, cf. Ainu *suy* 'again' > EOJ *su* 'id.' (14.3363), Ainu *nay* 'river' > EOJ *na* 'id.' (14.3401), and that this correspondence of Ainu *-y* to EOJ *-Ø* is regular. Thus, the first line can be interpreted as *atu-ka-ⁿ-gata* 'sea tideland', that makes much more sense than the otherwise unattested placename Aseka or Aⁿzeka. Aⁿze lake (安是湖) mentioned in Pitati Fudoki (Nakanishi 1985: 417) is certainly a poor equivalent for the identification.

OJ *kata* 'sea bed, tideland' is the part of the sea shore that is covered by water during the high tide and left exposed during the low tide.

On *ukera* flower and its metaphoric usage for the facial expression betraying one's feelings see the commentary to 14.3376.

The implied meaning of this poem is: 'Since I cannot think of you carefree, my love certainly will show in my facial color' (Mizushima 1986: 304).

14.3504

本文・*Original Text*
(1) 波流敝左久 (2) 布治能宇良葉乃 (3) 宇良夜須尓 (4) 左奴流夜曽奈伎 (5) 兒呂乎之毛倍婆

仮名の書き下し・*Kana Transliteration*
(1) はるへ₁さく (2) ふぢの₂うらばの₂ (3) うらやすに (4) さぬるよ₁そ₂なき₁ (5) こ₁ろ₂をしも₁へ₂ば

Romanization
(1) paru-ᵐ-be sak-u (2) puⁿdi-nə ura-ᵐ-BA-nə (3) ura yasu n-i (4) sa n-uru YO sə na-ki (5) KO-rə-wo si [o]mop-ɛ-ᵐba

Glossing with Morphemic Analysis
(1) spring-GEN-side bloom-ATTR (2) wisteria-GEN tip-GEN-leaf-COMP (3) heart easy COP-CONV (4) thus sleep-ATTR night FP exist.not-ATTR (5) girl-DIM-ACC EP think-EV-CON

Translation
(5) Because [I] think about [my] dear girl, (4) there is no night when [I] sleep (3) peacefully (2) like tip leaves of wisteria (1) that blooms in spring.

Commentary
The first two lines represent the poetic introduction (*jo*, 序) to the rest of the poem.

OJ *puⁿdi* 'wisteria' refers to a variety of this plant known as MDJ *nodafuji* (ノダフジ, *Wisteria floribunda*) 'Japanese wisteria', a deciduous plant that grows in the wild in fields and mountains, but also may be cultivated. It has a very long creeping stalk that winds dexterously around other things. It blooms from spring to early summer with purple flowers that are clustered in the bunches hanging down.

Leaves growing on the tip of a branch or a bunch are called *ura-ᵐ-ba* or *ure-pa*, where *ura-* is a bound form of *ure* 'top of a tree', 'tip of a branch'.

On EOJ diminutive suffix *-rə* see the commentary to 14.3351. This is the only EOJ feature in this poem.

14.3506

本文 · Original Text
(1) 尒比牟路能 (2) 許騰伎尒伊多礼婆 (3) 波太須酒伎 (4) 穂尒弖之伎美我 (5) 見延奴己能許呂

仮名の書き下し · Kana Transliteration
(1) にひ₁むろ₁の₂ (2) こ₂ど₂き₁にいたれば (3) はだすすき₁ (4) ほにでしき₁み₁が (5) み₁え₂ぬこ₂の₂こ₂ろ₂

Romanization
(1) nipi muro-nə (2) kəⁿdək-i-ni itar-e-ᵐba (3) paⁿda susuki (4) PO-ni [i]ⁿde-si kimi-ᵑga (5) MI-ye-n-u kənə kərə

Glossing with Morphemic Analysis
(1) new house-GEN (2) bless.with.words-NML-LOC reach-EV-CON (3) (*makura-kotoba*) (4) ear-LOC go.out(CONV)-PAST.ATTR lord-POSS (5) see-PASS-NEG-ATTR this time

Translation
(2) When [it] came to the blessing with words (1) the new house, (5) at this time [I] could not see (4) [my] lord who expressed [his feelings for me] openly (3) (*makura-kotoba*).

Commentary
OJ *muro* is a 'room' or a 'one-room house' in contrast to OJ *ipe* or OJ *ya* that could refer to multi-room houses as well.

Line two is hypermetric (*ji amari*, 字余り), but this is probably just a graphic illusion, since *kəⁿdək-i-ni itar-e-ᵐba* was in all probability pronounced as [kəⁿdəkinitareᵐba].

The major controversy in the interpretation of this poem concerns the word 許騰伎 *kəⁿdəki* in line two. The dominant school of thought believes that it reflects *kə-n[ə]-taki* 'time of silkworms' [feeding]' (Takagi et al. 1959: 443; Kojima et al. 1973: 488; Omodaka 1977.14: 207; Nakanishi 1981: 275; Mizushima 1986: 306; Itō 1997: 503; Satake et al. 2002: 360; Aso 2011: 433). The fact that *ko* 'silkworm' < 'child' is spelled as *kə* in this poem is not really a problem, because such a spelling occurs elsewhere in book fourteen (14.3361, 14.3369). What is much more bothersome is the fact that the existence of the custom of building a new house for silkworms is not textually confirmed for the Asuka or Nara periods. In addition, with this interpretation of *kəⁿdəki*, the phrase *nipi muro-nə kə-ⁿ-taki* 'silkworm time in a new room' is not an excitingly smooth construction to read (Mizushima 1986: 307). A minority of scholars believes that the word 許騰伎 *kəⁿdəki* is a contraction of WOJ *kətə-pok-* 'to bless with words' (Takeda 1966[1955]: 385; Kubota 1967: 237–238; Tsuchiya 1977.7: 357–358). Unlike the custom of building the new house for feeding silkworms, the custom of blessing new houses is textually attested (Takeda 1966 [1955]: 385). However, the phonetic contraction of *kətəpok-* to *kəⁿdək-* that is proposed by partisans of this hypothesis is completely impossible in the Nara period from the point of view of Japanese historical phonology. The context of this poem, however, strongly suggests that *kəⁿdək-* is indeed 'to bless with words' or something like that. We believe that the safest way is to assume that there was an EOJ verb *kəndək-* 'to bless with words'. We also think that the ultimate provenance of this EOJ word goes back to Ainu. Ainu *itak* 'word, speech, language, to speak', which also has magical connotations, cf. *itak-ko* 'shamaness', can be used in its directive form *ko-itak* 'to speak to, to address words to' that is normally contracted to *koytak*. Given the facts that syllable-final Ainu *-y* gives *-Ø* in EOJ (see the commentary to 14.3503), and that Ainu intervocalic voiced were normally borrowed into EOJ as prenasalized voiced (see the commentary to 14.3363), we expect Ainu *koytak* [koydak] ~ [koyDak] to be reflected in EOJ as *kəⁿdak. The only difference between *kəⁿdak- and our *kəⁿdək-* is the vocalism of the second syllable, but the form *kəⁿdək-* can be ultimately explained as resulting from the progressive assimilation *kəⁿdak- > kəⁿdək-*.

OJ *paⁿda susuki* is considered to be a permanent epithet (*makura-kotoba*, 枕詞) to the word *po* 'ear (of a plant)'.[46] OJ *susuki* is clearly 'Japanese pampas grass',[47] which has ears, but the situation with the first word is more complex. OJ *paⁿda susuki* occurs in the *Man'yōshū* nine times, with *paⁿda* spelled phonographically with *ongana* (波太, four times) and *kungana* (者田, once), and once either logographically with the character 皮 'skin' (if *paⁿda* really means 'skin' here), or using *kungana* here as well (if *paⁿda* does not mean 'skin'). In addition, there is probably a variant *pata susuki* with *pata* having a voiceless consonant /-t-/, which is attested twice in the *Man'yōshū*, but since both times the *pata* is spelled logographically with the character 旗 *pata* 'flag', it is difficult to say whether it is really meant to be /pata/ or is an imperfect *kungana* representation for *paⁿda*. Thus, the evidence for the interpretation that *pata susuki* actually implies that *susuki* 'pampas grass' is streaming in the wind like a flag is actually very slim even with the addition of one phonographic example from the *Izumo Fudoki* (Omodaka et al. 1967: 581). On the other hand, *paⁿda* 'skin' seems to make no sense: the varieties of *susuki* we are familiar with are somewhat rough and ticklish to the touch. Besides, as far as we can tell, OJ *paⁿda* 'skin' does not refer to the skin of animals, but only to the smooth skin of humans, especially women, therefore, *paⁿda susuki* cannot be understood as '*susuki*, rough and ticklish to the touch like the animal fur'. Consequently, the analysis of this *makura-kotoba* is better to be left on a back burner for the time being.

---

46   But see 14.3565 below where *paⁿda susuki* is used as a *makura-kotoba* for a specific mountain.

47   *Susuki* 'Japanese pampas grass' is a tall (1~2 m, 3ft 4in~6ft 8in) perennial grass which grows in the wild on river banks and mountains. In the autumn it develops long sword-like yellowish or purplish spikes. It is one of the 秋の七草 'seven autumnal plants', and is associated with autumn in Japanese traditional poetry.

196　　　　　　　　　　　　　　　　　　　　　　　　　CHAPTER 2

OJ idiomatic expression *po-ni i^nde-* lit.: 'to go out into the ear (of a plant)' means 'to show openly [one's feelings]'.

14.3509

本文・*Original Text*
(1) 多久夫須麻　(2) 之良夜麻可是能　(3) 宿奈敝杼母　(4) 古呂賀於曾伎能
(5) 安路許曾要志母

仮名の書き下し・*Kana Transliteration*
(1) たくぶすま　(2) しらやまかぜの₂　(3) ねなへ₁ど₂も₂　(4) こ₁ろ₂がおそ₂き₁の₂
(5) あろ₁こ₂そ₂え₂しも₂

Romanization
(1) taku-ᵐ-busuma (2) Sira yama kaⁿze-nə (3) NE-n-ap-e-ⁿdəmə (4) ko-rə-ⁿga osəki-nə (5) ar-o kəsə ye-si-mə

Glossing with Morphemic Analysis
(1) mulberry.tree-GEN-cover (2) White mountain wind-GEN (3) sleep-NEG-ITER-EV-CONC (4) girl-DIM-POSS garment-GEN (5) exist-ATTR FP good-FIN-EXCL

Translation
(3) Although [I] continue not to sleep (2) at the [cold] wind from the White Mountain, (1) [that is white like] covers [made] from the mulberry tree [bark cloth], (5) [it] is good to have (4) [my] dear girl's garment!

Commentary
On *taku* 'mulberry tree' and *taku-ᵐ-busuma* 'covers made from the mulberry tree [bark cloth]' see the commentary to 14.3432. The first line is considered to be a permanent epithet (*makura-kotoba*, 枕詞) to the word *sira* 'white' (Omodaka 1977.14: 210), but in this poem it can be incorporated into the translation.

Sira yama 'White mountain' can probably be identified as present-day Mt. Shirayama (白山, 2702 m) on the border of Ishikawa county (Ishikawa-gun, 石川郡) in Ishikawa prefecture and Ōno county (Ōno-gun, 大野郡) in Gifu prefecture (Omodaka 1977.14: 211), although Nakanishi is somewhat skeptical (1985: 454). Thus, if identification is correct, we can assign this poem either to Kaⁿga or Piⁿda province. Since this poem is in EOJ, this observation is important, as it demonstrates that EOJ was extending in the northern part of Chūbu or southern part of Hokuriku quite far to the west. Unfortunately, since we do not have any identified poems either from Kaⁿga or Pinda provinces that would have the same EOJ features, it is not possible to draw any definite conclusions.

The verbal form *ne-n-ap-* 'to continue not to sleep', with the iterative *-ap-* following negative, demonstrates typical EOJ order of morphemes, as in WOJ the order is reversed, with negative following the iterative. For more details see Vovin (2020.2: 738–745).

On EOJ diminutive suffix *-rə* see the commentary to 14.3351.

EOJ *osəki* 'garment' is a *hapax legomenon*. Modern commentators usually follow Keichū's explanation that equates WOJ *osupi* 'upper garment, cloak' and EOJ *osəki* (Omodaka 1977.14: 211). Mizushima further suggests that EOJ *osəki* represents a contraction from *osupi* + *tuk-i* 'attach-CONV' (1986: 312). Both suggestions, *osupi* > *osəki* and *osupi tuki* > *osəki* are impossible from the viewpoint of the historical phonology and morphophonology of the Old Japanese language.

On the EOJ verbal attributive *-o* see the commentary to 14.3395 and a brief description of EOJ special grammar in the introduction.

OJ *ye-* 'to be good' is a phonetic variant of OJ *yə-* 'id.'

14.3511

本文・*Original Text*
(1) 安乎祢呂尓 (2) 多奈毗久君母能 (3) 伊佐欲比尓 (4) 物能乎曾於毛布 (5) 等思乃許能己呂

仮名の書き下し・*Kana Transliteration*
(1) あをね₂ろ₂に (2) たなび₁くくも₂の₂ (3) いさよ₁ひ₁に (4) も₂の₂をそ₂おも₁ふ (5) と₂しの₂こ₂の₂こ₂ろ₂

Romanization
(1) awo ne-rə-ni (2) tanaᵐbik-u kumə-nə (3) isayop-i n-i (4) mənə-wo sə omop-u (5) təsi-nə kənə kərə

Glossing with Morphemic Analysis
(1) green peak-DIM-LOC (2) trail-ATTR cloud-COMP (3) hesitate/drift-NML COP-CONV (4) thing-ACC FP think-ATTR (5) year-GEN this time

Translation

(3) Hesitating/drifting (2) like clouds that are trailing (1) at the small green peaks, (4) [I] am deep in my thoughts (5) this time of the year.

Commentary

On EOJ diminutive suffix *-rə* see the commentary to 14.3351. This is the only EOJ feature in this poem.

There is an opinion that the first line represents a play on words (*kakekotoba*, 掛詞) *awo ne-rə* 'small green peak' and *a-wo ne-rə* 'sleep with me!' (Kojima et al. 1973: 490; Nakanishi 1981: 276; Mizushima 1986: 314). Content-wise it seems to be reasonable (a woman hesitates whether to accept man's proposal or not), but there is one serious grammatical problem: *ne-* 'to sleep' can be a transitive verb, but it cannot take animate nouns or personal pronouns as its object.

OJ *isayop-* can mean both 'to hesitate' and 'to drift' (Omodaka et al. 1967: 73), so it is likely that there is a play on words (*kakekotoba*, 掛詞) here.

14.3512

本文・*Original Text*

(1) 比登祢呂尓 (2) 伊波流毛能可良 (3) 安乎祢呂尓 (4) 伊佐欲布久母能 (5) 余曽里都麻波母

仮名の書き下し・*Kana Transliteration*

(1) ひ₁と₂ねろ₂に (2) いはるも₁の₂から (3) あをねろ₂に (4) いさよ₁ふくも₂の₂ (5) よ₂そ₂りつまはも₂

Romanization

(1) pitə ne-rə n-i (2) ip-ar-u monəkara (3) awo ne-rə-ni (4) isayop-u kumə-nə (5) yəsər-i tuma pa mə

Glossing with Morphemic Analysis

(1) one peak-DIM COP-CONV (2) say-PROG-ATTR CONJ (3) green peak-DIM-LOC (4) drift/hesitate-ATTR cloud-COMP (5) approach-CONV spouse TOP EP

Translation

(2) Although [they] say that (1) [we] are one peak, (5) ah, [she] is an intimate spouse [only in rumors] (4) who is like a cloud, drifting/hesitating (3) on green peaks.

Commentary

Kojima et al. build further on the hypothesis that *awo ne-rə* 'small green peaks' represents the play on words (*kakekotoba*, 掛詞) with *a-wo ne-rə* 'sleep with me!' (see the commentary to 14.3511), and speculate that the first two lines *pitə ne-rə n-i ip-ar-u monəkara* 'although [they] say that [we] are one peak' is also a play on words with 'although [other] person [says] sleep [with me]!' (1973: 490). Consequently, we have two suitors competing for the same woman. Similarly to *a-wo ne-rə* in 14.3511 (and this poem as well), this hypothesis also has a grammatical obstacle: we would expect *pitə ne-rə tə ip-ar-u monəkara* with the quotation verb *tə* 'to say', and not *pitə ne-rə n-i ip-ar-u monəkara* with the converb form *n-i* of the copula *n-* for the second variant to be grammatical (only *tə*, but not *ni* can be a quotation verb 'to say'). Mizushima also voices mild skepticism regarding this interpretation (1986: 316–317).

On EOJ diminutive suffix *-rə* see the commentary to 14.3351.

On the EOJ progressive suffix *-ar-* corresponding to WOJ *-er-* see the commentary to 14.3351.

OJ *yəsər-* 'to approach' may also have the meaning '[to be rumored] to have intimate relationship'.

On OJ *isayop-* 'to hesitate', 'to drift' see the commentary to 14.3511 above.

We follow Omodaka (1977.14: 213) in transcribing 都麻 as *tuma* 'spouse' rather than as *-ⁿ-duma*, preferred by the majority of modern commentators (Mizushima 1984a: 326), because there is no overt indication of prenasalized voicing in the *man'yōgana* script, and also because the converb in EOJ unlike WOJ can be used in an adnominal modifier function, see the commentary to 14.3415.

14.3513

本文 • Original Text
(1) 由布佐礼婆 (2) 美夜麻乎左良奴 (3) 尒努具母能 (4) 安是可多要牟等 (5) 伊比之兒呂婆母

仮名の書き下し • Kana Transliteration
(1) ゆふされば (2) み₁やまをさらぬ (3) にの₁ぐも₂の₂ (4) あぜかたえ₂むと₂ (5) いひ₁しこ₁ろ₂はも₂

Romanization
(1) yupu sar-e-ᵐba (2) mi-yama-wo sar-an-u (3) nino-ŋ-gumə-nə (4) aⁿze ka taye-m-u tə (5) ip-i-si KO-rə pa mə

Glossing with Morphemic Analysis

(1) evening come-EV-CON (2) HON-mountain-ACC go.away-NEG-ATTR (3) cloth-COMP-cloud-COMP (4) why IP be.broken.off-TENT-ATTR QV (5) say-CONV-PAST.ATTR girl-DIM TOP EP

Translation

(5) Ah, the girl who said: (4) 'Why should [our relationship] be broken off (3) like the cloth-like clouds (2) that do not leave mountains (1) when the evening comes?'

Commentary

The first three lines represent a metaphoric poetic introduction (*hiyuteki jo*, 比喩的序) to the rest of the poem (Omodaka 1977.14: 214).

Note the semantic ambivalence regarding the direction of moving of the verb *sar-* that can mean both 'to come' and 'to go'.

On EOJ *nino* 'cloth' see the commentary to 14.3351.
On EOJ *aⁿze* 'why' see the commentary to 14.3369.
On EOJ diminutive suffix *-rə* see the commentary to 14.3351.

14.3514

本文 • Original Text

(1) 多可伎袮介 (2) 久毛能都久能須 (3) 和礼左倍介 (4) 伎美介都吉奈那 (5) 多可袮等毛比弖

仮名の書き下し • Kana Transliteration

(1) たかき₁ねに (2) くも₁の₂つくの₂す (3) われさへ₂に (4) き₁み₁につき₁なな (5) たかねと₂も₁ひて

Romanization

(1) taka-ki ne-ni (2) kumo-nə tuk-u-nəsu (3) ware sapɛ n-i (4) kimi-ni tuk-i-n-ana (5) taka ne tə [o]mop-i-te

Glossing with Morphemic Analysis

(1) high-ATTR peak-LOC (2) cloud-GEN attach-ATTR-COMP (3) I RP COP-CONV (4) lord-DAT attach-CONV-PERF-DES (5) high peak QV think-CONV-SUB

Translation

(5) Thinking [of you] as a high peak, (3) I also (4) would have liked to cling to [my] lord (2) like clouds cling (1) to a high peak.

Commentary

Note the parallel usage of an inflected adjective *taka-* 'to be high' and its uninflected equivalent *taka* 'high'.

On EOJ comparative case marker *-nəsu* see the commentary to 14.3413.

Mizushima thinks that this poem is composed by a wife who was just visited by her husband, who does not live with her permanently, but she wants to live with him on an everyday basis (1986: 319). Needless to say, this analysis is no more than a possible speculation, based on the text's interpretation, and it is not supported by any textual evidence.

14.3515

本文・*Original Text*

(1) 阿我於毛乃 (2) 和須礼牟之太波 (3) 久尓波布利 (4) 祢尓多都久毛乎 (5) 見都追之努波西

仮名の書き下し・*Kana Transliteration*

(1) あがおも₁の₂ (2) わすれむしだは (3) くにはふり (4) ねにたつくも₁を (5) み₁つつしの₁はせ

Romanization

(1) a-ⁿga omo-nə (2) wasure-m-u siⁿda pa (3) kuni papur-i (4) ne-ni tat-u kumo-wo (5) MI-tutu sinop-as-e

Glossing with Morphemic Analysis

(1) I-POSS face-GEN (2) forget-TENT-ATTR time TOP (3) land spring-CONV (4) peak-LOC rise-ATTR cloud-ACC (5) look(CONV)-COOR long.for-HON-IMP

Translation

(2) When [you] forget (1) my face, (5) long for [me] while looking (3/4) at the clouds that spring [from] the earth and rise to the peaks.

Commentary

Due to the usage of the mild honorific suffix *-as-*, this poem is likely to be composed by a woman. In all probability it constitutes a sequence with the following 14.3516, which looks like a man's response to it.

There were two verbs meaning 'to forget' in OJ: the consonantal verb *wasur-* 'to forget intentionally' and the vowel verb *wasure-* 'to forget unintentionally, to fade from one's memory'.

On EOJ *siⁿda* 'time' see the commentary to 14.3363.

14.3516

本文・*Original Text*
(1) 對馬能祢波 (2) 之多具毛安良南敷 (3) 可牟能祢尓 (4) 多奈妣久君毛乎 (5) 見都追思努波毛

仮名の書き下し・*Kana Transliteration*
(1) つしま の₂ ねは (2) したぐも₁ あらなふ (3) かむ の₂ ねに (4) たなび₁く くも₁ を (5) み₁つつ しの₁は も₁

Romanization
(1) Tusima-nə ne pa (2) sita-ŋ-gumo ar-an-ap-u (3) kamu-nə ne-ni (4) tanaᵐbik-u kumo-wo (5) MI-tutu sinop-am-o

Glossing with Morphemic Analysis
(1) Tusima-GEN peak TOP (2) bottom-GEN-cloud exist-NEG-ITER-FIN (3) deity-GEN peak-LOC (4) trail-ATTR cloud-ACC (5) look(CONV)-COOR long.for-TENT-ATTR

Translation
(2) Low clouds never appear (1) at Tusima peaks. (5) [I] will long for [you] while looking (4) at the clouds that are trailing (3) over the deity's peak.

Commentary
This poem looks like a response by a man who went to serve as a border guard (OJ *sakimori*) at Tsushima island to the previous poem composed by his wife or lover (14.3515) (Omodaka 1977.14: 217; Mizushima 1986: 324).

WOJ Tusima (MDJ Tsushima, 對馬) is the island (now actually two islands since the canal was dug across its most narrow point in modern times) halfway between Korea and Japan. The island is of volcanic origin, composed predominantly of aqueous rock (*suiseigan*, 水成岩) and quartz porphyry (*sekieihangan*, 石英斑岩), and is mostly mountainous, with the average elevation above sea level at 200–300 m. The highest mountains on Tsushima are Yatateyama (矢立山, 649 m), Tatsurayama (竜良山, 559 m), Ariakeyama (有明山, 558 m), and Ōsimageyama (大島毛山, 555 m). It is possible that the reference to a Tukusi peak is made to one of these mountains, and more specifically to the Ariakeyama that is located in the south of the island, but Mizushima is skeptical about this latter identification (1986: 321).

Man'yōgana character 對 is a disyllabic phonogram standing for *tusi*. Both the vowel and the final *-si* probably indicate that this reading goes back to very old times, as the Late Han reading of the character 對 is *tuəs*, cf. EMC *twậi*[C] (Schuessler 2009: 313). It goes without saying that the EMC reading *twậi*[C] cannot possibly underlie *tusi*.

OJ *sita-ŋ-gumo* indicates the lower layer of clouds. Since Tsushima does not have high mountains, there is only one layer of clouds.

Line two is hypermetric (*ji amari*, 字余り), but this is probably just a graphic illusion, since *sita-ŋ-gumo ar-an-ap-u* was in all probability pronounced as [sitaŋgumaranapu] or [sitaŋgumoranapu].

There is a controversy over how to interpret 可牟 *kamu* in line three: 'top' or 'deity'. Following the lead of Keichū, Mizushima opts for 'top' believing that the author is looking at the upper layer of clouds, since there is no lower layer of clouds at Tsushima mountains (1986: 323). This point of view is apparently shared by the majority of modern commentators: Takagi et al. (1959: 445), Takeda (1966: 393), Kubota (1967: 243), Tsuchiya (1977.7: 364), Satake (2002: 363) offer the same interpretation, although, in contrast to Mizushima, none of them discusses any evidence. However, this interpretation faces a great difficulty, because WOJ *kami* 'top' has *kō-rui* vowel *i* in the second syllable, not the *otsu-rui* vowel *ï*. EOJ *u* can correspond only to WOJ *ï*, but not to WOJ *i*, cf. EOJ *tuku* 'moon' ~ WOJ *tukï* 'id.', EOJ *kopusi* 'be longing for' ~ WOJ *kopïsi* 'id.', etc. Consequently, EOJ *kamu* in this poem can correspond only to WOJ *kamï* 'deity' (Omodaka 1977.14: 216; Nakanishi 1981: 277). Itō (1997: 513–514) and Aso (2011: 443), mention both points of view, but remain non-committal. Kojima et al. treat *kamu* as a placename (1973: 490). We accept the Omodaka and Nakanishi interpretation, because unlike the Keichū-Mizushima explanation it does not violate language rules. We should also add that given the fact that Tsushima mountains are low, the reading *kamu-nə ne* 'upper peaks' does not make any sense, either.

The identification of *kamu-nə ne* 'deity's peak' is difficult. Presumably the author is standing on the top of the Ariakeyama, and looking in the direction of Kyūshū. On clear days some high mountains in Kyūshū can be seen from Tsushima, if one is standing on a top of a mountain (Omodaka 1977.14: 217). Then *kamu-nə ne* 'deity's peak' can be either Raizan (雷山, 955 m) or Sefurisan (背振山, 1,055 m) that straddle the present-day border between Fukuoka and Nagasaki prefectures, although neither identification is by any means certain.

On the EOJ verbal attributive *-o* see the commentary to 14.3395 and a brief description of EOJ special grammar in the introduction.

14.3517

本文・*Original Text*
(1) 思良久毛能 (2) 多要尓之伊毛乎 (3) 阿是西呂等 (4) 許己呂尓能里弖 (5) 許己婆可那之家

仮名の書き下し・*Kana Transliteration*
(1) しらくも₁の₂ (2) たえ₂にしいも₁を (3) あぜせろ₂と₂ (4) こ₂こ₂ろ₂₂にの₂りて (5) こ₂こ₂ばかなしけ₁

Romanization
(1) sira kumo-nə (2) taye-n-i-si imo-wo (3) aⁿze se-rə tə (4) kəkərə-ni nər-i-te (5) kəkəᵐba kanasi-ke

Glossing with Morphemic Analysis
(1) white cloud-COMP (2) be.broken.off(CONV)-PERF-CONV-PAST.ATTR beloved-ACC (3) how do-IMP QV (4) heart-LOC ride-CONV-SUB (5) extremely sad-ATTR

Translation
(5) [She] is extremely dear [to me], (4) so [it] weighs heavily on [my] heart (3) what (lit.: how) [should I] do about (2) [my] beloved who is separated [from me] (1) like a white cloud.

Commentary
The first line *sira kumo-nə* 'like a white cloud' is considered to be a permanent epithet (*makura-kotoba*, 枕詞) to the verb *taye-* 'to be broken' (Omodaka 1977.14: 218; Mizushima 1986: 325). However, since the metaphor is quite transparent here, we incorporate it into our translation. See details in the commentary to 14.3519 below.

On EOJ *aⁿze* 'why' see the commentary to 14.3369.

On EOJ diminutive suffix *-rə* see the commentary to 14.3351.

Kəkəᵐba 'extremely, so much' seems to be attested predominantly in EOJ, while its equivalent *kəkəⁿda* mostly occurs in WOJ. The forms are only partially related, since they exhibit different suffixation. For details see Vovin (2020.2: 1002–1003).

On EOJ attributive *-ke* in *kanasi-ke* see the commentary to 14.3412.

14.3518

本文・*Original Text*

(1) 伊波能倍尓 (2) 伊可賀流久毛能 (3) 可努麻豆久 (4) 比等曾於多波布 (5) 伊射祢之賣刀良

仮名の書き下し・*Kana Transliteration*

(1) いはの₂へ₂に (2) いかかるくも₁の₂ (3) かぬまづく (4) ひ₁と₂そ₂おたはふ (5) いざねしめ₁と₁ら

Romanization

(1) ipa-nə [u]pɛ-ni (2) i-kakar-u kumo-nə (3) ka-numa-ⁿ-duk-u (4) pitə sə otap-ap-u (5) iⁿza ne-sime tora

Glossing with Morphemic Analysis

(1) rock-GEN top-LOC (2) DLF-hang-ATTR cloud-GEN (3) top-marsh-LOC-arrive-FIN (4) person FP sing-ITER-ATTR (5) INTER sleep-CAUS(IMPER) together

Translation

(2) Clouds that hang (1) over the rocks (3) go down to the upper marsh. (4) People are singing all the time. (5) Hey, let [me] sleep together [with you]!

Commentary

This poem is clearly a textual variant of 14.3409, with lines three to five being practically identical. The only major difference is the focus particle *sə* in the fourth line of 14.3518 instead of its variant *tə* in 14.3409. Minor differences involve variant spellings, such as *ka-numa* 'upper marsh' spelled as 可奴麻 in 14.3409 and as 可努麻 in 14.3518, *tora* 'together' spelled as 刀羅 in 14.3409 and as 刀良 in 14.3518, and the causative suffix *-simɛ-* spelled correctly as 志米 in 14.3409 and misspelled as *-simɛ-* 之賣 in 14.3518. Neither of these spelling differences affect interpretation and translation.

Prefix *i-* is a marker of a directive-locative focus. For details see Vovin (2020.2: 505–512).

On the rest see the commentary to 14.3409.

14.3520

本文・*Original Text*
(1) 於毛可多能 (2) 和須礼牟之太波 (3) 於抱野呂尒 (4) 多奈婢久君母乎 (5) 見都追思努波牟

仮名の書き下し・*Kana Transliteration*
(1) おも₁かたの₂ (2) わすれむしだは (3) おほの₁ろ₂に (4) たなび₁くくも₂を (5) み₁つつしの₁はむ

Romanization
(1) omo-kata-nə (2) wasure-m-u siⁿda pa (3) opo NO-rə-ni (4) tana^mbik-u kumə-wo (5) MI-tutu sinop-am-u

Glossing with Morphemic Analysis
(1) face-shape-GEN (2) forget-TENT-ATTR time TOP (3) big field-DIM-LOC (4) trail-ATTR cloud-ACC (5) look(CONV)-COOR long.for-TENT-FIN

Translation
(2) When [I] forget (1) the shape of [your] face, (5) [I] will long for [you], looking (4) at the clouds that trail (3) over the big field.

Commentary
See 14.3515 and 14.3516 for some similar or even identical lines.

On OJ *wasure-* 'to forget unintentionally', 'to fade from one's memory' see the commentary to 14.3515. Note that the genitive marker *-nə* used on line one suggests that OJ *wasure-* is an intransitive verb 'to be forgotten' rather than a transitive 'to forget'.

On EOJ *siⁿda* 'time' see the commentary to 14.3363.

On EOJ diminutive suffix *-rə* see the commentary to 14.3351. In this poem, given *opo no* 'big field', *-rə* is unlikely to have a diminutive function, unless this is a placename. It can, however, have an endearment function (Vovin 2005: 211).

14.3521

本文・*Original Text*
(1) 可良須等布 (2) 於保乎曾杼里能 (3) 麻左侣尒毛 (4) 伎麻左奴伎美乎 (5) 許呂久等曾奈久

仮名の書き下し・*Kana Transliteration*

(1) からすと₂ふ (2) おほをそ₂ど₂りの₂ (3) まさでにも₁ (4) き₁まさぬき₁み₁を (5) こ₂ろ₂くと₂そ₂なく

Romanization

(1) karasu tə [i]p-u (2) opo wosə-ⁿ-dəri-nə (3) masaⁿde n-i mo (4) k-i-[i]mas-an-u kimi-wo (5) kərəku / kə-rə k-u tə sə nak-u

Glossing with Morphemic Analysis

(1) crow QV say-ATTR (2) big lying-COP(ATTR)-bird-GEN (3) really COP-CONV FP (4) come-CONV-HON-NEG-ATTR lord-ACC (5) caw-caw / lad-DIM come-FIN QV FP cry-ATTR

Translation

(2) A big lying bird, (1) which [they] call a crow, (5) cries 'caw-caw' / 'Your dear lad is coming' (3/4) about [my] lord who is not really coming.

Commentary

Poems 14.3521–14.3542 are love poems that involve mentioning birds or animals. Among these twenty-four poems (including two variants, 14.3537a and 14.3538a), eight are dealing with birds (14.3520–14.3528), one with a hare (14.3529), one with a deer (14.3530), one with game animals (14.3531), and the remaining thirteen (14.3532–14.3542) with horses (Mizushima 1986: 332).

OJ and MDJ *karasu* 'crow' (烏・鴉, *Corvus*) is a black bird with blue or purple sheen. It cries mostly at dawn. Crows are omnivores and very intelligent. They can be hunted as game, but their meat tastes awful (Nakanishi 1985: 292).

The interpretation of EOJ *wosə* in line two is a subject of controversy. All modern Japanese commentators, with the exception of Tsuchiya, follow the proposal of Takeda Yūkichi (Takeda 1966 [1955]: 396–397) who believes that EOJ *wosə* has the same meaning as WOJ *wosərə* 'hasty, rash, careless, thoughtless' (attested in 4.654 and 8.1548): (Takagi et al. 1959: 445; Kubota 1967: 245–246; Kojima et al. 1973: 492; Omodaka 1977.14: 220; Nakanishi 1981: 277; Mizushima 1986: 331; Itō 1997: 522; Satake et al. 2002: 364; Aso 2011: 449). This point of view claims that -*rə* in *wosərə* is a 'suffix', without explaining either its function or its meaning. We think that *wosərə* in 4.654 and 8.1458 can be analyzed as *wosə* 'rash' + *rə*, copula.[48] Besides most old commentators, with a

---

48   On copula *rə* see Vovin (2009a: 547–549).

notable exception of Keichū, see, e.g., Kamochi (1912.6: 136–137),[49] Tsuchiya is the only modern commentator who believes that EOJ *wosə* is cognate to EMDJ *uso* 'lie (n.)' (1977.7: 367). Although EOJ initial *wo-* can correspond to WOJ initial *u-*, cf., e.g. WOJ *usaⁿgi* 'hare' ~ EOJ *wosaⁿgi* 'id.' (see 14.3529 below), the problem is that EMDJ *uso* in the meaning 'lie' is a very late word. In addition, one may also bring the objection that the EOJ *wo-* ~ WOJ *u-* correspondence implies the pre-OJ **o > u* raising in WOJ, and consequently pre-WOJ form would be **woso*. Meanwhile, EOJ has *otsu-rui* vowel *ə* in *wosə*, and that implies pre-EOJ **wəsə*. However, one must not be fooled by EOJ orthography. As we have seen throughout this book, EOJ 'misspellings' reflecting the lack of different vowel contrasts found in WOJ are frequent, and there is no warranty that this is not another of these cases. Fortunately, we have compelling philological evidence coming from the *Nihon ryōiki* as described below:

本文・*Original Text from the Nihon ryōiki*
(1) 加良須等伊布 (2) 於保乎蘇止利能 (3) 去止乎能米 (4) 止母爾止伊比天 (5) 佐岐陀智伊奴留

仮名の書き下し・*Kana Transliteration*
(1) からすと₂いふ (2) おほをそ₁と₂りの₂ (3) こ₂と₂をの₂め₂ (4) と₂も₂にと₂いひ₁て (5) さき₁だちいぬる

Romanization
(1) karasu tə ip-u (2) opo woso təri-nə (3) kətə-wo nəmɛ (4) təmə n-i tə ip-i-te (5) saki-ⁿ-dat-i-in-uru

Glossing with Morphemic Analysis
(1) crow QV say-ATTR (2) big lying bird-GEN (3) word-ACC RP (4) together COP-CONV QV say-CONV-SUB (5) ahead-LOC-depart-CONV-go.away-ATTR

Translation
(2) A big lying bird, (1) which [they] call a crow, (3) [you] gave [me your] word that [we] will be together, (5) [but] departed [from this world] ahead [of me] (NR II.2)[50]

---

49 Mizushima lists Sengaku's commentary as also taking this point of view (1986: 332), but Sengaku actually says something very different: オホオソトリハカラス也 *opo oso tori pa karasu nari* 'big *oso* bird is a crow' (Sasaki 1981: 411).

50 I cite the *Nihon ryōiki* text according to the edition by Endō and Kasuga (1967: 176).

The first two lines in this poem are practically identical with the first two lines of 14.3521, and from the remaining lines it becomes apparent that 乎蘇 *woso* actually means 'lie, lying, liar', but not 'hasty'. Note also that this WOJ text has *kō-rui* vowel *o* in the second syllable of 乎蘇 *woso*. Someone could object, saying that the *Nihon ryōiki* is a late text from the early ninth century, and that consequently, its spelling system may not be reliable. However, this poem exhibits remarkable spelling conservatism,[51] and, thus such a possible objection can be overruled. Therefore, WOJ *wosə[rə]* 'hasty' and WOJ *woso* 'lie' are two different words, and the interpretation of EOJ *wosə* in 14.3521 as 'lie', which apparently corresponds to WOJ *woso* 'lie', becomes inescapable. Japanese scholars who are supporting 'hasty' interpretation are certainly aware of the existence of this poem in the *Nihon ryōiki*, but their objections to the interpretation of *woso* as 'lie' in this text or of *wosə* in 14.3521, are unfortunately devoid of any logic or presentation of any evidence: "there is an explanation of *woso* as 'lie', but it should be explained as 'rush, hasty, careless'" (Takeda 1966 [1955]: 397), "it looks like [we] should follow the old explanation B ('lie' – A.V.), but rather than explaining that the woman reproaches the man who promised to come, but does not come at all as *opo wosə təri*, and hears bird's crying *kərəku* as 'dear lad is coming', we followed explanation A" ('hasty' – A.V. and S.I-V.) (Mizushima 1986: 333). Given this level of argumentation on the side of supporters of 'hasty', the case should be really closed once and for all in favor of 'lie'. Having said all this, we really do not know whether there is any connection between WOJ *woso* ~ EOJ *wosə* 'lie' and MDJ *uso* 'id.' Phonologically such a relationship may be rather straightforward (the only problem being the absence of raising *o > u* in the first syllable of WOJ *woso*), but the late provenance of EMDJ *uso* presents a more serious problem.

On EOJ *masande n-i* 'surely, clearly, really' see the commentary to 14.3374.

EOJ *kərəku* 'caw-caw' is onomatopoeia for crow's cry. It also represents the play on words (*kakekotoba*, 掛詞) with *kə-rə k-u* '[your] dear lad is coming', where *ko* 'child, girl, lad' is misspelled as *kə*, but we have seen the same phenomenon in EOJ above in 14.3361. There are no WOJ cognates of EOJ *kərəku* 'caw-caw' attested.

On EOJ diminutive suffix *-rə* see the commentary to 14.3351.

---

51 Restrictive particle *nəmɛ* may be a misspelling of *nəmï*, but more likely it represents an alternative phonetic variant, cf. WOJ *kəmï-* and *kəmɛ-* 'to insert'.

14.3522

本文・*Original Text*
(1) 伎曾許曾波 (2) 兒呂等左宿之香 (3) 久毛能宇倍由 (4) 奈伎由久多豆乃 (5) 麻登保久於毛保由

仮名の書き下し・*Kana Transliteration*
(1) き₁そ₂こ₂そ₂は (2) こ₁ろ₂と₂さねしか (3) くも₁の₂うへ₂ゆ (4) なき₁ゆくたづの₂ (5) まと₂ほくおも₁ほゆ

Romanization
(1) kisə kəsə pa (2) KO-rə-tə sa-NE-sika (3) kumo-nə upɛ-yu (4) nak-i yuk-u taⁿdu-nə (5) ma-təpo-ku omop-oy-u

Glossing with Morphemic Analysis
(1) last.night FP TOP (2) girl-DIM-COM PREF-sleep(CONV)-PAST.EV (3) cloud-GEN top-ABL (4) cry-CONV go-ATTR crane-COMP (5) INT-far-CONV think-PASS-FIN

Translation
(2) [I] did sleep together with my dear girl (1) just last night. (5) [But it] suddenly seems to be very far away, (3/4) like cranes, who fly and cry along the top of the clouds.

Commentary
OJ *kisə* 'last night' is an obscure formation, although its first syllable *ki* is usually compared with *ki* of *kinəpu* 'yesterday', and the last syllable *sə* with ⁿ*zə* of *kəⁿzə* 'last year' (Omodaka et al. 1967: 241). Neither of these comparisons explain the etymology of the word.

On EOJ diminutive suffix *-rə* see the commentary to 14.3351. This is the only EOJ feature in this poem.

Lines three and five are hypermetric (*ji amari*, 字余り), but this is probably just a graphic illusion, since *kumo-nə upɛ-yu* and *ma-təpo-ku omop-oy-u* were in all probability pronounced as [kumonəpɛyu] and [matəpokumopoyu].

Ablative *-yu* has here a prolative function: *X-yu* 'along X'. For details see Itabashi (1989).

OJ *taⁿdu* 'crane' is a doublet of WOJ *turu* 'crane', with no apparent difference in meaning. Omodaka et al. note that *taⁿdu* is a word used in Old Japanese poetry, while *turu* does not appear in the poetry (1967: 428, 480). Since most Old Japanese texts are poetic, *turu* as a separate word is not attested, but we nevertheless have the evidence that it was present in the language, since the character 鶴 'crane' is used in the *Man'yōshū* on multiple occasions to write the attributive form *-t-uru* of the perfective auxiliary *-te-* (e.g., 1.81, 2.188, 3.248, etc.). The cognates of WOJ *turu* are well attested throughout the Japonic languages, including Ryūkyūan: Shuri *ciru* (OGJ 163), Nakijin *ciruu* (Nakasone 1983: 286), Miyako *cïru*, Iriomote *curu*, Kurojima *śiru*, Takebu *čiru* (Nakamatsu 1987: 117, 165, 207). MJ *turu* LF and Modern Kyōto *turu* LF belong to the accent class 2.5 that reflects Proto-Japanese (and in many cases Proto-Japonic) final *-m; therefore WOJ *turu* < PJ *turum. The striking similarity of this word to MK *turumi* HHH was noted long ago. The existence of doublets in Western Old Japanese would indicate that WOJ *turu* is a loan from Korean, but this is unlikely due to the widespread attestation of *turu* in Japonic. Possibly, MK *turumi* HHH represents a substratum Japonic word in Korean. OJ *ta^{n}du* 'crane', is on the other hand, a perfect candidate for being a loanword, since its attestation is limited to Western Old Japanese, Eastern Old Japanese, and Middle Japanese. Unfortunately, there seems to be no external etymology for this word. Certainly, one can speculate that it came from a language that was once spoken in Western Honshū, but then disappeared without trace, but there can be no proof for such a speculation.

14.3524

本文・*Original Text*
(1) 麻乎其母能 (2) 布能末知可久弖 (3) 安波奈敝波 (4) 於吉都麻可母能 (5) 奈氣伎曾安我須流

仮名の書き下し・*Kana Transliteration*
(1) まをご₂も₂の₂ (2) ふの₂まちかくて (3) あはなへ₁ば (4) おき₁つまかも₂の₂ (5) なげ₂き₁そ₂あがする

Romanization
(1) ma-woŋ-gəmə-nə (2) pu-nə ma tika-ku-te (3) ap-an-ap-e-ᵐba (4) oki-tu ma-kamə-nə (5) naŋgɛk-i sə a-ŋga s-uru

Glossing with Morphemic Analysis
(1) INT-DIM-wild.rice.mat-GEN (2) mesh-GEN space be.close-CONV-SUB (3) meet-NEG-ITER-EV-CON (4) offing-GEN/LOC INT-wild.duck-COMP (5) lament-NML FP I-POSS do-ATTR

Translation

(3) Because [we] do not meet (2) being close [to each other like] spaces between the meshes (1) of a mat [made from] wild rice, (5) I lament (4) like a wild duck in the offing.

Commentary

On OJ *kəmə* 'wild rice', 'mat made from wild rice' see the commentary to 14.3464.

On specific EOJ order of morphemes *-(a)n-ap-* 'NEG-ITER' see the commentary to 14.3375.

OJ *kamo*[52] 'wild duck' (鴨, *Anas*) is mostly a migratory bird. In the *Man'yōshū* times wild ducks came to Japan predominantly in winter. Nowadays there are wild ducks that stay in Japan all year round and do not migrate. Males and females have different feather colors. Wild ducks nest on the rivers and marshes, although some species do so on the sea. Wild ducks could be hunted as game. *Ma-kamo* 'real wild duck' is essentially the same species as *kamo* (Nakanishi 1985: 292).

The last two lines, 'I lament like a wild duck in the offing', may sound funny in English translation, but there is a reason for this imagery. OJ *naⁿgeki* 'lament' is derived from the combination of *naⁿga* 'long' + *iki* 'breath'. Wild ducks are well known for their ability to keep their breath for a long time while diving (Omodaka 1977.14: 223).

14.3525

本文・*Original Text*
(1) 水久君野尒 (2) 可母能波抱能須 (3) 兒呂我宇倍尒 (4) 許等乎呂波敝而 (5) 伊麻太宿奈布母

仮名の書き下し・*Kana Transliteration*
(1) み₁くくの₁に (2) かも₂の₂はほの₂す (3) こ₁ろ₂がうへ₂に (4) こ₂と₂をろ₂はへ₁て (5) いまだねなふも₂

Romanization
(1) Mikuku NO-ni (2) kəmə-nə pap-o-nəsu (3) KO-rə-ⁿga upɛ-ni (4) kətə-wo-rə pape-TE (5) imaⁿda NE-n-ap-umə

---

52 Etymological WOJ spelling.

Glossing with Morphemic Analysis
(1) Mikuku field-LOC (2) wild.duck-GEN crawl-ATTR-COMP (3) girl-DIM-POSS top-LOC (4) word-string-DIM spread(CONV)-SUB (5) yet sleep-NEG-ITER-EXCL

Translation
(4) Having made [my] promises reach (lit.: crawl) (3) to [my] dear girl, (2) like wild ducks crawling (1) at the field of Mikuku, (5) [I] continue not to sleep with [her]!

Commentary
Mikuku is probably a placename with unknown location, although there is a hypothesis that it was located in Titiᵐbu district (Titiᵐbu kəpori, 秩父郡) of Muⁿzasi province.[53] There is also a hypothesis that Mikuku is not a placename, but a compound *mi* 'water' + *kuk-u* 'to dive' (Itō et al. 1991: 370). Another etymological possibility would be *mi* 'water' + EOJ *kuku* 'stalk', that is 'water stalks', given the fact that EOJ *-u* corresponds to WOJ *-ï* (cf. WOJ *kukï* 'stalk'). In any case, it looks like this poem is from Muⁿzasi province, because it has EOJ specific order of morphemes *-(a)n-ap-* 'NEG-ITER' (vs. WOJ order *-ap-an-* 'ITER-NEG') also attested in another Muⁿzasi poem (14.3375).

On OJ *kamo* 'wild duck' see the commentary to 14.3524.

On the EOJ verbal attributive *-o* see the commentary to 14.3395 and a brief description of EOJ special grammar in the introduction.

On EOJ comparative case marker *-nəsu* see the commentary to 14.3413.

On EOJ diminutive suffix *-rə* see the commentary to 14.3351.

EOJ *kətə-wo* 'word-string' implies that words of a love promise are repeated for a long time.

OJ *papɛ-* is a transitive variant of the intransitive *pap-* 'to crawl'. It has the meaning 'to stretch, to make crawl', and also 'to make someone know of one's love intentions' (Omodaka et al. 1967: 590–591).

On the specific EOJ order of morphemes *-(a)n-ap-* 'NEG-ITER' see the commentary to 14.3375.

On OJ exclamative form *-umə* ~ *-mə* see the commentary to 14.3431.

---

53 It roughly corresponds to Chichibu county (Chichibu-gun, 秩父郡) in present-day Saitama prefecture.

14.3526

本文 • *Original Text*
(1) 奴麻布多都 (2) 可欲波等里我栖 (3) 安我己許呂 (4) 布多由久奈母等 (5) 奈与母波里曾祢

仮名の書き下し • *Kana Transliteration*
(1) ぬまふたつ (2) かよ₁はと₂りがす (3) あがこ₂こ₂ろ₂ (4) ふたゆくなも₂と₂ (5) なよ₂も₂はりそ₂ね

Romanization
(1) numa puta-tu (2) kayop-a təri-ᵑga su (3) a-ᵑga kəkərə (4) puta yuk-unam-ə tə (5) na-y-əmə p-ar-i-sə-n-e

Glossing with Morphemic Analysis
(1) marsh two-CL (2) visit-ATTR bird-POSS nest (3) I-POSS heart (4) two go-TENT2-ATTR QV (5) NEG-3pso-think-PROG-NML do-DES-IMP

Translation
(5) [I] wish [you] are not thinking (3) that my heart (4) would go [to] two [different places] (2) [like] nests of a bird that visits (1) two [different] marshes.

Commentary
Basically in this poem a man assures a woman that he does not have a second sweetheart, whom he also visits, unlike a bird that can go to two separate nests in two different marshes.

The -*a* in *kayop-a* is a special EOJ attributive (Mizushima 1986: 340), also attested in 14.3405, 14.3408, 14.3436, and 14.3457. Kupchik (2011: 696–697) proposed an alternative analysis of the first two lines:

> numa puta-tu / **kay-o** pa təri-ᵑga su
> marsh two-CL / **be.distant**-ATTR TOP bird-POSS nest
> As for [what] **are distant** [between] two marshes, [they are] a bird's nests.

The proposal is based on introducing a hypothetical EOJ consonant verb *kay*- (cf. WOJ *kaye*- 'be distant, be separated' (not attested in EOJ)) as a consonant verb. It must be noted, however, that consonant verbs with final -*y* are not attested either in WOJ or in EOJ. In addition, it remains unclear how Kupchik's version could fit with the remaining three lines and form a coherent context. Thus, we think that the traditional interpretation holds. Another possibility is that we might have here a unique EOJ attestation of an intentional form (志向形) in -a, widely attested in Ryūkyūan dialects. The translation of the first two lines then will be: (2) nests of a bird that would visit (1) two [different] marshes.

On EOJ tentative suffix -unam- see the commentary to 14.3366.

On the EOJ verbal attributive -o (misspelled as -ə in this poem) see the commentary to 14.3395 and a brief description of EOJ special grammar in the introduction.

On the EOJ progressive suffix -ar- corresponding to WOJ -er- see the commentary to 14.3351.

The EOJ -y- in na-y-əmap-ar-i-sə-n-e '[I] wish [you] are not thinking' in all probability reflects the Ainu third person indefinite object prefix i-, cf. the following Ainu phrases:

kuyku < *ku-i-ku* 1pss-**3pso**-drink 'I drink **it**'
wakka ku-ku water 1pss-drink 'I drink water'.

14.3527

本文・*Original Text*
(1) 於吉亦須毛 (2) 乎加母乃毛己呂 (3) 也左可杼利 (4) 伊伎豆久伊毛乎 (5) 於伎弖伎努可母

仮名の書き下し・*Kana Transliteration*
(1) おき₁にすも₁ (2) をかも₂の₂も₁こ₁ろ₂ (3) やさかど₂り (4) いき₁づくいも₁を (5) おき₁てき₁の₁かも₂

Romanization
(1) oki-ni sum-o (2) wo-kamə-nə mokərə (3) ya saka-ⁿ-dəri (4) ikiⁿduk-u imo-wo (5) ok-i-te k-i-n-o kamə

Glossing with Morphemic Analysis
(1) offing-LOC live-ATTR (2) DIM-wild.duck-GEN like (3) eight *saka*-GEN-bird (4) sigh-ATTR beloved-ACC (5) leave-CONV-SUB come-CONV-PERF-ATTR EP

Translation
(5) [I] came [here] leaving behind (4) [my] beloved, who sighs (2) like a small wild duck (1) that lives in the offing, (3) a bird with [breaths as long as] eight *saka*!

Commentary

This poem looks like a poem composed by a border guard (*sakimori*, 防人), and it was treated as such in all old commentaries, although some modern scholars raise their doubts based on a very impressionistic discussion (Tsuchiya 1977.7: 372; Mizushima 1986: 342–343). Together with the following 14.3528 it constitutes a two-poem Sakimori mini-sequence.

On the EOJ verbal attributive *-o* see the commentary to 14.3395 and a brief description of EOJ special grammar in the introduction.

On OJ *kamo* 'wild duck' see the commentary to 14.3524.

According to Nakanishi's opinion, OJ *wo-kamo* 'DIM-wild.duck' may be just an endearment form that does not mean 'small wild duck' (1985: 292). Unfortunately, the evidence is inconclusive for either a diminutive or an endearment hypothesis.

OJ *məkərə* is a postposition meaning 'like'. It occurs extremely rarely in the OJ texts. For details see Vovin (2020.2: 1204–1205).

OJ *saka* (尺) equals 0.32 m or roughly one foot. For more details see the commentary to the poem 14.3414.

Ya saka-ⁿ-dəri 'a bird with [breaths as long as] eight *saka*' is considered to be a permanent epithet (*makura-kotoba*, 枕詞) for the verb *ikiⁿduk-* 'to sigh' (Omodaka 1977.14: 225; Mizushima 1986: 342), but since the metaphor is quite clear, and since a bird is mentioned here, we believe it is possible to incorporate it into the translation. This is a similar metaphor to the one found in 14.3524 above: the ability of a wild duck to hold a long breath is compared to the intensity of lamenting or sighing of a human being.

On EOJ perfective attributive *-n-o* see the commentary to 14.3395.

14.3528

本文 • *Original Text*

(1) 水都等利能 (2) 多々武与曾比尓 (3) 伊母能良尓 (4) 毛乃伊波受伎尓弖 (5) 於毛比可祢都毛

仮名の書き下し • *Kana Transliteration*

(1) み₁づと₂りの₂ (2) たたむよ₂そ₂ひ₁に (3) いも₂の₂らに (4) も₁の₂いはずき₁にて (5) おも₁ひかねつも₁

Romanization

(1) MIⁿdu təri-nə (2) tat-am-u yəsəp-i n-i (3) imə-nə-ra-ni (4) monə ip-aⁿz-u k-i-n-i-te (5) omop-i-kane-t-umo

Glossing with Morphemic Analysis
(1) water bird-GEN/COMP (2) rise/depart-TENT-ATTR prepare-NML COP-CONV (3) wife-DIM-PLUR-DAT (4) thing say-NEG-CONV come-CONV-PERF-CONV-SUB (5) think-CONV-NEG.POT-EXCL

Translation
(5) [I] cannot bear the thought (4) [that I] have come here without saying good-bye (3) to [my] dear wives (2) because of preparations [for my] departure/flying away (1) like a water fowl!

Commentary
This poem looks like a poem composed by a border guard (*sakimori*, 防人), and it constitutes together with the previous 14.3527 a poetic mini-sequence.

Mi^ndu təri-nə 'like a water fowl' is considered to be a permanent epithet (*makura-kotoba*, 枕詞), but the imagery is quite transparent: the author's departure is as sudden as the rising of a scared water fowl into the air.

On EOJ diminutive suffix *-nə* see the commentary to 14.3402.

EOJ *imə-nə-ra-ni* 'to my dear wives' is an interesting form. We take the suffix *-ra* here to be the plural marker, not the diminutive, because in Azuma texts diminutive *-ra* occurs only in three cases, all of them after the word *ko* 'girl, child', and in two cases out of three in texts written in WOJ (Vovin 2005: 209). If *-ra* is a plural form, then this is a unique OJ example that gives us a combination of a diminutive, a plural, and a case marker in the same word form, and we can conclude on the basis of this example that the order was DIM-PLUR-CASE. Practically all examples we know of include only the combinations of DIM-CASE and PLUR-CASE, with two cases of DIM-DIM-CASE in 14.3446 and 14.3544. This linguistic example also provides us with important cultural evidence for the existence of polygamy, not only in the upper, but also in the lower classes.

The fourth line is hypermetric (*ji amari*, 字余り).

On OJ exclamative form *-umə ~ -mə* see the commentary to 14.3431.

In the *Nishi Honganji-bon* and the *Kishū-bon* 於毛比可祢都毛 *omop-i-kane-t-umo* is spelled as 於毛比可祢都母 *omop-i-kane-t-umə*. Although *omop-i-kane-t-umə* is etymologically correct, we leave the spelling *omop-i-kane-t-umo* found in the oldest manuscripts.

14.3529

本文・Original Text
(1) 等夜乃野尓 (2) 乎佐藝祢良波里 (3) 乎佐乎左毛 (4) 祢奈敝古由惠尓 (5) 波伴尓許呂波要

仮名の書き下し・Kana Transliteration
(1) と₂や の₂の₁に (2) をさぎ₁ねらはり (3) をさをさも₁ (4) ねなへ₁こ₁ゆゑに (5) ははにこ₂ろ₂はえ₂

Romanization
(1) Təya-nə NO-ni (2) wosaŋgi nerap-ar-i (3) wosa-wosa mo (4) ne-n-ape ko yuwe n-i (5) papa-ni kər-əp-aye

Glossing with Morphemic Analysis
(1) Təya-GEN field-LOC (2) hare watch-PROG-CONV (3) enough FP (4) sleep-NEG-ITER(CONV) girl reason COP-CONV (5) mother-DAT scold-ITER-PASS(CONV)

Translation
(4) Because of the girl with whom [I] am not sleeping (3) enough, (2) watching for hares (1) in Təya field, (5) [I] am scolded by [her] mother, and...

Commentary
Təya is considered to be a placename, with its location unknown. However, old commentaries[54] identify it with Təya village (鳥矢郷) in Inaᵐba district (Inaᵐba kəpori, 印幡郡) of Simotupusa province, the latter corresponding to Inaba county (Inaba-gun, 印幡郡) of present-day Chiba prefecture (Omodaka 1977.14: 226; Nakanishi 1985: 467; Mizushima 1986: 344). If this identification is correct, then this poem can be identified as a poem from Simotupusa province.[55] If we dispense with the speculation that Təya (鳥矢) is a contraction of təri 'bird' and ya 'arrow', then this placename is meaningless in OJ. Not so in Ainu, where toya means 'lake shore' < to 'lake' + ya 'shore, dry land'. It is worth mentioning that there was a big lake in the north of Inaᵐba district.

---

54 See, e.g. Kamochi (1912.6: 143–144).
55 The fourth line in this poem is identical to the fifth line in 14.3555, which has more evidence for being from Simotupusa province. Thus, given the same grammar present in both lines, it might be an additional proof that 14.3529 also comes from Simotupusa.

EOJ *wosaᵑgi* 'hare' corresponding to WOJ *usaᵑgi* is an important word, because it demonstrates that in proto-Japonic this word started with *w- and had *o, not *u in the first syllable. Cf. also a peninsular Japonic form attested in the pseudo-Koguryŏ placenames as *oseyam (烏斯含) 'hare' (SKSK 35.4b, 37.4a). EOJ *wosaᵑgi* ~ WOJ *usaᵑgi* 'hare' is a general term for various types of hares constituting the hare family (*Leporidae*, ウサギ科). Hares are herbivorous animals, with long pointed ears, and yellowish fur. The biggest type, *yabu no usagi* 'bush hare' reaches 50–76 cm in length. Hares live in fields and can run very fast. At night they can go to village fields and damage crops. Hares are game animals, and both their meat and fur skins are used by humans. In addition, writing brushes were made from hare's fur in the Asuka and Nara periods.

On the EOJ progressive suffix *-ar-* corresponding to WOJ *-er-* see the commentary to 14.3351.

EOJ *wosa-wosa* 'enough' is a *hapax legomenon* in OJ, but there are plenty of attestations in MJ. The following verb is always in the negative form (Omodaka et al. 1967: 833).

On specific EOJ order of morphemes *-(a)n-ap-* 'NEG-ITER' see the commentary to 14.3375.

EOJ iterative suffix *-ape-* is a variant of *-ap-*, and corresponds to WOJ *-apɛ-*, which is also a variant of *-ap-*. For details see Vovin (2020.2: 738–745).

On the adnominal function of the converb form in EOJ see the commentary to 14.3415.

OJ iterative *-əp-* is a phonetic variant of *-ap-*, found after certain stems containing vowels /ə/ and /u/ (Vovin 2020.2: 738).

14.3530

本文・*Original Text*
(1) 左乎思鹿能 (2) 布須也久草無良 (3) 見要受等母 (4) 兒呂我可奈門欲 (5) 由可久之要思母

仮名の書き下し・*Kana Transliteration*
(1) さをしかの₂ (2) ふすやくさむら (3) み₁え₂ず と₂も₂ (4) こ₁ろ₂がかなと₁よ₁ (5) ゆかくしえ₂しも₂

Romanization
(1) sa-wo-siKA-nə (2) pus-u ya kusa mura (3) MI-ye-ⁿz-u təmə (4) KO-rə-ᵑga kana-TO-yo (5) yuk-aku si ye-si-mə

Glossing with Morphemic Analysis
(1) PREF-male-deer-GEN/COMP (2) lie-ATTR EP grass group (3) see-PASS-NEG-FIN CONJ (4) girl-DIM-POSS metal-gate-ABL (5) go-NML EP good-FIN-EXCL

Translation
(3) Even though [I] do not see [her] (1) like a male deer (3) lying in the clump of grass, (5) it is good to go [inside] (4) through [my] dear girl's metal adorned gate!

Commentary
 This is probably one of the most sexually explicit and sexually graphic OJ poems. Besides the upper layer, which is rendered in the translation, there is very likely another layer, which was noticed by Gotō Toshio (後藤利雄) in his *Azuma uta nanka kō* (東歌難歌考) 'A commentary on difficult Eastern poems':[56] "Although I do not see her vulva hidden in her pubic hair (*kusa mura*), like one does not see a male deer lying in the clump of grass (*kusa mura*), I feel good going inside her through my dear girl's precious gate (= vulva)." Although Mizushima rather emphatically disagrees with this interpretation (1986: 347), it is more than likely, cf. also a reference to vulva as 'jade gate' (玉門). OJ *kana-to* 'metal adorned gate' certainly was precious gate as well. Without mentioning Gotō's name, Itō refers to his explanation as 'indecent' (きわどい) (1997: 532). Other modern commentators pass Gotō's theory in silence and discuss only the first layer of this poem.
 The deer endemic to Japan has a body length of approximately 1.5 m (5 ft) with the height of 90 cm (3 ft). Only the males have horns that are discarded in winter and then grow again in the spring. The horns can grow up to approximately 40 cm (1ft 3 in). The cry of a male deer calling for his female mate is a frequent theme in the *Man'yōshū* in particular and in traditional Japanese poetry in general. It symbolizes the author's longing for his beloved. The deer's cry is associated with the autumn. It is interesting that OJ *ka* also means 'deer', cf. also OJ *ka-ko* 'fawn' (lit. 'deer-child'), *me-ko* 'female deer'. This points to the analysis of *sika* 'deer' as a compound *si-ka*, where *-ka* means 'deer'. What could the first element *si-* mean? We think that the word *sisi* 'meat, flesh, game animals' (see 14.3531 below) could be a reduplication *si-si*. Since OJ *sisi* 'game animals' could be used to include both deer and wild boars, such an interpretation is more than probable. Then *si-* in *si-ka* may mean 'meat'. Then OJ *ka* probably was a generic term for a deer, while OJ *si-ka* 'meat-deer' might have indicated

---

56 Cited according to Mizushima (1986: 347), as this publication is unavailable to me.

'deer as a game animal'. It is necessary to conduct separate research to see whether such identification can be supported by textual evidence.

OJ *ya* in line two is an emphatic particle *ya*, not an interrogative particle *ya*. For details see Vovin (2020.2: 1166–1167).

On EOJ diminutive suffix *-rə* see the commentary to 14.3351.

OJ *kana-to*[57] 'metal adorned gate', an original form of OJ *kaⁿdo* and MDJ *kado* 'gate' is actually not a gate made entirely of metal, but a gate that was adorned with metal, and/or had some metal implements, like metal hinges. Presumably, only comparatively well-off people could afford to have such gates during the Asuka and Nara periods.

On OJ *ye-* 'to be good' see the commentary to 14.3509.

14.3531

本文・*Original Text*
(1) 伊母乎許曾 (2) 安比美尓許思可 (3) 麻欲婢吉能 (4) 与許夜麻敝呂能 (5) 思之奈須於母敝流

仮名の書き下し・*Kana Transliteration*
(1) いも₂を₂こ₂そ₂ (2) あひ₁み₁に₂しか (3) まよ₁び₁き₁の₂ (4) よ₂こ₂やまへ₁ろ₂の₂ (5) ししなすおも₂へ₁る

Romanization
(1) imə-wo kəsə (2) api-mi-ni kə-sika (3) mayo-ᵐ-bik-i-nə (4) yəkə yama pe-rə-nə (5) sisi-nasu oməp-er-u

Glossing with Morphemic Analysis
(1) beloved-ACC FP (2) REC-see(NML)-LOC come(CONV)-PAST.EV (3) eyebrow-GEN-draw-NML-COMP (4) horizontal mountain side-DIM-GEN (5) game.animal-COMP think-PROG-ATTR

Translation
(1) [I] did come to meet (2) with [my] beloved. (5) [But her parents] are thinking [of me] like [of] a game animal (4) from the mountains [stretched] horizontally (3) like painted eyebrows.

---

57 OJ *kana-* is a bound form of *kane* 'metal'.

Commentary

Note the irregular past tense evidential form *kə-sika* 'I did come'. For the details on irregular past tense forms see Vovin (2020.2: 828).

OJ *mayo-ᵐ-bik-i* is 'painted eyebrows' (lit.: 'eyebrow drawing'). OJ *mayo* 'eyebrow' reflects the original PJ *mayo 'id.' with a *kō-rui* /o/ that has not raised to /u/. Cf. MJ and MDJ *mayu* 'id.', where such a raising has already took place.

OJ expression *yəkə yama* 'horizontally [stretched] mountains' indicates the mountain chain that goes relatively evenly, without any dominating peaks suddenly protruding in the middle. Tateyama (立山) mountain chain in Eastern Toyama is a good example of *yəkə yama*.

On EOJ diminutive suffix *-rə* see the commentary to 14.3351.

OJ *sisi* 'game animal' refers to both deer and wild boars (as well as sometimes to some other representatives of fauna, in particular, some birds), either separately, or jointly. Thus, it can mean 'game deer', 'game wild boar', or 'deer and wild boars as game animals'. The original meaning of *sisi* appears to be 'flesh, meat', but the word itself is likely to be a reduplication. See the commentary to 14.3530 above.

OJ comparative case marker *-nasu* occurs mostly in WOJ, but there are also attestations in EOJ (Vovin 2020.1: 201, 203–205).

14.3532

本文 · *Original Text*

(1) 波流能野尒 (2) 久佐波牟古麻能 (3) 久知夜麻受 (4) 安乎思努布良武 (5) 伊敝乃兒呂波母

仮名の書き下し · *Kana Transliteration*

(1) はるの₂の₁に (2) くさはむこ₁まの₂ (3) くちやまず (4) あをしの₁ふらむ (5) い へ₁の₂こ₁ろ₂はも₂

Romanization

(1) paru-nə NO-ni (2) kusa pam-u koma-nə (3) kuti yam-aⁿz-u (4) a-wo sinop-uram-u (5) ipe-nə KO-rə pa mə

Glossing with Morphemic Analysis

(1) spring-GEN field-LOC (2) grass eat-ATTR stallion-GEN/COMP (3) mouth stop-NEG-CONV (4) I-ACC long.for-TENT2-ATTR (5) home-GEN girl-DIM TOP EP

Translation

(5) Ah, [my] dear girl from home, (4) who probably longs for me (3) without stopping [like] the mouth (2) of a stallion eating grass (1) in a spring field.

Commentary

Besides this interpretation, Japanese commentators also add a parallel one: 'my dear girl who probably longs for me talking [about me] all the time like a stallion who eats grass does not stop its mouth' (Omodaka 1977.14: 229; Mizushima 1986: 348–349). However, this is difficult to accept as such, because OJ *yam-* 'to stop' is an intransitive verb (its transitive counterpart is OJ *yamɛ-*). Therefore, *kuti yama*ⁿ*zu* does not mean 'not to stop one's mouth', but 'one's mouth does not stop'. The parallel interpretation then can be: 'my dear girl who probably longs for me without her mouth stopping like a stallion who eats grass'. Depending on the interpretation, case marker *-nə* after *koma* 'stallion' can be interpreted either as a genitive or as a comparative case marker. Consequently the metaphoric poetic introduction in this poem (*hiyuteki jo*, 比喩的序) can be limited to the first two lines (if the comparison is made with the stallion), or it can be extended, including the word *kuti* 'mouth' in the third line (if the comparison is made with the mouth of the stallion).

There were two basic words for 'to eat' in Western Old Japanese: *pam-* and *kup-*. The former seems to indicate the process of eating softer things, with a minimal amount of chewing involved, while the latter definitely indicates some good amount of chewing (Omodaka et al. 1967: 594).

On OJ *koma* 'stallion' see the commentary to 14.3387.

On EOJ diminutive suffix *-rə* see the commentary to 14.3351. This is the only EOJ feature in this poem, otherwise it looks as if written in WOJ.

14.3533

本文・Original Text

(1) 比登乃兒能 (2) 可奈思家之太波 (3) 波麻渚杼里 (4) 安奈由牟古麻能 (5) 乎之家口母奈思

仮名の書き下し・Kana Transliteration

(1) ひ₁と₂の₂こ₁の₂ (2) かなしけ₁しだは (3) はますど₂り (4) あなゆむこ₁まの₂ (5) をしけ₁くも₂なし

Romanization
(1) pitə-nə KO-nə (2) kanasi-ke siⁿda pa (3) pama SU-ⁿ-dəri (4) a nayum-u koma-nə (5) wosi-keku mə na-si

Glossing with Morphemic Analysis
(1) person-GEN girl-GEN (2) be.dear-ATTR time TOP (3) shore sandbar-GEN-bird (4) foot suffer-ATTR stallion-GEN (5) be.regrettable-ATTR/NML FP exist.not-FIN

Translation
(2) When [I] miss (1) [that] person's daughter, (5) [I] have no sorry feelings (4) for [my] stallion that will hurt [its] legs (3) [walking unsteadily like] birds on a shore sandbar.

Commentary
On OJ *pitə-nə ko* 'person's child' or 'person's girl' see the commentary to 14.3500.

On EOJ attributive *-ke* in *kanasi-ke* see the commentary to 14.3412.

On EOJ *siⁿda* 'time' see the commentary to 14.3363.

OJ *su* is 'sandbar' or 'sandbank' (Omodaka et al. 1967: 378).

OJ *pama su-ⁿ-dəri* 'birds on a shore sandbar' is considered to be a permanent epithet (*makura-kotoba,* 枕詞) for the word *a* 'foot, leg', because the birds that live on sandbars are considered to walk unsteadily on their legs. These birds probably are some type of plovers (*chidori,* 千鳥) (Mizushima 1986: 350–351).

On EOJ *a* 'foot, leg' see the commentary to 14.3387.

EOJ *nayum-* 'to suffer' corresponds to WOJ *nayam-* 'id.' EOJ *nayum-* is a *hapax legomenon*.

On OJ *koma* 'stallion' see the commentary to 14.3387.

On the OJ adjectival nominalized form *-keku* (which is essentially a WOJ form, the real EOJ form being *-k-aku*) is a nominalized form of OJ *yasu-* 'easy, peaceful', that consists of the root *yasu-*, attributive form *-ki* and nominalizer *-aku*. The latter two fused as *-keku* < *-ki-aku.

14.3536

本文 • Original Text
(1) 安加胡麻乎 (2) 宇知弖左乎妣吉 (3) 己許呂妣吉 (4) 伊可奈流勢奈可 (5) 和我理許武等伊布

仮名の書き下し・*Kana Transliteration*

(1) あかご₁まを (2) うちてさをび₁き₁ (3) こ₂こ₂ろ₂び₁き₁ (4) いかなるせなか (5) わがりこ₂むと₂いふ

Romanization

(1) aka-ŋ-goma-wo (2) ut-i-te sa-wo-ᵐ-bik-i (3) kəkərə-ᵐ-bik-i (4) ika nar-u se-na ka (5) wa-ŋgari kə-m-u tə ip-u

Glossing with Morphemic Analysis

(1) red-COP(ATTR)-stallion-ACC (2) hit-CONV-SUB PREF-reins-LOC-pull-CONV (3) heart-LOC-pull-CONV (4) how be-ATTR beloved-DIM IP (5) I-DIR come-TENT-FIN QV say-ATTR

Translation

(4) What kind of beloved is [he], (5) who says that [he] will come to me, (3) reining in [my] heart, (2) [like] reining in and hitting [with a whip] (1) [his] chestnut stallion?

Commentary

On OJ *koma* 'stallion' see the commentary to 14.3387.
   OJ *aka-ŋ-goma* lit. 'red stallion' is 'chestnut stallion' or 'brown stallion'.
   EOJ *wo* 'cord, string' here refers to horse reins.
   On EOJ diminutive suffix *-na* see the commentary to 14.3384.
   Case marker *-ŋgari* is a directive case marker that is attested in both WOJ and EOJ, but not in Classical Japanese. For details see Vovin (2020.1: 192–194).

14.3537

本文・*Original Text*

(1) 久敝胡之尓 (2) 武藝波武古宇馬能 (3) 波都々々尓 (4) 安比見之兒良之 (5) 安夜尓可奈思母

仮名の書き下し・*Kana Transliteration*

(1) くへ₁ご₂しに (2) むぎ₁はむこ₁うまの₂ (3) はつはつに (4) あひ₁み₁しこ₁らし (5) あやにかなしも₂

Romanization

(1) kupe-ŋ-gos-i-ni (2) muŋgi pam-u ko-uMA-nə (3) patu-patu n-i (4) api-MI-si KO-ra si (5) aya n-i kanasi-mə

Glossing with Morphemic Analysis
(1) fence-GEN-make.cross-NML-LOC (2) barley eat-ATTR DIM-horse-GEN (3) barely-barely COP-CONV (4) REC-see(CONV)-PAST.ATTR girl-DIM EP (5) extreme COP-CONV be.dear-EXCL

Translation
(3/4) [My] dear girl with whom [I] barely met, (2) [like] a little horse [that can barely] eat barley (1) when [it] makes [its neck] crane over a fence, (5) is extremely dear [to me]!

Commentary
The first two lines are a metaphoric introduction (*hiyuteki jo*, 比喩的序) to the rest of the poem (Omodaka 1977.14: 233; Mizushima 1986: 357).

Kupe is usually considered to be an EOJ *hapax legomenon* meaning 'fence' or 'pasture fence'. Omodaka et al. notice that in Uwajima region (Uwajima chihō, 宇和島地方) of present-day Ehime prefecture there is the word *kube* 'fence' (1967: 268). It is, however, unclear what relevance a North-Western Shikoku dialect word might have for establishing the EOJ nature of *kupe*. Although there are no other distinctive EOJ features in this poem, we tentatively assume on lexical grounds that it is written in EOJ.

OJ *muⁿgi* could refer to either wheat (*komugi*, 小麦) or barley (*ōmugi*, 大麦). Since in the *Man'yōshū* OJ *muⁿgi* is attested exclusively in the context *muⁿgi pam-u ko-uma/koma* 'stallion/little horse that eats *muⁿgi*' (12.3096, 14.3537, 14.3537a), we translate it as 'barley', which was a favorite staple of horses. Consequently, it is easy to imagine a horse that cranes its neck to get some of barley growing outside of the pasture fence. Both barley and wheat were planted in dry fields. There were annual and biennial varieties of *muⁿgi*, and it was included in the 'five cereals' (*gokoku*, 五穀). On the 'five cereals' see the commentary to 14.3451.

Presumably *ko-uma* in this poem is just 'little horse', and not the protoform *ko-uma of *koma* 'stallion'. On OJ *koma* 'stallion' see the commentary to 14.3387.

Line two is hypermetric (*ji amari*, 字余り), but this is probably just a graphic illusion, since *ko-uma* was in all probability pronounced as [koma], overlapping phonetically with *koma* 'stallion'.

Postscript to the Poem 14.3537

本文 • *Original Text*

或本歌曰

萬葉集巻第十四・MAN'YŌSHŪ BOOK FOURTEEN 227

Translation
In a certain book [a variant of this poem] says:

Commentary
We do not know what the book mentioned above is. The variant follows below as 14.3537a.

14.3537a

本文・Original Text
(1) 宇麻勢胡之 (2) 牟伎波武古麻能 (3) 波都々々尒 (4) 仁必波太布礼思 (5) 古呂之可奈思母

仮名の書き下し・Kana Transliteration
(1) うませご₁し (2) むぎ₁はむこ₁まの₂ (3) はつはつに (4) にひ₁はだふれし (5) こ₁ろ₂しかなしも₂

Romanization
(1) uma-se-ŋ-gos-i (2) muŋgi pam-u koma-nə (3) patu-patu n-i (4) nipi panda pure-si (5) ko-rə si kanasi-mə

Glossing with Morphemic Analysis
(1) horse-fence-LOC-make.cross-CONV (2) barley eat-ATTR stallion-GEN (3) barely-barely COP-CONV (4) new skin touch(CONV)-PAST.ATTR (5) girl-DIM EP be.dear-EXCL

Translation
(3/4/5) [My] dear girl whose skin [I] barely touched for the first time, (2) [like] a stallion [that can barely] eat barley (1) when [it] makes [its neck] crane over a fence, (5) is extremely dear [to me]!

Commentary
Similar to 14.3537, the first two lines are a metaphoric introduction (*hiyuteki jo*, 比喩的序) to the rest of the poem.

OJ *uma-se* is supposed to mean either 'fence' or 'pasture fence'. Mizushima notes that in modern dialects of Nagano, Ibaraki, and Yamanashi prefectures words *mase* or *masenbo* denote the horizontal bar that blocks the entrance to a stable, preventing a horse from getting out. However, if OJ *uma-se* meant this kind of a bar, then it would imply that barley is the food given to the horse.

The context of this poem, however, implies that the stallion is getting some extra food that is not given to it (1986: 357). OJ -*se* in *uma-se* is not attested independently.

The expression *nipi pa*ⁿ*da pure-* 'to touch new skin' implies that the author slept with his beloved for the first time.

On EOJ diminutive suffix *-rə* see the commentary to 14.3351. This is the only EOJ feature in this poem, otherwise it looks as if written in WOJ.

14.3538

本文・*Original Text*
(1) 比呂波之乎 (2) 宇馬古思我祢弖 (3) 己許呂能未 (4) 伊母我理夜里弖 (5) 和波己許尓思弖

仮名の書き下し・*Kana Transliteration*
(1) ひ₁ろ₂はしを (2) うまこ₁しがねて (3) こ₂こ₂ろ₂の₂み₂ (4) いも₂がりやりて (5) わはこ₂こ₂にして₂

Romanization
(1) pirə pasi-wo (2) uma kos-i-ⁿgane-te (3) kəkərə nəmï (4) imə-ⁿgari yar-i-te (5) wa pa kəkə-ni s-i-tɛ

Glossing with Morphemic Analysis
(1) oak bridge-ACC (2) horse make.cross-CONV-NEG.POT(CONV)-SUB (3) heart RP (4) beloved-DIR send-CONV-SUB (5) I TOP here-LOC do-CONV-SUB

Translation
(2) Failing to make [my] horse cross (1) the oak bridge, (5) I stay here, (3/4) sending just [my] heart to [my] beloved.

Commentary
OJ *pirə* in line one is usually interpreted as *pirə* 'wide', but the obvious problem that has been noted by all commentators is a semantic contradiction: why the rider cannot make his horse cross a *wide* bridge? Logically it should have been a *narrow* bridge that a horse would hesitate to cross. Takeda proposed that what is meant here is a bridge across a wide river (1966: 411). This explanation is also accepted by Omodaka (1977.14: 234). This is possible, but it remains unclear what the width of the river has to do with horse's fear. Mizushima follows the explanation by Kubota, who believes that the bridge is indeed wide, but it is the rider who fails to cross it, as he does not want to be seen going to

his beloved (Kubota 1967: 256; Mizushima 1986: 359). This is clearly an *ad hoc* theory, with no textual evidence to support it. There are also other explanations mentioned by Mizushima, but all of them violate either phonology or semantics, like, e.g. one that explains *piro pasi* as 'fathom bridge'. *Piro* 'fathom' is, of course, a measure of depth, not of width. There is, however, another possibility. We believe EOJ *pirə* here is a loanword from Ainu *pero* or *pero-ni*[58] 'a kind of oak', the same tree as MDJ *mizunara* (ミズナラ, *Quercus crispula*) (Chiri 1976: 176–177; Kayano 1996: 405). Its wood is known for its hardness, and is widely used in construction and manufacturing of tools. The vowel *i* in EOJ *pirə* 'oak' vs. Ainu *pero* 'id.' is easily explained as a result of OJ vowel raising: PJ *e > OJ *i*. Thus, EOJ *pirə pasi* is an 'oak bridge', quite possible just made out of two-to-four logs, on which a horse would be hesitant to step.

Negative potential auxiliary *ⁿgane-* is a rare phonetic variant of OJ *kane-*, with a secondary nasalization and voicing.

On OJ directive case marker *-ⁿgari* see the commentary to 14.3536.

The usage of an unextended stem *wa* 'I' in isolation is a distinctive EOJ feature. Such a usage does not occur in WOJ (Vovin 2020.1: 219–220).

Postscript to the Poem 14.3538

本文・*Original Text*
或本歌發句曰乎波夜之尒古麻乎波左佐氣

Translation
In a certain book the beginning stanza [of a variant of this poem] says: (1) *wo-payasi-ni* (2) *koma-wo pasasaⁿgɛ* '[I] made [my] stallion run into a small forest'.

Commentary
We do not know what the book mentioned above is. The variant with a different beginning stanza (lines one and two) follows below as 14.3538a.

14.3538a

本文・*Original Text*
(1) 乎波夜之尒 (2) 古麻乎波左佐氣 (3) 己許呂能未 (4) 伊母我理夜里弖 (5) 和波己許尒思天

---

58 Ainu *-ni* is 'tree'.

仮名の書き下し・*Kana Transliteration*
(1) をはやしに (2) こ₁まをはささげ₂ (3) こ₂こ₂ろ₂の₂み₂ (4) いも₂がりやりて (5) わはこ₂こ₂にして

Romanization
(1) wo-payasi-ni (2) koma-wo pas-as-aᵑgɛ (3) kəkərə nəmï (4) imə-ᵑgari yar-i-te (5) wa pa kəkə-ni s-i-te

Glossing with Morphemic Analysis
(1) DIM-forest-LOC (2) stallion-ACC make.run-CAUS-raise(CONV) (3) heart RP (4) beloved-DIR send-CONV-SUB (5) I TOP here-LOC do-CONV-SUB

Translation
(2) [I] have made my stallion run into (1) a small forest, (5) [so] I stay here, (3/4) sending just [my] heart to [my] beloved.

Commentary
EOJ *pasasaᵑgɛ-* is a *hapax legomenon* that is believed to mean 'to make [someone/something] run into', consisting of *pase-* 'to make run', a causative suffix *-ase-*, and an auxiliary *-aᵑgɛ-*, indicating that the movement is directed upwards (Omodaka et al. 1967: 575).

It remains unclear why the man makes his stallion run into the forest. Mizushima believes that this demonstrates that the man is making an excuse not to visit his beloved (1986: 359–360). Kojima et al. speculate that EOJ *pasasaᵑgɛ-* means 'to hurt' (1973: 496). Either of them might be right, but there is no textual or linguistic evidence to support their hypotheses.

On OJ directive case marker *-ᵑgari* see the commentary to 14.3536.

On the usage of an unextended stem *wa* 'I' in isolation see the commentary to 14.3538.

14.3539

本文・*Original Text*
(1) 安受能宇敝尓 (2) 古馬乎都奈伎弖 (3) 安夜抱可等 (4) 比等豆麻古呂乎 (5) 伊吉尓和我須流

仮名の書き下し・*Kana Transliteration*
(1) あずの₂う₁へ₁に (2) こ₁まをつなぎ₁て (3) あやほかど₂ (4) ひ₁と₂づまこ₁ろ₂を (5) いき₁にわがする

Romanization
(1) aⁿzu-nə upe-ni (2) koma-wo tunaᵑg-i-te (3) ayapo-ka-ⁿdə (4) pitə-ⁿ-duma ko-rə-wo (5) yik-i n-i wa-ᵑga s-uru

Glossing with Morphemic Analysis
(1) crumbling.cliff-GEN top-LOC (2) stallion-ACC tie-CONV-SUB (3) be.dangerous-EV-CONC (4) person-GEN-spouse girl-DIM-ACC (5) live-NML COP-CONV I-POSS do-ATTR

Translation
(3) Although [it] is [as] dangerous (2) [as] tying the stallion (1) to the top of the crumbling cliff, (5) I will risk [my] life (4) for [my] dear girl, [who is] the wife of [another] man.

Commentary
Line one is hypermetric (*ji amari*, 字余り), but this is probably just a graphic illusion, since *nə upe* was in all probability pronounced as [nəpe].

EOJ *aⁿzu* 'crumbling cliff' (see also 14.3541 below) is not attested in WOJ. A possible etymology is Hokkaidō Ainu *y-as-*, Sakhalin Ainu *nas-* 'to split'[59] (Hattori 1964: 136) + *so* 'rocky shore', 'hidden rocks in the sea' (Chiri 1956: 125–126; Kayano 1996: 288). Tentative Ainu **as-so* 'splitting rock' > EOJ *aⁿzu* involves expected EOJ raising of PJ **o > u* in the last syllable, cf. EOJ *kumu* 'cloud' ~ WOJ *kumo* 'id.' If this etymology is correct, EOJ -ⁿz- can be explained as a secondary nasalization.

EOJ *upe* 'top' corresponds to WOJ *upɛ* 'id.' This spelling probably indicates that the contrast between *e* and *ɛ* was lost in the EOJ dialect underlying this poem.

EOJ *ayapo-* 'to be dangerous' corresponds to MJ *ayapu-* 'id.' (OJ form is not attested). EOJ *ayapo-* preserves the original vowel *o*, which is raised to *u* in the MJ form.

On EOJ diminutive suffix *-rə* see the commentary to 14.3351.

On EOJ inflected adjectival evidential marker *-ka-* see the commentary to 14.3473.

---

59 There is no correspondence of Hokkaidō Ainu *y-* to Sakhalin Ainu *n-* attested otherwise, therefore we can suspect some morphology involved here. Since the verb is inherently transitive, Hokkaidō Ainu *y-* probably reflects the petrified object prefix *i-*. The nature of Sakhalin Ainu *n-* is obscure.

14.3540

本文・*Original Text*
(1) 左和多里能 (2) 手兒尓伊由伎安比 (3) 安可故麻我 (4) 安我伎乎波夜美 (5) 許等登波受伎奴

仮名の書き下し・*Kana Transliteration*
(1) さわたりの₂ (2) てご₁にいゆき₁あひ₁ (3) あかご₁まが (4) あがき₁をはやみ₁ (5) こ₂と₂と₂はずき₁ぬ

Romanization
(1) Sawatari-nə (2) TEŋgo-ni i-yuk-i ap-i (3) aka-ŋ-goma-ŋga (4) aŋgaki-wo paya-mi (5) kətətəp-aⁿz-u k-i-n-u

Glossing with Morphemic Analysis
(1) Sawatari-GEN (2) maiden-DAT DLF-go-CONV meet-CONV (3) red-COP(ATTR)-stallion-POSS (4) gallop-ABS be.fast-GER (5) talk.with-NEG-CONV come-CONV-PERF-FIN

Translation
(1/2) [I] went to the maiden in Sawatari and met [her], (3/4) [but] because the gallop of [my] chestnut stallion was fast, (5) [I] came back without talking [to her].

Commentary
Sawatari is a placename, but its exact location is unknown. It is alternatively identified as: (a) Sawatari hot springs (Sawatati onsen, 沢渡温泉) in Nakanojō town (Nakanojō machi, 中之条町) in Agatsuma county (Agatsuma-gun, 吾妻郡) in present-day Gunma prefecture, (b) Sawatari (沢渡) in Tokiwa town (Tokiwa-chō, 常盤町) of Mito city (Mito-shi, 水戸市) in present-day Ibaraki prefecture, (c) Miwa town (Miwa machi, 三和町), formerly Sawatari village (Sawatari mura, 沢渡村) of Iwaki city (いわき市) in present-day Fukushima prefecture (Nakanishi 1985: 450–51; Mizushima 1986: 361).

Line two is hypermetric (*ji amari*, 字余り), but this is probably just a graphic illusion, since *Teŋgo-ni i-yuk-i ap-i* was in all probability pronounced as [teŋgoniyukiapi] or [teŋgoniiyukapi].

On EOJ *teŋgo* 'maiden' see the commentary to 14.3384. The EOJ linguistic nature of this poem can only be established lexically on the basis of this word.

Prefix *i-* is a marker of a directive-locative focus. For details see Vovin (2020.2: 505–512).

On OJ *koma* 'stallion' see the commentary to 14.3387.

OJ *aka-ⁿ-goma* 'chestnut stallion' see the commentary to 14.3534.

OJ *aⁿgaki* 'gallop' has a transparent etymology *a* 'foot, leg' + *n[ə]*, genitive case marker + *kak-i* 'scratching', i.e. 'scratching [the ground surface] with legs' (Omodaka et al. 1967: 2).

On the absolutive case marker *-wo* see the commentary to 14.3426. For details, see Vovin (2020.1: 172–175).

OJ verb *kətatəp-* according to Mizushima is a polysemantic word with the following meanings: a) 'to say things', 'to speak', b) 'to talk [tenderly] with', 'to talk together' (usually between a man and a woman), c) 'to inquire', 'to ask', d) 'to visit' (1986: 313). However, Omodaka et al. present the examples that include only a), b), and c), but not d) (1967: 300–301). The verb occurs both as *kətatəp-* and *kətaⁿdəp-*, which indicates that the prenasalized voicing in *kətaⁿdəp-* is secondary. This makes the etymology of the word rather transparent: *kətə* 'word' or 'thing' + *təp-* 'to ask'. Omodaka et al. further note that although the verb 'to ask' occurs as both *top-* and *təp-*, the verb *kətaⁿdəp-* itself occurs only with *otsurui* vowel *ə* (1967: 300). This can be easily explained as a result of progressive vowel assimilation.

Some modern commentators believe that the man meets the maiden from Sawatari by chance (Mizushima 1986: 361–362; Itō 1997: 547; Aso 2011: 465, 467), but this is contradicted by the directive-locative verbal prefix *i-* that clearly demonstrates that the going and meeting was on purpose. Thus, the man had enough courage to go for a date with the maiden from Sawatari, but did not have the guts to talk with her and/or to talk her into going to bed.[60] When asked about the outcome of his experience, he put the blame on the speed of his stallion.

14.3541

本文 · *Original Text*
(1) 安受倍可良 (2) 古麻能由胡能須 (3) 安也波刀文 (4) 比登豆麻古呂乎 (5) 麻由可西良布母

仮名の書き下し · *Kana Transliteration*
(1) あずへ₂から (2) こ₁まの₂ゆこ₁の₂す (3) あやはと₁も (4) ひ₁と₂づまこ₁ろ₂を (5) まゆかせらふも₂

---

60 Tsuchiya believes that *kətatəp-* in this particular case indicates sexual relationship (1977.7: 383).

Romanization
(1) aⁿzu pɛ-kara (2) koma-nə yuk-o-nəsu (3) ayapa tomo (4) pitə-ⁿ-duma kǒ-rə-wo (5) ma-yuk-ase-[a]r-ap-umə

Glossing with Morphemic Analysis
(1) crumbling.cliff side-ABL (2) stallion-GEN go-ATTR-COMP (3) dangerous CONJ (4) person-GEN-wife girl-DIM-ACC (5) eye-go-CAUS-PROG-ITER-EXCL

Translation
(3) Even though [it] is as dangerous (2) as a stallion's going (1) through the vicinity of a crumbling cliff, (5) [I] let [my] eyes wander continuously over (4) the girl [who is] the wife of [another] man!

Commentary
On EOJ *aⁿzu* 'crumbling cliff' see the commentary to 14.3539.

EOJ spelling *pɛ* 'side' corresponds to WOJ *pe* 'id.', probably indicating that the contrast between *ɛ* and *e* did not exist in the EOJ dialect underlying this poem.

OJ *-kara* is an ablative case marker, here used in its prolative function (Omodaka 1977.14: 236).

On OJ *koma* 'stallion' see the commentary to 14.3387.

On the EOJ verbal attributive *-o* see the commentary to 14.3395 and a brief description of EOJ special grammar in the introduction.

On EOJ comparative case marker *-nəsu* see the commentary to 14.3413.

The *ayapa tomo* in the third line can be analyzed only tentatively, as this form is a *hapax legomenon*. We have seen EOJ *ayapo-* 'be dangerous' in 14.3539. The form *ayapa tomo* here looks like an uninflected adjective *ayapa* followed by the conjunction *tomo* (cf. WOJ *təmə*) 'even though, even if', with *ayapa* derived from *ayapo* by progressive assimilation. This analysis is not the only possibility now. One alternative would be to see otherwise unattested consonantal verb *ayap-* with attributive in *-a* (see 14.3526), followed by the conjunction *təmə*, but the problem is that the conjunction *təmə* follows the final and not attributive form of verbs. Another alternative would be to analyze this form as *ayap-a-ⁿdəmə* 'be.dangerous-EV-CONC', but there are two problems with this analysis as well. First, there are no cases in the *Man'yōshū* when the character 耳 is used for a syllable /ⁿdo/ or /ⁿdə/ with an initial prenasalized voiced /ⁿd/. Second, EOJ *a* can correspond to WOJ *e*, as for example EOJ *-kar-* vs. WOJ *-ker-* or EOJ *-ar-* vs. WOJ *-er-*, but the correspondence of EOJ *-a-* to WOJ *-ɛ-* in evidential forms of verbs is not attested. Thus, the first suggested analysis seems to be better off than the other two alternatives.

On EOJ diminutive suffix -rə see the commentary to 14.3351.

Omodaka after a rigorous analysis of various proposals comes to the conclusion that the last line is not analyzable and abstains from providing its translation into modern Japanese (1977.14: 236–237). The last line is indeed difficult to interpret, and there are practically as many hypotheses concerning its analysis as there are commentators. Since we cannot agree with any of them for various reasons, mostly of those concerning ungrammaticality, we propose our own here.

In Eastern Old Japanese the iterative -ap- follows progressive -[a]r- unlike Western Old Japanese where the iterative -ap- precedes progressive -er-.

14.3543

本文・*Original Text*
(1) 武路我夜乃 (2) 都留能都追美乃 (3) 那利奴賀尓 (4) 古呂波伊敝杼母 (5) 伊末太年那久尓

仮名の書き下し・*Kana Transliteration*
(1) むろ₁がやの₂ (2) つるの₂つつみ₁の₂ (3) なりぬがに (4) こ₁ろ₂はいへ₁ど₂も₂ (5) いまだねなくに

Romanization
(1) muro-ŋ-gaya-nə (2) Turu-nə tutumi-nə (3) nar-i-n-u ⁿgani (4) ko-rə pa ip-e-ⁿdəmə (5) imaⁿda ne-n-aku n-i

Glossing with Morphemic Analysis
(1) house-GEN-thatch.grass-GEN (2) Turu-GEN dam-GEN (3) become-CONV-PERF-FIN CONJ (4) girl-DIM TOP say-EV-CONC (5) yet sleep-NEG-NML COP-CONV

Translation
(4) Although [my] dear girl says that [our relationship is established solidly] (2/3) like the dam that is established on the Turu [river], (1) [where] thatch grass for houses [grows], (5) [we] have not yet slept together.

Commentary
On OJ *muro* 'room, house' see the commentary to 14.3506.

On OJ *kaya* 'kaya grass' see the commentary to 14.3499.

The first line *muro-ŋ-gaya-nə* is supposed to be a permanent epithet (*makura-kotoba*, 枕詞) (Mizushima 1986: 366), but to the best of my knowledge this '*makura-kotoba*' occurs only in this poem, so there is nothing 'permanent' about it.

The location of Turu [river] and especially the location of a dam on it is not known, although it is possible that Tsuru river (Tsurugawa, 鶴川) in Uenohara town (Uenohara machi, 上野原町)[61] of Northern Tsuru county (Kita Tsuru-gun, 北都留郡) in present-day Yamanashi prefecture corresponds to Turu in this poem (Nakanishi 1985: 465).

OJ *ŋgani* is a conjunction 'like, as if, so that' which follows the final form of verbs. For more examples of usage see Vovin (2020.2: 1055–1056).

On EOJ diminutive suffix -*rə* see the commentary to 14.3351.

EOJ *ip-e-ⁿdəmə* 'although [she] says' with the evidential form spelled with *e* instead of etymologically correct *ε* (cf. WOJ *ip-ε-ⁿdəmə*) is the only other feature in addition to diminutive suffix -*rə* that allows us to classify this poem as written in EOJ.

14.3544

本文・*Original Text*
(1) 阿須可河泊 (2) 之多尓其礼留乎 (3) 之良受思天 (4) 勢奈那登布多里 (5) 左宿而久也思母

仮名の書き下し・*Kana Transliteration*
(1) あすかがは (2) したにご₂れるを (3) しらずして (4) せななと₂ふたり (5) さねてくやしも₂

Romanization
(1) Asuka-ⁿ-GApa (2) sita niŋgər-er-u-wo (3) sir-aⁿz-u s-i-te (4) se-na-na-tə puta-ri (5) sa-NE-TE kuyasi-mə

Glossing with Morphemic Analysis
(1) Asuka-GEN-river (2) bottom be.muddy-PROG-ATTR-ACC (3) know-NEG-NML do-CONV-SUB (4) beloved-DIM-DIM-COM two-CL (5) PREF-sleep (CONV)-SUB be.regretful-EXCL

---

61 Uenohara town was incorporated into Uenohara city (Uenohara-shi, 上野原市) in 2005.

Translation
(4/5) [I] regret that [I] slept with you, (3) not knowing (2) that [the bottom of your heart] is [as] muddy [as] the bottom (1) of Asuka river!

Commentary
Together with the following 14.3545 this poem constitutes a poetic mini-sequence, since both mention Asuka river.

Opinions differ whether this is the same river as the famous Asuka river that flows through Asuka plain in Yamatə (Nakanishi 1985: 416). Omodaka is inclined to see this as an unidentified river in the East that has the same name (1977.14: 239–240). Mizushima is of the same opinion, although he painstakingly lists all the theories, some of them quite fantastic (1986: 368). We follow Omodaka and Mizushima's lead here and will define Asuka river in this poem and the following poem as a river in the East with an unknown location.

See the commentary to 14.3402 for the string of two diminutive suffixes *-na-na* in *se-na-na* 'dear beloved'. These diminutive suffixes represent the only EOJ feature in this poem.

This is clearly a woman's poem, because of *se* '[male] beloved' (lit.: 'elder brother') used towards the addressee.

The literal translation of line four *se-na-na-tə puta-ri* is 'with [my] dear beloved, two [of us]'.

14.3546

本文 · Original Text
(1) 安乎楊木能 (2) 波良路可波刀尓 (3) 奈乎麻都等 (4) 西美度波久末受 (5) 多知度奈良須母

仮名の書き下し · Kana Transliteration
(1) あをやぎ₂の₂ (2) はらろ₁かはと₁に (3) なをまつと₂ (4) せみ₁ど₁はくまず (5) たちど₁ならすも₂

Romanization
(1) awo YAᵑGÏ-nə (2) par-ar-o kapato-ni (3) na-wo mat-u tə (4) se miⁿdo pa kum-aⁿz-u (5) tat-i-ⁿ-do naras-umə

Glossing with Morphemic Analysis
(1) green willow-GEN (2) put.forth-PROG-ATTR ford-LOC (3) you-ACC wait-FIN QV (4) clear water TOP draw-NEG-CONV (5) stand-NML-GEN-place flatten-EXCL

Translation

(3) Saying that [I] will wait for you (1/2) at the ford, where green willows are putting forth [their buds], (5) [I] am flattening the place where [I] stand [by walking back and forth] (4) without drawing [any] clear water!

Commentary

On *yaⁿgï* 'willow', also probably *yanaⁿgï*, is a deciduous tree of a small to medium height. There are more than 300 species of it in the world, but only about seventy are found in Japan. The most typical Japanese willow is 枝垂れ柳 'weeping willow', which is believed to have been introduced from China during the Nara period. The name of the tree certainly points to a Chinese-Japanese hybrid origin: WOJ *kï* 'tree' is without any doubt the last component of this word, and the first and second components *ya*- and -*ŋ*- can certainly be equated to EMC 楊 *jiang* 'willow, poplar' and a compressed form of the genitive case marker -*nə*, respectively. The form *yanaⁿgï* is more complex, as it includes *ya*- < EMC *jiang* 'willow', a plural marker -*na*-, -*ŋ*-, a compressed form of the genitive case marker -*nə*, and -*kï* 'tree'.

On the EOJ progressive suffix -*ar*- corresponding to WOJ -*er*- see the commentary to 14.3351.

On the EOJ verbal attributive -*o* see the commentary to 14.3395 and a brief description of EOJ special grammar in the introduction.

OJ *kapato* 'ford' is a transparent compound consisting of *kapa* 'river' and *to* 'door, gate'.

EOJ uninflected adjective *se* 'clear' corresponds to WOJ *si* 'id.' EOJ form is more archaic as it preserves PJ *e, which raised to *i* in WOJ.

EOJ *miⁿdo* 'water' corresponds to WOJ *miⁿdu* 'id.' EOJ form is more archaic as it preserves PJ *o, which raised to *u* in WOJ.

On OJ *to* 'place' see the commentary to 14.3489.

This is certainly a woman's poem, as drawing water was not a man's job (Omodaka 1977.14: 241; Mizushima 1986: 371). Therefore, it clearly shows that the second person pronoun *na* 'you' could be used by a woman in a reference to a man. See also 14.3493 and the following commentary.

14.3548

本文 · *Original Text*

(1) 奈流世呂尒 (2) 木都能余須奈須 (3) 伊等能伎提 (4) 可奈思家世呂尒 (5) 比等佐敝余須母

仮名の書き下し・Kana Transliteration
(1) なるせ₂に (2) こ₂つの₂よ₂すなす (3) いと₂の₂き₁て (4) かなしけ₁せ₂に
(5) ひ₁と₂さへ₁よ₂すも₂

Romanization
(1) nar-u se-rə-ni (2) kətu-nə yəs-u-nasu (3) itə nəkite (4) kanasi-ke se-rə-ni
(5) pitə sape yəs-umə

Glossing with Morphemic Analysis
(1) sound-ATTR rapid-DIM-LOC (2) debris-GEN approach-ATTR-COMP (3) very extremely (4) be.dear-ATTR beloved-DIM-DAT (5) person RP approach-EXCL

Translation
(2) Like the debris approaching (1) in the singing rapids (5) [other] women, too, approach (3/4) [my] beloved, who is extremely dear [to me]!

Commentary
A play on words (*kakekotoba*, 掛詞) between *se* 'rapids' and *se* 'male beloved [lit.: elder brother]' is obviously involved in this poem.

On EOJ diminutive suffix -*rə* see the commentary to 14.3351.

EOJ *kətu* is usually glossed as 'debris', 'waste' (Omodaka et al. 1967: 296). The corresponding WOJ word is *kətumi*.

On OJ *itə nəkite* 'very extremely' is found in three other WOJ texts, with the first two examples *itə nəkite* MInZIKA-KI MƏNƏ-wo PASI kir-u 'to cut the edge of [already] *extremely* short thing' (MYS 5.892) and *itə nəkite* ITA-ki KInZU-ni pa KARA SIPO-wo SOSOK-U 'to sprinkle the pungent salt on an [already] *extremely* painful wound' (MYS 5.897) apparently coming from some proverbs. One more time *itə nəkite* 'very extremely' is attested in MYS 12.2903.

On EOJ attributive -*ke* in *kanasi-ke* see the commentary to 14.3412.

14.3549

本文・Original Text
(1) 多由比我多 (2) 志保弥知和多流 (3) 伊豆由可母 (4) 加奈之伎世呂我 (5) 和賀利可欲波牟

仮名の書き下し・Kana Transliteration
(1) たゆひ₁がた (2) しほみ₁ちわたる (3) いづゆかも₂ (4) かなしき₁せ₂が (5) わがりかよ₁はむ

Romanization
(1) Tayupi-ŋ-gata (2) sipo mit-i-watar-u (3) iⁿdu-yu kamə (4) kanasi-ki se-rə-ŋga (5) wa-ŋgari kayop-am-u

Glossing with Morphemic Analysis
(1) Tayupi-GEN-tideland (2) tide fill-CONV-cross-FIN (3) where-ABL EP (4) beloved-ATTR husband-DIM-POSS (5) I-DIR visit-TENT-ATTR

Translation
(2) The tide is rising over (1) the tideland of Tayupi. (3/4/5) Where will [my] dear beloved visit me from, I wonder?

Commentary
The location of Tayupi tideland is unknown, although it is alternatively identified with various placenames read as Tayupi. The problem is that all of them are located in Western Japan: present-day Kōchi prefecture, Hyōgo prefecture, Shimane prefecture, the easternmost being a part of Tsuruga bay in Fukui prefecture (Nakanishi 1985: 462; Mizushima 1986: 374–375). None of these proposals is likely, because we have here a poem in EOJ. In addition, Japanese character spellings 手結 'hand tied' and 田結 'paddy tied' for Tayupi are in all likelihood *ateji*, since neither 'hand tied' nor 'paddy tied' make good sense for a name of a tideland, if they make sense at all. We believe that this placename has rather transparent Ainu etymology: *tay* 'die'[62] + *yúpe* 'shark'. Given the expected raising of Ainu -*e* to EOJ -*i* and loss of final Ainu -*y* in EOJ loans (see the commentary to 14.3503), Ainu *tay-yúpe* 'dead shark' quite regularly becomes *ta-yupi* in EOJ.

On OJ *kata* 'sea bed, tideland' see the commentary to 14.3503.

EOJ *iⁿdu* 'where' is a *hapax legomenon* corresponding to WOJ *iⁿduku* 'id.' and WOJ bound form *iⁿdu-* 'where' found only in combination with the following locative case marker -*ra*.

On EOJ diminutive suffix -*rə* see the commentary to 14.3351.

14.3551

本文 • Original Text
(1) 阿遅可麻能 (2) 可多尓左久奈美 (3) 比良湍尓母 (4) 比毛登久毛能可 (5) 加奈思家乎於吉弖

---

62   Ainu *tay* 'to die' is Sakhalin Ainu form, corresponding to Hokkaidō Ainu *ray* 'id.', both derived from PA *day or *δay (Vovin 1993: 16–17).

仮名の書き下し・*Kana Transliteration*

(1) あぢかまの₂ (2) かたにさくなみ₁ (3) ひ₁らせにも₂ (4) ひ₁も₁と₂く₁も₁の₂か (5) かなしけ₁をおき₁て

Romanization

(1) Aⁿdikama-nə (2) kata-ni sak-u nami (3) pira sᴇ-ni mə / n-i mə (4) pimo tək-u monə ka (5) kanasi-ke-wo ok-i-te

Glossing with Morphemic Analysis

(1) Aⁿdikama-ɢᴇɴ (2) tideland-ʟᴏᴄ bloom-ᴀᴛᴛʀ/break.and.look.white-ᴀᴛᴛʀ wave (3) ordinary beloved-ᴅᴀᴛ / rapids ᴄᴏᴘ-ᴄᴏɴᴠ ꜰᴘ (4) cord untie-ᴀᴛᴛʀ thing ɪᴘ (5) be.dear-ᴀᴛᴛʀ-ᴀᴄᴄ leave-ᴄᴏɴᴠ-sᴜʙ

Translation

(5) Leaving my darling, (4) will [I] untie the cords [of my garment] (3) with an ordinary lover, [who] is [like] flat rapids, (2) where [the water] breaks and looks white [like] the waves that bloom in the tideland (1) of Aⁿdikama?

Commentary

The first two lines are considered to be a poetic introduction (*jo*, 序) to the rest of the poem that connects *sak-u* 'breaks and looks white' in line two to *pira* 'flat, ordinary' in line three (Omodaka 1977.14: 245–246). This poem is full of plays on words (*kakekotoba*, 掛詞): *sak-* 'to bloom' and 'to break and look like white (of waves)', *pira* 'flat' and 'ordinary', and *se* 'beloved/male lover' and 'rapids'. The last case is especially interesting, because it occurs in spite of the fact that *se* 'rapids' is written logographically as 湍. These word plays required double glossing on the forms that were affected. Also, two-layered translation as presented above was necessary to convey as close as possible these plays on words.

The location of Aⁿdikama is unknown (Nakanishi 1985: 417). Besides being interpreted as a placename (sometimes taken as 味鎌 'taste-sickle', which makes little sense as placename, or as *aⁿdikamo* 'a kind of a wild duck' that violates the principles of the phonetic change: *aⁿdikamo* > *aⁿdikama* is an impossible shift after a labial /m/), it is also explained alternatively as *aⁿdi* 'teal',[63] and *kama*, a tentative contraction of *kamamε* 'seagull', not otherwise attested

---

63 ᴏᴊ *aⁿdi* 'teal' is more exactly 'Baikal teal', ᴍᴅᴊ *tomoegamo* (トモエガモ, *Anas formosa*), which is a small migratory water fowl resembling a wild duck that comes to Japan in winter and lives in flocks at seashores. Male species have a comma-shaped spot (ᴍᴅᴊ *tomoe*) on their heads, hence the origin of ᴍᴅᴊ name (Nakanishi 1985: 288).

(Tsuchiya 1977.7: 392). Although the latter hypothesis might seem attractive at first glance because it allows one to interpret *a^ndi kama-nə kata* as 'the tideland where teals and seagulls [live]', the fact that *kama 'seagull' is not attested makes this interpretation unrealistic. On the contrary, if we follow the traditional interpretation of A^ndikama as a placename, and also dispense with the blinding shores of Japanese as the only possible vehicle of explaining placenames, we get a perfect interpretation via the prism of Ainu: *anci*[64] 'obsidian' (MDJ *kokuyōseki*, 黒曜石) + *kama* 'flat rock, rock' (Chiri 1956: 6, 39). Thus, *a^ndi kama* is 'obsidian [flat] rock', which unlike 'taste-sickle' appears to be quite appropriate for a placename.

On OJ *kata* 'sea bed, tideland' see the commentary to 14.3503.

On a custom among lovers of tying and untying the cords of their garments see the commentary to 14.3361.

On EOJ attributive *-ke* in *kanasi-ke* see the commentary to 14.3412. Note that in this poem the attributive *kanasi-ke* functions not as the adnominal form modifying a following noun, but as a nominalized form 'the dear one'.

14.3552

本文・*Original Text*
(1) 麻都我宇良尓 (2) 佐和惠宇良太知 (3) 麻比登其等 (4) 於毛抱須奈母呂 (5) 和賀母抱乃須毛

仮名の書き下し・*Kana Transliteration*
(1) まつがうらに (2) さわゑうらだち (3) まひ₁と₂ご₂と₂ (4) おも₁ほすなも₂ろ₂ (5) わがも₂ほの₂すも₁

Romanization
(1) Matu-ŋga ura-ni (2) sawaw-e ura-ⁿ-dat-i (3) ma-pitə-ŋ-gətə (4) omop-os-unam-ə rə (5) wa-ŋga [o]məp-o-nəsu mo

Glossing with Morphemic Analysis
(1) pine-POSS bay-LOC (2) make.noise-CONV(?) multitude(?)-COP(CONV)-rise-CONV (3) INT-person-GEN-word (4) think-HON-TENT2-ATTR EP (5) I-POSS think-ATTR-COMP FP

---

64   Ainu /ci/ < PA *ti (Vovin 1993: 12–15), therefore *anci* < *anti.

Translation

(4) [You] are probably thinking (3) about the rumors (2) that are rising noisily in multitude [like waves] (1) in the Pine bay, (5) like [I] am thinking [about them].

Commentary

Line one is hypermetric (*ji amari*, 字余り), but this is probably just a graphic illusion, since *matu-ŋga ura* was in all probability pronounced as [matuŋgara] or [matuŋgura].

Matu-ŋga ura may be either a placename with location unknown, or simply a 'bay where pines grow' (Mizushima 1986: 379). As a placename it is alternatively identified either as Matsukawa bay (松川浦) on the Ohama shore (尾浜) in Sōma city (相馬市) of present-day Fukushima prefecture, or as Matsugahama shore (松ヶ浜) in Shichigahama town (七ヶ浜町) in Miyagi county (宮城郡) of present-day Miyagi prefecture (Nakanishi 1985: 484).

The second line is the most difficult line to interpret: *sawaw-e* is believed to be an EOJ equivalent of WOJ *sawaŋg-i* 'make noise and' and *ura* an EOJ equivalent of WOJ *mura* 'many, multitude' (Mizushima 1986: 379). The obvious difficulties here are that there are no other examples where EOJ -*w*- corresponds to WOJ -*ŋg*-, EOJ -*e* to WOJ -*i* (as a converb marker), and EOJ *o*- to WOJ *m*-.

On EOJ tentative suffix -*unam*- see the commentary to 14.3366.

EOJ *rə* may be either a copula 'to be', or an emphatic particle corresponding to WOJ *yə*, in the same way as EOJ imperative -*rə* corresponds to WOJ -*yə*. The second solution seems to be more likely, since WOJ copula *rə* is a borrowing from Korean, attested independently (outside of compounds) only in early WOJ texts (Vovin 2009a: 547–549).

On the EOJ verbal attributive -*o* (misspelled as -*ə* in this poem) see the commentary to 14.3395 and a brief description of EOJ special grammar in the introduction.

On EOJ comparative case marker -*nəsu* see the commentary to 14.3413.

14.3553

本文 • Original Text

(1) 安治可麻能 (2) 可家能水奈刀尒 (3) 伊流思保乃 (4) 許弓多受久毛可 (5) 伊里弓祢麻久母

仮名の書き下し • Kana Transliteration

(1) あぢかまの₂ (2) かけ₁の₂み₁なと₁に (3) いるしほの₂ (4) こ₂てたずくも₁か (5) いりてねまくも₂

Romanization

(1) Aⁿdikama-nə (2) Kake-nə mIna-to-ni (3) ir-u sipo-nə (4) kətetaⁿzukumoka (5) ir-i-te ne-m-aku mə

Glossing with Morphemic Analysis

(1) Aⁿdikama-GEN (2) Kake-GEN water-door-LOC (3) enter-ATTR tide-COMP (4) ? (5) enter-CONV-SUB sleep-TENT-NML FP

Translation

(5) [I] would sleep entering (4) ? (3) like a tide that enters (2) the estuary of Kake (1) in Aⁿdikama.

Commentary

On Aⁿdikama see the commentary to 14.3551.

The location of Kake is unknown. It has been tentatively identified as a lowland between the Yokosuka (横須賀町) town and Ueno town (上野町) in Tōkai city (東海市) of present-day Aichi prefecture (Nakanishi 1985: 433). However, this seems to be too much of a stretch to the West for a poem that includes a clearly Ainu placename Aⁿdikama and a line that cannot be read in Japanese. Also, OJ Kake is meaningless as a placename, but possibly Ainu *ka-kes* 'upper end' underlies it (with an expected loss of *-s* as a syllable final consonant).

OJ *mina-to* 'water-gate' refers to an estuary, or an entrance to a lagoon. Consequently, if these places were good enough for anchoring boats, they could serve as a 'harbor', which is the only meaning surviving into MDJ.

OJ *mina* 'water' is an interesting word. It still survives in the compounds in the modern Japanese language, for example *mina-to* 'port' (< 'water-door'), *mina-giwa* 'waterfront' (< 'water-edge'), and *mina-moto* 'source', 'fountainhead' (< 'water-base'). The tradition holds that *-na* in *mina* is a genitive case marker, but Alexander Vovin has demonstrated before that this position is untenable, because *mina* 'water' is attested independently in WOJ:

美那許袁呂許袁呂爾
mina kəworə kəworə n-i
water churning churning COP-INF
water churning, churning (KK 100)

美那曾曾久淤美能袁登賣
mina səsək-u omi-nə wotəme
water pour-ATTR noble-GEN maiden
daughter of a noble, who pours **water** (KK 103)

The second example is especially important, because the word *mina* 'water' is found there in the object position, therefore, genitive case marking is not possible.[65] We have long maintained that the *-na* in OJ *mina* 'water' is a relic plural marker, and that the remaining portion *mi-* is cognate to OJ *mⁿdu* 'water' (Vovin 1994: 249; 2020.1: 119–123). However, now we believe that this position was mistaken for the following reason. OJ *mⁿdu* 'water' goes back to *me-ntu,[66] as Ryūkyūan reflexes, such as, e.g. Psara *midzï*, Amami *mïdzï*, etc. indicate PJ *me-, not *mi-. On the other hand, although Ryūkyūan did not preserve the cognate of OJ *mina* as an independent word, there are reflexes of *mina-to 'port' attested as *'Nnatu* in both Shuri and Yaeyama. Only PJ *mi- can go into *'N-* in Ryūkyūan, but not PJ *me-, which is reflected as *mi-*, cf. PJ *memensu 'earthworm' > Shuri *mimizi*. Therefore, OJ *mina* and Ryūkyūan *'Nna-* (in *'Nnatu*) must go back to PJ *mina, not PJ *mena. As a result, OJ *mⁿdu* 'water' and *mina* 'water' cannot be cognates. We suspect that OJ *mina* can indeed be analyzed as *mi-na*, but the real 'water' part in this word is *-na*, not *mi-*. OJ *na-* 'water' also appears in compounds: *na-ŋ-gï* 'water leek' < *na-nə-kï 'water-GEN-leek' and *naⁿduk-* 'to soak in water' < *na-ni-tuk- 'water-LOC-attach'. We believe that OJ *na* 'water' might be a possible borrowing from Tai-Kadai *r-nam 'water' (cf. Siamese *nam⁵* 'id.'), but the detailed discussion of this possibility falls outside of the scope of this book and will be undertaken elsewhere. The remaining part *mi-* in OJ *mi-na* 'water', we believe, can be identified with the honorific prefix *mi-* < PJ *mi-, cf. also OJ *miti* 'way, road' < *mi-ti* 'HON-road' (cf. WOJ *ti-mata* 'road fork'), WOJ *miki* 'rice wine' < *mi-kï*[67] 'HON-wine', etc. The honorific prefix should most likely be reconstructed as *mi- in Ryūkyūan as well (Serafim 2004: 318).

The fourth line seems to be completely resistant to any coherent explanation, although there is no lack of speculative explanations (Mizushima 1986: 381–382).

---

65 This example also demonstrates that the recent proposal of Unger to view *-na* in *mina* as *na* 'inside' (2009: 110–111) fares even worse: 'daughter of the noble pouring *inside* of water'?!

66 The morphological segmentation of the word *mⁿdu* as *mi-ⁿdu* < *me-ntu is supported by WOJ *iⁿdu-mi* 'spring' (< 'go out-water'), as well as by pseudo-Koguryŏ *me 'river, water'. The remaining suffix *-ⁿdu* is probably a collective, also found in *yərə-ⁿdu* 'many, 10,000'.

67 Quite likely from *mi-kï through the vowel assimilation of the second syllable (Murayama 1988: 251–253).

14.3555

本文・*Original Text*
(1) 麻久良我乃 (2) 許我能和多利乃 (3) 可良加治乃 (4) 於登太可思母奈 (5) 宿莫敝兒由惠尓

仮名の書き下し・*Kana Transliteration*
(1) まくらがの₂ (2) こ₂がの₂わたりの₂ (3) からかぢの₂ (4) おと₂だかしも₂な (5) ねなへ₁こ₁ゆゑに

Romanization
(1) Makuraŋga-nə (2) Kəŋga-nə watar-i-nə (3) Kara kaⁿdi-nə (4) otə-ⁿ-daka-si-mə na (5) NE-N-Ape KO yuwe n-i

Glossing with Morphemic Analysis
(1) Makuraŋga-GEN (2) Kəŋga-GEN cross-NML-GEN (3) Korea rudder-GEN (4) sound-GEN-high-FIN-EXCL EP (5) sleep-NEG-ITER(CONV) girl reason COP-CONV

Translation
(4) The [rumors] are loud [like] the sounds (3) of a Korean rudder (2) at Kəŋga crossing (1) in Makuraŋga! (5) [And all] is because of the girl with whom [I] am not sleeping.

Commentary
The exact location of Makuraŋga is not known, but it is supposed to be in the vicinity of Kəŋga (許我) that is believed to correspond to Furukawa city (Furukawa-shi, 古河市) in the part of present-day Ibaraki prefecture that belonged to Simotupusa province (Nakanishi 1985: 484; Mizushima 1986: 220). Given these two placenames, this poem is likely to be from Simotupusa province.

On Kara 'Korea, Korean' see the commentary to 14.3482a.

On OJ *kaⁿdi* is a 'rudder' (Kojima et al. 1975: 55; Nakanishi 1981: 304; Itō 1998: 91; Yoshii 1988: 100), and not an 'oar' (Omodaka 1984.15: 52). Omodaka et al. note that the difference between WOJ *kayi* 'oar' and *kaⁿdi* 'rudder' is not clear (1967: 197), but surely these are two different words. The rudder during this time was certainly a big oar, unlike rudders on modern boats. Although such a rudder does not splash water like an oar, it still can make a significant screeching noise.

On EOJ iterative suffix *-ape-* see the commentary to 14.3529.

On the adnominal function of the converb form in EOJ see the commentary to 14.3415.

14.3556

本文 • *Original Text*

(1) 思保夫祢能 (2) 於可礼婆可奈之 (3) 左宿都礼婆 (4) 比登其等思氣志 (5) 那乎杼可母思武

仮名の書き下し • *Kana Transliteration*

(1) しほぶねの₂ (2) おかればかなし (3) さねつれば (4) ひ₁と₂ご₂と₂しげ₂し (5) なをど₂か₂も₂しむ

Romanization

(1) sipo-ᵐ-bune-nə (2) ok-ar-e-ᵐba kanasi (3) sa-NE-t-ure-ᵐba (4) pitə-ⁿ-gətə siⁿgɛ-si (5) na-wo [a]ⁿ-də kamə si-m-u

Glossing with Morphemic Analysis

(1) tide-GEN-boat-COMP (2) leave-PROG-EV-CON be.sad(FIN) (3) PREF-sleep (CONV)-PERF-EV-CON (4) person-GEN-word be.dense-FIN (5) you-ACC what-QV EP do-TENT-ATTR

Translation

(1/2) When [I] leave [you] like a sea boat, [I] am sad. (3) When [we] sleep together, (4) people's rumors are dense. (5) What shall [I] do with you, I wonder?

Commentary

On *sipo-ᵐ-bune* 'tide-boat' see the commentary to 14.3450. It is believed that the first line represents the permanent epithet (*makura-kotoba*, 枕詞) to the verb *ok-* 'to put, to leave' (Omodaka 1977.14: 253; Mizushima 1986: 386), but this *makura-kotoba* does not occur anywhere else in the *Man'yōshū*. In addition, the comparison is quite transparent here: leaving one's beloved like a sea boat that one no longer uses, therefore we incorporate the first line into our translation.

On the EOJ progressive suffix *-ar-* corresponding to WOJ *-er-* see the commentary to 14.3351.

248　　　　　　　　　　　　　　　　　　　　　　　　　　　　CHAPTER 2

On EOJ interrogative pronoun *a^n-* 'what, why' see the commentary to 14.3379.

EOJ *si-* 'to do' corresponds to WOJ *se-* 'to do'. It is a strange example of raising of a secondary *e* to *i*.

14.3557

本文 • *Original Text*
(1) 奈夜麻思家 (2) 比登都麻可母与 (3) 許具布祢能 (4) 和須礼波勢奈那 (5) 伊夜母比麻須介

仮名の書き下し • *Kana Transliteration*
(1) なやましけ₁ (2) ひ₁と₂つまかも₂よ₂ (3) こ₂ぐふねの₂ (4) わすれはせなな (5) いやも₂ひ₁ますに

Romanization
(1) nayam-asi-ke (2) pitə-tuma kamə yə (3) kəᵑg-u pune-nə (4) wasure pa se-n-a-na (5) iya [o]məp-i mas-u-ni

Glossing with Morphemic Analysis
(1) suffer-ADJ-ATTR (2) person-spouse EP EP (3) row-ATTR boat-COMP (4) forget(NML) TOP do-NEG-ATTR-LOC (5) more.and.more think-NML increase-ATTR-LOC

Translation
(2) Oh, the wife of [another] man, (1) [for whom I] am suffering! (4) [I] will not forget [you] (3) like a boat that is rowing [away], (5) and [my] thoughts [for you] increase more and more, so …

Commentary
On EOJ attributive *-ke* in *nayam-asi-ke* see the commentary to 14.3412.

On *pitə-tuma* 'wife of another man' see the commentary to 14.3472.

On EOJ form in *V-(a)n-a-na* 'V-NEG-ATTR-LOC' see the commentary to 14.3408.

14.3560

本文 • *Original Text*
(1) 麻可祢布久 (2) 尒布能麻曾保乃 (3) 伊呂尒侶弖 (4) 伊波奈久能未曾 (5) 安我古布良久波

仮名の書き下し・*Kana Transliteration*

(1) まかねふく (2) にふの₂まそ₂ほの₂ (3) いろ₂にでて (4) いはなくの₂み₂そ₂ (5) あがこ₁ふらくは

Romanization

(1) ma-kane puk-u (2) Nipu-nə ma-səpo-nə (3) irə-ni [i]ⁿde-te (4) ip-an-aku nəmï sə (5) a-ŋga kop-ur-aku pa

Glossing with Morphemic Analysis

(1) INT-metal blow-ATTR (2) Nipu-GEN INT-red.earth-COMP (3) facial.color-LOC exit(CONV)-SUB (4) say-NEG-NML RP FP (5) I-POSS long.for-ATTR-NML TOP

Translation

(5) As for my longing for [you] (4) [I] just do not tell [you] about it, (3) as it shows in [my] face, (2) [red] like a red earth in Nipu, (1) where [they produce] iron [by] blowing [bellows].

Commentary

OJ *ma-kane*, lit.: 'true metal' is iron, alternatively also called *kuro-ŋ-gane* 'black metal'.

Nipu can be tentatively identified with Kami-nyū (上丹生) or Simo-nyū (下丹生) in Tomioka city (富岡市) in present-day Gunma prefecture (Nakanishi 1985: 473; Mizushima 1986: 391). Consequently, this poem must belong to the Kamitukɛno province. The etymology of the placename Nipu (丹生) could be Japanese (< *ni* 'red earth, red pigment' + *pu* 'thicket'), but it also could be from Ainu, where the placename Nipu 'storage in the forest on the river bank for storing frozen salmon' (< *ni* 'tree' + *pu* 'storage') is also attested (Chiri 1956: 66).

EOJ *səpo* 'red earth, red pigment' probably corresponds to WOJ *sopi* 'light red color'.[68] If so, then the presence of *ə* instead of *o* is the only feature that makes this poem to be in EOJ, and not WOJ. Both EOJ *səpo* and WOJ *sopi* fell out of use after the Nara period, but they might be connected to pseudo-Koguryǒ *sapu* (沙伏, SKSK 35.2a), *sapï* (沙非, SKSK 37.5b), and Paekche *sopi* (所比, SKSK 36.3b) all meaning 'red', either as loans from Old Korean, if these words belong to the Old Korean stratum of placenames recorded in the *Samkwuk saki*, or as

---

[68] It is believed that *səpo* is also present in WOJ (Omodaka et al. 1967: 405), but none of the *Man'yōshū* attestations are phonographic (16.3841 and 16.3843), so it may be that the reading of the character 朱 is either *sopi* or otherwise unattested *sopo. There is a later *kana* gloss そほ /sopo/ in the *Nihonshoki*, but it tells us nothing about the quality of the vowel. Certainly, it is likely that it is *səpə*, because the sequence *[C]oCo is not attested in WOJ, because the first /o/ in such a sequence would raise to /u/, resulting in [C]uCo.

cognates in the peninsular Japonic languages, if they belong to the Japonic stratum of these placenames.

The technique of producing iron in Ancient Japan involved placing a mixture of iron sand and charcoal into a kiln and putting it on the fire. Bellows were used to keep the fire going.

The verbal form *kop-ur-aku* demonstrates that the nominalizer *-aku* actually follows the attributive form of verbs, and not the bare stems. After consonantal verbs the attributive *-u* is lost before *-aku* according to the rules of OJ phonotactics. For details see Vovin (2020.2: 687–688).

14.3561

本文・*Original Text*
(1) 可奈刀田乎 (2) 安良我伎麻由美 (3) 比賀刀礼婆 (4) 阿米乎万刀能須 (5) 伎美乎等麻刀母

仮名の書き下し・*Kana Transliteration*
(1) かなと₁だを (2) あらがき₁まゆみ₁ (3) ひ₁がと₁れば (4) あめ₂をまと₁の₂す (5) き₁み₁をと₂まと₁も₂

Romanization
(1) kana-to-ⁿ-DA-wo (2) ara-ⁿ-gaki ma-yu mi (3) pi-ᵑga tor-e-ᵐba (4) amɛ-wo mat-o-nəsu (5) kimi-wo tə mat-o mə

Glossing with Morphemic Analysis
(1) metal-gate-GEN-paddy-ACC (2) rough-COP(ATTR)-fence space-ABL look (CONV) (3) sun-POSS shine-EV-CON (4) rain-ACC wait-ATTR-COMP (5) lord-ACC FP wait-ATTR FP

Translation
(5) [I] am waiting for [my] lord [to come] (4) like waiting for the rain (3) when the sun is shining (1/2) while looking at the paddy [in front] of the metal [adorned] gate through the spaces in the rough fence!

Commentary
On OJ *kana-to* 'metal adorned gate' see the commentary to 14.3530.

The interpretation of the second line is controversial. We follow here the interpretation adopted by Takeda (1966: 430–31), Kubota (1967: 269), Omodaka

(1977.14: 256–258), and Itō (1997: 574–575). A competing explanation interprets the second line as *ara-ŋ-gak-i ma-yumi* (rough-COP(CONV)-plough-CONV INT-taboo) 'roughly ploughing [the paddy], I cleansed my body (lit.: [cleansed] the taboo' (Takagi et al. 1973: 453; Tsuchiya 1977.7: 400; Nakanishi 1981: 285; Mizushima 1986: 391–392; Aso 2011: 489).[69] There are several major problems with this interpretation. First, to the best of my knowledge, the verb *kak-* 'to scratch' is not attested in the meaning 'to plough' in OJ. Second, EOJ *yumi 'taboo', which is alleged to be a 'corruption' of WOJ *imi* 'id.' is a ghost, not being attested in the texts. Finally, the author of this poem is clearly a woman. Why would she be ploughing a paddy?

EOJ *tor-* 'to shine' is a *hapax legomenon* corresponding to WOJ *ter-* 'id.'

On EOJ comparative case marker *-nəsu* see the commentary to 14.3413.

On the EOJ verbal attributive *-o* see the commentary to 14.3395 and a brief description of EOJ special grammar in the introduction.

On EOJ focus particle *tə* see the commentary to 14.3409.

EOJ *mə* in line five is an emphatic particle, which unlike the WOJ emphatic particle *mə* can follow attributive forms of verbs.

14.3562

本文・*Original Text*
(1) 安里蘇夜尓 (2) 於布流多麻母乃 (3) 宇知奈婢伎 (4) 比登里夜宿良牟 (5) 安乎麻知可祢弖

仮名の書き下し・*Kana Transliteration*
(1) ありそ₁やに (2) おふるたま₂の₂ (3) うちなび₁き₁ (4) ひ₁と₂りやぬらむ (5) あをまちかねて

Romanization
(1) ar-iso ya-ni (2) op-uru tama mə-nə (3) uti-naᵐbik-i (4) pitə-ri ya N-Uram-u (5) a-wo mat-i-kane-te

---

69 There are also modern commentators who mention both interpretations, but remain non-committal (Kojima et al. 1973: 501), and those who declare that the line is simply incomprehensible (Satake et al. 2002: 376).

Glossing with Morphemic Analysis

(1) rough-rock shore-LOC (2) grow-ATTR jewel seaweed-COMP (3) PREF-stretch.out-CONV (4) one-CL IP sleep-TENT2-ATTR (5) I-ACC wait-CONV-NEG.POT(CONV)-SUB

Translation

(4) Will [my beloved] sleep alone (3) stretching out (2) like jewel seaweed that grows (1) at the rough rocky shore, (5) because [she] cannot wait for me?

Commentary

OJ *ar-iso* is a contraction of *ara iso*. It is usually interpreted as 'rough rocky shore', but we should keep in mind that it also can mean 'rough rock', since OJ *iso* has the original meaning 'rock', which later developed the secondary meaning 'rocky shore' as well. This original meaning also appears in 14.3563 below, as well as in other poems.

The word *ya* in the first line is usually believed to be an emphatic particle *ya* (Omodaka 1977.14: 259; Mizushima 1986: 393), but the emphatic particle *ya* cannot precede locative case marker *-ni*. There is a much simpler explanation that does not violate OJ grammar if we take this *ya* to be a loanword from Ainu *ya*[70] 'shore, dry land' (Chiri 1956: 144; Hattori 1964: 212). This loanword is the only EOJ feature in this poem.

14.3563

本文 • Original Text

(1) 比多我多能 (2) 伊蘇乃和可米乃 (3) 多知美太要 (4) 和乎可麻都那毛 (5) 伎曾毛己余必母

仮名の書き下し • Kana Transliteration

(1) ひ₁たがたの₂ (2) いそ₁の₂わかめ₂の₂ (3) たちみ₁だえ₂ (4) わをかまつなも₁ (5) き₁そ₂も₁こ₂よ₂ひ₁も₂

Romanization

(1) Pita-ŋ-gata-nə (2) iso-nə wakamɛ-nə (3) tat-i-miⁿdaye (4) wa-wo ka mat-unam-o (5) kisə mo kə yəpi mə

---

70 From PA *yaa 'shore, dry land' (Vovin 1993: 153).

Glossing with Morphemic Analysis
(1) Pita-GEN-tideland-GEN (2) rock-GEN *wakamɛ*-COMP (3) rise-CONV-be.in.disorder(CONV) (4) I-ACC IP wait-TENT2-ATTR (5) last night FP this night FP

Translation
(4) Would [she] have waited for me, (5) both last night and tonight (3) [with her thoughts] rising in disorder (3) like *wakamɛ* on the rocks (1) in the tideland of Pita?

Commentary
The location of Pita is unknown with certainty, but it tentatively can be identified as a part of Kasumigaura bay (霞ヶ浦) in present-day Ibaraki prefecture (Nakanishi 1985: 478). If this identification is correct, then this poem is from Pitati province. The Ainu origin of this placename is rather transparent: Ainu *pitar* 'stone field' < *pit-tar* 'pebbles-continue one after another' (Chiri 1956: 96). EOJ has apparently borrowed the older form *pittar* < *pit-tar*, as this form in contrast to *pitar* explains the presence of -*t*- rather than -ⁿ*d*- in the EOJ form.

On OJ *kata* 'sea bed, tideland' see the commentary to 14.3503.

OJ *wakamɛ* (ワカメ (若布), *Undaria pinnatifida*) is an edible type of seaweed that is brown in color and grows on the seashore rocks everywhere in Japan with the exception of eastern Hokkaidō and Ryūkyūan islands. It normally ranges from 30 cm to 1 m in length, but can also reach up to 2m. Besides being directly used as an edible substance, *wakamɛ* is also used as an ingredient for making pickles.

EOJ *miⁿdaye-* 'to be in disorder' is a *hapax legomenon* corresponding to WOJ *miⁿdare-* 'id.'

On EOJ tentative suffix -*unam*- see the commentary to 14.3366.

On the EOJ verbal attributive -*o* see the commentary to 14.3395 and a brief description of EOJ special grammar in the introduction.

On OJ *kisə* 'last night' see the commentary to 14.3522.

14.3564

本文 • Original Text
(1) 古須氣呂乃 (2) 宇良布久可是能 (3) 安騰須酒香 (4) 可奈之家兒呂乎 (5) 於毛比須吾左牟

仮名の書き下し・*Kana Transliteration*

(1) こ₁すげ₂ろ₂の₂ (2) うらふくかぜの₂ (3) あど₂すすか (4) かなしけ₁こ₁ろ₂を (5) おも₁ひ₁すご₁さむ

Romanization

(1) ko-suᵑgɛ-rə-nə (2) ura puk-u kanze-nə (3) an-də su su ka (4) kanasi-ke ko-rə-wo (5) omop-i-suᵑgos-am-u

Glossing with Morphemic Analysis

(1) DIM-sedge-DIM-GEN (2) top blow-ATTR wind-COMP (3) why-QV again again IP (4) be.dear-ATTR girl-DIM-ACC (5) think-CONV-pass-TENT-ATTR

Translation

(3/5) Why would [I] pass again [and] again in [my] thoughts (4) [my] dear girl (2) like a wind [that passes] blowing [over] the tops (1) of little sedges?

Commentary

On OJ *suᵑgɛ* 'sedge' see the commentary to 14.3369.

On EOJ diminutive suffix *-rə* see the commentary to 14.3351.

On EOJ interrogative pronoun *an-* 'what, why' see the commentary to 14.3379.

EOJ *ura* 'top of a plant, upper branches [of a tree]' corresponds to WOJ *ure ~ ura-* 'id.', with the expected loss of PJ *-y in EOJ: PJ *uray > EOJ *ura*, cf. PJ *tukuy 'moon' > EOJ *tuku*, PJ *kopoy-* 'long for' > EOJ *kopu-*, etc.

Our interpretation of the first line as 'little sedge' and the word *ura* in the beginning of the second line as 'top of a plant' agrees with the minority's opinion (Kojima 1973: 501; Satake et al. 2002: 377). However, the majority of modern Japanese commentators interpret the word *ura* not as 'top of the plant', but as 'bay', and consequently the whole first line as a placename (Takagi et al. 1959: 455; Takeda 1966: 433; Kubota 1967: 271; Omodaka 1977.14: 260; Tsuchiya 1977.7: 402; Nakanishi 1981: 285; Mizushima 1986: 395; Itō 1997: 578–579; Aso 2011: 491–492). None of these scholars, however, backs this opinion with any detailed argumentation. We believe that two arguments can be made in favor of the minority opinion. First, while the placename Kosuᵑgɛ does indeed exist, there is no placename Kosuᵑgɛrə. In addition, it seems that having both prefixation and suffixation in placenames would be something unusual. Second, the poem is quite plain, if one reads it according to the majority's opinion, but it becomes a real masterpiece with unusual imagery if read in accordance with the minority's point of view.

On EOJ *su* 'again' < Ainu *suy* 'id.' see the commentary to 14.3363. See also 14.3487, especially on the reduplicated form *su su* < Ainu *suy suy*. Needless to say, this interpretation disagrees completely with the tradition, as all the commentators treat this *su su* as OJ *s-u s-u* 'do-FIN do-FIN'.

On EOJ attributive *-ke* in *kanasi-ke* see the commentary to 14.3412.

EOJ *suⁿgos-* 'to pass' is a *hapax legomenon* corresponding to WOJ *suⁿgus-*. The EOJ form is more archaic, as it represents the pre-raised form still preserving PJ *o. MDJ *sugos-* 'to pass' likewise preserves the form that is more archaic than WOJ *suⁿgus-*.

14.3565

本文・*Original Text*
(1) 可能古呂等 (2) 宿受夜奈里奈牟 (3) 波太須酒伎 (4) 宇良野乃夜麻尓 (5) 都久可多与留母

仮名の書き下し・*Kana Transliteration*
(1) かの₂こ₁ろ₂と₂ (2) ねずやなりなむ (3) はだすすき₁ (4) うらの₁の₂やまに (5) つくかたよ₂るも₂

Romanization
(1) kanə ko-rə-tə (2) NE-ⁿz-u ya nar-i-n-am-u (3) paⁿda susuki (4) UraNO-nə yama-ni (5) tuku katayər-umə

Glossing with Morphemic Analysis
(1) that girl-DIM-COM (2) sleep-NEG-CONV IP become-CONV-PERF-TENT-ATTR (3) (*makura-kotoba*) (4) Urano-GEN mountain-LOC (5) moon lean.down-EXCL

Translation
(2) Will it become [so that I] will not sleep (1) with that girl? (4/5) The moon is setting down at the Urano mountain (3) (*makura-kotoba*)!

Commentary
On the opaque permanent epithet (*makura-kotoba*, 枕詞) *paⁿda susuki* see the commentary to 14.3506. Note that in this poem *paⁿda susuki* refers not to the 'ear of rice', but to a specific mountain.

Mt. Urano is tentatively identified as a mountain in Urano town (Urano machi, 宇良野町) in Chiisagata county (Chiisagata-gun, 小県郡) of the present-day Nagano prefecture or as a mountain located almost between Ueda city (Ueda-shi, 上田市) and Matsumoto city (Matsumoto-shi, 松本市) in the same prefecture (Nakanishi 1985: 430; Mizushima 1986: 396). If this identification is correct, this poem is from Sinanu province. On Sinanu province see the commentary to 14.3399.

On EOJ *tuku* 'moon, month' corresponding to WOJ *tukï* 'id.' see the commentary to 14.3395.

14.3566

本文・*Original Text*
(1) 和伎毛古尓 (2) 安我古非思奈婆 (3) 曾和敝可毛 (4) 加未尓於保世牟 (5) 己許呂思良受弖

仮名の書き下し・*Kana Transliteration*
(1) わぎ₁も₁こ₁に (2) あがこ₁ひ₂しなば (3) そ₂わへ₁かも₁ (4) かみ₂におほせむ (5) こ₂こ₂ろ₂しらずて

Romanization
(1) wa-ᵑg-imo-ko-ni (2) a-ᵑga kopï-sin-aᵐba (3) səwape kamo (4) kamï-ni op-ose-m-u (5) kəkərə sir-aⁿz-u-te

Glossing with Morphemic Analysis
(1) I-POSS-beloved-DIM-DAT (2) I-POSS long.for(CONV)-die-COND (3) ? EP (4) deity-DAT carry-CAUS-TENT-ATTR (5) heart know-NEG-CONV-SUB

Translation
(2) If I die from longing (1) for my beloved (3/5) I wonder that [the people around] will not know (4) [my] heart that [I] will let deities carry [away].

Commentary
With the exception of the first two lines, this is a notoriously difficult poem to understand due to an unknown word *səwape* in the third line. There is no lack of explanations cited (Omodaka 1977.14: 262–263; Mizushima 1986: 399), but all of them are done with the complete disregard to the history of the Japanese language and the chronology of its phonological changes. Omodaka et al. mention three major hypotheses, but find them all suspicious (1967: 408). Therefore, there is no point in reviewing any of them. As far as we can tell, in terms of an explanation or an etymology, nothing can be deduced from Ainu, nor from any other neighboring language. The translation presented above is

extremely tentative and should be taken with a big pinch of salt. It partially follows Mizushima's interpretation (1986: 398–399), but not completely, as it takes the deities' curse out of the picture as something that is not substantiated by the text.

We tentatively classify this poem as being written in EOJ due to the mysterious word *səwape* on line three. Certainly WOJ has also its good share of *hapax legomenoi* with unknown meanings, but in the case of *səwape* we have here a very untypical for WOJ vowel sequence *ə – a*. It seems that this sequence occurs much more frequently in EOJ, for example, *ap-an-əpe-* 'continue not to meet' (MYS 14.3472), *kər-əp-aye-* 'be scolded' (MYS 14.3529), etc.

Preface to the Poems 14.3572–3576

本文 • *Original Text*
譬喩歌

Translation
Allegorical poems.

Commentary
This is the title for a short sub-sequence within the poems from unidentified provinces from the book fourteen of the *Man'yōshū*.

14.3572

本文 • *Original Text*
(1) 安杼毛敝可 (2) 阿自久麻夜末乃 (3) 由豆流波乃 (4) 布敷麻留等伎尓 (5) 可是布可受可母

仮名の書き下し • *Kana Transliteration*
(1) あど₂も₁へ₁か (2) あじくまやまの₂ (3) ゆづるはの₂ (4) ふふまると₂き₁に (5) かぜふかずかも₂

Romanization
(1) aⁿ-də [o]mop-e ka (2) Aⁿzikuma yama-nə (3) yuⁿduru pa-nə (4) pupum-ar-u təki-ni (5) kaⁿze puk-aⁿz-u kamə

Glossing with Morphemic Analysis
(1) what-QV think-EV IP (2) Aⁿzikuma mountain-GEN (3) *yuⁿduru* leaf-GEN (4) be.still.in.the.buds-PROG-ATTR time-LOC (5) wind blow-NEG-FIN EP

Translation
(5) [I] wonder whether the wind will not blow (4) when (3) *yuⁿduru* leaves (2) from Mt. Aⁿzikuma (4) are still in the buds – (1) what do [you] think?

Commentary
The allegorical meaning of this poem implies: 'Are you going to touch a girl who is still too young, are you not?' (Omodaka 1977.14: 269; Mizushima 1986: 408–409).

On EOJ interrogative pronoun *aⁿ-* 'what, why' see the commentary to 14.3379.

EOJ [*o*]*mop-e* 'think-EV' corresponds to WOJ *omop-ɛ* 'id.', with evidential -ɛ being misspelled as -*e*. This probably indicates the lack of the contrast between *e* : *ɛ* in the EOJ dialect that underlies this poem.

The exact location of Mt. Aⁿzikuma is unknown, but it is believed to be either Mt. Kokaiyama (Kokai yama, 子飼山) in Tsukuba town (Tsukuba machi, 筑波町)⁷¹ of Tsukuba county (Tsukuba-gun, 筑波郡) in present-day Ibaraki prefecture, or Mt. Hirasawa (Hirasawa yama, 平沢山) in Hirasawa village (Hirasawa mura, 平沢村) in the same township and county (Nakanishi 1985: 416). If either of these identifications is correct, then this poem is from Pitati province. This is further supported by the linguistic data, namely by the EOJ progressive suffix -*ar*- (corresponding to WOJ -*er*-), that occurs in another identified poems from Pitati (14.3351).

OJ *yuⁿduru-pa* is MDJ *yuzuri-ha* (譲り葉, *Daphniphyllum macropodum*), a tall evergreen tree that grows in the wild or can be planted. It is widespread in central and southern Honshū, Kyūshū, and Shikoku. The name of the plant is derived from the fact that when new leaves appear in the spring, old leaves fall off, giving their place (*yuⁿdur-* 'to hand over') for the new leaves. Leaves of *yuⁿduru-pa* are fleshy and smooth, with the underside having a white color. It blooms in summer with small yellowish green flowers that turn into purple fruits. The bark and leaves are used for medicinal purposes, and leaves are used for New Year decorations, especially being attached to *simenawa* 'sacred straw rope' or *kagami-moti* 'large rice cake offered to deities' (Nakanishi 1985: 332; Mizushima 1986: 408). OJ *yuⁿduru-* is an expected reflex in compounds of pre-OJ *yuⁿdurï < PJN *yuⁿduruy. In EOJ bound and free form is the same: *yuⁿduru* due to the regular *-y loss.

---

71   Tsukuba machi was incorporated into Tsukuba city (Tsukuba-shi, つくば市) in 1988.

OJ *pupum-* 'to hold inside [one's mouth]', 'to be still in buds' is believed to be a phonetic variant of OJ *pukum-*, although the latter is attested phonographically only in late *kana* glosses (Omodaka et al. 1967: 631).

On the EOJ progressive suffix *-ar-* corresponding to WOJ *-er-* see the commentary to 14.3351. EOJ progressive suffix *-ar-* occurs in other identified poems from Pitati (14.3351), therefore this poem should be classified as a poem from Pitati province.

There is an interesting morphosyntactic feature in this poem. While in WOJ emphatic particle *kamə* triggers the change of the final verbal form into attributive irrespective of whether it is found before or after the verb (Vovin 2009a: 1235), *puk-aⁿz-u kamə* 'blow-NEG-FIN EP' in line five demonstrates that in EOJ emphatic particle *kamə* does not necessarily trigger this change when it is found after the verb.

14.3576

本文 · *Original Text*
(1) 奈波之呂乃 (2) 古奈宜我波奈乎 (3) 伎奴尓須里 (4) 奈流留麻尓末仁 (5) 安是可加奈思家

仮名の書き下し · *Kana Transliteration*
(1) なはしろの₂ (2) こ₁なぎ₂がはなを (3) き₁ぬにすり (4) なるるまにまに (5) あぜかかなしけ₁

Romanization
(1) napa-sirə-nə (2) ko-naⁿgï-ⁿga pana-wo (3) kinu-ni sur-i (4) nar-uru manima n-i (5) aⁿze ka kanasi-ke

Glossing with Morphemic Analysis
(1) seedling-nursery-GEN (2) DIM-water.leek-POSS flower-ACC (3) garment-LOC rub-CONV (4) get.used/well.worn-ATTR according COP-CONV (5) why IP be.dear-ATTR

Translation
(4) As [I] am getting used [to her] as to well worn (3) garment to which [I] rub (2) the flower of water leek (1) from the seedling nursery, (5) why is [she] so dear to me?

Commentary

On OJ *na*ⁿ*gï* 'water leek' see the commentary to 14.3415. Its flowers are used for dyeing clothes.

OJ *nare-* represents a play on words (*kakekotoba*, 掛詞) between *nare-* 'to get used to' and *nare-* 'to wear clothes out'.

On EOJ *a*ⁿ*ze* 'why' see the commentary to 14.3369.

On EOJ attributive *-ke* in *kanasi-ke* see the commentary to 14.3412.

Postscript to the Poems 14.3438–3577

本文 · *Original Text*

以前歌詞未得勘知國土山川之名也

Translation

The names of lands, places, mountains, and rivers in the poems above still cannot be identified.

Commentary

This is a postscript to the whole unidentified section of Azuma poems in book fourteen of the *Man'yōshū*, meaning that the local origin of these poems is unknown. See, however, the Introduction to this volume on the possibility of determining the local origins of at least some of the poems 14.3438–3577 found in the unidentified section.

End of Book Fourteen

CHAPTER 3

萬葉集卷第十六・*Man'yōshū* Book Sixteen

16.3865

本文・*Orfiginal Text*
(1) 荒雄良者 (2) 妻子之産業乎波 (3) 不念呂 (4) 年之八歳乎 (5) 待騰來不座

仮名の書き下し・*Kana Transliteration*
(1) あらをらは (2) め₁こ₁の₂なりをば (3) おも₂はずろ₂ (4) と₂しの₂やと₂せを (5) まてど₂き₁まさず

Romanization
(1) Arawo-ra pa (2) ME KO-Nə NARI-woᵐba (3) OMƏP-Aⁿz-U rə (4) TƏSI-Nə YA-TƏSE-WO (5) MAT-E-ⁿdə K-I-mas-aⁿz-U

Glossing with Morphemic Analysis
(1) Arawo-DIM TOP (2) wife child-GEN daily.chores-ACC(EMPH) (3) think-NEG-FIN EP (4) year-GEN eight-CL-ACC (5) wait-EV-CONC come-CONV-HON-NEG-FIN

Translation
(1) [Our] dear Arawo (3) does not think (2) about his wife and children's livelihood. (5) [He] does not come back although [we] wait for [for him] (4) for eight years.

Commentary
On OJ *nari* 'daily chores' see the poem 5.801 (Vovin 2011: 30).

The emphatic particle *rə* on line three is the same as EOJ *rə*, attested, e.g. in 14.3552. Both correspond to WOJ emphatic particle *yə*.

Preface to the Poems 16.3878–3880

本文・*Original Text*
能登國歌三首

© ALEXANDER VOVIN AND SAMBI ISHISAKI-VOVIN, 2022 | DOI:10.1163/9789004471665_005

Translation

Three poems from Noto province.

Commentary

Noto province (Noto-no kuni, 能登國) had some turbulent history. It was created on the second day of the fifth lunar month of the second year of Yōrō (June 4, 718 AD) by separating it from Wettiu province (Wettiu-no kuni, 越中國). On the tenth day of the twelfth lunar month of the thirteenth year of Tenpyō (January 20, 742 AD), Noto province was merged again with Wettiu province, when it became Noto district (Noto-no kopori, 能登郡) of Wettiu province, which corresponds to present-day Nanao city (Nanao-shi, 七尾市) and Kashima county (Kashima-gun, 鹿島郡) of Ishikawa prefecture (石川県). On the ninth day of the fifth lunar month of the ninth year of Tenpyō-Shōhō[1] (May 31, 757 AD) it again became a separate province (Omodaka 1977.16: 221; Nakanishi 1985: 475; Hashimoto 1985: 302–303). Noto province was one of the Middle Provinces (Chūkoku, 中國) according to the *Ritsuryō* code. On the *Ritsuryō* code classification of Yamatə provinces see the commentary to the postscript to the poem 14.3349.

The place name Noto reflects Ainu *not* 'cape, promontory'. Attested also in the preface to the poems 17.4026–4027 and in the poem 17.4026. See also Vovin (2009b: 6).

16.3878

本文 • *Original Text*

(1) 階楯 (2) 熊來乃夜良尓 (3) 新羅斧 (4) 堕入和之 (5) 阿毛侶阿毛侶 (6) 勿鳴爲曾禰 (7) 浮出流夜登 (8) 將見和之

仮名の書き下し • *Kana Transliteration*

(1) はしたての₂ (2) くまき₁の₂やらに (3) しらき₂をの₂ (4) おと₂しいれわし (5) あも₁てあも₁て (6) ななかしそ₂ね (7) うき₁いづるやと₂ (8) み₁むわし

Romanization

(1) PASI tate-Nə (2) Kumaki-nə yara-ni (3) SIRAKÏ WONə (4) OTəS-I IRE wasi (5) a-mo-te a-mo-te (6) NA-NAK-AS-i-sə-n-e (7) UK-I-IⁿD-uru ya tə (8) MI-M-U wasi

---

1 The ninth year of Tenpyō-Shōhō is the same as the first year of Tenpyō-Hōji.

Glossing with Morphemic Analysis
(1) ladder make.stand(NML)-COMP (2) Kumaki-GEN sea-LOC (3) Silla ax (4) drop-CONV put.inside(CONV) INTERJ (5) 1ps-sleep-CAUS 1ps-sleep-CAUS (6) NEG-cry-HON-CONV-do-DES-IMP (7) float-CONV-go.out-ATTR IP QV (8) see-TENT-ATTR INTERJ

Translation
(4) [You] dropped, oh, no, (3) [your] Silla ax (2) into the sea of Kumaki, (1) [where rocks are steep] like ladders. (6) [I] wish [you] do not cry– (7/8) do [you] expect that [it] will float back up? – Oh, no – (5) [this] makes me asleep, [this] makes me asleep.

Commentary
Takeda defines this poem as *sedōka* (1957.11: 318), but since it has an extremely bizarre meter, it cannot be classified as either *sedōka* or any other known poetic form.

Note that this poem has considerable chunks written phonographically.

OJ *pasi tate-nə* 'like standing ladder' is a permanent epithet (*makurakotoba*, 枕詞) for storages and steep mountains, but its usage with the place name Kumaki is not clear (Omodaka et al. 1967: 577–578). The sea shore on the Eastern side of Noto peninsula is also quite flat and not steep at all, so it is a real mystery why OJ *pasi tate-nə* 'like standing ladder' is used in this poem. Maybe there were some steep rocks thirteen hundred years ago, which have crumbled since that time.

Kumaki village (Kumaki mura, 熊來村) corresponds to the present-day central part of Nakajima town (Nakajima machi, 中島町)[2] in Kashima county of Ishikawa prefecture (Hashimoto 1985: 302). Kumaki village is facing the sea, but there is also a Kumaki river, which has its picture in Omodaka (1977.16: 223).

The word *yara* (夜良) does not have a good Japonic explanation, e.g. Omodaka et al. list 'fish trap', 'marsh', and 'paddy' as possibilities (1967: 775), but all of them are highly unlikely in the given context. There is, however, a possible Ainu explanation:[3] Ainu *ya* is 'dry land', or 'to go up to the dry land from the water', and *ra* is 'low place'. Thus, *ya-ra* will be 'the low place from which one goes up to the dry land'. Consequently, *yara* in *Kumaki-nə yara* implies either a sea or a river. There is no way to tell with an absolute certainty which one is

---

2 Nakajima town was incorporated into Nanao city (Nanao-shi, 七尾市) in 2004.
3 Such a possibility was already suggested by Omodaka (1977.16: 224), but he used wrong Ainu words.

meant here, but since Ainu *ya* 'dry land' is most frequently used in opposition to Ainu *atuy* 'sea', and not to Ainu *pet* or *nay* 'river', we decided to use 'sea' here. This is also supported by the mention of the sea in the postscript to this poem.

OJ *Siraki͡wonə* is a 'Silla ax', that is a type of an ax made in Silla. Unfortunately, we do not know what type of an ax it was (Takeda 1957.11: 318). Siraki (or Siraŋgi, 新羅) is a Japanese name corresponding to OK Sela, the name of Silla, one of the Three Kingdoms (MDK Samguk, 三國) on Korean peninsula. Here, however, it apparently refers to United Silla (668–935 AD), which unified the peninsula in 668 AD.

The interjection *wasi* expresses disappointment (Vovin 2020.1.2: 1220). It is extremely rare, being attested only four times in two adjacent poems in the *Man'yōshū*: 16.3878 and 16.3879. The fact that it appears only in these two poems that are both from Noto province strongly suggests that it is a local word. Japanese scholars disagree how to interpret it, and some suggestions listed in Omodaka (1977.16: 224) are pretty wild, such as Kamo-no Mabuchi's hypothesis that it is a second person pronoun, resulting from a contraction *wa nusi* 'my master' > *wasi*. Certainly, such a contraction would not be possible in Old Japanese. Besides, addressing an ax as 'my master' would be very strange at least. Thus, we prefer our analysis of *wasi* as an interjection.

The extremely unreliable Ide and Mori publication claims that line five 阿毛侶阿毛侶 appears as such only in the *Ruijū koshū* and in the *Hirose-bon*, being 河毛侶河毛侶 in all other manuscripts (2012: 423). However, this is not true, since the *Amagasaki-bon* also has 阿毛侶阿毛侶. Thus, the evidence from two older manuscripts, the *Ruijū koshū* and *Amagasaki-bon* and the *Hirose-bon* from Teika line all offer evidence for 阿, and not 河, therefore I opt for 阿. Surprisingly, both Takeda (1957.11: 318) and especially Omodaka (1977.16: 221), who is usually very attentive to textological issues, both have opted for 河 without any explanation. Then there is a problem how to read 阿毛侶: *amote* or *akɛte*. Omodaka further notes that 毛 /ke/ is *kungana*, and mixing *ongana* with *kungana* is contradictory (1977.16: 224). Although, such cases of mixing exist, in this case we prefer to read 毛 as /mo/, because there are many more cases of 毛 usage as an *ongana* phonogram /mo/ than as a *kungana* sign /ke/. The resulting *amote* cannot be explained as Japonic, let alone Old Japanese, but it can be analyzed in Ainu as *a-*, storytelling first person singular prefix, *mo* 'to sleep', and *-te*, a causative suffix. The *amote* would mean '[it] made me sleepy', 'I was put to sleep'.

The usage of an honorific *-as-* on line six is apparently done in mockery of the stupid person who does not know that the iron cannot float.

Postscript to the Poem 16.3878

本文・*Original Text*
右歌一首傳云或有愚人斧墮海底而不解鐵沈無理浮水聊作此歌口吟爲喩也

Translation
[Here] is the story [they] tell about the above [poem]. There was a stupid man who dropped [his] ax to the sea bottom and did not know that [once] iron [object] submerges, [it] cannot float back to the water [surface]. [Then someone] composed this poem to make [him] realize [the truth].

Commentary
This story is an apparent allusion to a Chinese fable from the *Lüshi chūnqiū* (呂氏春秋)[4] about a man who dropped his sword into a river:

楚人有涉江者其劍自舟中墜於水遽刻其舟曰是吾劍所墜舟止從其所刻者入水求之舟已行矣而劍不行求劍若此不亦惑乎

There was a man from [the kingdom] of Chǔ who crossed a river. His sword fell from [his] boat into the water. Then [he] immediately cut a mark on his boat saying: "This is the place where my sword fell. After the boat [it] fell from stops, [I] will follow this mark and entering the water [I] will find it. Although the boat went away, the sword did not move. Finding [my] sword should be easy!"

Note that the folklore form of a poem, which also contains Ainu elements in it, may constitute contradiction with the knowledge of Chinese Classics. Could its author be a local aristocrat with an Ainu mother?

16.3879

本文・*Original Text*
(1) 堵楢 (2) 熊來酒屋尓 (3) 眞奴良留奴和之 (4) 佐須比立 (5) 率而來奈麻之乎 (6) 眞奴良留奴和之

---

[4] A collection of 160 stories in twenty-six books compiled by Lü Buwei (呂不韋), a famous politician of Qin in 239 BC.

仮名の書き下し・*Kana Transliteration*
(1) はしたての₂ (2) くまき₁さかやに (3) まぬらるやつこ₁わし (4) さすひ₁たて (5) ゐてき₁なましを (6) まぬらるやつこ₁わし

Romanization
(1) PASI tate-nə (2) Kumaki SAKA-YA-ni (3) ma-nur-ar-u YATUKO wasi (4) sasup-i-TATE (5) WI-TE K-I-n-amasi-wo (6) ma-nur-ar-u YATUKO wasi

Glossing with Morphemic Analysis
(1) ladder make.stand(NML)-COMP (2) Kumaki wine-shop-LOC (3) INT-scold-PASS-ATTR dude INTERJ (4) invite-CONV-make.stand(CONV) (5) take.along(CONV)-SUB come-CONV-SUBJ-ACC (6) INT-scold-PASS-ATTR dude INTERJ

Translation
(3) Oh, dude who was really scolded (2) in the wine shop of Kumaki, (1) [where rocks are steep] like ladders, (4) [I] would invite and (5) take [you] along [with me], but (6) oh, dude, [you] were really scolded.

Commentary
The poetic form of this poem unlike the previous poem 16.3878 looks more like a *sedōka*, but the *sedōka* meter of 5-7-7-5-7-7 is made hypermetric (*ji amari*, 字余り) in lines three and six by the interjection *wasi*.

On OJ *pasi tate-nə* see the commentary to the poem 16.3878.

On Kumaki see the commentary to the poem 16.3878.

The verbal form *ma-nur-ar-u* 'is really scolded' on lines three and six looks like an Eastern Old Japanese form, as one would expect WOJ *ma-nur-ar-uru.

Takeda believes that *yatuko* is a slave working in the wine shop (1957.11: 319). But certainly no one would invite a slave working there to drink, and we have strong doubts that slaves would have been allowed to drink in same wine shops with free folks. Therefore, *yatuko* here is probably nothing but a pejorative form of address like 'dude' to a fellow who might have been scolded because he initiated some fight or a drunken brawl at the wine shop.

On OJ interjection *wasi* see the commentary to the poem 16.3878.

Notice that *sasup-* 'to invite' may possibly look like an Eastern Old Japanese form. Unfortunately, we do not have *sasop- attested in Western Old Japanese, and MJ *sasop-* 'id.' may be just a form preserving archaic vocalism.

Postscript to the Poem 16.3879

本文・*Original Text*
右一首

Translation
The poem above ...

Commentary
Like the postscript to the poems 16.3851, 16.3852, 16.3858–3859, 16.3870, 16,3871, 16.3972–3873, 16.3874, and 16.3875, the postscript here also did not survive except for the three characters. Unfortunately, we have no means to reconstruct its original text that probably contained information on the story with which this poem is connected to, as well as the name of an author.

16.3880

本文・*Original Text*
(1) 所聞多禰乃 (2) 机之嶋能 (3) 小螺乎 (4) 伊拾持來而 (5) 石以 (6) 都追伎破夫利 (7) 早川尒 (8) 洗濯 (9) 辛塩尒 (10) 古胡登毛美 (11) 高坏尒盛 (12) 机尒立而 (13) 母尒奉都也 (14) 目豆兒乃刀自 (15) 父尒獻都也 (16) 身女兒乃刀自

仮名の書き下し・*Kana Transliteration*
(1) かしまねの₂ (2) つくゑの₂しまの₂ (3) しただみ₁を (4) いひり₁ひ₁も₂ちき₁て (5) いし₁も₂ち (6) つつき₁やぶり (7) はやかはに (8) あらひ₁すすき₁ (9) からしほに (10) こ₁ご₁と₂も₁み₁ (11) たかつき₁にもり (12) つくゑにたてて (13) ははにあへ₂つや (14) め₂づこ₁の₂と₁じ (15) ちちにあへ₂つや (16) み₂め₁ご₁の₂と₁じ

Romanization
(1) Kasima ne-nə (2) TUKUWE-Nə SIMA-nə (3) SITAⁿDAMI-WO (4) i-PIRIP-I-MƏT-I-K-I-TE (5) ISI MƏT-I (6) tutuk-i YAᵐbur-i (7) PAYA KAPA-ni (8) ARAP-I SUSUK-I (9) KARA SIPO-ni (10) koⁿgo tə mom-i (11) TAKA TUKI-ni MOR-I (12) TUKUWE-ni TATE-TE (13) PAPA-ni APƐ-t-u ya (14) MƐⁿD-U KO n-ə toⁿzi (15) TITI-ni APƐ-t-u ya (16) MÏ ME ᵑGO n-ə toⁿzi

Glossing with Morphemic Analysis
(1) Kasima peak-GEN (2) Tukuwe-GEN island-GEN (3) *sitaⁿdami*-ACC (4) DLF-gather-CONV-take-CONV-come-CONV-SUB (5) stone take-CONV (6) hit-CONV

break-CONV (7) rapid river-LOC (8) wash-CONV rinse-CONV (9) pungent salt-LOC (10) *koⁿgo* QV rub-CONV (11) high goblet-LOC put.up-CONV (12) tray. table-LOC make.stand(CON)-SUB (13) mother-DAT give(CONV)-PERF-FIN IP (14) love-ATTR girl COP-ATTR mistress (15) father-DAT offer(CONV)-PERF-FIN IP (16) body woman girl COP-ATTR mistress

Translation
(4) [You] gather and bring back [home] (3) *sitaⁿdami* seashells (2) from Tukuwe island (1) [in the area] of Kasima peaks, (6) hitting and breaking [them] (5) with a stone, and (8) washing and rinsing [them] (7) in a rapid river, and (10) rubbing [them] with a *koⁿgo* sound (9) in the pungent salt, and (12) placing [them] on table tray packed highly (11) being plentifully packed into a high goblet, (14) mistress [of the house], my beloved girl (13) did [you] give [them] to [my] mother? (16) [You, who are] the embodiment [of my] girl-wife, (15) did [you] offer [them] to [my] father?

Commentary
This *chōka* has even number of lines and not expected odd.

Kasima peak or peaks is/are probably the mountains facing Nanao bay (Nanao wan, 七尾湾) (Nakanishi 1985: 435).

WOJ *tukuwe* is a tray shaped like a low table. Tukuwe-nə sima is either Tukuejima (机島) in Nakajima town (Nakajima chō, 中島町) of Kashima county (Kashima gun, 鹿島郡) in present-day Ishikawa prefecture, or it is actually a couple of islands: Oshima 'Male Island' (雄島) and Meshima 'Female Island' (雌島) outside of Nanao harbor (Nakanishi 1985: 464).

WOJ *sitaⁿdami* (MDJ *gangara*, 小螺) is a general name for edible small size conch shellfish, which has almost circular shape. It attaches to rocks and moves around them (Nakanishi 1985: 295).

Lines five and six are hypometric (*ji tarazu*, 字足らず).

WOJ *koⁿgo* is onomatopoeia for squeezing the meat of *sitaⁿdami* (Takeda 1957.II: 322)

The verbal form *mɛⁿd-u* on line fourteen cannot be a final form. It is an attributive like in Eastern Old Japanese. One would expect WOJ *mɛⁿd-uru* as an attributive.

The character 召 is actually a combination of two ongana signs 刀 /to/ and 自 /ⁿzi/, put vertically one on another. Therefore, we treat it as a phonogram.

Preface to the Poems 16.3885–3886

本文 · *Original Text*
乞食者詠二首

Translation
Two poems composed by a beggar.

Commentary
Takeda believes that these two poems represent a prayer for longevity performed by a beggar in exchange for food (1957.11: 327–328). Omodaka expresses the same opinion (1977.16: 237). Certainly, we cannot tell for sure whether these two poems are composed by one and the same beggar or by two different beggars.

16.3885

本文 · *Original Text*
(1) 伊刀古 (2) 名兄乃君 (3) 居々而 (4) 物尓伊行跡波 (5) 韓國乃 (6) 虎云神乎 (7) 生取尓 (8) 八頭取持來 (9) 其皮乎 (10) 多々弥尓刺 (11) 八重疊 (12) 平群乃山尓 (13) 四月与 (14) 五月間尓 (15) 藥獦 (16) 仕流時尓 (17) 足引乃 (18) 此片山尓 (19) 二立 (20) 伊智比何本尓 (21) 梓弓 (22) 八多婆佐弥 (23) 比米加夫良 (24) 八多婆左弥 (25) 宍待跡 (26) 吾居時尓 (27) 佐男鹿乃 (28) 來立嘆久 (29) 頓尓 (30) 吾可死 (31) 王尓 (32) 吾仕牟 (33) 吾角者 (34) 御笠乃波夜詩 (35) 吾耳者 (36) 御墨坩 (37) 吾目良波 (38) 眞墨乃鏡 (39) 吾爪者 (40) 御弓乃弓波受 (41) 吾毛等者 (42) 御筆波夜斯 (43) 吾皮者 (44) 御箱皮尓 (45) 吾宍者 (46) 御奈麻須波夜志 (47) 吾伎毛母 (48) 御奈麻須波夜之 (49) 吾美義波 (50) 御塩乃波夜之 (51) 耆矣奴 (52) 吾身一尓 (53) 七重花佐久 (54) 八重花生跡 (55) 白賞尼 (56) 白賞尼

仮名の書き下し · *Kana Transliteration*
(1) いと₁こ₁ (2) なせの₂き₁み₁ (3) をりをりて (4) も₂の₂にいゆくと₂は (5) からくにの₂ (6) と₁らと₂いふかみ₂を (7) いけ₂と₂りに (8) やつと₂りも₂ちき₁ (9) そ₂の₂かはを (10) たたみ₁にさし (11) やへ₁たたみ₁ (12) へ₁ぐりの₂やまに (13) うづき₂と₂ (14) さつき₂の₂ほど₂に (15) くすりがり (16) つかふると₂き₁に (17) あしひ₁き₂の₂ (18) こ₂の₂かたやまに (19) ふたつたつ (20) いちひ₁がも₂と₂に (21) あづさゆみ₁ (22) やつたばさみ₁ (23) ひ₁め₂かぶら (24) やつたばさみ₁ (25) ししまつと₂ (26) わがをると₂き₁に (27) さをしかの₂ (28) き₁たちなげ₂かく (29) たちまちに (30) あれはしぬべ₂し (31) おほき₁

み₁に (32) あれはつか $ \mathrm{\hat{\wedge}}_{2} $ む (33) あがつの₁は (34) み₁かさのはやし (35) あがみ₁ み₁は (36) み₁すみ₁つぼ (37) あがめ₂らは (38) ますみ₁の₂かがみ₁ (39) あがつめ₂ は (40) み₁ゆみ₁の₂ゆはず (41) あがけ₂らは (42) み₁ふみ₁てはやし (43) あがかは は (44) み₁はこ₁の₂かはに (45) あがししは (46) み₁なますはやし (47) あがき₁も₁も₂ (48) み₁なますはやし (49) あがみ₁げ₂は (50) み₁しほの₂はやし (51) おいはての₁ (52) あがみ₂ひ₁と₂つに (53) なな $ \mathrm{\hat{\wedge}}_{1} $ はなさく (54) や $ \mathrm{\hat{\wedge}}_{1} $ はなさくと₂ (55) まうしはやさ ね (56) まうしはやさね

Romanization

(1) itoko (2) na SE n-ə KIMI (3) WOR-I WOR-I-TE (4) MƏNƏ-ni i-YUK-U tə pa (5) Kara KUNI-nə (6) TORA Tə IP-U KAMÏ-wo (7) IKƐ-ⁿ-DƏR-I n-i (8) YA-TU TƏR-I-MƏT-I-K-I (9) SƏNƏ KAPA-wo (10) tatami-ni SAS-I (11) YA PE TATAMI (12) Peⁿguri-nə YAMA-ni (13) UⁿDUKÏ-Tə (14) SATUKÏ-NƏ POⁿDƏ-ni (15) KUSURI-ᵑ-GARI (16) TUKAP-uru TƏKI-ni (17) ASI pikï n-ə (18) KƏNƏ kata YAMA-ni (19) PUTA-TU TAT-U (20) itipi-ᵑga MƏTƏ-ni (21) AⁿDUSA YUMI (22) YA-TU ta-ᵐ-basam-i (23) pimɛ kaᵐbura (24) YA-TU ta-ᵐ-basam-i (25) SISI MAT-U tə (26) WA-ᵑGA WOR-U TƏKI-ni (27) sa-wo SIKA-nə (28) K-I TAT-I NAᵑGƐK-Aku (29) TATIMATI n-i (30) ARE PA SIN-UᵐBƐ-SI (31) OPO KIMI-ni (32) ARE PA TUKAPƐ-m-u (33) A-ᵑGA TUNO pa (34) MI-KASA-nə payas-i (35) A-ᵑGA MIMI pa (36) MI-SUMI TUᵐBO (37) A-ᵑGA MƐ-ra pa (38) MA-sumi n-ə KAᵑGAMI (39) A-ᵑGA TUMƐ pa (40) MI-YUMI-nə YUpaⁿzu (41) A-ᵑGA KƐ-ra pa (42) MI-PUMITE payas-i (43) A-ᵑGA KAPA pa (44) MI-PAKO-nə KAPA n-i (45) A-ᵑGA sisi pa (46) MI-namasu payas-i (47) A-ᵑGA kimo mə (48) MI-namasu payas-i (49) A-ᵑGA miⁿgɛ pa (50) MI-SIPO-nə payas-i (51) OYI-PATE-n-o (52) A-ᵑGA MÏ PITƏ-TU-ni (53) NANA PE PANA sak-u (54) YA PE PANA SAK-U tə (55) MAWUS-I-PAYAS-An-e (56) MAWUS-I-PAYAS-An-e

Glossing with Morphemic Analysis

(1) dear (2) I beloved COP-ATTR lord (3) exist-CONV exist-CONV-SUB (4) thing-LOC DLF-go-FIN QV TOP (5) Korea land-GEN (6) tiger QV say-ATTR deity-ACC (7) make.alive(NML)-COP(ATTR)-catch-NML COP-CONV (8) eight-CL catch-CONV-bring-CONV-come-CONV (9) their pelt-ACC (10) mat-LOC spread-CONV (11) eight layer mat (12) Peⁿguri-GEN mountain-LOC (13) fourth.lunar.month-COM (14) fifth.lunar.month-GEN time-LOC (15) medicine-GEN-hunt (16) serve-ATTR time-LOC (17) foot low COP-ATTR (18) this one mountain-LOC (19) two-CL stand-ATTR (20) yew-POSS bottom-LOC (21) catalpa bow (22) eight-CL hand-LOC-squeeze-CONV (23) arrow arrow.tip (24) eight-CL hand-LOC-squeeze-CONV (25) game wait-FIN QV (26) we-POSS exist-ATTR time-LOC (27) PREF-male deer-GEN (28) come-CONV stand-CONV

lament-NML (29) immediate COP-CONV (30) I TOP die-DEB-FIN (31) Great Lord-DAT (32) I TOP serve-TENT-FIN (33) I-POSS horn TOP (34) HON-hat-GEN glorify-CONV (35) I-POSS ear TOP (36) HON-ink pot (37) I-POSS eye-PLUR TOP (38) INT-clear COP-ATTR mirror (39) I-POSS hoof TOP (40) HON-bow-GEN bow.string.notch (41) I-POSS hair-PLUR TOP (42) HON-writing.brush glorify-CONV (43) I-POSS hide TOP (44) HON-coffer-GEN hide COP-CONV (45) I-POSS meat TOP (46) HON-sashimi-GEN glorify-CONV (47) I-POSS liver FP (48) HON-sashimi-GEN glorify-CONV (49) I-POSS stomach TOP (50) HON-pickle-GEN glorify-CONV (51) become.old(CONV)-finish-PERF-ATTR (52) I-POSS body one-CL-LOC (53) seven layer flower bloom-FIN (54) eight layer flower bloom-FIN QV (55) say(HUM)-CONV-glorify-DES-IMP (56) say(HUM)-CONV-glorify-DES-IMP

Translation

(12) At Peⁿguri mountain (11) [that is like] eight-layered mat, where (1/2) my dear and beloved lord (3) after [he] sat and sat [at home], (8) brought back eight (7) captured alive tigers (6) whom [they] call deities in Korea, (4) after [he] went there on an expedition, and (9/10) spread their pelts on, (13/14) at the time of fourth lunar month and fifth lunar month, (15/16) at the time when [they] serve [doing] medicine hunt, (22) holding in [our] hands many (21) catalpa bows, and (24) holding in [our] hands many (23) arrows with [sharp] turnip-shaped arrowheads (19/20) under two yews standing (18) on this side of the mountain (17) with low feet, (25/26) at the time when [we] were waiting for game animals, (27) a male deer (28) came, stood [there], and lamented: "(30) I must die (29) right away. (32) [Therefore,] I will serve (31) to the Great Lord. (33) My horns (34) will decorate [his] hat, and (35) my ears (36) [his] inkpot. (37) My eyes [will decorate] (38) [his] clear mirror, [and] (39) my hooves (40) [his] bow string notches. (41) My hairs (42) will be the glory of [his] writing brush. (43) My hide (44) will cover [his] coffer. (45) My meat (46) will be [his] *sashimi* delicacy, and (47) my liver, too, (48) will be [his] *sashimi* delicacy. (49) My stomach (50) will be his pickled delicacy. (55) Glorify [me] saying, (56) glorify [me] saying (53) that seven layers of flowers will bloom, (54) eight layers of flowers will bloom (52) at my body alone (51) that has finally become old".

Commentary

This *chōka* has even number of lines and not expected odd. This might be due to the fact that line fifty-six is a repetition of line fifty-five. Note also that lines fifty-four, fifty-five, and fifty-six all have seven syllables.

Line one is hypometric (*ji tarazu*, 字足らず).

Although historically WOJ *itoko* apparently consists of *ito 'dear' and *ko* 'child', there is no synchronic evidence for drawing morphological boundary between these two words, because WOJ *ito is not attested by itself outside of the compound *itoko*.

Line two is hypometric (*ji tarazu*, 字足らず).

OJ *na* 'I' is a very rare pronoun. It was apparently borrowed from OK *na 'id.' (not attested phonographically, cf. MK *na* 'id.'). For details see Vovin (2005a: 245–246).

Line four is hypermetric (*ji amari*, 字余り). Note that there is no possibility that -*ni i*- would contract to [ni], because then the directive-locative prefix *i*- would be lost in recitation of this line.

On Kara 'Karak, Korea' see the commentary to the poem 14.3482a.

Line six is hypermetric (*ji amari*, 字余り), although there is a possibility that it is just a graphic illusion because *tə ip*- could have been contracted to *təp*-.

WOJ *tora* 'tiger' is a large feline carnivore animal with yellow hide that has black stripes. It is not endemic to Japan, and its hides were imported from Korea (Nakanishi 1985: 297). The reference to a tiger as a deity may be reminiscent of Ainu *kamúy*, which can mean both 'deity' and 'bear'. Apparently, a large strong animal that could be overcome by humans only with great difficulty could be perceived as a deity.

Peⁿguri mountains stretch from the South of Ikoma city (Ikoma shi, 生駒市) through Ikoma town (Ikoma chō, 生駒町) of Ikoma county (Ikoma gun, 生駒郡) and form Heguri valley (Heguri tani, 平郡谷), where Tatsuta river (Tatsutagawa, 龍田川) is flowing (Nakanishi 1985: 482).

Line thirteen is hypometric (*ji tarazu*, 字足らず).

OJ *kata yama* (lit.: 'one mountain') is 'one side of a mountain' (Omodaka 1977.10: 22).

OJ *itipi* 'Japanese yew' (MDJ *itiigasi*, 櫟) is a tall evergreen tree that could reach 30 m in height. It has a dark bark and its leaves are oval-shaped, but their tips are pointy. Hard edible fruits of *itipi* ripen in the fall. Because its wood is hard, it is used for building (Nakanishi 1985: 307).

On OJ *aⁿdusa* 'catalpa tree' (梓) and *aⁿdusa yumi* 'catalpa bow' see the commentaries to 14.3487 and 14.3489.

OJ *ya* 'eight' on line twenty-two simply means 'many'.

Lines twenty-two and twenty-four are hypometric (*ji tarazu*, 字足らず).

It is not clear what type of arrow WOJ *pimɛ kaᵐbura* is. Most likely it is an arrow with an arrow tip shaped like a turnip (*kaᵐbura*). Alternatively, it might be *kaᵐbura* 'whistling arrow'. Note that in any case the modifier *kaᵐbura* follows the head noun *pimɛ*, which contradicts the SOV word order.

On the analysis of *sa-wo sika* as 'PREF-male deer' with a possibility that *sawo* could be simply analyzed as 'male' see Vovin (2005a: 87–89).

On *opo kimi* 'Great Lord', which refers to the Emperor, see the commentary to 14.3480.

WOJ *payas-* 'to glorify' is historically a causative form *pay-as-* of the verb *paye-* 'to flourish'.

Line thirty-six is hypometric (*ji tarazu*, 字足らず).

WOJ *namasu* is a dish from thin slices of meat or fish. MDJ *sashimi* is probably the closest equivalent.

WOJ *miⁿgɛ* on line forty-nine is a 'cow's stomach' or a 'goat stomach'. It could never refer to a human stomach.

WOJ *sipo* might refer not only to the salt itself, but to pickled foodstuffs made with salt.

Line fifty-one 耆矣奴 *OYI-PATE-n-o* 'become.old(CONV)-finish-PERF-ATTR' has a problem that has been noted already by Kōnosu (1939.16: 2789). Namely, the standard attributive form of the perfective *-n-* in Western Old Japanese is *-n-uru*, and only the perfective attributive is possible here. Kōnosu comes up with an outlandish solution, proposing to read the character 奴 as *yatu* 'fellow', which would not fit either syntactically or semantically here. However, we should not forget that the character 奴 as a phonogram can stand for either /nu/ or /no/ in Old Japanese. We presume that it is perfective attributive *-n-o* that is used here. Certainly, attributive *-o* is an Eastern Old Japanese form, but one should not forget that it is also more archaic than WOJ *-uru*, which is an apparent innovation. Can it be possible that our form *oyi-pate-n-o* 'the one that has become old' is just an archaism here?

Postscript to the Poem 16.3885

本文 · *Original Text*
右歌一首爲鹿述痛作之也

Translation
The poem above was composed in order to narrate the pain of the deer.

Commentary
Although the deer in the poem above has willingly gave up his life, it is still supposed to feel the pain of being killed by hunters and dying.

CHAPTER 4

萬葉集卷第二十 • *Man'yōshū* Book Twenty

Preface to the Poems 20.4321–4424

本文 • *Original Text*
天平勝寶七歲乙未二月相替遣筑紫諸國防人等歌

Translation

Poems by *sakimori* sent in exchange to different provinces in Tukusi, and others, [composed] in the second lunar month of the seventh year of Tenpyō Shōhō.

Commentary

The poems in this poetic sequence were composed or collected by Opotəmə-nə Yakaməti, between the sixth day and twenty-ninth day of the second lunar month of the seventh year of Tenpyō Shōhō that is between March 23 and April 15, 755 AD. Among 104 poems in this sequence only eighty-four are composed by *sakimori*. These eighty-four poems were collected by Opotəmə-nə Yakaməti in Nanipa, where he was on official business at this time. There is also a theory that Tati^mbana-nə Naramarə, who was then the Minister of the Ministry of War, made Opotəmə-nə Yakaməti collect these poems on orders from his own father, Tati^mbana-nə Məraye, then the Minister of the Left (Kinoshita 1988: 59).

Tukusi is the old name for the island of Kyūshū.

OJ *sakimori* 'border guards' is the name for border guards that were sent to protect the Western border of Yamatə in Kyūshū, as well as in Tsushima and Iki islands. This name can also refer to the institution of border guards. The original meaning probably indicates 'promontory guards' or 'front guards', as the logographic spellings 埼守 'promontory guard' (MYS 16.3866) and 前守 'front guard' (NR 11.3) indicate. The logographic spelling 防人 indicates an imitation of Chinese border guard system from the Tang period (Kinoshita 1988: 58). The first mention of border guards dates back to the second year of Taika (646 AD), but the real posting of *sakimori* to the Western frontiers did not occur until the third year of Tenchi (664 AD). According to the military code, the term of service for *sakimori* was limited to three years, but it did not include the time required for the travel to and from the destination. The transportation of *sakimori* from their home provinces to Nanipa harbor was administered by their respective local governor offices who sent *sakimori* messengers (*Kətəriⁿdukapi*, 部領使) to accompany them, but from Nanipa harbor to Dazaifu in Kyūshū *sakimori* were transported by special messengers (*Senshi*, 專使). After the exchange between freshly arrived and departing *sakimori* took place, *sakimori* worked hard both for defense and to procure their own living under the jurisdiction of *sakimori* office (*Sakimori-nə tukasa*, 防人司) of Dazaifu. They had one day off in ten days. The general number of *sakimori* is believed to be 3,000, and the exchange between 1,000 new arrivals and 1,000 departing *sakimori* took place every year in the third lunar month. It is not clear when recruitment of *sakimori* started to be limited exclusively to the Eastern Provinces (東國, Aⁿduma), but in the tenth year of Tenpyō (738 AD) it is apparent that *sakimori* were recruited from the provinces starting from Təpotuapumi and further east in Tōkaidō (東海道) region and from Sinanu and further east in Tōsandō (東山道) region. This is most likely due to the fact that easterners had the reputation of being fierce and brave warriors at this time (see MYS 20.4331), although Kinoshita is inclined to see the reason more in a special connection between the Yamatə court and Aⁿduma (1988: 59), without, however, explaining what this special connection might have been.

20.4321

本文 • *Original Text*
(1) 可之古伎夜 (2) 美許等加我布理 (3) 阿須由利也 (4) 加曳我牟多祢牟 (5) 伊牟奈之尒志弖

仮名の書き下し • *Kana Transliteration*
(1) かしこ₁き₁や (2) み₁こ₂と₂かがふり (3) あすゆりや (4) かえ₂がむたねむ (5) いむなしにして

Romanization
(1) kasiko-ki ya (2) mi-kətə kaⁿgapur-i (3) asu-yuri ya (4) kaye-ⁿga muta ne-m-u (5) imu na-si n-i s-i-te

Glossing with Morphemic Analysis
(1) awesome-ATTR EP (2) HON-word receive(HUM)-CONV (3) tomorrow-ABL IP (4) reed-POSS together sleep-TENT-ATTR (5) beloved exist.not-FIN COP-CONV do-CONV-SUB

Translation

(1/2) [I] received the awesome order [from the sovereign], and (3) from tomorrow, (4) would [I] sleep together with reeds, (5) since [my] beloved is not [here]?

Commentary

This poem has two EOJ dialectal features: EOJ *kaye* 'reed, grass for thatching roofs' (cf. WOJ *kaya* 'id.') and EOJ *imu* 'beloved' (cf. WOJ *imo* 'id.'). Note, however, that the poem has *muta* 'with' identical with WOJ *muta* 'id.' as compared with EOJ *mita* 'id.' The EOJ form is probably more archaic, because it is easy to imagine *i* > *u* after *m*, but the reverse shift would have no phonetic motivation.

The first particle *ya* is an emphatic particle, and the second *ya* is an interrogative particle.

Postscript to the Poem 20.4321

本文 • *Original Text*

右一首國造丁長下郡物部秋持

Translation

The poem above [was composed] by Mənənᵊᵐbe-nə Akiməti, assistant commander from Naⁿga-nə simo district.

Commentary

Nothing is known about the biography of Mənənᵊᵐbe-nə Akiməti.

Commander (*Kuni-nə miyatuko, Kokuzō,* 國造) in pre-Taika ancient Japan was an official endowed with military and judicial powers. After the Taika reforms his role was essentially reduced to ceremonial religious functions. The term *yoporo ~ yoᵐboro* (丁), lit. 'muscle in the back of a leg' refers normally to a conscript to public works, but it also appears in *sakimori* rank names. We follow Omodaka, who believes that *Kuni-nə miyatuko-nə yoporo* (國造丁) is an Assistant Commander (1984.20: 37), although Kinoshita thinks that 國造 and 國造丁 were used synonymously (1988: 60). There was the following hierarchy among the *sakimori*, although there probably were slight individual differences between various provinces:

— Commander (*Kuni-nə miyatuko*, 國造)
— Assistant Commander (*Kuni-nə miyatuko-nə yoporo*, 國造丁)
— Captain (*Sukɛ-nə yoporo*, 助丁)

- Lieutenant (*Shuchō*, 主帳)
- Sergeant (*Shuchō-nə yoporo*, 主帳丁, or *Chō-nə yoporo*, 帳丁)
- Corporal (*Kachō*, 火長)
- Private (*Kami-nə yoporo*, 上丁)

Privates (*Kami-nə yoporo*, 上丁) were also sometimes mentioned just as *sakimori*, or given no indication of rank.

Naⁿga-nə simo district is found in Təpotuapumi province, and it corresponds to parts of Hamana county (Hamana-gun, 浜名郡) and Iwata county (Iwata-gun, 磐田郡) along Tenryū river (Tenryū-gawa, 天竜川) in present-day Shizuoka prefecture (Nakanishi 1985: 469). On Təpotuapumi province see the commentary to the postscript to 14.3353–3354.

Poems 20.4321–4327 are from Təpotuapumi province.

20.4322

本文・*Original Text*
(1) 和我都麻波 (2) 伊多久古非良之 (3) 乃牟美豆尓 (4) 加其佐倍美曳弖 (5) 余尓和須良礼受

仮名の書き下し・*Kana Transliteration*
(1) わがつまは (2) いたくこ₁ひ₂らし (3) の₂むみ₁づに (4) かご₂さへ₂み₁え₂て (5) よ₂にわすられず

Romanization
(1) wa-ŋga tuma pa (2) ita-ku kopï-rasi (3) nəm-u miⁿdu-ni (4) kaⁿgə sapɛ mi-ye-te (5) yə-ni wasur-are-ⁿz-u

Glossing with Morphemic Analysis
(1) I-POSS spouse TOP (2) extreme-CONV long.for(CONV)-SUP (3) drink-ATTR water-LOC (4) reflection RP see-PASS(CONV)-SUB (5) life-LOC forget-PASS-NEG-FIN

Translation
(1/2) It seems that my spouse longs for [me] dearly. (5) [I] will not be able to forget [her] in [my] life, (4) even seeing as much as [her] reflection (3) in the water [I] drink.

Commentary

This poem has two EOJ dialectal features: EOJ *kopï-rasi* (the corresponding WOJ form is *kop-urasi* 'love-SUP' with no converb form attested) and EOJ *kaŋgə* 'reflection' (cf. WOJ *kaŋgɛ*), with EOJ *ə* corresponding to WOJ *ɛ*.

Postscript to the Poem 20.4322

本文・*Original Text*
右一首主帳丁麁玉郡若倭部身麻呂

Translation
The poem above [was composed] by Wakayamatəmbe-nə Mïmarə, a sergeant from Aratama district.

Commentary
Nothing is known about the biography of Wakayamatəmbe-nə Mïmarə.

On sergeant (*Shuchō-nə yoporo*, 主帳丁) and other *sakimori* ranks see the commentary to the postscript to the poem 20.4321.

Aratama district (Aratama kəpori, 麁玉郡) was one of the districts of Təpotuapumi province. Its territory corresponds to the area along the Tenryū river (Tenryū-gawa, 天竜川) in present-day Hamakita city (Hamakita-shi, 浜北市) in Shizuoka prefecture (Nakanishi 1985: 420).

Poem 20.4322 is from Təpotuapumi province. On Təpotuapumi province see the commentary to the postscript to 14.3353–3354.

20.4323

本文・*Original Text*
(1) 等伎騰吉乃 (2) 波奈波佐家登母 (3) 奈尓須礼曾 (4) 波々登布波奈乃 (5) 佐吉泥己受祁牟

仮名の書き下し・*Kana Transliteration*
(1) と₂き₁ど₂き₁の₂ (2) はなはさけ₁ど₂も₂ (3) なにすれそ₂ (4) ははと₂ふはなの₂ (5) さき₁でこ₂ずけ₁む

Romanization
(1) təki-ⁿdəki-nə (2) pana pa sak-e-ⁿdəmə (3) nani s-ure sə (4) papa tə [i]p-u pana-nə (5) sak-i-[i]ⁿde-kə-ⁿz-u-kem-u

Glossing with Morphemic Analysis
(1) time-time-GEN (2) flower TOP bloom-EV-CONC (3) what do-EV FP (4) mother QV say-ATTR flower-GEN (5) bloom-CONV-exit(CONV)-come-NEG-CONV-PAST/TENT-ATTR

Translation
(1/2) Although the flowers of all [four] seasons bloom, (3) why (4/5) has the flower called 'Mother' not bloomed?

Commentary
There is a disagreement between Japanese scholars as to how to read 等伎騰吉: *təki-ⁿdəki* or *təki-təki*. Omodaka reads *təki-ⁿdəki*, but without providing any explanation (1984.20: 39). Kinoshita insists on reading *təki-təki*, because in Rodriguez's Japanese-Portuguese dictionary *toqidoqi* is 'sometimes', while *toqi toqi* means 'various times' (1988: 63). Mizushima is of the same opinion (2003: 103–104). It is certainly methodologically unsound to define an OJ reading on a usage in the language nine hundred years later. The character 騰 is predominantly used in OJ as a phonogram for the syllable ⁿdə, with a voiced prenasalized /ⁿd/. The exceptions of 騰 standing for the syllable *tə* with voiceless /t-/ are predominantly confined to book two. Moreover, what is important is that 騰 is always used for the syllable /ⁿdə/ in EOJ texts. Moreover, Opotəma-nə Yakaməti also uses 騰 for /ⁿdə/ in his poems with just one exception (20.4516). Given all this, we follow Omodaka, and read 等伎騰吉 as *təki-ⁿdəki*.

This poem has one certain EOJ dialectal feature: EOJ vowel *e* corresponds to WOJ vowel *ɛ* in EOJ *sakeⁿdəmə* 'although bloom' vs. WOJ *sakɛⁿdəmə* 'id.' This indicates that Təpotuapumi dialect unlike WOJ probably had no *e : ɛ* phonemic contrast. Another potential EOJ feature is *nani s-ure sə* used for 'why?'. As far as we are aware, this expression does not occur in WOJ texts.

Postscript to the Poem 20.4323

本文 · Original Text
右一首防人山名郡丈部眞麻呂

Translation
The poem above [was composed] by *sakimori* Pasetukaᵐbe-nə Mamarə from Yamana district.

Commentary

Nothing is known about the biography of Pasetuka ᵐbe-nə Mamarə. Since he is just called *sakimori*, without a rank, we can assume that he was a private. On private (*Kami-nə yoporo*, 上丁) and other *sakimori* ranks see the commentary to the postscript to 20.4321.

Yamana district (Yamana kəpori, 山名郡) included parts of Fukuroi city (Fukuroi-shi, 袋井市), Iwata city (Iwata-shi, 磐田市), and Iwata county (Iwata-gun, 磐田郡) in present-day Shizuoka prefecture (Nakanishi 1985: 494).

Poem 20.4323 is from Təpotuapumi province. On Təpotuapumi province see the commentary to the postscript to 14.3353–3354.

20.4324

本文・*Original Text*

(1) 等倍多保美 (2) 志留波乃伊宗等 (3) 尒閇乃宇良等 (4) 安比弖之阿良婆 (5) 己等母加由波牟

仮名の書き下し・*Kana Transliteration*

(1) と₂ヘ₂たほみ₁ (2) しるはの₂いそ₁と₂ (3) にヘ₂の₂うらと₂ (4) あひ₁てしあらば (5) こ₂と₂も₂かゆはむ

Romanization

(1) Təpɛtapomi (2) Sirupa-nə iso-tə (3) Nipɛ-nə ura-tə (4) ap-i-te si ar-ᵃmba (5) kətə mə kayup-am-u

Glossing with Morphemic Analysis

(1) Təpotuapumi (2) Sirupa-GEN rocky.shore-COM (3) Nipɛ-GEN bay-COM (4) meet-CONV-SUB EP exist-COND (5) word FP go.back.and.forth-TENT-FIN

Translation

(2/4) If Sirupa rocky shore and (3) Nipɛ bay (1) [in] Təpotuapumi (4) would have met [together], (5) [we] could also talk together.

Commentary

Təpɛtapomi is the EOJ name of the province corresponding to WOJ Təpotuapumi. On Təpotuapumi province see the commentary to the postscript to 14.3353–3354. The local name Təpɛtapomi is important, because in addition to the correspondence of EOJ ɛ : WOJ o < *ə¹ in təpɛ 'distant' part, which is opposite to the correspondence EOJ ə : WOJ ɛ that we have seen above in 20.4322, the EOJ -apomi 'fresh water sea' part corresponding to WOJ -apumi 'id.' also reverses the correspondence of EOJ u : WOJ o, which we have already seen above (EOJ imu 'beloved' in 20.4321) and also see in this poem: EOJ siru 'white' vs. WOJ siro 'id.' and EOJ kayup- 'go back and forth' vs. WOJ kayop- 'id.' This reversal, however, in all probability can be easily explained by the fact that in the placename compound Təpɛtapomi, the Təpotuapumi dialect of EOJ, has preserved -omi, the reflex of PJ *omi 'sea' (> WOJ umi).

Line three is hypermetric (*ji amari*, 字余り), but it is probably a graphic illusion, because the sequence Nipɛ-nə ura was most likely pronounced as [nipɛnura] or [nipɛnəra].

The exact location of Sirupa rocky shore is not known, although it is believed to be somewhere in either Iwata county (Iwata-gun, 磐田郡) or Hamamatsu city (Hamamatsu-shi, 浜松市) (Nakanishi 1985: 454). There are various other hypotheses, surveyed by Kinoshita (1988: 66–67), Omodaka (1984.20: 40–41), and Mizushima (2003: 117–118). We are inclined to agree with Mizushima that the location on the Omaezaki cape (Omaezaki, 御前崎) in Omaezaki city (Omaezaki-shi, 御前崎市) of Haibara county (Haibara-gun, 榛原郡) in present-day Shizuoka prefecture is the most persuasive, because Omaezaki cape represents a rocky shore, fully agreeing with *iso* 'rock, rocky shore' describing Sirupa in 20.4324. Meanwhile, two other locations most frequently believed to be the location of Sirupa *rocky shore*, shores in Toyota county (Toyota-gun, 豊田郡) and Fuchi county (Fuchi-gun, 敷知郡) are in fact *sand beaches*. Sirupa is believed to be an EOJ place name, literally meaning 'white feather' (白羽), with Təpotuapumi typical raising of o > u in *siru* 'white' (cf. WOJ *siro* 'id.'). However, Sirupa 'white feather' might as well be a later reinterpretation of an original Ainu placename. If the geographical identification with modern Omaezaki cape is correct, then Sirupa in all probability reflects Ainu *sirpa* 'cape, promontory'.²

There is even more disagreement about the exact location of Nipɛ bay (Nakanishi 1985: 474; Omodaka 1984.20: 41–42; Kinoshita 1988: 67; Mizushima 2003: 120–123). Unlike Sirupa discussed above, there are no exact land features

---

1 Although the earlier WOJ contrast between o and ə is not preserved in the *Man'yōshū* after the consonant /p/, WOJ o in Təpotuapumi could be only from an earlier *ə, because WOJ o and ə cannot coexist within the same morpheme, in this case the word təpo "distant" < *təpə.

2 Ainu *sirpa* 'cape' < *sir* 'land' + *pa* 'head'.

mentioned that would facilitate the choice – bays can be very different, after all. Therefore, we will follow Omodaka here and remain non-committal to any of the theories. Furthermore, like Omodaka (1984.20: 42), we think that Nipε bay must be sufficiently distant from Sirupa rocky shore, and not adjacent to it, otherwise the poem will make little sense. The placename Nipε is usually explained as WOJ *nipε* (贄) 'food offering for deities'. Takeda sees it as a place in present-day Tsu city (Tsu-shi, 津市) of Mie prefecture where fish and fowl were procured for the palace in the capital (1957.12: 377). As in the case of Sirupa, it could be a later reinterpretation of an original Ainu placename, whether it was indeed in Mie or elsewhere. It seems to me that a much simpler explanation for a placename than 'food offering for deities' is again possible: Ainu *nipet* 'wood river',[3] borrowed as EOJ *nipε* with the expected loss of the final *-t*.[4]

On EOJ dialectal features in this poem see the first paragraph in this commentary.

Postscript to the Poem 20.4324

本文 · *Original Text*
右一首同郡丈部川相

Translation
The poem above [was composed] by Pasetuka^mbe-nə Kapapi from the same district.

Commentary
Nothing is known about the biography of Pasetuka^mbe-nə Kapapi. Since he is mentioned without any rank, we can assume that he was a private. On private (*Kami-nə yoporo*, 上丁) and other *sakimori* ranks see the commentary to the postscript to 20.4321.

The same district is Yamana district (Yamana-gun, 山名郡), on which see the commentary to the postscript to the poem 20.4323.

---

3 Ainu *nipet* < *ni* 'tree, wood' + *pet* 'river'.
4 There is one slight problem with the Ainu etymology. We would expect Ainu *nipet* being borrowed as OJ *ni^mbε*, with a prenasalized voiced -^mb-, reflecting Ainu intervocalic [-b-]. However, there is no special sign for ^mbε in *man'yōgana*. It seems that the character 閇 is used only for *pε* in the *Man'yōshū*, but it is rare, being mostly found in books five and twenty, so a possibility that it could be used for ^mbε cannot be completely excluded.

20.4325

本文・*Original Text*
(1) 知々波々母 (2) 波奈尓母我毛夜 (3) 久佐麻久良 (4) 多妣波由久等母 (5) 佐々己弖由加牟

仮名の書き下し・*Kana Transliteration*
(1) ちちははも₂ (2) はなにも₂がも₁や (3) くさまくら (4) たび₁はゆくと₂も₂ (5) ささご₂てゆかむ

Romanization
(1) titi papa mə (2) pana n-i məᵑgamo ya (3) kusa makura (4) taᵐbi pa yuk-u təmə (5) sasaᵑgə-te yuk-am-u

Glossing with Morphemic Analysis
(1) father mother FP (2) flower COP-CONV DP EP (3) grass pillow (4) journey TOP go-FIN CONJ (5) lift.up.in.hands(CONV)-SUB go-TENT-FIN

Translation
(1/2) [I] wish [my] father and mother were flowers! (4) Although [I] will go on a journey (3) [where I will sleep using] grass [as my] pillow, (5) [I] would go carrying [them] high up in my hands.

Commentary
This poem has only one EOJ feature: the correspondence of EOJ ə : WOJ ɛ in EOJ *sasaᵑgə-* 'lift up in one's hands' (cf. WOJ *sasaᵑgɛ-* 'id.'). We have already seen above the same correspondence in 20.4322 above: EOJ *kaᵑgə* 'reflection' : WOJ *kaᵑgɛ* 'id.'

Kusa makura 'grass pillow' is a permanent epithet (*makura-kotoba*, 枕詞) that is normally applied to a land journey (implying that a traveler has hardships on his journey such as sleeping in the open using grass as his pillow), but here it is used for the journey on the sea[5] that is considered to be as difficult as a journey on land.

---

5 At least one leg of the *sakimori* journey from Azuma to Northern Kyūshū must have been by the sea, namely from Naniwa (OJ Nanipa) to Northern Kyūshū.

Postscript to the Poem 20.4325

本文・*Original Text*
右一首佐野郡丈部黒當

Translation
The poem above [was composed] by Pasetuka{ᵐ}be-nə Kurota from Saya district.

Commentary
Nothing is known about the biography of Pasetuka{ᵐ}be-nə Kurota. Since he is mentioned without any rank, we can assume that he was a private. It is not clear whether his given name 黒當 should be read as Kuromasa (Kōnosu 1939: 3284) or Kurota (Takagi et al. 1962: 411). Because there is a female name Kurotame (written as 黒多賣 or 黒太賣), appearing in the population census of the second year of Taihō (大寶, 702 AD), we believe that the reading Kurota is more likely.

Saya district corresponds to the northern part of Ogasa county (Ogasa-gun, 小笠郡) in present-day Shizuoka prefecture (Nakanishi 1985: 450).

20.4327

本文・*Original Text*
(1) 和我都麻母 (2) 畫尒可伎等良無 (3) 伊豆麻母加 (4) 多妣由久阿礼波 (5) 美都々志努波牟

仮名の書き下し・*Kana Transliteration*
(1) わがつま母$_2$ (2) ゑにかき$_1$と$_2$らむ (3) いつま母$_2$が (4) たび$_1$ゆくあれは (5) み$_1$つつしの$_1$はむ

Romanization
(1) wa-ŋga tuma mə (2) we-ni kak-i-tər-am-u (3) ituma məŋga (4) ta{ᵐ}bi yuk-u are pa (5) mi-tutu sinop-am-u

Glossing with Morphemic Analysis
(1) I-POSS spouse FP (2) picture-LOC paint-CONV-take-TENT-ATTR (3) free.time DP (4) journey go-ATTR I TOP (5) look-COOR long.for-TENT-FIN

Translation

(3) [I] want free time (1/2) to paint my spouse in a picture. (4) I, who will go on a journey, (5) will long for her while looking at [it].

Commentary

This poem has just one EOJ feature: raising of *o > u in the word *ituma* 'free time' (cf. WOJ *itoma* 'id.'). See also 20.4321 and 20.4324 for other examples of this process.

The last character in the *Genryaku kōhon* is 可, and not 波 as in other old manuscripts. However, even the *Genryaku kōhon* has also 波イ written on the right of the character 可. Thus, we follow the majority of the manuscripts.

On the other hand, we follow the *Genryaku kōhon* that uniquely uses the spelling 多妣 for the word *ta*ᵐ*bi* 'journey', while other old manuscripts use the spelling 多比 *tapi*. The first spelling is etymological, and the second is not, therefore it is reasonable to believe that the *Genryaku kōhon* preserves the original text more faithfully in this respect.

Omodaka reads the word 伊豆麻 'free time' as *i*ⁿ*duma* (1984.20: 45), and not as *ituma* as all other commentators do. While the character is indeed predominantly used as a phonogram for the syllable ⁿ*du*, there are also some cases where it can stand for *tu*. Given the fact that there is no other independent evidence for the secondary nasalization *ituma* > *i*ⁿ*duma* in Təpotuapumi dialect, we follow the reading *ituma*.

Postscript to the Poem 20.4327

本文 · Original Text
右一首長下郡物部古麻呂

Translation

The poem above [was composed] by Mənənəᵐbe-nə Komarə from Naŋga-nə simo district.

Commentary

Nothing is known about the biography of Mənənəᵐbe-nə Komarə. Since he is mentioned without any rank, we can assume that he was a private. On private (*Kami-nə yoporo*, 上丁) and other *sakimori* ranks see the commentary to the postscript to 20.4321–4327. It is not inconceivable that Mənənəᵐbe-nə

Akiməti, the author of 20.4321, and Mənənəmbe-nə Komarə are somehow related, but we have no proof of this.

On Naŋga-nə simo district see the commentary to the postscript to 20.4321.

Postscript to the Poems 20.4321–4327

本文 • *Original Text*
二月六日防人部領使遠江國史生坂本朝臣人上進歌數十八首但有拙劣歌十一首不取載之

Translation
On the sixth day of the second lunar month [of the seventh year of Tenpyō Shōhō], Sakamətə-nə asəmi Pitəkami, secretary of Təpotuapumi province, and *sakimori* messenger, presented [to me] eighteen poems. However, eleven of them were of inferior [quality], so I did not include them here.

Commentary
The sixth day of the second lunar month of the seventh year of Tenpyō Shōhō corresponds to March 23, 755 AD.

Besides this postscript, Sakamətə-nə asəmi Pitəkami is mentioned once in a Shōsōin document. Around 749 AD he had no rank and worked for the office of Tōdaiji construction. It is also recorded that he was used as a messenger ten times (Kinoshita 1988: 76; Omodaka 1984.20: 45).

Shishō (史生) is a provincial secretary.

On *sakimori* messengers, see the commentary to the preface to poems 20.4321–4424.

On Təpotuapumi province see the commentary to the postscript to 14.3353–3354.

Pierson in his translation mistook this postscript for the preface to the poem 20.4328, which of course, makes no sense, because the next poem is from Saŋgamu province.

One can only wonder what were Opotəmə-nə Yakaməti's criteria for inferior quality. See the introduction for a possible solution.

20.4328

本文・*Original Text*
(1) 於保吉美能 (2) 美許等可之古美 (3) 伊蘇尓布理 (4) 宇乃波良和多流 (5) 知々波々乎於伎弖

仮名の書き下し・*Kana Transliteration*
(1) おほき₁み₁の₂ (2) み₁こ₂と₂かしこ₁み₁ (3) いそ₁にふり (4) うの₂はらわたる (5) ちちははをおき₁て

Romanization
(1) opo kimi-nə (2) mi-kətə kasiko-mi (3) iso-ni pur-i (4) unə-para watar-u (5) titi papa-wo ok-i-te

Glossing with Morphemic Analysis
(1) Great Lord-GEN (2) HON-word be.awesome-GER (3) rocky.shore-LOC touch-CONV (4) sea-plain cross-FIN (5) father mother-ACC leave.behind-CONV-SUB

Translation
(1/2) Because the command of the Great Lord is awesome, (4) [I] will cross the sea plain, (3) going along the rocky shores, (5) having left [my] father and mother behind.

Commentary
This poem has just one EOJ feature: EOJ *unəpara* 'sea plain' (cf. WOJ *unapara*). Although Kinoshita believes that the consonantal verb *pur-* 'to touch' might be an EOJ feature (1988: 77), there are rare examples of WOJ *pur-* as well, e.g. see KK 78. The usual WOJ verb is the vowel verb *pure-* 'to touch'.

On *opo kimi* 'Great Lord' which refers to the Emperor see the commentary to 14.3480.

On *mi-kətə* 'honorable word', 'imperial order/edict' see the commentary to 14.3480.

Line four is hypermetric (*ji amari*, 字余り), but it is probably a graphic illusion, because *titi papa-wo okite* was most likely pronounced as [titipapawokite].

Postscript to the Poem 20.4328

本文 • *Original Text*
右一首助丁丈部造人麻呂

Translation
The poem above [was composed] by captain Pasetukaᵐbe-nə miyatuko Pitəmarə.

Commentary
Nothing is known about the biography of captain Pasetukaᵐbe-nə miyatuko Pitəmarə except what is apparent from this postscript. Kinoshita notes that in the case of captains their place of origin is usually not recorded (1988: 77).

On captain (*Sukɛ-nə yoporo*, 助丁) and other *sakimori* ranks see the commentary to the postscript to 20.4321.

Miyatuko is an old *kabane* title which was converted to *mura*ⁿ*zi* in the thirteenth year of Emperor Tenmu rule (685 AD).

Poems 20.4328–4330 are from Saⁿgamu province. On Saⁿgamu province see the commentary to the postscript to the poems 14.3431–3433.

20.4329

本文 • *Original Text*
(1) 夜蘇久尓波 (2) 那尓波尓都度比 (3) 布奈可射里 (4) 安我世武比呂乎
(5) 美毛比等母我毛

仮名の書き下し • *Kana Transliteration*
(1) やそくには (2) なにはにつど₁ひ₁ (3) ふなかざり (4) あがせむひ₁ろ₂を
(5) み₁も₁ひ₁と₂も₂がも₁

Romanization
(1) yaso kuni pa (2) Nanipa-ni tuⁿdop-i (3) puna-kaⁿzar-i (4) a-ⁿga se-m-u pi-rə-wo (5) mi-m-o pitə məⁿgamo

Glossing with Morphemic Analysis
(1) eighty province TOP (2) Nanipa-LOC gather-CONV (3) boat-decorate-NML
(4) I-POSS do-TENT-ATTR day-DIM-ACC (5) see-TENT-ATTR person DP

Translation

(1) Many provinces (2) gather at Nanipa, and (5) [I] wish someone would see (3/4) the day when I decorate [my] boat.

Commentary

OJ *yaso* 'eighty' is used here metaphorically to indicate 'many'. It cannot be taken literally, because Yamatə never had as many as eighty provinces.

Nanipa refers to the seashore that was situated along the Uemachi daichi (上町台地) section of present-day Ōsaka city (Nakanishi 1985: 470). Nowadays, the sea line has receded further to the West, and Uemachi daichi is found inland.

Decorating a boat indicates preparations for departure.

There are two EOJ features in this poem: diminutive suffix *-rə* (cf. WOJ *-ra*) and special EOJ attributive form *-o*. On the diminutive suffix *-rə* see the commentary to 14.3351. On the EOJ verbal attributive *-o* see the commentary to 14.3395 and brief description of EOJ special grammar in the introductions to book fourteen and this volume.

Postscript to the Poem 20.4329

本文 · Original Text

右一首足下郡上丁丹比部國人

Translation

The poem above [was composed] by private Taⁿdipiᵐbe-nə Kunipitə from Lower Asiŋgara district.

Commentary

Nothing is known about the biography of private Taⁿdipiᵐbe-nə Kunipitə except what is apparent from this postscript. Kinoshita suggests that the given name 國人 should be read as Təkipitə rather than Kunipitə (1988: 79), but his argument is based on the name 馬國人 appearing in the preface to 20.4457, which he reads as Uma-nə Təkipitə, which has a much later *kana* gloss Tokipito in a rather late manuscript.

On private (*Kami-nə yoporo*, 上丁) and other *sakimori* ranks see the commentary to the postscript to the poem 20.4321.

足下郡 is an abbreviation for 足柄下郡 'Lower Asiŋgara district'. On Asiŋgara see the commentary to 14.3361.

20.4330

本文・Original Text

(1) 奈尒波都尒 (2) 余曾比余曾比弖 (3) 氣布能比夜 (4) 伊田弓麻可良武 (5) 美流波々奈之尒

仮名の書き下し・Kana Transliteration

(1) なにはつに (2) よ₂そ₂ひ₁よ₂そ₂ひ₁て (3) け₂ふの₂ひ₁や (4) いでてまからむ (5) み₁るははなしに

Romanization

(1) Nanipa tu-ni (2) yəsəp-i yəsəp-i-te (3) kɛpu-nə pi ya (4) iⁿde-te makar-am-u (5) mi-ru papa na-si-ni

Glossing with Morphemic Analysis

(1) Nanipa harbor-LOC (2) decorate-CONV adorn-CONV-SUB (3) today-GEN day IP (4) go.out(CONV)-SUB go.far.away-TENT-ATTR (5) see-ATTR mother exist.not-FIN-LOC

Translation

(2) Having thoroughly decorated [my boat] (1) in Nanipa harbor, (3) shall [I] go far away today? (5) Because [my] mother, who [could] see [it], is not [here] ...

Commentary

Nanipa tu 'Nanipa harbor', the biggest and the most important of all Japanese harbors, was located in a former lagoon, connected to the sea by an artificial canal that led to the Nanipa seashore, on which see the commentary to 20.4329 above. Incidentally, this represents further evidence against a fantastic theory by Unger that OJ *tu* originally meant not a 'harbor', but a 'river', because Japanese harbors were mostly located in estuaries (2009: 111), which also does not stand on many other accounts. Although several rivers used to flow into Nanipa lagoon, the port itself was not connected with any of the estuaries.

This poem has only one EOJ feature: the word 'today' is spelled as *kɛpu* (cf. WOJ *kepu*).

Postscript to the Poem 20.4330

本文・Original Text

右一首鎌倉郡上丁丸子連多麻呂

萬葉集卷第二十 · MAN'YŌSHŪ BOOK TWENTY 291

Translation

The poem above [was composed] by private Marəko-nə muraⁿzi Opomarə from Kamakura district.

Commentary

Nothing is known about the biography of private Taⁿdipiᵐbe-nə Kunipitə except what is apparent from this postscript.

Muraⁿzi is a (姓) *kabane* title. *Kabane* titles are appellations of court offices and ranks. There were many of them during the Kofun and Asuka periods, the main being *omi* (臣), *muraⁿzi* (連), *miyatuko* (造), *kimi* (君), *atapi* (値), *puᵐbitə* (史), *aⁿgatanusi* (県主), and *suⁿguri* (村主). In 684 AD Emperor Tenmu reorganized *kabane* into eight types (*yakusa*, 八色). In descending order, these were: *mapitə* (眞人), *asəmi* (朝臣), *sukune* (宿彌), *imiki* (忌寸), *mitinəsi* (道師), *omi* (臣), *muraⁿzi* (連), and *inaⁿgi* (稲置). The *kabane* rank was placed between the family name and the given name, as Marəko-nə muraⁿzi Opomarə and some other names of *sakimori* demonstrate.

On private (*Kami-nə yoporo*, 上丁) and other *sakimori* ranks see the commentary to the postscript to 20.4321.

On Kamakura district see the commentary to 14.3366.

Postscript to the Poems 20.4328–4330

本文 · *Original Text*
二月七日相模國防人部領使守從五位下藤原朝臣宿奈麻呂進歌數八首但拙劣歌五首者不取載之

Translation

On the seventh day of the second lunar month [of the seventh year of Tenpyō Shōhō], Puⁿdipara-nə asəmi Sukunamarə (Junior Fifth Rank, Lower Grade), governor of Saⁿgamu province, and *sakimori* messenger, presented [to me] eight poems. However, five of them were of inferior [quality], so I did not include them here.

Commentary

The seventh day of the second lunar month of the seventh year of Tenpyō Shōhō corresponds to March 24, 755 AD.

Puⁿdipara-nə asəmi Sukunamarə is the second son of Puⁿdipara-nə Umakapi (藤原馬養・藤原宇合), and the grandson of Puⁿdipara-nə Puᵐbitə. Due to the rebellion of his elder brother Puⁿdipara-nə Pirotuⁿgu (藤原広嗣) in the twelfth year of Tenpyō (740 AD), he was exiled to I^ndu province (伊豆國), but pardoned and appointed Junior Secretary (*Shōhanji*, 少判事) of Dazaifu in the fourteenth year of Tenpyō (742 AD). In the eighteenth year of Tenpyō (746 AD) he was promoted to Junior Fifth Rank, Lower Grade. He had an illustrious career, reaching the position of the Great Minister of the Center (*Naidaijin*, 内大臣) with Junior Second Rank. He died in the eighth year of Hōki (777 AD) and was posthumously promoted to the Junior First Rank.

On *sakimori* messengers, see the commentary to the preface to poems 20.4321–4424.

On Sa^ngamu province see the commentary to the postscript to the poems 14.3431–3433.

20.4337

本文 • *Original Text*
(1) 美豆等利乃 (2) 多知能已蘇岐尓 (3) 父母尓 (4) 毛能波須價尓弖 (5) 已麻叙久夜志伎

仮名の書き下し • *Kana Transliteration*
(1) み₁づと₂りの₂ (2) たちの₂いそ₁ぎ₁に (3) ちちははに (4) も₁の₂はずけ₁にて (5) いまぞ₂くやしき₁

Romanization
(1) mi^ndu təri-nə (2) tat-i-nə iso^ng-i n-i (3) TITI PAPA-ni (4) monə-[i]p-a^nz-u ke-n-i-te (5) ima ^nzə kuyasi-ki

Glossing with Morphemic Analysis
(1) water fowl-COMP (2) rise/depart-NML-GEN hurry-NML COP-CONV (3) father mother-DAT (4) thing-say-NEG-CONV come(CONV)-PERF-CONV-SUB (5) now FP be.regretful-ATTR

Translation
(5) [I] now regret (4) that [I] have come [here] without saying anything (3) to [my] father and mother (2) because of the haste of [my] departure/flying away (1) like a water fowl.

Commentary

On *miⁿdu təri* 'water fowl' and the imagery associated with it, see the commentary to 14.3528.

Omodaka believes that EOJ *kenite* 'has come and' in line four is a result of the vowel shift *i* > *e* in Suruⁿga dialect of EOJ (1984.20: 59). Omodaka apparently thought that EOJ *kenite* should be analyzed as *k-e-n-i-te* 'come-CONV-PERF-CONV-SUB', being a corruption of WOJ *k-i-n-i-te* As we will see below, while the vowel raising *e* > *i* indeed takes place in Suruⁿga, the vowel lowering *i* > *e* is an artifact of incorrect analysis and as a matter of fact does not exist. Another problem is that there are no other examples of converb form *-e-* and not *-i-* in EOJ corpus. Given all this, it is much simpler to analyze EOJ *kenite* as a product of a different line of development: while in WOJ the root vowel **ə* elided, but the following converb was left untouched, thus PJ **kə-i-n-i-te* > WOJ *k-i-n-i-te*, in EOJ the process was opposite: the converb suffix *-i-* was dropped, but the root vowel remained: PJ **kə-i-n-i-te* > **kə-n-i-te* > EOJ *ke-n-i-te*. The correspondence of WOJ *ə* to Suruⁿga EOJ *e* is well attested otherwise, see the examples in the following Suruⁿga poems.

Poems 20.4337–4346 are by *sakimori* from Suruⁿga province.

Postscript to the Poem 20.4337

本文 · Original Text

右一首上丁有度部牛麻呂

Translation

The poem above [was composed] by private Uⁿdo^mbe-nə Usimarə.

Commentary

On private (*Kami-nə yoporo*, 上丁) and other *sakimori* ranks, see the commentary to the postscript to 20.4321.

Nothing is known about the biography of Uⁿdo^mbe-nə Usimarə. Takeda notes that there is no mention of his district of origin in Suruⁿga province, but that there was Uⁿdo district (Uⁿdo kəpori, 有度郡) in this province, which corresponds to a part of Abe county (Abe-gun, 安部郡) in present-day Shizuoka prefecture. Takeda further conjectures that there might have been a connection between his family name and Uⁿdo district (1957: 392).

20.4338

本文 • *Original Text*
(1) 多々美氣米 (2) 牟良自加已蘇乃 (3) 波奈利蘇乃 (4) 波々乎波奈例弖 (5) 由久我加奈之佐

仮名の書き下し • *Kana Transliteration*
(1) たたみ₁け₂め₂ (2) むらじがいそ₁の₂ (3) はなりそ₁の₂ (4) ははをはなれて (5) ゆくがかなしさ

Romanization
(1) tatami kɛmɛ (2) Muraⁿzi-ŋga iso-nə (3) panar-iso-nə (4) papa-wo panare-te (5) yuk-u-ŋga kanasi-sa

Glossing with Morphemic Analysis
(1) rice.straw.mat wild.rice.straw.mat (2) Muraⁿzi-POSS rocky.shore-GEN (3) be.separated(CONV)-rock-COMP (4) mother-ACC be.separated(CONV)-SUB (5) go-ATTR-POSS be.sad-NML

Translation
(5) Sadness of going, (4) being separated from [my] mother, (3) like rocks [in the sea] are separated (2) from Muraⁿzi rocky shore (1) (*makura-kotoba*).

Commentary
Although the permanent epithet (*makura-kotoba*, 枕詞) *tatami kɛmɛ* 'mats made from rice straw and mats made from wild rice straw' is etymologically transparent, it is not clear how it is connected to the rest of the poem, therefore we left it untranslated.

EOJ *kɛmɛ* 'mat made from wild rice straw' corresponds etymologically to WOJ *kəmə* 'id.' In the Suruŋga dialect of EOJ the vowels *ɛ* and *e* (probably there was no phonemic contrast between the two) may correspond to WOJ *ə*, especially after velars and labials, see 20.4337 above. We have seen above that the same correspondence is found in the Təpotuapumi dialect of EOJ, see the commentary to 20.4324.

The exact location of Muraⁿzi rocky shore in Suruŋga province is not known (Nakanishi 1985: 491).

EOJ *panar-iso* 'rocks in the sea not connected to the shore' corresponds to WOJ *panare-so* 'id.', but the EOJ form cannot be used as evidence for the raising *e > i*, because although EOJ *panar-iso* and WOJ *panare-so* are both derived from the PJ *panare-iso, they follow two different paths of development, with EOJ losing the first vowel in the vowel cluster *e+i*, and WOJ losing the second one in the same cluster.

Note that in this poem both meanings of the OJ word *iso* are used: 'rock' and 'rocky shore'.

The first three lines represent a poetic introduction (*jo*, 序) to the rest of the poem.

Postscript to the Poem 20.4338

本文 · *Original Text*
右一首助丁生部道麻呂

Translation
The poem above [was composed] by captain Opusimbe-nə Mitimarə.

Commentary
Nothing is known about the biography of captain Opusimbe-nə Mitimarə. Kinoshita notes that in the case of captains their district of origin is usually not recorded (1988: 77).

On captain (*Sukɛ-nə yoporo*, 助丁) and other *sakimori* ranks, see the commentary to the postscript to 20.4321.

20.4339

本文 · *Original Text*
(1) 久尓米具留 (2) 阿等利加麻氣利 (3) 由伎米具利 (4) 加比利久麻弖尓 (5) 已波比弖麻多祢

仮名の書き下し · *Kana Transliteration*
(1) くにめ₂ぐる (2) あと₂りかまけ₂り (3) ゆき₁め₂ぐり (4) かひ₁りくまでに (5) いはひ₁てまたね

Romanization
(1) kuni mɛⁿgur-u (2) atəri kama kɛri (3) yuk-i-mɛⁿgur-i (4) kapir-i-k-u-maⁿde-ni (5) ipap-i-te mat-an-e

Glossing with Morphemic Analysis

(1) land go.around-ATTR (2) brambling wild.duck gray.headed.lapwing (3) go-CONV-go.around-CONV (4) return-CONV-come-ATTR-TERM-LOC (5) pray-CONV-SUB wait-DES-IMP

Translation

(5) Pray and wait [for me] (4) until [I] return (3) [after] going around (2) like bramblings, wild ducks, and lapwings (1) that go around the lands.

Commentary

EOJ *atəri* 'brambling' (MDJ *atori,* 獦子鳥, Lat. *Fringilla montifringilla*) is a small migratory bird the size of a sparrow (it belongs to the order of sparrow) that comes to Japan in late autumn in large flocks and stays through winter. It is colored black and red-brownish, with a light yellow beak and white belly (Nakanishi 1985: 288).

EOJ *kama* 'wild duck' corresponds to WOJ *kamo* 'id.' (also attested in EOJ). On OJ *kamo* 'wild duck' see the commentary to 14.3524.

EOJ *kɛri* 'gray-headed lapwing' (MDJ *keri,* 鳬, Lat. *Vanellus cinereus*) is a migratory bird from the plover order, that leaves Japan for the winter and migrates to the South. It is the size of a pigeon, but has long legs of yellow color. Its back is a light brown color, its belly is white and its wings are black. It mostly lives in grassy meadows near the water, as it hunts small fish in Central and Northern Japan.

Since all three birds are migratory, the word *kuni* in line one apparently indicates different lands or countries, and not provinces of Japan.

EOJ *kapir-* 'to return' corresponds to WOJ *kaper-* 'id.', demonstrating the raising *e > i* in Suruⁿga dialect of EOJ.

The suffix *-u* in *k-u-maⁿde* 'come-ATTR-TERM' can be interpreted as final form if we look at it through the prism of WOJ. However, it would be highly unusual to have a case marker after a final, and not an attributive form of a verb. We believe that this suffix *-u* represents a reflex of the EOJ attributive form in *-o* that underwent raising *-o > -u*, therefore *k-u-maⁿde* should be interpreted as 'come-ATTR-TERM'. Note that *k-uru-maⁿde with attributive *-uru* is not attested in EOJ texts.

Postscript to the Poem 20.4339

本文・*Original Text*

右一首刑部虫麻呂

Translation

The poem above [was composed] by Osakaᵐbe-nə Musimarə.

Commentary

Nothing is known about the biography of Osakaᵐbe-nə Musimarə. Since his rank is not mentioned, he probably was a private. On private (*Kami-nə yoporo*, 上丁) and other *sakimori* ranks, see the commentary to the postscript to 20.4321.

20.4340

本文 · Original Text

(1) 等知波々江 (2) 已波比弓麻多祢 (3) 豆久志奈流 (4) 美豆久白玉 (5) 等里弓久麻弓尒

仮名の書き下し · Kana Transliteration

(1) と₂ちははえ₂ (2) いはひ₁てまたね (3) つくしなる (4) み₁づくしらたま (5) と₂りてくまでに

Romanization

(1) təti papa ye (2) ipap-i-te mat-an-e (3) Tukusi-n-ar-u (4) mi-ⁿ-duk-u SIRA TAMA (5) tər-i-te k-u-maⁿde-ni

Glossing with Morphemic Analysis

(1) father mother EP (2) pray-CONV-SUB wait-DES-IMP (3) Tukusi-LOC-exist-ATTR (4) water-LOC-soak-ATTR white pearl (5) take-CONV-SUB come-ATTR-TERM-LOC

Translation

(1) Oh, father and mother! (2) Pray and wait for [me], (5) until [I] come back, bringing [with me] (4) white pearls that soak in water (5) in Tukusi.

Commentary

Suruᵑga EOJ *təti* 'father' corresponds to WOJ *titi* 'father', although Suruᵑga *titi* 'id.' is also attested, see 20.4344 below. The correspondence of Suruᵑga *ə* to WOJ *i* is difficult to explain, especially in light of Simotukɛno EOJ *sisi* 'id.' that clearly shows palatalization $t > s / \_i$.

EOJ *ye* is an emphatic particle, corresponding to WOJ *ya*. Note the correspondence of Suruᵑga EOJ *e* : WOJ *ə* that we have already seen above (see 20.4337, 20.4338 and the commentary to 20.4338).

Tukusi is the old name of Kyūshū.

The OJ compound *mi-ⁿ-duk-* 'to soak in water' consists of the root *mi-* of the word *miⁿdu* 'water', special compressed locative case marker *-n-* and verb *tuk-* 'to soak'. It is a relatively rare case of using *mi-* 'water' not for fresh water, but for sea water. Cf. WOJ *na-ⁿ-duk-* 'to soak in water' (Omodaka et al. 1967: 524), which include OJ *mi* 'water' < PJ *me and OJ *na* 'id.' < *na that have different origin. *na 'water' was borrowed from proto-Tai *r-nam 'id.' when speakers of PJ were still living in their notherland in Southern China or not far from it, and before they moved away towards the North.

OJ *sira tama*, lit. 'white jewel' usually refers to pearls.

On special reduced form *-n-* and special compressed form *-ⁿ-* of the locative case marker *-ni*, see Vovin (2020.1: 149–150).

On attributive *-u* in *k-u-maⁿde-ni* 'until I come back' in line five, see the commentary to 20.4339 above.

Postscript to the Poem 20.4340

本文・*Original Text*
右一首川原虫麻呂

Translation
The poem above [was composed] by Kapara-nə Musimarə.

Commentary
Nothing is known about the biography of Kapara-nə Musimarə. Since his rank is not mentioned, he probably was a private. On private (*Kami-nə yoporo*, 上丁) and other *sakimori* ranks, see the commentary to the postscript to 20.4321.

20.4341

本文・*Original Text*
(1) 多知波奈能 (2) 美袁利乃佐刀尒 (3) 父乎於伎弖 (4) 道乃長道波 (5) 由伎加弖努加毛

仮名の書き下し・*Kana Transliteration*
(1) たちばなの₂ (2) み₁をりの₂さと₁に (3) ちちをおき₁て (4) み₁ちの₂ながちは (5) ゆき₁かての₁かも₁

Romanization
(1) Tati^mbana-nə (2) Miwori-nə sato-ni (3) TITI-wo ok-i-te (4) MITI-nə NA^NGAti pa (5) yuk-i-kate-n-o kamo

Glossing with Morphemic Analysis
(1) Tati^mbana-GEN (2) Miwori-GEN village-LOC (3) father-ACC leave-CONV-SUB (4) road-GEN length TOP (5) go-CONV-POT-NEG-ATTR EP

Translation
(5) [I] cannot go (4) [all the] length of the road, (3) leaving my father [behind] (2) in Miwori village (1) of Tati^mbana!

Commentary
The location of Miwori village of Tati^mbana is not known precisely, but it might have been located in Tati^mbana (立花) district in the north-eastern part of Shimizu city (清水市) in present-day Shizuoka prefecture (Nakanishi 1985: 490; Kinoshita 1988: 102).

Line three is hypermetric (*ji amari*, 字余り), but it is probably a graphic illusion, because *titi-wo ok-i-te* was most likely pronounced as [titiwokite].

The word for 'father' in line three is written logographically with the character 父. In the previous poem 20.4340 we have Suru^nga EOJ *təti* 'father', but in the poem 20.4344 Suru^nga EOJ *titi* 'id.' is attested. Thus, the underlying reading of the character 父 in this poem remains unknown: it can be *titi*, or it can be *təti*.

Most Japanese scholars treat 長道 in 道乃長道 in line four as 'long road' (Inoue 1928: 4029; Kōnosu 1939: 3299; Takeda 1957: 395; Tsuchiya 1977: 295; Kubota 1967: 438; Kojima et al. 1975: 387; Omodaka 1984.20: 63; Kinoshita 1988: 102; Itō 1999: 468; Satake et al. 2003: 399; Mizushima 2003: 228). However, Takagi et al. (1962: 417) and Nakanishi (1983: 297) read 長道 as *na^ngate* 'length'. There is WOJ *na^ngate* 'length' that specifically occurs in the expression *miti-nə na^ngate* 'length of the road', which makes sense, while *miti-nə na^nga miti* 'the long road of the road' does not. We trust that Takagi et al. and the Nakanishi's semantic interpretation is correct, but not their phonetic reading. First, the character 道 'road, way' is used in the *Man'yōshū* as a phonogram for the syllable *ti*, but not for the syllable *te*. Second, the word *ti* 'road, way' is attested in OJ only in compounds, that is it is essentially a bound noun, therefore its appearance after the uninflected adjective *na^nga* 'long' would be strange, because only free nouns occur in this position. We believe that we are dealing here with EOJ *na^ngati* 'length' (with last syllable written phonographically with the character 道 as *ti*), which corresponds to WOJ *naⁿgate* 'id.' EOJ form resulted from raising *e* > *i*. On WOJ *naⁿgate*, see the commentary to 15.3724.

On the EOJ verbal attributive *-o*, see the commentary to 14.3395 and a brief description of EOJ special grammar in the introductions to books fourteen and twenty.

Postscript to the Poem 20.4341

本文・*Original Text*
右一首丈部足麻呂

Translation
The poem above [was composed] by Pasetukaᵐbe-nə Tarimarə.

Commentary
Nothing is known about the biography of Pasetukaᵐbe-nə Tarimarə. Since his rank is not mentioned, he probably was a private. On private (*Kami-nə yoporo*, 上丁) and other *sakimori* ranks see the commentary to the postscript to the poem 20.4321.

20.4342

本文・*Original Text*
(1) 麻氣婆之良 (2) 寶米弖豆久礼留 (3) 等乃能其等 (4) 已麻勢波々刀自 (5) 於米加波利勢受

仮名の書き下し・*Kana Transliteration*
(1) まけ₂ばしら (2) ほめ₂てつくれる (3) と₂の₂の₂ご₂と₂ (4) いませはは と₁じ (5) おめ₂がはりせず

Romanization
(1) ma-kɛ-ᵐ-basira (2) pomɛ-te tukur-er-u (3) tənə-nə ⁿgətə (4) imas-e papa toⁿzi (5) omɛ-ⁿ-gapar-i se-ⁿz-u

Glossing with Morphemic Analysis
(1) INT-tree-GEN-pillar (2) bless(CONV)-SUB make-PROG-ATTR (3) mansion-GEN like (4) exist(HON)-IMP mother mistress.of.the.house (5) face-GEN-change-NML do-NEG-CONV

Translation

(5) Without changing [your] looks, (4) [my] dear mother, live [a long time] (3) like mansion (2) that [they] have built, blessing (1) the pillars [made] of true trees!

Commentary

EOJ *kɛ* 'tree' corresponds to WOJ *kï* 'id.' Pillars were made from 'true trees' (WOJ *ma-kï*, EOJ *ma-kɛ*) that were either cryptomeria (OJ *suᵑgi*) or cypress (OJ *pi, pi-nə kï*), namely tall straight trees. Contrary to Pierson's translation of this poem that includes 'pillars of pine' (1963: 49), it would be impossible to make pillars from crooked and bent Japanese pines.

OJ *toⁿzi* is a 'mistress of the house', which was frequently used in reference to older women, although it could also be used as an honorific address for younger women. OJ *toⁿzi* is a contraction of *to* 'gate, door' and *nusi* 'master'. By the extension of the meaning, the word also acquired later the meaning 'wife'.

EOJ *omɛ* 'face' corresponds to WOJ *omə* 'id.' Note the correspondence of Suruᵑga EOJ *e* : WOJ *ə* that we have already seen above (see 20.4337, 20.4338 and 20.4340).

EOJ *omɛᵑgapari* (WOJ *oməᵑgapari*) 'facial change, change in the looks' often referred to emaciation or worn-out appearance.

Postscript to the Poem 20.4342

本文 · *Original Text*

右一首坂田部首麻呂

Translation

The poem above [was composed] by Sakataᵐbe-nə Oᵐbitə Marə.

Commentary

Nothing is known about the biography of Sakataᵐbe-nə Oᵐbitə Marə. Since his rank is not mentioned, he probably was a private. On private (*Kami-nə yoporo*, 上丁) and other *sakimori* ranks, see the commentary to the postscript to the poem 20.4321. Oᵐbitə (首) can be either a part of the given name Oᵐbitəmarə (Tsuchiya 1977: 296), or a *kabane* title *oᵐbitə* (首) (Kōnosu 1939: 3300), in which case the given name is just Marə. There is compelling evidence for both solutions, so it is really difficult to decide (Mizushima 2003: 238). We will tentatively follow the *kabane* solution here.

20.4343

本文・*Original Text*
(1) 和呂多比波 (2) 多比等於米保等 (3) 已比尒志弖 (4) 古米知夜須良牟 (5) 和加美可奈志母

仮名の書き下し・*Kana Transliteration*
(1) わろ₂たび₁は (2) たび₁と₂おめ₂ほど₂ (3) いひ₁にして (4) こ₁め₂ちやすらむ (5) わがみ₁かなしも₂

Romanization
(1) warə taᵐbi pa (2) taᵐbi tə omɛp-o-ⁿdə (3) ipi n-i s-i-te (4) ko mɛt-i yas-uram-u (5) wa-ŋga mi kanasi-mə

Glossing with Morphemic Analysis
(1) I journey TOP (2) journey QV think-EV-CONC (3) house COP-CONV do-CONV-SUB (4) child hold-CONV be.emaciated-TENT2-ATTR (5) I-POSS wife be.dear-EXCL

Translation
(1/2) Although I think that [my] journey is [just an unpleasant] journey, (5) [I] think tenderly of my wife (4) who is probably losing weight taking care of children (3) at home!

Commentary
EOJ *warə* 'I' corresponds to WOJ *ware* 'id.', although Suruŋga EOJ *ware* 'I' is also attested (see 20.4344 below). The correspondence Suruŋga EOJ *ə* : WOJ *e* is opposite to the correspondence Suruŋga EOJ *e* : WOJ *ə* that we have seen so far (see 20.4338, 20.4340, and 20.4342). Another example of the same correspondence of Suruŋga EOJ *ə* : WOJ *ɛ* in this poem is in the third syllable of Suruŋga EOJ *omɛpoⁿdə* (*o* < *ə*) 'although [I] think' in line three.

EOJ *omɛpoⁿdə* 'although [I] think' corresponds to WOJ *omopɛⁿdə* 'id.' We have already seen in other Suruŋga poems the example of the correspondence Suruŋga EOJ *ɛ* : WOJ *ə* in the second syllable (see 20.4337, 20.4338, 20.4340, and 20.4342). Another example in this poem of the same correspondence is Suruŋga EOJ *mɛt-* 'to hold', cf. its cognate WOJ *mət-* 'id.'[6] Both Suruŋga EOJ *ipi*

---

6 Since *po* : *pə* contrast is preserved only in the Kojiki, Suruŋga EOJ *omɛpoⁿdə* 'although [I] think' demonstrates the neutralization of this contrast: the underlying historical form of Suruŋga EOJ *omɛpoⁿdə* is *əmɛpəndə.

'house' corresponding to WOJ *ipe* 'id.' and Suruŋga EOJ *mi* 'wife' corresponding to WOJ *me* exhibit the same raising *e > i* in Suruŋga, as we have already seen above in 20.4339.

On *-umə ~ -mə* as a special Old Japanese exclamative form, see the commentary to 14.3431.

Postscript to the Poem 20.4343

本文・*Original Text*
右一首玉作部廣目

Translation
The poem above [was composed] by Tamatukuri^mbe-nə Pirəmɛ.

Commentary
Nothing is known about the biography of Tamatukuri^mbe-nə Pirəmɛ. Since his rank is not mentioned, he probably was a private. On private (*Kami-nə yoporo*, 上丁) and other *sakimori* ranks, see the commentary to the postscript to the poem 20.4321. Kinoshita notes that in the Suruŋga district (駿河郡) of Suruŋga province there was a Tamatukuri sato (玉造郷) 'Jade-carving village', which is likely to be the place where jade-carvers (*tamatukuri*) lived (1988: 105).

20.4344

本文・*Original Text*
(1) 和須良牟弓 (2) 努由伎夜麻由伎 (3) 和例久礼等 (4) 和我知々波々波 (5) 和須例勢努加毛

仮名の書き下し・*Kana Transliteration*
(1) わすらむて (2) の₁ゆき₁やまゆき₁ (3) われくれど₂ (4) わがちちははは (5) わすれせの₁かも₁

Romanization
(1) wasur-am-u te (2) no yuk-i yama yuk-i (3) ware k-ure-ⁿdə (4) wa-ⁿga titi papa pa (5) wasure se-n-o kamo

Glossing with Morphemic Analysis
(1) forget-TENT-FIN QV (2) field go-CONV mountain go-CONV (3) I come-EV-CONC (4) I-POSS father mother TOP (5) forget(NML) do-NEG-ATTR EP

Translation
(3) Although I came [here] (2) going through fields and mountains (1) intending to forget, (5) [how] can [I] forget (4) my father and mother?!

Commentary
There is an interesting problem in line one, since none of the old manuscripts has the phonogram 弖 /te/. Instead, we find 豆 /ⁿdu/ in the *Genryaku kōhon*, 等 /tə/ in the *Ruijū koshū*, and 砡 /to/ in the *Nishi Honganji-bon* and most other manuscripts. We believe that the line of reasoning in modern Japanese scholarship that views 豆 /ⁿdu/ in the *Genryaku kōhon* as a mistake of 弖 /te/ due to the similar forms in *sōsho*, 等 /tə/ in the *Ruijū koshū* as an attempt to 'explain' unfamiliar EOJ form, and 砡 /to/ in the *Nishi Honganji-bon* with an addition of the radical 石 'stone' to the phonogram 弖 /te/ as a correction of the text is misleading. The usage of the character 砡 /to/ 'whetstone' with *kō-rui* vowel *o* for the quotation verb *tə* with *otsu-rui* vowel *ə* would be highly unlikely in the eighth century, so it must be a late false correction (Omodaka 1984.20: 67; Kinoshita 1988: 105–106; Mizushima 2003: 255–256, 259–260). It must be further noted that both the *Genryaku kōhon* and the *Nishi Honganji-bon* gloss their respective 豆 /ⁿdu/ and 砡 /to/ with hiragana と /to/ and katakana ト /to/. Among all the manuscripts, the *Hirose-bon* is the only one that preserves 弖 /te/ (X: 60a), and this evidence alone is strong enough to support 弖 /te/ as being original. Finally, historical linguistics also lends us a hand in this matter: we have already seen in other Suruⁿga poems the example of the correspondence Suruⁿga EOJ *e* : WOJ *ə* (see 20.4337, 20.4338, 20.4340, 20.4342, and 20.4343), therefore Suruⁿga EOJ quotation verb *te* corresponding to WOJ *tə* should not be a surprising form. There is another example of Suruⁿga EOJ quotation verb *te* in poem 20.4346 below.

There are two verbs for 'to forget' in OJ that both appear in this poem: consonantal verb *wasur-* 'to forget intentionally' and vowel verb *wasure-* 'to forget unintentionally'.

On the EOJ verbal attributive *-o*, see the commentary to 14.3395 and a brief description of EOJ special grammar in the introductions to books fourteen and twenty.

Postscript to the Poem 20.4344

本文 • *Original Text*
右一首商長首麻呂

MAN'YŌSHŪ BOOK TWENTY

Translation
The poem above [was composed] by Akinəwosa-nə O{m}bitə Marə.

Commentary
Nothing is known about the biography of Akinəwosa-nə O{m}bitə Marə. Since his rank is not mentioned, he probably was a private. On private (*Kami-nə yoporo*, 上丁) and other *sakimori* ranks, see the commentary to the postscript to the poem 20.4321. There is a hypothesis connecting this person with Akinəwosa-nə O{m}bitə mentioned in the *Sinsen shōji roku* (新選姓氏録), compiled in 815 AD by the order of Emperor Saga (嵯峨天皇) (Kinoshita 1988: 106; Mizushima 2003: 257–258).

On O{m}bitə, see the commentary to the postscript to 20.4342.

20.4345

本文・*Original Text*
(1) 和伎米故等 (2) 不多利和我見之 (3) 宇知江須流 (4) 須流河乃祢良波 (5) 苦不志久米阿流可

仮名の書き下し・*Kana Transliteration*
(1) わぎめ₂こ₁と₂ (2) ふたりわがみ₁し (3) うちえ₂する (4) するがの₂ねらは (5) くふしくめ₂あるか

Romanization
(1) wa-ŋg-imɛ-ko-tə (2) puta-ri wa-ŋga MI-si (3) ut-i-yes-uru (4) Suruŋga-nə ne-ra pa (5) kupusi-ku mɛ ar-u ka

Glossing with Morphemic Analysis
(1) I-POSS-beloved-DIM-COM (2) two-CL we-POSS see(CONV)-PAST.ATTR (3) hit-CONV-approach-ATTR (4) Suruŋga-GEN peak-PLUR TOP (5) be.longing-CONV FP exist-ATTR EP

Translation
(5) Oh, how [I] long for (4) peaks in Suruŋga, (3) washed [by the waves], (1) [the peaks] that my beloved (2) two of us, looked at [together].

Commentary
The correspondence Suruŋga EOJ *e* : WOJ *ə* is attested in this poem in two examples: Suruŋga EOJ *yese-* 'to approach' (cf. WOJ *yəse-* 'id.') and Suruŋga EOJ

mɛ, focus particle (cf. WOJ *mə*). See also 20.4337, 20.4338, 20.4340, 20.4342, 20.4343, and 20.4344 for other examples. Interestingly enough, there is another example in this poem, where Suruᵑga EOJ *e* corresponds historically not to WOJ *ə*, but to WOJ *o*: Suruᵑga *imɛ* 'beloved' ~ WOJ *imo* 'id.' (this, of course, rests on the assumption that the contrast ɛ : e was neutralized in Suruᵑga EOJ).

Line three *utiyesuru* is considered to be a permanent epithet (*makura-kotoba*, 枕詞) to Suruᵑga (Omodaka 1984: 20: 68), but since it is quite transparent, we translate it. Kinoshita also suggests that there might be a play on sound with /suru/ of *utiyesuru* and **Suru**ᵑga (Kinoshita 1988: 107).

Line five is hypermetric (*ji amari*, 字余り), but it is probably a graphic illusion, because *kupusiku mɛ aru ka* was most likely pronounced as [kupusikumaruka] or [kupusikumɛruka].

Omodaka speculates that Suruᵑga-nə ne-ra 'Suruᵑga peaks' might refer to Mt. Fuji (1984.20: 68). But the plural marker -ra contradicts this hypothesis. We treat this phrase simply as 'Suruᵑga peaks'.

Suruᵑga EOJ *kupusi* 'to be longing' corresponds to early WOJ *koposi* and late WOJ *kopïsi* 'id.' Suruᵑga EOJ *kupusi* 'to be longing' is a result of raising of PJ *o > u. Cf. also EOJ *kopusi* in 14.3476.

Postscript to the Poem 20.4345

本文 • *Original Text*
右一首春日部麻呂

Translation
The poem above [was composed] by Kasuᵑgaᵐbe-nə Marə.

Commentary
Nothing is known about the biography of Kasuᵑgaᵐbe-nə Marə. Since his rank is not mentioned, he probably was a private. On private (*Kami-nə yoporo*, 上丁) and other *sakimori* ranks, see the commentary to the postscript to the poem 20.4321.

20.4346

本文 • *Original Text*
(1) 知々波々我 (2) 可之良加伎奈弖 (3) 佐久安礼天 (4) 伊比之氣等婆是 (5) 和須礼加祢豆流

仮名の書き下し・*Kana Transliteration*

(1) ちちははが (2) かしらかき₁なで (3) さくあれて (4) いひ₁しけ₂と₂ばぜ (5) わすれかねつる

Romanization

(1) titi papa-ⁿga (2) kasira kaki-naⁿde (3) sa-ku ar-e te (4) ip-i-si kɛtəᵐba ⁿze (5) wasure-kane-t-uru

Glossing with Morphemic Analysis

(1) father mother-POSS (2) head PREF-stroke(CONV) (3) safe-CONV exist-IMP QV (4) say-CONV-PAST.ATTR word FP (5) forget(CONV)-NEG.POT(CONV)-PERF-ATTR

Translation

(4/5) [I] cannot forget the words: (3) "Be safe!" that (1) [my] father and mother (4) said, (2) stroking [my] head.

Commentary

OJ *kasira* may refer either to the head itself, or to the head hair. It is quite possible that the author was actually patted on the head hair. In any case, stroking one's head or hair indicated strong emotional attachment and/or empathy (Kinoshita 1988: 108).

Suruⁿga EOJ *sa-ku* 'safely' corresponds to WOJ *saki-ku* 'id.' and Pitati EOJ *sake-ku ~ sakɛ-ku* 'id.' (see 20.4368 and 20.4372).

For Suruⁿga EOJ quotation verb *te* 'to say, to think' see the commentary to 20.4344.

Suruⁿga EOJ *kɛtəᵐba* 'word' corresponds to WOJ *kətəᵐba* 'id.'

Suruⁿga EOJ focus particle ⁿze corresponds to WOJ *sə ~ ⁿzə* 'id.' Thus, this poem provides three additional examples for the correspondence of Suruⁿga EOJ *e* : WOJ *ə*.

Postscript to the Poem 20.4346

本文・*Original Text*

右一首丈部稲麻呂

Translation

The poem above [was composed] by Pasetukaᵐbe-nə Inamarə.

308　　　　　　　　　　　　　　　　　　　　　　CHAPTER 4

Commentary

Nothing is known about the biography of Pasetuka^(m)be-nə Inamarə. Since his rank is not mentioned, he probably was a private. On private (*Kami-nə yoporo*, 上丁) and other *sakimori* ranks, see the commentary to the postscript to the poem 20.4321.

Postscript to the Poems 20.4337–4346

本文 • *Original Text*

二月七日駿河國防人部領使守從五位下布勢朝臣人主實進九日歌數廿首但拙劣歌者不取載之

Translation

On the seventh day of the second lunar month [of the seventh year of Tenpyō Shōhō], Puse-nə asəmi Pitənusi (Junior Fifth Rank, Lower Grade), governor of Suruŋga province, and *sakimori* messenger, [collected *sakimori* poems], but in reality presented [to me] twenty poems on ninth day. However, I did not include [here] the poems of inferior [quality].

Commentary

The seventh and ninth days of the second lunar month of the seventh year of Tenpyō Shōhō correspond to March 24 and 26, 755 AD.

Several additional facts are known about Puse-nə asəmi Pitənusi's biography. In the sixth year of Tenpyō Shōhō (754 AD) he came back to Dazaifu as a member of the embassy to Tang China. At that time he had Senior Sixth Rank, Upper Grade. In the third year of Tenpyō Hōji (759 AD) he was appointed Minor Controller of the Right (*Ushōben*, 右少辨). In the fourth year of Tenpyō Hōji (760 AD) Puse-nə asəmi Pitənusi served as an Inspector (*Junsatushi*, 巡察使) of the San'indō region. In the seventh year of Tenpyō Hōji (763 AD) he was promoted to Junior Fifth Rank, Upper Grade and appointed the Officer of the Public Affairs of the Left Capital Ward (*Sakyōryō*, 左京亮). In the eighth year of Tenpyō Hōji (764 AD) he was appointed the governor of Kamitupusa province. In the first year of Jingo Keiun (767 AD) he was made Senior Assistant Minister (*Tayū*, 大輔) of the Ministry of Ceremonial Affairs (*Shikibushō*, 式部省), and in the third year of Jingo Keiun (769 AD) Puse-nə asəmi Pitənusi was appointed the governor of I^(n)dumo province. We do not know when he was born or passed away.

On Suruŋga province, see the commentary to 14.3359.

20.4347

本文 · Original Text
(1) 伊閇尓之弖 (2) 古非都々安良受波 (3) 奈我波氣流 (4) 多知尓奈里弖母 (5) 伊波非弖之加母

仮名の書き下し · Kana Transliteration
(1) いへ₂にして (2) こ₁ひ₂つつあらずは (3) ながはけ₂る (4) たちになりても₂ (5) いはひ₂てしかも₂

Romanization
(1) ipɛ n-i s-i-te (2) kopï-tutu ar-aⁿz-u pa (3) na-ⁿga pak-ɛr-u (4) tati n-i nar-i-te mə (5) ipap-ï-te-si kamə

Glossing with Morphemic Analysis
(1) house COP-CONV do-CONV-SUB (2) long.for(CONV)-COOR exist-NEG-CONV TOP (3) thou-POSS carry-PROG-ATTR (4) long.sword COP-CONV become-CONV-SUB FP (5) protect-CONV-PERF(CONV)-PAST.ATTR EP

Translation
(4/5) [I] want to become the long sword (3) that you are carrying (5) and protect [you], (2) without longing for [you] (1) at home.

Commentary
This poem could be a poem in impeccable WOJ, but there are three misspellings impossible in WOJ that betray its EOJ origin: *ipɛ* 'house' vs. *ipe*, *pakɛru* 'are carrying' vs. *pakeru*, and *ipap-ï-te-si* vs. *ipap-i-te-si*. Since this poem is composed by the father of an upper-class *sakimori*, it is no wonder that we find only minor phonetic discrepancies between EOJ and WOJ. These misspellings probably indicate that unlike WOJ in Kamitupusa EOJ there was no distinction between *kō-rui* vowels *i, e* and *otsu-rui* vowels *ï, ɛ*.

Line two is hypermetric (*ji amari*, 字余り), but it is probably a graphic illusion, because *kopï-tutu ar-aⁿz-u* was most likely pronounced as [kopïtutaraⁿzu] or [kopïtuturaⁿzu].

On OJ *tati* 'long sword' see the commentary to 14.3485.

Besides the main meaning 'to pray', 'to perform purification/abstinence rituals', OJ verb *ipap-* has also the meaning 'to protect', 'to treat with care' (Mizushima 2003: 277).

Poems 20.4347–4359 are from Kamitupusa province.

Postscript to the Poem 20.4347

本文・*Original Text*
右一首國造丁日下部使主三中之父歌

Translation
The poem above [was composed] by the father of Assistant Commander Kusaka^(m)be-nə omi Minaka.

Commentary
Nothing is known about the biographies of Kusaka^(m)be-nə omi Minaka or his father. Kinoshita notes that the *kabane* title *omi* with the spelling 使主 was frequently encountered among immigrants from the mainland (1988: 110).

On Assistant Commander (*Kuni-nə miyatuko-nə yoporo*, 國造丁) and other *sakimori* ranks, see the commentary to the postscript to 20.4321.

This is the only poem composed by the father of a *sakimori*, although there are five poems composed by *sakimori* wives.

20.4348

本文・*Original Text*
(1) 多良知祢乃 (2) 波々平和加例弖 (3) 麻許等和例 (4) 多非乃加里保尓 (5) 夜須久祢牟加母

仮名の書き下し・*Kana Transliteration*
(1) たらちねの₂ (2) ははをわかれて (3) まこ₂と₂われ (4) たび₂の₂かりほに (5) やすくねむかも₂

Romanization
(1) tara t-ine n-ə (2) papa-wo wakare-te (3) ma-kətə ware (4) ta^(m)bï-nə kari-[i]po-ni (5) yasu-ku ne-m-u kamə

Glossing with Morphemic Analysis
(1) blood HON-mother COP-ATTR (2) mother-ACC be.separated(CONV)-SUB (3) INT-matter I (4) journey-GEN temporary-hut-LOC (5) easy-CONV sleep-TENT-ATTR EP

Translation
(3/5) I really wonder whether [I] would sleep easily (4) in the temporary hut on [my] journey, (2) being separated from my mother (1) who is [my own] blood mother.

Commentary
The only EOJ feature of this poem is the misspelling of the word *ta^mbi* 'journey' as *ta^mbï* that could not happen in WOJ. This misspelling indicates that there was no contrast between *kō-rui* vowel *i* and *otsu-rui* vowel *ï* in Kamitupusa EOJ. Since this poem is composed by an upper-class *sakimori*, it is no wonder that we find only a minor phonetic discrepancy between EOJ and WOJ.

OJ *taratine-nə* is an opaque permanent epithet (*makura-kotoba*, 枕詞) applied to OJ *papa* 'mother' see also MYS 15.3688. It has no coherent etymology in Japanese, although several have been suggested. It might possibly reflect the long-sought Austronesian substratum in Japanese. As Alexander Vovin has recently demonstrated, it consists of tara 'blood' < PAN *daraq 'id.', *t-, a PAN honorific prefix, *ine* < Western Malayo-Polynesian *inay 'mother', and OJ *n-ə*, COP-ATTR, with an overall meaning 'one's own blood mother' (2021, forthcoming).

Postscript to the Poem 20.4348

本文 • Original Text
右一首國造丁日下部使主三中

Translation
The poem above [was composed] by Assistant Commander Kusaka^mbe-nə omi Minaka.

Commentary
On Kusaka^mbe-nə omi Minaka, see the commentary to the postscript to 20.4347.

On Assistant Commander (*Kuni-nə miyatuko-nə yoporo*, 國造丁) and other *sakimori* ranks, see the commentary to the postscript to 20.4321.

20.4349

本文 • *Original Text*
(1) 毛母久麻能 (2) 美知波紀尒志乎 (3) 麻多佐良尒 (4) 夜蘇志麻須義弖 (5) 和加例加由可牟

仮名の書き下し • *Kana Transliteration*
(1) も₁も₂くまの₂ (2) み₁ちはき₂にしを (3) またさらに (4) やそ₁しますぎ₂て (5) わかれかゆかむ

Romanization
(1) momə kuma-nə (2) miti pa k-ï-n-i-si-wo (3) mata sara n-i (4) yaso sima suŋgï-te (5) wakare ka yuk-am-u

Glossing with Morphemic Analysis
(1) hundred bend-GEN (2) road TOP come-CONV-PERF-CONV-PAST.ATTR- ACC
(3) again again COP-CONV (4) eighty island pass(CONV)-SUB (5) part(CONV) IP go-TENT-ATTR

Translation
(2) Although [I] came along the road (1) with one hundred bends, (5) should [I] go farther away [from home] (3/4) passing again and again many islands?

Commentary
The only EOJ feature in this poem is the misspelling of *k-i-n-i-si* 'came' as *k-ï-n-i-si*, which would be impossible in WOJ and which probably indicates that there was no contrast between *kō-rui* vowel *i* and *otsu-rui* vowel *ï* in Kamitupusa EOJ. See also 20.4347 and 20.4348 above.

OJ *yaso* 'eighty' is used here metaphorically to indicate 'many'. See also 20.4329 for the similar usage.

Postscript to the Poem 20.4349

本文 • *Original Text*
右一首助丁刑部直三野

Translation
The poem above [was composed] by Captain Osakaᵐbe-nə atapi Mino.

萬葉集卷第二十・MAN'YŌSHŪ BOOK TWENTY

Commentary

Nothing is known about the biography of Osaka^mbe-nə atapi Mino. Atapi (直) is a *kabane* title.

On captain (*Sukɛ-nə yoporo*, 助丁) and other *sakimori* ranks, see the commentary to the postscript to the poem 20.4321.

20.4350

本文・Original Text
(1) 尒波奈加能 (2) 阿須波乃可美尒 (3) 古志波佐之 (4) 阿例波伊波々牟 (5) 加倍理久麻泥尒

仮名の書き下し・Kana Transliteration
(1) にはなかの₂ (2) あすはの₂かみ₁に (3) こ₁しばさし (4) あれはいははむ (5) か へ₂りくまでに

Romanization
(1) nipa naka-nə (2) Asupa n-ə kami-ni (3) ko-si^mba sas-i (4) are pa ipap-am-u (5) kapɛr-i-k-u-ma^nde-ni

Glossing with Morphemic Analysis
(1) garden inside-GEN (2) Asupa COP-ATTR deity-DAT (3) DIM-small.branch insert-CONV (4) I TOP pray-TENT-FIN (5) return-CONV-come-ATTR-TERM-LOC

Translation
(5) Until [you] come back, (4) I will pray (3) sticking into [the ground] small branches (2) for deity Asupa (1) in the garden.

Commentary

This poem was probably composed either by a wife or a parent of the *sakimori* named as an author in the postscript to this poem, otherwise the poem would not make any sense.

The only EOJ features in this poem are misspellings of *kamï* 'deity' as *kami* and of *kapɛr-* 'to return' as *kapɛr-*, which would be impossible in WOJ and which probably indicates that there was no contrast between *kō-rui* vowels *i, e* and *otsu-rui* vowels *ï, ɛ* in Kamitupusa EOJ. See also 20.4347, 20.4348, and 20.4349 above.

Omodaka et al. assign to OJ *nipa* three meanings: a) 'a place for conducting matters', b) 'open space in front or behind a house', 'garden', c) 'sea surface', 'open water surface', but at the same time they express reservation whether gardens during the Nara period were really called *nipa* besides *sənə* (1967: 546). We believe that this reservation is unfounded: the sequence of locative case marker *-ni* and topic marker *pa* is written in 1.2 with the character 庭 'garden': 山常庭 *Yamatə-ni pa* 'in Yamatə', and in the poem 15.3609 by Kakinəmətə-nə asəmi Pitəmarə 庭 /nipa/ is used as a *kungana* for 'sea surface'. So it is quite clear that *nipa* meant garden in the Nara period. It is, however, a different matter whether *nipa* 'sea surface' and *nipa* 'garden', 'open space in front or behind a house' are one and the same word. Most likely they are just homonyms.

The deity Asupa (阿須波) is mentioned in the *Kojiki* as one of the children of deity Opə təsi-nə kamï (大年神) (KJK I: 38a.8), and is also listed in the *Norito* (NT 1.388.7). Nothing is really clear about this deity, although there are attempts to define him as a household deity (Kinoshita 1988: 113). The much later character spellings 足羽 /Asipa/ 'leg feathers' and 足岩 /Asipa/ 'foot rock' demonstrate with certainty only two things: first, that they really do not fit with the name (/u/ vs. /i/), and second, that the name of this deity in all probability is not Japanese. The context of the poem suggests that it was a deity somehow associated with safe travel and/or return.

Sticking small branches in the ground probably indicates constructing the boundaries for the sacred space where the deity Asupa was worshipped.

OJ *si^mba* could refer either to a bush or a small tree, or to small branches.

On attributive *-u* in *k-u-ma^nde-ni* 'until I come back' in line five see the commentary to 20.4339.

Postscript to the Poem 20.4350

本文・*Original Text*
右一首帳丁若麻續部諸人

Translation
The poem above [was composed] by sergeant Wakawomi^mbe-nə Mərəpitə.

Commentary
Nothing is known about the biography of Wakawomi^mbe-nə Mərəpitə. The author of this poem is not him, but either his wife or parent, as mentioned above in commentary to 20.4350. Therefore, characters 妻 'spouse', 母 'mother', or 父 'father' probably were lost after his name.

On sergeant (*Chō-no yoporo*, 帳丁) and other *sakimori* ranks see the commentary to the postscript to 20.4321.

20.4351

本文・*Original Text*
(1) 多妣己呂母 (2) 夜倍伎可佐祢弖 (3) 伊努礼等母 (4) 奈保波太佐牟志 (5) 伊母尓志阿良祢婆

仮名の書き下し・*Kana Transliteration*
(1) たび₁こ₂ろ₂も₂ (2) や へ₂き₁かさねて (3) い の₁れど₂も₂ (4) なほはださむし (5) いも₂にしあらねば

Romanization
(1) ta^mbi kərəmə (2) ya-pɛ ki-kasane-te (3) i n-ore-^ndəmə (4) napo pa^nda samu-si (5) imə n-i si ar-an-e-^mba

Glossing with Morphemic Analysis
(1) travel garment (2) eight-CL wear(CONV)-pile.up(CONV)-SUB (3) sleep sleep-EV-CONC (4) still skin cold-FIN (5) beloved COP-CONV EP exist-NEG-EV-CON

Translation
(3) Although [I] sleep, (2) putting on eight layers (1) [of] travel garments, (4) it is still cold, (5) because [they] are not [my] beloved.

Commentary
This poem has two EOJ features: misspelling of *pe* 'layer' as *pɛ*, which should indicate the absence of distinction between *kō-rui* vowel *e* and *otsu-rui* vowel *ɛ* in Kamitupusa EOJ; and EOJ-specific evidential suffix *-ore-* (cf. WOJ *-ure-*). Like Omodaka (1984.20: 75), and unlike other Japanese scholars, we think that 伊努礼等母 should be read *i n-ore-^ndəmə*, and not *i n-ure-^ndəmə*, because the character 努 is used to write the syllable /no/, and not the syllable /nu/ not only in all *sakimori* poems, but specifically also in other *sakimori* poems from Kamitupusa province, see EOJ 和努 *wano* 'I' in 20.4358.

Line five is hypermetric (*ji amari*, 字余り), but it is probably a graphic illusion, because *imə n-i si ar-an-e-^mba* was most likely pronounced as [imənisarane^mba].

Postscript to the Poem 20.4351

本文・*Original Text*
右一首望陀郡上丁玉作部國忍

Translation
The poem above [was composed] by private Tamatukuri^(m)be-nə Kuniosi from Umaŋguta district.

Commentary
Nothing is known about the biography of Tamatukuri^(m)be-nə Kuniosi.

On private (*Kami-nə yoporo*, 上丁) and other *sakimori* ranks, see the commentary to the postscript to the poem 20.4321.

On Umaŋguta district, see the commentary to 14.3382.

20.4352

本文・*Original Text*
(1) 美知乃倍乃 (2) 宇万良能宇礼尓 (3) 波保麻米乃 (4) 可良麻流伎美乎 (5) 波可礼加由加牟

仮名の書き下し・*Kana Transliteration*
(1) み₁ちの₂へ₂の₂ (2) うまらの₂うれに (3) はほまめ₂の₂ (4) からまるき₁み₁を (5) はかれかゆかむ

Romanization
(1) miti-nə pɛ-nə (2) umara-nə ure-ni (3) pap-o mamɛ-nə (4) karamar-u kimi-wo (5) pakare ka yuk-am-u

Glossing with Morphemic Analysis
(1) road-GEN side-GEN (2) thorny.tree-GEN top-LOC (3) crawl-ATTR bean-COMP (4) entwine-ATTR lord-ACC (5) be.separated(CONV) IP go-TENT-ATTR

Translation
(5) Will [I] go away separating [myself] (4) from you, who is entwined [around me] (3) like beans that crawl (2) on the top of a thorny tree (1) at the side of a road?

Commentary
This poem is easy to understand, but difficult to interpret. It seems to be a love poem composed by a man to a woman, but the pronominal usage of *kimi* 'lord', which is always used by women toward men, and not *vice versa*, is difficult to explain. Among premodern Japanese scholars, Sengaku offers a brief commentary on this poem, but his comments deal only with unusual vocabulary or grammar and do not offer any insight to this problem (Satake 1981: 493). Keichū

does not comment on the oddity of *kimi* used as a second person pronoun in a reference to a woman in this poem (1690.20: 28a–29a), and Kamochi does not comment on it either (1912.7: 341–342). Therefore, it seems that premodern Japanese commentators either did not perceive this strange usage of *kimi* as an issue, or were completely oblivious to it. We trust that the first explanation is more likely, because all three premodern commentaries comment on EOJ form *pap-o* 'crawl-ATTR', which was apparently perceived as a grammatical irregularity vis-à-vis WOJ *pap-u* 'id.' This illustrates that premodern scholars were not oblivious to the grammar rules, and consequently it does not explain why the ungrammatical pronominal usage of *kimi* escaped their attention. The only possible answer to this puzzle is that this usage apparently did not violate the grammatical rules. Contrary to premodern scholars, modern Japanese scholars seem to be preoccupied with the task of explaining this odd usage of *kimi*. Among the earlier modern scholars, Inoue just provides a comment that *kimi* is used towards a woman in this poem (1928.7: 4040), which is echoed by others in a more probabilistic tone (Kōnosu 1939: 3309; Takeda 1957: 406). Takagi et al. agree with this point of view as well, but indicate that the usage of *kimi* in reference to a woman is rare, and also speculate further that this might be an EOJ usage (1962: 420). The majority of modern scholars adopt the explanation proposed by Saeki Umetomo (1959: 85) that the woman in question might be the young mistress of the main house to whom the author is especially close (Nakanishi 1983: 301; Omodaka 1984.20: 77; Kinoshita 1988: 117; Itō 1999: 478; Satake et al. 2003: 404). Kubota plainly states that *kimi* is a honorific term designating one's wife (1967: 445). Others remain non-committal (Tsuchiya 1977: 303; Kojima et al. 1975: 391). However, we believe that the usage of the verb *karamar-* 'to be entwined' is likely to indicate embrace, and therefore has sexual connotations. Consequently, Saeki Umetomo's explanation is unlikely. Mizushima in his monumental study of *sakimori* poems takes the position that the pronominal usage of *kimi* by a man towards a woman was possible in OJ and provides references to twelve poems in the *Man'yōshū* (4.495 4.668, 4.697, 6.915, 6.947, 6.953, 8.1428, 8.1641, 11.2579, 11.2586, 12.3136, and 14.3365), where such a usage can be observed according to his opinion (2003: 314–316). However, we trust that all these cases can be interpreted either as poems addressed to male friends or male superiors to whom they are close, as poems where males assume the voice of females, or as humorous or playful poems – we normally encounter these kinds of interpretation in the commentaries by other *Man'yōshū* scholars who do not agree with Mizushima. Therefore, we still feel that something is amiss here that we cannot explain.

This leads me to another hypothesis, which alone can explain this oddity. The author of this poem is called Pasetuka^mbe-nə Təri (丈部鳥). Although *təri* (鳥) 'bird' as a component of male names occurs in modern Japan, in the Nara period male name *tǝri* seems to be odd: we know of no such examples. On the other hand, in Mino province census of 702 AD there is a female name Ma-tǝri-me (眞鳥賣), lit. 'true-bird-female' that belongs to a four year-old girl (SSI 2.24.8.10). A connection between birds in general and females can also be supported by the following passage in the *Kojiki kayō* that represents the speech of a female:

> 伊麻許曾婆和杼理迩阿良米能知波那杼理迩阿良牟遠
> ima kǝsǝ pa wa-ⁿdǝri n-i ar-am-ɛ nǝti pa na-ⁿdǝri n-i ar-am-u-wo
> now FP TOP I-OSM-bird COP-CONV exist-TENT-EV later TOP thou-OSM-bird COP-CONV exist-TENT-ATTR-ACC
> Right now [I] am my bird. But because later [I] will be thy bird ...
> (KK 3)

Consequently, we dare to suggest that Pasetukaᵐbe-nǝ Tǝri was in fact a faithful wife of a *sakimori*, who went together with her husband to Tukusi.[7] Thus, the probability that Pasetukaᵐbe-nǝ Tǝri was a female, and that, therefore, this poem was composed by a woman is quite high.

OJ *umara* (also *uᵐbara*) is a generic name for low thorny trees as well for a thorn itself.

This poem has two EOJ features: misspelling of *pe* 'side' as *pɛ*, which should indicate the absence of distinction between *kō-rui* vowel *e* and *otsu-rui* vowel *ɛ* in Kamitupusa EOJ; and special EOJ attributive -*o* in *pap-o* < *pap-o*, on which see the commentary to 14.3395 and a brief description of EOJ special grammar in the introductions to book fourteen and this volume.

The initial alternation of *p*- with *w*- as in *pakare* ~ *wakare* 'be separated' is a rare correspondence, but it also occurs in a couple of other words, such as *pasir-* ~ *wasir-* 'to run, to move fast', *patuka n-i* ~ *waⁿduka n-i* 'barely' (Kinoshita 1988: 117). Given also the fact that the syllable /ka/ in *pakare* is spelled with the character 可 {ka}, not {ⁿga}, this explanation is preferable to Omodaka's attempt to read *pakare* as *paⁿgare* (1984.20: 77), an otherwise unattested intransitive counterpart of the transitive *paⁿgas-* 'to take off'. The intransitive counterpart would also make no sense syntactically, as *kimi* is marked by the accusative case marker -*wo*.

---

7 Many thanks to Karl Friday who dissuaded me from my originally crazy idea that this person was a female *sakimori*, and suggested that the author might be a daughter of a *sakimori*, as well as providing me with a wealth of other information on *sakimori*. We still perceive this poem as having, however, at least some sexual overtones, so we are more inclined towards the 'wife version'. *Sakimori* were allowed to take with them their families, at least in theory, although very few probably actually used this privilege. Still, the problem remains why the wife or the daughter is given the rank of a private?

Postscript to the Poem 20.4352

本文 · *Original Text*
右一首天羽郡上丁丈部鳥

Translation
The poem above [was composed] by private Pasetuka^mbe-nə Təri from Amapa district.

Commentary
Nothing is known about the biography of Pasetuka^mbe-nə Təri. See the commentary above on the possible gender of Pasetuka^mbe-nə Təri.

On private (*Kami-nə yoporo*, 上丁) and other *sakimori* ranks, see the commentary to the postscript to the poem 20.4321.

Amapa district corresponds to an area in the southern part of Futtsu city (Futtsu-shi, 富津市) in present-day Chiba Prefecture (Nakanishi 1985: 420).

20.4353

本文 · *Original Text*
(1) 伊倍加是波 (2) 比尓々々布氣等 (3) 和伎母古賀 (4) 伊倍其登母遲弖 (5) 久流比等母奈之

仮名の書き下し · *Kana Transliteration*
(1) いへ₂かぜは (2) ひ₁にひ₁にふけ₂ど₂ (3) わぎ₁も₂こ₁が (4) いへ₂ご₂と₂も₂ちて (5) くるひ₁と₂も₂なし

Romanization
(1) ipɛ kaⁿze pa (2) pi-ni pi-ni puk-ɛ-ⁿdə (3) wa-ŋg-imə-ko-ŋga (4) ipɛ-ŋ-gətə mət-i-te (5) k-uru pitə mə na-si

Glossing with Morphemic Analysis
(1) home wind TOP (2) day-LOC day-LOC blow-EV-CONC (3) I-POSS-beloved-DIM-POSS (4) home-GEN-word hold-CONV-SUB (5) come-ATTR person FP exist.not-FIN

Translation
(1/2) Although the wind from home blows every day, (4/5) there is nobody who will bring the message about home (3) from my dear beloved.

Commentary

Wind from home is the wind blowing from the direction where home is, which for *sakimori* was the Eastern wind.

This poem has just one EOJ feature: 'misspelling' of *ipe* 'home' as *ipɛ* (on lines one and four), which should indicate the absence of distinction between *kō-rui* vowel *e* and *otsu-rui* vowel *ɛ* in Kamitupusa EOJ.

The second syllable /ti/ in OJ *matite* 'hold and' is spelled with the character 遅 that is believed to be used in the *man'yōgana* for the syllable /ⁿdi/ with a prenasalized initial [ⁿd]. Nakanishi consequently reads *məⁿdite* (1983: 301), but Kinoshita speculates that it was misheard as prenasalized voiced (1988: 118). However, as Alexander Vovin have demonstrated elsewhere, 遅 could be used for the syllable /ti/ as well (2009b: 29–30).

Postscript to the Poem 20.4353

本文 • *Original Text*
右一首朝夷郡上丁丸子連大歳

Translation
The poem above [was composed] by private Maroko-nə muraⁿzi Opotəsi from Asapina district.

Commentary

Nothing is known about the biography of Maroko-nə muraⁿzi Opotəsi.

On private (*Kami-nə yoporo*, 上丁) and other *sakimori* ranks, see the commentary to the postscript to the poem 20.4321.

Asapina district (Asapina kəpori, 朝夷郡) corresponds to an area in Minamibōsō city (Minamibōsō-shi, 南房総市) in present-day Chiba prefecture (Nakanishi 1985: 420). Before the integration into big cities in 2006 it was a part of Chikura town (Chikura machi, 千倉町) of Awa county (Awa-gun, 安房郡) of Chiba prefecture. Historically, Apa province (Apa-nə kuni, 安房國), to which Asapina district belonged, was separated from Kamitupusa province in the second year of Yōrō (養老) (718 AD), then integrated back into Kamitupusa province in the thirteenth year of Tenpyō (741 AD), and then made a separate province again in the first year of Tenpyō Hōji (757 AD). In the seventh year of Tenpyō Shōhō (755 AD) it was a part of Kamitupusa province (Kinoshita 1988: 118).

20.4354

本文・*Original Text*
(1) 多知許毛乃 (2) 多知乃佐和伎尒 (3) 阿比美弖之 (4) 伊母加己々呂波 (5) 和須礼世奴可母

仮名の書き下し・*Kana Transliteration*
(1) たちこ₂も₁の₂ (2) たちの₂さわき₁に (3) あひ₁み₁てし (4) いも₂がこ₂こ₂ろ₂は (5) わすれせぬかも₂

Romanization
(1) tat-i kəmo-nə (2) tat-i-nə sawak-i-ni (3) api-mi-te-si (4) imə-ⁿga kəkərə pa (5) wasure se-n-u kamə

Glossing with Morphemic Analysis
(1) rise-CONV wild.duck-COMP (2) depart-NML-GEN make.noise-NML-LOC (3) REC-see(CONV)-PERF(CONV)-PAST.ATTR (4) beloved-POSS heart TOP (5) forget(NML) do-NEG-ATTR EP

Translation
(5) [I] will not forget (4) the feelings of [my] beloved, (3) with whom [I] met (2) during the noise of [my] departure (1) that was like a wild duck rising.

Commentary
This poem has just one EOJ feature: Kamitupusa EOJ *kəmo* 'wild duck' corresponding to WOJ *kamo* 'id.' (also attested in EOJ). Cf. also EOJ *kama* 'wild duck' in 20.4339. On OJ *kamo* 'wild duck' see the commentary to 14.3524. Both EOJ *kəmo* and *kama* are likely to be results of vowel assimilations: regressive in the former case (if the contrast between *o* and *ə* was lost), and progressive in the latter.

Japanese scholars believe that *tat-i* 'rise-CONV' in *tat-i kəmo* 'rising wild duck' is not an converb, but an attributive form that corresponds to WOJ *tat-u* 'rise-ATTR' (Kinoshita 1988: 119), but since there are no other examples where EOJ imagined attributive *-i would correspond to WOJ attributive *-u*, this usage can be rather compared to MJ usage of the converb form in the attributive function (Vovin 2003: 232).

There is certainly a play on words involved on *tat-* 'to rise' in line one and *tat-* 'to depart' in line two. Although there is a tendency to treat the first line as a permanent epithet (*makura-kotoba*, 枕詞) (Kinoshita 1988: 119), this is highly unlikely, since a flock of wild ducks, or even a single wild duck are likely to produce significant noise when rising into the air.

The hypothesis that EOJ *kəmo* means 'mat made from the straw of wild rice' (WOJ *kəmə*, EOJ *kɛmɛ*) and not 'wild duck' was advanced by Takeda (1957: 408), but Omodaka has demonstrated very persuasively that this hypothesis should be rejected (1984.20: 79).

Postscript to the Poem 20.4354

本文・*Original Text*
右一首長狭郡上丁丈部与呂麻呂

Translation
The poem above [was composed] by private Pasetuka ^mbe-nə Yərəmarə from Na ^ŋgasa district.

Commentary
Nothing is known about the biography of Pasetuka ^mbe-nə Yərəmarə.

On private (*Kami-nə yoporo*, 上丁) and other *sakimori* ranks, see the commentary to the postscript to the poem 20.4321.

Like Asapina district that appears in 20.4353 above, Na ^ŋgasa district (Na ^ŋgasa kəpori, 長狭郡) was also originally a district of Apa province (Apa-nə kuni, 安房國), that was located to the North of Asapina district mentioned in poem 20.4353 above. It corresponds to an area including Kamogawa city (Kamogawa-shi, 鴨川市), Amatukominato town (Amatukominato-chō, 天津小湊町), and an area around Kamo river (Kamogawa, 加茂川) basin in present-day Chiba prefecture (Nakanishi 1985: 468).

20.4355

本文・*Original Text*
(1) 余曾尒能美 (2) 美弖夜和多良毛 (3) 奈尒波我多 (4) 久毛爲尒美由流 (5) 志麻奈良奈久尒

仮名の書き下し・*Kana Transliteration*
(1) よ₂そ₂にの₂み₁ (2) み₁てやわたらも₁ (3) なにはがた (4) くも₁ゐにみ₁ゆる (5) しまならなくに

Romanization
(1) yəsə-ni nəmi (2) mi-te ya watar-am-o (3) Nanipa-ŋ-gata (4) kumowi-ni mi-y-uru (5) sima nar-an-aku n-i

Glossing with Morphemic Analysis
(1) outside-LOC RP (2) see(CONV)-SUB IP cross-TENT-ATTR (3) Nanipa-GEN-lagoon (4) distance-LOC see-PASS-ATTR (5) island be-NEG-NML COP-CONV

Translation
(3/5) Although Nanipa lagoon is not an island (4) that is seen in the distance, (2) will [I] cross over [to Tukusi] seeing [it] (5) only from afar?

Commentary
This poem has two EOJ features. The first is the misspelling of *nəmï* 'only' as *nəmi*, which should indicate the absence of distinction between *kō-rui* vowel *i* and *otsu-rui* vowel *ï* in Kamitupusa EOJ. The second is the special EOJ attributive form *-o*, on which see the commentary to 14.3395 and a brief description of EOJ special grammar in the introductions to book fourteen and this volume.

On Nanipa and Nanipa lagoon, see the commentaries to poems 20.4329 and 20.4330.

Postscript to the Poem 20.4355

本文 · Original Text
右一首武射郡上丁丈部山代

Translation
The poem above [was composed] by private Pasetuka{m}be-nə Yamasirə from Mu{n}za district.

Commentary
Nothing is known about the biography of Pasetuka{m}be-nə Yamasirə.

On private (*Kami-nə yoporo*, 上丁) and other *sakimori* ranks, see the commentary to the postscript to the poem 20.4321.

Mu{n}za district corresponds to the northern part of present-day Sanbu county in Chiba prefecture (Omodaka 1984.20: 82; Nakanishi 1985: 491; Kinoshita 1988: 120). This placename is apparently of Ainu origin: Munsa < *mun-sa (Aini *mun* 'unedible grass' + *sa* 'plain') 'plain of unedible grass'. Cf. also related placename

Muⁿzasi < *mun-sa-si < Ainu *mun sa-hi* 'unedible.grass plain-POSS'. For details on Muⁿzasi see the list of Ainu words in the introduction to this volume and Vovin (2009b: 2–3).

20.4356

本文 • *Original Text*
(1) 和我波々能 (2) 蘇弖母知奈弖氏 (3) 和我可良尒 (4) 奈伎之許己呂乎 (5) 和須良延努可毛

仮名の書き下し • *Kana Transliteration*
(1) わがははの₂ (2) そ₁でも₂ちなでて (3) わがからに (4) なき₁しこ₂こ₂ろ₂を (5) わすらえ₂の₁かも

Romanization
(1) wa-ⁿga papa-nə (2) soⁿde mət-i naⁿde-te (3) wa-ⁿga karani (4) nak-i-si kəkərə-wo (5) wasur-aye-n-o kamo

Glossing with Morphemic Analysis
(1) I-POSS mother-GEN (2) sleeve hold-CONV caress(CONV)-SUB (3) I-POSS CONJ (4) weep-CONV-PAST.ATTR heart-ACC (5) forget-PASS-NEG-ATTR EP

Translation
(5) [I] cannot forget (1/4) my mother's feelings when [she] wept (3) because of me (2) caressing me with [her] sleeve!

Commentary
We follow here Itō's and Mizushima's reading of the verb *wasur-aye-n-o* in line five and the reconstruction of its script archetype as 和須良延努 with the character 努 (Itō 1999: 472, 474, 485; Mizushima 2003: 341, 343). We disagree with other Japanese scholars on their reading of the verb, where they unanimously read *wasurayenu*, notwithstanding whether they reconstruct the script archetype as 和須良延努 with the character 努 (Kōnosu 1939: 3313; Takagi et al. 1962: 421; Kubota 1967: 448; Nakanishi 1983: 302), or as 和須良延奴 with the character 奴 (Takeda 1957: 409; Kojima et al. 1975: 392; Tsuchiya 1977: 306; Omodaka 1984.20: 82; Kinoshita 1988: 121; Satake 2003: 406). Among the oldest manuscripts, the character 奴 appears only in the *Genryaku kōhon*, all other have the character 努. In addition, the *Hirose-bon*, the only manuscript that comes from the independent lineage of the now lost *Teika-bon*, also has the

character 努. This heavily tips the balance in favor of the character 努. As we can see elsewhere, the character 努 is used to write predominantly the syllable *no*, not the syllable *nu* (see 20.4341, 20.4344, 20.4351 above and 20.4358 below). Consequently, this poem turns out to have just one EOJ feature: the special EOJ attributive form *-o*, on which see the commentary to 14.3395 and a brief description of EOJ special grammar in the introductions to book fourteen and this volume.

It is not quite clear whose sleeve it is; in other words, is it the author's sleeve that his mother holds and caresses, or is it his mother's sleeve that she holds to caress him? In our translation we follow the second interpretation adopted by the majority of modern Japanese scholars.

Postscript to the Poem 20.4356

本文 • *Original Text*
右一首山邊郡上丁物部乎刀良

Translation
The poem above [was composed] by private Mənəᵐbe-nə Wotora from Yamanəpe district.

Commentary
Nothing is known about the biography of Mənəᵐbe-nə Wotora.

On private (*Kami-nə yoporo*, 上丁) and other *sakimori* ranks, see the commentary to the postscript to the poem 20.4321.

Yamanəpe district corresponds to the southern part of Sanbu county (Sanbu-gun, 山武郡) in present-day Chiba prefecture (Omodaka 1984.20: 83; Nakanishi 1985: 494; Kinoshita 1988: 121).

20.4358

本文 • *Original Text*
(1) 於保伎美乃 (2) 美許等加志古美 (3) 伊弖久礼婆 (4) 和努等里都伎弖 (5) 伊比之古奈波毛

仮名の書き下し • *Kana Transliteration*
(1) おほき₁み₁の₂ (2) み₁こ₂と₂かしこ₁み₁ (3) いでくれば (4) わの₁と₂りつき₁て (5) いひ₁しこ₁なはも₁

Romanization
(1) opo kimi-nə (2) mi-kətə kasiko-mi (3) iⁿde-k-ure-ᵐba (4) wano tər-i-tuk-i-te (5) ip-i-si ko-na pa mo

Glossing with Morphemic Analysis
(1) Great Lord-GEN (2) HON-word be.awesome-GER (3) exit(CONV)-come-EV-CON (4) I grab-CONV-attach-CONV-SUB (5) say-CONV-PAST.ATTR girl-DIM TOP EP

Translation
(3) When [I] left [the house], (1/2) because the command of the Great Lord is awesome, (4/5) oh, [that] girl who grabbed me and pleaded [with me not to go].

Commentary
There are two EOJ features in this poem: Kamitupusa EOJ first personal singular pronoun *wano* 'I' (cf. *wano* 'id.' in 14.3476 and 14.3476a), and EOJ diminutive suffix *-na* corresponding to WOJ *-ra* [for details see Vovin (2005: 208–210, 212–213)].

On *opo kimi* 'Great Lord' which refers to the Emperor, see the commentary to 14.3480.

On *mi-kətə* 'honorable word', 'imperial order/edict', see the commentary to 14.3480.

Postscript to the Poem 20.4358

本文 • *Original Text*
右一首種泍郡上丁物部龍

Translation
The poem above [was composed] by private Mənənəᵐbe-nə Tatu from Supi district.

Commentary
Nothing is known about the biography of Mənənəᵐbe-nə Tatu.

On private (*Kami-nə yoporo*, 上丁) and other *sakimori* ranks, see the commentary to the postscript to the poem 20.4321.

All modern scholars correct the name of Supi district (Supi kəpori, 種泍郡) to Suwe district (Suwe kəpori, 種淮郡), see, e.g. Omodaka 1984.20: 85; Kinoshita

1988: 124; Mizushima 2003: 356–57. There are two problems with this revision of the text. First, all the oldest manuscripts and the *Hirose-bon* have Supi district (種沚郡), and not Suwe district (種淮郡), which appears only in the much later *Hosoi-bon* and wood-block printed editions. Second, the earliest attestation of this placename spelled as Suwe is found only in the early tenth century dictionary *Wamyōshō* (和名抄).[8] But this is too late, as by this time medial -*p*- and -*w*- merged as -*w*-. Also, we must keep in mind that MJ is much more conservative than OJ regarding the raising of original PJ vowels *e and *o to high vowels *i* and *u* respectively. The form Supi suggests EOJ origin, since EOJ raises *e and *o to *i* and *u* in the last syllable of a disyllabic noun, while WOJ tends to keep them there in most cases (Hayata 1998). The otherwise unattested WOJ form was in all probability *Supe that had its expected development into MJ Suwe. *Supe district corresponds to Kimitsu city (Kimitsu-shi, 君津市) and northern part of Futtsu city (Futtsu-shi, 富津市) in present-day Chiba prefecture (Nakanishi 1985: 456; Kinoshita 1988: 124).

20.4359

本文 • *Original Text*
(1) 都久之閇尓 (2) 敝牟加流布祢乃 (3) 伊都之加毛 (4) 都加敝麻都里弖 (5) 久尓々閇牟可毛

仮名の書き下し • *Kana Transliteration*
(1) つくしへ₂に (2) へ₁むかるふねの₂ (3) いつしかも₁ (4) つかへ₁まつりて (5) くにに へ₂むかも₁

Romanization
(1) Tukusi-pɛ-ni (2) pe muk-ar-u pune-nə (3) itu si kamo (4) tukape-matur-i-te (5) kuni-ni pɛ muk-am-o

Glossing with Morphemic Analysis
(1) Tukusi-side-LOC (2) bow direct-PROG-ATTR boat-GEN (3) when EP EP (4) serve(CONV)-HUM-CONV-SUB (5) province-LOC bow turn-TENT-ATTR

---

8 I believe that *suwe* (末) appearing in preface and text of 9.1738 is not the alternative spelling of this placename, but a reference to 'edge, end', in other words, the seashore, where the land ends.

Translation
(3) I wonder when (2) the boat which is [now] directing [its] bow (1) towards Tukusi (5) will turn its bow towards [my home] province, (4) after [I finish my] service?

Commentary
Tukusi is the old name for the island of Kyūshū.

It is quite clear that unlike WOJ, Kamitupusa EOJ did not have a phonemic contrast between *e* and *ɛ*. OJ *pɛ* 'ship's bow' (with etymological *ɛ*) is spelled incorrectly as *pe* in line two, but correctly as *pɛ* in line five. In addition, *pe* 'side' is misspelled as *pɛ* in line one, and *tukapɛ-* 'to serve' as *tukape-* in line four.

EOJ progressive suffix *-ar-* corresponds to WOJ *-er-*.

On EOJ special attributive form *-o*, see the commentary to 14.3395 and a brief description of EOJ special grammar in the introductions to book fourteen and this volume.

Postscript to the Poem 20.4359

本文 • Original Text
右一首長柄郡上丁若麻續部羊

Translation
The poem above [was composed] by private Wakawomi ᵐbe-nə Pituⁿzi from Naᵑgara district.

Commentary
Nothing is known about the biography of Wakawomiᵐbe-nə Pituⁿzi.

On private (*Kami-nə yoporo*, 上丁) and other *sakimori* ranks, see the commentary to the postscript to the poem 20.4321.

Naᵑgara district corresponds to the northern part of Chōsei county (長生郡) and Mobara city (茂原市) in present-day Chiba prefecture (Kinoshita 1988: 126).

Postscript to the Poems 20.4347–4359

本文 • Original Text
二月九日上総国防人部領使少目従七位下茨田連沙弥麻呂進歌數十九首但拙劣歌者不取載之

Translation

On the ninth day of the second lunar month [of the seventh year of Tenpyō Shōhō], Mamu{{n}}da-nə mura{{n}}zi Samimarə (Junior Seventh Rank, Lower Grade), Junior Clerk and *sakimori* messenger of Kamitupusa province, presented [to me] nineteen poems. However, I did not include [here] the poems of inferior [quality].

Commentary

The ninth day of the second lunar month of the seventh year of Tenpyō Shōhō corresponds to March 26, 755 AD.

Nothing is known about the biography of Mamu{{n}}da-nə mura{{n}}zi Samimarə. Mura{{n}}zi is a *kabane* title.

On Kamitupusa province, see the commentary to the postscript to the poems 14.3382–3383.

Shō-sakan (少目) 'junior clerk' is the junior clerical position in provincial offices of Great Provinces. It corresponded to Junior Eighth Rank, Lower Grade. Thus, Mamu{{n}}da-nə mura{{n}}zi Samimarə had a rank that exceeded his actual position.

On *sakimori* messengers, see the commentary to the preface to poems 20.4321–4424.

Although Opotəmə-nə Yakaməti received nineteen poems, he included only thirteen.

20.4363

本文・*Original Text*

(1) 奈尓波都尓 (2) 美布祢於呂須惠 (3) 夜蘇加奴伎 (4) 伊麻波許伎奴等 (5) 伊母尓都氣許曾

仮名の書き下し・*Kana Transliteration*

(1) なにはつに (2) み₁ふねおろ₂すゑ (3) やそ₁かぬき₁ (4) いまはこ₂ぎ₁ぬと₂ (5) いも₂につげ₂こ₂そ₂

Romanization

(1) Nanipa tu-ni (2) mi-pune or-ə suwe (3) yaso ka nuk-i (4) ima pa kəŋg-i-n-u tə (5) imə-ni tuŋgɛ-kəs-ə

Glossing with Morphemic Analysis

(1) Nanipa harbor-LOC (2) HON-boat place-POSS place(CONV) (3) eighty rudder pierce-CONV (4) now TOP row-CONV-PERF-FIN QV (5) beloved-DAT report(CONV)-BEN-IMP

Translation

(5) Please tell [my] beloved (4) that [we] have rowed out now (3) piercing [the waves with] many rudders (2) [after] putting [our] beautiful boats in their place (1) in Nanipa harbor.

Commentary

On Nanipa and Nanipa harbor, see the commentaries to poems 20.4329 and 20.4330.

OJ honorific prefix *mi-* in line two has the beautification function in this poem, although there is also an opinion that it has honorification meaning because the boats that *sakimori* took to Kyūshū were dispatched by imperial order (Kinoshita 1988: 134; Mizushima 2003: 370).

The only problem with the interpretation of this poem lies with 於呂須惠 *orəsuwe* in line two. Omodaka believes that *orəsuwe* is a contraction of *orəs-i-suwe* 'lower-CONV-place(CONV)' and that it describes the situation of lowering beached boats into the sea, and he also cites *pune uke-suwete* 'lowering the boat and letting it float' from 17.3991 (1984.20: 93). Other Japanese scholars express the same opinion (Takagi et al. 1962: 424; Kinoshita 1988: 134; Kojima et al. 1975: 395; Mizushima 2003: 370), etc. There is, however, a fundamental flaw in this explanation, due to the presumption that *orəs-i-suwe* 'lower-CONV-place(CONV)' contracted into *orəsuwe*: there are no other examples of either EOJ or WOJ phonetic sequence [-sis-] to be contracted just to a single fricative [-s-].[9] Similar to the cases we have already observed in book fourteen, we believe that there is a much more solid phonetic interpretation of line two, if we are willing to leave the perennial shores of interpreting everything in EOJ texts as Japanese. Namely, we think that while *suwe* is indeed EOJ *suwe* 'place/put(CONV)', the preceding *orə* reflects Ainu *or-o* 'place-POSS', or 'its place', which refers to *pune* 'boats' in the previous line. Thus, *pune or-ə* means

---

9 Sven Osterkamp (p.c.) pointed out to me that there might be one exception in WOJ: "a possible case for /sis/ > /ss/ > /s/ would be Osisaka > *Ossaka > Osaka: KK 9 for instance has Osaka 於佐箇, but the name is usually written 忍坂 (thus e.g. in MYS 13.3331), indicating original Osisaka. The latter is probably also what is meant by 意柴沙加 on the Suda Hachiman shrine (Suda Hachiman gū, 須田八幡宮) mirror inscription." The inscription is dated by 443 AD (– A.V. and S.I-V.).

'the place of boats', which probably refers to the docking place before departure. The presence of an Ainu loanword is the only evidence for this poem to be classified as EOJ, and not WOJ.

Yaso 'eighty' in line three is used in the metaphoric sense for 'many'.

OJ *ka* 'rudder' is either a contraction of *ka*ⁿ*di* 'id.', or it is its original unsuffixed form. However, in the latter case -ⁿ*di* becomes an unaccounted segment, since its meaning or function are obscure. On WOJ *ka*ⁿ*di* 'rudder', see the commentary to 14.3555.

OJ benefactive auxiliary *-kəse-* has a contracted form *-kəs-* before the imperative suffix *-ə* and the negative imperative suffix *-una*. For details see Vovin (2020.2: 899–902).

20.4364

本文・*Original Text*
(1) 佐伎牟理尓 (2) 多々牟佐和伎尓 (3) 伊敝能伊牟何 (4) 奈流弊伎己等乎 (5) 伊波須伎奴可母

仮名の書き下し・*Kana Transliteration*
(1) さき₁むりに (2) たたむさわき₁に (3) い へ₁の₂いむが (4) なるべ₁き₁こ₂と₂を (5) いはずき₁ぬかも₂

Romanization
(1) sakimuri n-i (2) tat-am-u sawak-i n-i (3) ipe-nə imu-ⁿga (4) nar-uᵐbe-ki kətə-wo (5) ip-aⁿz-u k-i-n-u kamə

Glossing with Morphemic Analysis
(1) border.guard COP-CONV (2) depart-TENT-ATTR clamor-NML COP-CONV (3) home-GEN beloved-POSS (4) manage.household.affairs-DEB-ATTR matter-ACC say-NEG-CONV thing-ACC (5) say-NEG-CONV come-CONV-PERF-ATTR EP

Translation
(5) [I] have come here without saying (3/4) anything about how [my] beloved at home should manage household affairs (2) due to the clamor at my departure (1) to be a border guard!

Commentary
This poem has three EOJ features: raising of *o* > *u* in *sakimuri* 'border guard' and *imu* 'beloved', the perfective attributive *-n-u* instead of WOJ *-n-uru*, and the

misspelling of -u^mbɛ- as -u^mbe-. The latter probably indicates that there was no distinction between /e/ and /ɛ/ in Pitati EOJ.

Line three is hypermetric (*ji amari*, 字余り).

Postscript to the Poems 20.4363–4364

本文・*Original Text*
右二首茨城郡若舍人部廣足

Translation
Two poems above [were composed] by Wakatəneri^mbe-nə Pirətari from U^mbarakï district.

Commentary
Nothing is known about the biography of Wakatəneri^mbe-nə Pirətari. Since his rank is not mentioned, he probably was a private. On private (*Kami-nə yoporo*, 上丁) and other *sakimori* ranks see the commentary to the postscript to the poem 20.4321. Wakatəneri^mbe-nə Pirətari is one of only three *sakimori* who are authors of two poems each in the *Man'yōshū* along with the authors of 20.4365–4366 and 20.4369–4370. All three are *sakimori* from Pitati province.

Until recently U^mbarakï district corresponded to Niihari county (Niihari-gun, 新治郡) and parts of Eastern Ibaraki county (Higasi Ibaraki-gun, 東茨城郡) and Western Ibaraki county (Nisi Ibaraki-gun, 西茨城郡) to the northeast of Niihari county in present-day Ibaraki prefecture (Nakanishi 1985: 430; Omodaka 1984.20: 94). On March 19, 2006 Western Ibaraki county was dissolved and incorporated into Kasama city (Kasama-shi, 笠間市). On March 27, 2006 Niihari county was dissolved and incorporated into Omitama city (Omitama-shi, 小美玉市).

20.4365

本文・*Original Text*
(1) 於之弖流夜 (2) 奈尓波能都由利 (3) 布奈与曾比 (4) 阿例波許藝奴等 (5) 伊母尓都岐許曾

仮名の書き下し・*Kana Transliteration*
(1) おしてるや (2) なにはの₂つゆり (3) ふなよ₂そ₂ひ₁ (4) あれはこ₂ぎ₁ぬと₂ (5) いも₂につぎ₁こ₂そ₂

Romanization
(1) os-i-ter-u ya (2) Nanipa-nə tu-yuri (3) puna-yəsəp-i (4) are pa kəᵑg-i-n-u tə (5) imə-ni tuᵑgi-kəs-ə

Glossing with Morphemic Analysis
(1) push-CONV-shine-ATTR EP (2) Nanipa-GEN harbor-ABL (3) boat-equip-CONV (4) I TOP row-CONV-PERF-FIN QV (5) beloved-DAT report(CONV)-BEN-IMP

Translation
(5) Please tell [my] beloved (3) that having equipped [my] boat, (4) I rowed [out] (2) from the harbor of Nanipa, (1) on which [the sun] shines.

Commentary
Lines four and five are almost identical to the same lines in 20.4363.

On OJ *ositeru*, see the commentary to 20.4360. OJ *ya* after *ositeru* is an emphatic particle *ya*, not to be confused with the interrogative particle *ya*.

On Nanipa and Nanipa harbor, see the commentaries to poems 20.4329 and 20.4330.

This poem has one EOJ feature: Pitati EOJ *tuᵑgi-* 'to report', cf. WOJ *tuᵑgɛ-* 'id.' Note that in a similar poem 20.4363 above, also from Pitati, *tuᵑgɛ-*, not *tuᵑgi-* is used. This variation probably indicates that Pitati EOJ had a different vowel from WOJ /ɛ/, probably /e/ or /ï/.

On the contracted form *-kəs-* of the OJ benefactive auxiliary *kəse-*, see the commentary to 20.4363.

20.4366

本文・Original Text
(1) 比多知散思 (2) 由可牟加里母我 (3) 阿我古比乎 (4) 志留志弖都祁弖 (5) 伊母尒志良世牟

仮名の書き下し・Kana Transliteration
(1) ひ₁たちさし (2) ゆかむかりも₂が (3) あがこ₁ひ₁を (4) しるしてつけ₁て (5) いも₂にしらせむ

Romanization
(1) Pitati sas-i (2) yuk-am-u kari məᵑga (3) a-ᵑga kopi-wo (4) sirus-i-te tuke-te (5) imə-ni sir-ase-m-u

Glossing with Morphemic Analysis
(1) Pitati point-CONV (2) go-TENT-ATTR wild.goose DP (3) I-POSS long(NML)-ACC (4) describe-CONV-SUB attach(CONV)-SUB (5) beloved-DAT know-CAUS-TENT-FIN

Translation
(2) [I] want a wild goose that would go (1) to Pitati. (5) [I] would inform [my] beloved (4) by attaching to [the goose a letter] describing (3) my longing [for her].

Commentary
This poem looks like an allusion to an episode in the biography of Sū Wǔ (蘇武), found in volume fifty-four of the Chinese dynastic history Hànshū (漢書). Sū Wǔ was sent as the Hàn ambassador to Xiong-nu, but Xiong-nu detained him and did not allow him to return. Then, he wrote a letter and attached it to a wild goose's foot. The Emperor in China was able to receive this letter. Omodaka notes that some scholars voice skepticism as to whether this story was known in Azuma (1984.20: 95), but like Omodaka we see no reason why it should not have reached the Eastern provinces.

This poem has three EOJ features: Pitati EOJ *kopi* 'longing' (see also the same spelling in 20.4371 below), cf. WOJ *kopï* 'id.' and Pitati EOJ *tuke-* 'to attach', cf. WOJ *tukɛ-* 'id.' The former probably indicates that there was no /i/ : /ï/ contrast in Pitati; on the latter cf. also the variation between /ɛ/ and /i/ in EOJ *tuⁿgɛ- ~ tuⁿgi-* 'to inform' (20.4363 and 20.4365) also after a velar, which probably points to a different vowel here (/e/ or /ï/) as compared to WOJ /ɛ/. The third feature is discussed below.

On Pitati province see the commentary to the postscript to 14.3350–3351.

The usage of EOJ *sas-i* 'point-CONV' is highly reminiscent of a case marker. Cf. *-wo sas-i-te* 'pointing to' used in the same context and function in 20.4374. Although *-wo sas-i-te* is amply attested in WOJ as well, the usage of *sas-i* alone seems to be purely EOJ. We wonder whether this *sas-i* could be a predecessor of the locative/directive case marker *-sa* widespread in modern Tōhoku dialects.

OJ *kari* 'wild geese' are migratory birds that come to Japan, Korea, and China in the autumn to escape the colder climate in the north, and return to their places of original habitat in Siberia to nest in the spring. Their cry (WOJ *kari-ⁿga ne*) evokes the feeling of sadness – this cultural perception was probably borrowed from Chinese poetry. OJ *kari* 'wild goose' is associated with autumn in Japanese traditional poetry.

Postscript to the Poems 20.4365–4366

本文 • *Original Text*
右二首信太郡物部道足

Translation
Two poems above [were composed] by Mənənᵐbe-nə Mititari from Siⁿda district.

Commentary
Nothing is known about the biography of Mənənᵐbe-nə Mititari. Since his rank is not mentioned, he probably was a private. On private (*Kami-nə yoporo*, 上丁) and other *sakimori* ranks see the commentary to the postscript to the poem 20.4321. Mənənᵐbe-nə Mititari is one of only three *sakimori* who are authors of two poems each in the *Man'yōshū* along with the authors of 20.4363–4364 and 20.4369–4370. All three are *sakimori* from Pitati province.

Siⁿda district corresponds to the southern part of Inashiki county (Inashiki-gun, 稲敷郡) in present-day Ibaraki prefecture (Omodaka 1984.20: 95; Nakanishi 1985: 452).

20.4367

本文 • *Original Text*
(1) 阿我母弓能 (2) 和須例母之太波 (3) 都久波尼乎 (4) 布利佐氣美都々 (5) 伊母波之奴波尼

仮名の書き下し • *Kana Transliteration*
(1) あが母₂て の₂ (2) わすれも₂しだは (3) つくはねを (4) ふりさけ₂み₁つつ (5) いも₂はしぬはね

Romanization
(1) a-ⁿga [o]məte-nə (2) wasure-m-ə siⁿda pa (3) Tukupa ne-wo (4) purisakɛ-mi-tutu (5) imə pa sinup-an-e

Glossing with Morphemic Analysis
(1) I-POSS face-GEN (2) forget-TENT-ATTR time TOP (3) Tukupa peak-ACC (4) look.up(CONV)-look(CONV)-COOR (5) beloved TOP yearn- DES-IMP

Translation

(2/5) When [you, my] beloved will be forgetting (1) my face, (5) please yearn [for me], (4) looking up (3) at the Tukupa peak.

Commentary

Two similar poems are 14.3515 and 14.3520.

On EOJ special attributive form -*o*, see the commentary to 14.3395 and a brief description of EOJ special grammar in the introductions to book fourteen and this volume.

On EOJ *siⁿda* 'time' < Ainu *hi-ta* 'time, when', see the commentary to 14.3363.
On Mt. Tukupa, see the commentary to FK 2.

Postscript to the Poem 20.4367

本文・*Original Text*
右一首茨城郡占部小龍

Translation

The poem above [was composed] by Ura^mbe-nə Wotatu from U^mbarakï district.

Commentary

Nothing is known about the biography of Ura^mbe-nə Wotatu. Since his rank is not mentioned, he probably was a private. On private (*Kami-nə yoporo*, 上丁) and other *sakimori* ranks, see the commentary to the postscript to the poem 20.4321.

On U^mbarakï district see the commentary to the postscript to 20.4363–4364.

20.4368

本文・*Original Text*
(1) 久自我波々 (2) 佐氣久阿利麻弖 (3) 志富夫祢尓 (4) 麻可知之自奴伎 (5) 和波可敝里許牟

仮名の書き下し・*Kana Transliteration*
(1) くじがはは (2) さけ₂くありまて (3) しほぶねに (4) まかぢしじぬき₁ (5) わはかへ₁りこ₂む

Romanization
(1) Kuⁿzi-ŋ-gapa pa (2) sakɛ-ku ari-mat-e (3) sipo-ᵐ-bune-ni (4) ma-kaⁿdi siⁿzi nuk-i (5) wa pa kaper-i-kə-m-u

Glossing with Morphemic Analysis
(1) Kuⁿzi-GEN-river TOP (2) safe-CONV ITER-wait-IMP (3) tide-GEN-boat- LOC (4) INT-rudder constantly pierce-CONV (5) I TOP return-CONV-come-TENT-FIN

Translation
(2) Wait for [me] all this time safely (1) at Kuⁿzi river! (5) I will come back (4) constantly piercing [the waves with] a great rudder (3) in the sea boat.

Commentary
There are two EOJ features in this poem: the usage of the unextended stem *wa* of the first person pronoun in isolation (Vovin 2020.1: 219, 224–225), and Pitati EOJ *sakɛku* 'safely' vs. WOJ *sakiku* 'id.' Pitati EOJ *sakɛku* 'safely' reflects the form before the raising *e > i*.

Kuⁿzi river is the same as modern Kuji river (Kujigawa, 久慈川), which originates in present-day Fukushima prefecture and flows through Kuji county (Kuji-gun, 久慈郡) and Naka county (Naka-gun, 那珂郡) in present-day Ibaraki prefecture, reaching the sea in the south of Kuji town (Kuji-chō, 久慈町) of Hitachi city (Hitachi-shi, 日立市) (Omodaka 1984.20: 97; Nakanishi 1985: 443). Its length without tributaries is 124 km. Kuⁿzi does not seem to be a meaningful Japanese placename. Possibly, it is from Ainu *kus* 'to flood' (Hattori 1964: 217; Izutsu 2006: 244), with the secondary nasalization, on which see the commentary to 14.3539.

On *sipo-ᵐ-bune* 'sea boat' (lit. 'tide-boat'), see the commentary to 14.3450.

On WOJ *kaⁿdi* 'rudder', see the commentary to 14.3555.

Cf. identical or similar lines to *ma-kaⁿdi siⁿzi nuk-i* 'constantly piercing [the waves with] great oars' in WOJ: MYS 15.3611, 15.3627, 15.3679, and 20.4331.

Postscript to the Poem 20.4368

本文 • Original Text
右一首久慈郡丸子部佐壯

Translation
The poem above [was composed] by Marokoᵐbe-nə Sukɛwo from Kuⁿzi district.

Commentary

Nothing is known about the biography of Marokoⁿbe-nə Sukɛwo. Since his rank is not mentioned, he probably was a private. On private (*Kami-nə yoporo*, 上丁) and other *sakimori* ranks see the commentary to the postscript to the poem 20.4321.

Kuⁿzi district corresponds to Kuji county (Kuji-gun, 久慈郡) and Hitatiōta city (Hitatiōta-shi, 常陸太田市) of present-day Ibaraki prefecture (Kinoshita 1988: 140). Nakanishi also mentions that it corresponds to an area of Hitati city (Hitachi-shi, 日立市) in the same prefecture (1985: 443).

20.4369

本文・*Original Text*
(1) 都久波祢乃 (2) 佐由流能波奈能 (3) 由等許尒母 (4) 可奈之家伊母曾 (5) 比留毛可奈之祁

仮名の書き下し・*Kana Transliteration*
(1) つくはねの₂ (2) さゆるの₂はなの₂ (3) ゆと₂こ₂にも₂ (4) かなしけ₁いも₂そ₂ (5) ひ₁るもかなしけ₁

Romanization
(1) Tukupa ne-nə (2) sa-yuru-nə pana-nə (3) yu təkə-ni mə (4) kanasi-ke imə sə (5) piru mo kanasi-ke

Glossing with Morphemic Analysis
(1) Tukupa peak-GEN (2) PREF-lily-GEN flower-COMP (3) night bed-LOC FP (4) be.dear-ATTR beloved FP (5) day.time FP be.dear-ATTR

Translation
(4) [My] beloved, who is (2) like a lily flower (1) on the Tukupa peak, (4) is dear [to me] (3) in the bed at night, (5) as well as in day time.

Commentary
There are three EOJ features in this poem. First, Pitati EOJ *yuru* 'lily' corresponds to WOJ *yuri* 'id.' (both derived from PJ *yuru-y) with the expected loss of PJ *-y in final or preconsonantal position, on which see the commentary to 14.3564. Second, Pitati EOJ *yu* 'night' is the result of raising of *o > u*, cf. WOJ *yo* 'id.' Third, there is EOJ adjectival attributive *-ke* corresponding to WOJ *-ki*.

On Mt. Tukupa, see the commentary to FK 2.

EOJ *yuru*, WOJ *yuri* 'lily' is a perennial grass that grows in the wild. There are several varieties of it, and the one that appears in Old Japanese poetry is usually the mountain lily (MDJ *yamayuri*, Lat. *Lilium auratum*), which is endemic to the Hokkaidō, Kantō, and Kinki (with the exception of Hokuriku) regions in Japan. It has a long stalk and blooms in summer with large six-petal flowers that have red spots. Its bulb is edible (Nakanishi 1985: 332).

20.4370

本文 • Original Text
(1) 阿良例布理 (2) 可志麻能可美乎 (3) 伊能利都々 (4) 須米良美久佐尒 (5) 和例波伎尒之乎

仮名の書き下し • Kana Transliteration
(1) あられふり (2) かしまの₂かみ₁を (3) いの₂りつつ (4) すめ₂らみ₁くさに (5) われはき₁にしを

Romanization
(1) arare pur-i (2) Kasima-nə kami-wo (3) inər-i-tutu (4) sumɛra mi-[i]kusa n-i (5) ware pa k-i-n-i-si-wo

Glossing with Morphemic Analysis
(1) hail fall-CONV (2) Kasima-GEN deity-ACC (3) pray-CONV-COOR (4) Emperor HON-warrior COP-CONV (5) I TOP come-CONV-PERF-CONV-PAST.ATTR-ACC

Translation
(3) Praying (2) to the deity of Kasima (1) [that is rambling like] a falling hail, (5) I have come [here] (4) as an imperial warrior, (5) but [I miss my beloved]...

Commentary
There are two EOJ features in this poem: Pitati EOJ *kami* 'deity' vs. WOJ *kamï* 'id.' and Pitati EOJ *sumɛra* 'Emperor' vs. WOJ *sumera* 'id.' Both 'misspellings' indicate that Pitati EOJ in all probability did not have WOJ phonemic contrasts /i/ : /ï/ and /e/ : /ɛ/.

Arare puri 'it hails and' is considered to be a permanent epithet (*makura-kotoba*, 枕詞) for Kasima, that is based on the play on words because falling hail is noisy (OJ *kasimasi*, MDJ *kashimashii*) (Kinoshita 1988: 142). Still, it is transparent, and, therefore, we chose to translate it here.

Kasima deity is a tutelary deity of Pitati province that resides in Kasima shrine (鹿島神宮) in Kashima town (Kashima-chō, 鹿島町) in Kashima county (Kashima-gun, 鹿島郡) of present-day Ibaraki prefecture. It is considered to be a deity of thunder, and a patron of military affairs (Omodaka 1984.20: 89).

Omodaka believes that -wo in kinisi-wo in line five is an emphatic particle (1984.20: 98–99), but this is incorrect, because there is no emphatic particle wo in EOJ, and WOJ emphatic particle wo does not occur in a sentence-final position (Vovin 2020.2: 1177–1178). We think that Kinoshita, who believes that this is a case marker -wo that is used as a conjunction with the concessive function (1988: 143) is right here. Thus, kinisi-wo 'I have come, but ...' makes a point of reference to the preceding poem, indicating that although the author is here, he misses his beloved.

Postscript to the Poems 20.4369–4370

本文 • *Original Text*
右二首那賀郡上丁大舎人部千文

Translation
Two poems above [were composed] by private Opotəneri^{m}be-nə Tipumi from Naka district.

Commentary
Nothing is known about the biography of Opotəneri^{m}be-nə Tipumi. He is one of only three *sakimori* who are authors of two poems each in the *Man'yōshū* along with the authors of 20.4363–4364 and 20.4365–4366. All three are *sakimori* from Pitati province.

On private (*Kami-nə yoporo*, 上丁) and other *sakimori* ranks see the commentary to the postscript to the poem 20.4321.

Naka district (Naka kəpori, 那賀郡) corresponds to Naka county (Naka-gun, 那珂郡), northern part of Eastern Ibaraki county (Higashi Ibaraki-gun, 東茨城郡), and a section of Mito city (Mito-shi, 水戸市) in present-day Ibaraki prefecture (Nakanishi 1985: 468).

20.4371

本文 • *Original Text*
(1) 多知波奈乃 (2) 之多布久可是乃 (3) 可具波志伎 (4) 都久波能夜麻乎 (5) 古比須安良米可毛

仮名の書き下し・*Kana Transliteration*
(1) たちばなの₂ (2) したふくかぜの₂ (3) かぐはしき₁ (4) つくはの₂やまを (5) こ₁ひ₁ずあらめ₂かも₁

Romanization
(1) tati^mbana-nə (2) sita puk-u ka^nze-nə (3) ka^ngupasi-ki (4) Tukupa-nə yama-wo (5) kopï-^nz-u ar-am-ɛ kamo

Glossing with Morphemic Analysis
(1) mandarin.orange-GEN (2) below blow-ATTR wind-GEN (3) be.fragrant-ATTR (4) Tukupa-GEN mountain-ACC (5) long.for-NEG-CONV exist-TENT-EV EP

Translation
(5) Will [I] not long (4) for Mt. Tukupa, (3) where the fragrant (2) wind blows under (1) the mandarin oranges [flowers]? [– Certainly I will!]

Commentary
There are two EOJ features in this poem. One is the 'misspelling' of WOJ *kopï-* 'to long for' as Pitati EOJ *kopi-* 'id.', indicating lack of phonemic contrast between /i/ and /ï/ in Pitati EOJ, see also 20.4366 above, where the same spelling is used. Another is purely morphosyntactic: while in WOJ the irony questions are formed with tentative evidential *-(a)m-ɛ* + interrogative particle *ya*, in EOJ they are formed with tentative evidential *-(a)m-ɛ* + emphatic particle *kamə* (Omodaka 1984.20: 99–100).

On OJ *tati^mbana* 'mandarin orange', see the commentary to 14.3496.

On Mt. Tukupa, see the commentary to FK 2.

Postscript to the Poem 20.4371

本文・*Original Text*
右一首助丁占部廣方

Translation
The poem above [was composed] by captain Ura^mbe-nə Pirəkata.

Commentary
Nothing is known about the biography of Ura^mbe-nə Pirəkata.

On captain (*Sukɛ-nə yoporo*, 助丁) and other *sakimori* ranks, see the commentary to the postscript to the poem 20.4321.

The districts of origin for captains are usually not recorded (Omodaka 1984.20: 100).

20.4372

本文 • *Original Text*

(1) 阿志加良能 (2) 美佐可多麻波理 (3) 可閇理美須 (4) 阿例波久江由久 (5) 阿良志乎母 (6) 多志夜波婆可流 (7) 不破乃世伎 (8) 久江弖和波由久 (9) 牟麻能都米 (10) 都久志能佐伎尓 (11) 知麻利爲弖 (12) 阿例波伊波々牟 (13) 母呂々々波 (14) 佐祁久等麻乎須 (15) 可閇利久麻弖尓

仮名の書き下し • *Kana Transliteration*

(1) あしがらの₂ (2) み₁さかたまはり (3) か へ₂りみ₁ず (4) あれはくえ₂ゆく (5) あらしをも₂ (6) たしやはばかる (7) ふはの₂せき₁ (8) くえ₂てわはゆく (9) むまの₂つめ₂ (10) つくしの₂さき₁に (11) ちまりゐて (12) あれはいははむ (13) も₂ろ₂も₂ろ₂は (14) さけ₁くと₂まをす (15) か へ₂りくまでに

Romanization

(1) Asiⁿgara-nə (2) mi-saka tamapar-i (3) kapɛr-i-mi-ⁿz-u (4) are pa kuye-yuk-u (5) ara-si wo mə (6) tas-i ya paᵐbakar-u (7) Pupa-nə seki (8) kuye-te wa pa yuk-u (9) muma-nə tumɛ (10) Tukusi-nə saki-ni (11) timar-i wi-te (12) are pa ipap-am-u (13) mərə-mərə pa (14) sake-ku tə mawos-u (15) kapɛr-i-k-u-maⁿde-ni

Glossing with Morphemic Analysis

(1) Asiⁿgara-GEN (2) HON-slope receive(HUM)-CONV (3) return-CONV-look-NEG-CONV (4) I TOP cross.over(CONV)-go-FIN (5) tough-FIN man FP (6) depart-NML IP hesitate-ATTR (7) Pupa-GEN barrier (8) cross.over(CONV)-SUB I TOP go-FIN (9) horse-GEN hoof (10) Tukusi-GEN cape-LOC (11) stay-CONV dwell(CONV)-SUB (12) I TOP pray-TENT-FIN (13) all-all TOP (14) safe-CONV QV say(HUM)-FIN (15) return-CONV-come-ATTR-TERM-LOC

Translation

(1/2) [I] received [the permission of the deity to cross] the Asiⁿgara slope, and (4) I will cross over [it] (3) without looking back. (5) Will a tough man (6) hesitate to depart? (7/8) I will go crossing Pupa barrier. (11) [I] will stay and dwell (10) at the cape in Tukusi (9) [that is easy to wear off like] a horse's hoof, (12) and I will pray (13/14) [and I] will ask [the deities] that everybody [at home would be] safe (15) until [I] return.

Commentary

This is the only *chōka* written in EOJ in the whole *Man'yōshū*.

There are several EOJ features in this poem that will be described in the commentary below in order of their occurrence.

On Asiŋgara, see the commentary to 14.3361.

Asiŋgara-nə mi-saka 'Asiŋgara slope' refers to the mountain pass (795 m high) that leads from Yagura station (Yagura eki, 矢倉駅) in Minami Asigara city (Minami Asigara-shi, 南足柄市) in present-day Kanagawa prefecture to Oyama town (Oyama-chō, 小山町) in Eastern Suruga county (Suruga Higasi-gun, 駿河東郡) of present-day Shizuoka prefecture.[10] There was a belief in ancient Japan that mountain and river deities could prevent the passage of travelers, hence the honorific reference to this pass with the honorific prefix *mi-* (Kinoshita 1988: 145).

There are two interpretations of *tamapar-* in line two. One of them takes it as *ta-mapar-* 'to go around', and another one as *tamapar-* 'to be granted, to receive'. The first one hardly makes any sense, because one does not go *around* a slope or a mountain pass when travelling from one point to another point. Thus, we follow the second interpretation that is also adapted by Omodaka (1984.20: 101), Kinoshita (1988: 146), and Mizushima (2003: 444).

Pitati EOJ *kapɛr-* 'to return' is a misspelling of WOJ *kaper-* 'id.', demonstrating lack of the phonemic contrast between /e/ and /ɛ/ in Pitati EOJ.

Pitati EOJ *kuye-* 'to cross over' is a result of *o* > *u* raising. It corresponds to WOJ *koye-* 'id.'

The usage of the unextended stem *wa* of the first person pronoun in isolation is an EOJ feature (Vovin 2005: 220–221, 226).

Following the lead of Hashimoto Shirō (no citation provided), Omodaka interprets line five not as *ara-si wo mo* 'tough-FIN man FP', but as *arasi-wo mo* 'storm-ACC FP' (1984.20: 101–102). This seems to be stretched grammatically, as **arasi-ni mə tas-i ya pa*ᵐ*bakar-u* 'will [I] hesitate to depart in the storm?' and not *arasi-wo mə tas-i ya pa*ᵐ*bakar-u* will be required. In addition, *arasi* 'storm' appears to be completely out of context. In addition, *ara-si wo* 'tough-FIN man' is attested in both WOJ (17.3962) and EOJ (20.4330), but *arasi-wo 'storm-ACC' is not found in the *Man'yōshū*. Therefore, we are going to follow the traditional interpretation of *ara-si wo mo* 'tough-FIN man FP' (Kinoshita 1988: 146; Mizushima 2003: 446).

---

10   Oyama town is located just at the foot of Mt. Fuji.

OJ -*si* in *ara-si wo mo* 'tough-FIN man FP' is an example of a special OJ usage of the final form -*si* in the attributive function. For more details and examples see Vovin (2009a: 461–65).

EOJ *tas-i* 'depart-NML' corresponding to WOJ *tat-i* 'id.' is an example of EOJ palatalization *t > s/_i*, on which also see the commentary to 14.3395.

Pupa barrier was in Mino province. Nowadays its remains are located to the west of Sekigahara station (Sekigahara eki, 関ヶ原駅) in present-day Gifu prefecture (Kinoshita 1988: 146).

Before the Edo period horses in Japan were not provided with horseshoes, therefore their hoofs were easy to damage or wear off. *Muma-nə tumɛ* is a permanent epithet (*makura-kotoba*, 枕詞) that is based on the play on words for Tukusi 'old name for Kyūshū' and the verb *tukus-* 'to exhaust'.

Tukusi is the old name for the island of Kyūshū.

Pitati EOJ *timar-* 'to stay' corresponds to WOJ *təmar-*. The correspondence of EOJ *i* to WOJ *ə* is difficult to explain.

Pitati EOJ *sake-ku* 'safely' (also spelled as *sakɛ-ku* in 20.4368) corresponds to Suruⁿga EOJ *sa-ku* 'id.' and WOJ *saki-ku* 'id.'

On EOJ attributive -*u* in *k-u-maⁿde-ni* 'until I come back', see the commentary to 20.4339.

Postscript to the Poem 20.4372

本文 • *Original Text*
右一首倭文部可良麻呂

Translation
The poem above [was composed] by Sitoriᵐbe-nə Karamarə.

Commentary
Nothing is known about the biography of Sitoriᵐbe-nə Karamarə. Since his rank is not mentioned, he probably was a private. On private (*Kami-nə yoporo*, 上丁) and other *sakimori* ranks, see the commentary to the postscript to the poem 20.4321. Although for privates the district of his origin is usually recorded, it is not done here.

Postscript to the Poems 20.4363–4372

本文 • *Original Text*
二月十四日常陸國部領防人使大目正七位上息長眞人國嶋進歌數廿七首但拙劣歌者不取載之

Translation
On the fourteenth day of the second lunar month [of the seventh year of Tenpyō Shōhō], Okinaŋga-nə mapitə Kunisima (Senior Seventh Rank, Upper Grade), senior clerk and *sakimori* messenger of Pitati province, presented [to me] twenty-seven poems. However, I did not include [here] the poems of inferior [quality].

Commentary
The fourteenth day of the second lunar month of the seventh year of Tenpyō Shōhō corresponds to March 31, 755 AD.

Okinaŋga-nə mapitə Kunisima is mentioned in the *Shoku Nihongi* as person of the Senior Sixth Rank, Upper Grade, who has been promoted to a Junior Fifth Rank, Lower Grade on the fourth day of the first lunar month of the sixth year of Tenpyō Hōji (February 1, 762 AD). Nothing else is known of his biography. Mapitə is a *kabane* title.

On Pitati province, see the commentary to the postscript to the poems 14.3350–3351.

Dai-sakan (大目) 'Senior Clerk' is the senior clerical position in provincial offices of Great Provinces. It corresponded to Junior Eighth Rank, Upper Grade. Thus, Okinaŋga-nə mapitə Kunisima had a rank that exceeded his actual position.

On *sakimori* messengers, see the commentary to the preface to poems 20.4321–4424.

Only the *Genryaku kōhon* and the *Koyō ryaku ruijū shō* mention twenty-seven (廿七) original poems. All other manuscripts indicate only seventeen (十七) original poems (Omodaka 1984.20: 103). However, the *Hirose-bon*, the only manuscript that comes from the independent lineage of the now lost *Teika-bon*, also has twenty-seven (10: 69b). This heavily tips the balance in favor of twenty-seven. Thus, although Opotəmə-nə Yakaməti received twenty-seven poems, he included only ten.

20.4373

本文・*Original Text*
(1) 祁布与利波 (2) 可敝里見奈久弖 (3) 意富伎美乃 (4) 之許乃美多弖等 (5) 伊弖多都和例波

仮名の書き下し・*Kana Transliteration*
(1) け₁ふよ₂りは (2) かへ₁りみ₁なくて (3) おほき₁み₁の₂ (4) しこ₂の₂み₁たてと₂ (5) いでたつわれは

Romanization
(1) kepu-yəri pa (2) kaper-i-MI na-ku-te (3) opo kimi-nə (4) sikə n-ə mi-tate tə (5) iⁿde-tat-u ware pa

Glossing with Morphemic Analysis
(1) today-ABL TOP (2) return-CONV-look(NML) exist.not-CONV-SUB (3) Great Lord-GEN (4) unworthy COP-ATTR HON-shield COP (5) exit(CONV)-leave-ATTR I TOP

Translation
(5) I leave (1) today (2) without looking back (4) to be an unworthy shield (3) of the Great Lord.

Commentary
There is only one EOJ feature in this poem: misspelling of the ablative case marker *-yori* as *-yəri*, which probably indicates that there was no phonemic distinction between /o/ and /ə/ in Simotukeno EOJ. Otherwise it looks like a poem written in WOJ. Also note that EOJ *siko* 'stupid, unworthy, disgusting' spelled with /o/ in FK 5, here appears as *sikə*, identical to the regular WOJ spelling.

On *opo kimi* 'Great Lord' which refers to the Emperor, see the commentary to 14.3480.

The more literal translation of this poem would be: 'I, who leave today without looking back to be an unworthy shield of the Great Lord'.

Postscript to the Poem 20.4373

本文・*Original Text*
右一首火長今奉部与曾布

Translation
The poem above [was composed] by corporal Imamaturi^mbe-nə Yəsəpu.

Commentary
Nothing is known about the biography of Imamaturi^mbe-nə Yəsəpu. His district of origin is not recorded.

Corporal (*Kachō*, 火長) had under his command ten men according to the Military Code (*Gunbōryō*, 軍防令) (Omodaka 1984.20: 104). On corporal (*Kachō*, 火長) and other *sakimori* ranks see the commentary to the postscript to the poem 20.4321.

20.4374

本文 • *Original Text*
(1) 阿米都知乃 (2) 可美乎伊乃里弖 (3) 佐都夜奴伎 (4) 都久之乃之麻乎 (5) 佐之弖由久和例波

仮名の書き下し • *Kana Transliteration*
(1) あめ₂つち乃₂ (2) かみ₁をいの₂りて (3) さつやぬき₁ (4) つくしの₂しまを (5) さしてゆくわれは

Romanization
(1) amɛ tuti-nə (2) kami-wo inər-i-te (3) satu-ya nuk-i (4) Tukusi-nə sima-wo (5) sas-i-te yuk-u ware pa

Glossing with Morphemic Analysis
(1) heaven earth-GEN (2) deity-ACC pray-CONV-SUB (3) luck-arrow insert-CONV (4) Tukusi-GEN island-ACC (5) point-CONV-SUB go-ATTR I TOP

Translation
(5) I will go to (4) the island of Tukusi (2) after praying to the deities (1) of Heaven and Earth, (3) and putting lucky arrows inside [my quiver].

Commentary
• There is only one EOJ feature in this poem: the 'misspelling' of the word *kamï* 'deity' as *kami*, which probably indicates that the phonemic contrast between /i/ and /ï/ did not exist in Simotukɛno EOJ.

There are three hypotheses regarding the meaning of *satu-ya* in line three: (a) 'lucky arrow' (Mizushima 2003: 472–474; c) (b) 'war arrow' (Kinoshita 1988: 149; c) (c) 'arrow' (in general) (Omodaka 1984.20: 104–105). Although the primary meaning of *satu-ya* is 'hunting arrow', it appears that no one has suggested this interpretation.[11] Probably it is due to the fact that it might seem strange that a warrior in military service would carry hunting arrows, and not fighting arrows. However, we should not forget that *sakimori* were not fed by the government in Tukusi, and were required to provide their own subsistence. In addition, since there is a special word *sə-ya* for 'fighting arrows', it is difficult to imagine that *satu-ya* simply meant 'fighting arrows'. Omodaka mentions that there was a ritual, where a warrior took out arrowheads and presented them as an offering for a deity when praying for a safe passage on a journey (1988: 105). Although Omodaka himself is inclined to follow Motoori Norinaga's hypothesis that *satu-ya* is just a general term for arrows, this is unlikely, since then the distinction between *ya* 'arrow' and *satu-ya* remains unclear. Both the existence of the ritual and clear reference to the prayer to deities in the poem itself make me believe that in this given context *satu-ya* refers to 'lucky arrows', presumably those blessed by the deities of Heaven and Earth.

Tukusi is the old name for the island of Kyūshū.

Postscript to the Poem 20.4374

本文 · *Original Text*
右一首火長大田部荒耳

Translation
The poem above [was composed] by corporal Opota ͫ be-nə Aramimi.

Commentary
Nothing is known about the biography of Opota ͫ be-nə Aramimi. His district of origin is not recorded.

Corporal (*Kachō*, 火長) had under his command ten men according to the Military Code (*Gunbōryō*, 軍防令) (Omodaka 1984.20: 104). On corporal (*Kachō*, 火長) and other *sakimori* ranks see the commentary to the postscript to the poem 20.4321.

---

11 Presumably the difference between hunting arrows and fighting arrows was that while the latter had barbed arrow heads, the former did not.

20.4375

本文・Original Text
(1) 麻都能氣乃 (2) 奈美多流美礼婆 (3) 伊波妣等乃 (4) 和例乎美於久流等 (5) 多々理之母己呂

仮名の書き下し・Kana Transliteration
(1) まつ₂け₂の₂ (2) なみ₁たるみ₁れば (3) いはび₁と₂の₂ (4) われをみ₁おくると₂ (5) たたりしも₂こ₂ろ₂

Romanization
(1) matu n-ə kɛ-nə (2) nam-i-tar-u mi-re-ᵐba (3) ipa-ᵐ-bitə-nə (4) ware-wo mi-okur-u tə (5) tat-ar-i-si məkərə

Glossing with Morphemic Analysis
(1) pine COP-ATTR tree-GEN (2) stand.in.line-CONV-PERF/PROG-ATTR see-EV-CON (3) home-GEN-person-GEN (4) I-ACC see(CONV)-send-FIN QV (5) stand-PROG-CONV-PAST.ATTR like

Translation
(1/2) When [I] see that the pine trees are standing in line, (3/5) [they are] like [my] home folks [who] were standing [in a row] (4) going to see me off.

Commentary
Simotukɛno EOJ *kɛ* 'tree' corresponds to WOJ *kï* 'id.' See also 20.4342 for the same form in Suruⁿga EOJ.

EOJ *ipa* 'house' corresponds to WOJ *ipe* 'id.' The vowel correspondence EOJ *a* : WOJ *e* also appears in EOJ *tatarisi* 'were standing' below. See also 20.4406, 20.4416, 20.4419, 20.4423, and 20.4427.

Simotukɛno EOJ *tat-ar-i-si* 'were standing' corresponds to WOJ *tat-er-i-si* 'id.' Note the same vowel correspondence of EOJ *a* to WOJ *e* as above.

Line four is hypermetric (*ji amari*, 字余り).

Postscript to the Poem 20.4375

本文・Original Text
右一首火長物部眞嶋

Translation
The poem above [was composed] by corporal Mənənəᵐbe-nə Masima.

Commentary

Nothing is known about the biography of Mənənəᵐbe-nə Masima. His district of origin is not recorded.

Corporal (*Kachō*, 火長) had under his command ten men according to the Military Code (*Gunbōryō*, 軍防令) (Omodaka 1984.20: 104). On corporal (*Kachō*, 火長) and other *sakimori* ranks see the commentary to the postscript to the poem 20.4321.

20.4376

本文・*Original Text*

(1) 多妣由岐尓 (2) 由久等之良受弖 (3) 阿母志々尓 (4) 己等麻乎佐受弖 (5) 伊麻叙久夜之氣

仮名の書き下し・*Kana Transliteration*

(1) たび₁ゆき₁に (2) ゆくと₂しらずて (3) あも₂ししに (4) こ₂と₂まをさずて (5) いまぞ₂くやしけ₂

Romanization

(1) taᵐbi-yuk-i-ni (2) yuk-u tə sir-aⁿz-u-te (3) amə sisi-ni (4) kətə mawos-aⁿz-u-te (5) ima ⁿzə kuyasi-kɛ

Glossing with Morphemic Analysis

(1) journey-go-NML-LOC (2) go-FIN QV know-NEG-CONV-SUB (3) mother father-DAT (4) word say(HUM)-NEG-CONV-SUB (5) now FP be.regretful-ATTR

Translation

(1/2) Without knowing that [I] will go on a journey, (5) now [I] regret that (4) [I] did not tell (3) [my] mother and father.

Commentary

This poem is interesting because instead of the more usual OJ *titi papa* 'father [and] mother' it has it in the reverse order: *amə sisi* 'mother [and] father'. The usual point of view of modern Japanese scholars is that 'father and mother' reflects a patrilineal society, while 'mother and father' reflects matrilineal one (Kinoshita 1988: 151–152). We are afraid that this kind of reasoning is pretty much influenced by the European syntactic model, where the most important member is mentioned first due to the SVO structure. However, the Japanese language throughout its written history has always been SOV, so we should expect that the most important member is the one that is the closest to the verb, not the farthest from it. Thus, in the context of Japanese, *titi papa* 'father [and] mother' in all probability reflects the matrilineal organization, while *amə sisi* 'mother [and] father' reflects the patrilineal one. The choice of words for 'mother' in these sequences also may not be coincidental: while WOJ *omə titi* 'mother [and] father' is attested as well, there is no *papa titi* 'mother [and] father' in OJ texts. We know quite well that the traditional Western Japanese society was essentially matrilineal, and that the vestiges of this organization well survived even into the Heian period. On the other hand, Korean society has always been patrilineal, and the same is applicable to Ainu society. While the Korean influence may not be completely responsible for EOJ word order *amə sisi* 'father [and] mother', in spite of the fact that many immigrants from Korea settled in Kantō region after the fall of Paekche and Koguryǒ in 660s AD, the Ainu influence most certainly is, given the amount of Ainu influence documented in book fourteen of the *Man'yōshū*. As additional food for thought in the same direction, one can only wonder why the transition from the traditional matrilineal society to the patrilineal society occurred so easily after the Easterners ascended to power at the end of the Heian period. This should not have happened if the Eastern Japanese society was traditionally matrilineal, as Kinoshita (1988: 152), Mizushima (2003: 486) and others have claimed.

EOJ *amə* 'mother' probably corresponds to WOJ *omə* 'id.', although the cognacy might be in question, since there is one example of WOJ *amə* 'mother' (NK 82). For details see Vovin (2010: 234–235).

Simotukəno EOJ *sisi* 'father', cognate to OJ *titi* 'id.' represents the palatalization of *t* > *s/_i*, see also 20.4372 and introduction to this volume.

EOJ adjectival attributive *-kɛ* (more frequently spelled as *-ke*) corresponds to WOJ *-ki*.

Postscript to the Poem 20.4376

本文 · *Original Text*
右一首寒川郡上丁川上臣老

Translation
The poem above [was composed] by private Kapakami-nə omi Oyu from Samukapa district.

Commentary

Nothing is known about the biography of Kapakami-nə omi Oyu. Omi is a *kabane* title.

On private (*Kami-nə yoporo*, 上丁) and other *sakimori* ranks, see the commentary to the postscript to the poem 20.4321.

Samukapa district corresponds to the southern part of Shimotsuga county (Shimotsuga-gun, 下都賀郡), and includes Tochigi city (栃木市) and Oyama city (小山市) of present-day Tochigi prefecture (Kinoshita 1988: 152).

20.4377

本文 · *Original Text*

(1) 阿母刀自母 (2) 多麻尓母賀母夜 (3) 伊多太伎弖 (4) 美都良乃奈可尓 (5) 阿敝麻可麻久母

仮名の書き下し · *Kana Transliteration*

(1) あも₂と₁じも₂ (2) たまにも₂がも₂や (3) いただき₁て (4) み₁づらの₂なかに (5) あへ₁まかまくも₂

Romanization

(1) amə toⁿzi mə (2) tama n-i mə^ŋgamə ya (3) itaⁿdak-i-te (4) miⁿdura-nə naka-ni (5) ape-mak-am-aku mə

Glossing with Morphemic Analysis

(1) mother mistress.of.the.house FP (2) jewel COP-CONV DP EP (3) put.on.the.top.of.the.head-CONV-SUB (4) miⁿdura-GEN inside-LOC (5) COOP-roll-TENT-NML FP

Translation

(1/2) [I] want my dear mother to be a jewel! (3) [I] would put [her] on the top of [my] head, (4/5) and roll [her] together [with my hair] into my *miⁿdura*.

Commentary

On EOJ *amə* 'mother' see the commentary to 20.4376.

On OJ *toⁿzi* 'mistress of the house', see the commentary to 20.4342.

OJ *miⁿdura* is a name of a male hairstyle, which was made by dividing hair at the top of the head and letting it drop down at ears to the left and right. These two locks were tied in the middle by a cord (Omodaka et al. 1967: 710).

There was a variation of the same hairstyle for boys, where these two locks were made into loops (Mizushima 2003: 493).

Simotukɛno EOJ reciprocal-cooperative prefix *ape-* corresponds to WOJ *api-*, id.

Postscript to the Poem 20.4377

本文・*Original Text*
右一首津守宿祢小黒栖

Translation
The poem above [was composed] by Tumori-nə sukune Wokurosu.

Commentary
Nothing is known about the biography of Tumori-nə sukune Wokurosu. Since his rank is not mentioned, he probably was a private. On private (*Kami-nə yoporo,* 上丁) and other *sakimori* ranks, see the commentary to the postscript to the poem 20.4321. Sukune is a *kabane* title. No district of origin is recorded.

20.4378

本文・*Original Text*
(1) 都久比夜波 (2) 須具波由氣等毛 (3) 阿母志々可 (4) 多麻乃須我多波 (5) 和須例西奈布母

仮名の書き下し・*Kana Transliteration*
(1) つくひ₁やは (2) すぐはゆけ₂ど₂も₁ (3) あも₂ししが (4) たまの₂すがたは (5) わすれせなふも₂

Romanization
(1) tuku pi ya pa (2) suŋgu pa yuk-ɛ-ⁿdəmo (3) amə sisi-ŋga (4) tama-nə suŋgata pa (5) wasure se-n-ap-umə

Glossing with Morphemic Analysis
(1) month day EP TOP (2) grow.old year go-EV-CONC (3) mother father-POSS (4) jewel-COMP appearance TOP (5) forget(NML) do-NEG-ITER-EXCL

Translation

(1/2) Although months and days pass and past years go away, (5) [I] will never forget (4) jewel-like appearance (3) of [my] father and mother!

Commentary

There is a disagreement on how to read the character 夜 'night' in the first line 都久比夜波. Some scholars considered it to represent phonogram *ya* (Omodaka 1984.20: 107–108), while others prefer to see it as a semantogram 'night' and read it as *yo* accordingly (Kinoshita 1988: 154). While Kinoshita is right that a combination of emphatic particle *ya* + topic marker *pa* is not attested in OJ texts (1988: 154), neither is the expression *tuku pi yo* in EOJ or *tukï pi yo* in WOJ. Meanwhile the expression *tukï pi* is amply attested, so we agree with Omodaka here.

On EOJ *tuku* 'moon, month' corresponding to WOJ *tukï* 'id.' see the commentary to 14.3395.

The first three characters 須具波 are traditionally explained as EOJ *suⁿgu pa*, nominalized form of the verb *suⁿgï-* 'to pass' + topic marker *pa* (Kinoshita 1988: 154; Mizushima 2003: 498). However, there are no other attestations of a nominalized or converb form *suⁿgu* in EOJ, and, as a matter of fact, only converb *suⁿgï* is attested in EOJ. In addition, the construction 'passing TOP go away' seems very strange. We suspect that *suⁿgu* and *pa* are really two Ainu loanwords: *sukup* [suGup] 'to live [through]', 'to grow [old]' and *pa* 'year'. If one adopts this point of view, any clumsiness in the reading of the poem will disappear. Ainu intervocalic voiced were normally borrowed into EOJ as prenasalized voiced (see the commentary to 14.3363), so Ainu *-k-* [-G-] > EOJ *-ⁿg-*, and the loss of the Ainu syllable final *-p* in EOJ *suⁿgu* < Ainu *sukup* is also regular, since OJ does not have any syllable-final consonants.

On EOJ *amə sisi* 'mother [and] father', see the commentary to 20.4376.

On specific EOJ order of morphemes *-(a)n-ap-* 'NEG-ITER', see the commentary to 14.3375.

On *-umə ~ -mə* as a special Old Japanese exclamative form, see the commentary to 14.3431.

Postscript to the Poem 20.4378

本文 • *Original Text*

右一首都賀郡上丁中臣部足國

Translation

The poem above [was composed] by private Nakatəmiᵐbe-nə Tarikuni from Tuⁿga district.

Commentary

Nothing is known about the biography of Nakatəmiᵐbe-nə Tarikuni.

On private (*Kami-nə yoporo*, 上丁) and other *sakimori* ranks, see the commentary to the postscript to the poem 20.4321.

Tuⁿga district corresponds to Upper Tsuga county (Kami Tsuga-gun, 上都賀郡), northern part of Lower Tsuga county (Shimo Tsuga-gun, 下都賀郡), and to Nikkō city (Nikkō-shi, 日光市), Imaichi city (Imaichi-shi, 今市市), and Kanuma city (Kanuma-shi, 鹿沼市) that are administratively separate in present-day Tochigi prefecture (Kinoshita 1988: 154).

20.4379

本文・*Original Text*
(1) 之良奈美乃 (2) 与曽流波麻倍尓 (3) 和可例奈婆 (4) 伊刀毛須倍奈美 (5) 夜多妣蘇弖布流

仮名の書き下し・*Kana Transliteration*
(1) しらなみ₁の₂ (2) よ₂そ₂るはまへ₂に (3) わかれなば (4) いと₁も₁すべ₂なみ₁ (5) やたび₁そ₁でふる

Romanization
(1) sira nami-nə (2) yəsər-u pama pɛ-ni (3) wakare-n-aᵐba (4) ito mo suᵐbɛ na-mi (5) ya taᵐbi soⁿde pur-u

Glossing with Morphemic Analysis
(1) white wave-GEN (2) approach-ATTR seashore side-LOC (3) be.separated(CONV)-PERF-COND (4) very FP way exist.not-GER (5) eight time sleeve wave-FIN

Translation
(3) If [I] am separated (1/2) from the seashore, washed by white waves, (4) [I] will wave my sleeves many times, (4) because nothing at all can be done.

356　　　　　　　　　　　　　　　　　　　　　　　　　　　CHAPTER 4

Commentary

The only EOJ feature of this poem is the 'misspelling' of *pe* 'side' and *su*ᵐ*be* 'way [to do]' as *pɛ* and *su*ᵐ*bɛ*. This indicates that there was probably no phonemic contrast between /e/ and /ɛ/ in Simotukɛno EOJ.

OJ *ya* 'eight' is used here metaphorically in the meaning 'many'.

On the sleeve-waving ritual by women, see the commentary to 14.3389. Presumably, the sleeve-waving ritual by men had the same or similar function.

Postscript to the Poem 20.4379

本文 • *Original Text*
右一首足利郡上丁大舍人部祢麻呂

Translation
The poem above [was composed] by private Opotəneriᵐbe-nə Nemarə from Asikaᵑga district.

Commentary
Nothing is known about the biography of Opotəneriᵐbe-nə Nemarə.

On private (*Kami-nə yoporo*, 上丁) and other *sakimori* ranks, see the commentary to the postscript to the poem 20.4321.

Asikaᵑga district corresponds to Sano city (佐野市) and a part of Ashikaga city (Ashikaga-shi, 足利市) in present-day Tochigi prefecture (Kinoshita 1988: 156). Asikaᵑga in all probability is the Ainu placename: < Ainu *askan-*[12] 'beautiful' + *kat* 'view, appearance'. Thus, *asikan-kat* 'beautiful view' > EOJ Asikaᵑga. The first *-k-* is reflected as EOJ voiceless *-k-*, and not prenasalized voiced *-ᵑg-* due to the fact that it is a part of the cluster *-sk-* in Ainu, in which voicing of *-k-* did not occur.

20.4380

本文 • *Original Text*
(1) 奈尓波刀乎　(2) 己岐埿弖美例婆　(3) 可美佐夫流　(4) 伊古麻多可祢尓
(5) 久毛曾多奈妣久

12　　Attested as *asikan-ne* in modern Ainu, where *-ne* is clearly a copula.

仮名の書き下し・*Kana Transliteration*

(1) なにはと₁を (2) こ₂ぎ₁でてみ₁れば (3) かみ₁さぶる (4) い こ₁またかねに (5) くも₁そ₂たなび₁く

Romanization
(1) Nanipa to-wo (2) kəᵑg-i-[i]ⁿde-te mi-re-ᵐba (3) kami saᵐb-uru (4) Ikoma taka ne-ni (5) kumo sə tanaᵐbik-u

Glossing with Morphemic Analysis
(1) Nanipa harbor-ACC (2) row-CONV-exit(CONV)-SUB look-EV-CON (3) deity be.like-ATTR (4) Ikoma high peak-LOC (5) cloud FP trail-ATTR

Translation
(1/2) When [one] rows out of the Nanipa harbor and looks, (5) clouds are trailing over (4) the high peak of Ikoma [mountain] (3) that is like a deity.

Commentary
The only EOJ feature of this poem is the 'misspelling' of *kamï* 'deity' as *kami*. This indicates that there was probably no phonemic contrast between /i/ and /ï/ in Simotukɛno EOJ. See also the same misspelling of the same word in 20.4374 above.

On Nanipa and Nanipa harbor, see the commentaries to poems 20.4329 and 20.4330.

OJ *to* 'door' could be used as a synonym of *minato* 'harbor'.

Mt. Ikoma (642 m) is located between the present Ikoma district of Ikoma city of Nara prefecture and Eastern Ōsaka. In Ancient Japan, Ikoma crossing served as a shortcut between Yamatə and Kapati provinces compared to the easier but longer Tatuta crossing to the south. The name of the mountain (as well as of the city and of the district) is spelled today in Chinese characters as 生駒 'living stallion', but this is apparently a late phonographic spelling since it is written as 胆駒 in the *Nihonshoki* (24.199.8), and *Fudoki* (FK 434.10).[13] In the *Man'yōshū* it is written phonographically in *on-yomi* spelling as 伊故麻 in 15.3589 and the next 15.3590, in *kun-yomi* spelling as 射駒 (6.1047, 10.2201), or in the mixed *on-kun-yomi* phonographic spelling as 伊駒 (12.3032). In the latter two cases 駒 /koma/ 'stallion' is likely to be used as a *kun-yomi* character, but not as a semantogram. Even if it were a semantogram, it still remains unclear

---

13   This place name is not attested in the *Kojiki, Shoku Nihongi*, and other minor Old Japanese texts, as far as I can tell.

what the first syllable /i/ would mean. Theoretically, it could be *i* 'sacred', but 'sacred stallion' seems to be a strange name for a mountain. It is quite possible that this placename is non-Japanese in origin. One possibility might be Ainu *e-ko-oman* 'INSTR-DIR-go' or *e-ko-oma* 'INSTR-DIR-enter' 'the place by which [one] passes toward' that is 'crossing' that became *ikoma* after *e > i raising that took place in pre-Old Japanese.

Postscript to the Poem 20.4380

本文・*Original Text*
右一首梁田郡上丁大田部三成

Translation
The poem above [was composed] by private Opota︎ᵐbe-nə Minari from Yanata district.

Commentary
Nothing is known about the biography of Opota︎ᵐbe-nə Minari.

On private (*Kami-nə yoporo*, 上丁) and other *sakimori* ranks, see the commentary to the postscript to the poem 20.4321.

Yanata district corresponds to the western part of Ashikaga city (Ashikaga-shi, 足利市) in present-day Tochigi prefecture, but one part of it was incorporated into Kiryū city (Kiryū-shi, 桐生市) in present-day Gunma prefecture (Kinoshita 1988: 156).

20.4381

本文・*Original Text*
(1) 久爾具爾乃 (2) 佐岐毛利都度比 (3) 布奈能里弖 (4) 和可流乎美礼婆 (5) 伊刀母須敝奈之

仮名の書き下し・*Kana Transliteration*
(1) くにぐにの₂ (2) さき₁も₁りつど₁ひ₁ (3) ふ␣なの₂りて (4) わかるをみ₁れば (5) いと₁も₂すべ₁なし

Romanization
(1) kuni-ⁿguni-nə (2) sakimori tuⁿdop-i (3) puna-nər-i-te (4) wakar-u-wo mi-re-ᵐba (5) ito mə suᵐbe na-si

Glossing with Morphemic Analysis
(1) province-province-GEN (2) border.guard gather-CONV (3) boat-embark-CONV-SUB (4) part-ATTR-ACC see-EV-CON (5) extremely FP way no-FIN

Translation
(4) When [I] see that (1/2) border guards from [different] provinces gather and (4) then part, (3) embarking on the boats, (5) [it is sad, but] there is absolutely nothing [that] can be done.

Commentary
The only EOJ feature of this poem is the fact that the verb *wakar-* 'to part' is consonantal. In WOJ it is a vowel verb *wakare-* 'id.', so in WOJ the attributive form *wakar-uru*, and not *wakar-u* would be expected.

Postscript to the Poem 20.4381

本文 • Original Text
右一首河内郡上丁神麻續部嶋麻呂

Translation
The poem above [was composed] by private Kamuwomimbe-nə Simamarə from Kaputi district.

Commentary
Nothing is known about the biography of Kamuwomimbe-nə Simamarə. We follow both Omodaka (1984.20: 110) and Mizushima (2003: 515) in reading 神麻續部 as Kamuwomimbe. Kinoshita reads this family name as Miwawomimbe (1988: 157).

On private (*Kami-nə yoporo*, 上丁) and other *sakimori* ranks, see the commentary to the postscript to the poem 20.4321.

Kaputi district corresponds to Kawati county (Kawati-gun, 河内郡) and a part of Utsunomiya city (Utsunomiya-shi, 宇都宮市) in present-day Tochigi prefecture (Kinoshita 1988: 156).

20.4382

本文・Original Text
(1) 布多富我美 (2) 阿志氣比等奈里 (3) 阿多由麻比 (4) 和我須流等伎尓 (5) 佐伎母里尓佐須

仮名の書き下し・Kana Transliteration
(1) ふたほがみ₁ (2) あしけ₂ひ₁と₂なり (3) あたゆまひ₁ (4) わがする と₂き₁に (5) さき₁ も₂りにさす

Romanization
(1) Puta [o]po-ŋ-gami (2) asi-kɛ pitə nar-i (3) ata yumapi (4) wa-ŋga s-uru təki-ni (5) sakiməri n-i sas-u

Glossing with Morphemic Analysis
(1) Puta great-COP(ATTR)-head (2) be.bad-ATTR person be-FIN (3) sudden sickness (4) I-POSS do-ATTR time-LOC (5) border.guard COP-CONV appoint-FIN

Translation
(1) The governor [in] Puta (2) is a bad person. (3/4) When I suddenly became sick, (5) [he] appointed [me] as a border guard.

Commentary
There are two basic competing hypotheses regarding 布多富我美 *putapoŋgami* in line one. One takes *puta* as 'two' and *poŋgami* as 'lower abdomen', while the other sees Puta as a placename and *poŋgami* as [o]po-ŋ-gami 'great head', that is the governor of the province. While 'Two lower abdomens' could be a person's name, the second explanation makes much more sense, because Puta is the name of the village in Tuŋga district where the seat of the provincial government in Simotukɛno province was located (Takeda 1957: 437–438; Omodaka 1984.20: 111–112; Kinoshita 1988: 158).

EOJ adjectival attributive *-kɛ* (more frequently spelled as *-ke*) corresponds to WOJ *-ki*.

Simotukɛno EOJ *ata* 'sudden' has no WOJ cognate, but there are many cognates in Ryūkyūan and some mainland Japanese dialects (Omodaka 1984.20: 112–113; Kinoshita 1988: 159).

Simotukɛno EOJ *yumapi* 'sickness' corresponds to WOJ *yamapi* 'id.' For the same correspondence EOJ *u* : WOJ *a* cf. EOJ *nayum-* 'to suffer, to be hurt' in 14.5333 and WOJ *nayam-* 'id.'

Postscript to the Poem 20.4382

本文 · *Original Text*
右一首那須郡上丁大伴部廣成

Translation
The poem above [was composed] by private Opotəməmbe-nə Pirənari from Nasu district.

Commentary
Nothing is known about the biography of Opotəməmbe-nə Pirənari.

On private (*Kami-nə yoporo*, 上丁) and other *sakimori* ranks, see the commentary to the postscript to the poem 20.4321.

Until recently, Nasu district corresponded to Nasu county (Nasu-gun, 那須郡) and Ōtawara city (Ōtawara-shi, 大田原市) in present-day Tochigi prefecture (Kinoshita 1988: 159), but on October 1, 2005 Nasu district was incorporated into Ōtawara city.

20.4383

本文 · *Original Text*
(1) 都乃久尓乃 (2) 宇美能奈岐佐尓 (3) 布奈餘曾比 (4) 多志弖毛等伎尓 (5) 阿母我米母我母

仮名の書き下し · *Kana Transliteration*
(1) つの₂くにの₂ (2) うみ₁の₂なぎ₁さに (3) ふなよ₂そ₂ひ₁ (4) たしでも₁と₂き₁に (5) あも₂がめ₂も₂がも₂

Romanization
(1) Tu-nə kuni-nə (2) umi-nə naⁿgisa-ni (3) puna-yəsəp-i (4) tas-i-[i]ⁿde-m-o təki-ni (5) amə-ⁿga mɛ məⁿgamə

Glossing with Morphemic Analysis
(1) Tu-GEN province-GEN (2) sea-GEN shore-LOC (3) boat-equip-CONV (4) depart-CONV-exit-TENT-ATTR time-LOC (5) mother-POSS eye DP

Translation
(5) [I] want [my] mother to see [me] (4) when I am going to depart, (3) having equipped [my] boat (2) at the seashore (1) of Tu province.

Commentary

Tu province (Tu kuni, 津國, Settu kuni, 攝津國) was one of the Upper Provinces (Jōkoku, 上國) according to the *Ritsuryō* code. It corresponds to a part of Ōsaka prefecture and southeastern part of Hyōgo prefecture (Nakanishi 1985: 463). On the *Ritsuryō* code classification of Yamatə provinces see the commentary to the postscript to the poem 14.3349.

EOJ *tas-i* 'depart-NML' corresponding to WOJ *tat-i* 'id.' is an example of EOJ palatalization $t > s/\_i$, on which see the commentary to 14.3395.

On EOJ special attributive form -*o*, see also the commentary to 14.3395 and a brief description of EOJ special grammar in the introductions to book fourteen and this volume.

On EOJ *amə* 'mother', see the commentary to 20.4376.

There are different interpretations of line five: 'I want to see my mother's face' (Omodaka 1984.20: 113), 'I want to meet my mother' (Takeda 1957: 438; Kojima et al. 1975: 401; Kinoshita 1988: 160), 'I want to meet my mother just for a moment' (Mizushima 2003: 533), 'I want my mother to see me' (Takagi et al. 1962: 430). We think that the Takagi et al. interpretation makes the most sense, because the author has equipped and decorated his boat, and apparently expresses the desire for his mother to see this boat and him on this boat.

Postscript to the Poem 20.4383

本文 • *Original Text*
右一首塩屋郡上丁丈部足人

Translation
The poem above [was composed] by private Pasetuka^mbe-nə Taripitə from Siponəya district.

Commentary
Nothing is known about the biography of Pasetuka^mbe-nə Taripitə.

On private (*Kami-nə yoporo*, 上丁) and other *sakimori* ranks, see the commentary to the postscript to the poem 20.4321.

Siponəya district corresponds to Shioya county (Shioya-gun, 塩谷郡) and Yaita city (Yaita-shi, 矢板市) in present-day Tochigi prefecture (Kinoshita 1988: 160).

Postscript to the Poems 20.4373–4383

本文 • *Original Text*
二月十四日下野國防人部領使正六位上田口朝臣大戸進歌數十八首但拙劣歌者不取載之

Translation
On the fourteenth day of the second lunar month [of the seventh year of Tenpyō Shōhō], Tanəkuti-nə asəmi Opoto[14] (Senior Sixth Rank, Upper Grade), *sakimori* messenger of Simotukɛno province, presented [to me] eighteen poems. However, I did not include [here] the poems of inferior [quality].

Commentary
The fourteenth day of the second lunar month of the seventh year of Tenpyō Shōhō corresponds to March 31, 755 AD.

Tanəkuti-nə asəmi Opoto is mentioned several times in the *Shoku Nihongi*. He was promoted to Junior Fifth Rank, Lower Grade on the fourth day of the first lunar month of the sixth year of Tenpyō Hōji (February 1, 762 AD). On the ninth day of the first lunar month of the sixth year of Tenpyō Hōji (February 6, 762 AD) he was appointed as the governor of Pimuka province. He was further appointed as the Head (*tō*, 頭) of War Horses Bureau (*Heibashi*, 兵馬司) on the ninth day of the first lunar month of the seventh year of Tenpyō Hōji (February 25, 763 AD) and Assistant Governor of Kamitukɛno province on the twenty-first day of the first lunar month of the eighth year of Tenpyō Hōji (February 27, 764 AD). On the seventh day of the first lunar month of the eighth year of Hōki (February 6, 770 AD) Tanəkuti-nə asəmi Opoto was promoted to Junior Fifth Rank, Upper Grade. Nothing else is known of his biography. Asəmi is a *kabane* title.

On Simotukɛno province, see the commentary to 14.3424.

On *sakimori* messengers, see the commentary to the preface to poems 20.4321–4424.

The *Genryaku kōhon* mentions sixteen (十六) original poems, but all other manuscripts indicate eighteen (十八) original poems (Omodaka 1984.20: 103). Since the *Hirose-bon*, the only manuscript that comes from the independent lineage of the now lost *Teika-bon*, also has eighteen poems (10: 73a), the *Genryaku kōhon* most likely has a mistake. Thus, although Opotəmə-nə Yakaməti received eighteen poems, he included only eleven.

---

14   Opoto is alternatively read as Opopɛ (Omodaka 1984.20: 114; Kinoshita 1988: 160).

20.4384

本文・Original Text
(1) 阿加等伎乃 (2) 加波多例等枳尓 (3) 之麻加枳乎 (4) 己枳尓之布祢乃 (5) 他都枳之良須母

仮名の書き下し・Kana Transliteration
(1) あかと₂き₁の₂ (2) かはたれと₂き₁に (3) しまかぎ₁を (4) こ₂ぎ₁にしふねの₂ (5) たづき₁しらずも₂

Romanization
(1) akatəki-nə (2) ka pa tare təki-ni (3) sima kaⁿgi-wo (4) kəⁿg-i-n-i-si pune-nə (5) taⁿduki sir-aⁿz-umə

Glossing with Morphemic Analysis
(1) dawn-GEN (2) that TOP who time-LOC (3) island shadow-ACC (4) row-CONV-PERF-CONV-PAST.ATTR boat-GEN (5) clue know-NEG-EXCL

Translation
(5) [I] have no clue (4) about the boat that rowed (3) under the shadow of the island (2) at the dim time (1) of dawn!

Commentary
OJ *ka pa tare* is literally 'that [is] who?' It introduces the play on words in this poem: in the dimly-lit time at dawn one cannot clearly see who is who, hence this playful expression to indicate this time (Omodaka 1984.20: 115).

Simotupusa EOJ *kaⁿgi* 'shadow' corresponds to WOJ *kaⁿgɛ* 'id.' This is a case of a raising of a secondary /ɛ/ to /i/.

On EOJ and WOJ *taⁿduki* and WOJ *taⁿdoki ~ taⁿdəki* 'clue', see the commentary to 15.3777.

On *-umə ~ -mə* as a special Old Japanese exclamative form, see the commentary to 14.3431.

Postscript to the Poem 20.4384

本文・Original Text
右一首助丁海上郡海上國造他田日奉直得大理

Translation

The poem above [was composed] by commander Wosaⁿda-nə Pimaturi-nə atapi Təkətari from Unakami district.

Commentary

It seems that the text of this postscript is corrupted. After the usual 右一首 'the poem above' we find the *sakimori* rank of Captain (*Sukɛ-nə yoporo*, 助丁), not followed by any name, but by the placename 海上郡 'Unakami district'. This is again followed just by 海上 'Unakami' with the omission of the character 郡 'district'. And only then comes the rank of commander (*Kuni-nə miyatuko*, 國造), followed by the name of the author. We presume that the reconstruction of the original text that would make sense and would correspond to the translation offered above should be something like:

右一首海上郡國造他田日奉直得大理

The poem above [was composed] by commander Wosaⁿda-nə Pimaturi-nə atapi Təkətari from Unakami district.

We have used this reconstruction for the translation above.

Nothing is known about the biography of Wosaⁿda-nə Pimaturi-nə atapi Təkətari. Atapi is a *kabane* title.

On commander (*Kuni-nə miyatuko*, 國造) and other *sakimori* ranks, see the commentary to the postscript to the poem 20.4321.

Unakami district corresponds to Kaijō county (Kaijō-gun, 海上郡), Chōshi city (Chōshi-shi, 銚子市), and Asahi city (Asahi-shi, 旭市) in present-day Chiba prefecture (Kinoshita 1988: 162).

20.4385

本文・*Original Text*

(1) 由古作枳尓 (2) 奈美奈等惠良比 (3) 志流敝尓波 (4) 古乎等都麻乎等 (5) 於枳弖等母枳奴

仮名の書き下し・*Kana Transliteration*

(1) ゆこ₁さき₁に (2) なみ₁なと₂ゑらひ (3) しるへ₁には (4) こ₁をと₂つまをと₂ (5) おき₁てと₂も₂き₁ぬ

Romanization
(1) yuk-o saki-ni (2) nami na təwerap-i (3) siru-pe-ni pa (4) ko-wo-tə tuma-wo-tə (5) ok-i-te tə mə k-i-n-u

Glossing with Morphemic Analysis
(1) go-ATTR ahead-LOC (2) wave NEG/IMP surge-CONV (3) behind-side-LOC TOP (4) child-ACC-COM spouse-ACC-COM (5) leave.behind-CONV-SUB FP EP come-CONV-PERF-FIN

Translation
(2) Waves, do not surge (1) at the destination [I] am going to! (5) [I] have come [here] leaving (4) [my] children and spouse (3) behind me.

Commentary
On EOJ special attributive form -*o* see the commentary to 14.3395 and a brief description of EOJ special grammar in the introductions to book fourteen and this volume.

Simotupusa EOJ *təwerap-* 'to surge, to swell (of waves)' is a *hapax legomenon* that corresponds to WOJ *təworap-* 'to rock (of a boat on waves)' (MYS 9.1740), also a *hapax legomenon* (Omodaka 1984.20: 116).

Simotupusa EOJ *siru* 'behind' corresponds to WOJ *siri* 'id.' Both are derivations from PJ *siruy, with a regular loss of final *-y in EOJ.

A combination of accusative and comitative case markers -*wo-tə* repeated twice in the phrase *ko-wo-tə tuma-wo-tə* 'children and spouse' in line four is unusual. It is not attested anywhere else in OJ texts, and the expected construction would be *ko-tə tuma-wo* or *ko-tə tuma-tə-wo* 'children and spouse'. Possibly *ko-wo-tə tuma-wo-tə* 'children and spouse' represents Simotupusa EOJ usage, but without the second independent piece of evidence it is impossible to prove it.

The word *təmə* in line five is a puzzle. It cannot be an OJ conjunction *təmə* 'even though', because it would make no sense in the given context, and because OJ *təmə* follows the final form of a verb, not the subordinative gerund *-te*. It may seem at first glance that it is also unlikely to be a combination of a focus particle *mə* with a preceding EOJ focus particle *tə*,[15] cognate to WOJ *sə*, id., as believed by Omodaka (1984.20: 116) and Mizushima (2003: 551) because we then would expect the final verb to be in attributive form *k-i-n-uru* or

---

15 Attested in 14.3409, 14.3425, 14.3561, and 20.4430.

k-i-n-o,[16] due to *kakari-musubi* rules. But the final verb is *k-i-n-u*, in the final form. In addition, among the four attestations of EOJ focus particle *tə*, it is attested once in Kamitukɛno EOJ (14.3409), once in Simotukɛno EOJ (14.3425), and twice in poems without geographic identification (14.3561 and 20.4330). None of the attestations is from Simotupusa, but it is interesting that poem 14.4357, where the violation of the *kakari-musubi* rule with the verb in final form following EOJ particle *sə* occurs, is from Itipara district in Kamitupusa province. Itipara district is adjacent to Simotupusa province, and although it does not have a common border with Kaⁿdusika district in Simotupusa province, it is quite close. On the other hand, Kaⁿdusika district shares a common border with Simotukɛno province. Consequently, it would not come as a surprise that its dialect may have common features with both Kamitupusa and Simotukɛno. Therefore, we do not share Kinoshita's skepticism about the equation of EOJ *tə* with WOJ *sə* in this poem (1988: 164), and follow Omodaka and Mizushima's proposal.

Postscript to the Poem 20.4385

本文 · *Original Text*
右一首葛餝郡私部石嶋

Translation
The poem above [was composed] by Kisaki^mbe-nə Isosima from Kaⁿdusika district.

Commentary
Nothing is known about the biography of Kisaki^mbe-nə Isosima. He probably was a private, since his rank is not mentioned. On private (*Kami-nə yoporo*, 上丁) and other *sakimori* ranks, see the commentary to the postscript to the poem 20.4321.

On Kaⁿdusika district see the commentary to 14.3349.

---

[16] Kinoshita provides two examples when the focus particle *sə* is followed in EOJ not by a verb in the attributive form, but by a verb in the final form: 20.4357 and 20.4401 (1988: 164). While the first example is valid, the second is not, because the script actually indicates EOJ *k-i-n-o* 'come-INF-PERF-ATTR'.

20.4386

本文・*Original Text*
(1) 和加々都乃 (2) 以都母等夜奈枳 (3) 以都母以都母 (4) 於母加古比須々 (5) 奈理麻之都之母

仮名の書き下し・*Kana Transliteration*
(1) わがかづの₂ (2) いつも₂と₂やなぎ₁ (3) いつも₂いつも₂ (4) おも₂がこ₁ひ₁すす (5) なりましつしも₂

Romanization
(1) wa-ⁿga kaⁿdu-nə (2) itu-mətə yanaⁿgi (3) itu mə itu mə (4) omə-ⁿga kopi-susu (5) nar-i-[i]mas-i-tusi-mə

Glossing with Morphemic Analysis
(1) I-POSS gate-GEN (2) five-CL willow (3) when FP when FP (4) mother- POSS long.for(CONV)-COOR (5) do.house.work-CONV-HON-COOR-EXCL

Translation
(2) Five willow trees (1) at my gate ... (3/4) [My] mother always, always longs for [me] and (5) is doing [her] house work!

Commentary

The first two lines are the introduction (*jo*, 序) to the rest of the poem based on phonetic word play between *itu-mətə*, lit. 'five roots' and *itu mə* 'always'.

Simotupusa EOJ *kaⁿdu* 'gate' corresponds to WOJ and EOJ *kaⁿdo* 'id.' < *kana-to* 'metal [adorned] gate', on which see the commentary to 14.3530. This example illustrates that in Simotupusa EOJ primary PJ *o underwent raising to /u/ in final syllables.

EOJ 'misspellings' *yanaⁿgi* 'willow' for WOJ *yanaⁿgï* 'id.' and *kopi-* for WOJ *kopï-* 'to long for' indicate that there was no phonemic contrast between /i/ and /ï/ in Simotupusa.

Line three is hypermetric (*ji amari*, 字余り).

This poem includes two different forms of coordinative gerund -*susu* and -*tusi* (the second of them in the function of the final predicate) corresponding to WOJ -*tutu*, id.

Both Omodaka (1984.20: 117) and Mizushima (2003: 561) believe that the OJ verb *nar-* in this particular poem means 'to do agricultural work'. Neither of these two scholars provide any argumentation as to why we simply cannot take it here in its usual meanings 'to do house work', to 'manage household affairs', so we disregard their opinion in our glossing and translation.

On -umə ~ -mə as a special Old Japanese exclamative form, see the commentary to 14.3431.

Postscript to the Poem 20.4386

本文 • *Original Text*
右一首結城郡矢作部眞長

Translation
The poem above [was composed] by Yapaⁿgiᵐbe-nə Manaŋga from Yupukï district.

Commentary
Nothing is known about the biography of Yapaⁿgiᵐbe-nə Manaŋga. He probably was a private, since his rank is not mentioned. On private (*Kami-nə yoporo*, 上丁) and other *sakimori* ranks see the commentary to the postscript to the poem 20.4321.

Yupukï district corresponds to Yūki county (結城郡) and a part of Yūki city (結城市) in present-day Ibaraki prefecture (Nakanishi 1985: 495; Kinoshita 1988: 166).

20.4387

本文 • *Original Text*
(1) 知波乃奴乃 (2) 古乃弖加之波能 (3) 保々麻例等 (4) 阿夜尓加奈之美 (5) 於枳弖他加枳奴

仮名の書き下し • *Kana Transliteration*
(1) ちばの₂ぬの₂ (2) こ₁の₂てかしはの₂ (3) ほほまれど₂ (4) あやにかなしみ₁ (5) おき₁てたかき₁ぬ

Romanization
(1) Tiᵐba-nə nu-nə (2) ko-nə te kasipa-nə (3) popom-ar-e-ⁿdə (4) aya n-i kanasi-mi (5) ok-i-te ta-ka k-i-n-u

Glossing with Morphemic Analysis
(1) Tiᵐba-GEN field-GEN (2) child-GEN hand oak-GEN (3) be.still.in.the.buds-PROG-EV-CONC (4) extreme COP-CONV be.dear-GER (5) leave.behind-CONV-SUB here-DIR come-CONV-PERF-FIN

Translation

(1/2) Although the oak [with leaves like] child's hand at the fields of Ti^mba (3) has [its leaves] still in the buds, (4) [she] is extremely dear [to me], (5) [I] left [her] behind and have come here.

Commentary

Ti^mba refers to an area around modern Chiba city (Nakanishi 1985: 463).

The first three lines are the introduction (*jo*, 序) to the rest of the poem. The girl that the author has left behind is compared here to the oak with young leaves that are still in the buds.

It is unclear what kind of tree is *ko-nə te kasipa* 'oak [with leaves like] child's hand', although it is certainly some kind of oak (Omodaka 1984.20: 118–119; Kinoshita 1988: 167–168; Mizushima 2003: 567).

Simotupusa EOJ *popom-* is the unraised from of OJ *pupum-* 'to hold inside [one's mouth]', 'to be still in buds', on which see the commentary to 14.3572.

On the EOJ progressive suffix *-ar-* corresponding to WOJ *-er-*, see the commentary to 14.3351.

The word *taka* in line five is considered to be of unknown meaning (Omodaka 1984.20: 119). Kinoshita (1988: 169) and Mizushima (2003: 570) believe that it is *taka* 'high' used in the sense 'far', but this interpretation, although it is based on Sengaku's authority, hardly makes any sense, because *taka* 'high' is never used in the meaning 'far' anywhere else in OJ texts. We think that in fact we are dealing here with two Ainu loanwords: *ta* < Ainu *ta* 'this, here' and Ainu *-ke*, directive case particle. The usage of Ainu *ta ke* 'here to' survives in Yakumo and Osamanpe Ainu *take'áni ~ takáni* 'here' (Hattori 1964: 311; Izutu 2006: 326).

Postscript to the Poem 20.4387

本文 • *Original Text*
右一首千葉郡大田部足人

Translation

The poem above [was composed] by Opota^mbe-nə Taripitə from Ti^mba district.

Commentary

Nothing is known about the biography of Opota^mbe-nə Taripitə. He probably was a private, since his rank is not mentioned. On private (*Kami-nə yoporo,*

上丁) and other *sakimori* ranks see the commentary to the postscript to the poem 20.4321.

Ti^mba district corresponds to a part of Chiba county (千葉郡), Chiba city (千葉市), and Narashino city (習志野市) in present-day Chiba prefecture (Nakanishi 1985: 495; Kinoshita 1988: 166).

20.4388

本文・*Original Text*
(1) 多妣等弊等 (2) 麻多妣尓奈理奴 (3) 以弊乃母加 (4) 枳世之己呂母尓 (5) 阿加都枳尓迦理

仮名の書き下し・*Kana Transliteration*
(1) たび₁と₂へ₁ど₂ (2) またび₁になりぬ (3) いへ₁の₂も₂が (4) き₁せしこ₂ろ₂も₂に (5) あかつき₁にかり

Romanization
(1) ta^mbi tə [i]p-e-^ndə (2) ma-ta^mbi n-i nar-i-n-u (3) ipe-nə [i]mə-^nga (4) ki-se-si kərəmə-ni (5) aka tuk-i-n-i-kar-i

Glossing with Morphemic Analysis
(1) journey QV say-EV-CONC (2) INT-journey COP-CONV become-CONV-PERF-FIN (3) home-GEN beloved-POSS (4) wear-CAUS(CONV)-PAST.ATTR garment-LOC (5) dirt attach-CONV-PERF-CONV-RETR-FIN

Translation
(1) Although [I] spoke about a journey, (2) [it] has become a really [long] journey. (5) The dirt stuck (3/4) to the garment that my beloved at home made [me] wear.

Commentary
The 'misspelling' of evidential suffix as -*e*- instead of WOJ -*ɛ*- probably indicates that there was no phonemic contrast between /e/ and /ɛ/ in Simotupusa.

Simotupusa EOJ retrospective auxiliary -*kar*- corresponds to WOJ -*ker*-, id.

A similar poem is found in the *Man'yōshū* book fifteen: 15.3667.

Postscript to the Poem 20.4388

本文・Original Text
右一首占部虫麻呂

Translation
The poem above [was composed] by Uraᵐbe-nə Musimarə.

Commentary
Nothing is known about the biography of Uraᵐbe-nə Musimarə. He probably was a private, since his rank is not mentioned. On private (*Kami-nə yoporo*, 上丁) and other *sakimori* ranks, see the commentary to the postscript to the poem 20.4321.

Uraᵐbe-nə Musimarə's district of origin is not mentioned. Kamochi suggests that it might be because he was from the same Tiᵐba district as the author of the previous poem (1912.7: 379).

20.4389

本文・Original Text
(1) 志保不尼乃 (2) 弊古祖志良奈美 (3) 尒波志久母 (4) 於不世他麻保加 (5) 於母波弊奈久尒

仮名の書き下し・Kana Transliteration
(1) しほふねの₂ (2) へ₁こ₁そ₁しらなみ₁ (3) にはしく も₂ (4) おふせたまほか (5) おも₂はへ₁なくに

Romanization
(1) sipo pune-nə (2) pe kos-o sira nami (3) nipasi-ku mə (4) opuse-tamap-o ka (5) oməp-ape-n-aku n-i

Glossing with Morphemic Analysis
(1) tide boat-GEN (2) bow cross.over-ATTR white wave (3) sudden-CONV FP (4) give.order-HON-ATTR IP (5) think-dare-NEG-NML COP-CONV

Translation
(5) Although [I] could not [even] think [about it], (4) did [the Emperor] give [me] an order (3) as sudden as (2) white waves crossing the bow (1) of a sea boat?

Commentary

The order that is meant here is certainly the order to become a *sakimori*.

On *sipo pune* 'sea boat' (lit. 'tide boat'), see the commentary to 14.3450.

The 'misspelling' of *pɛ* 'bow' as *pe* and of *apɛ-* 'to dare' as *ape-* probably indicates that there was no phonemic contrast between /e/ and /ɛ/ in Simotupusa.

On EOJ special attributive form *-o*, see the commentary to 14.3395 and a brief description of EOJ special grammar in the introductions to book fourteen and this volume.

Simotupusa EOJ *nipasi* 'to be sudden' is a *hapax legomenon*, but since WOJ *nipaka* 'sudden' is attested (16.3811), the meaning is easily understood.

Simotupusa EOJ *opuse-* 'to speak (honorific), to give an order' corresponds to WOJ *opose-* 'id.'

Simotupusa EOJ *oməp-ape-* 'to be able to think' is contraction of *oməp-i-ape-*, with the expected EOJ *-a-* in place of *-i+a-*.

Postscript to the Poem 20.4389

本文・*Original Text*

右一首印波郡丈部直大麻呂

Translation

The poem above [was composed] by Pasetukaᵐbe-nə atapi Opomarə from Inipa district.

Commentary

Nothing is known about the biography of Pasetukaᵐbe-nə atapi Opomarə. He probably was a private, since his rank is not mentioned. On private (*Kami-nə yoporo*, 上丁) and other *sakimori* ranks, see the commentary to the postscript to the poem 20.4321. Atapi is a *kabane* title.

Inipa district corresponds to Inba county (Inba-gun, 印旛郡), Narita city (Narita-shi, 成田市), and Sakura city (Sakura-shi, 佐倉市) in present-day Chiba prefecture (Kinoshita 1988: 171).

20.4390

本文・*Original Text*

(1) 牟浪他麻乃 (2) 久留尓久枳作之 (3) 加多米等之 (4) 以母加去々里波 (5) 阿用久奈米加母

仮名の書き下し・*Kana Transliteration*

(1) むらたまの₂ (2) くるにくぎ₁さし (3) かため₂と₂し (4) いも₂がこ₂こ₂ろ₂は (5) あよ₁くなめ₂かも₂

Romanization

(1) mura tama-nə (2) kuru-ni kuᵑgi sas-i (3) katamɛ-tə-si (4) imə-ᵑga kəkərə pa (5) ayok-unam-ɛ kamə

Glossing with Morphemic Analysis

(1) many jewel-COMP (2) pivot-LOC nail insert-CONV (3) make.strong. promise (CONV)-PERF(CONV)-PAST.ATTR (4) beloved-POSS heart TOP (5) waver-TENT2-EV EP

Translation

(4) The heart of my beloved (3) who has promised strongly (2) [like] a nail is driven [strongly] into a pivot (1) that [rotates] like multiple jewels, (5) will [it] waver? [− Certainly not!]

Commentary

Mura tama-nə in line one is considered to be a permanent epithet (*makura-kotoba*, 枕詞) for *kuru* 'pivot'. Although the *makura-kotoba* itself is transparent, the way of its connection to *kuru* 'pivot' is not quite clear, although several explanations exist. We followed in our translation Keichū's hypothesis that points out the connection between *kuru* 'pivot' and *kur-* 'to rotate, to spin' (1690.20: 45a). This hypothesis is essentially adopted by almost all modern commentators.

Simotupusa EOJ perfective auxiliary -*tə*- corresponds to WOJ -*te*-.

There is a problem how to read the word 去々里 'heart': *kəkərə* or *kəkəri*. The reading *rə* (attested in Suiko era inscriptions) for the character 里 is based on Late Han Chinese *liə^B, but its more usual reading *ri* in the eighth century is based on EMC *li^B. Since there are other cases in the *Man'yōshū* when Late Old Chinese readings are used for *man'yōgana* phonograms, like *ki* < *ke for 支, at the first glance 里 /rə/ would not seem to be impossible, but the problem is that while 支 /ki/ is widespread in the *Man'yōshū*, 里 /rə/ is extremely rare. However, within Simotupusa the usage of 里 as /rə/ is somewhat consistent, see also 20.4391. It is quite possible that the archaic phonographic usage survived on periphery in Azuma. If so, this incidentally provides us a perspective on both literacy in Azuma, and on the fact that the poems were transcribed by *sakimori* themselves, and not by *sakimori* messengers, who presented them to Opotəmə-nə Yakamətı, because it is more likely that *sakimori* messengers, being themselves born and bred in Kansai would use a more up-to-date spelling system.

On EOJ tentative suffix *-unam-* see the commentary to 14.3366.

The tentative evidential *-unam-ɛ* + particle *kamə* expresses an irony question in EOJ. See the commentary to 20.4371.

Postscript to the Poem 20.4390

本文 • *Original Text*
右一首偲嶋郡刑部志加麻呂

Translation
The poem above [was composed] by Osaka^mbe-nə Sikamərə from Sasima district.

Commentary
Nothing is known about the biography of Osaka^mbe-nə Sikamərə. He probably was a private, since his rank is not mentioned. On private (*Kami-nə yoporo*, 上丁) and other *sakimori* ranks, see the commentary to the postscript to the poem 20.4321.

Sasima district corresponds to Sashima county (Sashima-gun, 猿島郡) and a part of Koga city (Koga-shi, 古河市) in present-day Ibaraki prefecture (Kinoshita 1988: 173).

20.4391

本文 • *Original Text*
(1) 久尓具尓乃 (2) 夜之里乃加美尓 (3) 奴佐麻都理 (4) 阿加古比須奈牟 (5) 伊母賀加奈志作

仮名の書き下し • *Kana Transliteration*
(1) くにぐにの₂ (2) やしろ₂の₂かみ₁に (3) ぬさまつり (4) あがこ₁ひ₁すなむ (5) いも₂がかなしさ

Romanization
(1) kuni-ⁿguni-nə (2) yasirə-nə kami-ni (3) nusa matur-i (4) a-ⁿga kopi s-unam-u (5) imə-ⁿga kanasi-sa

Glossing with Morphemic Analysis
(1) province-province-GEN (2) shrine-GEN deity-DAT (3) *nusa* present(HUM)-CONV (4) I-POSS long.for-NML do-TENT2-ATTR (5) beloved-POSS dear-NML

Translation
(5) Oh, [the feeling of] endearment for [my] beloved, (4) who probably longs for [me] (3) and presents the *nusa* offerings (2) to the shrine deities (1) of many provinces.

Commentary
There are several interpretations of this poem. The main problem is who is longing for whom and who is making offerings – the author or his beloved? I follow here Kinoshita's interpretation that maintains that it is the beloved of the author who performs both actions (1988: 174–175). It is easy to demonstrate that longing is indeed done by the woman – the tentative *-unam-* will not be used by the author in reference to his own action. Omodaka's hypothesis that the function of *-unam-* in this poem is not that of tentative, but of assertion (1984.20: 125) has no foundation, because there are no other examples of the assertive usage of *-unam-*. It is more difficult to justify that the woman is making offerings: as Kinoshita himself notes, there are both textual examples of a traveler making offerings and a person who stayed at home doing the same (1988: 174). The justification of Kinoshita's point of view would be easier if we could prove that there was indeed a shrine dedicated to deities of various provinces in the author's home village or district.

On the spelling of syllable /rə/ with the phonogram 里 see the commentary to 20.4390.

The 'misspelling' of *kamï* 'deity' as *kami* and of *kopï-* 'to long for' as *kopi-* probably indicates that there was no phonemic contrast between /i/ and /ï/ in Simotupusa.

OJ *nusa* are paper or cloth offerings for deities (Omodaka et al. 1967: 553).

On EOJ tentative suffix *-unam-*, see the commentary to 14.3366.

Postscript to the Poem 20.4391

本文 • *Original Text*
右一首結城郡忍海部五百麻呂

Translation

The poem above [was composed] by Osinəmiᵐbe-nə Ipomarə from Yupukï district.

Commentary

Nothing is known about the biography of Osinəmiᵐbe-nə Ipomarə. He probably was a private, since his rank is not mentioned. On private (*Kami-nə yoporo*, 上丁) and other *sakimori* ranks see the commentary to the postscript to the poem 20.4321.

On Yupukï district see the commentary to the postscript to 20.4386.

20.4392

本文 · Original Text

(1) 阿米都之乃 (2) 以都例乃可美乎 (3) 以乃良波加 (4) 有都久之波々尓 (5) 麻多己等刀波牟

仮名の書き下し · Kana Transliteration

(1) あめ₂つしの₂ (2) いづれの₂かみ₁を (3) いの₂らばか (4) うつくしははに (5) またこ₂と₂と₁はむ

Romanization

(1) amɛ tusi-nə (2) iⁿdure n-ə kami-wo (3) inər-aᵐba ka (4) utukusi papa-ni (5) mata kətə top-am-u

Glossing with Morphemic Analysis

(1) heaven earth-GEN (2) which COP-ATTR deity-ACC (3) pray-COND IP (4) dear mother-DAT (5) again word ask-TENT-ATTR

Translation

(2) Which deities (1) of Heaven and Earth (3) should [I] pray, (5) [so I] would [be able to] (5) talk to [my] dear mother again?

Commentary

Simotupusa EOJ *tusi* 'earth' corresponds to EOJ *tuti* 'id.' The EOJ form exhibits the palatalization $t > s/\_i$. See also 20.4426 for another example of EOJ *tusi*.

Simotupusa EOJ *kami* 'deity' corresponds to WOJ *kamï* 'id.' This probably indicates that there was no phonemic distinction between /i/ and /ï/ in Simotupusa.

Postscript to the Poem 20.4392

本文 • *Original Text*
右一首埴生郡大伴部麻与佐

Translation
The poem above [was composed] by Opotəmə^mbe-nə Mayəsa from Panipu district.

Commentary
Nothing is known about the biography of Opotəmə^mbe-nə Mayəsa. He probably was a private, since his rank is not mentioned. On private (*Kami-nə yoporo*, 上丁) and other *sakimori* ranks, see the commentary to the postscript to the poem 20.4321.

Panipu district corresponds to parts of Inba county (Inba-gun, 印旛郡), Narita city (Narita-shi, 成田市), and Sakura city (Sakura-shi, 佐倉市) in present-day Chiba prefecture (Kinoshita 1988: 176).

20.4393

本文 • *Original Text*
(1) 於保伎美能 (2) 美許等尓作例波 (3) 知々波々乎 (4) 以波比弊等於枳弖 (5) 麻爲弖枳尓之乎

仮名の書き下し • *Kana Transliteration*
(1) おほき₁み₁の₂ (2) み₁こ₂と₂にされば (3) ちちははを (4) いはひ₁へ₁と₂おき₁て (5) まゐでき₁にしを

Romanization
(1) opo kimi-nə (2) mi-kətə n-i s[i]-ar-e-^mba (3) titi papa-wo (4) ipap-i-pe-tə ok-i-te (5) mawi-[i]ⁿde-k-i-n-i-si-wo

Glossing with Morphemic Analysis
(1) great lord-GEN (2) HON-word COP-CONV EP-exist-EV-CON (3) father mother-ACC (4) pray-NML-vessel-COM leave-CONV-SUB (5) come(HUM)(CONV)-go.out(CONV)-come-CONV-PERF-CONV-PAST.ATTR-ACC

Translation
(2) Because [it] had been the command (1) of the Great Lord, (5) [I] came out here, (3/4) leaving behind [my] father and mother together with a praying vessel.

Commentary
On *opo kimi* 'Great Lord' which refers to the Emperor, see the commentary to 14.3480.

On *mi-kətə* 'honorable word', 'imperial order/edict', see the commentary to 14.3480.

Line four is hypermetric (*ji amari*, 字余り), but it is probably a graphic illusion, because *ipap-i-pe-tə ok-i-te* was most likely pronounced as [ipapipetəkite].

Simotupusa EOJ *pe* 'vessel for prayer' corresponds to WOJ *pɛ* 'id.' The 'misspelling' of *pɛ* as *pe* probably indicates that there was no phonemic contrast between /e/ and /ɛ/ in Simotupusa. OJ *pɛ ~ pe* is a ritual vessel in which *sake* or food were offered to deities. It was a precious and sacred commodity, hence its mention alongside with one's parents.

Postscript to the Poem 20.4393

本文 • Original Text
右一首結城郡雀部廣嶋

Translation
The poem above [was composed] by Sanzakimbe-nə Pirəsima from Yupukï district.

Commentary
Nothing is known about the biography of Sanzakimbe-nə Pirəsima. He probably was a private, since his rank is not mentioned. On private (*Kami-nə yoporo*, 上丁) and other *sakimori* ranks, see the commentary to the postscript to the poem 20.4321.

On Yupukï district, see the commentary to the postscript to 20.4386.

20.4394

本文・*Original Text*
(1) 於保伎美能 (2) 美己等加之古美 (3) 由美乃美他 (4) 佐尼加和多良牟 (5) 奈賀氣己乃用乎

仮名の書き下し・*Kana Transliteration*
(1) おほき₁み₁の₂ (2) み₁こ₂と₂かしこ₁み₁ (3) ゆみ₁の₂みた (4) さねかわたらむ (5) なग़け₂こ₂の₂よ₁を

Romanization
(1) opo kimi-nə (2) mi-kətə kasiko-mi (3) yumi-nə mita (4) sa-ne ka watar-am-u (5) naⁿga-kɛ kənə yo-wo

Glossing with Morphemic Analysis
(1) great lord-GEN (2) HON-word be.awesome-GER (3) bow-GEN together (4) PREF-sleep(CONV) IP cross.over-TENT-ATTR (5) be.long-ATTR this night-ACC

Translation
(1/2) Because the command of the Great Lord is awesome, (4) will [I] sleep through (5) this long night [alone] (4) with [my] bow?

Commentary
On *opo kimi* 'Great Lord' which refers to the Emperor, see the commentary to 14.3480.

On *mi-kətə* 'honorable word', 'imperial order/edict', see the commentary to 14.3480.

Simotupusa EOJ *mita* 'together' corresponds to WOJ *muta* 'id.' The latter form is more innovative due to the progressive assimilation *i > u* after *m*.

EOJ adjectival attributive *-kɛ* (more frequently spelled as *-ke*) corresponds to WOJ *-ki*.

Postscript to the Poem 20.4394

本文・*Original Text*
右一首相馬郡大伴部子羊

Translation

The poem above [was composed] by Opotəmə^mbe-nə Kopituⁿzi from Sauma district.

Commentary

Nothing is known about the biography of Opotəmə^mbe-nə Kopituⁿzi. He probably was a private, since his rank is not mentioned. On private (*Kami-nə yoporo*, 上丁) and other *sakimori* ranks, see the commentary to the postscript to the poem 20.4321.

Sauma district corresponds to Northern Sōma county (Kita Sōma-gun, 北相馬郡) of present-day Ibaraki prefecture and to a part of Eastern Katushika county (Higashi Katsushika-gun, 東葛飾郡) of present-day Chiba prefecture (Kinoshita 1988: 179).

Postscript to the Poems 20.4384–4394

本文 • Original Text

二月十六日下総國防人部領使少目従七位下縣犬養宿祢浄人進歌數廿二首但拙劣歌者不取載之

Translation

On the sixteenth day of the second lunar month [of the seventh year of Tenpyō Shōhō], Aⁿgatainukapi-nə sukune Kiyopitə (Junior Seventh Rank, Lower Grade), Junior Clerk and *sakimori* messenger of Simotupusa province, presented [to me] twenty-two poems. However, I did not include [here] the poems of inferior [quality].

Commentary

The sixteenth day of the second lunar month of the seventh year of Tenpyō Shōhō corresponds to April 2, 755 AD.

Nothing is known about the biography of Aⁿgatainukapi-nə sukune Kiyopitə. Sukune is a *kabane* title.

On Simotupusa province, see the commentary to 14.3349.

Shō-sakan (少目) 'Junior Clerk' is the junior clerical position in provincial offices of Great Provinces. It corresponded to Junior Eighth Rank, Lower Grade. Thus, Aⁿgatainukapi-nə sukune Kiyopitə had a rank that exceeded his actual position.

On *sakimori* messengers, see the commentary to the preface to poems 20.4321–4424.

Although Opotəmə-nə Yakamətɨ received twenty-two poems, he included only eleven.

20.4401

本文・*Original Text*
(1) 可良己呂武 (2) 須宗尒等里都伎 (3) 奈苦古良乎 (4) 意伎弖曾伎怒也 (5) 意母奈之尒志弖

仮名の書き下し・*Kana Transliteration*
(1) からこ₂ろ₂む (2) すそ₁にと₂りつき₁ (3) なくこ₁らを (4) おき₁てそ₂き₁の₁や (5) おも₂なしにして

Romanization
(1) Kara kərəmu (2) suso-ni tər-i-tuk-i (3) nak-u ko-ra-wo (4) ok-i-te sə k-i-n-o ya (5) omə na-si n-i s-i-te

Glossing with Morphemic Analysis
(1) Korea garment (2) hem-LOC take-CONV-attach-CONV (3) cry-ATTR child-PLUR-ACC (4) leave.behind-CONV-SUB FP come-CONV-PERF-ATTR EP (5) mother exist.not-FIN COP-CONV do-CONV-SUB

Translation
(4) [I] have come [here] leaving behind (3) [my] crying children (2) who held on to the hem (1) [of my] Korean garment (5) [in spite of the fact that they] have no mother.

Commentary
Kara 'Korea' here refers to United Silla. Since the author of the poem is a commander, he certainly could afford to purchase imported goods. See also the commentary on Kara 'Korea, Karak' to 15.3688.

Sinanu EOJ *kərəmu*[17] 'garment' represents a strange case of *ə* > *u* raising (cf. WOJ *kərəmə* 'id.'). Normally, PJ *ə (> OJ ə) does not raise to *u*, unlike PJ *o

---

17 Mizushima corrects this 己呂武 /kərəmu/ to 己呂茂 /kərəmo/, considering 武 to be the scribal mistake for 茂 (2003: 636), but this is highly speculative at best, because all manuscripts, including the *Hirose-bon* have 武.

(> WOJ *o*). We suppose that this example probably points to the fact that ə and *o* merged in Sinanu EOJ as /o/ while the raising of *o* > *u* was still an active process in this dialect. See also Sinanu EOJ *kamu*, emphatic particle vs. WOJ *kamə* in 20.4403 below.

We follow Takeda (1957: 458) and Nakanishi (1983: 319) in reading 伎怒 as *k-i-n-o* 'come-CONV-PERF-ATTR', not as *k-i-n-u* 'come-CONV-PERF-FIN', which is done by all other Japanese scholars, both premodern and modern. This reading is supported both by the usage of the character 怒 /no/ in the spelling, as well as by the fact that we would expect attributive form after the preceding focus particle *sə*. See also 20.4403 below. The spelling 伎怒 *k-i-n-o* is found in the oldest manuscripts, the *Genryaku kōhon* and the *Ruijū koshū*, while the spelling 伎奴 *k-i-n-u* is found only in later manuscripts starting from the *Nishi Honganji-bon*. There is further supporting evidence from the *Hirose-bon* that has the spelling 伎努 *k-i-n-o* (10: 79a)[18] as well, where /no/ is spelled with the character 努.

On EOJ perfective attributive *-n-o*, see the commentary to 14.3395.

OJ *ya* in line four is an emphatic particle *ya*, not to be confused with the interrogative particle *ya*.

Postscript to the Poem 20.4401

本文 • *Original Text*
右一首國造小縣郡他田舍人大嶋

Translation
The poem above [was composed] by commander Wosaⁿda-nə təneri Oposima from Tipisaⁿgata district.

Commentary
Nothing is known about the biography of Wosaⁿda-nə təneri Oposima. Təneri 'retainer' is a title of an official, but it is not a *kabane* title.

On commander (*Kuni-nə miyatuko,* 國造) and other *sakimori* ranks, see the commentary to the postscript to the poem 20.4321.

Tipisaⁿgata district corresponds to Chiisagata county (小縣郡) and Ueda city (上田市) in present-day Nagano prefecture (Kinoshita 1988: 192).

---

18 The *Hirose-bon* has the *katakana* gloss *kinuru*, which is, of course, unwarranted because the character 努 cannot be read as *nuru*. It is indicative, however, that the attributive form was really meant here.

20.4402

本文・*Original Text*
(1) 知波夜布留 (2) 賀美乃美佐賀尒 (3) 奴佐麻都理 (4) 伊波布伊能知波 (5) 意毛知々我多米

仮名の書き下し・*Kana Transliteration*
(1) ちはやぶる (2) かみ₁の₂み₁さかに (3) ぬさまつり (4) いはふいの₂ちは (5) おも₁ちちがため₂

Romanization
(1) ti-[i]pa ya^mbur-u (2) kami-nə mi-saka-ni (3) nusa matur-i (4) ipap-u inəti pa (5) omo titi-ⁿga tamɛ

Glossing with Morphemic Analysis
(1) thousand-rock crush-ATTR (2) deity-GEN HON-slope-LOC (3) *nusa* offer-CONV (4) pray-ATTR life TOP (5) mother father-POSS for

Translation
(2) At the slope of the deity (1) who crushes thousand rocks (3) [I] offered *nusa* and (4) prayed for the life (5) of my mother and father.

Commentary
OJ *tipaya*ᵐ*buru* is a permanent epithet (*makura-kotoba*, 枕詞) for *kamï* 'deity'. There are two possible interpretations of it: *ti-[i]pa ya*ᵐ*bur-u* 'crushing thousand rocks', adopted here, and *ti paya-*ᵐ*-buru* strength fast-COP(CONV) swing-ATTR 'swinging with a fast strength' (Omodaka 1958.2: 59). Out of sixteen examples of *tipaya*ᵐ*buru* attested in the *Man'yōshū*, eight are spelled logographically as 千磐破 'crushing thousand rocks'.

Sinanu EOJ word for 'deity' is spelled as *kami* (cf. WOJ *kamï*), which probably indicates that there was no phonemic contrast between /i/ and /ï/.

OJ *nusa* are paper or cloth offerings for deities (Omodaka et al. 1967: 553). Offering *nusa* at the slope of a mountain for the mountain deity was a ritual that insured that the deity would offer a safe passage across the mountain.

On the order of *omə titi* 'mother [and] father', see the commentary to 20.4376.

Postscript to the Poem 20.4402

本文・*Original Text*
右一首主帳埴科郡神人部子忍男

Translation
The poem above [was composed] by lieutenant Kamutᵊbe-nə Koosiwo from Panisina district.

Commentary
Nothing is known about the biography of Kamutᵊbe-nə Koosiwo.

On lieutenant (*Shuchō*, 主帳) and other *sakimori* ranks, see the commentary to the postscript to the poem 20.4321.

On Panisina district, see the commentary to 14.3398.

20.4403

本文・*Original Text*
(1) 意保枳美能 (2) 美己等可之古美 (3) 阿乎久牟乃 (4) 等能妣久夜麻乎 (5) 古与弖伎怒加牟

仮名の書き下し・*Kana Transliteration*
(1) おほき₁み₁の₂ (2) み₁こ₂と₂かしこ₁み₁ (3) あをくむの₂ (4) と₂の₂び₁くやまを (5) こ₁よ₂てき₁の₁かむ

Romanization
(1) opo kimi-nə (2) mi-kətə kasiko-mi (3) awo kumu-nə (4) tənᵊmbik-u yama-wo (5) koyə-te k-i-n-o kamu

Glossing with Morphemic Analysis
(1) Great Lord-GEN (2) HON-word awesome-GER (3) blue cloud-GEN (4) trail-ATTR mountain-ACC (5) cross(CONV)-SUB come-CONV-PERF-ATTR EP

Translation
(1/2) Because the order of [my] Great Lord is awesome, (5) [I] came [here] crossing (3/4) the mountains where dark clouds trail!

Commentary

On *opo kimi* 'Great Lord' which refers to the Emperor, see the commentary to 14.3480.

On *mi-kətə* 'honorable word', 'imperial order/edict', see the commentary to 14.3480.

Sinanu EOJ *kumu* 'cloud' resulted from the raising of PJ *o (> WOJ *o*) to *u* (cf. WOJ *kumo* 'id.').

Sinanu EOJ *tənᵐbik-* 'to trail' corresponds to WOJ *tanᵐbik-* 'id.'

Sinanu EOJ *koyə-* 'cross' (cf. WOJ *koye-* 'id.') exhibits the same correspondence of EOJ ə : WOJ ɛ (ɛ becomes *e* after *y*) found in Təpotuapumi EOJ *sasaᵑgə-* 'lift up in one's hands' (cf. WOJ *sasaᵑge-* 'id.') in 20.4325 and *kaᵑgə* 'reflection' (cf. WOJ *kaᵑgɛ* 'id.') in 20.4322.

We follow Takeda (1957: 460), Itō (1999: 565, 569), and Mizushima (2003: 654) in reading 伎怒 as *k-i-n-o* 'come-CONV-PERF-ATTR', not as *k-i-n-u* 'come-CONV-PERF-FIN', which is done by all other Japanese scholars, both premodern and modern. It must be noted that Nakanishi (1983: 319), Itō (1999: 565, 569), and Mizushima (2003: 654) are inconsistent, because they read the same verbal form as *k-i-n-u* in 20.4401. The inconsistency of both Itō and Mizushima results from their overreliance on the *Nishi Honganji-bon*, which has 伎奴 *k-i-n-u* in 20.4401, but 伎怒 *k-i-n-o* in 20.4403. We see no tangible explanation for the inconsistency of Nakanishi. The reading of 伎怒 as *k-i-n-o* is supported both by the usage of the character 怒 /no/ in the spelling, as well as by the fact that we would expect attributive form before the following emphatic particle *kamu*. The spelling 伎怒 *k-i-n-o* is found in all other manuscripts, including the *Hirose-bon*.

On EOJ perfective attributive *-n-o*, see the commentary to 14.3395.

Sinanu EOJ *kamu*, emphatic particle represents a strange case of ə > *u* raising (cf. WOJ *kamə*, id.). Normally, PJ *ə (> OJ ə) does not raise to *u*, unlike PJ *o (> WOJ *o*). We suppose that this example probably points to the fact that ə and *o* merged in Sinanu EOJ as /o/ while the raising of *o* > *u* was still an active process in this dialect. See also Sinanu EOJ *kərəmu* 'garment' vs. WOJ *kərəmə* 'id.' in 20.4401 above. There is also a single attestation of *kamu* in WOJ: WOJ emphatic particle *kamu* (可儺) attested in the last line of MYS 5.813 is a *hapax legomenon*, like EOJ *kamu*. Its original form is *kamə*, and since /ə/ in contrast to /o/ does not raise to /u/, we might be dealing here with a scribal error, but in the light of EOJ *kamu* in 20.4403 such an explanation becomes very unlikely. Omodaka et al. tried to 'fix' this problem by reading this particle as *kamo* in this particular poem, which goes against all other commentaries, but it is symptomatic that

Postscript to the Poem 20.4403

本文 · *Original Text*
右一首小長谷部笠麻呂

Translation
The poem above [was composed] by Wopatuse^mbe-nə Kasamarə.

Commentary
Nothing is known about the biography of Wopatuse^mbe-nə Kasamarə. He probably was a private, since his rank is not mentioned. On private (*Kami-nə yoporo*, 上丁) and other *sakimori* ranks, see the commentary to the postscript to the poem 20.4321.

The district of origin is not recorded. It might have been the same Panisina district as in 20.4402 above, but there is no proof for it (Kinoshita 1988: 194).

Postscript to the Poems 20.4401–4403

本文 · *Original Text*
二月廿二日信濃國防人部領使上道得病不來進歌數十二首但拙劣歌者不取載之

Translation
On the twenty-second day of the second lunar month [of the seventh year of Tenpyō Shōhō], the *sakimori* messenger of Sinanu province, presented [to me] twelve poems, [although he] became sick on his way and did not come. However, I did not include [here] the poems of inferior [quality].

---

[19] Omodaka et al. present this particle as *kamo* with an unspecified vowel /o/ (1967: 226), apparently disregarding the evidence from the *Kojiki kayō*, where this particle is spelled as *kamö* (and not otherwise) fourteen times.

Commentary

The twenty-second day of the second lunar month of the seventh year of Tenpyō Shōhō corresponds to April 9, 755 AD.

The name of the *sakimori* messenger from Sinanu province is not recorded. It could possibly mean that his rank was very low, therefore his name was not worth even mentioning.

On Sinanu province see the commentary to 14.3399.

On *sakimori* messengers, see the commentary to the preface to poems 20.4321–4424.

Although Opotəmə-nə Yakamətɨ received twelve poems, he included only three.

20.4404

本文 • *Original Text*
(1) 奈尓波治乎 (2) 由伎弖久麻弖等 (3) 和藝毛古賀 (4) 都氣之非毛我乎 (5) 多延尓氣流可母

仮名の書き下し • *Kana Transliteration*
(1) なにはぢを (2) ゆき₁てくまでと₂ (3) わぎ₁も₁こ₁が (4) つけ₂しひ₂も₁がを (5) たえ₂にけ₂るかも₂

Romanization
(1) Nanipa-ⁿ-di-wo (2) yuk-i-te k-u-maⁿde tə (3) wa-ŋg-imo-ko-ŋga (4) tukɛ-si pïmo-ŋga wo (5) taye-n-i-kɛr-u kamə

Glossing with Morphemic Analysis
(1) Nanipa-GEN-road-ACC (2) go-CONV-SUB come-ATTR-TERM QV (3) I-POSS-beloved-DIM-POSS (4) attach(CONV)-PAST.ATTR cord-POSS cord (5) break(CONV)-PERF-CONV-RETR-ATTR EP

Translation
(3/4) The cords [of my garment] that my beloved tied, (1/2) saying: "[Keep them tied] until [you] go [all] the way to Nanipa and come back", (5) broke off!

Commentary
On the custom of tying and untying the cords of one's garment, see the commentary to 14.3361.

On Nanipa and Nanipa harbor, see the commentaries to poems 20.4329 and 20.4330.

On EOJ attributive -*u* in *k-u-ma*ⁿ*de* 'until [you] come back', see the commentary to 20.4339.

Kamitukɛno EOJ *pïmo* 'cord' corresponds to WOJ *pimo* 'id.' This spelling probably indicates that there was no phonemic contrast between /i/ and /ï/ in Kamitukɛno. See also 20.4405 below for the same spelling of the same word.

Kamitukɛno EOJ *-kɛr-*, retrospective auxiliary corresponds to WOJ *-ker-*, id. This spelling probably indicates that there was no phonemic contrast between /e/ and /ɛ/ in Kamitukɛno.

Postscript to the Poem 20.4404

本文 • *Original Text*
右一首助丁上毛野牛甘

Translation
The poem above [was composed] by captain Kamitukɛno-nə Usikapi.

Commentary
Nothing is known about the biography of Kamitukɛno-nə Usikapi.

On captain (*Sukɛ-nə yoporo*, 助丁) and other *sakimori* ranks, see the commentary to the postscript to the poem 20.4321.

The districts of origin for captains are usually not recorded (Omodaka 1984.20: 100).

20.4405

本文 • *Original Text*
(1) 和我伊母古我 (2) 志濃比尓西餘等 (3) 都氣志非毛 (4) 伊刀尒奈流等毛 (5) 和波等可自等余

仮名の書き下し • *Kana Transliteration*
(1) わがいも₂こ₁が (2) しぬひ₁にせよ₂と₂ (3) つけ₂しひ₂も₁ (4) いと₁になると₂も₁ (5) わはと₂かじと₂よ₂

Romanization

(1) wa-ⁿga imə-ko-ⁿga (2) sinup-i n-i se-yə tə (3) tukɛ-si pïmo (4) ito n-i nar-u təmo (5) wa pa tək-aⁿzi tə yə

Glossing with Morphemic Analysis

(1) I-POSS beloved-DIM-POSS (2) yearn-NML COP-CONV do-IMP QV (3) attach (CONV)-PAST.ATTR (4) thread COP-CONV become-FIN CONJ (5) I TOP untie-NEG/TENT QV EP

Translation

(5) [I] think that I would not untie (1/3) the cords [of my garment] that [my] beloved tied, (2) telling [me]: "Treat [them] as a reminder [of me]" (4) even if [they] become [thin] threads!

Commentary

On the custom of tying and untying the cords of one's garment, see the commentary to 14.3361.

Line one is hypermetric (*ji amari*, 字余り), but it is most certainly a graphic illusion, because *wa-ⁿga imo-ko* was most likely pronounced as [waⁿgimoko], as evidenced by 20.4404 above and many other examples in the *Man'yōshū*.

Kamitukɛno EOJ *pïmo* 'cord' corresponds to WOJ *pimo* 'id.' This spelling probably indicates that there was no phonemic contrast between /i/ and /ï/ in Kamitukɛno. See also 20.4404 above for the same spelling of the same word.

The usage of the unextended stem *wa* of the first person pronoun in isolation is an EOJ feature (Vovin 2020.1: 219, 224–225).

Postscript to the Poem 20.4405

本文・*Original Text*

右一首朝倉益人

Translation

The poem above [was composed] by Asakura-nə Masupitə.

Commentary

Nothing is known about the biography of Asakura-nə Masupitə. He probably was a private, since his rank is not mentioned. On private (*Kami-nə yoporo*, 上丁) and other *sakimori* ranks see the commentary to the postscript to the poem 20.4321.

The district of origin is not recorded.

20.4406

本文・Original Text
(1) 和我伊波呂尓 (2) 由加毛比等母我 (3) 久佐麻久良 (4) 多妣波久流之等 (5) 都氣夜良麻久母

仮名の書き下し・Kana Transliteration
(1) わがいはろ₂に (2) ゆかも₁ひ₁と₂も₂が (3) くさまくら (4) たび₁はくるしと₂ (5) つげ₂やらまくも₂

Romanization
(1) wa-ŋga ipa-rə-ni (2) yuk-am-o pitə məŋga (3) kusa makura (4) taᵐbi pa kurusi tə (5) tuŋgɛ-yar-am-aku mə

Glossing with Morphemic Analysis
(1) I-POSS house-DIM-LOC (2) go-TENT-ATTR person DP (3) grass pillow (4) journey TOP hard(FIN) QV (5) inform(CONV)-send-TENT-NML FP

Translation
(2) [I] want someone who would go (1) to my home. (5) [He] would tell [my home folks] that (3/4) [my] travel [where I use] grass [for my] pillow is hard.

Commentary
Line one is hypermetric (*ji amari*, 字余り), but it is most certainly a graphic illusion, because *wa-ŋga ipa-rə-ni* was most likely pronounced as [waŋgiparəni].

EOJ *ipa* 'house' corresponds to WOJ *ipe* 'id.' See also 20.4375, 20.4416, 20.4419, 20.4423, and 20.4427.

On EOJ special attributive form -*o*, see the commentary to 14.3395 and a brief description of EOJ special grammar in the introductions to book fourteen and this volume.

On the permanent epithet (*makura-kotoba*, 枕詞) *kusa makura* 'grass pillow', see the commentary to 20.4325.

Postscript to the Poem 20.4406

本文・Original Text
右一首大伴部節麻呂

Translation
The poem above [was composed] by Opotəməᵐbe-nə Pusimarə.

Commentary

Nothing is known about the biography of Opotəmə ᵐbe-nə Pusimarə. He probably was a private, since his rank is not mentioned. On private (*Kami-nə yoporo*, 上丁) and other *sakimori* ranks, see the commentary to the postscript to the poem 20.4321.

The district of origin is not recorded.

20.4407

本文・*Original Text*

(1) 比奈久母理 (2) 宇須比乃佐可乎 (3) 古延志太尓 (4) 伊毛賀古比之久 (5) 和須良延奴加母

仮名の書き下し・*Kana Transliteration*

(1) ひ₁なくも₂り (2) うすひ₁の₂さかを (3) こ₁え₂しだに (4) いも₁がこ₁ひ₁しく (5) わすらえ₂ぬかも₂

Romanization

(1) pi-na kumər-i (2) Usupi-nə saka-wo (3) koye siⁿda-ni (4) imo-ŋga kopisi-ku (5) wasur-aye-n-u kamə

Glossing with Morphemic Analysis

(1) sun-LOC be.cloudy-CONV (2) Usupi-GEN slope-ACC (3) cross(CONV) time-LOC (4) beloved-POSS be.longing.for-CONV (5) forget- PASS-NEG-ATTR EP

Translation

(3) When [I] crossed the slope of Usupi, (1) where the sun is obscured by clouds, (4) [I] felt longing for [my] beloved, and (5) [I] cannot forget [her].

Commentary

Pina kuməri is considered to be a permanent epithet (*makura-kotoba*, 枕詞) for the placename Usupi. There is nothing permanent about it, because *pina kuməri* occurs only once in the OJ corpus. It is quite transparent, so we chose to translate it.

EOJ *-na* in *pi-na* is a locative case marker specific for EOJ. For details see Vovin (2005: 151–152).

On Usupi mountain pass, see the commentary to 14.3402.

The converb form *koye* 'crossing' on line three has the typical EOJ attributive function, modifying the following *siⁿda* 'time', 'when'. However, in this particular case it is not impossible to suppose that *koye si^{n}da* 'when [I] crossed' is a result of the hapology of *koye-si si^{n}da*.

On EOJ *si^{n}da* 'time' < Ainu *hi-ta* 'time, when', see the commentary to 14.3363.

The spelling of Kamitukɛno EOJ *kopisi* to be longing for' (cf. WOJ *kopïsi* 'id.') probably indicates that there was no phonemic contrast between /i/ and /ï/ in Kamitukɛno EOJ.

Postscript to the Poem 20.4407

本文 • Original Text
右一首他田部子磐前

Translation
The poem above [was composed] by Wosa^{n}da-nə Koyipasaki.

Commentary
Nothing is known about the biography of Wosa^{n}da-nə Koyipasaki. He probably was a private, since his rank is not mentioned. On private (*Kami-nə yoporo*, 上丁) and other *sakimori* ranks, see the commentary to the postscript to the poem 20.4321.

The district of origin is not recorded.

Postscript to the Poems 20.4404–4407

本文 • Original Text
二月廿三日上野國防人部領使大目正六位下上毛野君駿河進歌數十二首但拙劣歌者不取載之

Translation
On the twenty-third day of the second lunar month [of the seventh year of Tenpyō Shōhō], Kamitukɛno-nə kimi Suru^{n}ga (Senior Sixth Rank, Lower Grade), Senior Clerk and *sakimori* messenger of Kamitukɛno province, presented [to me] twelve poems. However, I did not include [here] the poems of inferior [quality].

Commentary
The twenty-third day of the second lunar month of the seventh year of Tenpyō Shōhō corresponds to April 9, 755 AD.

Kimi 'lord' in Kamitukɛno-nə kimi Suruⁿga is probably an old pre-684 AD *kabane* title. Kamitukɛno-nə kimi Suruⁿga is mentioned in the *Shoku Nihongi* as Tanəᵐbe-nə Puᵐbitə, an immigrant by origin who has been granted the family name of Kamitukɛno on the tenth day of the third lunar month of the second year of Tenpyō Shōhō (April 20, 750 AD) (Omodaka 1984.20: 143; Kinoshita 1988: 199). Nothing else is known of his biography.

On Kamitukɛno province, see the commentary to 14.3404. Kinoshita notes that Kamitukɛno province was not officially upgraded to the Great Province until 811 AD, but the presence of *Dai-sakan* (大目) 'senior clerk' among its officials certainly indicates that it was a Great Province *de facto* (Kinoshita 1988: 199).

Dai-sakan (大目) 'Senior Clerk' is the senior clerical position in provincial offices of Great Provinces. It corresponded to Junior Eighth Rank, Upper Grade. Thus, Kamitukɛno-nə kimi Suruⁿga had a rank that exceeded his actual position.

On *sakimori* messengers, see the commentary to the preface to poems 20.4321–4424.

Although Opotəmə-nə Yakaməti received twelve poems, he included only four.

20.4413

本文・*Original Text*

(1) 麻久良多之 (2) 己志尓等里波伎 (3) 麻可奈之伎 (4) 西呂我馬伎己無 (5) 都久乃之良奈久

仮名の書き下し・*Kana Transliteration*

(1) まくらたし (2) こ₂しにと₂りはき₁ (3) まかなしき₁ (4) せろ₂がまき₁こ₂む (5) つくの₂しらなく

Romanization

(1) makura tasi (2) kəsi-ni tər-i-pak-i (3) ma-kanasi-ki (4) se-rə-ⁿga mak-i kə-m-u (5) tuku-nə sir-an-aku

Glossing with Morphemic Analysis

(1) head.rest long.sword (2) waist-LOC hold-CONV-wear-CONV (3) INT-be.dear-ATTR (4) beloved-DIM-POSS back-POSS come-TENT-ATTR (5) month-GEN know-NEG-NML

Translation

(5) [I] do not know [which] month (3) [my] dear (4) beloved (2) who wears at [his] waist (1) [his] long sword [that he usually keeps] at the headrest, (4) will come back.

Commentary

Muⁿzasi EOJ *tasi* 'long sword' corresponds to WOJ *tati* 'id.' The EOJ form exhibits the palatalization *t > s/_i*.

On the predominantly EOJ diminutive suffix *-rə*, see the commentary to 14.3351.

The characters 馬伎 in line four are read as either *mek-i* and treated as an unknown EOJ verb *mek-* (Omodaka 1984.20: 153), or as *mak-i* and explained as the root of the OJ verb *makar-* 'to go, to depart' (Kinoshita 1988: 211). Neither of the explanations is satisfactory, the first one for obvious reasons, and the second one because only the verbs *makar-* 'to go, to depart' and *mak-* ~ *makɛ-* 'to send, to appoint' are attested (Omodaka et al. 1967: 667, 669). We believe that *mak-i* is a loanword from Ainu: Muⁿzasi EOJ *mak-i* 'its-back' < Ainu *mak* 'back' + Ainu 3rd person possessive suffix *-i*.

On EOJ *tuku* 'moon, month' corresponding to WOJ *tukï* 'id.', see the commentary to 14.3395.

Postscript to the Poem 20.4413

本文 • Original Text

右一首上丁那珂郡檜前舍人石前之妻大伴部眞足女

Translation

The poem above [was composed] by Opotəmə^mbe-nə Matarime, the wife of Pïnəkuma-nə təneri Ipasaki, a private from Naka district.

Commentary

Nothing is known about the biographies of Opotəmə^mbe-nə Matarime and Pïnəkuma-nə təneri Ipasaki. Note that wife and husband normally had different family (clan) names, as was the custom at this time, like in modern China or Korea, but unlike modern Japan. In the censuses of different provinces from Shōsōin, wives and mothers of a master of the house have different family names, while children carry their father's family name. The fact that a husband and a wife that are authors of 20.4421 and 20.4422 below share the same family name is a rare occasion (Kinoshita 1988: 212).

It is interesting that the poem by Pïnəkuma-nə tǝneri Ipasaki is not included. Possibly it was one of these eight poems that were not included by Opotǝmǝ-nǝ Yakamǝti due to their inferior quality.

On private (*Kami-nə yoporo*, 上丁) and other *sakimori* ranks, see the commentary to the postscript to the poem 20.4321.

Təneri 'retainer' is a title of an official, but it is not a *kabane* title. This title in Nara period was very different from *toneri* in the Heian period, which indicated the closest advisers to the Emperor. A partial, but not quite complete Nara period equivalent to the Heian period *toneri* would be *uti təneri* 'inside retainers'.

Naka district corresponds to the south-eastern part of Kodama county (Kodama-gun, 児玉郡) in present-day Saitama prefecture (Kinoshita 1988: 211).

20.4414

本文 · *Original Text*
(1) 於保伎美乃 (2) 美己等可之古美 (3) 宇都久之氣 (4) 麻古我弖波奈利 (5) 之末豆多比由久

仮名の書き下し · *Kana Transliteration*
(1) おほき₁み₁の₂ (2) み₁こ₂と₂かしこ₁み₁ (3) うつくしけ₂ (4) まこ₁がてはなり (5) しまづたひ₁ゆく

Romanization
(1) opo kimi-nə (2) mi-kətə kasiko-mi (3) utukusi-kɛ (4) ma-ko-ⁿga te panar-i (5) sima-ⁿ-dutap-i yuk-u

Glossing with Morphemic Analysis
(1) Great Lord-GEN (2) HON-word be.awesome-GER (3) be.dear-ATTR (4) INT-girl-POSS hand be.separated-CONV (5) island-LOC-pass.along-CONV go-FIN

Translation
(1/2) Because the command of the Great Lord is awesome, (3/4) [I] separated [myself] from the hands of [my] dear girl, and (5) will go [away] passing along the islands.

Commentary
On *opo kimi* 'Great Lord' which refers to the Emperor, see the commentary to 14.3480.

On OJ *mi-kətə* 'honorable word', 'imperial order/edict', see the commentary to 14.3480.

EOJ adjectival attributive *-kɛ* (more frequently spelled as *-ke*) corresponds to WOJ *-ki*.

Mu^{n}zasi EOJ *panar-* 'to be separated' is a consonantal verb, which corresponds to WOJ vowel verb *panare-* 'id.'

Postscript to the Poem 20.4414

本文・*Original Text*

右一首助丁秩父郡大伴部小歳

Translation

The poem above [was composed] by captain Opotəmə^{m}be-nə Wotəsi from Titi^{m}bu district.

Commentary

Nothing is known about the biography of Opotəmə^{m}be-nə Wotəsi. It is interesting that a poem by a captain is placed after the poem of a wife of a private. Usually poems of *sakimori* of higher ranks precede those of lower ranks. Another exception of the same kind is 20.4338, also a poem by a captain, which is placed after a poem by a private.

On captain (*Sukɛ-nə yoporo*, 助丁) and other *sakimori* ranks, see the commentary to the postscript to the poem 20.4321.

Titi^{m}bu district corresponds to Chichibu county (Chichibu-gun, 秩父郡) and Chichibu city (Chichibu-shi, 秩父市) in present-day Saitama prefecture (Kinoshita 1988: 214).

20.4415

本文・*Original Text*

(1) 志良多麻乎 (2) 弖尒刀里母之弖 (3) 美流乃須母 (4) 伊弊奈流伊母乎 (5) 麻多美弖毛母也

仮名の書き下し・*Kana Transliteration*

(1) しらたまを (2) てにと$_{1}$りも$_{2}$して (3) み$_{1}$るの$_{2}$すも$_{2}$ (4) いへ$_{1}$なるいも$_{2}$を (5) またみ$_{1}$ても$_{1}$も$_{2}$や

Romanization
(1) sira tama-wo (2) te-ni tor-i-məs-i-te (3) mi-ru-nəsu mə (4) ipe-n-ar-u imə-wo (5) mata mi-te-m-o mə ya

Glossing with Morphemic Analysis
(1) white pearl-ACC (2) hand-LOC take-CONV-hold-CONV-SUB (3) see-ATTR-COMP FP (4) home-LOC-exist-ATTR beloved-ACC (5) again see(CONV)-PERF-TENT-ATTR FP EP

Translation
(3) Like [one] looks at (1) a white pearl (2) holding [it] in hands (5) [I] would like to see again (4) [my] beloved who is at home!

Commentary
Muⁿzasi EOJ *məs-i* 'hold and' corresponds to WOJ *mət-i* 'id.' The EOJ form exhibits the palatalization $t > s/\_i$. See also 20.4420.

EOJ *-nəsu* is a comparative case marker corresponding to WOJ *-nasu*. For details see Vovin (2005: 199–206).

On EOJ special attributive form *-o*, see the commentary to 14.3395 and a brief description of EOJ special grammar in the introductions to book fourteen and this volume.

Postscript to the Poem 20.4415

本文 · Original Text
右一首主帳荏原郡物部歳徳

Translation
The poem above [was composed] by lieutenant Mənənəmbe-nə Təsitəkə from E^mbara district.

Commentary
Nothing is known about the biography of Mənənəmbe-nə Təsitəkə.

On lieutenant (*Shuchō*, 主帳) and other *sakimori* ranks, see the commentary to the postscript to the poem 20.4321.

E^mbara district corresponds to Ōta ward (Ōta-ku, 大田区), Shinagawa ward (Shinagawa-ku, 品川区), Meguro ward (Meguro-ku, 目黒区), and Setagaya ward (Setagaya-ku, 世田谷区) in present-day Tokyo city (Kinoshita 1988: 215).

20.4416

本文・*Original Text*
(1) 久佐麻久良 (2) 多比由苦世奈我 (3) 麻流祢世婆 (4) 伊波奈流和礼波 (5) 比毛等加受祢牟

仮名の書き下し・*Kana Transliteration*
(1) くさまくら (2) たび₁ゆくせなが (3) まるねせば (4) いはなるわれは (5) ひ₁も₁と₂かずねむ

Romanization
(1) kusa makura (2) ta^mbi yuk-u se-na-ŋga (3) maru ne se-^mba (4) ipa-n-ar-u ware pa (5) pimo tək-aⁿz-u ne-m-u

Glossing with Morphemic Analysis
(1) grass pillow (2) journey go-ATTR beloved-DIM-POSS (3) round sleep(NML) do-COND (4) home-LOC-exist-ATTR I TOP (5) cord untie-NEG-CONV sleep-TENT-FIN

Translation
(2) If [my] beloved, who goes on a journey (1) where [he will use] grass [as his] pillow, (3) sleeps in his clothes, (4) I, who is at home, (5) will sleep without untying the cords [of my garment].

Commentary
On the permanent epithet (*makura-kotoba*, 枕詞) *kusa makura* 'grass pillow', see the commentary to 20.4325.

On EOJ diminutive suffix *-na,* see the commentary to 14.3384.

EOJ *maru ne* (cf. WOJ *maro ne*), lit. 'round sleep' refers to sleeping in one's clothes without taking them off. See also 20.4420.

EOJ *ipa* 'house' corresponds to WOJ *ipe* 'id.' See also 20.4375, 20.4406, 20.4419, 20.4423, and 20.4427.

On the custom of tying and untying the cords of one's garment, see the commentary to 14.3361.

Overall, this is a very interesting poem conveying the psychology that is much more in accord with the twenty-first century than with the eighth: if you do not cheat on me, I will not cheat on you. But maybe human nature in this respect has not really evolved this much in the last thirteen hundred years – this is also a possibility that cannot be denied.

Postscript to the Poem 20.4416

本文 · *Original Text*
右一首妻椋椅部刀自賣

Translation
The poem above [was composed by] Kurapasi^(m)be-nə To^(n)zime, the wife [of lieutenant Mənənəmbe-nə Təsitəkə].

Commentary
Nothing is known about the biography of Kurapasi^(m)be-nə To^(n)zime, except the fact that she must have been really concerned about her husband's fidelity while he was performing his *sakimori* duties.

Lieutenant Mənənəmbe-nə Təsitəkə is the author of the previous poem 20.4415. It is interesting enough that his poem refers to his desire to see his wife again, but the imagery employed uses no reference to the usual symbols of fidelity, like the garment cords that cannot be untied. Could Mənənəmbe-nə Təsitəkə be an Eastern Japanese playboy? Unfortunately, there is no evidence to confirm it or to deny it ...

20.4417

本文 · *Original Text*
(1) 阿加胡麻乎 (2) 夜麻努尓波賀志 (3) 刀里加尔弖 (4) 多麻能余許夜麻 (5) 加志由加也良牟

仮名の書き下し · *Kana Transliteration*
(1) あかご₁まを (2) やまの₁にはがし (3) と₁りかにて (4) たまの₂よこ₂やま (5) かしゆかやらむ

Romanization
(1) aka-ŋ-goma-wo (2) yama no-ni paŋgas-i (3) tor-i-kani-te (4) Tama-nə yəkə yama (5) kasi-yu ka yar-am-u

Glossing with Morphemic Analysis
(1) red-COP(ATTR)-stallion-ACC (2) mountain field-LOC turn.out.to.graze-CONV (3) take-CONV-NEG.POT(CONV)-SUB (4) Tama-GEN horizontal mountain (5) walking-ABL IP send-TENT-ATTR

Translation

(5) Will [I] send [my beloved] walking (4) [across] horizontally stretched mountain in Tama (3) as [I] could not catch (1) [our] chestnut stallion (2) after turning [it] out to graze in mountain fields.

Commentary

On OJ *koma* 'stallion', see the commentary to 14.3387.

OJ *aka-ⁿ-goma* lit. 'red stallion' is 'chestnut stallion' or 'brown stallion'.

Muⁿzasi EOJ negative potential auxiliary *-kani-* corresponds to WOJ *-kane-*, id. Muⁿzasi EOJ *-kani-* shows an interesting secondary raising *e > i*.

Tama region is an area along the basin of Tama river (Tamagawa, 多摩川) in the west of present-day Tokyo prefecture. Tama horizontal mountains refers to the chain of hills in this region (Nakanishi 1985: 461).

On OJ expression *yəkə yama* 'horizontally [stretched] mountains', see the commentary to 14.3531.

Muⁿzasi EOJ *kasi* 'walking' corresponds to WOJ *kati* 'id.', and ultimately is a loan (via WOJ) from OK form that would be a predecessor of MK *kèlí* 'id.' (< *keti). For details see Vovin (2010: 150).

The underlying idea of this poem (fictional, of course) is that the wife pretends to be unable to let her husband go because she cannot provide him with a horse to ride to his destination.

Postscript to the Poem 20.4417

本文 • *Original Text*

右一首豊嶋郡上丁椋椅部荒虫之妻宇遅部黒女

Translation

The poem above [was composed] by Uⁿdⁱᵐbe-nə Kurome, the wife of Kurapasiᵐbe-nə Aramusi, a private from Təsima district.

Commentary

Nothing is known about the biographies of Uⁿdⁱᵐbe-nə Kurome and Kurapasiᵐbe-nə Aramusi.

On husband and wife having different family names see the commentary to the postscript to the poem 20.4413.

It is interesting that the poem by Kurapasiᵐbe-nə Aramusi is not included. Possibly it was one of these eight poems that were not included by Opotəmə-nə Yakaməti due to their inferior quality.

On private (*Kami-nə yoporo*, 上丁) and other *sakimori* ranks, see the commentary to the postscript to the poem 20.4321.

Təsima district corresponds to Toshima ward (Toshima-ku, 豊島区), Arakawa ward (Arakawa-ku, 荒川区), Northern ward (Kita-ku, 北区), Itabashi ward (Itabashi-ku, 板橋区), and Bunkyō ward (Bunkyō-ku, 文京区) of the present-day Tokyo city (Kinoshita 1988: 218).

20.4418

本文 · *Original Text*
(1) 和我可度乃 (2) 可多夜麻都婆伎 (3) 麻己等奈礼 (4) 和我弖布礼奈々 (5) 都知尓於知母加毛

仮名の書き下し · *Kana Transliteration*
(1) わがかど₁の₂ (2) かたやまつばき₁ (3) ま己₂と₂なれ (4) わがてふれなな (5) つちにおち母₂か母₁

Romanization
(1) wa-ⁿga kaⁿdo-nə (2) kata yama tuᵐbaki (3) ma-kətə nare (4) wa-ⁿga te pure-n-a-na (5) tuti-ni oti-m-ə kamo

Glossing with Morphemic Analysis
(1) I-POSS gate-GEN (2) side mountain camellia (3) INT-thing you (4) I-POSS hand touch-NEG-ATTR-LOC (5) ground-LOC fall-TENT-ATTR EP

Translation
(2) [Oh,] camellia [flowers] at the mountain near (1) my gate, (3/5) I wonder whether you would really fall to the ground, (4) when my hand does not touch [you]?

Commentary
Camellia flowers in this poem serve as a metaphorical reference to the author's beloved (Omodaka 1984.20: 157).

On OJ *kaⁿdo* 'gate' < *kana-to* 'metal [adorned] gate', see the commentary to 14.3530.

OJ *tuᵐbaki* 'camellia' (MDJ *yamatsubaki, yabutsubaki*, 椿; Lat. *Camellia japonica*) is a tall evergreen tree that grows in warm areas in the wild. It has oval leaves that are glossy and feel thick to the touch. Camellia blooms with red flowers in early spring. It is considered to be an auspicious flower. The *tsubaki* oil (*tsubaki abura*, 椿油), which is considered to be good for one's hair, is made from its seeds (Nakanishi 1985: 321).

On EOJ form in *V-(a)n-a-na* 'V-NEG-ATTR-LOC', see the commentary to 14.3408. On EOJ special attributive *-a*, see the commentary to 14.3526 and the sketch of the EOJ grammar in the introduction to this volume.

On EOJ special attributive form *-o* (here misspelled as *-ə*), see the commentary to 14.3395 and a brief description of EOJ special grammar in the introductions to book fourteen and this volume.

Line five is hypermetric (*ji amari*, 字余り).

Postscript to the Poem 20.4418

本文・*Original Text*
右一首荏原郡上丁物部廣足

Translation
The poem above [was composed] by private Mənənᵃᵐbe-nə Pirətari from Eᵐbara district.

Commentary
Nothing is known about the biography of Mənənᵃᵐbe-nə Pirətari.

On private (*Kami-nə yoporo*, 上丁) and other *sakimori* ranks, see the commentary to the postscript to the poem 20.4321.

On Eᵐbara district, see the commentary to the postscript to the poem 20.4415.

20.4419

本文・*Original Text*
(1) 伊波呂尓波 (2) 安之布多氣騰母 (3) 須美与氣平 (4) 都久之尓伊多里弖 (5) 古布志氣毛波母

仮名の書き下し・*Kana Transliteration*
(1) いはろ₂には (2) あしふたけ₂ど₂も₂ (3) すみ₁よ₂け₂を (4) つくしにいたりて (5) こ₁ふしけ₂も₁はも₂

Romanization
(1) ipa-rə-ni pa (2) asi pu tak-ɛ-ⁿdəmə (3) sum-i yə-kɛ-wo (4) Tukusi-ni itar-i-te (5) kopusi-kɛ-mo pa mə

Glossing with Morphemic Analysis
(1) house-DIM-LOC TOP (2) reed fire burn-EV-CONC (3) live-NML good-ATTR-ACC (4) Tukusi-LOC reach-CONV-SUB (5) be.longing-ATTR-EXCL TOP EP

Translation
(2) Although [we] make a fire out of reeds (1) at [my] house, (3) the living [there] is good, so (5) [I] will be longing for it (4) when I reach Tukusi!

Commentary
EOJ *ipa* 'house' corresponds to WOJ *ipe* 'id.' See also 20.4375, 20.4406, 20.4416, 20.4423, and 20.4427.

Fire made out of reeds certainly symbolizes life in poverty (Omodaka 1984.20: 159).

Muⁿzasi EOJ *pu* 'fire' corresponds to WOJ *pï ~ po-* 'id.' that indicate PJ form *poy, not *pəy, as is frequently believed. For details see Vovin (2011b).

EOJ adjectival attributive *-kɛ* (more frequently spelled as *-ke*) corresponds to WOJ *-ki*.

Line four is hypermetric (*ji amari*, 字余り), but it is probably a graphic illusion, because *Tukusi-ni itar-i-te* was most likely pronounced as [Tukusinitarite].

Tukusi is the old name for the island of Kyūshū.

On EOJ *kopusi* 'to be longing', see the commentary to 14.3476.

Postscript to the Poem 20.4419

本文 • Original Text
右一首橘樹郡上丁物部眞根

Translation
The poem above [was composed] by private Mənənəᵐbe-nə Mane from Tatiᵐbana district.

Commentary
Nothing is known about the biography of Mənənəᵐbe-nə Mane.

On private (*Kami-nə yoporo*, 上丁) and other *sakimori* ranks, see the commentary to the postscript to the poem 20.4321.

Tati^mbana district corresponds to Kawasaki city (Kawasaki-shi, 川崎市) and most of Yokohama city (Yokohama-shi, 横浜市) with the exception of Totuka ward (Totuka-ku, 戸塚区) in present-day Kanagawa prefecture (Kinoshita 1988: 220).

20.4420

本文・*Original Text*
(1) 久佐麻久良 (2) 多妣乃麻流祢乃 (3) 比毛多要婆 (4) 安我弖等都氣呂 (5) 許礼乃波流母志

仮名の書き下し・*Kana Transliteration*
(1) くさまくら (2) たび₁の₂まるねの₂ (3) ひ₁も₁たえ₂ば (4) あがてと₂つけ₂ろ₂ (5) こ₂れの₂はるも₂し

Romanization
(1) kusa makura (2) ta^mbi-nə maru ne-nə (3) pimo taye-^mba (4) a-ŋga te tə tukɛ-rə (5) kəre n-ə paru məs-i

Glossing with Morphemic Analysis
(1) grass pillow (2) journey-GEN round sleep(NML)-GEN (3) cord tear-COND (4) I-POSS hand QV attach-IMP (5) this COP-ATTR needle hold-CONV

Translation
(3) If the cords [of your garment] break (2) when [you] sleep in your clothes on a journey (1) where [you will use] grass [as your] pillow, (4/5) attach [them] holding this needle, and thinking that [it is] my hand.

Commentary
On the permanent epithet (*makura-kotoba*, 枕詞) *kusa makura* 'grass pillow', see the commentary to 20.4325.

EOJ *maru ne* (cf. WOJ *maro ne*), lit. 'round sleep' refers to sleeping in one's clothes without taking them off. See also 20.4416.

On the symbolism of tying and untying the cords of one's garment, as well as on cords getting loose, see the commentary to 14.3361.

Since OJ personal pronouns do not have reflexive function typical for MJ pronouns, the interpretation of Omodaka (1984.20: 159–160) and Kinoshita (1988: 221) of 安我弖等 as *a-ŋga te tə* 'thinking that it is my hand' is preferable to the Takagi et al. interpretation as *a-ŋga te-tə* 'with one's own hand' (1962: 445).

EOJ -rə is imperative suffix, corresponding to WOJ -yə. See also 14.3465.

OJ adnominal construction kəre n-ə 'this' instead of kənə 'id.' is unusual and very rare. Besides this poem it is also attested in phonographic script in MYS 3.245 and in *Bussoku seki-no uta*.

Muⁿzasi EOJ *paru* 'needle' corresponds to WOJ *pari* 'id.' Both reflect PJ *paruy or *paroy, with different paths of development of *uy or *oy in EOJ, where *uy/*oy > *uy > *u*, and WOJ, where *uy/*oy > *ï > *i* (after dentals).

Muⁿzasi EOJ *məs-i* 'hold and' corresponds to WOJ *mət-* 'id.' The EOJ form exhibits the palatalization $t > s/\_i$. See also 20.4415.

Postscript to the Poem 20.4420

本文 • Original Text
右一首妻椋椅部弟女

Translation
The poem above [was composed by] Kurapasi^mbe-nə Otəme, the wife [of private Mənənə^mbe-nə Mane].

Commentary
Nothing is known about the biography of Kurapasi^mbe-nə Toⁿzime.

Private Mənənə^mbe-nə Mane is the author of the previous poem 20.4419.

20.4421

本文 • Original Text
(1) 和我由伎乃 (2) 伊伎都久之可婆 (3) 安之我良乃 (4) 美祢波保久毛乎 (5) 美等登志努波祢

仮名の書き下し • Kana Transliteration
(1) わがゆき₁の₂ (2) いき₁づくしかば (3) あしがらの₂ (4) み₁ねはほくも₁を (5) み₁と₂と₂し の₁はね

Romanization
(1) wa-^ŋga yuk-i-nə (2) ikiⁿdukusi-ka-^mba (3) Asi^ŋgara-nə (4) mi-ne pap-o kumo-wo (5) mi-tətə sinop-an-e

Glossing with Morphemic Analysis
(1) I-POSS go-NML-GEN (2) be.regrettable-EV-COND (3) Asiⁿgara-GEN (4) HON-peak crawl-ATTR cloud-ACC (5) look(CONV)-COOR yearn-DES-IMP

Translation
(2) If [you] regret (1) that I went [away], (5) yearn [for me] while looking (3/4) at the clouds crawling at the Asiⁿgara peak.

Commentary
Muⁿzasi EOJ *ikiⁿdukusi* 'to be regrettable, to be lamentable' corresponds to WOJ *ikiⁿdukasi* 'id.'

   EOJ inflected adjectival evidential marker *-ka-* corresponds to WOJ *-ke-*.

   On Asiⁿgara, see the commentary to 14.3361.

   On EOJ special attributive form *-o* (neutralized to *-o* after /p/), see the commentary to 14.3395 and a brief description of EOJ special grammar in the introductions to book fourteen and this volume.

   Muⁿzasi EOJ coordinative gerund *-tətə* corresponds to WOJ *-tutu*, id. Possibly, *-tətə* is a misspelling for *-toto*, because OJ *ə* does not raise to *u*. There is a bedazzling array of different phonetic shapes of EOJ shapes of a coordinative gerund: *-tətə* (20.4421), *-susu* (20.4386), *-tusi* (20.4386), *-tutu* (20.4314, etc.). If the original form was *-toto it is difficult to explain palatalizations in *-susu* and *-tusi*.

Postscript to the Poem 20.4421

本文 · Original Text
右一首都筑郡上丁服部於田

Translation
The poem above [was composed] by private Patoriᵐbe-nə Upɛⁿda from Tutuki district.

Commentary
Nothing is known about the biography of Patoriᵐbe-nə Upɛⁿda. There is a disagreement between scholars whether to rely on the *Genryaku kōhon* and the majority of other manuscripts that have 於田, traditionally glossed as Upɛⁿda, or on the *Nishi Honganji-bon*, which has it glossed as Oyu. We follow the first opinion (Omodaka 1984.20: 161).

On private (*Kami-nə yoporo*, 上丁) and other *sakimori* ranks, see the commentary to the postscript to the poem 20.4321.

Tutuki district corresponds to the northern part of Yokohama city (横浜市) in present-day Kanagawa prefecture (Omodaka 1984.20: 161).

20.4422

本文・*Original Text*
(1) 和我世奈乎 (2) 都久之倍夜里弖 (3) 宇都久之美 (4) 於妣波等可奈々 (5) 阿也尔加母祢毛

仮名の書き下し・*Kana Transliteration*
(1) わがせなを (2) つくしへ₂やりて (3) うつくしみ₁ (4) おび₁はと₂かなな (5) あやにかも₂ね₁も₁

Romanization
(1) wa-ⁿga se-na-wo (2) Tukusi-pɛ yar-i-te (3) utukusi-mi (4) oᵐbi pa tək-an-a-na (5) aya n-i kamə ne-m-o

Glossing with Morphemic Analysis
(1) I-POSS beloved-DIM-ACC (2) Tukusi-side send-CONV-SUB (3) be.longing-GER (4) sash TOP untie-NEG-ATTR-LOC (5) unusual COP-CONV EP sleep-TENT-ATTR

Translation
(3) Because [I] long for [him], (1/2) after sending my beloved to Tukusi, (5) [I] will sleep in an unusual manner (4) without untying [my] sash!

Commentary
This poem is practically identical to poem 20.4428 below.

On EOJ diminutive suffix *-na* see the commentary to 14.3384.

Tukusi is the old name for the island of Kyūshū.

Muⁿzasi EOJ *-pɛ* 'side' corresponds to WOJ *-pe* 'id.' Here, it functions as a directive case marker. The misspelling of *-pe* as *-pɛ* probably indicates that there was no phonemic contrast between /e/ and /ɛ/ in Muⁿzasi EOJ. Cf. *-pa* in 20.4428 below.

On EOJ form in *V-(a)n-a-na* 'V-NEG-ATTR-LOC', see the commentary to 14.3408. On EOJ special attributive *-a*, see the commentary to 14.3526 and the sketch of the EOJ grammar in the introduction to this volume.

On EOJ special attributive form -*o*, see the commentary to 14.3395 and a brief description of EOJ special grammar in the introductions to book fourteen and this volume.

Postscript to the Poem 20.4422

本文 • *Original Text*
右一首妻服部呰女

Translation
The poem above [was composed by] Patori^mbe-nə A^nzame, the wife [of private Patori^mbe-nə Upɛ^nda].

Commentary
Nothing is known about the biography of Patori^mbe-nə A^nzame.
 Private Patori^mbe-nə Upɛ^nda is the author of the previous poem 20.4421.
 The fact that a husband and a wife that are authors of 20.4421 and 20.4422 share the same family name is a rare occasion (Kinoshita 1988: 212). See also the commentary to the postscript to the poem 20.4413.

20.4423

本文 • *Original Text*
(1) 安之我良乃 (2) 美佐可尒多志弓 (3) 蘇埿布良婆 (4) 伊波奈流伊毛波 (5) 佐夜尒美毛可母

仮名の書き下し • *Kana Transliteration*
(1) あしがらの₂ (2) み₁さかにたして (3) そ₁でふらば (4) いはなるいも₁は (5) さやにみ₁も₁かも₂

Romanization
(1) Asi^ŋgara-nə (2) mi-saka-ni tas-i-te (3) so^nde pur-a^mba (4) ipa-n-ar-u imo pa (5) saya n-i mi-m-o kamə

Glossing with Morphemic Analysis
(1) Asi^ŋgara-GEN (2) HON-slope-LOC stand-CONV-SUB (3) sleeve wave-COND (4) home-LOC-exist-ATTR beloved TOP (5) clear COP-CONV see-TENT-ATTR EP

Translation

(3) If [I] wave [my] sleeve (2) standing on the slope (1) of Asiŋgara, (4/5) I wonder whether my beloved who is at home would see [it] clearly.

Commentary

On Asiŋgara see the commentary to 14.3361.

On Asiŋgara-nə mi-saka 'Asiŋgara slope', see the commentary to 20.4372.

EOJ *tas-i* 'stand-NML' corresponding to WOJ *tat-i* 'id.' is an example of EOJ palatalization *t > s/_i*, on which also see the commentary to 14.3395.

On the sleeve-waving ritual by women, see the commentary to 14.3389. Presumably, the sleeve-waving ritual by men had the same or similar function.

EOJ *ipa* 'house' corresponds to WOJ *ipe* 'id.' See also 20.4375, 20.4406, 20.4416, 20.4419, and 20.4427.

On EOJ special attributive form *-o*, see the commentary to 14.3395 and a brief description of EOJ special grammar in the introductions to book fourteen and this volume.

Postscript to the Poem 20.4423

本文 • *Original Text*

右一首埼玉郡上丁藤原部等母麻呂

Translation

The poem above [was composed] by private Puⁿdiparaᵐbe-nə Təməmarə from Sakitama district.

Commentary

Nothing is known about the biography of Puⁿdiparaᵐbe-nə Təməmarə.

On private (*Kami-nə yoporo*, 上丁) and other *sakimori* ranks, see the commentary to the postscript to the poem 20.4321.

Sakitama district corresponds to Northern Saitama county (Kita Saitama-gun, 北埼玉郡), Southern Saitama county (Minami Saitama-gun, 南埼玉郡), Gyōda city (Gyōda-shi, 行田市), Hanyū city (Hanyū-shi, 羽生市), Kazo city (Kazo-shi, 加須市), Kuki city (Kuki-shi, 久喜市), Hasuda city (Hasuda-shi, 蓮田市), Kasukabe city (Kasukabe-shi, 春日部市), Iwatsuki city (Iwatsuki-shi, 岩槻市), Kosigaya city (Koshigaya-shi, 越谷市), and Yashio city (Yashio-shi, 八潮市) in present-day Saitama prefecture (Kinoshita 1988: 226).

20.4424

本文・*Original Text*

(1) 伊呂夫可久 (2) 世奈我許呂母波 (3) 曾米麻之乎 (4) 美佐可多婆良婆 (5) 麻佐夜可尓美無

仮名の書き下し・*Kana Transliteration*

(1) い ろ₂ ぶ か く (2) せ な が こ₂ ろ₂ も₂ は (3) そ₂ め₂ ま し を (4) み₁ さ か た ば ら ば (5) ま さ や か に み₁ む

Romanization

(1) irə-ᵐ-buka-ku (2) se-na-ŋga kərəmə pa (3) səmɛ-masi-wo (4) mi-saka taᵐbar-aᵐba (5) ma-sayaka n-i mi-m-u

Glossing with Morphemic Analysis

(1) color-GEN-be.deep-CONV (2) beloved-DIM-POSS garment TOP (3) dye-SUBJ-ACC (4) HON-slope receive(HUM)-COND (5) INT-clear COP-CONV see-TENT-FIN

Translation

(3) [I] wish [I] would dye (2) the clothes of my dear beloved (1) [in] deep [bright] color! (4) if [you] were to receive [the permission of the deity to cross] the [Asiŋgara] slope, (5) [I] would see [you] clearly.

Commentary

Kinoshita notes that low-ranked *sakimori* probably wore black clothes dyed with a juice of acorn of *kunuŋgï* (櫟) 'a kind of oak' (MDJ *kunugi*, Lat. *Quercus acutissima*) (1988: 227).

On EOJ diminutive suffix *-na*, see the commentary to 14.3384.

On Asiŋgara-nə mi-saka 'Asiŋgara slope', see the commentary to 20.4372.

OJ *taᵐbar-* 'to receive' is a contraction of OJ *tamapar-* 'id.'

Postscript to the Poem 20.4424

本文・*Original Text*

右一首妻物部刀自賣

Translation
The poem above [was composed by] Mənənəmbe-nə Tonzime, the wife [of private Pundiparambe-nə Təməmarə].

Commentary
Nothing is known about the biography of Mənənəmbe-nə Tonzime.
　Private Pundiparambe-nə Təməmarə is the author of the previous poem 20.4423.

Postscript to the Poems 20.4413–4424

本文 • *Original Text*
二月廿九日武蔵國部領防人使掾正六位上安曇宿祢三國進歌數廿首但拙劣歌者不取載之

Translation
On the twenty-ninth day of the second lunar month [of the seventh year of Tenpyō Shōhō], Andumi-nə sukune Mikuni (Senior Sixth Rank, Upper Grade), Assistant Official and *sakimori* messenger of Munzasi province, presented [to me] twenty poems. However, I did not include [here] the poems of inferior [quality].

Commentary
The sequence of *sakimori* poems from Munzasi is the most unusual one, because it includes the poems of not only *sakimori*, but also their wives, and also sometimes the poems of *sakimori* wives only without preceding poems by their husbands. One notable exception in other sequences may be the poem 20.4352 in the sequence of poems from Kamitupusa, which might have been composed by a wife or a daughter of a *sakimori*, accompanying her husband or father.
　The twenty-ninth day of the second lunar month of the seventh year of Tenpyō Shōhō corresponds to April 15, 755 AD.
　On Munzasi province, see the commentary to 14.3374.
　On *sakimori* messengers, see the commentary to the preface to poems 20.4321–4424.
　Assistant Official (*En*, 掾) is the position in provincial offices of Upper and Middle Provinces immediately below Assistant Governor (*Sukɛ*, 介) in Upper Provinces and below the Governor in Middle Provinces. It corresponded to Junior Seventh Rank, Upper Grade (for Upper Provinces) and to Junior Eighth Rank, Upper Grade (for Middle Provinces). We have a clear discrepancy in this

case, because Muⁿzasi was a Great Province that was supposed to have the positions of both Senior Assistant Official (*Daien*, 大掾) and Junior Assistant Official (*Shōen*, 少掾), but not just Assistant Official like Upper and Middle Provinces. In any case, Aⁿdumi-nə sukune Mikuni had a rank that exceeded his actual position.

Aⁿdumi-nə sukune Mikuni is mentioned in the *Shoku Nihongi* as a person who was promoted from the Senior Sixth Rank, Upper Grade to the Junior Fifth Rank, Lower Grade on the seventh day of the tenth lunar month of the eighth year of Tenpyō Hōji (November 4, 764 AD). Nothing else is known about his biography.

Although Opotəmə-nə Yakaməti received twenty poems, he included only twelve.

20.4426

本文 • *Original Text*
(1) 阿米都之乃 (2) 可未尒奴佐於伎 (3) 伊波比都々 (4) 伊麻世和我世奈 (5) 阿礼乎之毛波婆

仮名の書き下し • *Kana Transliteration*
(1) あめ₂つしの₂ (2) かみ₂にぬさおき₁ (3) いはひ₁つつ (4) いませわがせな (5) あれをしも₁はば

Romanization
(1) ame tusi-nə (2) kamï-ni nusa ok-i (3) ipap-i-tutu (4) imas-e wa-ⁿga se-na (5) are-wo si [o]mop-amba

Glossing with Morphemic Analysis
(1) heaven earth-GEN (2) deity-DAT *nusa* place-CONV (3) pray-CONV-COOR (4) go(HON)-IMP I-POSS beloved-DIM (5) I-ACC EP love-COND

Translation
(5) If [you] love me, (4) my beloved, go (2) after making *nusa* offerings to the deities (1) of heaven and earth, (3) and continue to be [ritually] pure!

Commentary
This poem is composed by a wife of a *sakimori*.

EOJ *tusi* 'earth' corresponds to WOJ *tuti* 'id.' The EOJ form exhibits the palatalization *t* > *s*/_*i*. Since EOJ *tusi* is attested only in Simotupusa province (see 20.4392), this poem may be a poem from the same province, but this is not certain, since the palatalization of *t > s/_i* is also attested in other Azuma provinces: Simotukɛno, Pitati, and Muⁿzasi.

OJ *nusa* are paper or cloth offerings for deities (Omodaka et al. 1967: 553).

OJ *ipap-* is usually translated as 'to pray'. This tag translation works in most cases, but not in all of them, because the primary meaning of OJ *ipap-* appears 'to be ritually pure while praying' or 'to implore deities while in the ritually pure state'.

On EOJ diminutive suffix *-na*, see the commentary to 14.3384.

20.4427

本文・*Original Text*
(1) 伊波乃伊毛呂 (2) 和乎之乃布良之 (3) 麻由須比尓 (4) 由須比之比毛乃 (5) 登久良久毛倍婆

仮名の書き下し・*Kana Transliteration*
(1) いはの₂いも₁ろ₂ (2) わをしの₂ふらし (3) まゆすひ₁に (4) ゆすひ₁しひ₁も₁の₂ (5) と₂くらくも₁へ₂ば

Romanization
(1) ipa-nə imo-rə (2) wa-wo sinəp-urasi (3) ma-yusup-i-ni (4) yusup-i-si pimo-nə (5) tək-ur-aku [o]mop-ɛ-ᵐba

Glossing with Morphemic Analysis
(1) home-GEN beloved-DIM (2) I-ACC yearn-SUP (3) INT-tie-NML-LOC (4) tie-CONV-PAST.ATTR cord-GEN (5) untie-ATTR-NML think-EV-COND

Translation
(3/4/5) When [I] think that the cords [of my garment] tied in a really [good] knot got untied [by themselves], (1/2) it seems that my dear beloved at home yearns for me.

Commentary
Line one is hypermetric (*ji amari*, 字余り).

EOJ *ipa* 'house' corresponds to WOJ *ipe* 'id.' See also 20.4375, 20.4406, 20.4416, 20.4419, and 20.4423.

On the EOJ diminutive suffix *-rə*, see the commentary to 14.3351.

OJ *sinəp-* 'to yearn' corresponding to WOJ *sinop-* 'id.' cannot be taken as an EOJ form, contrary to Omodaka's suggestion (1984.20: 166), because the same misspelling of the same word also occurs in late WOJ texts, for example in *Bussoku seki-no uta* (several examples).

EOJ *yusup-* 'to tie', which occurs twice in this poem, seems to be related to WOJ *musu^mb-* 'id.', but the correspondence of EOJ *y-* to WOJ *m-* is unique and hard to explain. As a working hypothesis, we would like to propose that EOJ *y-* might reflect Ainu third person indefinite direct object prefix *i-*, which is also attested as *-y-* in 14.3526. Thus, *yusup-* < *i-usup- < *i-musup-. The condition for the loss of *-m-* is not clear.

On the symbolism of tying and untying the cords of one's garment, as well on cords getting loose, see the commentary to 14.3361.

20.4428

本文 • Original Text
(1) 和我世奈乎 (2) 都久志波夜利弖 (3) 宇都久之美 (4) 叡比波登加奈々 (5) 阿夜尓可毛祢牟

仮名の書き下し • Kana Transliteration
(1) わがせなを (2) つくしはやりて (3) うつくしみ₁ (4) え₂ひ₁はと₂かなな (5) あやにかも₁ねむ

Romanization
(1) wa-ⁿga se-na-wo (2) Tukusi-pa yar-i-te (3) utukusi-mi (4) yepi pa tək-an-a-na (5) aya n-i kamo ne-m-u

Glossing with Morphemic Analysis
(1) I-POSS beloved-DIM-ACC (2) Tukusi-side send-CONV-SUB (3) be.longing-GER (4) sash TOP untie-NEG-ATTR-LOC (5) unusual COP-CONV EP sleep-TENT-ATTR

Translation
(3) Because [I] long for [him], (1/2) after sending my beloved to Tukusi, (5) [I] will sleep in an unusual manner (4) without untying [my] sash.

Commentary
This poem is composed by a wife of a *sakimori*. It is practically identical to the poem 20.4422 above.

On EOJ diminutive suffix *-na*, see the commentary to 14.3384.

Tukusi is the old name for the island of Kyūshū.

EOJ -*pa* 'side' corresponds to WOJ -*pe* 'id.' Here it functions as a directive case marker. Cf. -*pɛ* in 20.4422 above.

On the custom of tying and untying the cords see the commentary to 14.3361.

EOJ *yepi* 'sash' corresponds to WOJ *o^mbi* 'id.' (also found in 20.4422 above). The correspondence of EOJ *y*- to WOJ *o*- is unique and difficult to explain. We believe that EOJ *yepi* < *i-epi, where *i- is Ainu prefix 'thing-', attested, e.g., in Chitose dialect (Nakagawa 1995: 26) and Kushiro dialect (Masuno et al. 2004: 45). The correspondence EOJ *e* : WOJ *ə* that we have seen so far (see 20.4338, 20.4340, 20.4342, 20.4343, and 20.4345) is typical for Suruŋga EOJ, so this poem may be from Suruŋga.

On EOJ form in *V-(a)n-a-na* 'V-NEG-ATTR-LOC', see the commentary to 14.3408. On EOJ special attributive -*a*, see the commentary to 14.3526 and the sketch of the EOJ grammar in the introduction to this volume.

20.4429

本文・*Original Text*
(1) 宇麻夜奈流 (2) 奈波多都古麻乃 (3) 於久流我弁 (4) 伊毛我伊比之乎 (5) 於岐弖可奈之毛

仮名の書き下し・*Kana Transliteration*
(1) うまやなる (2) なはたつこ₁ま の₂ (3) おくるがへ₁ (4) いも₁がいひ₁しを (5) おき₁てかなしも₁

Romanization
(1) umaya-n-ar-u (2) napa tat-u koma-nə (3) okur-u ŋgape (4) imo-ŋga ip-i-si-wo (5) ok-i-te kanasi-mo

Glossing with Morphemic Analysis
(1) stables-LOC-exist-ATTR (2) rope break-ATTR stallion-COMP (3) be.left.behind IP (4) beloved-POSS say-CONV-PAST.ATTR-ACC (5) leave.behind-CONV-SUB be.sad-EXCL

Translation
(4) Although [my] beloved said: (3) "Will [I] be left behind?", (5) [I] am sad after [I] left [her] behind (2) like a stallion that [would] break [his] rope (1) in the stables!

Commentary

The first two lines represent a poetic introduction (*jo*, 序), introducing a metaphor that a stallion left behind will break his halter in order to join his master.

OJ *umaya* 'stable' is a transparent compound: *uma* 'horse' + *ya* 'house'.

OJ *okure-* 'to be left behind' is an intransitive verb that contrasts with the transitive OJ verb *ok-* 'to leave behind'.

On EOJ interrogative particle *ŋgape*, see the commentary to 14.3420 (spelled as *ŋgapɛ* in 14.3420 and 14.3502).

On *-umə ~ -mə* as a special Old Japanese exclamative form, see the commentary to 14.3431.

20.4430

本文・*Original Text*
(1) 阿良之乎乃 (2) 伊乎佐太波佐美 (3) 牟可比多知 (4) 可奈流麻之都美 (5) 伊埿弖登阿我久流

仮名の書き下し・*Kana Transliteration*
(1) あらしをの₂ (2) いをさたばさみ₁ (3) むかひ₁たち (4) かなるましづみ₁ (5) いでてと₂あがくる

Romanization
(1) ara-si wo-nə (2) i-wo-sa-ta-ᵐ-basam-i (3) mukap-i-tat-i (4) ka nar-u ma siⁿdum-i (5) iⁿde-te tə a-ŋga k-uru

Glossing with Morphemic Analysis
(1) tough-FIN man-GEN (2) OBJ-DIM-arrow-hand-LOC-hold.between-CONV (3) face-CONV-stand-CONV (4) voice sound-ATTR interval become.quiet-CONV (5) go.out(CONV)-SUB FP I-POSS come-ATTR

Translation
(4) At the time when voices became quiet (1) [similarly to the scene when] tough men (3) stand facing [their targets] (2) holding arrows in their hands, (5) [I] went out and came here.

Commentary
OJ *-si* in *ara-si wo mo* 'tough-FIN man FP' is an example of a special OJ usage of the final form *-si* in the attributive function. For more details and examples see Vovin (2020.1: 406–410).

There is no satisfactory internal Japanese explanation of the prefix *i-* in line two (Kinoshita 1988: 234). It certainly cannot be directive-locative prefix *i-*, because *i-* cannot be separated from a verb by two or even one noun. We believe it is a loan of Ainu *e-*, indirect object prefix, with the expected raising **e- > i-* in EOJ. This indirect object prefix is simultaneously playing a function of an incorporation marker, because two nouns, *sa* 'arrow' and *ta-* 'hand' are found between it and the stem of the verb *pasam-* 'to hold between'.

OJ *sa* 'arrow' is a loanword from Korean (via WOJ), cf. MK *sál* 'arrow'. For details see Vovin (2010: 173).

Line four also occurs in its entirety as line four in 14.3361, see the commentary to this poem for details. Unlike all other scholars, we read *kanaru* as *unaru* (reflecting Ainu *hunar* 'to search') on the basis of the *Genryaku kōhon* script, but there is no such possibility for 20.4430, because all manuscripts, including the *Genryaku kōhon*, clearly have the phonogram 可 /ka/, not the phonogram 宇 /u/. Given the formulaic nature of Old Japanese poetry, we should expect that the lines would be the same, but it is not necessarily so. Consequently, we do not know whether my reading of line four in 14.3361 was mistaken or not. After all, the contexts are very different: there is no search for traps here in contrast to 14.3361. We think that *kanaru* in line four of 20.4430 is difficult to interpret entirely in Japanese, and, therefore it is highly likely that it should partially involve Ainu. Namely, we presume that while *nar-u* 'sounds' is Japanese, *ka* in all probability represents a loanword of Ainu *háw* 'voice'.

Line five is hypermetric (*ji amari*, 字余り).

On EOJ focus particle *tə*, corresponding to WOJ *sə*, see the commentary to 14. 3409. In book twenty it also occurs in 20.4385.

20.4431

本文 • *Original Text*
(1) 佐左賀波乃 (2) 佐也久志毛用尒 (3) 奈々弁加流 (4) 去呂毛尒麻世流 (5) 古侶賀波太波毛

仮名の書き下し • *Kana Transliteration*
(1) ささがはの₂ (2) さやぐしも₁よ₁に (3) ななへ₁かる (4) こ₂ろ₂も₁にませる (5) こ₁ろ₂がはだはも₁

Romanization
(1) sasa-ⁿga pa-nə (2) sayaⁿg-u simo yo-ni (3) nana pe k-ar-u (4) kərəmo-ni mas-er-u (5) ko-rə-ⁿga paⁿda pa mə

Glossing with Morphemic Analysis
(1) bamboo.grass-POSS leaf-GEN (2) rustle.softly-ATTR frost night-LOC (3) seven layer wear-PROG-ATTR (4) garment-LOC be.superior-PROG-ATTR (5) girl-DIM-POSS skin TOP EP

Translation
(5) The skin of [my beloved] girl (3/4) is superior to the seven-layered garment that [I] am wearing (1/2) on a frosty night, when the leaves of the bamboo grass are rustling softly!

Commentary
The usage of the possessive case marker -*ŋga* after OJ *sasa* 'bamboo grass' may indicate that this word once belonged to the animate class. Or it might be a result of confusion between the possessive -*ŋga* and the genitive -*nə* that is already present in OJ.

EOJ *k-ar-u* 'wear-PROG-ATTR' corresponds to WOJ *k-er-u* 'id.' On the EOJ progressive suffix -*ar*- corresponding to WOJ -*er*- see the commentary to 14.3351. It is interesting that both progressive -*ar*- and -*er*- co-occur in this poem.

On the predominantly EOJ diminutive suffix -*rə*, see the commentary to 14.3351.

20.4432

本文・Original Text
(1) 佐弁奈弁奴 (2) 美許登尓阿礼婆 (3) 可奈之伊毛我 (4) 多麻久良波奈礼 (5) 阿夜尓可奈之毛

仮名の書き下し・Kana Transliteration
(1) さへ₁なへ₁ぬ (2) み₁こ₂と₂にあれば (3) かなしいも₁が (4) たまくらはなれ (5) あやにかなしも₁

Romanization
(1) sape-n-ape-n-u (2) mi-kətə n-i ar-e-ᵐba (3) kanasi imo-ŋga (4) ta-makura panare (5) aya n-i kanasi-mo

Glossing with Morphemic Analysis
(1) obstruct(NML)-LOC-dare-NEG-ATTR (2) HON-word COP-CONV exist-EV-CON (3) dear beloved-POSS (4) arm-pillow be.separated(CONV) (5) unusual COP-CONV be.sad-EXCL

Translation

(2) Because [it] is [my sovereign's] command (1) that [I] cannot refuse, (3/4) [I] separated [myself] from the arms of [my] dear beloved that [I used as] a pillow, (5) and [I] am unusually sad.

Commentary

This poem is very close textually to 14.3480, which also seems to be a poem written by a *sakimori*.

On *mi-kətə* 'honorable word', 'imperial order/edict', see the commentary to 14.3480.

This poem could have been perceived as a poem written in WOJ if not for two features. First, WOJ /ɛ/ is misspelled as /e/ twice in the first line. Second, as far as we can tell, the construction V(NML)-LOC + *ape-* 'to dare' is not attested in WOJ texts.

The third line is hypermetric (*ji amari*, 字余り), but this is probably just a graphic illusion, since *kanasi imo* was in all probability pronounced as [kanasimo].

On *-umə ~ -mə* as a special Old Japanese exclamative form, see the commentary to 14.3431.

Postscript to the Poems 20.4425–4432

本文・*Original Text*
右八首昔年防人歌矣主典刑部少録正七位上磐余伊美吉諸君抄寫贈兵部少輔大伴宿祢家持

Translation

Eight poems above are poems by *sakimori* from the past years. Ipare-nə imiki Mərəkimi (Senior Seventh Rank, Upper Grade), the official of the fourth class, and Junior Secretary of the Ministry of Justice selected and recorded [these poems], and presented [them] to Opətəmə-no sukune Yakaməti, the Junior Assistant Minister of the Ministry of War.

Commentary

Poems 20.4425–4432 are poems by *sakimori* and their wives from the past years that were collected by Ipare-nə imiki Mərəkimi as becomes clear from this postscript. All eight poems are anonymous. They are also not dated nor have any record of a location where their authors come from. This constitutes a sharp contrast to all preceding *sakimori* poems that were collected by Opotəmə-nə Yakaməti.

Nothing is known about the biography of Ipare-nə imiki Mərəkimi, except the information provided in the postscript to the poems 20.4425–4432. Imiki is a *kabane* title (hereditary nobility title).

Officials of the fourth class (*Sakwan*, 主典) were bureaucrats in charge of documents and records in ministries and offices (Kinoshita 1988: 238).

Under the Ritsuryō code, Ministry of Justice (*Gyōbu[shō]*, 刑部[省]) is one of the four Ministries under the Controlling Board of the Right (*Ubenkan*, 右弁官).

Junior Secretary (*Shōroku*, 少録) position corresponds to Senior Eighth Rank, Upper Grade. Thus, the rank of Ipare-nə imiki Mərəkimi exceeded his actual position. There were two Junior Secretary positions per Ministry.

On Opotəmə-nə Yakaməti's biography, see the Introduction to book twenty of the *Man'yōshū*.

On the Junior Assistant Minister (*Shōyū*, 少輔) and the Ministry of War (*Hyōbu[shō]*, 兵部[省]), see the commentary to the postscript to 20.4315–4320.

End of Book Twenty

CHAPTER 5

東遊び歌 • *Azuma asobi uta*

Preface to the First Poem

本文 • *Original Text*
一歌

Translation
The first poem.

Commentary
There are altogether thirteen poems in the *Azuma asobi uta*, but only the first two show clear EOJ features.

AAU 1

本文 • *Original Text*
(1) 乎乎乎乎 (2) 者礼奈 (3) 天平止々乃部呂奈 (4) 宇太止止乃部无奈 (5) 左加无乃祢 (6) 乎々々乎

仮名の書き下し • *Kana Transliteration*
(1) をををを (2) はれな (3) てをと₂と₂の₂へ₂ろ₂な (4) うたと₂と₂の₂へ₂むな (5) さがむの₂ね (6) をををを

Romanization
(1) wo wo wo wo (2) parena (3) te-wo tətənəpɛ-rə na (4) uta tətənəpɛ-m-u na (5) Saŋgamu-nə ne (6) wo wo wo wo

Glossing with Morphemic Analysis
(1) yes yes yes yes (2) *hayashi-kotoba* (3) hand-ACC arrange-IMP EP (4) poem arrange-TENT-FIN EP (5) Saŋgamu-GEN peak (6) yes yes yes yes

Translation
(1) Yes, yes, yes, yes (2) *hayashi-kotoba* (3) Arrange [you] hands! (4) [We] should prepare the poems! (5) [Oh,] peaks of Saŋgamu! (6) Yes, yes, yes, yes.

Commentary

Contextually and content-wise all poems from the *Azuma Asobi Uta* are very difficult to understand because they are connected to rituals we know next to nothing about.

Arranging hands and preparing poems probably has something to do with the fact that these poems were recited under the music accompaniment and during dances.

As in this and other poems from the *Azuma Asobi Uta*, the distinction between voiceless and renasalized voiced consonants is not really reflected in the script.

The usage of the repetition sign 々 is very inconsistent.

Parena on line two is believed to be a *hayashi-kotoba* (囃子詞, 囃子言葉) (Konishi 1957: 422). Hayashi-kotoba are meaningless utterances added to maintain the meter of a poem, although in this poem as well as in other poems from the *Azuma Asobi Uta* there is not much to maintain because the meter is highly irregular.

There is only one EOJ feature in this poem: imperative form -rə vs. WOJ -yə.

On Saⁿgamu province see the commentary to the postscript to the poems 14.3431–3433.

Preface to the Second Poem

本文 · *Original Text*

二歌

Translation

The second poem.

Commentary

See above the commentary to the first poem.

AAU 2

本文 · *Original Text*

(1) 衣 (2) 和賀世古加 (3) 介左乃古止天者 (4) 奈奈川乎乃 (5) 也川乎乃古止乎 (6) 之良部太留古止也 (7) 奈乎加介也末乃 (8) 可川乃介也 (9) 乎々々々

仮名の書き下し・*Kana Transliteration*
(1) え₁ (2) わがせこ₁が (3) け₁さの₂こ₁と₂では (4) ななつをの₂ (5) やつをの₂こ₁と₂を (6) しらべ₂たるご₁と₂や (7) なをかけ₁やまの₂ (8) かづの₂け₁や (9) ををを

Romanization
(1) e (2) wa-ⁿga se-ko-ⁿga (3) kesa-nə kotaⁿde pa (4) nana-tu wo-nə (5) ya-tu wo-nə kotə-wo (6) siraᵐbɛ-tar-u ⁿgotə ya (7) na-wo Kake yama-nə (8) kaⁿdu-nə ke ya (9) wo wo wo wo

Glossing with Morphemic Analysis
(1) INTERJ (2) I-POSS beloved-DIM-POSS (3) this.morning-GEN talk TOP (4) seven CL string-GEN (5) eight-CL string-GEN *koto*-ACC (6) examine(CONV)-PERF/PROG-ATTR like EP (7) you-ACC Kake mountain-GEN (8) paper.mulberry-GEN tree EP (9) yes yes yes yes

Translation
(1) Oh, (3) this morning's story (2) of my beloved (6) [is] like examining (4) seven string [or] (5) eight string *koto*. (8) Paper mulberry trees (7) on Kake mountain that is like you. (9) Yes, yes, yes, yes.

Commentary
OJ *kətaⁿde* 'talk', 'conversation' is a nominalization of *kətaⁿde-* 'to talk'.

Although Konishi maintains that there were no eight-string *koto* (1957: 422), he is mistaken. Three types of *koto* (a term for a stringed musical instrument that can be tentatively translated as 'zither', although the analogy is far from being accurate) were used during Asuka and Nara periods: *Yamatə-ⁿ-gətə* 'Japanese *koto*' (mentioned in this poem), *Siraⁿgï-ⁿ-gətə* 'Silla *koto*', and *Kuⁿdara-ⁿ-gətə* 'Paekche *koto*'. The number of strings on the Japanese *koto* seems to be fluctuating between eight and five, although it subsequently settled to six in the later Nara period. The Japanese *koto*, unlike other types of *koto*, was used not only for entertainment, but also in sacred rituals to summon deities. *Siraⁿgï-ⁿ-gətə* 'Silla *koto*' had twelve strings, and *Kuⁿdara-ⁿ-gətə* 'Paekche *koto*' had thirteen. It is quite interesting that it is only the Paekche type of *koto* that has survived today in Japan. In any case, WOJ *kətə* seems to be a loanword from Korean: cf. MK *kó* 'koto' < OK *kotV.[1]

Mt. Kake is one of the mountains in Asiⁿgari range. It possibly corresponds to present-day Yagura peak (Yagura dake, 870 m, 矢倉岳) (Nakanishi 1985: 433) in Kanagawa prefecture. Mizushima thinks that *wawokake* in the second line

---
[1] For phonetic development cf. MK *hyé* 'tongue' < EMK *hyet* < OK *hitV.

represents the mountain name and not *wa-wo* 'I-ACC' plus the name of the mountain, or that at least a word play (*kakekotoba*, 掛詞) may be involved here (1986: 195).

On EOJ *ka^{n}du-nə kï* ~ *ka^{n}du-nə ke* 'paper mulberry tree' see the commentary to MYS 14.3432.

There is just one EOJ feature in this poem: EOJ *ke* 'tree' vs. WOJ *kï* 'id.' Cf. EOJ *kɛ* 'id.' in MYS 20.4342 and MYS 20. 4375 above.

CHAPTER 6

古今和歌集 • *Kokin wakashū*

Preface to the Poems 1097–1098

本文 • *Original Text*
かひうた

Translation
Kapi poems.

Commentary
Kapi province (WOJ Kapï-nə kuni, 甲斐國) was one of the Upper Provinces (Jōkoku, 上國) according to the *Ritsuryō* code. It corresponds to present-day Yamanashi prefecture. On the *Ritsuryō* code classification of Yamatə provinces see the commentary to the postscript to the poem 14.3349.

    KKWKS 1098 has no EOJ features, therefore it is not included here.

KKWKS 1097

本文 • *Original Text*
(1) かひがねを (2) さやに見しか (3) けけれなく (4) よこはりふせる (5) さやのなか山

Romanization
(1) Kapi-ŋga ne-wo (2) saya n-i MI-si ka (3) kekere na-ku (4) yokopar-i pus-er-u (5) Saya-no Nakayama

Glossing with Morphemic Analysis
(1) Kapi-POSS peak-ACC (2) clear COP-CONV see(CONV)-PAST.ATTR EP (3) heart not.exist-CONV (4) lie.down-CONV lie-PROG-ATTR (5) Saya-GEN Nakayama

Translation
(2) I want to see clearly (1) the peaks of Kapi. (5) [But] Mt. Nakayama in Saya (4) lies [between us] (3) heartlessly.

Commentary

On Kapï province see the commentary to the preface to KKWKS 1097–1098 above.

Saya and Mt. Nakayama are believed to be placenames located in present-day Shizuoka prefecture, which corresponds to four Ancient Japanese provinces: Saᵑgamu (相模), Iⁿdu (伊豆), Suruᵑga (駿河), and Təpotuapumi (遠江). Since Kapï province had common border only with Saᵑgamu and Suruᵑga, and also because of the context of KKWKS 1097 one would expect Saya and Mt. Nakayama to be located in either one of them on the border with Kapï, or its close proximity

There are three EOJ features in this poem. First it is EOJ *kekere* 'heart' vs. WOJ *kəkərə* 'id.' Second, it is verb *yokopar-* 'to lie down', which has no WOJ or MJ cognates. EOJ *yokopar-* is apparently from *yəkə* 'horizontal' + *par-* 'to stretch'. Third, it is the form expressing the wish of a speaker: EOJ *-si ka* vs. WOJ *-te-si ka*.

PART 2

Dictionary of Eastern Old Japanese

∴

Dictionary of Eastern Old Japanese

Some Preliminary Notes

Alphabetical order adopted in the dictionary:

a, ᵐb, ⁿd, e, ɛ, ə, ⁿg, i, ï, k, m, n, o, p, r, s, t, u, w, y, ⁿz

This is not an etymological dictionary, but a dictionary to the EOJ texts. Some minimal etymological notes are sometimes included, but the detailed ones can be found in the corpus.

The writing system in most texts is predominantly phonographic. The major exception is the *Man'yōshū* book sixteen, which is heavily logographic, with some poem mostly logographic like MYS 16.3885. The difference between phonographic and logographic spellings is not marked in the dictionary, but it is consistently shown in the corpus.

A

a 'foot, leg'. Attested in: MYS 14.3387 (Simotupusa), MYS 14.3533 (unidentified). Cf. WOJ, *asi, a-* (in compounds only) 'id.'

a 'I'. Attested in: MYS 14.3404 (Kamitukɛno), MYS 14.3501 (unidentified), MYS 14.3515 (unidentified), MYS 14.3526 (unidentified), MYS 14.3532 (unidentified), MYS 14.3560 (unidentified), MYS 14.3562 (unidentified), MYS 14.3566 (unidentified), MYS 16.3885 (unidentified), MYS 20.4366 (Pitati), MYS 20.4367 (Pitati), MYS 20.4391 (Simotupusa), MYS 20.4420 (Muⁿzasi), MYS 20.4430 (unidentified). Cf. WOJ *a* 'id.'

aⁿ- 'what, why'. Attested in: MYS 14.3379 (Muⁿzasi), MYS 14.3397 (Pitati), 3404 (Kamitukɛno), MYS 14.3465 (unidentified), MYS 14.3494 (unidentified), MYS 14.3556 (unidentified), MYS 14.3564 (unidentified), MYS 14.3572 (unidentified). Possibly related to WOJ *nani* 'id.', see Vovin (2020.1: 295–297). Cf. WOJ *nani* 'id.'

Aⁿdatara (p.n.). Attested in: MYS 14.3437 (Mitinəku).

Aⁿdikama (p.n.) < Ainu: *anci* 'obsidian' + *kama* 'flat rock, rock'. Attested in: MYS 14.3551 (unidentified), MYS 14.3553 (unidentified).

aⁿdusa 'catalpa tree'. Attested in: MYS 14.3487 (unidentified), MYS 14.3489 (unidentified), MYS 16.3885 (unidentified). Cf. WOJ *aⁿdusa* 'id.'

aᵑgaki 'gallop'. Attested in: MYS 14.3540 (unidentified). Cf. WOJ *aᵑgaki* 'id.'

ak- 'to satisfy'. Attested in: MYS 14.3404 (Kamitukɛno), MYS 20.4329 (Saᵑgamu). Cf. WOJ *ak-* 'id.'

© ALEXANDER VOVIN AND SAMBI ISHISAKI-VOVIN, 2022 | DOI:10.1163/9789004471665_009

aka 'dirt'. Attested in: MYS 20.4388 (Simotupusa). Cf. WOJ *aka* 'id.'

aka 'red'. Attested in: MYS 14.3536 (unidentified), MYS 14.3540 (unidentified), MYS 20.4417 (Muⁿzasi). Cf. WOJ *aka* 'id.'

akatəki 'dawn'. Attested in: MYS 20.4384 (Simotupusa). Cf. WOJ *akatəki*, MJ *akatuki* 'id.'

akɛ- ~ ake- 'dawn'. Attested in: FK 3 (Pitati), MYS 14.3461 (unidentified). Cf. WOJ *akɛ-* 'id.'

Akina (p.n.) < Ainu *ay-kina* 'arrow grass'. Attested in: MYS 14.3431 (Saⁿgamu).

amɛ ~ ama- 'heaven'. Attested in: MYS 14.3409 (Kamitukɛno), MYS 20.4374 (Simotukɛno), MYS 20.4392 (Simotupusa), MYS 20.4426 (unidentified). Cf. WOJ *ama ~ ama-* 'id.'

amɛ 'rain'. Attested in: MYS 14.3561 (unidentified). Cf. WOJ *amɛ ~ ama-, -samɛ* 'id.'

amə 'mother'. Attested in: MYS 20.4376 (Simotukɛno), MYS 20.4377 (Simotukɛno), MYS 20.4378 (Simotukɛno), MYS 20.4383 (Simotukɛno). Cf. WOJ *omə, amə* (the latter is attested only once) 'id.'

Ano (p.n.). Attested in: MYS 14.3447 (unidentified).

ap- 'to meet'. Attested in: FK 2 (Pitati), MYS 14.3358b (Suruⁿga), MYS 14.3375 (Muⁿzasi), MYS 14.3401 (Sinanu), MYS 14.3405 (Kamitukɛno), MYS 14.3405a (Kamitukɛno), MYS 14.3413 (Kamitukɛno), MYS 14.3426 (Simotukɛno), MYS 14.3461 (unidentified), MYS 14.3463 (unidentified), MYS 14.3478 (unidentified), MYS 14.3482a (unidentified), MYS 14.3483 (unidentified), MYS 14.3493 (unidentified), MYS 14.3524 (unidentified), MYS 14.3531 (unidentified), MYS 14.3540 (unidentified), MYS 20.4324 (Təpotuapumi). Cf. WOJ *ap-*, MDJ *aw-* 'id.'

apa 'foxtail millet'. Attested in: MYS 14.3405a (Kamitukɛno), MYS 14.3451 (unidentified). Cf. WOJ *apa* 'id.'

Apa (p.n.). Attested in: MYS 14.3501 (unidentified).

ape- 'to dare'. Attested in: MYS 20.4432 (unidentified). Cf. WOJ *apɛ-* 'id.'

ape- 'to give'. Attested in: MYS 16.3880 (Noto). No apparent WOJ cognates with a possible exception of *apɛ-* 'to treat'.

apiⁿda 'interval'. Attested in: MYS 14.3395 (Pitati). Cf. WOJ *apiⁿda* 'id.'

Apiⁿdu (p.n.). Attested in: MYS 14.3426 (Mitinəku).

ar- ~ -ar- 'to exist'. Attested in: MYS 14.3376a (Muⁿzasi), MYS 14.3385 (Simotupusa), MYS 14.3397 (Pitati), MYS 14.3400 (Sinanu), MYS 14.3401 (Sinanu), MYS 14.3407 (Kamitukɛno), MYS 14.3408 (Kamitukɛno), MYS 14.3445 (unidentified), MYS 14.3472 (unidentified), MYS 14.3476 (unidentified), MYS 14.3482a (unidentified), MYS 14.3485 (unidentified), MYS 14.3509 (unidentified), MYS 14.3516 (unidentified), MYS 20.4324 (Təpotuapumi), MYS 20.4340 (Suruⁿga), MYS 20.4345 (Suruⁿga), MYS 20.4346 (Suruⁿga), MYS 20.4347 (Kamitupusa), MYS 20.4351 (Kamitupusa), MYS 20.4371 (Pitati), MYS 20.4393 (Simotupusa), MYS 20.4415 (Muⁿzasi), MYS 20.4416 (Muⁿzasi), MYS 20.4423 (Muⁿzasi), MYS 20.4429 (unidentified), MYS 20.4432 (unidentified). Cf. WOJ *ar- ~ -ar-* 'id.'

ara ~ ar- 'rough, tough'. Attested in: MYS 14.3447 (unidentified), MYS 14.3561 (unidentified), MYS 14.3562 (unidentified), MYS 20.4372 (Pitati), MYS 20.4430 (unidentified). Cf. WOJ *ara ~ -ar-* 'id.'

arap- 'to wash'. Attested in: FK 9 (Pitati), MYS 16.3880 (Noto). Cf. WOJ *arap-* 'id.'

arapar- 'to appear'. Attested in: MYS 14.3414 (Kamitukɛno). Cf. WOJ *arapare-* 'id.'

arare 'hail'. Attested in: MYS 20.4370 (Pitati). Cf. WOJ *arare* 'id.'

arasop- 'to resist'. Attested in: MYS 14.3456 (unidentified). Cf. WOJ *arasop-* 'to compete', 'to argue'.

are 'I'. Attested in: MYS 14.3361 (Saŋgamu), MYS 14.3496 (unidentified), MYS 16.3885 (unidentified), MYS 20.4327 (Təpotuapumi), MYS 20.4350 (Kamitupusa), MYS 20.4365 (Pitati), MYS 20.4372 (Pitati), MYS 20.4426 (unidentified). Cf. WOJ *are* 'id.'

arikinu-nə (makura-kotoba). Attested in: MYS 14.3481 (unidentified). Cf. WOJ *arikinu-nə-* 'id.'

asa 'morning'. Attested in: MYS 14.3407 (Kamitukɛno). Cf. WOJ *asa* 'id.'

asa 'hemp'. Attested in: MYS 14.3484 (unidentified). Cf. WOJ *asa* 'id.'

asaⁿgapo 'morning glory' < *asa-nə kapo 'morning face'. Attested in: MYS 14.3502 (unidentified). Cf. WOJ *asaⁿgapo* 'id.'

asi 'foot'. Attested in: MYS 14.3399 (Sinanu), MYS 16.3885 (unidentified). Cf. WOJ *asi* 'id.'

asi 'reed'. Attested in: MYS 14.3445 (unidentified), MYS 14.3446 (unidentified), MYS 20.4419 (Muⁿzasi). Cf. WOJ *asi* 'id.'

asi 'to be bad'. Attested in: MYS 20.4382 (Simotukɛno). Cf. WOJ *asi* 'id.'

Asikaŋga (p.n.) < Ainu *askan(-ne)* '(be) beautiful' + *kat* 'view, appearance'. Attested in: MYS 20.4379.[1] This poem is in WOJ.

Asiⁿgara ~ Asiⁿgari (p.n.) < Ainu *askar-i* 'clear place'. Attested in: MYS 14.3361 (Saŋgamu), MYS 14.3363 (Saŋgamu), MYS 14.3368 (Saŋgamu), MYS 14.3369 (Saŋgamu), MYS 14.3370 (Saŋgamu), MYS 14.3431 (Saŋgamu), MYS 14.3432 (Saŋgamu), MYS 20.4372 (Pitati), MYS 20.4421 (Muⁿzasi), MYS 20.4432 (Muⁿzasi).

Aso (p.n.). Attested in: MYS 14.3404 (Kamitukɛno), MYS 14.3425 (Simotukɛno), MYS 14.3434 (Kamitukɛno).

asu 'tomorrow'. Attested in: MYS 14.3484 (unidentified), MYS 20.4321 (Təpotuapumi). Cf. WOJ *asu* 'id.'

Asuka (p.n.). Attested in: MYS 14.3544 (unidentified).

Asupa (p.n.). Attested in: MYS 20.4350 (Kamitupusə).

ata 'sudden'. Attested in: MYS 20.4382 (Simotukɛno). No WOJ cognates.

atari 'vicinity'. Attested in: MYS 14.3423 (Kamitukɛno). Cf. WOJ *atari* 'id.'

atəri 'brambling'. Attested in: MYS 20.4339 (Suruŋga). WOJ examples are in the logographic script. Cf. MJ *atori* 'id.'

atu- 'sea' < Ainu *atuy* 'id.' Attested in: MYS 14.3503 (unidentified).

awo 'green, blue'. Attested in: MYS 14.3511 (unidentified), MYS 14.3512 (unidentified), MYS 14.3546 (unidentified), MYS 20.4403 (Sinanu). Cf. WOJ *awo* 'id.'

---

1 It would be ironic if the family name of the Ashikaga shoguns might be also of Ainu provenance.

aya 'strange, unusual'. Attested in: MYS 14.3408 (Kamitukɛno), MYS 20.4422 (Muⁿzasi), MYS 20.4428 (unidentified), MYS 20.4432 (unidentified). Cf. WOJ *aya* 'id.'

aya 'extreme'. Attested in: MYS 14.3465 (unidentified), MYS 14.3537 (unidentified), MYS 20.4387 (Simotupusa). No WOJ cognates.

ayapa 'dangerous'. Attested in: MYS 14.3541 (unidentified). No WOJ cognates, unless related to *aya* 'strange'.

ayapo- 'to be dangerous'. Attested in: MYS 14.3539 (unidentified). No WOJ cognates, unless related to *aya* 'strange'. Cf. MJ *ayapu-* 'id.'

ayok- 'to waver'. Attested in: MYS 20.4390 (Simotupusa). No reliable WOJ cognates.

aⁿze 'why, how'. Attested in: MYS 14.3369 (Saⁿgamu), MYS 14.3434 (Saⁿgamu), MYS 14.3461 (unidentified), MYS 14.3469 (unidentified), MYS 14.3472 (unidentified), MYS 14.3513 (unidentified), MYS 14.3517 (unidentified), MYS 14.3576 (unidentified). Possibly related to WOJ *naⁿde ~ naⁿzə* 'id.', see Vovin (2020.1: 316–319).

Aⁿze (p.n.). Attested in: FK 7 (Pitati).

Aⁿzikuma (p.n.). Attested in: MYS 14.3572 (unidentified).

aⁿzu 'crumbling cliff' < ? Ainu **-as-* 'to split' + *so* 'rocky shore', 'hidden rocks in the sea'. Attested in: MYS 14.3539 (unidentified), 14.3541 (unidentified).

E

e, interjection. Attested in: AAU 2.

ə

-əmap- 'to think'. Attested in: MYS 14.3526 (unidentified). See *omap-*. Cf. WOJ *omap-* 'id.'

ⁿG

ⁿgətə 'like'. Attested in: MYS 20.4342 (Suruⁿga). Cf. WOJ *ⁿgətə* 'like'.

ⁿgotə 'like'. Attested in: AAU 2 (Saⁿgamu). Cf. WOJ *ⁿgətə* 'like'.

ⁿgure 'sunset'. Attested in: MYS 14.3402 (Kamitukɛno). Cf. WOJ *kure* 'id.'

ⁿgupasi 'beautiful'. Attested in: MYS 14.3407 (Kamitukɛno), MYS 14.3424 (Simotukɛno). Cf. WOJ *kupasi* 'id.'

I

i- 'to sleep'. Attested in: MYS 20.4351 (Kamitupusa). Cf. WOJ *i* 'sleep' (n.)

i-, indirect object prefix < Ainu *e-* 'id.' Attested in: MYS 20.4430 (unidentified).

i-, nominal prefix 'thing-' < Ainu *i-* 'id.' Attested in: MYS 20.4428 (unidentified).

iⁿd- ~ iⁿde- ~ [i]ⁿd- ~ -[i]ⁿde- 'to go out, to exit'. Attested in: MYS 14.3368 (Saŋgamu), MYS 14.3374 (Muⁿzasi), MYS 14.3376 (Muⁿzasi), MYS 14.3376a (Muⁿzasi), MYS 14.3401 (Sinanu), MYS 14.3466 (unidentified), MYS 14.3474 (unidentified), MYS 14.3488 (unidentified), MYS 14.3503 (unidentified), MYS 14.3506 (unidentified), MYS 14.3560 (unidentified), MYS 20.4323 (Təpotuapumi), MYS 20.4330 (Saŋgamu), MYS 16l3878 (Noto), MYS 20.4358 (Kamitupusa), MYS 20.4373 (Simotukɛno), MYS 20.4380 (Simotukɛno), MYS 20.4383 (Simotukɛno), MYS 20.4393 (Simotupusa), MYS 20.4430 (unidentified). Cf. WOJ *iⁿd- ~ iⁿde- ~ [i]ⁿd- ~ -[i]ⁿde-* 'id.'

iⁿdu 'where'. Attested in: MYS 14.3549 (unidentified). Cf. WOJ *iⁿdu* 'id.' and WOJ bound form *iⁿdu-* 'where' found only in combination with the following locative case marker *-ra*.

iⁿdure 'which'. Attested in: MYS 20.4392 (Simotupusa). Cf. WOJ *iⁿdure* 'id.'

iⁿdusi 'where'. Attested in: MYS 14.3474 (unidentified). Cf. WOJ *iⁿduti* 'id.'

ik- 'to live'. Attested in: MYS 14.3539 (unidentified). Cf. WOJ *ik-* 'id.'

ika 'how'. Attested in: MYS 14.3376a (Muⁿzasi), MYS 14.3418 (Kamitukɛno), MYS 14.3536 (unidentified). Cf. WOJ *ika* 'id.'

Ikapo (p.n.). Attested in: MYS 14.3409 (Kamitukɛno), MYS 14.3410 (Kamitukɛno), MYS 14.3414 (Kamitukɛno), MYS 14.3415 (Kamitukɛno), MYS 14.3419 (Kamitukɛno), MYS 14.3423 (Kamitukɛno), MYS 14.3435 (Kamitukɛno).

ikɛ- 'to make alive'. Attested in: MYS 16.3885 (unidentified). Cf. WOJ *ikɛ-* 'to leave alive', 'to let live'.

ikiⁿduk- 'to sigh', 'to catch one's breath, to breathe with difficulty'. Attested in: MYS 14.3388 (Pitati), MYS 14.3458 (unidentified), MYS 14.3527 (unidentified). Cf. WOJ *ikiⁿduk-* 'id.'

ikiⁿdukusi 'to be regrettable, to be lamentable'. Attested in: MYS 20.4421 (Muⁿzasi). Cf. WOJ *ikiⁿdukasi* 'id.' The WOJ form can be easily analyzed as *ikiⁿduk-* 'to sigh' + adjectivizer *-asi*, but EOJ form is opaque. Probably we deal here with a vowel assimilation /a/ > /u/: *ikiⁿdukasi* > *ikiⁿdukusi*.

Ikoma (p.n.). Attested in: MYS 20.4380 (Simotukɛno).

ikusa ~ [i]kusa 'warrior'. Attested in: MYS 20.4370 (Pitati). Cf. WOJ *ikusa* 'id.'

ima 'now'. Attested in: MYS 14.3399 (Sinanu), MYS 14.3418 (Kamitukɛno), MYS 20.4363 (Pitati), MYS 20.4376 (Simotukɛno). Cf. WOJ *ima* 'id.'

imaⁿda 'yet'. Attested in: MYS 14.3525 (unidentified), MYS 14.3543 (unidentified), MYS 20.4337 (Suruŋga). Cf. WOJ *imaⁿda* 'id.'

imas- 'to exist (HON)'. Attested in: MYS 20.4342 (Suruŋga). Cf. WOJ *imas-* 'id.'

imas- 'to go (HON)'. Attested in: MYS 20.4426 (unidentified). Cf. WOJ *imas-* 'id.'

imasi 'you'. Attested in: MYS 14.3359 (Suruŋga), MYS 14.3359a (Suruŋga). Cf. WOJ *imasi ~ mimasi* 'id.'

imə 'beloved, wife'. Attested in: MYS 14.3528 (unidentified), MYS 20.4351 (Kamitupusa), MYS 20.4353 (Kamitupusa), MYS 20.4354 (Kamitupusa), MYS 20.4363 (Pitati), MYS 20.4365 (Pitati), MYS 20.4366 (Pitati), MYS 20.4367 (Pitati), MYS 20.4369 (Pitati), MYS 20.4388 (Simotupusa), MYS 20.4390 (Simotupusa), MYS 20.4391 (Simotupusa), MYS 20.4405 (Kamitukɛno), MYS 20.4415 (Muⁿzasi). Cf. WOJ *imo* 'id.'

imɛ 'beloved, wife'. Attested in: MYS 20.4345 (Suruŋga). See also *imu*. Cf. WOJ *imo* 'id.'

imo 'beloved, wife'. Attested in: FK 5 (Pitati), MYS 14.3354 (Təpotuapumi), MYS 14.3376a (Muⁿzasi), MYS 14.3389 (Pitati), MYS 14.3423 (Kamitukɛno), MYS 14.3446 (unidentified), MYS 14.3474 (unidentified), MYS 14.3480 (unidentified), MYS 14.3481 (unidentified), MYS 14.3485 (unidentified), MYS 14.3488 (unidentified), MYS 14.3489 (unidentified), MYS 14.3517 (unidentified), MYS 14.3527 (unidentified), MYS 14.3531 (unidentified), MYS 14.3538 (unidentified), MYS 14.3538a (unidentified), MYS 14.3566 (unidentified), MYS 20.4404 (Sinanu), MYS 20.4407 (Kamitukɛno), MYS 20.4423 (Muⁿzasi), MYS 20.4427 (unidentified), MYS 20.4429 (unidentified), MYS 20.4432 (unidentified). Cf. WOJ *imo* 'id.'

imu 'beloved, wife'. Attested in: MYS 20.4321 (Təpotuapumi), MYS 20.4364 (Pitati). See also *imɛ*. Cf. WOJ *imo* 'id.'

in- 'to go away'. Attested in: MYS 14.3375 (Muⁿzasi), MYS 14.3474 (unidentified). Cf. WOJ *in-* 'id.'

ina 'no'. Attested in: MYS 14.3351 (Pitati). Cf. WOJ *ina* 'id.'

Inasa (p.n.) < Ainu *inaw-san* 'the place where *inaw* [are offered]'. Attested in: MYS 14.3429.

inər- 'to pray'. Attested in: MYS 20.4370 (Pitati), MYS 20.4374 (Simotukɛno), MYS 20.4392 (Simotupusa). Cf. WOJ *inər-* 'id.'

inəti 'life'. Attested in: MYS 20.4402 (Sinanu). Cf. WOJ *inəti* 'life', 'life force' < *i* 'gall bladder' + *-nə*, genitive case marker + *ti* 'force'.

ipa ~ ipapo ~ [i]pa 'rock'. Attested in: MYS 14.3392 (Pitati), MYS 14.3495 (unidentified), MYS 14.3518 (unidentified), MYS 20.4402 (Sinanu). Cf. WOJ *ipa* 'id.'

ipa 'house, home'. Attested in: MYS 20.4375 (Simotukɛno), MYS 20.4406 (Kamitukɛno), MYS 20.4416 (Muⁿzasi), MYS 20.4419 (Muⁿzasi), MYS 20.4423 (Muⁿzasi), MYS 20.4427 (unidentified). See also *ipi*. Cf. WOJ *ipe* 'id.'

ipap- 'to pray, to purify oneself, to protect, to treat with care'. Attested in: MYS 14.3460 (unidentified), MYS 20.4339 (Suruŋga), MYS 20.4340 (Suruŋga), MYS 20.4347 (Kamitupusa), MYS 20.4350 (Kamitupusa), MYS 20.4372 (Pitati), MYS 20.4393 (Simotupusa), MYS 20.4402 (Sinanu), MYS 20.4426 (unidentified). Cf. WOJ *ipap-* 'id.'

ipe 'house, home'. Attested in: MYS 14.3423 (Kamitukɛno), MYS 14.3481 (unidentified), MYS 14.3532 (unidentified), MYS 20.4364 (Pitati), MYS 20.4388 (Simotupusa), MYS 20.4415 (Muⁿzasi). Cf. WOJ *ipe* 'id.'

ipɛ 'house, home'. Attested in: MYS 20.4347 (Kamitupusa), MYS 20.4353 (Kamitupusa). Cf. WOJ *ipe* 'id.'

ipawi 'rock(?)'. Attested in: MYS 14.3378 (Muⁿzasi). Cf. WOJ *ipa* 'id.'

ipi 'house'. Attested in: MYS 20.4343 (Suruⁿga). See also *ipa*. Cf. WOJ *ipe* 'id.'

ipi- ~ ip- 'to say'. Attested in: FK2 (Pitati), FK3 (Pitati), FK8 (Pitati), MYS 14.3368 (Saⁿgamu), MYS 14.3379 (Muⁿsasi), MYS 14.3384 (Simotupusa), MYS 13.3461 (unidentified), MYS 14.3472 (unidentified), MYS 14.3478 (unidentified), MYS 14.3481 (unidentified), MYS 14.3499 (unidentified), MYS 14.3512 (unidentified), MYS 14.3513 (unidentified), MYS 14.3521 (unidentified), MYS 14.3528 (unidentified), MYS 14.3536 (unidentified), MYS 14.3543 (unidentified), MYS 14.3560 (unidentified), MYS 16.3885 (unidentified), MYS 20.4323 (Təpotuapumi), MYS 20.4337 (Suruⁿga), MYS 20.4346 (Suruⁿga), MYS 20.4358 (Kamitsupusa), MYS 20.4364 (Pitati), MYS 20.4388 (Simōtsupusa), MYS 20.442 9 (unidentified). Cf. WOJ *ip-* 'id.'

ipo ~ -[i]po 'hut'. Attested in: MYS 20.4348 (Kamitupusa). Cf. WOJ *ipo* 'id.'

ipor- 'to lodge'. Attested in: FK3 (Pitati). Cf. WOJ *ipor-* 'id.'

ir- 'to enter'. Attested in: MYS 14.3354 (Təpotuapumi), MYS 14.3553 (unidentified). Cf. WOJ *ir-* 'id.'

ire- 'to put inside'. Attested in: MYS 16.3878 (Noto). Cf. WOJ *ire-* 'id.'

Irima (p.n.). Attested in: MYS 14.3378 (Muⁿzasi).

irə 'color'. Attested in: MYS 14.3376 (Muⁿzasi), MYS 14.3376a (Muⁿzasi), MYS 14.3503 (unidentified), MYS 14.3560 (unidentified), MYS 20.4424 (Muⁿzasi). Cf. WOJ *irə* 'id.'

isayop- 'to hesitate, to drift'. Attested in: MYS 14.3511 (unidentified), MYS 14.3512 (unidentified). Cf. WOJ *isayop-* 'id.'

isi 'stone'. Attested in: MYS 14.3425 (Simotukɛno), MYS 16.3880 (Noto). Cf. WOJ *isi* 'id.'

Isiwi (p.n.). Attested in: MYS 14.3398 (Sinanu).

iso 'rock, rocky shore'. Attested in: MYS 14.3563 (unidentified), MYS 20.4324 (Təpotuapumi), MYS 20.4328 (Saⁿgamu), MYS 20.4338 (Suruⁿga). Cf. WOJ *iso* 'id.'

isoⁿg- 'to hurry'. Attested in: MYS 20.4337 (Suruⁿga). Cf. WOJ *isoⁿg-* 'id.'

ita- 'extreme'. Attested in: MYS 20.4322 (Təpotuapumi). Cf. WOJ *ita* 'extremely'.

ita- 'to be painful'. Attested in: MYS 14.3482 a (unidentified). Cf. WOJ *ita-* 'id.'

itaⁿdak- 'to put on the head'. Attested in: MYS 20.4377 (Simotukɛno). Cf. WOJ *itaⁿdak-* 'id.'

itar- 'to reach'. Attested in: MYS 14.3506 (unidentified), MYS 20.4419 (Muⁿzasi). Cf. WOJ *itar-* 'id.'

itə nəkite 'very extremely'. Attested in: MYS 14.3548 (unidentified). Cf. WOJ *itə nəkite* 'id.'

itipi 'yew'. Attested in: MYS 16.3885 (unidentified). Cf. WOJ *itipi* 'id.'

ito 'thread'. Attested in: MYS 20.4405 (Kamitukɛno). Cf. WOJ *itə ~ ito* 'id.'

ito 'very, extremely'. Attested in: MYS 20.4379 (Simotukɛno), MYS 20.4381 (Simotukɛno). Cf. WOJ *itə ~ ito* 'id.'

itoko 'dear' (n.). Attested in: MYS 16.3885 (unidentified). Cf. WOJ *itoko* 'id.'

itu 'when'. Attested in: MYS 20.4359 (Kamitupusa), MYS 20.4386 (Simotupusa). Cf. WOJ *itu* 'id.'

itu- 'five'. Attested in: MYS 20.4386 (Simotupusa). Cf. WOJ *itu-* 'id.'

ituma 'free time'. Attested in: MYS 20.4327 (Təpotuapumi). Cf. WOJ *itoma* 'id.'

iya 'more and more'. Attested in: MYS 14.3389 (Pitati), MYS 14.3412 (Kamitukɛno), MYS 14.3557 (unidentified). Cf. WOJ *iya* 'id.'

iya^{n}zeru 'excellent, well noticeable' (?). Attested in FK 7 (Pitati). No WOJ cognates.

K

ka 'top' < Ainu *ka* 'id.' Attested in: MYS 14.3409 (Kamitukɛno), MYS 14.3503 (unidentified), MYS 14.3518 (unidentified).

ka 'voice' < Ainu *háw* 'id.' Attested in: MYS 20.4430 (unidentified).

ka 'rudder'. A contraction of *ka^{n}di* 'id.' Attested in: MYS 20.4363 (Pitati). Cf. WOJ *ka^{n}di* 'id.' See *ka^{n}di*.

ka ~ ka- 'thus'. Attested in: MYS 14.3377 (Mu^{n}zasi), MYS 14.3383 (Kamitupusa), MYS 14.3415 (Kamitukɛno), MYS 14.3487 (unidentified). Cf. WOJ *ka* 'id.'

ka 'that'. Attested in: MYS 20.4384 (Simotupusa). Cf. WOJ *kare* 'id.' Attested in phonographic script only once in MYS 18.4045.

ka, focus particle < Ainu *ka*, id. Attested in: MYS 14.3361 (Sa^{n}gamu), MYS 20.4386 (Simotupusa).

ka^{m}bura 'arrow tip type'. Attested in: MYS 16.3885 (unidentified). Cf. WOJ *ka^{m}bura* 'id.'

ka^{n}di 'rudder'. Attested in: MYS 14.3555 (unidentified), MYS 20.4368 (Pitati). Cf. WOJ *ka^{n}di* 'id.'

ka^{n}do 'gate'. Attested in: MYS 14.3389 (Pitati), MYS 20.4418 (Mu^{n}zasi). Cf. WOJ *ka^{n}do* 'id.' < *kana-to* 'metal [adorned] gate'.

ka^{n}du 'gate'. Attested in: MYS 20.4386 (Simotupusa). Cf. WOJ and EOJ *ka^{n}do* 'id.'

ka^{n}du-nə ke 'paper mulberry tree'. Attested in: AAU 2 (Sa^{n}gamu). Cf. WOJ *ka^{n}di* 'id.'

ka^{n}dunəkï 'paper mulberry tree'. Attested in: MYS 14.3431 (Sa^{n}gamu), MYS 14.3432 (Sa^{n}gamu). Cf. WOJ *ka^{n}di* 'id.'

ka^{n}dus- 'to abduct' (?). Attested in: MYS 14.3432 (Sa^{n}gamu). No WOJ cognates.

Ka^{n}dusika (p.n.) < Ainu *ka-n-toska* < *ka-ne-toska* *top-COP-low.cliffs* 'low cliffs that are above'. Attested in: MYS 14.3349 (Simotupusa), MYS 14.3350 (Pitati), MYS 14.3353 (Təpotuapumi), MYS 14.3384 (Simotupusa), MYS 14.3385 (Simotupusa), 3386, MYS 14.3387 (Simotupusa).

kaⁿgami 'mirror'. Attested in: MYS 14.3468 (unidentified), MYS 16.3885 (unidentified). Cf. WOJ *kaⁿgami* 'id.'

kaⁿgapur- 'to receive'. Attested in: MYS 20.4321 (Təpotuapumi). Cf. WOJ *kaⁿgapur-*.

kaⁿgɛ 'shadow, reflection'. Attested in: MYS 14.3447 (unidentified). Cf. WOJ *kaⁿgɛ* 'id.'

kaⁿgə 'shadow, reflection'. Attested in: MYS 20.4322 (Təpotuapumi). Cf. WOJ *kaⁿgɛ* 'id.'

kaⁿgi 'shadow'. Attested in: MYS 20.4384 (Simotupusa). Cf. WOJ *kaⁿgɛ* 'id.'

kaⁿgir- 'to limit'. Attested in: MYS 14.3495 (unidentified). Cf. WOJ *kaⁿgir-* 'id.'

kaⁿgupasi- 'to be fragrant'. Attested in: MYS 20.4371 (Pitati). Cf. WOJ *kaⁿgupasi-* 'id.'

kak- 'to draw, to paint'. Attested in: MYS 20.4327 (Təpotuapumi). Cf. WOJ *kak-* 'id.'

kakar- 'to hang'. Attested in: MYS 14.3518 (unidentified). Cf. WOJ *kakar-* 'id.'

kake- 'to call'. Attested in: MYS 14.3394 (Pitati). Cf. WOJ *kakɛ-* 'id.'

kake- 'to hang'. Attested in: MYS 14.3468 (unidentified). Cf. WOJ *kakɛ-* 'id.'

Kake (p.n.) < Ainu *ka-kes* 'upper end'. Attested in: MYS 14.3553 (unidentified).

Kake yama (p.n.). Attested in: MYS 14.3432 (Saⁿgamu), AAU 2 (Saⁿgamu).

kaki ~ -ⁿ-gaki 'fence'. Attested in: MYS 14.3561 (unidentified).

kakur- 'to hide, to be hidden'. Attested in: FK 8 (Pitati), MYS 14.3383 (Kamitupusa), MYS 14.3389 (Pitati). Cf. WOJ *kakur-* 'id.'

kama 'wild duck'. Attested in: MYS 20.4339 (Suruⁿga). See also *kamə*, cf. also EOJ *kama* 'id.' Cf. WOJ *kamo* 'id.'

Kamakura (p.n.). Attested in: MYS 14.3366 (Saⁿgamu).

kamə 'wild duck'. Attested in: MYS 14.3524 (unidentified), MYS 14.3525 (unidentified), MYS 14.3527 (unidentified). Cf. WOJ *kamo* 'id.'

kami ~ -ⁿ-gami 'head'. Attested in: MYS 20.4382 (Simotukɛno). Cf. WOJ *kami* 'head hair'.

kami 'deity'. Attested in: MYS 16.3885 (unidentified), MYS 20.4370 (Pitati), MYS 20.4391 (Simotupusa), MYS 20.4350 (Kamitupusa), MYS 20.4374 (Simotukɛno), MYS 20.4380 (Simotukɛno), MYS 20.4392 (Simotupusa), MYS 20.4402 (Sinanu). Cf. WOJ *kamï* 'id.' < *kamuy.

kamï 'deity'. Attested in: MYS 14.3566 (unidentified), MYS 20.4426 (unidentified). Cf. WOJ *kamï* 'id.' < *kamuy.

Kamitukɛno (p.n.). Attested in: MYS 14.3404 (Kamitukɛno), MYS 14.3405 (Kamitukɛno), MYS 14.3405a (Kamitukɛno), MYS 14.3407 (Kamitukɛno), MYS 14.3412 (Kamitukɛno), MYS 14.3415 (Kamitukɛno), MYS 14.3418 (Kamitukɛno), MYS 14.3420 (Kamitukɛno), MYS 14.3423 (Kamitukɛno), MYS 14.3434 (Kamitukɛno).

kamu 'deity'. Attested in: MYS 14.3516 (unidentified). Cf. WOJ *kamï* 'id.' < *kamuy.

kamu, emphatic particle. Attested in: MYS 20.4403. Cf. WOJ *kamə* 'id.'

kana 'metal'. Attested in: MYS 14.3530 (unidentified), MYS 14.3561 (unidentified). Cf. WOJ *kane* 'id.' < *kanay.

kana-to 'metal adorned gate'. Attested in: MYS 14.3530 (unidentified), MYS 14.3561 (unidentified). Cf. WOJ *kanato* 'id.'

kanasi- 'dear, lovely, beloved, sad'. Attested in: MYS 14.3351 (Pitati), MYS 14.3366 (Saⁿgamu), MYS 14.3408 (Kamitukɛno), MYS 14.3412 (Kamitukɛno), MYS 14.3451 (unidentified), MYS 14.3465 (unidentified), MYS 14.3466 (unidentified), MYS 14.3480 (unidentified), MYS 14.3500 (unidentified), MYS 14.3517 (unidentified), MYS 14.3533 (unidentified), MYS 14.3537 (unidentified), MYS 14.3537a (unidentified), MYS 14.3548 (unidentified), MYS 14.3549 (unidentified), MYS 14.3551 (unidentified), MYS 14.3556 (unidentified), MYS 14.3564 (unidentified), MYS 14.3576 (unidentified), MYS 20.4338 (Suruⁿga), MYS 20.4343 (Suruⁿga), MYS 20.4369 (Pitati), MYS 20.4387 (Simotupusa), MYS 20.4391 (Simotupusa), MYS 20.4413 (Muⁿzasi), MYS 20.4429 (unidentified), MYS 20.4432 (unidentified). Cf. WOJ *kanasi-* 'id.'

kane 'metal'. Attested in: MYS 14.3560 (unidentified). Cf. WOJ *kane* 'id.' < *kanay.

kane- 'to think about future, to worry about future'. Attested in: MYS 14.3410 (Kamitukɛno). Cf. WOJ *kane-* 'id.'

kanə 'that'. Attested in: MYS 14.3565 (unidentified). Cf. WOJ *kare* 'id.' WOJ *kare* is attested in phonographic script only once in MYS 18.4045.

Kanipa (p.n.) < Ainu *ka-ne-pa* 'upper bank' (lit. 'top-COP-bank'). Attested in MYS 20.4456. This place name occurs in a WOJ poem.

kap- 'river'. Attested in: MYS 14.3368 (Saⁿgamu).

kapa 'river'. Attested in: MYS 14.3366 (Saⁿgamu), MYS 14.3400 (Sinanu), MYS 14.3405 (Kamitukɛno), MYS 14.3413 (Kamitukɛno), MYS 14.3446 (unidentified), MYS 14.3544 (unidentified), MYS 16.3880 (Noto), MYS 20.4368 (Pitati). Cf. WOJ *kapa* 'id.'

kapa 'pelt, hide'. Attested in: MYS 16.3885 (unidentified). Cf. WOJ *kapa* 'id.'

kapar- ~ -ⁿ-*kapar-* 'to change'. Attested in: MYS 20.4342 (Suruⁿga). Cf. WOJ *kapar-* 'id.'

kapara 'river bed'. Attested in: MYS 14.3425 (Simotukɛno). Cf. WOJ *kapara* 'id.'

kapato 'ford'. Attested in: MYS 14.3546 (unidentified). Cf. WOJ *kapato* 'harbor, ford'.

kaper- 'to return'. Attested in: MYS 20.4368 (Pitati), MYS 20.4373 (Simotukɛno). See also *kapir-*. Cf. WOJ *kaper-* 'id.'

kaperute 'maple'. Attested in: MYS 14.3494 (unidentified). Cf. WOJ *kaperute* 'maple'.

kapɛr- 'to return'. Attested in: 20.4350 (Kamitupusa), MYS 20.4372 (Pitati). Cf. WOJ *kaper-* 'id.'

Kapi (p.n.). Attested in: KKWKS 1097. Cf. WOJ Kapï.

kapir- 'to return'. Attested in: MYS 20.4339 (Suruⁿga). Cf. WOJ *kaper-* 'id.'

kapo 'face'. Attested in: MYS 14.3411 (Kamitukɛno). Cf. WOJ *kapo* 'id.'

kar- 'to cut'. Attested in: MYS 14.3445 (unidentified). Cf. WOJ *kar-* 'id.'

kar- 'to borrow'. Attested in: MYS 14.3472 (unidentified), MYS 14.3499 (unidentified). Cf. WOJ *kar-* 'id.'

Kara 'Korea, Korean'. Attested in: MYS 14.3482a (unidentified), MYS 14.3555 (unidentified), MYS 16.3885 (unidentified), MYS 20.4401 (Sinanu). Cf. WOJ Kara 'id.', 'China', 'Mimana'.

DICTIONARY OF EASTERN OLD JAPANESE 441

kara 'pungent'. Attested in: MYS 16.3880 (Noto). Cf. WOJ *kara* 'id.'

karamar- 'to be entwined'. MYS 20.4352 (Kamitupusa). No direct WOJ cognates.

karasu 'crow'. Attested in: MYS 14.3521 (unidentified). Cf. MJ *karasu* 'id.'

kare- 'to wither'. MYS 14.3436 (Kamitukɛno). Cf. WOJ *kare-* 'id.'

kari 'wild goose'. Attested in: MYS.3466 (Pitati). Cf. WOJ *kari* 'id.'

kari 'hunt'. Attested in: MYS 16.3885 (unidentified). Cf. WOJ *kari* 'id.'

kari 'temporary'. Attested in: MYS 20.4348 (Kamitupusa). Cf. WOJ *kari* 'id.'

kariᵐba 'sakura' < Ainu *karinpa* 'sakura [bark]'. Attested in: MYS 14.3399 (Sinanu). Cf. WOJ *kaniᵐba* 'id.'

kasa 'hat'. Attested in: MYS 16.3885 (unidentified). Cf. WOJ *kasa* 'id.'

kasane- 'to pile up'. Attested in: MYS 20.4351 (Kamitupusa). Cf. WOJ *kasane-* 'id.'

kasi- 'to walk'. Attested in: MYS 20.4417 (Muⁿzasi). Cf. WOJ *kati* 'id.' < otherwise unattested OK form *kati, a predecessor of MK *kèlí* 'id.'

kasiko- 'awesome'. Attested in: MYS 14.3480 (unidentified), MYS 20.4321 (Təpotuapumi), MYS 20.4328 (Saⁿgamu), MYS 20.4358 (Kamitupusa), MYS 20.4394 (Simotupusa), MYS 20.4403 (Sinanu), MYS 20.4414 (Muⁿzasi). Cf. WOJ *kasiko-* 'id.'

Kasima (p.n.). Attested in: MYS 20.4370 (Pitati), MYS 16.3880 (Noto).

kasipa 'oak'. Attested in: MYS 20.4387 (Simotupusa). Cf. WOJ *kasipa* 'id.'

kasira 'head'. Attested in: MYS 20.4346 (Suruⁿga). Cf. WOJ *kasira* 'id.'

kasumi 'mist'. Attested in: MYS 14.3388 (Pitati). Cf. WOJ *kasumi* 'id.'

kat- 'to win'. Attested in: MYS 14.3450 (unidentified). Cf. WOJ *kat-* 'id.'

kata 'side'. Attested in: MYS 20.4418 (Muⁿzasi). Cf. WOJ *kata* 'id.'

kata 'one'. Attested in: MYS 16.3885 (unidentified). Cf. WOJ *kata* 'id.' < OK *hʌtaŋ* 'id.'

kata 'tideland, lagoon'. Attested in: MYS 14.3503 (unidentified), MYS 14.3549 (unidentified), MYS 14.3551 (unidentified), MYS 14.3563 (unidentified), MYS 20.4355 (Kamitupusa). Cf. WOJ *kata* 'id.'

kata 'shape'. Attested in: MYS 14.3520 (unidentified). Cf. WOJ *kata* 'id.'

kata 'vine'. Attested in: MYS 14.3412 (Kamitukɛno). Cf. WOJ *kata* 'id.'

kata 'shoulder'. Attested in: MYS 14.3374 (Muⁿzasi), MYS 14.3488 (unidentified). Cf. WOJ *kata* 'id.'

kata- 'difficult', 'hard'. Attested in: MYS 14.3431 (Saⁿgamu), MYS 14.3401 (Sinanu). WOJ *kata* 'id.'

katamɛ- 'to make a strong promise'. Attested in: MYS 20.4390 (Simotupusa). Cf. WOJ *katamɛ-* 'to harden', 'to make strong', *katamɛ-* 'to make a strong promise'.

katar- 'to talk'. MYS 14.3446 (unidentified). Cf. WOJ *katar-* 'id.'

katayər- 'to lean down, to set'. Attested in: MYS 14.3565 (unidentified). Cf. WOJ *katayər-* 'id.'

kaya 'kaya grass'. Attested in: MYS 14.3499 (unidentified), MYS 14.3543 (unidentified). Cf. WOJ *kaya* 'id.'

kaye 'generic name for reeds and grasses used to thatch roofs of houses'. Cf. WOJ *kaya* 'id.' Attested in: MYS 20.4321 (Təpotuapumi). Cf. WOJ *kaya* 'id.'

kayop- 'to visit'. Attested in: MYS 14.3387 (Simotupusa), MYS 14.3526 (unidentified), MYS 14.3549 (unidentified). Cf. WOJ *kayop-* 'id.'

kayup- 'to go back and forth'. Attested in MYS 20.4324 (Təpotuapumi). Cf. WOJ *kayop-* 'id.'

kaⁿzar- 'to decorate'. Attested in: MYS 20.4329 (Sa^ŋgamu). Cf. WOJ *kaⁿzar-* 'id.'

kaⁿze 'wind'. Attested in FK5 (Pitati), MYS 14.3509 (unidentified), MYS 14.3564 (unidentified), MYS 14.3572 (unidentified), MYS 20.4353 (Kamitupusa), MYS 20.4371 (Pitati). Cf. WOJ *kaⁿze* 'id.'

ke 'food container'. Attested in: MYS 14.3424 (Simotukɛno). Cf. WOJ *kɛ* 'id.'

ke 'hair'. Attested in: MYS 16.3885 (unidentified). Cf. WOJ *kɛ* 'id.'

ke 'tree'. Attested in: AAU 2 (Sa^ŋgamu). See also EOJ *kɛ*, *kï* and *kə* 'id.' Cf. WOJ *kï* 'id.' < PJ *kəy.

ke- 'to come'. Attested in MYS 20.4337 (Suru^ŋga). Cf. WOJ *kə-* id.'

kekere 'heart'. Attested in: KKWKS 1097. See also EOJ *kəkərə* 'id.' Cf. WOJ *kəkərə* 'id.'

-kem-, past tentative auxiliary. Attested in: MYS 14.3415 (Kamitukɛno), MYS 14.3468 (unidentified), MYS 20.4323 (Təpotuapumi EOJ). See also *-kɛm-*. Cf. WOJ *-kem-*.

-kɛm-, past tentative auxiliary. Attested in: FK 2 (Pitati). See also *-kem-*. Cf. WOJ *-kem-*.

kepu 'today'. Attested in: MYS 14.3401 (Sinanu), MYS 20.4373 (Simotukɛno). Cf. WOJ *kepu* 'id.'

kesa 'this morning'. Attested in: AAU 2 (Sa^ŋgamu). Cf. WOJ *kesa* 'id.'

kɛ 'tree'. Attested in: MYS 20.4342 (Suru^ŋga), MYS 20.4375 (Simotukɛno). See also EOJ *ke*, *kï* and *kə* 'id.' Cf. WOJ *kï* 'id.' < PJ *kəy.

kɛmɛ 'mat made from wild rice straw'. Attested in: MYS 20.4338 (Suru^ŋga). Cf. WOJ *kəmə* 'id.'

kɛpu 'today'. Attested in: MYS 20.4330 (Sa^ŋgamu). Cf. WOJ *kepu* 'id.'

kɛri 'lapwing'. Attested in MYS 20.4339 (Suru^ŋga). Not attested in WOJ or MJ, but cf. EMDJ *keri* 'id.'

kɛtə^mba 'word'. Attested in: MYS 20.4346 (Suru^ŋga). Cf. WOJ *kətə^mba* 'id.'

kə 'beloved'. Attested in: MYS 14.3361 (Sa^ŋgamu). Cf. WOJ *ko* 'id', 'child', 'babe'.

kə 'tree'. Attested in: MYS 14.3363 (Sa^ŋgamu). See also EOJ *ke*, *kɛ*, and *kï* 'id.' Cf. WOJ *kï* 'id.' < PJ *kəy.

kə 'this'. Attested in: MYS 14.3469 (unidentified), MYS 14.3563 (unidentified). Cf. WOJ *kə* 'id.'

kə- 'to come'. Attested in: MYS 14.3382 (Kamitupusa), MYS 14.3394 (Pitati), MYS 14.3411 (Kamitukɛno), MYS 14.3412 (Kamitukɛno), MYS 14.3425 (Simotukɛno), MYS 14.3431 (Sa^ŋgamu), MYS 14.3437 (Mitinəku), MYS 14.3445 (unidentified), MYS 14.3461 (unidentified), MYS 14.3469 (unidentified), MYS 14.3480 (unidentified), MYS 14.3481 (unidentified), MYS 14.3495 (unidentified), MYS 14.3521 (unidentified), MYS 14.3527 (unidentified), MYS 14.3528 (unidentified), MYS 14.3531 (unidentified),

MYS 14.3536 (unidentified), MYS 14.3540 (unidentified), MYS 16.3865 (unidentified), MYS 16.3879 (Noto), MYS 16.3880 (Noto), MYS 16.3885 (unidentified), MYS 20.4323 (Təpotuapumi), MYS 20.4339 (Suruŋga), MYS 20.4340 (Suruŋga), MYS 20.4344 (Suruŋga), MYS 20.4349 (Kamitupusa), MYS 20.4350 (Kamitupusa), MYS 20.4353 (Kamitupusa), MYS 20.4358 (Kamitupusa), MYS 20.4364 (Pitati), MYS 20.4368 (Pitati), MYS 20.4370 (Pitati), MYS 20.4372 (Pitati), MYS 20.4385 (Simotupusa), MYS 20.4387 (Simotupusa), MYS 20.4393 (Simotupusa), MYS 20.4401 (Sinanu), MYS 20.4403 (Sinanu), MYS 20.4404 (Kamitukɛno), MYS 20.4413 (Muⁿzasi), MYS 20.4430 (unidentified). Cf. WOJ kə- 'id.'

kəⁿdək- 'to bless with words' < Ainu ko-itak 'to speak to, to address words to' (normally contracted to koytak). Attested in: MYS 14.3506 (unidentified).

Kəŋga (p.n.). Attested in: MYS 14.3555 (unidentified).

kəŋg- 'to row'. Attested in: MYS 14.3349 (Simotupusa), MYS 14.3401 (Sinanu), MYS 14.3557 (unidentified), MYS 20.4363 (Pitati), MYS 20.4365 (Pitati), MYS 20.4380 (Simotukɛno), MYS 20.4384 (Simotupusa). Cf. WOJ kəŋg- 'id.'

kəŋgətə 'many'. Attested in: MYS 14.3502 (unidentified). Cf. WOJ kəkəⁿda 'id.', which is unlikely to be related.

kəkə 'here'. Attested in: MYS 14.3538 (unidentified), MYS 14.3538a (unidentified). Cf. WOJ kəkə 'id.'

kəkəᵐba 'extremely, so much'. Attested in: MYS 14.3431 (Saŋgamu), MYS 14.3517 (unidentified). Cf. WOJ kəkəⁿda 'id.'

kəkərə 'heart'. Attested in: MYS 14.3425 (Simotukɛno), MYS 14.3463 (unidentified), MYS 14.3466 (unidentified), MYS 14.3496 (unidentified), MYS 14.3517 (unidentified), MYS 14.3526 (unidentified), MYS 14.3536 (unidentified), MYS 14.3538 (unidentified), MYS 14.3538a (unidentified), MYS 14.3566 (unidentified), MYS 20.4354 (Kamitupusa), MYS 20.4356 (Kamitupusa), MYS 20.4390 (Simotupusa), KKWKS 1097 (Kapi). Cf. WOJ kəkərə 'id.'

kəmə 'wild rice'. Attested in: MYS 14.3464 (unidentified), MYS 14.3524 (unidentified). See also EOJ kəmo 'id.' Cf. WOJ kəmə 'id.'

kəmo 'wild duck'. Attested in: MYS 20.4354 (Kamitupusa). See also EOJ kama 'id.' Cf. WOJ kamo 'id.'

Kəma (p.n. 'Koguryo'). MYS 14.3465 (unidentified). Cf. WOJ Kəma (p.n. 'Koguryo').

kənə 'this'. Attested in: MYS 14.3361 (Saŋgamu), MYS 14.3445 (unidentified), MYS 14.3448 (unidentified), MYS 14.3448 (unidentified), MYS 14.3460 (unidentified), MYS 14.3488 (unidentified), MYS 14.3506 (unidentified), MYS 14.3511 (unidentified), MYS 16.3885 (unidentified), MYS 20.4394 (Simotupusa). Cf. WOJ kənə 'id.'

kər- 'to scold'. Attested in: MYS 14.3529 (unidentified). No WOJ cognates.

kəre 'this'. Attested in: MYS 20.4420 (Muⁿzasi). Cf. WOJ kəre 'id.'

kərə 'time'. Attested in: MYS 14.3506 (unidentified), MYS 14.3511 (unidentified). Cf. WOJ kərə 'id.'

kəraku 'caw-caw (onomatopoeia for crow's cry)'. Attested in: MYS 14.3521 (unidentified). No WOJ cognates attested.

kərəmə 'garment'. Attested in: MYS 14.3482a (unidentified), MYS 20.4351 (Kamitupusa), MYS 20.4388 (Simotupusa), MYS 20.4424 (Muⁿzasi). See also EOJ kərəmo, kərəmu 'id.' Cf. WOJ kərəmə 'id.'

kərəmo 'garment'. Attested in: MYS 14.3394 (Pitati), MYS 20.4431 (unidentified). See also EOJ kərəmə, kərəmu 'id.' Cf. WOJ kərəmə 'id.'

kərəmu 'garment'. Cf. WOJ kərəmə 'id.' Attested in: MYS 20.4401 (Sinanu). See also EOJ kərəmə, kərəmo 'id.' Cf. WOJ kərəmə 'id.'

kəsi 'waist'. Attested in: MYS 20.4413 (Muⁿzasi). Cf. WOJ kəsi 'id.'

kətu '[wooden] debris, trash'. Attested in: MYS 14.3548 (unidentified). Cf. WOJ kətumi 'id.'

kətə 'matter'. Attested in: MYS 14.3384 (Simotupusa), MYS 14.3401 (Sinanu), MYS 14.3418 (Kamitukɛno), MYS 14.3499 (unidentified), MYS 20.4348 (Kamitupusa), MYS 20.4364 (Pitati), MYS 20.4418 (Muⁿzasi). Cf. WOJ kətə 'id.'

kətə 'word'. Attested in: MYS 14.3398 (Sinanu), MYS 14.3446 (unidentified), MYS 14.3456 (unidentified), MYS 14.3464 (unidentified), MYS 14.3466 (unidentified), MYS 14.3480 (unidentified), MYS 14.3482a (unidentified), MYS 14.3501 (unidentified), MYS 14.3525 (unidentified), MYS 14.3552 (unidentified), MYS 14.3556 (unidentified), MYS 20.4321 (Təpotuapumi), MYS 20.4324 (Təpotuapumi), MYS 20.4328 (Saⁿgamu), MYS 20.4353 (Kamitupusa), MYS 20.4358 (Kamitupusa), MYS 20.4376 (Simotukɛno), MYS 20.4392 (Simotupusa), MYS 20.4393 (Simotupusa), MYS 20.4394 (Simotupusa), MYS 20.4403 (Sinanu), MYS 20.4414 (Muⁿzasi), MYS 20.4432 (unidentified). Cf. WOJ kətə 'id.'

kətətəp- 'to talk with'. Attested in: MYS 14.3540 (unidentified), MYS 20.4392 (Simotupusa). Cf. WOJ kətətəp- 'id.'

ki- 'to wear'. Attested in: MYS 14.3472 (unidentified), MYS 14.3484 (unidentified), MYS 20.4351 (Kamitupusa), MYS 20.4388 (Simotupusa), MYS 20.4431 (unidentified). Cf. WOJ ki- 'id.'

kik- 'to listen'. Attested in: FK2 (Pitati). Cf. WOJ kik- 'id.'

Kiᵐbe (p.n.) < Ainu kimpe 'bear' (< kim-pe 'mountain thing'). Attested in: MYS 14.3353, MYS 14.3354 (Təpotuapumi).

kimi 'lord'. Attested in: MYS 14.3374 (Muⁿzasi), MYS 14.3377 (Muⁿzasi), MYS 14.3388 (Pitati), MYS 14.3400 (Sinanu), MYS 14.3413 (Kamitukɛno), MYS 14.3448 (unidentified), MYS 14.3480 (unidentified), MYS 14.3495 (unidentified), MYS 14.3506 (unidentified), MYS 14.3514 (unidentified), MYS 14.3521 (unidentified), MYS 14.3561 (unidentified), MYS 16.3885 (unidentified), MYS 20.4328 (Saⁿgamu), MYS 20.4352 (Kamitupusa), MYS 20.4358 (Kamitupusa), MYS 20.4373 (Simotukɛno), MYS 20.4393 (Simotupusa), MYS 20.4394 (Simotupusa), MYS 20.4403 (Sinanu), MYS 20.4414 (Muⁿzasi). Cf. WOJ kimi 'id.'

kimo 'liver'. Attested in: MYS 16.3885 (unidentified). Cf. WOJ *kimo* 'id.'

kinu 'garment'. Attested in: MYS 14.3435 (Kamitukɛno), MYS 14.3472 (unidentified), MYS 14.3576 (unidentified). Cf. WOJ *kinu* 'id.'

kiⁿgisi 'pheasant'. Attested in: MYS 14.3375 (Muⁿzasi). Cf. WOJ *kiⁿgisi* 'id.'

Kipatuku (p.n.). Attested in: MYS 14.3444 (unidentified).

kisə 'last night'. Attested in: MYS 14.3522 (unidentified), MYS 14.3563 (unidentified). Cf. WOJ *kisə* 'id.'

kï 'tree'. Attested in: MYS 14.3432 (Saⁿgamu). See also EOJ *ke, kɛ, kə* 'id.' Cf. WOJ *kï* 'id.' < PJ *kəy.

ko 'child, girl, daughter, beloved'. Attested in: FK2 (Pitati), FK7 (Pitati), FK8 (Pitati), MYS 14.3351 (Pitati), MYS 14.3368 (Saⁿgamu), MYS 14.3369 (Saⁿgamu), MYS 14.3405 (Kamitukɛno), MYS 14.3408 (Kamitukɛno), MYS 14.3412 (Kamitukɛno), MYS 14.3424 (Simotukɛno), MYS 14.3458 (unidentified), MYS 14.3473 (unidentified), MYS 14.3476 (unidentified), MYS 14.3476a (unidentified), MYS 14.3485 (unidentified), MYS 14.3500 (unidentified), MYS 14.3504 (unidentified), MYS 14.3509 (unidentified), MYS 14.3513 (unidentified), MYS 14.3522 (unidentified), MYS 14.3525 (unidentified), MYS 14.3529 (unidentified), MYS 14.3530 (unidentified), MYS 14.3532 (unidentified), MYS 14.3533 (unidentified), MYS 14.3537 (unidentified), MYS 14.3537a (unidentified), MYS 14.3539 (unidentified), MYS 14.3541 (unidentified), MYS 14.3543 (unidentified), MYS 14.3555 (unidentified), MYS 14.3564 (unidentified), MYS 14.3565 (unidentified), MYS 16.3865 (unidentified), MYS 16.3880 (Noto), MYS 20.4343 (Suruⁿga), MYS 20.4358 (Kamitupusa), MYS 20.4385 (Simotupusa), MYS 20.4387 (Simotupusa), MYS 20.4401 (Sinanu), MYS 20.4414 (Muⁿzasi), MYS 20.4431 (unidentified). cf. WOJ *ko* 'id.'

ko 'basket'. Attested in: MYS 14.3444 (unidentified). WOJ *ko* 'id.'

koma 'stallion'. Attested in: MYS 14.3387 (Simotupusa), MYS 14.3451 (unidentified), MYS 14.3532 (unidentified), MYS 14.3533 (unidentified), MYS 14.3536 (unidentified), MYS 14.3537a (unidentified), MYS 14.3538a (unidentified), MYS 14.3539 (unidentified), MYS 14.3540 (unidentified), MYS 14.3541 (unidentified), MYS 20.4417 (Muⁿzasi), MYS 20.4429 (unidentified). WOJ *koma* 'id.'

Koᵐba (p.n.). Attested in: MYS 14.3496 (unidentified).

Komoti (p.n.). Attested in: MYS 14.3494 (unidentified).

Kona (p.n.). Attested in: MYS 14.3478 (unidentified).

koⁿgo (onomatopoeia for squeezing the meat of *sitaⁿdami*). Attested in: MYS 16.3880 (Noto). No WOJ cognates.

kopi- 'to long for'. Attested in: FK 5 (Pitati), MYS 20.4366 (Pitati), MYS 20.4371 (Pitati), MYS 20.4386 (Simotupusa), MYS 20.4391 (Simotupusa). See also EOJ *kopï-* 'id.' Cf. WOJ *kopi-* 'id.'

kopï- 'to long for'. Attested in: MYS 14.3358b (Suruⁿga), MYS 14.3376a (Muⁿzasi), MYS 14.3382 (Kamitupusa), MYS 14.3415 (Kamitukɛno), MYS 14.3560 (unidentified), MYS

14.3566 (unidentified), MYS 20.4322 (Təpotuapumi), MYS 20.4347 (Kamitupusa). See also *kopi-* 'id.' Cf. WOJ *kopï-* 'id.'

kopisi- 'be longing for'. Attested in: MYS 20.4407 (Kamitukɛno). See also EOJ *kopïsi-, kopusi-, kupusi-* 'id.' Cf. WOJ *koposo- ~ kopïsi-* 'id.'

kopïsi- 'be longing for'. Attested in: MYS 14.3376 (Muⁿzasi). See also EOJ *kopisi-, kopusi-, kupusi-* 'id.' Cf. WOJ *koposo- ~ kopïsi-* 'id.'

kopusi- 'be longing for, be missing (someone)'. Cf. WOJ *koposi ~kopïsi* 'id.' Attested in: MYS 14.3476 (unidentified), MYS 20.4419 (Muⁿzasi). See also EOJ *kopisi-, kopïsi-, kupusi-* 'id.' Cf. WOJ *koposo- ~ kopïsi-* 'id.'

kos- ~ -ⁿ-kos- 'to make something cross over'. Attested in: MYS 14.3537 (unidentified), MYS 14.3537a (unidentified), MYS 14.3538 (unidentified), MYS 20.4389 (Simotupusa). Cf. WOJ *kos-* 'id.'

kotə 'koto (stringed musical instrument)'. Attested in: AAU 2 (Saⁿgamu). Cf. WOJ *kətə* 'id.' < MK *kó* 'koto' < OK *kotV.[2]

kotəⁿde 'talk'. Attested in: AAU 2 (Saⁿgamu).

koyə- 'to cross, to cross over'. Attested in: FK 9 (Pitati), MYS 14.3402 (Kamitukɛno), MYS 20. 4403 (Kamitukɛno), MYS 20.4407 (Kamitukɛno). See also EOJ *kuye-* 'id.' Cf. WOJ *koye-* 'id.'

kuⁿgi 'nail'. Attested in: MYS 20.4390 (Simotupusa). Cf. WOJ *kuⁿgi* 'id.'

kukï 'stalk'. Attested in: MYS 14.3375 (Muⁿzasi). See also EOJ *kuku* 'id.' Cf. WOJ *kukï* 'id.'

kuku 'stalk'. Attested in: MYS 14.3444 (unidentified). See also EOJ *kukï* 'id.' Cf. WOJ *kukï* 'id.'

kum- 'to draw (water)'. Attested in: MYS 14.3546 (unidentified). Cf. WOJ *kum-* 'id.'

kuma 'bend'. Attested in: MYS 20.4349 (Kamitupusa). Cf. WOJ *kuma* 'id.'

Kumaki (p.n.). Attested in: MYS 16.3878 (Noto), MYS 16.3879 (Noto).

kumə 'cloud'. Attested in: MYS 14.3409 (Kamitukɛno), MYS 14.3511 (unidentified), MYS 14.3512 (unidentified), MYS 14.3513 (unidentified), MYS 14.3520 (unidentified). See also EOJ *kumo, kumu* 'id.' Cf. WOJ *kumo* 'id.'

kumər- 'be cloudy'. Attested in: MYS 20.4407 (Kamitukɛno).

kumo 'cloud'. Attested in: MYS 14.3514 (unidentified), MYS 14.3515 (unidentified), MYS 14.3516 (unidentified), MYS 14.3517 (unidentified), MYS 14.3518 (unidentified), MYS 14.3522 (unidentified), MYS 20.4380 (Simotukɛno), MYS 20.4421 (Muⁿzasi). See also EOJ *kumə, kumu* 'id.' Cf. WOJ *kumo* 'id.'

kumowi 'distant'. Attested in: MYS 20.4355 (Kamitupusa). Cf. WOJ *kumowi* 'id.'

kumu 'cloud'. Cf. WOJ *kumo* 'id.' Attested in: MYS 20.4403 (Sinanu). See also EOJ *kumə, kumo* 'id.' Cf. WOJ *kumo* 'id.'

kuni 'province', 'land'. Attested in: MYS 14.3383 (Kamitupusa), MYS 14.3426 (Mitinəku), MYS 14.3515 (unidentified), MYS 16.3885 (unidentified), MYS 20.4329 (Saⁿgamu),

---

[2] For phonetic development cf. MK *hyé* 'tongue' < EMK *hyet* < OK *hitV.

MYS 20.4339 (Suruⁿga), MYS 20.4359 (Kamitupusa), MYS 20.4381 (Simotukɛno), MYS 20.4383 (Simotukɛno), MYS 20.4392 (Simotupusa). Cf. WOJ *kuni* 'id.'

kupe 'fence'. No WOJ cognates. Attested in: MYS 14.3537 (unidentified). No WOJ cognates.

kupusi 'be longing for, be missing (someone)'. Attested in: MYS 20.4345 (Suruⁿga). See also EOJ *kopïsi-, kopusi-, kopisi-* 'id.' Cf. WOJ *koposi- ~ kopïsi-* 'id.'

kure- 'to grow dark'. Attested in: MYS 14.3461 (unidentified). Cf. WOJ *kure-* 'id.'

Kuropo (p.n.). Attested in: MYS 14.3412 (Kamitukɛno).

kuru 'pivot'. Attested in: MYS 20.4390 (Simotupusa). Cf. MJ *kuru* 'id.'

kurusi- 'hard'. Attested in: MYS 14.3481 (unidentified), MYS 20.4406 (Kamitukɛno). Cf. WOJ *kurusi-* 'id.'

kusa 'grass'. Attested in: MYS 14.3370 (Saⁿgamu), MYS 14.3377 (Muⁿzasi), MYS 14.3447 (unidentified), MYS 14.3452 (unidentified), MYS 14.3530 (unidentified), MYS 14.3532 (unidentified), MYS 20.4325 (Təpotuapumi), MYS 20.4406 (Kamitukɛno), MYS 20.4416 (Muⁿzasi), MYS 20.4420 (Muⁿzasi). Cf. WOJ *kusa* 'id.'

kusuri 'medicine'. Attested in: MYS 16.3885 (unidentified). Cf. WOJ *kusuri* 'id.'

kuti 'mouth'. Attested in: MYS 14.3532 (unidentified). Cf. WOJ *kuti* 'id.'

kutu 'shoes'. Attested in: MYS 14.3399 (Sinanu). Cf. WOJ *kutu* 'id.'

kuyasi- 'to be regretful'. Attested in: MYS 14.3544 (unidentified), MYS 20.4337 (Suruⁿga), MYS 20.4376 (Simotukɛno). Cf. WOJ *kuyasi-* 'id.'

kuye- 'to cross over'. Attested in: 4372 (Pitati). See also EOJ *koyə-* 'id.' Cf. WOJ *koye-* 'id.'

Kuⁿzi (p.n.) < Ainu *kus* 'to overflow'. Attested in: MYS 20.4368 (Pitati).

kuⁿzu 'kudzu, arrowroot (Puetaria thunbergiana)'. Attested in: MYS 14.3412 (Kamitukɛno). Cf. WOJ *kuⁿzu* 'id.'

M

ma 'wife' < Ainu *mat* 'woman, wife'. Attested in: MYS 14.3502 (unidentified).

ma 'eye'. Attested in: MYS 14.3541 (unidentified). Cf. WOJ *ma-* 'id.'

ma 'space', 'interval'. Attested in: FK 9 (Pitati), MYS 14.3361 (Saⁿgamu), MYS 14.3363 (Saⁿgamu), MYS 14.3524 (unidentified), MYS 14.3561 (unidentified), MYS 20.4430 (unidentified). Cf. WOJ *ma* 'id.'

ma 'true'. Attested in: MYS 14.3384 (Simotupusa), MYS 14.3499 (unidentified), MYS 14.3560 (unidentified), MYS 20.4342 (Suruⁿga), MYS 20.4348 (Kamitupusa). Cf. WOJ *ma* 'id.'

maⁿdara 'spotted'. Attested in: MYS 14.3354 (Təpotuapumi). No WOJ phonographic attestations.

mak- 'to wrap, to roll'. Attested in: MYS 14.3487 (unidentified), MYS 20.4377 (Simotukɛno). Cf. WOJ *mak-* 'id.'

mak- 'to use as a pillow'. Attested in: MYS 14.3369 (Saⁿgamu), MYS 14.3464 (unidentified). Cf. WOJ *mak-* 'id.'

mak- 'to sow'. Attested in: MYS 14.3451 (unidentified). Cf. WOJ *mak-*, EMDJ *mak-* 'id.'

mak-i 'back-POSS' < Ainu *mak* 'back' + 3rd person possessive suffix *-i*. Attested in: MYS 20.4413 (Muⁿzasi).

makar- 'to go far away'. Attested in: MYS 20.4330 (Saⁿgamu). Cf. WOJ *makar-* 'id.'

makirapasi- 'to be blinding'. MYS 14.3407 (Kamitukɛno). No WOJ cognates.

makura 'headrest', 'pillow'. Attested in: MYS 14.3369 (Saⁿgamu), MYS 14.3464 (unidentified), MYS 14.3480 (unidentified), MYS 20.4325 (Təpotuapumi), MYS 20.4406 (Kamitukɛno), MYS 20.4413 (Muⁿzasi), MYS 20.4416 (Muⁿzasi), MYS 20.4420 (Muⁿzasi), MYS 20.4432 (unidentified). Cf. WOJ *makura* 'id.'

Makuraⁿga (p.n.). Attested in: MYS 14.3555 (unidentified).

mama 'cliff'. Attested in: MYS 14.3349 (Simotupusa), MYS 14.3369 (Saⁿgamu), MYS 14.3384 (Simotupusa), MYS 14.3385 (Simotupusa), MYS 14.3387 (Simotupusa). Cf. Hachijō *mama* 'id.' No WOJ cognates.

mamɛ 'bean'. MYS 20.4352 (Kamitupusa). Cf. WOJ *mamɛ* 'id.'

manima 'according'. Attested in: MYS 14.3377 (Muⁿzasi), MYS 14.3576 (unidentified). Cf. WOJ *manima* 'id.'

map- 'dance'. Attested in: FK 7 (Pitati). Cf. WOJ *map-* 'id.'

maru 'round'. Attested in: MYS 20.4416 (Muⁿzasi), MYS 20.4420 (Muⁿzasi). Cf. WOJ *maro ~ maru* 'id.'

maru ne- 'to sleep in one's clothes'. Attested in: MYS 20.4416 (Muⁿzasi), MYS 20.4420 (Muⁿzasi). Cf. WOJ *marə ne-* 'id.'

mas- 'to increase'. Attested in: MYS 14.3557 (unidentified). Cf. WOJ *mas-* 'id.'

mas- 'to be superior'. Attested in: MYS 20.4431 (unidentified). Cf. WOJ *mas-* 'id.'

masaⁿde n- 'clear, sure, real'. Attested in: MYS 14.3374 (Muⁿzasi), MYS 14.3521 (unidentified). No WOJ cognates.

masaka 'now'. Attested in: MYS 14.3410 (Kamitukɛno). Cf. WOJ *masaka* 'id.'

mat- 'to wait'. Attested in: MYS 14.3363 (Saⁿgamu), MYS 14.3493 (unidentified), MYS 14.3546 (unidentified), MYS 14.3561 (unidentified), MYS 14.3562 (unidentified), MYS 14.3563 (unidentified), MYS 16.3865 (unidentified), MYS 16.3885 (unidentified), MYS 20.4339 (Suruⁿga), MYS 20.4340 (Suruⁿga), MYS 20.4368 (Pitati). Cf. WOJ *mat-* 'id.'

mata 'again'. Attested in: MYS 14.3395 (Pitati), MYS 20.4349 (Kamitupusa), MYS 20.4392 (Simotupusa), MYS 20.4415 (Muⁿzasi). Cf. WOJ *mata* 'id.'

mato 'girl' < Ainu *mat-po* 'girl' (< *mat* 'woman, wife', *po* 'child'). Attested in: MYS 14.3407 (Kamitukɛno).

matu 'pine'. Attested in: MYS 14.3495 (unidentified), MYS 14.3552 (unidentified), MYS 20.4375 (Simotukɛno). Cf. WOJ *matu* 'id.'

matur- 'to present', 'to offer (HUM)'. MYS 20.4391 (Simotupusa), MYS 20.4402 (Sinanu). Cf. WOJ *matur-* 'id.'

mayo 'eyebrow'. Attested in: MYS 14.3531 (unidentified). Cf. WOJ *mayo* 'id.'

mawi- 'to come (HUM)'. Attested in: MYS 14.4393 (Simotupusa). Cf. WOJ *mawi-* 'id.'

mawos- 'to say (HUM)'. Attested in: MYS 20.4372 (Pitati), MYS 20.4376 (Simotukɛno). Cf. WOJ *mawos-* 'id.'

mawus- 'to say (HUM)'. Attested in: MYS 16.3885 (unidentified). Cf. WOJ *mawus-* 'id.'

maⁿzir- 'to get mixed'. Attested in: MYS 14.3452 (unidentified). Cf. MJ *maⁿzir* 'id.'

me 'woman', 'wife'. Attested in: MYS 16.3865 (unidentified), MYS 16.3880 (Noto). See also EOJ *mi* 'id.' Cf. WOJ *me* 'id.'

mɛ 'eye'. Attested in: MYS 14.3383 (Kamitupusa), MYS 16.3885 (unidentified), MYS 20.4383 (Simotukɛno). Cf. WOJ *mɛ* 'id.'

mɛ, focus particle. Attested in: MYS 14.4345. Cf. WOJ *mə* 'id.'

mɛⁿd- or *mɛⁿde-* 'to love'.³ Attested in: MYS 14.3502 (unidentified), MYS 16.3880 (Noto). Cf. WOJ *mɛⁿde-* 'id.'

mɛⁿgur- 'to go around'. Attested in: MYS 20.4339 (Suruŋga). Cf. WOJ *mɛⁿgur-* 'id.'

mɛt- 'to hold'. Attested in: MYS 20.4343 (Suruŋga). See also EOJ *mət-* and *məs-* 'id.' Cf. WOJ *mət-*. 'id.'

mə 'side'. Attested in: MYS 14.3361 (Saŋgamu). Cf. WOJ *ma ~ mo* 'id.'

məkərə 'like' (postposition). Attested in: MYS 20.4375 (Simotukɛno). Cf. WOJ *məkərə* 'id.'

mənə 'thing'. Attested in: MYS 14.3511 (unidentified). See also EOJ *monə* and *mono* 'id.' Cf. WOJ *mənə* 'id.'

mərə 'all'. Attested in: 14.3377 (Muⁿzasi), MYS 20.4372 (Pitati).

məs- 'to hold'. Attested in: MYS 20.4415 (Muⁿzasi), MYS 20.4420 (Muⁿzasi). See also EOJ *mɛt-* and *mət-* 'id.' Cf. WOJ *mət-* 'id.'

mət- 'to hold, to take, to bring'. Attested in: MYS 14.3424 (Simotukɛno), MYS 16.3880 (Noto), MYS 16.3885 (unidentified), MYS 20.4353 (Kamitupusa), MYS 20.4356 (Kamitupusa). See also EOJ *mɛt-* and *məs-* 'id.' Cf. WOJ *mət-* 'id.'

mətə 'base', 'bottom'. Attested in: MYS 14.3488 (unidentified), MYS 16.3885 (unidentified), MYS 20.4386 (Simotupusa). See also EOJ *motə* 'id.' Cf. WOJ *mətə* 'id.'

mi 'wife'. Attested in: MYS 20.4343 (Suruŋga). See also EOJ *me* 'id.' Cf. WOJ *me* 'id.'

mi 'water'. Attested in: MYS 20.4340 (Suruŋga).

mi- 'to see, to look'. Attested in: FK 7 (Pitati), FK 8 (Pitati), MYS 14.3405a (Kamitukɛno), MYS 14.3407 (Kamitukɛno), MYS 14.3450 (unidentified), MYS 14.3473 (unidentified), MYS 14.3485 (unidentified), MYS 14.3506 (unidentified), MYS 14.3515 (unidentified), MYS 14.3516 (unidentified), MYS 14.3520 (unidentified), MYS 14.3530 (unidentified), MYS 14.3531 (unidentified), MYS 14.3537 (unidentified), MYS 14.3561 (unidentified), MYS 16.3878 (Noto), MYS 20.4322 (Təpotuapumi), MYS 20.4327 (Təpotuapumi), MYS 20.4329 (Saŋgamu), MYS 20.4330 (Saŋgamu), MYS 20.4345 (Suruŋga), MYS 20.4354 (Kamitupusa), MYS 20.4355 (Kamitupusa), MYS 20.4367

---

3 It is impossible to tell on the basis of attested forms whether it was a consonantal or a vowel verb in EOJ.

(Pitati), MYS 20.4372 (Simotukɛno), MYS 20.4373 (Simotukɛno), MYS 20.4375 (Simotukɛno), MYS 20.4380 (Simotukɛno), MYS 20.4381 (Simotukɛno), MYS 20.4415 (Muⁿzasi), MYS 20.4421 (Muⁿzasi), MYS 20.4423 (Muⁿzasi), MYS 20.4424 (Muⁿzasi), KKWKS 1097 (Kapi). Cf. WOJ *mi-* 'id.'

miⁿdaye- 'to be in disorder'. Attested in: MYS 14.3563 (unidentified). Cf. WOJ *miⁿdare-* 'id.'

miⁿdo 'water'. Attested in: MYS 14.3546 (unidentified). See also EOJ *miⁿdu* 'id.' Cf. WOJ *miⁿdu* 'id.'

miⁿdu 'water'. Attested in: MYS 14.3392 (Pitati), MYS 14.3528 (unidentified), MYS 20.4322 (Təpotuapumi), MYS 20.4337 (Suruⁿga). See also EOJ *miⁿdo* 'id.' Cf. WOJ *miⁿdu* 'id.'

miⁿdura 'a male hairstyle'. MYS 20.4377 (Simotukɛno). Cf. WOJ *miⁿdura* 'id.'

miᵑgɛ 'cow's stomach, goat's stomach'. Attested in: MYS 16.3885 (unidentified). Cf. WOJ *miᵑgɛ* 'id.'

Mikamə (p.n.). Attested in: MYS 14.3424 (Simotukɛno).

Mikuku (p.n.). Attested in: MYS 14.3525 (unidentified).

mimi 'ear'. Attested in: MYS 16.3885 (unidentified). Cf. WOJ *mimi* 'id.'

mina 'water'. Attested in: MYS 14.3553 (unidentified). Cf. WOJ *mina* 'id.'

minato 'harbor'. Attested in: MYS 14.3445 (unidentified), MYS 14.3553 (unidentified). Cf. WOJ *minato* 'id.'

Minanəse (p.n.). Attested in: MYS 14.3366 (Saᵑgamu).

mi-ne 'peak'. Attested in: FK 2 (Pitati), MYS 20.4421 (Muⁿzasi). See also EOJ *ne* 'id.' Cf. WOJ *mi-ne* 'id.'

mira 'leek'. Attested in: MYS 14.3444 (unidentified). Cf. WOJ *mira* 'id.'

mit- 'to rise', 'to fill', 'to become full'. Attested in: MYS 14.3366 (Saᵑgamu), MYS 14.3549 (unidentified). Cf. WOJ *mit-* 'id.'

mita 'with' (postposition). Attested in: MYS 20.4394 (Simotupusa). See also EOJ *muta* 'id.' Cf. WOJ *muta* 'id.'

miti 'road'. Attested in: MYS 14.3399 (Sinanu), MYS 14.3447 (unidentified), MYS 20.4341 (Suruᵑga), MYS 20.4349 (Kamitupusa), MYS 20.4352 (Kamitupusa). See also EOJ *ti* 'id.' Cf. WOJ *miti* 'id.'

Mitinəku (p.n.). Attested in: MYS 14.3437 (Mitinəku).

Miwori (p.n.). Attested in: MYS 20.4341 (Suruᵑga).

mï 'body'. Attested in: MYS 14.3485 (unidentified), MYS 16.3880 (Noto), MYS 16.3885 (unidentified). Cf. WOJ *mï* 'id.'

mï- 'to turn around'. Attested in: MYS 14.3349 (Simotupusa). Cf. WOJ *mï-* 'id.'

mïna 'all'. Attested in: MYS 14.3398 (Sinanu).

mo 'side'. Attested in: MYS 14.3361 (Saᵑgamu). See also EOJ *mə* 'id.' Cf. WOJ *mo ~ mə* 'id.'

mo 'seaweed'. Attested in: MYS 14.3397 (Pitati), MYS 14.3562 (unidentified). Cf. WOJ *mo* 'id.'

mo- 'to sleep'. Attested in: MYS 16.3878 (Noto). Cf. Ainu *mo* 'id.'

mokərə 'like' (postposition). Attested in: MYS 14.3527 (unidentified). See also EOJ *məkərə* (postposition 'like'). Cf. WOJ *məkərə* 'id.' and OJ *məkərə* 'id.'

mom- 'to rub'. Attested in: MYS 16.3880 (Noto). Cf. WOJ *mom-* 'id.'

momə 'hundred'. Attested in: MYS 20.4349 (Kamitupusa). Cf. WOJ *momo* 'id.'

momit- 'to turn red/yellow (of leaves)'. Attested in: MYS 14.3494 (unidentified). Cf. WOJ *momit-* 'id.'

monə 'thing'. Attested in: MYS 14.3481 (unidentified), MYS 14.3528 (unidentified), MYS 14.3551 (unidentified), MYS 20.4337 (Suruⁿga). See also EOJ *mono* and *mənə* 'id.' Cf. WOJ *mənə* 'id.'

mono 'thing'. Attested in: MYS 16.3885 (unidentified). See also EOJ *mənə* and *monə* 'id.' Cf. WOJ *mənə* 'id.'

mor- 'to protect'. Attested in: MYS 14.3436 (Kamitukɛno). Cf. WOJ *mor-* 'id.'

mor- 'to pile up'. Attested in: MYS 16.3880 (Noto). Cf. WOJ *mor-* 'id.'

motə 'root', 'base'. Attested in: MYS 14.3474 (unidentified), MYS 14.3495 (unidentified). See also EOJ *mətə* 'id.' Cf. WOJ *mətə* 'id.'

motəmɛ- 'to look for'. Attested in: MYS 14.3415 (Kamitukɛno). Cf. WOJ *motəmɛ-* 'to look for', 'to find [out]'.

muⁿdak- 'to embrace'. Attested in: MYS 14.3404 (Kamitukɛno). Cf. WOJ *uⁿdak-* and MJ *iⁿdak-* 'id.'

muŋgi 'barley', 'wheat'. Attested in: MYS 14.3537 (unidentified), MYS 14.3537a (unidentified). Cf. WOJ *muŋgi* 'id.'

muk- 'to face', 'to direct', 'to turn'. Attested in: MYS 14.3377 (Muⁿzasi), MYS 14.3474 (unidentified), MYS 20.4359 (Kamitupusa). Cf. WOJ *muk-* 'id.'

muka-tu 'opposite side'. Attested in: MYS 14.3448 (unidentified), MYS 14.3493 (unidentified). Cf. WOJ *muka-tu* 'id.'

mukap- 'to face'. Attested in: MYS 20.4430 (unidentified). Cf. WOJ *mukap-* 'to meet', 'to face an enemy'.

muma 'horse'. Attested in: MYS 20.4372 (Pitati). Cf. WOJ *muma* 'id.'

mura 'many', 'bundle', 'group'. Attested in: MYS 14.3404 (Kamitukɛno), MYS 14.3530 (unidentified), MYS 20.4390 (Simotupusa). Cf. WOJ *mura* 'id.'

muranapɛ- 'to perform divination'. Attested in: MYS 14.3418 (Kamitukɛno). Cf. WOJ *uranap(ɛ)-*, MJ *uranape-* 'id.' The correspondence EOJ *m-* : MJ *Ø-* is irregular.

murasaki 'gromwell'. Attested in: MYS 14.3500 (unidentified). Cf. WOJ *murasaki* 'id.'

Muraⁿzi (p.n.). Attested in: MYS 20.4338 (Suruⁿga).

muro 'room, one-room house'. Attested in: MYS 14.3506 (unidentified), MYS 14.3543 (unidentified). Cf. WOJ *muro* 'id.'

musumb- 'to tie'. Attested in: MYS 14.3426 (Mitinəku). Cf. WOJ *musumb-* 'id.'

muta 'with' (postposition). Attested in: MYS 20.4321 (Təpotuapumi). See also EOJ *mita* 'id.' Cf. WOJ *muta* 'id.'

Muⁿza (p.n.) < Ainu *mun* 'unedible grass' + *sa* 'shore, plain'. Attested in: postscript to MYS 20.4355 (Kamitupusa). See also Muⁿzasi.

Muⁿzasi (p.n.) < Ainu *mun* 'unedible grass'[4] + *sa* 'shore, plain' + *-hi* third person singular possessive, i.e. 'grass plain' or 'grass shore'. Attested in: 14.3362a (Saŋgamu), MYS 14.3374 (Muⁿzasi), MYS 14.3375 (Muⁿzasi), MYS 14.3376 (Muⁿzasi), MYS 14.3376a (Muⁿzasi), MYS 14.3377 (Muⁿzasi), MYS 14.3379 (Muⁿzasi). See also Muⁿza.

N

na 'name'. Attested in: MYS 14.3374 (Muⁿzasi), MYS 14.3394 (Pitati). Cf. WOJ *na* 'id.'

na 'you'. Attested in: FK 8 (Pitati), MYS 14.3382 (Kamitupusa), MYS 14.3383 (Kamitupusa), MYS 14.3425 (Simotukɛno), MYS 14.3468 (unidentified), MYS 14.3478 (unidentified), MYS 14.3493 (unidentified), MYS 14.3494 (unidentified), MYS 14.3546 (unidentified), MYS 14.3556 (unidentified), MYS 20.4347 (Kamitupusa), AAU 2 (Saŋgamu). Cf. WOJ *na* 'id.' < OK *ne* 'id.' (cf. MK *ne* 'id.')

na 'I'. Attested in: MYS 14.3450 (unidentified), MYS 16.3885 (unidentified). Cf. WOJ *na* 'id.' < OK *na* 'id.' (cf. MK *na* 'id.')

na 'river' < Ainu *nay* 'id.' Attested in: MYS 14.3401 (Kamitukɛno).

na- 'not exist, no'. Attested in: FK 3 (Pitati), MYS 14.3379 (Muⁿzasi), MYS 14.3405a (Kamitukɛno), MYS 14.3463 (unidentified), MYS 14.3495 (unidentified), MYS 14.3504 (unidentified), MYS 14.3533 (unidentified), MYS 20.4321 (Təpotuapumi), MYS 20.4330 (Saŋgamu), MYS 20.4353 (Kamitupusa), MYS 20.4373 (Simotukɛno), MYS 20.4379 (Simotukɛno), MYS 20.4381 (Simotukɛno), MYS 20.4401 (Sinanu), KKWKS 1097 (Kapi). Cf. WOJ *na-* 'id.'

naᵐbik- 'to stretch out'. Attested in: MYS 14.3562 (unidentified). Cf. WOJ *naᵐbik-* 'id.'

naⁿde- 'to stroke'. Attested in: MYS 20.4346 (Suruŋga), MYS 20.4356 (Kamitupusa). Cf. WOJ *naⁿde-* 'to stroke', 'to pat'.

naŋga- 'to be long'. Attested in: MYS 20.4394 (Simotupusa). Cf. WOJ *naŋga-* 'id.'

naŋgati 'length'. Attested in: MYS 20.4341 (Suruŋga). Cf. WOJ *naŋgate* 'id.'

naŋgɛk- 'to lament'. Attested in: MYS 14.3474 (unidentified), MYS 14.3524 (unidentified), MYS 16.3885 (unidentified). Cf. WOJ *naŋgɛk-* 'id.'

naŋgəya 'soft'. Attested in: MYS 14.3499 (unidentified). Cf. WOJ *naŋgo ~ naŋgoya* 'id.'

naŋgisa 'shore'. Attested in: MYS 20.4383 (Simotukɛno). Cf. WOJ *naŋgisa* 'id.'

naŋgï 'water leek'. Attested in: MYS 14.3415 (Kamitukɛno), MYS 14.3576 (unidentified). Cf. WOJ *naŋgï* 'id.'

nak- 'to cry'. MYS 16.3878 (Noto). Cf. WOJ *nak-* 'id.'

---

4 Ainu strictly differentiates between two types of grass: *kina* 'edible grass' and *mun* 'unedible grass'.

naka 'middle', 'inside'. Attested in: MYS 14.3445 (unidentified), MYS 14.3458 (unidentified), MYS 14.3463 (unidentified), MYS 20.4350 (Kamitupusa), MYS 20.4377 (Simotukɛno). Cf. WOJ *naka* 'id.'

Nakayama (p.n.). Attested in: KKWKS 1097 (Kapi).

nakɛ- 'to cry', to weep', 'to make someone cry'. MYS 14.3458 (unidentified), MYS 14.3485 (unidentified), MYS 14.3521 (unidentified), MYS 14.3522 (unidentified), MYS 20.4356 (Kamitupusa), MYS 20.4401 (Sinanu). Cf. WOJ *nakɛ-* 'id.'

nam- 'to stand in line'. Attested in: MYS 20.4375 (Simotukɛno). Cf. WOJ *nam-* 'id.'

namasu 'sashimi'. Attested in: MYS 16.3885 (unidentified). No reliable phonographic examples of WOJ *namasu* 'id.'

nami 'wave' (n.). Attested in: MYS 14.3349 (Simotupusa), MYS 14.3385 (Simotupusa), MYS 14.3413 (Kamitukɛno), MYS 14.3551 (unidentified), MYS 20.4379 (Simotukɛno), MYS 20.4385 (Simotupusa), MYS 20.4389 (Simotupusa). Cf. WOJ *nami* 'id.'

namï- 'to lick', 'to taste'. Attested in: 14.3460 (unidentified). Cf. WOJ *namɛ-* 'id.'

nana 'seven'. Attested in: MYS 16.3885 (unidentified), MYS 20.4431 (unidentified), AAU 2 (Saŋgamu). Cf. WOJ *nana* 'id.'

nani 'what'. Attested in: MYS 20.4323 (Təpotuapumi). Cf. WOJ *nani* 'id.'

Nanipa (p.n.). Attested in: MYS 20.4329 (Saŋgamu), MYS 20.4330 (Saŋgamu), MYS 20.4355 (Kamitupusa), MYS 20.4363 (Pitati), MYS 20.4365 (Pitati), MYS 20.4380 (Simotukɛno), MYS 20.4404 (Kamitukɛno).

napa 'rope'. Attested in: MYS 20.4429 (unidentified). Cf. WOJ *napa* 'id.'

napɛ ~ napa- 'seedling'. Attested in: MYS 14.3418 (Kamitukɛno), MYS 14.3576 (unidentified). Cf. WOJ *napɛ* 'id.'

napo 'still'. Attested in: MYS 20.4351 (Kamitupusa). Cf. WOJ *napo* 'id.'

nar- 'to become', 'to be'. Attested in: MYS 14.3370 (Saŋgamu), MYS 14.3395 (Pitati), MYS 14.3487 (unidentified), MYS 14.3536 (unidentified), MYS 14.3543 (unidentified), MYS 14.3565 (unidentified), MYS 20.4347 (Kamitupusa), MYS 20.4355 (Kamitupusa), MYS 20.4382 (Simotukɛno), MYS 20.4388 (Simotupusa), MYS 20.4405 (Kamitukɛno). Cf. WOJ *nar-* 'id.'

nar- 'to sound'. Attested in: MYS 14.3548 (unidentified), MYS 20.4430 (unidentified). Cf. WOJ *nar-* 'id.'

nar- 'to get used', 'to be well worn'. Attested in: MYS 14.3576 (unidentified). Cf. WOJ *nar-* 'id.'

nar- 'to manage household affairs'. Attested in: MYS 20.4364 (Pitati), MYS 20.4386 (Simotupusa). Cf. WOJ *nar-* 'id.'

nara 'oak'. Attested in: MYS 14.3424 (Simotukɛno). Cf. WOJ *nara* 'id.'

nara^mbe- 'to stand side by side'. Cf. WOJ *nara^mbe-* 'id.' Attested in: MYS 14.3450 (unidentified). Cf. WOJ *nara^mbɛ-* 'id.'

naras- 'to flatten'. Attested in: MYS 14.3546 (unidentified). Cf. WOJ *naras-* 'id.'

nare 'you'. Attested in: MYS 20.4418 (Mu{ⁿ}zasi). Cf. WOJ *nare* 'id.'

nari 'daily chores'. Attested in: MYS 16.3865 (unidentified). Cf. WOJ *nari* 'id.'

nas- 'to make'. Attested in: MYS 14.3456 (unidentified). Cf. WOJ *nas-* 'id.'

Nasaka (p.n.). Attested in: MYS 14.3397 (Pitati).

nayam- 'to suffer'. Attested in: MYS 14.3557 (unidentified). See also EOJ *nayum-* 'id.' Cf. WOJ *nayam-* 'id.'

nayum- 'to suffer'. Attested in: MYS 14.3533 (unidentified). See also EOJ *nayam-* 'id.' Cf. WOJ *nayam-* 'id.'

ne 'peak', 'summit'. Attested in: FK 2 (Pitati), FK 3 (Pitati), MYS 14.3351 (Pitati), MYS 14.3358b (Suruⁿga), MYS 14.3370 (Saⁿgamu), MYS 14.3382 (Kamitupusa), MYS 14.3383 (Kamitupusa), MYS 14.3388 (Pitati), MYS 14.3392 (Pitati), MYS 14.3394 (Pitati), MYS 14.3395 (Pitati), MYS 14.3408 (Kamitukɛno), MYS 14.3411 (Kamitukɛno), MYS 14.3412 (Kamitukɛno), MYS 14.3423 (Kamitukɛno), MYS 14.3426 (Simotukɛno), MYS 14.3448 (Kamitukɛno), MYS 14.3478 (unidentified), MYS 14.3511 (unidentified), MYS 14.3512 (unidentified), MYS 14.3514 (unidentified), MYS 14.3515 (unidentified), MYS 14.3516 (unidentified), MYS 16.3880 (Noto), MYS 20.4345 (Suruⁿga), MYS 20.4367 (Pitati), MYS 20.4369 (Pitati), MYS 20.4380 (Simotukɛno), MYS 20.4421 (Mu{ⁿ}zasi), AAU 1 (Saⁿgamu), KKWKS 1097 (Kapi). Also attested as *mi-ne* 'HON-peak' with an honorific prefix *mi-*. Cf. WOJ *ne*, MDJ *mine* (with a petrified honorific prefix *mi-*) 'id.'

ne 'root'. Attested in: MYS 14.3399 (Sinanu), MYS 14.3408 (Kamitukɛno), MYS 14.3500 (unidentified). Cf. WOJ *ne* 'id.'

ne 'sound'. Attested in: MYS 14.3458 (unidentified), MYS 14.3485 (unidentified). Cf. WOJ *ne* 'id.'

ne- 'to sleep'. Attested in: FK3 (Pitati), MYS 14.3366 (Saⁿgamu), MYS 14.3370 (Saⁿgamu), MYS 14.3388 (Pitati), MYS 14.3404 (Kamitukɛno), MYS 14.3408 (Kamitukɛno), MYS 14.3409 (Kamitukɛno), MYS 14.3414 (Kamitukɛno), MYS 14.3461 (unidentified), MYS 14.3465 (unidentified), MYS 14.3466 (unidentified), MYS 14.3473 (unidentified), MYS 14.3482a (unidentified), MYS 14.3487 (unidentified), MYS 14.3489 (unidentified), MYS 14.3494 (unidentified), MYS 14.3395 (Pitati), MYS 14.3499 (unidentified), MYS 14.3500 (unidentified), MYS 14.3504 (unidentified), MYS 14.3509 (unidentified), MYS 14.3514 (unidentified), MYS 14.3518 (unidentified), MYS 14.3522 (unidentified), MYS 14.3525 (unidentified), MYS 14.3529 (unidentified), MYS 14.3543 (unidentified), MYS 14.3544 (unidentified), MYS 14.3553 (unidentified), MYS 14.3555 (unidentified), MYS 14.3556 (unidentified), MYS 14.3562 (unidentified), MYS 14.3565 (unidentified), MYS 20.4321 (Təpotuapumi), MYS 20.4348 (Kamitupusa), MYS 20.4351 (Kamitupusa), MYS 20.4380 (Simotukɛno), MYS 20.4394 (Simotupusa), MYS 20.4416 (Mu{ⁿ}zasi), MYS 20.4420 (Mu{ⁿ}zasi), MYS 20.4422 (Mu{ⁿ}zasi), MYS 20.4428 (unidentified). Cf. WOJ *ne-* 'id.'

nemokərə 'cordial'. Attested in: MYS 14.3410 (Kamitukɛno). Cf. WOJ *nemokərə* 'id.'

nerap- 'to watch'. Attested in: MYS 14.3529 (unidentified). Cf. WOJ *nerap-* 'id.'

nəm- 'to drink'. Attested in: MYS 20.4322 (Təpotuapumi). Cf. WOJ *nəm-* 'id.'

nər- 'to say', 'to tell'. Attested in: MYS 14.3374 (Muⁿzasi), MYS 14.3425 (Simotukɛno), MYS 3469 (unidentified), MYS 14.3488 (unidentified). Cf. WOJ *nər-* 'id.'

nər- 'to ride, to embark'. Attested in: MYS 14.3466 (unidentified), MYS 14.3517 (unidentified), MYS 20.4381 (Simotukɛno). Cf. WOJ *nər-* 'id.'

nət- 'to fill'. Attested in: 14.3444 (unidentified). No apparent WOJ cognates (cf. WOJ *mit-* 'id.'[5]).

niⁿgər- 'to be muddy'. Attested in: MYS 14.3544 (unidentified). Cf. WOJ *niⁿgər-* 'id.'

niko 'soft'. Attested in: MYS 14.3370 (Saⁿgamu). Cf. WOJ *niko, niki* < *nikoy 'soft', 'gentle'.

nino 'cloth'. Attested in: MYS 14.3351 (Pitati), MYS 14.3513 (unidentified). Cf. MJ *nuno* 'id.'

nipa 'garden'. Attested in: MYS 20.4350 (Kamitupusa).

nipasi- 'to be sudden'. Attested in: MYS 20.4389 (Simotupusa). Cf. WOJ *nipaka* 'sudden'.

Nipɛ (p.n.) < Ainu *nipet* 'wood river' (*ni* 'tree, wood' + *pet* 'river'). Attested in MYS 20.4324 (Təpotuapumi).

nipi 'new'. Attested in: MYS 14.3452 (unidentified), MYS 14.3506 (unidentified), MYS 14.3537a (unidentified). Cf. WOJ *nipi* 'id.'

Nipita (p.n.). Attested in: MYS 14.3408 (Kamitukɛno), MYS 14.3436 (Kamitukɛno).

Nipu (p.n.) < Ainu place name Nipu 'storage in the forest on the river bank for storing frozen salmon' (< *ni* 'tree' + *pu* 'storage'). Attested in: MYS 14.3560 (unidentified).

nipu 'new'. Attested in: 14.3460 (unidentified). The vowel correspondence in the second syllable is puzzling, but it could potentially point to PJ *mipoy 'new' (initial *m- reconstructed on the basis of Ryūkyūan data). Cf. WOJ *nipi* 'id.'

nisiki 'brocade'. Attested in: MYS 14.3465 (unidentified). Cf. WOJ *nisiki* 'id.'

no 'field'. Attested in: MYS 14.3374 (Muⁿzasi), MYS 14.3375 (Muⁿzasi), MYS 14.3376 (Muⁿzasi), MYS 14.3376a (Muⁿzasi), MYS 14.3377 (Muⁿzasi), MYS 14.3379 (Muⁿzasi), MYS 14.3434 (Kamıtukɛno), MYS 14.3452 (unidentified), MYS 14.3463 (unidentified), MYS 14.3520 (unidentified), MYS 14.3525 (unidentified), MYS 14.3529 (unidentified), MYS 14.3532 (unidentified), MYS 20.4344 (Suruⁿga), MYS 20.4417 (Muⁿzasi). See also EOJ *nu* 'id.' Cf. WOJ *no* 'id.'

noⁿgan-ape- 'to flow constantly'. Attested in: MYS 14.3476 (unidentified), 14.3476a (unidentified). Cf. WOJ *naⁿgar-apɛ-* 'to flow constantly, to pass [of time]'.

noⁿzi 'rainbow'. Attested in: MYS 14.3414 (Kamitukɛno). Cf. WOJ *niⁿzi* 'id.'

nu 'field'. Attested in: MYS 20.4387 (Simotupusa). See also EOJ *no* 'id.' Cf. WOJ *no* 'id.'

nuk- 'to pierce', 'to insert'. Attested in: MYS 20.4363 (Pitati), MYS 20.4368 (Pitati), MYS 20.4374 (Simotukɛno). Cf. WOJ *nuk-* 'id.'

numa 'marsh'. Attested in: MYS 14.3409 (Kamitukɛno), MYS 14.3415 (Kamitukɛno), MYS 14.3518 (unidentified), MYS 14.3526 (unidentified). Cf. WOJ *nu, numa* 'id.'

---

5 Although the palatalization *m- > n- /_i* is possible, the vowel shift *i > ə* remains unexplained.

nur- 'to scold'. Attested in: MYS 16.3879 (Noto). No WOJ cognates.

nure- 'to get wet'. Attested in: MYS 14.3382 (Kamitupusa). Cf. WOJ *nure-* 'id.'

nuru-nuru 'slippery'. Attested in: MYS 14.3378 (Muⁿzasi), MYS 14.3501 (unidentified). No WOJ cognates.

nusa 'paper or cloth offerings for deities'. Attested in: MYS 20.4391 (Simotupusa), MYS 20.4402 (Sinanu), MYS 20.4426 (unidentified). Cf. WOJ *nusa* 'id.'

O

o-, locative prefix < Ainu *o-* 'id.' Attested in 3473.

oᵐbi 'sash'. Attested in: MYS 20.4422 (Muⁿzasi). See also EOJ *yepi* 'id.' Cf. WOJ *oᵐbi* 'id.'

ok- 'to put', 'to place', 'to leave', 'to leave behind'. Attested in: MYS 14.3437 (Mitinəku), MYS 14.3527 (unidentified), MYS 14.3551 (unidentified), MYS 14.3556 (unidentified), MYS 20.4328 (Saⁿgamu), MYS 20.4341 (Suruⁿga), MYS 20.4385 (Simotupusa), MYS 20.4387 (Simotupusa), MYS 20.4393 (Simotupusa), MYS 20.4401 (Sinanu), MYS 20.4426 (unidentified), MYS 20.4429 (unidentified). Cf. WOJ *ok-* 'id.'

oki 'offing'. Attested in: MYS 14.3524 (unidentified), MYS 14.3527 (unidentified). Cf. WOJ *oki* 'id.'

oku 'future'. Attested in: MYS 14.3410 (Kamitukɛno), MYS 14.3487 (unidentified). Cf. WOJ *oku* 'id.'

okur- 'to send'. Attested in: MYS 20.4375 (Simotukɛno). Cf. WOJ *okur-* 'id.'

okure- 'to be left behind'. Attested in: MYS 20.4429 (unidentified). Cf. WOJ *okure-* 'id.'

omɛ 'face'. Attested in: MYS 20.4342 (Suruⁿga). See also EOJ *omo* and *oməte* 'id.' Cf. WOJ *omə* and *oməte* 'id.'

omə 'mother'. Attested in: MYS 20.4386 (Simotupusa), MYS 20.4401 (Sinanu). See also EOJ *omo* 'id.' Cf. WOJ *omə* 'id.'

omo 'face'. Attested in: MYS 14.3515 (unidentified), MYS 14.3520 (unidentified). See also EOJ *omɛ* and *oməte* 'id.' Cf. WOJ *omə* and *oməte* 'id.'

omo 'mother'. Attested in: MYS 20.4402 (Sinanu). See also EOJ *omə* 'id.' Cf. WOJ *omə* / *amə* 'id.'

omɛp- 'to think', 'to love'. Cf. WOJ *oməp-* 'id.' Attested in: MYS 20.4343 (Suruⁿga). See also EOJ *oməp-* and *omop-* 'id.' Cf. WOJ *oməp-* 'id.'

oməp- 'to think', 'to love'. Attested in: MYS 14.3531 (unidentified), MYS 14.3552 (unidentified), MYS 14.3557 (unidentified), MYS 20.4389 (Simotupusa). See also EOJ *omɛp-* and *omop-* 'id.' Cf. WOJ *oməp-* 'id.'

omop- ~ *[o]mop-* 'to think, to love'. Attested in: MYS 14.3392 (Pitati), MYS 14.3419 (Kamitukɛno), MYS 14.3435 (Kamitukɛno), MYS 14.3451 (unidentified), MYS 14.3481 (unidentified), MYS 14.3494 (unidentified), MYS 14.3496 (unidentified), MYS 14.3503 (unidentified), MYS 14.3504 (unidentified), MYS 14.3511 (unidentified), MYS 14.3514 (unidentified), MYS 14.3522 (unidentified), MYS 14.3528 (unidentified), MYS 14.3552 (unidentified), MYS 14.3564 (unidentified), MYS 14.3572 (unidentified), MYS 16.3865 (unidentified), MYS 20.4426 (Təpotuapumi), MYS 20.4427 (unidentified). See also EOJ oməp- and omɛp- 'id.' Cf. WOJ oməp- 'id.'

omopiⁿdoro (impossible to analyze). Attested in: MYS 14.3419 (Kamitukɛno). No WOJ cognates.

omosiro- 'charming'. Attested in: MYS 14.3452 (unidentified). Cf. WOJ oməsirə- 'id.'

oməte 'face'. Attested in: MYS 20.4367 (Pitati). See also EOJ omɛ and omo 'id.' Cf. WOJ omə and oməte 'id.'

op- 'to grow'. Attested in: MYS 14.3359 (Suruŋga), MYS 14.3359a (Suruŋga), MYS 14.3452 (unidentified), MYS 14.3488 (unidentified), MYS 14.3501 (unidentified), MYS 14.3526 (unidentified). Cf. WOJ opï- 'id.'

op- 'to carry'. Attested in: MYS 14.3566 (unidentified). Cf. WOJ op- 'id.'

opo ~ -[o]po 'big', 'great'. Attested in: MYS 14.3480 (unidentified), MYS 14.3520 (unidentified), MYS 14.3521 (unidentified), MYS 16.3885 (unidentified), MYS 20.4328 (Saŋgamu), MYS 20.4358 (Kamitupusa), MYS 20.4373 (Simotukɛno), MYS 20.4393 (Simotupusa), MYS 20.4394 (Simotupusa), MYS 20.4403 (Sinanu), MYS 20.4414 (Muⁿzasi). Cf. WOJ opo 'id.'

opo kimi 'great lord', 'Emperor'. Attested in: MYS 14.3480 (unidentified), MYS 16.3885 (unidentified), MYS 20.4328 (Saŋgamu), MYS 20.4358 (Kamitupusa), MYS 20.4373 (Simotukɛno), MYS 20.4382 (Simotukɛno), MYS 20.4393 (Simotupusa), MYS 20.4394 (Simotupusa), MYS 20.4403 (Sinanu), MYS 20.4414 (Muⁿzasi). Cf. WOJ opo kimi 'id.'

Opoya (p.n.). Attested in: MYS 14.3378 (Muⁿzasi).

opuse- 'to give order (HON)'. Attested in: MYS 20.4389 (Simotupusa). Cf. WOJ opose- 'id.'

or-ə 'its place' < Ainu or-o 'place-POSS'. Attested in: MYS 20.4363 (Pitati).

os- 'to push'. Attested in: MYS 20.4365 (Pitati). Cf. WOJ os- 'id.'

osə 'late'. Attested in: MYS 14.3493 (unidentified). Cf. WOJ osə 'id.'

osəki 'garment'. Attested in: MYS 14.3509 (unidentified). No apparent WOJ cognates.

osi 'rock', 'rocky shore'. Attested in: MYS 14.3359 (Suruŋga), MYS 14.3359a (Suruŋga). Cf. WOJ isi 'stone', iso 'rock, rocky shore'.

oso^mbur- 'to push and shake'. Attested in: MYS 14.3460 (unidentified). Cf. WOJ oso^mbur- 'id.'

osu 'rock', 'rocky shore'. Attested in: MYS 14.3385 (Simotupusa). Cf. WOJ iso 'id.'

otap- 'to sing'. Attested in: MYS 14.3409 (Kamitukɛno), MYS 14.3518 (unidentified). Cf. WOJ utap- 'id.'

otə 'sound'. Attested in: MYS 14.3387 (Simotupusa), MYS 14.3473 (unidentified), MYS 14.3555 (unidentified). Cf. WOJ otə 'id.'

otəs- 'to drop'. Attested in: MYS 16.3878 (Noto). Cf. WOJ otəs– 'id.'

oti- 'to fall'. Attested in: MYS 14.3392 (Pitati), MYS 20.4418 (Muⁿzasi). Cf. WOJ oti- 'id.'

oya 'parent'. Attested in: MYS 14.3359a (Suru^ŋga), MYS 14.3420 (Muⁿzasi). Cf. WOJ *oya* 'id.'

oyaⁿzi 'same'. Attested in: MYS 14.3464 (unidentified). Cf. WOJ *oyaⁿzi, onaⁿzi* 'id.'

oyi- 'become old'. Attested in: MYS 16.3885 (unidentified). Cf. WOJ *oyi-* 'id.'

P

pa 'side'. Attested in: MYS 20.4428 (unidentified). Cf. WOJ *pe* 'id.'

pa 'wing'. Attested in: FK 9 (Pitati). Cf. WOJ *pa* 'id.', 'feather'.

pa 'year' < Ainu *pa* 'id.' Attested in: MYS 20.4378 (Simotukɛno).

pa 'to find' < Ainu *pa* 'id.' Attested in: 14.3499 (unidentified).

pa 'leaf'. Attested in: MYS 14.3382 (Kamitupusa), MYS 14.3412 (Kamitukɛno), MYS 14.3436 (Kamitukɛno), MYS 14.3504 (unidentified), MYS 14.3572 (unidentified), MYS 20.4431 (unidentified). Cf. WOJ *pa* 'id.'

pa^mbakar- 'to hesitate'. Attested in: MYS 20.4372 (Pitati). Cf. WOJ *pa^mbakar-* 'id.'

paⁿda 'skin'. Attested in: MYS 14.3537a (unidentified), MYS 20.4351 (Kamitupusa), MYS 20.4431 (unidentified). Cf. WOJ *paⁿda* 'id.'

paⁿda susuki (makura-kotoba) Attested in: MYS 14.3506 (unidentified), MYS 14.3565 (unidentified). Cf. WOJ *paⁿda susuki* 'id.'

pa^ŋgas- 'to turn out to graze'. Attested in: MYS 20.4417 (Muⁿzasi). No apparent WOJ cognates.

pak- 'to put', 'to wear', 'to carry'. Attested in: MYS 14.3399 (Sinanu), MYS 14.3437 (Mitinəku), MYS 20.4347 (Kamitupusa), MYS 20.4413 (Muⁿzasi). Cf. WOJ *pak-* 'id.'

paka 'rumor', 'gossip' < Ainu *páhaw* 'id.' Attested in: MYS 14.3385 (Simotupusa).

pakare- 'to be separated'. Attested in: MYS 20.4352 (Kamitupusa). See also EOJ *wakare- ~ wakar-*. Cf. WOJ *wakare-* id.'

pako 'coffer'. Attested in: MYS 16.3885 (unidentified). Cf. WOJ *pako* 'id.', 'box'.

Pakone (p.n.). Attested in: MYS 14.3370 (Sa^ŋgamu).

pam- 'to eat'. Attested in: MYS 14.3532 (unidentified), MYS 14.3537 (unidentified), MYS 14.3537a (unidentified). Cf. WOJ *pam-* 'id.'

pama 'shore', 'seashore'. Attested in: MYS 14.3359 (Suru^ŋga), MYS 14.3359a (Suru^ŋga), MYS 14.3533 (unidentified), MYS 20.4379 (Simotukɛno). Cf. WOJ *pama* 'id.'

pana 'flower'. Attested in: MYS 14.3370 (Sa^ŋgamu), MYS 14.3376 (Muⁿzasi), MYS 14.3376a (Muⁿzasi), MYS 14.3379 (Muⁿzasi), MYS 14.3448 (unidentified), MYS 14.3503 (unidentified), MYS 14.3576 (unidentified), MYS 16.3885 (unidentified), MYS 20.4323 (Təpotuapumi), MYS 20.4325 (Təpotuapumi), MYS 20.4369 (Pitati). Cf. WOJ *pana* 'id.'

panar- ~ *panare* 'to be separated'. Attested in: MYS 14.3480 (unidentified), MYS 20.4338 (Suruⁿga), MYS 20.4414 (Muⁿzasi), MYS 20.4414 (Muⁿzasi), MYS 20.4432 (unidentified). Cf. WOJ *panare-* 'id.'

panari 'maiden'. Attested in: MYS 14.3496 (unidentified). Cf. WOJ *panare* 'id.'

panar-iso 'rocks in the sea not connected to the shore'. Attested in: MYS 20.4338 (Suruⁿga). Cf. WOJ *panare-so* 'id.'

panas- 'to separate'. Attested in: MYS 14.3420 (Kamitukɛno). Cf. WOJ *panas-* 'id.'

Panisina (p.n.). Attested in: MYS 14.3398 (Sinanu).

pap- 'to crawl'. Attested in: MYS 14.3434 (Kamitukɛno), MYS 14.3525 (unidentified), MYS 20.4352 (Kamitupusa), MYS 204421 (Muⁿzasi). Cf. WOJ *pap-* 'id.'

papa 'mother'. Attested in: MYS 14.3359 (Suruⁿga), MYS 14.3529 (unidentified), MYS 16.3880 (Noto), MYS 20.4323 (Təpotuapumi), MYS 20.4325 (Təpotuapumi), MYS 20.4328 (Saⁿgamu), MYS 20.4330 (Saⁿgamu), MYS 20.4337 (Suruⁿga), MYS 20.4338 (Suruⁿga), MYS 20.4340 (Suruⁿga), MYS 20.4342 (Suruⁿga), MYS 20.4344 (Suruⁿga), MYS 20.4346 (Suruⁿga), MYS 20.4348 (Kamitupusa), MYS 20.4356 (Kamitupusa), MYS 20.4392 (Simotupusa), MYS 20.4393 (Simotupusa). Cf. WOJ *papa* 'id.'

papɛ- 'to stretch', 'to make crawl', 'to make someone know of one's love intentions'. Attested in: MYS 14.3411 (Kamitukɛno). Cf. WOJ *papɛ-* 'id.'

papur- 'to spring'. Attested in: MYS 14.3515 (unidentified). Cf. WOJ *papur-* 'to overflow'.

par- 'to clear'. Attested in: MYS 14.3399 (Sinanu), MYS 14.3447 (unidentified). Cf. WOJ *pare-* 'to clear up'.

par- 'to put forth', 'to stretch'. Attested in: MYS 14.3546 (unidentified). Cf. WOJ *par-* 'id.'

para 'field'. Attested in: MYS 14.3378 (Muⁿzasi), MYS 14.3410 (Kamitukɛno), MYS 14.3435 (Kamitukɛno). Cf. WOJ *para* 'id.'

parap- 'to clear'. Attested in: MYS 14.3489 (unidentified). Cf. WOJ *parap-* 'id.'

pari 'alder'. Attested in: MYS 14.3410 (Kamitukɛno), MYS 14.3435 (Kamitukɛno). Cf. WOJ *pari* 'id.'

paru 'needle'. Attested in: 20.4420 (Muⁿzasi). Cf. WOJ *pari* 'id.'

paru 'spring'. Attested in: MYS 14.3504 (unidentified), MYS 14.3532 (unidentified). Cf. WOJ *paru* 'id.'

pasam- 'to hold between', 'to squeeze'. Attested in: MYS 16.3885 (unidentified), MYS 20.4430 (unidentified). Cf. WOJ *pasam-* 'id.'

pasasaⁿgɛ- 'to make someone/something run into'. Attested in: MYS 14.3538a (unidentified). Cf. WOJ *pasase-* 'to make (a horse) run'.

pasi 'bridge'. Attested in: MYS 14.3387 (Simotupusa), MYS 14.3420 (Kamitukɛno), MYS 14.3538 (unidentified). Cf. WOJ *pasi* 'id.'

pasi 'ladder'. Attested in: MYS 16.3878 (Noto), MYS 16.3879 (Noto). Cf. WOJ *pasi* 'id.'

pasi 'middle'. Attested in: MYS 14.3408 (Kamitukɛno). Cf. WOJ *pasi* 'interval', 'between'.

pasira 'pillar'. Attested in: MYS 20.4342 (Suruⁿga). Cf. WOJ *pasira* 'id.'

pate- 'to finish'. Attested in: MYS 16.3885 (unidentified). Cf. WOJ *pate-* 'id.'

patu 'first'. Attested in: MYS 14.3468 (unidentified). Cf. WOJ *patu* 'id.'

patu-patu 'barely'. Attested in: MYS 14.3537 (unidentified), MYS 14.3537a (unidentified). Cf. WOJ *patu-patu* 'id.'

paya 'fast', 'early'. Attested in: FK3 (Pitati), MYS 14.3493 (unidentified), MYS 14.3540 (unidentified), MYS 16.3880 (Noto). Cf. WOJ *paya* 'id.'

payas- 'to glorify'. Attested in: MYS 16.3885 (unidentified). Cf. WOJ *payas-* 'id.'

payasi 'forest'. Attested in: MYS 14.3538a (unidentified). Cf. WOJ *payasi* 'id.'

paⁿzik- 'to take off (a bow-string)'. Attested in: MYS 14.3437 (Mitinəku). Cf. WOJ *paⁿzik-* 'to hit with force', 'to repel'

pe 'side', 'shore'. Attested in: MYS 14.3359 (Suruⁿga), MYS 14.3359a (Suruⁿga), MYS 14.3489 (unidentified), MYS 14.3504 (unidentified), MYS 14.3531 (unidentified), MYS 20.4385 (Simotupusa). See also EOJ *pɛ, pi* 'id.' Cf. WOJ *pe* 'id.'

pe 'leaf'. Attested in: MYS 14.3456 (unidentified). Cf. WOJ *pa* 'id.'

pe 'ship's bow'. Attested in: MYS 20.4359 (Kamitupusa), MYS 20.4389 (Simotupusa). See also EOJ *pɛ* 'id.' Cf. WOJ *pɛ* 'id.'

pe 'vessel'. Attested in: MYS 20.4393 (Simotupusa). Cf. WOJ *pɛ* 'id.'

pe 'layer'. Attested in: MYS 16.3885 (unidentified), MYS 20.4431 (unidentified). Cf. WOJ *pe* 'id.'

peⁿdas- 'to be separated'. Attested in: MYS 14.3445 (unidentified). Cf. WOJ *peⁿdat-* 'id.'

Peⁿguri (p.n.). Attested in: MYS 16.3885 (unidentified).

pɛ 'side', 'shore'. Attested in: MYS 14.3541 (unidentified), MYS 20.4352 (Kamitupusa), MYS 20.4359 (Kamitupusa), MYS 20.4379 (Simotukɛno), MYS 20.4422 (Muⁿzasi). See also EOJ *pe, pi* 'id.' Cf. WOJ *pe* 'id.'

pɛ 'ship's bow'. Attested in: MYS 20.4359 (Kamitupusa). See also EOJ *pe* 'id.' Cf. WOJ *pɛ* 'id.'

pi 'side', 'shore'. Attested in: MYS 14.3385 (Simotupusa). See also EOJ *pe, pɛ* 'id.' Cf. WOJ *pe* 'id.'

pi 'sun', 'day'. Attested in: MYS 14.3402 (Kamitukɛno), MYS 14.3407 (Kamitukɛno), MYS 14.3461 (unidentified), MYS 14.3561 (unidentified), MYS 20.4329 (Saⁿgamu), MYS 20.4330 (Saⁿgamu), MYS 20.4353 (Kamitupusa), MYS 20.4378 (Simotukɛno), MYS 20.4407 (Kamitukɛno). Cf. WOJ *pi* 'id.'

pik- 'to pull', 'to invite', 'to drag', 'to draw'. Attested in: MYS 14.3378 (Muⁿzasi), MYS 14.3397 (Pitati), MYS 14.3431 (Saⁿgamu), MYS 14.3501 (unidentified), MYS 14.3531 (unidentified), MYS 14.3536 (unidentified). Cf. WOJ *pik-* 'id.'

pikï 'low'. Attested in: MYS 16.3885 (unidentified). Cf. WOJ *piku-* 'id.'

pimə 'cord'. Attested in: MYS 14.3370 (Saⁿgamu). See also EOJ *pimo, pïmo* 'id.' Cf. WOJ *pimo* 'id.'

pimo 'cord'. Attested in: MYS 14.3361 (Saⁿgamu), MYS 14.3426 (Mitinəku), MYS 14.3465 (unidentified), MYS 14.3483 (unidentified), MYS 14.3551 (unidentified), MYS 20.4416

(Muⁿzasi), MYS 20.4420 (Muⁿzasi), MYS 20.4427 (unidentified). See also EOJ *pimə, pümo* 'id.' Cf. WOJ *pimo* 'id.'

pimɛ 'arrow'. Attested in: MYS 16.3885 (unidentified). No WOJ cognates.

pinzi 'sandbank' < Ainu *pis* 'shore', *pis-i* 'its shore'. Attested in: MYS 14.3448 (unidentified).

pira 'flat', 'ordinary'. Attested in: MYS 14.3551 (unidentified). WOJ *pira* 'id.'

pirə 'oak' < Ainu *pero* or *pero-ni* 'id.' Attested in: MYS 14.3538 (unidentified).

pirə- 'to be wide'. Attested in: MYS 14.3434 (Kamitukɛno). WOJ *pirə* 'id.'

pirəp- 'to pick up', 'to gather'. Attested in: MYS 14.3400 (Sinanu). See also EOJ *pirip-* 'id.' Cf. WOJ *pirip-* 'id.'

pirip- 'to pick up', 'to gather'. Attested in: MYS 16.3880 (Noto). See also EOJ *pirəp-* 'id.' Cf. WOJ *pirip-* 'id.'

piru 'day time'. Attested in: MYS 14.3483 (unidentified), MYS 20.4369 (Pitati). Cf. WOJ *piru* 'id.'

Pita (p.n.) < Ainu *pitar* 'stone field' < *pit-tar* 'pebbles-continue one after another'. Attested in: MYS 14.3563 (unidentified).

pita 'one'. Attested in: MYS 14.3435 (Kamitukɛno). See also EOJ *pitə* 'id.' Cf. WOJ *pitə* 'id.'

Pitati (p.n.). Attested in: MYS 14.3397 (Pitati), MYS 20.4366 (Pitati).

pitə 'one'. Atteted in: MYS 14.3405 (Kamitukɛno), MYS 14.3512 (unidentified), MYS 14.3562 (unidentified), MYS 16.3885 (unidentified). See also EOJ *pita* 'id.' Cf. WOJ *pitə* 'id.'

pitə 'person'. Attested in: MYS 14.3349 (Simotupusa), MYS 14.3354 (Təpotuapumi), MYS 14.3398 (Sinanu), MYS 14.3405a (Kamitukɛno), MYS 14.3409 (Kamitukɛno), MYS 14.3446 (unidentified), MYS 14.3464 (unidentified), MYS 14.3472 (unidentified), MYS 14.3500 (unidentified), MYS 14.3502 (unidentified), MYS 14.3518 (unidentified), MYS 14.3533 (unidentified), MYS 14.3539 (unidentified), MYS 14.3541 (unidentified), MYS 14.3548 (unidentified), MYS 14.3552 (unidentified), MYS 14.3556 (unidentified), MYS 14.3557 (unidentified), MYS 20.4329 (Saŋgamu), MYS 20.4353 (Kamitupusa), MYS 20.4375 (Simotukɛno), MYS 20.4382 (Simotukɛno), MYS 20.4406 (Kamitukɛno). Cf. WOJ *pitə* 'id.'

pï 'dry'. Attested in: MYS 14.3503 (unidentified). WOJ *pï-* 'to dry'.

pümo 'cord'. Attested in: MYS 20.4404 (Kamitukɛno), MYS 20.4405 (Kamitukɛno). See also EOJ *pimo, pimə* 'id.' Cf. WOJ *pimo* 'id.'

po 'ear (of a plant)'. Attested in: MYS 14.3506 (unidentified). Cf. WOJ *po* 'id.'

poⁿdo 'time'. Attested in: MYS 16.3885 (unidentified). See also EOJ *poto* 'id.' Cf. WOJ *poⁿdo* 'id.'

pomɛ- 'to bless'. Attested in: MYS 20.4342 (Suruŋga). Cf. WOJ *pomɛ-* 'id.'

popom- 'to hold inside [one's mouth]', 'to be still in the buds'. Attested in: MYS 20.4387 (Simotupusa). See also EOJ *pupum-* 'id.' Cf. WOJ *pupum-* 'id.'

por- 'to want'. Attested in: MYS 14.3383 (Kamitupusa). Cf. WOJ *por-* 'id.'

pos- 'to dry'. Attested in: MYS 14.3351 (Pitati). Cf. WOJ *pos-* 'id.'

poto 'time'. Attested in: MYS 14.3389 (Pitati). See also EOJ *poⁿdo* 'id.' Cf. WOJ *poⁿdo* 'id.'

pu 'fire'. Attested in: MYS 20.4419 (Muⁿzasi). Cf. WOJ *pï ~ po-* 'id.'

pu 'mesh'. Attested in: MYS 14.3524 (unidentified). Cf. WOJ *pu* 'id.'

puⁿdi 'wisteria'. Attested in: MYS 14.3504 (unidentified). Cf. WOJ *puⁿdi* 'id.'

puk- 'to blow'. Attested in: MYS 14.3560 (unidentified), MYS 14.3564 (unidentified), MYS 14.3572 (unidentified), MYS 20.4353 (Kamitupusa), MYS 20.4371 (Pitati). Cf. WOJ *puk-* 'id.'

puka- 'to be deep'. Attested in: MYS 20.4424 (Muⁿzasi). Cf. WOJ *puka-* 'id.'

pum- 'to step', 'to tread'. Attested in: MYS 14.3399 (Sinanu), MYS 14.3400 (Sinanu), MYS 14.3425 (Simotukɛno). Cf. WOJ *pum-* 'id.'

pumite 'writing brush'. Attested in: MYS 16.3885 (unidentified). Cf. WOJ *pumite* 'id.'

puna 'boat'. Attested in: MYS 14.3349 (Simotupusa), MYS 14.3420 (Kamitukɛno), MYS 20.4329 (Saⁿgamu), MYS 20.4365 (Pitati), MYS 20.4381 (Simotukɛno), MYS 20.4383 (Simotukɛno). See also EOJ *pune* 'id.' Cf. WOJ *pune, puna-* 'id.'

pune 'boat'. Attested in: MYS 14.3349 (Simotupusa), MYS 14.3401 (Sinanu), MYS 14.3431 (Saⁿgamu), MYS 14.3450 (unidentified), MYS 14.3556 (unidentified), MYS 14.3557 (unidentified), MYS 20.4359 (Kamitupusa), MYS 20.4363 (Pitati), MYS 20.4368 (Pitati), MYS 20.4384 (Simotupusa), MYS 20.4389 (Simotupusa). See also EOJ *puna* 'id.' Cf. WOJ *pune, puna-* 'id.'

Pupa (p.n.). Attested in: MYS 20.4372 (Pitati).

pupum- 'to hold inside [one's mouth]', 'to be still in the buds'. Attested in: MYS 14.3572 (unidentified). See also EOJ *popom-* 'id.' Cf. WOJ *pupum-* 'id.'

pur- 'to wave'. Attested in: FK 7 (Pitati), MYS 14.3376 (Muⁿzasi), MYS 14.3389 (Simotupusa), MYS 14.3402 (Kamitukɛno), MYS 20. 4379 (Simotukɛno), MYS 20.4423 (Muⁿzasi). Cf. WOJ *pur-* 'id.'

pur- 'to fall (of precipitation)'. Attested in: MYS 14.3358b (Suruⁿga), MYS 14.3351 (Pitati), MYS 14.3423 (Kamitukɛno), MYS 20.4370 (Pitati). Cf. WOJ *pur-* 'id.'

pur- 'to touch'. Attested in: MYS 20.4328 (Saⁿgamu). See also EOJ *pure-* 'id.' See also EOJ *pure-* 'id.' Cf. WOJ *pur-* 'id.'

pure- 'to touch'. Attested in: MYS 14.3537a (unidentified), MYS 20.4418 (Muⁿzasi). See also EOJ *pur-* 'id.' Cf. WOJ *pure-* 'id.'

purisakɛ- 'to look up'. Attested in: MYS 20.4367 (Pitati). Cf. WOJ *purisakɛ-* 'id.'

puru 'old'. Attested in: MYS 14.3452 (unidentified). Cf. WOJ *puru* 'id.'

pus- 'to lie down'. Attested in: MYS 14.3530 (unidentified), KKWKS 1097 (Kapï). Cf. WOJ *pus-* 'id.'

pusuma 'cover'. Attested in: MYS 14.3354 (Təpotuapumi), MYS 14.3509 (unidentified). Cf. WOJ *pusuma* 'id.'

pususa 'many'. Attested in: MYS 14.3484 (unidentified). No WOJ cognates.

Puta (p.n.). Attested in: MYS 20.4382 (Simotukɛno).

puta- 'two'. Attested in: MYS 14.3526 (unidentified), MYS 14.3544 (unidentified), MYS 16.3885 (unidentified), MYS 20.4345 (Suruⁿga). Cf. WOJ *puta* 'id.'

Puⁿzi (p.n.) < EOJ *pu* 'fire' + *nusi* 'master'. Attested in: MYS 14.3355 (Suruⁿga), MYS 14.3356 (Suruⁿga), MYS 14.3357 (Suruⁿga), MYS 14.3358, MYS 14.3358b (Suruⁿga).⁶

S

sa 'arrow'. Attested in: MYS 20.4430 (unidentified). Cf. WOJ *sa* < MK *sál* 'arrow'.
sa- 'fifth' (lunar month). Attested in: MYS 14.3394 (Pitati). Cf. WOJ *sa-* 'id.'
sa 'thus'. Attested in: MYS 14.3504 (unidentified). Cf. WOJ *sa* 'id.'
saᵐbï- 'to be like'. Attested in: MYS 20.4380 (Simotukɛno). Cf. WOJ *saᵐbï-* 'id.'
saⁿdamɛ- 'to decide'. Attested in: MYS 14.3418 (Kamitukɛno). Cf. WOJ *saⁿdamɛ-* 'id.'
Saⁿgamu (p.n.). Attested in: AAU 1 (Saⁿgamu).
sak- 'to bloom'. MYS 14. 3504 (unidentified), MYS 14.3551 (unidentified), MYS 16.3885 (unidentified), MYS 20.4323 (Təpotuapumi). Cf. WOJ *sak-* 'id.'
sak- ~ sakɛ- 'to separate'. Attested in: MYS 14.3420 (Kamitukɛno), MYS 14.3465 (unidentified), MYS 14.3502 (unidentified). Cf. WOJ *sak- ~ sakɛ-* 'id.'
saka 'slope'. Attested in: MYS 20.4372 (Pitati), MYS 20.4402 (Sinanu), MYS 20.4407 (Kamitukɛno), MYS 20.4423 (Muⁿzasi), MYS 20.4424 (Muⁿzasi). Cf. WOJ *saka* 'id.'
saka- 'rice wine'. Attested in: MYS 16.3879 (Noto). Cf. WOJ *sakɛ ~ saka-* 'id.'
saka (a measure of length). Attested in: MYS 14.3414 (Kamitukɛno), MYS 14.3527 (unidentified). Cf. WOJ *saka* 'id.'
sakar- 'to be separated'. Attested in: MYS 14.3412, 14.3420 (Kamitukɛno), MYS 14.3502 (unidentified). Cf. WOJ *saka* 'id.'
sake-ku 'safely'. Attested in: MYS 20.4372 (Pitati). See also EOJ *sakɛ-ku, sa-ku* 'id.' Cf. WOJ *saki-ku* 'id.'
sakɛ-ku 'safely'. Attested in: MYS 20.4368 (Pitati). See also EOJ *sake-ku, sa-ku* 'id.' Cf. WOJ *saki-ku* 'id.'
saki 'protrusion, cape'. Attested in: MYS 14.3394 (Pitati), MYS 20.4372 (Pitati). Cf. WOJ *saki* 'id.'
saki 'ahead'. Attested in: MYS 20.4385 (Simotupusa). WOJ *saki* 'id.'
sakiməri 'borderguard'. Attested in: MYS 20.4382 (Simotukɛno). See also EOJ *sakimori, sakimuri*. Cf. WOJ *sakimori* 'id.'
sakimori 'borderguard'. Attested in: MYS 20.4381 (Simotukɛno). See also EOJ *sakiməri, sakimuri*. Cf. WOJ *sakimori* 'id.'

---

6 This etymology for Mt. Fuji (OJ *puⁿzi*) was provided in the introduction to book fourteen (Vovin 2012: 12). However, now I think that there is a better EOJ etymology: EOJ *pu* 'fire' (20.4419) + *-ⁿzi* < *-nusi* 'master', i.e. 'master of the fire'. The details of argumentation are in Vovin (2018: 85–86).

sakimuri 'borderguard'. Attested in: MYS 20.4364 (Pitati). See also EOJ *sakiməri, sakimori*. Cf. WOJ *sakimori* 'id.'

sa-ku 'safely'. Attested in: MYS 20.4346 (Suruⁿga). See also *sake-ku ~ sakɛ-ku* 'id.' Cf. WOJ *saki-ku* 'id.'

samu- 'be cold'. Attested in: MYS 20.4351 (Kamitupusa). Cf. WOJ *samu-* 'id.'

Sanatura (p.n.). Attested in: MYS 14.3451 (unidentified).

Sano (p.n.). Attested in: MYS 14.3418 (Kamitukɛno), MYS 14.3420 (Kamitukɛno), MYS 14.3473 (unidentified).

sapaⁿda 'many'. Attested in: MYS 14.3354 (Təpotuapumi), MYS 14.3395 (Pitati). Cf. WOJ *sapa* 'id.'

sape- 'to obstruct'. Attested in: MYS 20.4432 (unidentified). Cf. WOJ *sapɛ-* 'id.'

sar- 'to leave', 'to go', 'to come'. Attested in: MYS 14.3513 (unidentified). Cf. WOJ *sar-* 'id.'

sara 'again'. Attested in: MYS 20.4349 (Kamitupusa). Cf. WOJ *sara* 'in addition'.

sas- 'to set'. Attested in: MYS 14.3361 (Simotupusa). No apparent WOJ cognates.

sas- 'to spread'. Attested in: MYS 16.3885 (unidentified). Cf. WOJ *sas-* 'id.'

sas- 'to point', 'to insert', 'to appoint'. Attested in: MYS 14.3407 (Kamitukɛno), MYS 20.4350 (Kamitupusa), MYS 20.4366 (Pitati), MYS 20.4374 (Simotukɛno), MYS 20.4382 (Simotukɛno), MYS 20.4390 (Simotupusa). Cf. WOJ *sas-* 'id.'

sasa 'bamboo grass'. Attested in: MYS 14.3382 (Kamitupusa), MYS 20.4431 (unidentified). Cf. WOJ *sasa* 'id.'

sasaⁿgə- 'to lift up high in one's hands'. Attested in: MYS 20.4325 (Təpotuapumi). Cf. WOJ *sasaⁿgɛ-* 'id.'

sasara 'small'. Attested in: MYS 14.3446 (unidentified). Cf. WOJ *sasara, saⁿzare* 'id.'

sasup- 'to invite'. Attested in: MYS 16.3879 (Noto). Cf. MJ *sasop-* 'id.'

sato 'village'. Attested in: MYS 14.3463 (unidentified), MYS 20.4341 (Suruⁿga). Cf. WOJ *sato* 'id.'

satu-ya 'lucky arrow'. Attested in: MYS 20.4374 (Simotukɛno). Cf. WOJ *satu-ya* 'hunting arrow'.

satuki 'fifth month'. Attested in: MYS 16.3885 (unidentified). Cf. WOJ *satukï* 'id.'

sawak- 'to make noise, to clamour'. Attested in: MYS 14.3349 (Simotupusa), MYS 20.4354 (Kamitupusa), MYS 20.4364 (Pitati). Cf. WOJ *sawak-* 'id.'

Sawatari (p.n.). Attested in: MYS 14.3540 (unidentified).

sawaw- 'to make noise'. Attestd in: MYS 14.3552 (unidentified). Cf. WOJ *sawak-* 'id.'

sawe-sawe 'hustle and bustle'. Attested in: MYS 14.3481 (unidentified). Cf. WOJ *sawi-sawi* 'id.'

Saya (p.n.). Attested in: KKWKS 1097 (Kapi).

saya 'clear'. Attested in: MYS 14.3402 (Kamitukɛno), MYS 20.4423 (Muⁿzasi), KKWKS 1097 (Kapi). See also EOJ *sayaka* 'id.' Cf. WOJ *saya* 'id.'

sayaka 'clear'. Attested in: MYS 20.4424 (Muⁿzasi). See also EOJ *saya* 'id.' Cf. WOJ *sayaka* 'id.'

sayaⁿg- 'to rustle softly', 'to be noisy'. Attested in: FK5 (Pitati), MYS 20.4431 (Suruⁿga). Cf. WOJ *sayaⁿg-* 'id.'

saⁿzaresi 'pebble'. Attested in: MYS 14.3400 (Sinanu). Cf. WOJ *saⁿzare isi* 'id.'

se 'beloved', 'husband'. Attested in: FK 8 (Pitati), MYS 14.3363 (Saⁿgamu), MYS 14.3375 (Muⁿzasi), MYS 14.3379 (Muⁿzasi), MYS 14.3399 (Sinanu), MYS 14.3402 (Kamitukɛno), MYS 14.3405a (Kamitukɛno), MYS 14.3419 (Kamitukɛno), MYS 14.3444 (Kamitukɛno), MYS 14.3445 (unidentified), MYS 14.3458 (unidentified), MYS 14.3460 (unidentified), MYS 14.3463 (unidentified), MYS 14.3469 (unidentified), MYS 14.3483 (unidentified), MYS 14.3536 (unidentified), MYS 14.3544 (unidentified), MYS 14.3548 (unidentified), MYS 14.3549 (unidentified), MYS 14.3551 (unidentified), MYS 16.3885 (unidentified), MYS 20.4413 (Muⁿzasi), MYS 20.4416 (Muⁿzasi), MYS 20.4422 (Muⁿzasi), MYS 20.4424 (Muⁿzasi), MYS 20.4426 (unidentified), MYS 20.4428 (unidentified), AAU2 (Saⁿgamu). Cf. WOJ *se* 'id.'

se 'rapids'. Attested in: MYS 14.3413 (Kamitukɛno), MYS 14.3419 (Kamitukɛno), MYS 14.3548 (unidentified), MYS 14.3551 (unidentified). Cf. WOJ *se* 'id.'

se 'fence'. Attested in: MYS 14.3537a (unidentified). No WOJ cognates.

se 'clear'. Attested in: MYS 14.3546 (unidentified). Cf. WOJ *si* 'id.'

se- 'to do'. Attested in: MYS 14.3369 (Saⁿgamu), MYS 14.3376a (Muⁿzasi), MYS 14.3378 (Muⁿzasi), MYS 14.3383 (Kamitupusa), MYS 14.3387 (Simotupusa), MYS 14.3397 (Pitati), MYS 14.3398 (Sinanu), MYS 14.3404 (Kamitukɛno), MYS 14.3405 (Kamitukɛno), MYS 14.3410, MYS 14.3418 (Kamitukɛno), MYS 14.3419 (Kamitukɛno), MYS 14.3426 (Simotukɛno), MYS 14.3434 (Kamitukɛno), MYS 14.3436 (Kamitukɛno), MYS 14.3452, MYS 14.3465 (unidentified), MYS 14.3484 (unidentified), MYS 14.3517 (unidentified), MYS 14.3524 (unidentified), MYS 14.3526 (unidentified), MYS 14.3538 (unidentified), MYS 14.3538a (unidentified), MYS 14.3539 (unidentified), MYS 14.3544 (unidentified), MYS 14.3556 (unidentified), MYS 14.3557 (unidentified), MYS 16.3878 (Noto), MYS 20.4321 (Təpotuapumi), MYS 20.4323 (Təpotuapumi), MYS 20.4329 (Saⁿgamu), MYS 20.4342 (Suruⁿga), MYS 20.4343 (Suruⁿga), MYS 20.4344 (Suruⁿga), MYS 20.4347 (Kamitupusa), MYS 20.4354 (Kamitupusa), MYS 20.4378 (Simotukɛno), MYS 20.4382 (Simotukɛno), MYS 20.4391 (Simotupusa), MYS 20.4401 (Sinanu), MYS 20.4405 (Kamitukɛno), MYS 20.4416 (Muⁿzasi). Cf. WOJ *se-* 'id.'

seki 'barrier'. Attested in: MYS 20.4372 (Pitati). Cf. WOJ *seki* 'id.'

ser- 'to bend'. Attested in: MYS 14.3437 (Mitinəku). Cf. MJ *sor-* 'id.'

sə- 'she'. Attested in: MYS 14.3472 (unidentified). Cf. WOJ *sə* 'he'.

sək- 'to become distant'. Attested in: MYS 14.3389 (Pitati). Cf. WOJ *sək-* 'id.'

səmə 'not' < Ainu *somo* 'id.' Attested in: MYS 14.3382 (Kamitupusa).

səmɛ- 'to dye'. Attested in: MYS 20.4424 (Muⁿzasi). Cf. WOJ *səmɛ-* 'id.'

sənə 'that'. Attested in: MYS 14.3411 (Kamitukɛno), MYS 16.3885 (unidentified). Cf. WOJ *sənə* 'id.'

sǝpo 'red earth', 'red pigment'. Attested in: MYS 14.3560 (unidentified). Cf. WOJ sopi 'light red color'.

sǝwape, meaning unknown. Attested in: MYS 14.3566 (unidentified). No WOJ cognates.

si^mba 'brushwood', 'small branch'. Attested in: MYS 14.3488 (unidentified), MYS 20.4350 (Kamitupusa). Cf. WOJ si^mba 'id.'

si^mba 'frequently'. Attested in: MYS 14.3488 (unidentified). Cf. WOJ si^mba 'id.'

si^nda 'time', 'when' < Ainu hi 'time, occasion' + ta, locative case marker. Attested in: MYS 14.3363 (Saŋgamu), MYS 14.3461 (unidentified), MYS 14.3478 (unidentified), MYS 14.3515 (unidentified), MYS 14.3520 (unidentified), MYS 14.3533 (unidentified), MYS 20.4367 (Pitati), MYS 20.4407 (Kamitukɛno).

si^nduk- 'to submerge'. Attested in: MYS 14.3411 (Kamitukɛno). Cf. WOJ si^nduk- 'id.'

si^ndum- 'to become quiet'. Attested in MYS 14.3361 (Saŋgamu), MYS 14.3481 (unidentified), MYS 20.4430 (unidentified). Cf. WOJ si^ndum- 'id.'

si^ŋge- 'overgrown', 'thick', 'dense'. Attested in: MYS 14.3489 (unidentified). See also EOJ si^ŋgɛ-. Cf. WOJ si^ŋge- 'id.'

si^ŋgɛ- 'overgrown', 'thick', 'dense'. Attested in: MYS 14.3456 (unidentified), MYS 14.3464 (unidentified), MYS 14.3556 (unidentified). See also EOJ si^ŋge-. Cf. WOJ si^ŋgɛ- 'id.'

sik- 'to reach'. Attested in: MYS 14.3358b (Suruŋga). Cf. WOJ sik- 'id.'

sika 'deer'. Attested in: MYS 14.3530 (unidentified), MYS 16.3885 (unidentified). Cf. WOJ sika 'id.'

sika 'so'. Attested in: MYS 14.3472 (unidentified). Cf. WOJ sika 'id.'

sikǝ ~ siko 'unworthy', 'repugnant', 'disgusting'. Attested in: FK 5 (Pitati), MYS 20.4373 (Simotukɛno). Cf. WOJ sikǝ 'id.'

sima 'island'. Attested in: FK 8 (Pitati), MYS 16.3880 (Noto), MYS 20.4349 (Kamitupusa), MYS 20.4355 (Kamitupusa), MYS 20.4374 (Simotukɛno), MYS 20.4384 (Simotupusa), MYS 20.4414 (Mu^nzasi). Cf. WOJ sima 'id.'

simǝtǝ ~ simotǝ 'small branch'. Attested in: MYS 14.3488 (unidentified). Cf. WOJ simǝtǝ 'id.', 'whip'.

Simǝtukeno (p.n.). Attested in: MYS 14.3424 (Simotukɛno), MYS 14.3425 (Simotukɛno).

simo ~ simǝ 'frost'. Attested in: MYS 14.3382 (Kamitupusa), MYS 20.4431 (unidentified). Cf. WOJ simo 'id.'

sin- 'to die'. Attested in: MYS 14.3566 (unidentified), MYS 16.3885 (unidentified). Cf. WOJ sin- 'id.'

Sinanu (p.n.) < Ainu sinam (< sir-nam) 'to be cold' + nup 'mountain field'. Attested in: MYS 14.3352 (Sinanu), MYS 14.3399 (Sinanu), MYS 14.3400 (Sinanu).

sinǝp- 'to yearn'. Attested in: MYS 20.4427 (unidentified). See also EOJ sinop- ~ sinup- 'id.' Cf. WOJ sinop- 'id.'

sinop- 'to long for', 'to yearn'. Attested in: MYS 14.3426 (Mitinǝku), MYS 14.3515 (unidentified), MYS 14.3516 (unidentified), MYS 14.3520 (unidentified), MYS 14.3532 (unidentified), MYS 20.4327 (Təpotuapumi), MYS 20.4421 (Muⁿzasi). See also EOJ *sinəp-* ~ *sinup-* 'id.' Cf. WOJ *sinop-* 'id.'

sinup- 'to yearn'. Attested in: MYS 20.4367 (Pitati), MYS 20.4405 (Kamitukɛno). See also EOJ *sinəp-* ~ *sinop-* 'id.' Cf. WOJ *sinop-* 'id.'

sipi 'chinquapin'. Attested in: MYS 14.3493 (unidentified). Cf. WOJ *sipi* 'id.'

sipo 'tide'. Attested in: MYS 14.3366 (Saⁿgamu), MYS 14.3450 (unidentified), MYS 14.3503 (unidentified), MYS 14.3549 (unidentified), MYS 14.3553 (unidentified), MYS 14.3556 (unidentified), MYS 20.4368 (Pitati), MYS 20.4389 (Simotupusa). Cf. WOJ *sipo* 'id.'

sipo 'salt'. Attested in: MYS 16.3880 (Noto). Cf. WOJ *sipo* 'id.'

sipo 'pickle'. Attested in: MYS 16.3885 (unidentified). Cf. WOJ *sipo* 'id.'

sir- 'to know'. Attested in: FK 8 (Pitati), MYS 14.3413 (Kamitukɛno), MYS 14.3544 (unidentified), MYS 14.3566 (unidentified), MYS 20.4366 (Pitati), MYS 20.4376 (Simotukɛno), MYS 20.4384 (Simotupusa), MYS 20.4413 (Muⁿzasi). Cf. WOJ *sir-* 'id.'

sira 'white'. Attested in: MYS 14.3478 (unidentified), MYS 14.3509 (unidentified), MYS 14.3517 (unidentified), MYS 20.4340 (Suruⁿga), MYS 20.4379 (Simotukɛno), MYS 20.4389 (Simotupusa), MYS 20.4415 (Muⁿzasi). See also EOJ *siro, siru* 'id.' Cf. WOJ *sira* 'id.'

siraᵐbɛ- 'to examine'. Attested in: AAU 2 (Saⁿgamu). Cf. WOJ *siraᵐbɛ-* 'id.'

Sirakï (p.n. 'Silla'). Attested in: MYS 16.3878 (Noto).

siratəpopu (permanent epithet to Mr. Nipita). Attested in: MYS 14.3436 (Kamitukɛno). Cf. WOJ *siratəpopu* 'id.'

sirə 'nursery (for plants)'. Attested in: MYS 14.3576 (unidentified). Cf. WOJ *sirə* 'substitute'.

siri 'behind', 'back', 'ass'. Attested in: MYS 14.3431 (Saⁿgamu). Cf. WOJ *siri* 'id.'

siro 'white'. Attested in: FK 9 (Pitati). See also EOJ *sira, siru* 'id.' Cf. WOJ *siro* 'id.'

siru 'behind'. Attested in: MYS 20.4385 (Simotupusa). Cf. WOJ *siri* 'id.'

siru 'white'. Attested in: MYS 20.4324 (Təpotuapumi). See also EOJ *sira, siro* 'id.' Cf. WOJ *siro* 'id.'

Sirupa (p.n.) < Ainu *sirpa* 'cape' (*sir* 'land' + *pa* 'head'). Attested in: MYS 20.4324 (Təpotuapumi).

sirus- 'to describe'. Attested in: MYS 20.4366 (Pitati). Cf. WOJ *sirus-* 'to mark'.

sisi 'father'. Attested in: MYS 20.4376 (Simotukɛno), MYS 20.4378 (Simotukɛno). See also EOJ *təti, titi* 'id.' Cf. WOJ *titi* 'id.'

sisi 'game animal', 'meat'. Attested in: MYS 14.3531 (unidentified), MYS 16.3885 (unidentified). Cf. WOJ *sisi* 'id.'

sita 'bottom', 'below'. Attested in FK5 (Pitati), MYS 14.3516 (unidentified), MYS 14.3544 (unidentified), MYS 20.4371 (Pitati). Cf. WOJ *sita* 'id.'

sitaⁿdami '*sitaⁿdami* seashells (edible small size conch shellfish)'.[7] Attested in: MYS 16.3880 (Noto). Cf. WOJ *sitaⁿdami* 'id.'

---

[7] MDJ *gangara*, 小螺 'id.'

situ 'lowly'. Attested in: FK 5 (Pitati). Cf. WOJ *si^ndu-* 'low' in *si^ndu-ye* 'low branches'.

si^nzi 'constantly'. Attested in: MYS 20.4368 (Pitati). Cf. WOJ *si^nzi* 'id.'

so 'rock'. Attested in: MYS 14.3562 (unidentified). Cf. WOJ *iso* 'id.'

-so 'hemp'. Attested in: MYS 14.3404 (Kamitukɛno). Cf. WOJ *-so* 'id.'

so 'shoo'. Attested in: MYS 14.3451 (unidentified). Cf. WOJ *so* 'id.'

so^nde 'sleeve'. MYS 14.3376 (Mu^nzasi), MYS 14.3389 (Pitati), MYS 14.3402 (Kamitukɛno), MYS 20.4356 (Kamitupusa), MYS 20.4379 (Simotukɛno), MYS 20.4423 (Mu^nzasi). Cf. WOJ *so^nde* 'id.' < OK *son* 'hand' + *tʌy* 'place' (MK *swon* + *tʌy*).

sop- 'to go along', 'to be close'. Attested in: MYS 14.3410 (Kamitukɛno), MYS 14.3435 (Kamitukɛno), MYS 14.3485 (unidentified), MYS 14.3495 (unidentified). Cf. WOJ *sop-* 'id.'

sora 'sky'. Attested in: MYS 14.3425 (Simotukɛno). Cf. WOJ *sora* 'id.'

su 'nest'. Attested in: MYS 14.3526 (unidentified). Cf. WOJ *su* 'id.'

su 'sandbar', 'sandbank'. Attested in: MYS 14.3533 (unidentified). Cf. WOJ *su* 'id.'

su 'again' < Ainu *suy* 'id.' Attested in: MYS 14.3363 (Sa^ngamu), MYS 14.3487 (unidentified), MYS. 14.3564 (unidentified).

su^mbe ~ su^mbɛ 'way'. Attested in: MYS 20.4379 (Simotukɛno), MYS 20.4381 (Simotukɛno). Cf. WOJ *su^mbe* 'id.'

su^ngata 'appearance'. Attested in: MYS 20.4378 (Simotukɛno). Cf. WOJ *su^ngata* 'id.'

su^ngɛ ~ su^nga- 'sedge'. Attested in: MYS 14.3369 (Sa^ngamu), MYS 14.3445 (unidentified), MYS 14.3564 (unidentified). Cf. WOJ *su^ngɛ* 'id.'

su^ngï 'cryptomeria'. Attested in: MYS 14.3363 (Sa^ngamu). Cf. WOJ *su^ngï* 'id.'

su^ngï- 'to pass'. Attested in: MYS 14.3388 (Pitati), MYS 14.3423 (Kamitukɛno), MYS 20.4349 (Kamitupusa). Cf. WOJ *su^ngï-* 'id.'

su^ngos- 'to pass'. Attested in: MYS 14.3564 (unidentified). Cf. WOJ *su^ngus-* 'id.'

su^ngu 'to grow old' < Ainu *sukup* 'id.' Attested in: MYS 20.4378 (Simotukɛno).

suke 'assistant'. Cf. *sukɛ* 'id.' Attested in: MYS 14.3450 (unidentified). Cf. WOJ *suke* 'id.'

sum- 'to live'. Attested in: MYS 14.3527 (unidentified), MYS 20.4419 (Mu^nzasi). Cf. WOJ *sum-* 'id.'

sumɛra 'Emperor'. Attested in: MYS 20.4370 (Pitati). Cf. WOJ *sumera* 'id.'

sumi 'ink'. Attested in: MYS 16.3885 (unidentified). Cf. WOJ *sumi* 'id.'

sumi 'clear'. Attested in: MYS 16.3885 (unidentified). Cf. WOJ *sumi* 'id.'

sur- 'to rub'. Attested in: MYS 14.3576 (unidentified). Cf. WOJ *sur-* 'id.'

Suru^nga (p.n.). Attested in: MYS 14.3359 (Suru^nga), MYS 14.3359a (Suru^nga), MYS 20.4345 (Suru^nga).

suso 'hem'. Attested in: MYS 14.3482 (unidentified), MYS 20.4401 (Sinanu). Cf. WOJ *suso* 'id.'

susuk- 'to rinse'. Attested in: MYS 16.3880 (Noto). Cf. WOJ *susuk-* 'id.'

suwe 'end'. Attested in: MYS 14.3487 (unidentified). Cf. WOJ *suwe* 'id.'

suwe- 'to place'. Attested in: MYS 20.4363 (Pitati). Cf. WOJ *suwe-* 'id.'

T

ta 'paddy'. Attested in: MYS 14.3418 (Kamitukɛno), MYS 14.3501 (unidentified), MYS 14.3561 (unidentified). Cf. WOJ *ta* 'id.'

ta 'arm', 'hand'. Attested in: MYS 14.3369 (Saᵑgamu), MYS 14.3480 (unidentified), MYS 16.3885 (unidentified), MYS 20.4430 (unidentified), MYS 20.4432 (unidentified). See also EOJ *te* 'id.' Cf. WOJ *te* 'id.' < *tɛ < *tay

ta 'who'. Attested in: FK 2 (Pitati), MYS 14.3424 (Simotukɛno). See also EOJ *tare* 'id.' Cf. WOJ *ta-* 'id.'

ta 'here' < Ainu *ta* 'this, here'. Attested in: MYS 20.4386 (Simotupusa).

taᵐbar- 'to receive (HUM)'. Attested in: MYS 20.4424 (Muⁿzasi). See also EOJ *tamapar-* 'id.' Cf. WOJ *taᵐbar-* 'id.' A contraction of *tamapar-*. Cf. also OJ *tamapar-* 'id.'

taᵐbi 'journey', 'travel'. Attested in: MYS 20.4325 (Təpotuapumi), MYS 20.4327 (Təpotuapumi), MYS 20.4343 (Suruᵑga), MYS 20.4351 (Kamitupusa), MYS 20.4376 (Simotukɛno), MYS 20.4388 (Simotupusa), MYS 20.4406 (Kamitukɛno), MYS 20.4416 (Muⁿzasi), MYS 20.4420 (Muⁿzasi). See also EOJ *taᵐbï* 'id.' Cf. WOJ *taᵐbi* 'id.'

taᵐbï 'journey'. Attested in: MYS 20.4348 (Kamitupusa). See also EOJ *taᵐbi* 'id.' Cf. WOJ *taᵐbi* 'id.'

taᵐbi 'time'. Attested in: MYS 20.4379 (Simotukɛno). Cf. WOJ *taᵐbi* 'id.'

taⁿda 'directly'. Attested in: MYS 14.3413 (Kamitukɛno). Cf. WOJ *taⁿda* 'id.'

Taⁿdəri (p.n.). Attested in: MYS 14.3405 (Kamitukɛno), MYS 14.3405a (Kamitukɛno).

taⁿdu 'crane'. Attested in: MYS 14.3522 (unidentified). Cf. WOJ *taⁿdu* 'id.'

taⁿduki 'clue'. Attested in: MYS 20.4384 (Simotupusa). Cf. WOJ *taⁿdoki ~ taⁿdəki* 'id.'

tane 'seed'. Attested in: MYS 14.3415 (Kamitukɛno). Cf. WOJ *tane* 'id.'

taᵑg- 'to eat'. Attested in: MYS 14.3451 (unidentified). Cf. WOJ *taᵑg-* 'id.'

taᵑgap- 'to go against', 'to differ'. Attested in: MYS 14.3359 (Suruᵑga), MYS 14.3359a (Suruᵑga), MYS 14.3493 (unidentified). Cf. WOJ *taᵑgap-* 'id.'

Taᵑgo (p.n.). Attested in: MYS 14.3411 (Kamitukɛno).

taka 'high'. Attested in: MYS 14.3358b (Suruᵑga), MYS 14.3514 (unidentified), MYS 14.3555 (unidentified), MYS 16.3880 (Noto), MYS 20.4380 (Simotukɛno). Cf. WOJ *taka* 'id.'

Takapama (p.n.). Attested in FK5 (Pitati).

takɛ 'bamboo'. Attested in: MYS 14.3474 (unidentified). Cf. WOJ *takɛ* 'id.'

tak- 'to burn'. Attested in: MYS 20.4419 (Muⁿzasi). Cf. WOJ *tak-* 'id.'

taku 'mulberry tree'. Attested in: MYS 14.3509 (unidentified). Cf. WOJ *taku* 'id.' < OK *tak[v] (MK *tàk*) 'id.'

tama 'jewel', 'pearl'. Attested in: MYS 14.3358b (Suruᵑga), MYS 14.3397 (Pitati), MYS 14.3400 (Sinanu), MYS 14.3445 (unidentified), MYS 14.3487 (unidentified), MYS 14.3562 (unidentified), MYS 20.4340 (Suruᵑga), MYS 20.4377 (Simotukɛno), MYS 20.4378 (Simotukɛno), MYS 20.4390 (Simotupusa), MYS 20.4415 (Muⁿzasi). Cf. WOJ *tama* 'id.'

Tama (p.n.). Attested in: MYS 20.4417 (Muⁿzasi).

tamapar- 'to be granted', 'to receive (HUM)'. Attested in: MYS 20.4372 (Pitati). See also EOJ *ta^mbar-* 'id.' Cf. WOJ *tamapar-* 'id.'

tana^mbik- 'to trail'. Attested in: MYS 14.3511 (unidentified), MYS 14.3516 (unidentified), MYS 14.3520 (unidentified), MYS 20.4380 (Simotukɛno). See also EOJ *tənə^mbik-* 'id.' Cf. WOJ *tana^mbik-* 'id.'

tanəm- 'to trust'. Attested in: MYS 14.3359 (Suruᵑga), MYS 14.3359a (Suruᵑga). Cf. WOJ *tanəm-* 'id.'

tamɛ 'for'. Attested in: MYS 14.4402 (Sinanu). Cf. WOJ *tamɛ* 'id.'

tapam- 'to bend'. Attested in: MYS 14.3501 (unidentified). No apparent WOJ cognates.

taratinen-ə (makura-kotoba) Attested in: MYS 20.4348 (Kamitupusa). Cf. WOJ *taratinen-ə* 'id.' *tara t-ine n-ə* 'blood HON-mother COP-ATTR' < PAN *daraq t-inay 'blood mother'.

tare 'who'. Attested in: MYS 14.3460 (unidentified), MYS 20.4384 (Simotupusa). See also EOJ *ta* 'id.' Cf. WOJ *tare* 'id.'

tas- 'to rise', 'to depart', 'to stand'. Attested in: MYS 14.3395 (Pitati), MYS 20.4372 (Pitati), MYS 20.4383 (Simotukɛno), MYS 20.4423 (Muⁿzasi). Cf. WOJ *tat-* 'id.'

tasi 'long sword'. Attested in: MYS 20.4413 (Muⁿzasi). Cf. WOJ *tati* 'id.'

tat- 'to break'. Attested in: MYS 20.4429 (unidentified). Cf. WOJ *tat-* 'id.'

tat- 'to stand', 'to rise', 'to depart', 'to leave'. Attested in: FK 8 (Pitati), MYS 14.3349 (Simotupusa), MYS 14.3375 (Muⁿzasi), MYS 14.3414 (Kamitukɛno), MYS 14.3447 (unidentified), MYS 14.3476 (unidentified), MYS 14.3476a (unidentified), MYS 14.3480 (unidentified), MYS 14.3515 (unidentified), MYS 14.3528 (unidentified), MYS 14.3546 (unidentified), MYS 14.3552 (unidentified), MYS 14.3563 (unidentified), MYS 16.3885 (unidentified), MYS 20.4337 (Suruᵑga), MYS 20.4354 (Kamitupusa), MYS 20.4364 (Pitati), MYS 20.4373 (Simotukɛno), MYS 20.4375 (Simotukɛno), MYS 20.4430 (unidentified). Cf. WOJ *tat-* 'id.'

tatami 'rice straw mat'. Attested in: MYS 16.3885 (unidentified), MYS 20.4338 (Suruᵑga). Cf. WOJ *tatami* 'id.'

tatami kɛmɛ (makura-kotoba) Attested in: MYS 20.4338 (Suruᵑga). Cf. WOJ *tatami kəmə* 'id.'

tate 'shield'. Attested in: MYS 20.4373 (Simotukɛno). Cf. WOJ *tate* 'id.'

tate- 'to make something stand'. Attested in: MYS 14.3489 (unidentified), MYS 16.3878 (Noto), MYS 16.3879 (Noto), MYS 16.3880 (Noto). Cf. WOJ *tate* 'id.'

tati 'long sword'. Attested in: MYS 14.3485 (unidentified), MYS 20.4347 (Kamitupusa). See also EOJ *tasi* 'id.' Cf. WOJ *tati* 'id.'

Tati^mbana (p.n.). Attested in: MYS 14.3496 (unidentified), MYS 20.4341 (Suruᵑga).

tati^mbana 'mandarin orange'. Attested in: MYS 20.4371 (Pitati). Cf. WOJ *tati^mbana* 'id.'

tatimati 'immediate'. Attested in: MYS 16.3885 (unidentified). Cf. WOJ *tatimati* 'id.'

taye- 'to break', 'to stop', 'to cease'. Attested in: MYS 14.3378 (Muⁿzasi), MYS 14.3397 (Pitati), MYS 14.3398 (Sinanu), MYS 14.3434 (Kamitukɛno), MYS 14.3501 (unidentified), MYS

14.3513 (unidentified), MYS 14.3517 (unidentified), MYS 20.4404 (Kamitukɛno), MYS 20.4420 (Muⁿzasi). Cf. WOJ *taye-* 'id.'

tayor- 'to cease'. Attested in MYS 14.3368 (Saŋgamu), MYS 14.3392 (Pitati). Cf. WOJ *taye-* 'to break, to stop, to cease'.

Tayupi (p.n.) < Ainu *tay-yúpe* 'dead shark' (*tay*⁸ 'die' + *yúpe* 'shark'). Attested in: MYS 14.3549 (unidentified).

tawore 'mountain saddle'. Attested in: MYS 14.3458 (unidentified). Cf. WOJ *tawori* 'id.'

te 'hand'. Attested in: MYS 20.4387 (Simotupusa), MYS 20.4415 (Muⁿzasi), MYS 20.4418 (Muⁿzasi), MYS 20.4420 (Muⁿzasi), AAU 1 (Saŋgamu). See also EOJ *ta* 'id.' Cf. WOJ *te* 'id.'

te, quotation verb 'to say', 'to think'. Attested in: MYS 20.4344, MYS 20.4346. Cf. WOJ *tə* 'id.'

teŋgo~ teŋgo-na 'maiden', 'beloved' < Ainu *tek* 'hand, arm' + *o* 'take in, embrace'. Attested in: MYS 14.3384 (Simotupusa), MYS 14.3385 (Simotupusa), MYS 14.3398 (Pitati), MYS 14.3442, MYS 14.3485 (unidentified), MYS 14.3540 (unidentified). No WOJ cognates.

ter- 'to shine'. Attested in: MYS 20.4365 (Pitati). See also EOJ *tor-* 'id.' Cf. WOJ *ter-* 'id.'

tə, focus particle. Attested in: MYS 14.3409, MYS 14.3425, MYS 14.3561, MYS 20.4385, MYS 20.4430. See also EOJ *sə* 'id.' Cf. WOJ *sə* 'id.'

təⁿdərə 'roaring'. Attested in: MYS 14.3385 (Simotupusa), MYS 14.3392 (Pitati). Cf. WOJ *təⁿdərə* 'roaring'.

tək- 'to untie'. Attested in: MYS 14.3361 (Saŋgamu), MYS 14.3370 (Saŋgamu), MYS 14.3465 (unidentified), MYS 14.3483 (unidentified), MYS 14.3551 (unidentified), MYS 20.4405 (Kamitukɛno), MYS 20.4416 (Muⁿzasi), MYS 20.4422 (Muⁿzasi), MYS 20.4427 (unidentified), MYS 20.4428 (unidentified). Cf. WOJ *tək-* 'id.'

təke- 'to get untied'. Attested in: MYS 14.3483 (unidentified). Cf. WOJ *təkɛ-* 'id.'

təki 'time'. Attested in: MYS 14.3379 (Muⁿzasi), MYS 14.3572 (unidentified), MYS 16.3885 (unidentified), MYS 20.4323 (Təpotuapumi), MYS 20.4382 (Simotukɛno), MYS 20.4383 (Simotukɛno), MYS 20.4384 (Simotupusa). Cf. WOJ *təki* 'id.'

təkə 'bed'. Attested in: MYS 14.3354 (Təpotuapumi), MYS 14.3445 (unidentified), MYS 14.3484 (unidentified), MYS 20.4369 (Pitati). Cf. WOJ *təkə* 'id.'

təkə 'eternal'. Attested in: MYS 14.3436 (Kamitukɛno). Cf. WOJ *təkə* 'id.'

təme 'old woman'. Attested in: FK 5 (Pitati). Cf. WOJ *tome* 'id.'

tənə 'mansion'. Attested in: MYS 20.4342 (Suruŋga). Cf. WOJ *tənə* 'id.'

tənəᵐbik- 'to trail'. Cf. WOJ *tanaᵐbik-* 'id.' Attested in: MYS 20.4403 (Sinanu). See also EOJ *tanaᵐbik-* 'id.' Cf. WOJ *tanaᵐbik-* 'id.'

Təpotuapumi (p.n.). Attested in: MYS 20.4324 (Təpotuapumi).

təpo- 'be far'. Attested in: MYS 14.3383 (Kamitupusa), MYS 14.3389 (Pitati), MYS 14.3426 (Mitinəku), MYS 14.3463 (unidentified), MYS 14.3473 (unidentified), MYS 14.3478 (unidentified), MYS 14.3522 (unidentified). Cf. WOJ *təpo-* 'id.'

---

8 *tay* is a Sakhalin Ainu form corresponding to *ray* in Hokkaidō Ainu. Both reflect PA *ðay.

tər- 'to take', 'to grab', 'to hold'. Attested in: MYS 14.3420 (Kamitukɛno), MYS 14.3485 (unidentified), MYS 20.4327 (Təpotuapumi), MYS 20.4340 (Suruŋga), MYS 20.4358 (Kamitupusa), MYS 20.4401 (Sinanu), MYS 20.4413 (Munzasi). See also EOJ tor- 'id.' Cf. WOJ tər- 'to take, to grab', WOJ tor- 'to hold'.

təri 'bird'. Attested in: FK 9 (Pitati), MYS 14.3468 (unidentified), MYS 14.3521 (unidentified), MYS 14.3526 (unidentified), MYS 14.3527 (unidentified), MYS 14.3528 (unidentified), MYS 14.3533 (unidentified), MYS 20.4337 (Suruŋga). Cf. WOJ təri 'id.'

Təri (p.n.). Attested in: MYS 14.3458 (unidentified).

təsi 'year'. Attested in: MYS 14.3502 (unidentified), MYS 14.3511 (unidentified). MYS 16.3865 (unidentified). Cf. WOJ təsi 'id.'

təti 'father'. Attested in: MYS 20.4340 (Suruŋga). See also EOJ sisi. Cf. WOJ titi 'id.'

tətənəpɛ- 'to arrange'. AAU 1 (Saŋgamu). Cf. WOJ tətənəpɛ- 'id.'

təwerap- 'to surge, to swell (of waves)'. Attested in: MYS 20.4385 (Simotupusa). Cf. WOJ təworap- 'to rock (of boats on the top of waves)'.

Təya (p.n.) < Ainu to-ya 'lake shore' (to 'lake' + ya 'shore, dry land'). Attested in: 14.3529 (unidentified).

təyəm- 'to sound'. Attested in: MYS 14.3474 (unidentified). Cf. WOJ təyəm- 'id.'

ti 'road'. Attested in: MYS 14.3378 (Munzasi), MYS 14.3399 (Sinanu), MYS 14.3405 (Kamitukɛno), MYS 14.3405a (Kamitukɛno), MYS 14.3458 (unidentified), MYS 20.4404 (Kamitukɛno). Cf. WOJ ti 'id.'

ti 'thousand'. Attested in: MYS 20.4402 (Sinanu). Cf. WOJ ti 'id.'

ti-[i]pa yambur-u (permanent epithet) Attested in: MYS 20.4402 (Sinanu). Cf. WOJ ti-[i]pa yambur-u 'id.'

tika- 'to be close'. Attested in: MYS 14.3524 (unidentified). Cf. WOJ tika- 'id.'

Tiŋguma (p.n.). Attested in: MYS 14.3400 (Sinanu), MYS 14.3401 (Sinanu).

timar- 'to stay'. Attested in: MYS 20.4372 (Pitati). Cf. WOJ təmar- 'id.'

Timba (p.n.). Attested in: MYS 20.4387 (Simotupusa).

tir- ~ -n-dir- 'to fall (of flowers)'. Attested in: MYS 14.3448 (unidentified). Cf. WOJ tir- 'id.'

titi 'father'. Attested in: MYS 16.3880 (Noto), MYS 20.4325 (Təpotuapumi), MYS 20.4328 (Saŋgamu), MYS 20.4337 (Suruŋga), MYS 20.4341 (Suruŋga), MYS 20.4344 (Suruŋga), MYS 20.4346 (Suruŋga), MYS 20.4393 (Simotupusa), MYS 20.4402 (Sinanu). See also EOJ sisi, təti 'id.' Cf. WOJ titi 'id.'

to 'door', 'harbor'. Synonym of minato 'harbor'. Attested in: MYS 14.3460 (unidentified), MYS 14.3530 (unidentified), MYS 14.3553 (unidentified), MYS 14.3561 (unidentified), MYS 20.4380 (Simotukɛno). Cf. WOJ to 'id.'

to 'place'. Attested in: MYS 14.3489 (unidentified), MYS 14.3546 (unidentified). Cf. WOJ təkərə 'id.' with /ə/ caused by regressive assimilation. WOJ to 'id.'

tonap- 'to recite'. MYS 14.3468 (unidentified). Cf. WOJ tonap- 'id.'

tonari 'neighbor'. Attested in: MYS 14.3472 (unidentified). Cf. WOJ tonari 'id.'

Tone (p.n.). Attested in: MYS 14.3413 (Kamitukɛno).

tor- 'to shine'. Attested in: MYS 14.3561 (unidentified). See also EOJ *ter-* 'id.' Cf. WOJ *ter-* 'id.'

tor- 'to take', 'to catch'. Attested in: MYS 14.3419 (Kamitukɛno), MYS 16.3885 (unidentified), MYS 20.4415 (Muⁿzasi), MYS 20.4417 (Muⁿzasi). See also EOJ *tər-* 'to take', 'to catch', 'to grab', 'to hold'. Cf. WOJ *tor-* 'to hold', 'to support'.

tora 'tiger'. Attested in: MYS 16.3885 (unidentified). Cf. WOJ *tora* 'id.'

tora 'together' < Ainu *tura* 'id.' Attested in: MYS 14.3409 (Kamitukɛno), MYS14.3518 (unidentified), MYS 14.3561 (unidentified).

top- 'to ask'. Attested in: MYS 20.4392 (Simotupusa). Cf. WOJ *top-* 'id.'

Topi (p.n.). Attested in MYS 14.3368 (Saŋgamu).

toⁿzi 'mistress of the house'. Attested in: MYS 16.3880 (Noto), MYS 20.4342 (Suruŋga), MYS 20.4377 (Simotukɛno). Cf. WOJ *toⁿzi* 'id.' < *to 'door' + *nusi 'master', 'mistress'.

Tu (p.n.). Attested in: MYS 20.4383 (Simotukɛno).

tu 'harbor'. Attested in: MYS 14.3446 (unidentified), MYS 20.4330 (Saŋgamu), MYS 20.4363 (Pitati), MYS 20.4365 (Pitati). Cf. WOJ *tu* 'id.'

tuᵐbaki 'camellia'. MYS 20.4418 (Muⁿzasi). Cf. WOJ *tuᵐbaki* 'id.'

tuᵐbo 'pot'. Attested in: MYS 16.3885 (unidentified) in logographic spelling. Cf. WOJ *tupo* 'id.'

tuⁿdop- 'to gather'. Attested in: MYS 20.4329 (Saŋgamu), MYS 20.4381 (Simotukɛno). Cf. WOJ *tuⁿdop-* 'id.'

tuⁿdura 'vine'. Attested in: MYS 14.3359 (Suruŋga), MYS 14.3559a (Suruŋga), MYS 14.3434 (Kamitukɛno). Cf. WOJ *tuⁿdura* 'id.'

tuŋg- 'to join'. Attested in: MYS 14.3387 (Simotupusa). Cf. WOJ *tuŋg-* 'id.'

tuŋg- 'to follow'. Attested in: MYS 14.3409 (Kamitukɛno). Cf. WOJ *tuŋg-* 'id.'

tuŋgɛ- 'to report'. Attested in: MYS 20.4363 (Pitati), MYS 20.4406 (Kamitukɛno). Cf. WOJ *tuŋgɛ-* 'id.'

tuŋgi- 'to report'. Attested in MYS 20.4365 (Pitati). Cf. WOJ *tuŋgɛ-* 'id.'

tuk- 'to reach', 'to arrive', 'to attach'. Attested in: MYS 14.3408 (Kamitukɛno), MYS 14.3409 (Kamitukɛno), MYS 14.3435 (Kamitukɛno), MYS 14.3448 (unidentified), MYS 14.3514 (unidentified), MYS 14.3518 (unidentified), MYS 20.4358 (Kamitupusa), MYS 20.4388 (Simotupusa), MYS 20.4401 (Sinanu). Cf. WOJ *tuk-* 'id.'

tuk- 'to be soaked'. Attested in: MYS 14.3446 (unidentified), MYS 20.4340 (Suruŋga). Cf. WOJ *tuk-* 'id.'

tukap- ~ *tukape-* 'to serve'. Attested in: MYS 16.3885 (unidentified), MYS 20.4359 (Kamitupusa). Cf. WOJ *tukapɛ-* 'id.'

tuke- 'to attach'. Attested in: MYS 20.4366 (Pitati). See also EOJ *tukɛ-* 'id.' Cf. WOJ *tukɛ-* 'id.'

tukɛ- 'to attach'. Attested in: MYS 20.4404 (Kamitukɛno), MYS 20.4405 (Kamitukɛno), MYS 20.4420 (Muⁿzasi). See also EOJ *tuke-* 'id.' Cf. WOJ *tukɛ-* 'id.'

tuki 'goblet'. Attested in: MYS 16.3880 (Noto). Cf. WOJ *tuki* 'id.'

tuku 'moon', 'month'. Attested in: MYS 14.3395 (Pitati), MYS 14.3476 (unidentified), MYS 14.3476a (unidentified), MYS 14.3565 (unidentified), 20.4378 (Simotukɛno), MYS 20.4413 (Muⁿzasi). Cf. WOJ *tukï* 'id.'

Tukupa (p.n.). WOJ *Tukupa*, MDJ *Tsukuba*. Name of a mountain in Pitati province. Attested in: FK 2 (Pitati), FK 3 (Pitati), MYS 14.3351 (Pitati), MYS 14.3388 (Pitati), MYS 14.3389 (Pitati), MYS 14.3392 (Pitati), MYS 14.3394 (Pitati), MYS 14.3395 (Pitati), MYS 20.4367 (Pitati), MYS 20.4369 (Pitati), MYS 20.4371 (Pitati). Probably from Ainu *tuk* 'small mountain' + *pa* 'head, top'.

tukur- 'to make'. Attested in: MYS 20.4342 (Suruⁿga). Cf. WOJ *tukur-* 'id.'

Tukusi (p.n.). Attested in: MYS 20.4359 (Kamitupusa), MYS 20.4372 (Pitati), MYS 20.4340 (Suruⁿga), MYS 20.4374 (Simotukɛno), MYS 20.4419 (Muⁿzasi), MYS 20.4422 (Muⁿzasi), MYS 20.4428 (unidentified).

Tukuwe (p.n.). Attested in: MYS 16.3880 (Noto).

tukuwe 'tray table'. Attested in: MYS 16.3880 (Noto). Cf. WOJ *tukuwe* 'id.'

tum- 'to gather (fruits, etc.)'. Attested in: MYS 14.3444 (unidentified). Cf. WOJ *tum-* 'id.'

tuma 'spouse', 'wife'. Attested in: FK3 (Pitati), FK5 (Pitati), MYS 14.3370 (Saⁿgamu), MYS 14.3472 (unidentified), MYS 14.3502 (unidentified), MYS 14.3512 (unidentified), MYS 14.3539 (unidentified), MYS 14.3541 (unidentified), MYS 14.3557 (unidentified), MYS 20.4322 (Təpotuapumi), MYS 20.4327 (Təpotuapumi), MYS 20.4385 (Simotupusa). Cf. WOJ *tuma* 'id.'

tumɛ 'hoof'. Attested in: MYS 16.3885 (unidentified), MYS 20.4372 (Pitati). Cf. WOJ *tumɛ* 'id.'

Tumu (p.n.) < Ainu *tum* 'middle (of water, land, or grassy area)'. Attested in: MYS 14.3438. This is a poem in WOJ.

tuna 'rope'. Attested in: MYS 14.3411 (Kamitukɛno). Cf. WOJ *tuna* 'id.'

tuna ⁿg- 'to tie'. Attested in: MYS 14.3539 (unidentified). Cf. WOJ *tunaⁿg-* 'id.'

tuno 'horn'. Attested in: MYS 16.3885 (unidentified). Cf. WOJ *tuno* 'id.'

tura 'vine'. Attested in: MYS 14.3378 (Muⁿzasi), MYS 14.3437 (Mitinəku), MYS 14.3501 (unidentified). Cf. WOJ *tura* 'id.'

Turu (p.n.). Attested in: MYS MYS 14.3543 (unidentified).

turuki 'double edge sword'. Attested in: MYS 14.3485 (unidentified). Cf. WOJ *turuki* 'id.'

tusi 'earth'. Attested in: MYS 20.4392 (Simotupusa), MYS 20.4426 (unidentified). See also EOJ *tuti* 'id.' Cf. WOJ *tuti* 'id.'

Tusima (p.n.). Attested in: MYS 14.3516 (unidentified).

tutap- 'to pass along'. Attested in: MYS 20.4414 (Muⁿzasi). Cf. WOJ *tutapɛ-* 'id.'

tuti 'ground', 'earth'. Attested in: MYS 20.4374 (Simotukɛno), MYS 20.4418 (Muⁿzasi). See also EOJ *tusi* 'id.' Cf. WOJ *tuti* 'id.'

tutuk- 'to hit'. Attested in: MYS 16.3880 (Noto). Cf. WOJ *tutuk-* 'id.'

tutumi 'dam'. Attested in: FK 9 (Pitati), MYS 14.3543 (unidentified). Cf. WOJ *tutumi* 'id.'

tutum- 'to wrap'. Attested in: FK 9 (Pitati). Cf. WOJ *tutum-* 'id.'

tuyu 'dew'. Attested in: MYS 14.3382 (Kamitupusa). Cf. WOJ *tuyu* 'id.'

U

uᵐbɛ 'indeed'. Attested in: MYS 14.3476 (unidentified), MYS 14.3476a (unidentified). Cf. WOJ *uᵐbɛ* 'id.'

uⁿduki 'fourth month'. Attested in: MYS 16.3885 (unidentified). Cf. WOJ *uⁿduki* 'id.'

uk- 'to float'. Attested in: MYS 14.3401 (Sinanu), MYS 16.3878 (Noto). Cf. WOJ *uk-* 'id.'

ukera '*ukera* flower'. Cf. MJ *wokera* 'id.' Attested in: MYS 14.3376 (Muⁿzasi), MYS 14.3376a (Muⁿzasi), MYS 14.3379 (Muⁿzasi), MYS 14.3503 (unidentified).

ukï- 'to make float'. Attested in: FK 9 (Pitati). Cf. WOJ *ukï-* 'id.'

um- 'to spin'. Attested in: MYS 14.3484 (unidentified). Cf. WOJ *um-* 'id.' (no reliable phonographic attestations).

uma 'horse'. Attested in: MYS 14.3537 (unidentified), MYS 14.3537a (unidentified), MYS 14.3538 (unidentified). Cf. WOJ *uma* 'id.'

umaya 'stable'. Attested in: MYS 20.4429 (unidentified). Cf. WOJ *umaya* 'id.'

Umaⁿguta (p.n.). Attested in: MYS 14.3382 (Kamitupusa), MYS 14.3383 (Kamitupusa).

umara 'thorny tree'. Attested in: MYS 20.4352 (Kamitupusa). Cf. WOJ *uᵐbara ~ umara* 'id.'

uma-se 'fence', 'pasture fence'. Attested in: MYS 14.3537a (unidentified). No apparent WOJ cognates.

umi 'sea'. Attested in: MYS 14.3359 (Suruⁿga), MYS 14.3359a (Suruⁿga), MYS 14.3397 (Pitati), MYS 20.4383 (Simotukɛno). Cf. WOJ *umi* 'sea'.

unaru 'to search' < Ainu *hunar* 'id.' Attested in: MYS 14.3361 (Saⁿgamu).

unəpara 'sea plain'. Cf. WOJ *unapara* 'id.' Attested in: MYS 20.4328 (Saⁿgamu).

upe 'top' Attested in: MYS 14.3539 (unidentified). See also EOJ *upɛ* 'id.' Cf. WOJ *upɛ* 'id.'

upɛ 'top'. Attested in: MYS 14.3465 (unidentified), MYS 14.3518 (unidentified), MYS 14.3522 (unidentified), MYS 14.3525 (unidentified). See also EOJ *upe* 'id.' Cf. WOJ *upɛ* 'id.'

ura 'bay'. Attested in MYS 14.3349 (Simotupusa), MYS 14.3552 (Sinanu), MYS 20.4324 (Təpotuapumi).

ura 'top branch', 'top of a tree', 'top of a plant'. Attested in: MYS 14.3436 (Kamitukɛno), MYS 14.3504 (unidentified), MYS 14.3564 (unidentified). See also EOJ *ure* 'id.' Cf. WOJ *ure ~ ura-* 'id.'

ura 'divination'. Attested in: MYS 14.3374 (Muⁿzasi). Cf. WOJ *ura* 'id.'

ura 'inside', 'back', 'heart'. Attested in: MYS 14.3495 (unidentified). MYS 14.3500 (unidentified), MYS 14.3504 (unidentified). Cf. WOJ *ura* 'id.'

Urano (p.n.). Attested in: MYS 14.3565 (unidentified).

ura-pe 'divination clan'. Attested in: MYS 14.3374 (Muⁿzasi). Cf. WOJ *uraᵐbe* 'id.'

ure 'top branch', 'top of a tree', 'top of a plant'. Attested in: MYS 20.4352 (Kamitupusa). See also EOJ *ura* 'id.' Cf. WOJ *ure* 'id.'

usipo 'receding tide'. Attested in: FK 8 (Pitati). Cf. WOJ *usipo* 'id.'

Usupi (p.n.). Attested in: MYS 14.3402 (Kamitukɛno), MYS 20.4407 (Kamitukɛno).

ut- 'to hit'. Attested in: MYS 14.3473 (unidentified), MYS 14.3536 (unidentified), MYS 20.4345 (Suruⁿga). Cf. WOJ *ut-* 'id.'

uta 'poem'. Attested in: AAU 1 (Saⁿgamu). Cf. WOJ *uta* 'id.'

uti 'inside'. Attested in: MYS 14.3368 (Saⁿgamu). Cf. WOJ *uti* 'id.'

uti-kap- 'to cross over'. Attested in: MYS 14.3482a (unidentified). No WOJ cognates.

utukusi 'adorable', 'dear'. Attested in: MYS 14.3496 (unidentified), MYS 20.4392 (Simotupusa), MYS 20.4414 (Muⁿzasi). Cf. WOJ *utukusi* 'id.'

utukusi- 'be longing for'. Attested in: MYS 20.4422 (Muⁿzasi), MYS 20.4428 (unidentified). Cf. WOJ *utukusi-* 'id.'

utu semi 'ephemeral cicada'. Attested in: MYS 14.3456 (unidentified). Cf. WOJ *utu semi* 'id.'

uwe- 'to plant'. Attested in: MYS 14.3415 (Kamitukɛno), MYS 14.3474 (unidentified). Cf. WOJ *uwe-* 'id.'

W

wa 'I'. Attested in: FK 3 (Pitati), FK 7 (Pitati), FK 8 (Pitati), MYS 14.3363 (Saⁿgamu), MYS 14.3377 (Muⁿzasi), MYS 14.3378 (Muⁿzasi), MYS 14.3379 (Muⁿzasi), MYS 14.3382 (Kamitupusa), MYS 14.3392 (Pitati), MYS 14.3399 (Sinanu), MYS 14.3408 (Kamitukɛno), MYS 14.3420 (Kamitukɛno), MYS 14.3432 (Saⁿgamu), MYS 14.3435 (Kamitukɛno), MYS 14.3445 (unidentified), MYS 14.3451 (unidentified), MYS 14.3456 (unidentified), MYS 14.3458 (unidentified), MYS 14.3460 (unidentified), MYS 14.3464 (unidentified), MYS 14.3469 (unidentified), MYS 14.3483 (unidentified), MYS 14.3494 (unidentified), MYS 14.3499 (unidentified), MYS 14.3502 (unidentified), MYS 14.3536 (unidentified), MYS 14.3538 (unidentified), MYS 14.3538a (unidentified), MYS 14.3539 (unidentified), MYS 14.3549 (unidentified), MYS 14.3552 (unidentified), MYS 14.3563 (unidentified), MYS 14.3566 (unidentified), MYS 20.4322 (Tǝpotuapumi), MYS 20.4327 (Tǝpotuapumi), MYS 20.4343 (Suruⁿga), MYS 20.4344 (Suruⁿga), MYS 20.4345 (Suruⁿga), MYS 20.4353 (Kamitupusa), MYS 20.4356 (Kamitupusa), MYS 20.4368 (Pitati), MYS 20.4372 (Pitati), MYS 20.4382 (Simotukɛno), MYS 20.4386 (Simotupusa), MYS 20.4404 (Kamitukɛno), MYS 20.4405 (Kamitukɛno), MYS 20.4406 (Kamitukɛno), MYS 20.4418 (Muⁿzasi), MYS 20.4421 (Muⁿzasi), MYS 20.4422 (Muⁿzasi), MYS 204426 (unidentified), MYS 20.4427 (unidentified), MYS 20.4428 (unidentified), AAU 2 (Saⁿgamu). See also EOJ *wano, ware, warǝ,* 'id.' Cf. WOJ *wa, ware* 'I, we'.

wa 'we'. Attested in: MYS 16.3885 (unidentified). See also EOJ *ware, warǝ, wano* 'I'. Cf. WOJ *wa, ware* 'I, we'.

waka 'young'. Attested in: MYS 14.3494 (unidentified), MYS 14.3495 (unidentified). Cf. WOJ *waka* 'id.'

wakamɛ 'seaweed'. Attested in: MYS 14.3563 (unidentified). Cf. WOJ *wakamɛ* 'id.'

wakare- ~ *wakar-* 'to part, to be separated'. Attested in: MYS 14.3375 (Muⁿzasi), MYS 20.4348 (Kamitupusa), MYS 20.4349 (Kamitupusa), MYS 20.4379 (Simotukɛno), MYS 20.4381 (Simotukeno). See also EOJ *pakare* 'id.' Cf. WOJ *wakare-* 'id.'

wana 'trap'. Attested in MYS 14.3361 (Saⁿgamu). Cf. WOJ *wana* 'id.'

wano 'I'. Attested in: MYS 14.3476 (unidentified), 14.3476a (unidentified), MYS 20.4358 (Kamitupusa). See also EOJ *wa, ware, warə* 'I', 'we'. Cf. WOJ *wa[-], waⁿ-, ware* 'I, we'.

ware 'I'. Attested in: MYS 14.3384 (Simotupusa), MYS 14.3444 (unidentified), MYS 14.3514 (unidentified), MYS 20.4344 (Suruⁿga), MYS 20.4348 (Kamitupusa), MYS 20.4370 (Pitati), MYS 20.4373 (Simotukeno), MYS 20.4374 (Simotukeno), MYS 20.4375 (Simotukeno), MYS 20.4416 (Muⁿzasi). See also EOJ *wa, wano, warə* 'I', 'we'. Cf. WOJ *wa, ware* 'I, we'.

warə 'I'. Cf. WOJ *ware* 'I, we'. Attested in: MYS 20.4343 (Suruⁿga). See also EOJ *wa, wano, ware* 'I', 'we'. Cf. WOJ *wa, ware* 'I, we'.

wasur- 'to forget intentionally'. Attested in: MYS 20.4322 (Təpotuapumi), MYS 20.4344 (Suruⁿga), MYS 20.4356 (Kamitupusa), MYS 20.4407 (Kamitukeno). Cf. WOJ *wasur-* 'id.'

wasura- 'to forget unintentionally'. Attested in: MYS 14.3394 (Pitati). See also EOJ *wasure-* 'id.' Cf. WOJ *wasure-* 'id.'

wasure- 'to forget unintentionally', 'to fade from one's memory'. Attested in: MYS 14.3419 (Kamitukeno), MYS 14.3515 (unidentified), MYS 14.3520 (unidentified), MYS 14.3557 (unidentified), MYS 20.4344 (Suruⁿga), MYS 20.4346 (Suruⁿga), MYS 20.4354 (Kamitupusa), MYS 20.4367 (Pitati), MYS 20.4378 (Simotukeno). See also EOJ *wasura-* 'id.' Cf. WOJ *wasure-* 'id.'

wata 'cotton'. Attested in: MYS 14.3354 (Təpotuapumi). Cf. WOJ *wata* 'id.'⁹

watar- 'to cross'. Attested in: MYS 14.3413 (Kamitukeno), MYS 14.3549 (unidentified), MYS 14.3555 (unidentified), MYS 20.4328 (Saⁿgamu), MYS 20.4355 (Kamitupusa), MYS 20.4394 (Simotupusa). Cf. WOJ *watar-* 'id.'

we 'picture'. Attested in: MYS 20.4327 (Təpotuapumi). Cf. WOJ *we* 'picture' < EMC *ɣwâi^C* (繪) 'picture'.

wi- 'to dwell', 'to sit'. Attested in: MYS 14.3383 (Kamitupusa), MYS 14.3388 (Pitati), MYS 20.4372 (Pitati). Cf. WOJ *wi-* 'id.'

wi- 'to bring'. Attested in: MYS 14.3388 (Pitati). Cf. WOJ *wi-* 'id.'

wi- 'to take along'. Attested in: MYS 16.3879 (Noto). Cf. WOJ *wi-* 'id.'

wiⁿde 'dam'. Attested in: MYS 14.3414 (Kamitukeno). Cf. WOJ *wiⁿde* 'id.'

wo 'male'. Attested in: MYS 14.3530 (unidentified), MYS 16.3885 (unidentified), MYS 20.4372 (Pitati), MYS 20.4430 (unidentified). Cf. WOJ *wo* 'id.'

---

9 Phonographic spelling occurs only once: the character 綿 'cotton' is used as a *kungana* for *wata* in *wataru* 'to cross'.

wo 'cord', 'string', 'rein'. Attested in: MYS 14.3358b (Suruⁿga), MYS 14.3466 (unidentified), MYS 14.3525 (unidentified), MYS 14.3536 (unidentified), MYS 20.4404 (Kamitukɛno), AAU 2 (Saⁿgamu). Cf. WOJ *wo* 'id.'

wo 'mountain ridge', 'peak', 'hill'. Attested in: MYS 14.3448 (unidentified), MYS 14.3493 (unidentified), MYS 14.3501 (unidentified). Cf. WOJ *wo* 'id.'

wo 'tail'. Attested in: MYS 14.3468 (unidentified). Cf. WOJ *wo* 'id.'

wo 'hemp', 'hemp thread'. Attested in: MYS 14.3468 (unidentified), MYS 14.3484 (unidentified). Cf. WOJ *wo* 'id.'

wo 'yes'. Attested in: MYS 14.3351 (Pitati). Cf. WOJ *wo* 'id.'

Woⁿdo (p.n.). Attested in: MYS 14.3405 (Kamitukɛno).

woⁿgï 'common reed'. MYS 14.3446 (unidentified). No reliable WOJ phonographic attestations.

Woⁿgusa (p.n.). Attested in: MYS 14.3450 (unidentified).

woka 'hill'. Attested in: MYS 14.3444 (unidentified), MYS 14.3451 (unidentified), MYS 14.3458 (unidentified), MYS 14.3499 (unidentified). Cf. WOJ *woka* 'id.'

wo-ke 'hemp container'. Attested in: MYS 14.3484 (unidentified). Cf. WOJ *wo-kɛ* 'id.'

Wokusa (p.n.). Attested in: MYS 14.3450 (unidentified).

Wona (p.n.). Attested in: MYS 14.3448 (unidentified).

wonə 'ax'. Attested in: MYS 14.3473 (unidentified), MYS 16.3878 (Noto). Cf. WOJ *wonə* 'id.'

Wono (p.n.). Attested in: MYS 14.3405a (Kamitukɛno).

wope- 'to finish'. Attested in: MYS 14.3500 (unidentified). Cf. WOJ *wope-* 'id.'

wor- 'to exist'. Attested in: MYS 14.3401 (Sinanu), MYS 16.3885 (unidentified). Cf. WOJ *wor-* 'id.'

wosaⁿgi 'hare'. Attested in: MYS 14.3529 (unidentified). Cf. WOJ *usaⁿgi* 'id.'

wosa-wosa 'enough'. Attested in: MYS 14.3529 (unidentified). No WOJ cognates.

wosə 'lie'. Misspelling of WOJ *woso* 'lie'. Attested in: MYS 14.3521 (unidentified). Cf. WOJ *woso* 'lie'.

wosi- 'be regrettable'. Attested in: MYS 14.3533 (unidentified). Cf. WOS *wosi-* 'id.'

wote 'that'. Attested in MYS 14.3361 (Saⁿgamu). Cf. WOJ *woti, wote, wotə* 'id.' (Vovin 2020.1: 282–284).

Y

-y-, indefinite direct object prefix < Ainu *i-* 'id.' Attested in: MYS 14.3526 (unidentified), MYS 20.4427 (unidentified).

ya 'shore' < Ainu *ya* 'shore, dry land'. Attested in: MYS 14.3562 (unidentified).

ya 'eight'. Attested in: MYS 14.3414 (Kamitukɛno), MYS 14.3527 (unidentified), MYS 16.3865 (unidentified), MYS 16.3885 (unidentified), MYS 20.4351 (Kamitupusa), MYS 20.4379 (Simotukɛno), AAU 2 (Saⁿgamu). Cf. WOJ *ya* 'id.'

ya 'house'. Attested in: MYS 14.3460 (unidentified). Cf. WOJ *ya* 'id.'

ya 'arrow'. Attested in: MYS 20.4374 (Simotukɛno). Cf. WOJ *ya* 'id.'

ya 'shop' < 'house'. Attested in: MYS 16.3879 (Noto). Cf. WOJ *ya* 'id.' in the entry for *ya* 'house'.

yaᵐbur- 'to crush', 'to break'. Attested in: MYS 20.4402 (Sinanu), MYS 16.3880 (Noto). Cf. WOJ *yaᵐbur-* 'id.'

yaⁿde 'branch'. Cf. WOJ *ye, yeⁿda* 'id.' Attested in: MYS 14.3493 (unidentified). Cf. WOJ *yeⁿda* 'id.'

yaᵑgï 'willow'. Attested in: MYS 14.3546 (unidentified). Cf. WOJ *yaᵑgï* 'id.'

yak- 'to burn'. Attested in: MYS 14.3374 (Muⁿzasi), MYS 14.3452 (unidentified). Cf. WOJ *yak-* 'id.'

yam- 'to stop'. Attested in: MYS 14.3387 (Simotupusa), MYS 14.3532 (unidentified). Cf. WOJ *yam-* 'id.'

yama 'mountain'. Attested in MYS 14.3363 (Saᵑgamu), MYS 14.3389 (Pitati), MYS 14.3394 (Pitati), MYS 14.3402 (Kamitukɛno), MYS 14.3408 (Kamitukɛno), MYS 14.3424 (Simotukɛno), MYS 14.3431 (Saᵑgamu), MYS 14.3432 (Saᵑgamu), MYS 14.3434 (Kamitukɛno), MYS 14.3436 (Kamitukɛno), MYS 14.3468 (unidentified), MYS 14.3473 (unidentified), MYS 14.3488 (unidentified), MYS 14.3489 (unidentified), MYS 14.3494 (unidentified), MYS 14.3509 (unidentified), MYS 14.3513 (unidentified), MYS 14.3531 (unidentified), MYS 14.3565 (unidentified), MYS 14.3572 (unidentified), MYS 16.3885 (unidentified), MYS 20.4344 (Suruᵑga), MYS 20.4371 (Pitati), MYS 20.4403 (Sinanu), MYS 20.4417 (Muⁿzasi), MYS 20.4418 (Muⁿzasi), AAU 2 (Saᵑgamu). Cf. WOJ *yama* 'id.'

Yamatə (p.n.). Attested in: MYS 14.3363 (Saᵑgamu).

yanaᵑgï 'willow'. Attested in: MYS 20.4387 (Simotupusa). Cf. WOJ *yanaᵑgï* 'id.'

yar- 'to send', 'to send away'. Attested in: MYS 14.3363 (Saᵑgamu), MYS 14.3388 (Pitati), MYS 14.3460 (unidentified), MYS 14.3538 (unidentified), MYS 14.3538a (unidentified), MYS 20.4406 (Kamitukɛno), MYS 20.4417 (Muⁿzasi), MYS 20.4422 (Muⁿzasi), MYS 20.4428 (unidentified). Cf. WOJ *yar-* 'id.'

yara 'sea', 'river'. Cf. Ainu *ya-ra* 'the low pace from which one goes up to the dry land'. Attested in: MYS 16.3878 (Noto). Cf. Ainu *ya-ra* 'the low pace from which one goes up to the dry land'.

yase- 'to be emaciated'.[10] Attested in: MYS 20.4343 (Suruᵑga). Cf. WOJ *yase-* 'id.'

yasirə 'shrine'. Attested in: MYS 20.4391 (Simotupusa). Cf. WOJ *yasirə* 'shrine'.

yaso 'eighty'. Attested in: FK 8 (Pitati), MYS 14.3456 (unidentified), MYS 20.4329 (Təpotuapumi), MYS 20.4349 (Kamitupusa), MYS 20.4363 (Pitati). WOJ *yaso* 'id.'

yasu- 'be easy'. Attested in: MYS 14.3483 (unidentified), MYS 14.3504 (unidentified), MYS 20.4348 (Kamitupusa). Cf, WOJ *yasu-* 'be easy'.

yatuko 'dude'. Attested in: MYS 16.3879 (Noto). Cf. WOJ *yatuko* 'id.'

---

10 EOJ verb can be either vowel verb or consonantal, because the attested tentative form *yas-uram-* does not offer us any clue regarding its paradigm.

ye 'life time'. Attested in: MYS 14.3368 (Saᵑgamu), MYS 14.3392 (Pitati). See also EOJ *yə* 'life'. Cf. WOJ *yə* 'id.'

ye- 'to be good'. Attested in: MYS 14.3509 (unidentified), MYS 14.3530 (unidentified). See also EOJ *yə-* 'id.' Cf. WOJ *yə-* 'id.'

ye, emphatic particle. Attested in: MYS 20.4340. Cf. WOJ *yə* 'id.'

yepi 'sash'. Attested in: MYS 20.4428 (unidentified). See also EOJ *oᵐbi* 'id.' Cf. WOJ *oᵐbi* 'id.'

yes- ~ *yese-* 'to approach'. Attested in: MYS 14.4345 (unidentified), 14.4346 (unidentified). See also EOJ *yər-* 'id.' Cf. WOJ *yəse-* 'id.'

yik- 'to go'. Attested in: MYS 14.3496 (unidentified). See also EOJ *yuk-* 'id.' Cf. WOJ *yik-* ~ *yuk-* 'id.'

yə 'life'. Attested in: MYS 14.3368 (Saᵑgamu), MYS 14.3392 (Pitati), MYS 14.3448 (unidentified), MYS 20.4322 (Təpotuapumi). See also EOJ *ye* 'life time'. Cf. WOJ *yə* 'id.'

yə- 'to be good'. Attested in: MYS 14.3410 (Kamitukɛno), MYS 14.3411 (Kamitukɛno), MYS 20.4419 (Muⁿzasi). See also EOJ *ye-* 'id.' Cf. WOJ *yə-* 'id.'

yəki 'snow'. Attested in: MYS 14.3423 (Kamitupusa), MYS 14.3523 (unidentified). See also EOJ *yuki* 'id.' Cf. WOJ *yuki* 'id.' and Old Okinawan *yoki* 'id.'

yəkə 'horizontal'. Attested in: MYS 14.3531 (unidentified), MYS 20.4417 (Muⁿzasi). Cf. WOJ *yəkə* 'id.'

yəkə yama 'horizontally [stretched] montains'. Attested in: MYS 14.3531 (unidentified), MYS 20.4417 (Muⁿzasi). Cf. WOJ *yəkə yama* 'id.'

yəpi 'early night'. Attested in: MYS 14.3375 (Muⁿzasi), MYS 14.3461 (unidentified), MYS 14.3469 (unidentified), MYS 14.3563 (unidentified). Cf. WOJ *yəpi* 'id.'

yər- 'to approach'. Attested in: MYS 14.3377 (Muⁿzasi), MYS 14.3435 (Kamitukɛno), MYS 14.3446 (unidentified), MYS 14.3483 (unidentified). Cf. WOJ *yər-* 'id.'

yər- 'to be based', 'to rely'. Attested in: MYS 14.3464 (unidentified). Cf. WOJ *yər-* 'id.'

yəs- ~ *yəse-* 'to make something approach', to 'draw'. Attested in: MYS 14.3384 (Simotupusa), MYS 14.3499 (unidentified), MYS 14.3411 (Kamitukɛno), MYS 14.3548 (unidentified), MYS 20.4345 (Suruⁿga). Cf. WOJ *yəse-* 'id.'

yəsar- 'to be attracted', 'to give one's heart'. See also EOJ *yəsər-* 'id.' Attested in: 14.3478 (unidentified). See also EOJ *yəsər-* and *yəsira-* 'to approach'. Cf. WOJ *yəsər-* 'id.'

yəsə 'outside'. Attested in: MYS 20.4355 (Kamitupusa). Cf. WOJ *yəsə* 'id.'

yəsər- 'to approach', 'to give one's heart'. Attested in: MYS 14.3408 (Kamitukɛno), MYS 14.3468 (unidentified), MYS 14.3512 (unidentified), MYS 20.4379 (Simotukɛno). See also EOJ *yəsar-* 'to be attracted', 'id.' and EOJ *yəsira-* 'id.' Cf. WOJ *yəsər-* 'id.'

yəsəp- 'to prepare', 'to decorate', 'to adorn', 'to equip'. Attested in: MYS 14.3528 (unidentified), MYS 20.4330 (Saᵑgamu), MYS 20.4365 (Pitati), MYS 20.4383, (Simotukɛno). Cf. WOJ *yəsəp-* 'id.'

yəsira- 'to approach'. Attested in: MYS 14.3469 (unidentified). See also EOJ *yəsar-* 'to be attracted', 'id.' and *yəsar-* 'id.' Cf. WOJ *yəsər-* 'id.'

yo 'night'. Attested in: FK 3 (Pitati), MYS 14.3395 (Pitati), MYS 14.3480 (unidentified), MYS 14.3504 (unidentified), MYS 20.4394 (Simotupusa), MYS 20.4431 (unidentified). See also EOJ *yu* 'id.' Cf. WOJ *yo* 'id.'

yokopar- 'to lie down'. Attested in: KKWKS 1097 (Kapï). No WOJ cognates.

Yora (p.n.). Attested in: MYS 14.3489 (unidentified).

yoru 'night time'. Attested in: MYS 14.3483 (unidentified). Cf. WOJ *yoru* 'id.'

yu 'hot spring'. Attested in: MYS 14.3368 (Saᵑgamu). Cf. WOJ *yu* 'id.'

yu 'night'. Attested in: MYS 20.4369 (Pitati). See also EOJ *yo* 'id.' Cf. WOJ *yo* 'id.'

yuⁿduru-pa 'Daphniphyllum macropodum'. Attested in: MYS 14.3572 (unidentified). Cf. MDJ *yuzuri-ha* 'id.'

yuk- 'to go'. Attested in: MYS 14.3366 (Saᵑgamu), MYS 14.3387 (Simotupusa), MYS 14.3423 (Kamitukɛno), MYS 14.3447 (unidentified), MYS 14.3476 (unidentified), MYS 14.3476a (unidentified), MYS 14.3522 (unidentified), MYS 14.3526 (unidentified), MYS 14.3530 (unidentified), MYS 14.3540 (unidentified), MYS 14.3541 (unidentified), MYS 16.3885 (unidentified), MYS 20.4325 (Təpotuapumi), MYS 20.4327 (Təpotuapumi), MYS 20.4338 (Suruᵑga), MYS 20.4339 (Suruᵑga), MYS 20.4341 (Suruᵑga), MYS 20.4344 (Suruᵑga), MYS 20.4349 (Kamitupusa), MYS 20.4352 (Kamitupusa), MYS 20.4366 (Pitati), MYS 20.4372 (Pitati), MYS 20.4374 (Simotukɛno), MYS 20.4376 (Simotukɛno), MYS 20.4378 (Simotukɛno), MYS 20.4385 (Simotupusa), MYS 20.4404 (Kamitukɛno), MYS 20.4406 (Kamitukɛno), MYS 20.4414 (Muⁿzasi), MYS 20.4416 (Muⁿzasi), MYS 20.4421 (Muⁿzasi). See also EOJ *yik-* 'id.' Cf. WOJ *yik-* ~ *yuk-* 'id.'

yuki 'snow'. Attested in: MYS 14.3351 (Pitati), MYS 14.3358b (Suruᵑga). See also EOJ *yəki* 'id.' Cf. WOJ *yuki* 'id.' and Old Okinawan *yoki* 'id.'

yumapi 'sickness'. Attested in: MYS 20.4382 (Simotukɛno). Cf. WOJ *yamapi* 'id.'

yumi 'bow'. Attested in: MYS 14.3437 (Mitinəku), MYS 14.3487 (unidentified), MYS 14.3489 (unidentified), MYS 16.3885 (unidentified), MYS 20.4394 (unidentified). Cf. WOJ *yumi* 'id.'

yun- 'to sleep'. Attested in: MYS 14.3473 (unidentified), MYS 14.3476a (unidentified). Cf. late MJ *o-yor-* 'id.'

yupaⁿzu 'bow string notch'. Attested in: MYS 16.3885 (unidentified). Cf. WOJ *yupaⁿzu* 'id.' (only *-paⁿzu* part is attested phonographically).

yupu 'evening'. Attested in: MYS 14.3469 (unidentified), MYS 14.3513 (unidentified). Cf. WOJ *yupu* 'id.'

yupu kɛ 'evening divination'. Attested in: MYS 14.3469 (unidentified). Cf. WOJ *yupu kɛ* 'id.'

yupu siⁿde 'white bark strip hanging'. Attested in: FK 7 (Pitati). Cf. WOJ *yupu siⁿde* 'id.'

yume 'at all'. Attested in: MYS 14.3376 (Muⁿzasi). Cf. WOJ *yumɛ* 'id.'

yuru 'lily'. Attested in: MYS 20.4369 (Pitati). Cf. WOJ *yuri* 'id.' < *yuruy.

yusup- 'to tie'. Attested in: MYS 20.4427 (unidentified). No apparent WOJ cognates.

yuta 'carefree'. Attested in: MYS 14.3503 (unidentified). Cf. WOJ *yutaka* 'gentle', 'relaxed'.

yuwe 'reason'. Attested in: MYS 14.3529 (unidentified), MYS 14.3555 (unidentified). Cf. WOJ *yuwe* 'id.'

ⁿZ

ⁿze, focus particle. Cf. WOJ *sə* ~ *ⁿzə*, id. Attested in: MYS 20.4346.

Bibliography

Akimoto Kichirō (ed.). 1958. *Fudoki* [*Gazetteers*]. Nihon Koten Bungaku Taikei [Series of the Japanese Classical Literature], vol. 2. Tokyo: Iwanami shoten.

Aso Mizue (ed.). 2007. *Man'yōshū zenka kōgi. Kan daigo ~ kan dairoku* [*A commentary on all Man'yōshū poems. Books five and six*]. Tokyo: Kasama shoin.

Aso Mizue (ed.). 2011. *Man'yōshū zenka kōgi. Kan daijūsan ~ kan daijūyon* [*A commentary on all Man'yōshū poems. Books thirteen and fourteen*]. Tokyo: Kasama shoin.

Bentley, John R. 1997. *MO and PO in Old Japanese*. Unpublished MA thesis. University of Hawai'i at Mānoa.

Bentley, John R. 1999. 'The Verb *TORU* in Old Japanese.' *Journal of East Asian Linguistics* 8: 131–146.

Bentley, John R. 2001a. 'The Origin of the Man'yōgana.' *Bulletin of the School of Oriental and African Studies* 64.1: 59–73.

Bentley, John R. 2001b. *A Descriptive Grammar of Early Old Japanese Prose*. Leiden: Brill.

Bentley, John R. 2002. 'The spelling of /MO/ in Old Japanese.' *Journal of East Asian Linguistics* 11.4: 349–374.

Chiri Mashiho. 1956. *Chimei Ainu go shō jiten* [*A Mini-dictionary of Ainu placenames*]. Sapporo: Hokkaidō shuppan kiga sentā.

Chiri Mashiho. 1975. *Bunrui Ainu go jiten. Ningen hen* [*Classified dictionary of the Ainu language. Humans*]. Tokyo: Heibonsha.

Chiri Mashiho. 1976. *Bunrui Ainu go jiten. Shokubutsu hen. Dōbutsu hen* [*Classified dictionary of the Ainu language. Plants. Animals*]. Tokyo: Heibonsha.

Endō Yoshimoto, and Kasuga Kazuo (eds.). 1967. *Nihon ryōiki* [*Japanese Tales of Wonders*]. *Nihon koten bungaku taikei, vol. 70.* Tokyo: Iwanami.

Frellesvig, Bjarke and John B. Whitman. 2012. 'On the origin of *shimo nidan* conjugation.' Lecture at the conference on Japanese linguistics, NINJAL, Summer 2012.

Fukuda Yoshisuke. 1965. *Nara jidai Azuma hōgen no kenkyū* [*A Study of the Eastern Japanese Dialects in the Nara Period*]. Tokyo: Kazama shoin.

Gluskina, Anna E. 1971–73. *Man"yosiu*. t. 1–3. Moscow: Nauka [reprinted: Moscow: Izdatel'stvo ACT, 2001].

Gluskina, Anna E. 1979. 'O prefikse sa- v pesniakh Man"yoshu [About the prefix sa- in the Man'yōshū songs].' In: Gluskina, A. *Zametki o iaponskoi literature i teatre* [*Notes on the Japanese literature and theater*], pp. 99–110. Moscow: Nauka, Glavnaia redakciia vostochnoi literatury.

Hashimoto Shinkichi. 1917. 'Kokugo kanazukai kenkyū shi jō no ichi hakken – Ishizuka Tatsumaro no Kanazukai oku no yama michi ni tsuite [A Discovery in the Field of Japanese Kana Usage Research Concerning Ishizuka Tatsumaro's The Mountain Road into the Secrets of Kana Usage].' *Teikoku bungaku* 23.5 [reprinted in Hashimoto 1949: 123–163].

Hashimoto Shinkichi. 1931. 'Jōdai no bunken ni sonsuru tokushu no kanazukai to tōji no gohō [The Special Kana Usage of Old Japanese Texts and the Grammar of the Period].' *Kokugo to kokubungaku* 8.9 [reprinted in Hashimoto 1949: 164–191].

Hashimoto Shinkichi. 1938. 'Kokugo on'in no hensen [Changes in Japanese Phonology].' *Kokugo to kokubungaku* 10: 3–40.

Hashimoto Shinkichi. 1949. *Moji oyobi kanazukai no kenkyū* [*Studies on Characters and Kana Usage*]. Tokyo: Iwanami shoten.

Hattori Shirō (ed.). 1964. *Ainu go hōgen jiten* [*An Ainu dialect dictionary*]. Tokyo: Iwanami shoten.

Hayashi Tsutomu. 1990. 'Man'yōshū no shohon [The manuscripts of the Man'yōshū].' In: Inaoka, Kōji (ed.), *Man'yōshū hikkei* [*A Handbook of the Man'yōshū*], pp. 9–19. Tokyo: Gakutōsha.

Hayashi Tsutomu. 1994. 'Man'yōshū no shohon [The manuscripts of the Man'yōshū].' In: Inaoka, Kōji (ed.), *Man'yōshū jiten* [*An Encyclopedia on the Man'yōshū*], pp. 403–414. Tokyo: Gakutōsha.

Hayata Teruhiro. 1998. 'Jōdai Nihongo no onsetsu kōzō to o-retsu kō-otsu no betsu [The structure of Old Japanese syllables and the kō-otsu distinction in the o-line].' *Onsei kenkyū* 2.1: 25–33.

Hendriks, Peter. 1994. 'Adverbial Modification in Old Japanese.' *Japanese/Korean Linguistics*, vol. 4, ed. by Noriko Akatsuka, pp. 120–136. Stanford University: Center for the Study of Language and Information.

Higashi Mitsuharu. 1942. *Man'yō dōbutsu* [*Man'yōshū animals*]. Tokyo: Sanseidō.

Hino Sukenari. 2003. 'Nihon sogo no boin taikei – Jōdai Azuma hōgen shiryō ni yoru saikō [A Reconstruction of the Proto-Japanese Vowel System on the Basis of the Data from Eastern Old Japanese].' In: Osada, Toshiki and Alexander Vovin (eds.), *Nihongo keitōron no genzai/Perspectives on the Origins of the Japanese Language*, pp. 187–206. Kyoto: Kokusai Nihon bunka kenkyū sentā.

Hirayama Teruo. 1966. *Ryūkyū hōgen no sōgōteki kenkyū* [*A Comprehensive Study of the Ryūkyūan dialects*]. Tokyo: Meiji shoin.

Hirose Sutezō, Satake Akihiro, Kinoshita Masatosi, Kanbori Shinobu, and Kudō Rikio. 1994. *Kōtei Man'yōshū. Bessatu 3* (*The Revised Man'yōshū. Additional volume 3*). Tokyo: Iwanami.

Hōjō Tadao. 1966. *Jōdai Azuma hōgen no kenkyū* [*A Study of the Eastern Japanese Dialects*]. Tokyo: Nihon gakujutsu shinkōkai.

Hokama Shuzen, et al. (eds.). 1995. *Okinawa kogo daijiten* (*A Big Dictionary of the Old Okinawan Language*). Tokyo: Kadokawa shoten.

Honda, Heihachirō. 1967. *The Man'yōshū: A New and Complete Translation*. Tokyo: The Hokuseido Press.

Hoshino Yukihiko (ed.). 1976. *Sakimori uta ko kun chūshaku shūsei* [*A collection of Old Readings and Commentaries on Border Guards Poems*]. Tokyo: Kyōiku shuppan sentā.

Imura Tetsuo. 1983. *Man'yōshū zenchū. Kan dai 5*. [*The Man'yōshū completely annotated, vol. 5*]. Tokyo: Yūhikaku.

Inagaki, Hisao. 1989. *A Dictionary of Japanese Buddhist Terms*. Union City: Heian International.

Inaoka Kōji (ed.). 1990. *Man'yōshū hikkei* [*A Handbook on the Man'yōshū*]. Tokyo: Gakutōsha.

Inaoka Kōji (ed.). 1994. *Man'yōshū jiten* [*The Man'yōshū Encyclopedia*]. Tokyo: Gakutōsha.

Inoue Michiyasu (ed.). 1928. *Man'yōshū shinkō* [*A New commentary on the Man'yōshū*]. Tokyo: Kokumin tosho kabushiki kaisha.

Itabashi, Yoshizō. 1989. 'The Origin of the Old Japanese Prosecutive Case Suffix yuri.' *Central Asiatic Journal*, vol. 33: 47–66.

Itō Haku. 1995–2000. *Man'yōshū shakuchū* [The Annotated *Man'yōshū*]. Tokyo: Shūeisha.

Itō Haku, Nakanishi Susumu, Hashimoto Tatsuo, Mitani Eiichi, and Watase Masatada. 1991 (1975, 1981). *Man'yōshū jiten* [*The Man'yōshū Encyclopedia*]. Tokyo: Yūseidō.

Izutsu Katsunobu (ed.). 2006. *I/Yay-pakasnu: Ainugo no gakushū to kyōiku no tame ni* [*Teaching it to ourselves: for the pedagogy and acquisition of the Ainu language*]. Asahikawa: Hokkaidō kyōiku daigaku Asahikawa kō.

Jarosz, Aleksandra and Alfred F. Majewicz. 2013. *Nikolay Nevskiy's Miyakoan Dictionary as Recovered from its Manuscript by Aleksandra Jarosz*. Stęszew: International Institute of Ethnolinguistic and Oriental Studies.

Kamochi Masazumi. 1912. *Man'yōshū kogi* [*The old meaning of the Man'yōshū*]. Vol. 7. Tokyo: Kokusho kankōkai.

Karlgren, Berhnard. 1950. *The Book of Odes*. Stockholm: Museum of Far Eastern Antiquities.

Kayano Shigeru. 1996. *Kayano Shigeru no Ainugo jiten* [*An Ainu dictionary by Kayano Shigeru*]. Tokyo: Sanseidō.

Keichū. 1690 (1974). Man'yō daishōki. In: *Keichū zenshū*, dai 3 kan. Hisamatsu Sen'ichi (ed.). Tokyo: Iwanami shoten.

Keichū. 1690 (1974). Man'yō daishōki. In: *Keichū zenshū*, dai 6 kan. Hisamatsu Sen'ichi (ed.). Tokyo: Iwanami shoten.

Keichū. 1690 (1974). Man'yō daishōki. In: *Keichū zenshū*, dai 7 kan. Hisamatsu Sen'ichi (ed.). Tokyo: Iwanami shoten.

Kim Congchel. 1983. *Hyangka-wa Man'yepcip ka-uy phyokipep pikyo yenkwu* [*A Comparative Study on the Writing Systems in Hyangka and the Man'yōshū*]. Seoul: Cipmuntang.

Kim Sayep. 1984–91. *Man'yepcip* [*Man'yōshū*]. Tokyo: Seikō shobō.

Kinoshita Masatoshi. 1988. *Man'yōshū zenchū. Kan dai 20*. [*The Man'yōshū Completely Annotated, vol. 20*]. Tokyo: Yūhikaku.

Kinoshita Masatoshi (ed.). 2001. *Man'yōshū CD-ROM-han* [*Man'yōshū: The CD-ROM edition*]. Tokyo: Hanawa shobō.

Kinoshita Masatoshi, et al. (eds.). 2003. *Man'yōshū sakuin* [*The Index to the Man'yōshū*]. Tokyo: Hanawa shobō.

Kitagawa Kazuhide. 1982. *Shoku Nihongi Senmyō. Kōhon. Sōsakuin* [*Imperial Edicts from the 'Shoku Nihongi.' Critical text. General index*]. Tokyo: Yoshikawa Kōbunkan.

Kojima Noriyuki, Kinoshita Masatoshi, and Satake Akihiro (eds.). 1971–1975. *Man'yōshū 1–4*. *Nihon koten bungaku zenshū* [*A Complete Collection of the Japanese Classical Literature*], vol. 2–5. Tokyo: Shōgakukan.

Konishi, Jin'ichi (ed.). 1957. Commentary and edition of the 'Kagura uta', 'Saibara uta', 'Azuma asobi uta', 'Fuzoku uta', and 'Zōka.' In: *Kodai kayōshū, Nihon Koten Bungaku Taikei* [*Series of Japanese Classical Literature*], vol. 3. Tokyo: Iwanami shoten.

Kōnosu Morihiro (ed.). 1930–39. *Man'yōshū zenshaku* [*The Man'yōshū fully annotated*]. Tokyo: Kōbundō.

KSDJT = *Kokushi daijiten* [*A Large Dictionary of the National History*], vol. 11. Tokyo: Yoshikawa kōbunkan, 1990.

Kubota Utsuho (ed.). 1943–52 (1967). *Man'yōshū hyōshaku VII* [*A Commentary on the Man'yōshū, vol. VII*]. Tokyo: Tōkyōdō.

Kunaichō Shōsōin jimusho (eds.). *Shōsōin komonjo einin shūsei 2* [*Collection of Facsimiles of Documents from Shōsōin, vol. 2*]. Tokyo: Yagi shoten.

Kupchik, John. 2011. *A Grammar of the Eastern Old Japanese Dialects*. Unpublished Ph.D. dissertation. Department of Linguistics, University of Hawai'i at Mānoa.

Kurano Kenji (ed.). 1958. *Kojiki* [*Records of Ancient Matters*]. *Nihon Koten Bungaku Taikei* [*Series of the Japanese Classical Literature*], vol. 1. Tokyo: Iwanami shoten.

Kuroita Katsumi and Matsuyama Jirō (ed.). 1965–66. *Nihonshoki* [*Annals of Japan*]. *Shintei zōho kokushi taikei* [*The newly corrected and enlarged series on Japanese history*], vol. 1a and 1b. Tokyo: Yoshikawa kōbunkan.

Mabuchi Kazuo. 2000. *Kodai Nihongo no sugata* [*The appearance of Old Japanese*]. Tokyo: Musashino shoin.

Majtczak, Tomasz. 2008. *Japońskie klasy czasownikowe v perspektiwie diachronicznej*. Kraków: Wydawnictwo Uniwersytetu Jagiellońskiego.

Man'yōshū ko chūshaku shūsei henshū iinkai (eds.). 1989–91. *Man'yōshū ko chūshaku shūsei. Kinsei hen* [*A Collection of Old Commentaries on the Man'yōshū. Edo period*]. vol. 1–20. Tokyo: Nihon tosho sentā.

Martin, Samuel E. 1987. *The Japanese Language Through Time*. New Haven and London: Yale University Press.

Masamune Atsuo. 1974. *Man'yōshū sōsakuin* [*General index to the 'Man'yōshū'*], vol. 1 *tango hen* [*vocabulary*], vol. 2 *kanji hen* [*characters*]. Tokyo: Heibonsha.

Masuno Mitsunori, et al. 2004. *Ainugo Kushiro hōgen goi* [*A vocabulary of the Kushiro dialect of the Ainu language*]. Kushiro: Kushiro Ainugo no kai.

Miyajima Tatsuo. 1971. *Koten taishō goi hyō* [*A Comparative Chart of Classical Vocabulary*]. Tokyo: Kasama shoin.

Miyajima Tatsuo. 2014. *Nihon koten taishō bunrui goi hyō* [*A Comparative and Classified Table of Japanese Classics Vocabulary*]. Tokyo: Kasama shoin.

Miyake, Marc H. 1999. *The Phonology of Eighth Century Japanese Revisited: Another Reconstruction Based upon Written Sources*, University of Hawaii Ph.D. dissertation.

Miyake, Marc H. 2003a. *Old Japanese: A phonetic reconstruction*. London: Routledge/Curzon.

Miyake, Marc H. 2003b. 'Philological evidence for *e and *o in Pre-Old Japanese.' *Diachronica* XX.1: 81–137.

Miyara Tōsō. 1980. *Yaeyama goi* [*The lexicon of Yaeyama*]. *Miyara Tōsō zenshū* [*Complete Works of Miyara Tōsō*], vol. 8a. Tokyo: Daiichi shobō.

Miyara Tōsō. 1981. *Yaeyama goi sakuin* [*The index to the lexicon of Yaeyama*]. *Miyara Tōsō zenshū* [*Complete Works of Miyara Tōsō*], vol. 8b. Tokyo: Daiichi shobō.

Mizushima Yoshiharu. 1984a. *Man'yōshū Azuma uta honbun kenkyū narabi ni sōsakuin* [*Indexes to and Research on the Original Text of Eastern Poems in the 'Man'yōshū'*]. Tokyo: Kasama shoin.

Mizushima Yoshiharu. 1984b *Man'yōshū Azuma uta no kokugogaku teki kenkyū* [*A Linguistic Study of the Ma'yōshū's Eastern Poems*]. Tokyo: Kasama shoin.

Mizushima Yoshiharu. 1986. *Man'yōshū zenchū. Kan dai 14.* [*The Man'yōshū Completely Annotated, vol. 14*]. Tokyo: Yūhikaku.

Mizushima Yoshiharu. 1996 (1972). *Man'yōshū Azuma uta sakimori uta* [*Eastern Poems and Border Guards Poems from the Man'yōshū*]. Revised and enlarged edition. Tokyo: Kasama shoin.

Mizushima Yoshiharu. 2003. *Man'yōshū sakimori uta zen chūshaku* [*A Complete Commentary on the Border Guards Poems in the Man'yōshū*]. Tokyo: Kasama shoin.

Monier-Williams, Monier. 1899. *A Sanskrit-English Dictionary*. Oxford: Clarendon Press.

Mori Hiromichi. 1991. *Kodai no on'in to Nihonshoki no seiritsu* [*The Phonology of Old Japanese and Origins of the 'Nihonshoki'*]. Tokyo: Daishūkan.

Murayama Shichirō. 1988. *Nihongo no kigen to gogen* [*The Origins and Etymology of the Japanese language*]. Tokyo: San'ichi shobō.

Nakagawa Hiroshi. 1995. *Ainugo Chitose hōgen jiten* [*A dictionary of the Chitose dialect of the Ainu language*]. Tokyo: Sōfūkan.

Nakamatsu Takeo. 1987. *Ryūkyū hōgen jiten* [*A Dictionary of Ryūkyūan Dialects*]. Naha: Naha shuppansha.

Nakanishi Susumu. 1978–83. *Man'yōsū zen chūshaku genbun tsuki* [*Man'yōshū with the Complete Commentary and the Original Text*]. Tokyo: Kadokawa.

Nakanishi Susumu. 1984. *Man'yōshū zen chūshaku genbun tsuki* [*'Man'yōshū' with the Complete Commentary and the Original Text*]. Tokyo: Kōdansha.

Nakanishi Susumu. 1985. *Man'yōshū jiten* [The *Man'yōshū* Encyclopedia]. Tokyo: Kōdansha.

Nakasone Seizen. 1983. *Okinawa Nakijin hōgen jiten* [*A Dictionary of the Nakijin Dialect in Okinawa*]. Tokyo: Kadokawa.

Narita Shūichi (ed.). 1986. *Kinsei no Ezo goi* [*Edo period Ainu vocabularies*]. IV. *Ezo go hen* [*Edition of 'Ezo language'*]. Narita Shūichi, privately published.

OGJ 1976 = *Okinawa go jiten* [*A dictionary of the Okinawan language*]. Tokyo: Ōkurashō insatsu kyoku.

Omodaka Hisataka. 1984 (1960, 1977). *Man'yōshū chūshaku* [*The Annotated Man'yōshū*]. Tokyo: Chūōkōronsha.

Omodaka Hisataka, et al. (eds.). 1967. *Jidai betsu kokugo dai jiten (Jōdai hen)* [*A Large Dictionary of the National Language by Periods (Old Japanese)*]. Tokyo: Sanseidō.

Ōno Susumu. 1953. *Jōdai kanazukai no kenkyū* [*A Research on the Old Japanese Orthography*]. Tokyo: Iwanami.

Origuchi Shinobu (ed.). 1917–18. *Kōyaku Man'yōshū* [*The Translation of the Man'yōshū into colloquial Japanese*]. Tokyo: Bunkaidō shoten.

Ōtsuka Rie, et al. (eds.). 2008. *Saharin Ainugo jiten* (*A Dictionary of Sakhalin Ainu*). Asahikawa: Hokkaidō kyōiku daigaku.

Pierson, Jan L. 1929–63. *The Manyośû Translated and Annotated*, vol. 1–20. Leiden: E.J. Brill.

Pierson, Jan L. 1964. *The Makura-kotoba of the Manyośû*. Leiden: E.J. Brill.

Pierson, Jan L. 1967. *Character Dictionary of the Manyośū*. Leiden: E.J. Brill.

Pierson, Jan L. 1969. *General Index of the Manyośū*. Leiden: E.J. Brill.

Robinson, Jeremy R. 2004. *The Tsukushi Man'yōshū Poets and the Invention of Japanese Poetry*. Unpublished Ph.D. dissertation, University of Michigan.

Russell, Kerri L. 2006. *A Reconstruction of Proto-Japonic Verbal Morphology*. Unpublished Ph.D. dissertation, Department of East Asian Languages and Literatures, University of Hawai'i at Mānoa.

Saeki Umetomo. 1959 (1950). *Nara jidai no kokugo* [*The Japanese Language of the Nara Period*]. Tokyo: Sanseidō.

Saeki Umetomo, Ishii Shōji, Fujimori Tomoo (eds.). 1947–55. *Man'yōshū*. Tokyo: Asahi shinbunsha.

Saeki Umetomo and Mabuchi Kazuo. 1969. *Kōdansha kogo jiten* (*Kōdasha's Premodern Japanese Dictionary*). Tokyo: Kōdansha.

Sakakura Atsuyoshi. 1955. Kan nijū [Volume twenty]. In: *Man'yōshū taisei 4* [*A variorum edition of the Man'yōshū, vol. 4*]. Kunkitsu ge [*Analysis of kun-yomi readings, part 2*]. Tokyo: Heibonsha, pp. 375–407.

Sakamoto Nobuyuki, Nishihata Yukio, Hasegawa Chiaki, Suzuki Eiichi (eds.). 2002–2006. *Man'yō Shūsui shō eiin honkoku (fu eiin CD-ROM)* [*The Reproduction and Transliteration of the Man'yō Shūsui shō (with the Reproduction on the Attached CD-ROM)*]. Tokyo: Hanawa shobō.

Sasaki Nobutsuna (ed.). 1925. *Sengaku zenshū* [*Complete Works of Sengaku*]. Tokyo: Kokin shoin.

Sasaki Nobutsuna (ed.). 1948–1954. *Hyōshaku Man'yōshū* [*The annotated Man'yōshū*]. Tokyo: Gaizōsha.

Sasaki Nobutsuna. 1983 [1956]. *Man'yōshū jiten* [*The Man'yōshū Encyclopedia*]. Tokyo: Heibonsha.

Satake Akihiro (ed.). 1981. *Ninnaji-zō Man'yōshū chūshaku. Sengaku shō* [*Sengaku's Selected Commentary on the Man'yōshū from the Ninnaji Temple Collection*]. Kyōto: Rinsen shoten.

Satake Akihiro, Yamada Hideo, Kudō Rikio, Ōtani Masao, and Yamazaki Yoshiyuki (eds.). 1999–2003. *Man'yōshū* [*Ten thousand leaves (of words)*], 1–4. *Shin Nihon koten bungaku taikei* [*New Series on the Classical Japanese Literature*] vols. 1–4. Tokyo: Iwanami shoten.

Schuessler, Axel. 2009. *Minimal Old Chinese and Later Han Chinese*. Honolulu: University of Hawai'i Press.

Seeley, Christopher. 1991. *A History of Writing in Japan*. Leiden: E.J. Brill.

Serafim, Leon A. 2004. 'The Shuri Ryūkyūan Exalting Prefix *myi- and the Japanese connection.' *Japanese Language and Literature* 38.2: 301–322.

Shirafuji Noriyuki. 1987. *Nara jidai no kokugo* [*The Japanese Language of the Nara Period*]. Tokyo: Tōkyōdō.

Sieffert, René. 1997–2003. *Man.yoshū*. v. 1–5. Editions UNESCO: Publications Orientalistes de France.

Song, Kicwung. 2004. *Kotay kwuke ehwi phyoki hanca-uy capyel yonglyey yenkwu* [*A Study of Examples of Character-by-Character Usage in Old Korean Vocabulary*]. Seoul: Seoul tayhakkyo chwulphanpu.

Soothill, William E. and Hodous, Lewis. 1937. *A Dictionary of Chinese Buddhist Terms with Sanskrit and English Equivalents*. London: Kegan Paul.

Suga, Teruo. 1991. *The Man'yo-shu. A Complete English Translation in 5-7 Rhythm*. Vol. 1–3. Tokyo: Kanda Institute of Foreign Languages.

Tachibana Chikage. 1796 (1929). *Man'yōshū ryakuge* [*An Abbreviated Commentary on the Man'yōshū*]. Ed. by Masamune Atsuo. Tokyo: Nagashima Tōichi.

Takagi Ichinosuke, Gomi Tomohide, and Ōno Susumu (eds.). 1957–62. *Man'yōshū* [*Ten thousand leaves (of words)*], vol. 1–4, Nihon koten bungaku taikei [Series of Japanese Classical Literature], vol. 4–7, Tokyo: Iwanami shoten.

Takagi Ichinosuke and Toyama Tamizō. 1974a. *Kojiki sōsakuin/sōsakuin hen*. Kojiki taisei 8 [*Index to the 'Kojiki' index volume*. The complete series on 'Kojiki']. Tokyo: Heibonsha.

Takagi Ichinosuke and Toyama Tamizō. 1974b. *Kojiki sōsakuin/honbun hen*. Kojiki taisei 7 [*Index to the 'Kojiki' Text Volume*. The Complete Series on 'Kojiki']. Tokyo: Heibonsha.

Takagi Ichinosuke and Toyama Tamizō. 1977. *Kojiki sōsakuin/hoi. Kojiki taisei* [*Index to the 'Kojiki' Supplement. The Complete Series on 'Kojiki'*]. Tokyo: Heibonsha.

Takeda Yūkichi (ed.). 1948–51. *Man'yōshū zenchūshaku* [*The Man'yōshū completely annotated*]. Tokyo: Kadokawa shoten.

Takeda Yūkichi (ed.). 1966 [1955]. *Zōtei Man'yōshū zenchūshaku, dai 13–14 kan* [*The Man'yōshū Completely Annotated, Revised and Enlarged, vol. 13–14*]. Tokyo: Kadokawa shoten.

Takeda Yūkichi (ed.). 1955. *Man'yōshū zenkō, jō – ge* [*Complete Explanation of the Man'ōshū, vol. 1–3*]. Tokyo: Meiji shoin.

Takeda Yūkichi (ed.). 1916. Kishimoto Yuzura. *Man'yōshū kōshō* [*A Study of the Man'yōshū by Kishimoto Yuzura*]. Reprinted 1971: *Man'yōshū sōsho, dai go shū* [*The Man'yōshū Compendium, Fifth Collection*]. 4 vols. Kyoto: Nozomikawa shoten.

Tanabe Ikuo. 1997. *Heijō-kyō: mati to kurasi* [*The capital of Nara: streets and life*]. Tokyo: Tōkyō-dō shuppansha.

Thorpe, Maner L. 1983. *Ryūkyūan Language History*. An unpublished Ph.D. dissertation, University of South California.

Tōjō Misao. 1951. *Zenkoku hōgen jiten* [*A Japanese Dialect Dictionary*]. Tokyo: Tōkyōdō.

Tokieda Motoki. 1989 (1954). *Nihon bunpō. Bungo hen* [*A Japanese Grammar. Written Language*]. Tokyo: Iwanami.

Tsuchihashi, Yutaka (ed.). 1957. Commentary and edition of the 'Kojiki kayō', 'Nihonshoki kayō', 'Shoku Nihongi kayō', 'Fudoki kayō', and 'Bussoku seki no uta.' In: *Kodai kayōshū, Nihon Koten Bungaku Taikei* [*Series of Japanese Classical Literature*], vol. 3. Tokyo: Iwanami shoten.

Tsuchiya Fumiaki (ed.). 1975–77. *Man'yōshū shichū* [*A Private Commentary on the 'Man'yōshū'*]. vols. 1–10. Tokyo: Chikuma shobō.

Uchima Chokujin and Arakaki Kumiko. 2000. *Okinawa hokubu nanbu hōgen no kijutsuteki kenkyū* [*A Descriptive Study of Northern and Southern Ryūkyūan dialects*]. Tokyo: Kazama shobō.

Unger, J. Marshall. 2009. *The Role of Contact in the Origins of the Japanese and Korean Languages*. Honolulu: University of Hawai'i Press.

Vance, Timothy J. 2007. 'Have we learned anything about rendaku that Lyman already didn't know?' In: Frellesvig, Bjarke; Shibatani, Masayoshi; Smith, John Charles (eds.), *Current Issues in the History and Structure of Japanese*, pp. 153–170. Tokyo: Kurosio Publishers.

Vovin, Alexander. 1993. *A Reconstruction of Proto-Ainu*. Leiden: E.J. Brill.

Vovin, Alexander. 1994. 'Genetic affiliation of Japanese and methodology of linguistic comparison.' *Journal de la Société Finno-Ougrienne* 85: 241–256.

Vovin, Alexander. 1997. 'On the syntactic typology of Old Japanese.' *Journal of East Asian Linguistics* 6: 273–290.

Vovin, Alexander. 2003. *A Reference Grammar of Classical Japanese Prose*. London: Routledge/Curzon.

Vovin, Alexander. 2005. *The Descriptive and Comparative Grammar of Western Old Japanese*. Part 1: Sources, Script and Phonology, Lexicon, Nominals. Folkestone: Global Oriental.

Vovin, Alexander. 2008. 'Shinsei no ken to mahō no hire: gengogaku to rekishigaku no setten' [Sacred swords and magical long scarves: the interaction between linguistics and history]. In: Wang, Wei-kun and Uno, Takao (eds.), *Kodai Higashi Ajia kōryū no sōgōteki kenkyū* [*A Comprehensive Study of Exchanges in Ancient East Asia*]. *Nichubunken sōsho* 42: 455–467. Kyoto: International Center for Japanese Studies.

Vovin, Alexander. 2009a. *The Descriptive and Comparative Grammar of Western Old Japanese*. Part 2: Adjectives, Verbs, Adverbs, Conjunctions, Particles, Postpositions. Folkestone: Global Oriental.

Vovin, Alexander. 2009b. *Man'yōshū to Fudoki ni mirareru fushigina kotoba to jōdai Nihon rettō ni okeru Ainu go no bunpu* [*Strange Words in the Man'yōshū and Fudoki and the Distribution of the Ainu language in the Japanese Islands in Prehistory*]. Kyoto: Kokusai Nihon bunka kenkyū sentā.

Vovin, Alexander. 2009c. *Man'yōshū. Book 15. A New English Translation Containing the Original Text, Kana Transliteration, Romanization, Glossing, and Commentary*. Folkestone: Global Oriental.

Vovin, Alexander. 2010. *Koreo-Japonica: A critical study in the proposed language relationship*. Honolulu: University of Hawai'i Press.

Vovin, Alexander. 2011a. *Man'yōshū. Book 5. A New English Translation Containing the Original Text, Kana Transliteration, Romanization, Glossing, and Commentary*. Folkestone: Global Oriental.

Vovin, Alexander. 2011b. 'On one more source for Old Japanese otsu-rui /I$_2$/.' *Journal of East Asian Linguistics* 20: 219–228.

Vovin, Alexander. 2012. *Man'yōshū. Book 14. A New English Translation Containing the Original Text, Kana Transliteration, Romanization, Glossing, and Commentary*. Folkestone/Leiden: Global Oriental/Brill.

Vovin, Alexander. 2013. *Man'yōshū. Book 20. A New English Translation Containing the Original Text, Kana Transliteration, Romanization, Glossing, and Commentary*. Folkestone/Leiden: Global Oriental/Brill.

Vovin, Alexander. 2016a. *Man'yōshū. Book 17. A New English Translation Containing the Original Text, Kana Transliteration, Romanization, Glossing, and Commentary*. Leiden & Boston: Brill.

Vovin, Alexander. 2016b (work in progress). 'Out of South China? Looking for the *Urheimat* of the Japonic language family.'

Vovin, Alexander. 2016c. *Man'yōshū. Book 18. A New English Translation Containing the Original Text, Kana Transliteration, Romanization, Glossing, and Commentary*. Leiden & Boston: Brill.

Vovin, Alexander. 2018a. *Man'yōshū. Book 1. A New English Translation Containing the Original Text, Kana Transliteration, Romanization, Glossing, and Commentary*. Leiden & Boston: Brill.

Vovin, Alexander. 2018b. 'An Interpretation of the Khüis Tolgoi Inscription.' *Journal Asiatique* 306.2: 303–313.

Vovin, Alexander. 2018c. 'On the etymology of the name of Mt. Fuji.' In: Vovin, Alexander and William McClure (eds.), *Studies in Japanese/Korean historical and theoretical linguistics and beyond. A Festschrift for John B. Whitman on the Occasion of his Sixtieth Birthday*. Folkestone & Leiden: Global Oriental/Brill, pp. 80–89.

Vovin, Alexander. 2019a. 'Groping in the Dark: The First Attempt to Interpret the Bugut Brāhmī Inscription.' *Journal Asiatique* 307.1: 121–134.

Vovin, Alexander. 2019b. 'A Sketch of the Earliest Mongolic Language: The Brāhmī Bugut and Khüis Tolgoi Inscriptions.' International Journal of Eurasian Linguistics 1.1: 162–197.

Vovin, Alexander. 2020.1. *The Descriptive and Comparative Grammar of Western Old Japanese*. Volume 1: Sources, Script and Phonology, Lexicon, Nominals, Adjectives. 2nd edition. Handbuch der Orientalistik. Leiden and Boston: Brill.

Vovin, Alexander. 2020.2. *The Descriptive and Comparative Grammar of Western Old Japanese*. Volume 2: Verbs, Adverbs, Conjunctions, Particles, Postpositions, Interjections. 2nd edition. Handbuch der Orientalistik. Leiden and Boston: Brill.

Vovin, Alexander. 2021, forthcoming. 'Austronesians in the Northern Waters?' *International Journal of Eurasian Linguistics* 3.2.

Yamada Takuzō and Nakajima Shintarō. 1995. *Man'yō shokubutsu jiten* [*The Encyclopedia of Plants in the Man'yōshū*]. Tokyo: Hokuryūkan.

Yamada Yasuei, Itō Chikara, Bunden Masaaki (eds.). 1911–14. *Man'yōshū kogi* [*The Old Meaning of the Man'yōshū*]. vols. 1–7. Tokyo: Kokusho kōkan kai.

Yamada Yoshio. 1954 (1912). *Nara chō bunpō shi* [*A History of Japanese Grammar in the Nara Period*]. Tokyo: Hōbunkan.

Yanagida, Yuko and Whitman, John B. 2009. 'Alignment and Word Order in Old Japanese.' *Journal of East Asian Linguistics* 18: 101–144.

Yanai Shigeshi, Murafusi Shinsuke, Ōasa Yūji, Suzuki Hideo, Fujii Sadakazu, Imanishi Yūichirō (eds.). 1933–97. *Genji monogatari* [*A Tale of Genji*]. vols. 1–5. *Shin Nihon koten bungaku taikei* [*New Series of Japanese Classical Literature*], vols. 19–23. Tokyo: Iwanami.

Yi Swungnyeng. 1961/1997. *Cwungsey kwuke munpep* [*A Grammar of Middle Korean*]. Seoul: Ulyu munhwasa.

Yosano Yutaka, et al. (eds.). 1925–26. *Man'yōshū ryakuge. Nihon koten zenshū*. Tokyo: Nihon koten zenshū kankōkai.

Yoshii Iwao (ed.). 1988. *Man'yōshū zenchū, kan dai 15* [*The Man'yōshū completely annotated, vol. 15*]. Tokyo: Yūhikaku.

Zachert, Herbert. 1950. *Semmyo: Die kaiserlichen Erlasse des Shoku-Nihongi*. Berlin: Akademie-Verlag.

Index

abduct 438
according 448
adorable 476
adorn 480
again 448, 464, 468
ahead 463
alder 459
all 449, 450
Aⁿdatara (p.n.) 431
Aⁿdikama (p.n.) 431
Ano (p.n.) 432
Aⁿze (p.n.) 434
Aⁿzikuma (p.n.) 434
Apa (p.n.) 432
Apiⁿdu (p.n.) 432
appear 433
appearance 468
appoint 464
approach 480
arikinu-nə (makura-kotoba) 433
arm 469
arrange 472
arrive 473
arrow 461, 463, 479
arrow grass 432
arrowroot 447
arrow tip type 438
Aɛikaⁿga (p.n.) 433
Asiⁿgara ~ Asiⁿgari (p.n.) 433
ask 473
Aso (p.n.) 433
ass 467
assistant 468
Asuka (p.n.) 433
Asupa (p.n.) 433
at all 481
attach 473
awesome 441
ax 478

back 467, 475
bad 433
bamboo 469
bamboo grass 464
barely 460

barley 451
barrier 465
base 449, 451
basket 445
bay 475
be 453
be attracted 480
be based 480
be blinding 448
be emaciated 479
be granted 470
be in disorder 450
be left behind 456
be like 463
be longing for 446, 447, 476
be missing (someone) 447
be regretful 447
be separated 463, 477
be still in the buds 461, 462
bean 448
bear 444
beautiful 434
become 453
become distant 465
become full 450
become quiet 466
bed 471
behind 467
beloved 436, 440, 442, 445, 465, 471
below 467
bend 446, 465, 470
big 457
bird 472
bless 461
bless with words 443
bloom 463
blow 462
blue 433
boat 462
body 450
borderguard 463–464
borrow 440
bottom 449, 467
bow 481
bow string notch 481

brambling   433
break   470, 479
breathe with difficulty   435
bridge   459
bring   449, 477
brocade   455
brushwood   466
bundle   451
burn   469, 479

call   439
camellia   473
cape   463
carefree   482
carry   457, 458
catalpa tree   431
catch   473
catch one's breath   435
caw-caw   444
cease   470, 471
change   440
charming   457
child   445
chinquapin   467
clamour   464
clear   448, 459, 464, 465, 468
cliff   448
close   468, 472
cloth   455
cloud   446
cloudy   446
clue   469
coffer   458
cold   464
color   437
come   442, 464
come (HUM)   449
common reed   478
constantly   468
cord   460–461, 478
cordial   454
cotton   477
cover   462
cow's stomach   450
crane   469
crawl   459
cross   446, 477
cross over   446, 447, 476

crow   441
crumbling cliff   434
crush   479
cry   452, 453
cryptomeria   468
cut   440

daily chores   454
dam   474, 477
dance   448
dangerous   434
Daphniphyllum macropodum   481
dare   432
daughter   445
dawn   432
day   460
day time   461
dear   438, 440, 476
debris   444
decide   463
decorate   442, 480
deep   462
deer   466
deity   439
dense   466
depart   470
describe   467
dew   474
die   466
differ   469
difficult   441
direct   451
directly   469
dirt   432
disgusting   466
distant   446
divination   475
divination clan   475
do   465
door   472
double edge sword   474
drag   460
draw   439, 460, 480
draw (water)   446
drift   437
drink   455
drop   457
dry   461

INDEX

dude   479
dwell   477
dye   465

ear   450
early   460
early night   480
ear (of a plant)   461
earth   474
easy   479
eat   458, 469
eight   478
eighty   479
embark   455
embrace   451
Emperor   457, 468
emphatic particle   439, 480
end   468
enough   478
enter   437
entwined   441
ephemeral cicada   476
equip   480
eternal   471
evening   481
evening divination   481
examine   467
excellent   438
exist   432, 478
exist (HON)   436
exit   435
extreme   434, 437
extremely   438
extremely, so much   443
eye   447, 449
eyebrow   449

face   440, 451, 456, 457
fade from one's memory   477
fall   457
fall (of flowers)   472
fall (of precipitation)   462
far   471
fast   460
father   467, 472
fence   439, 447, 465, 475
field   455, 459
fifth   463

fill   450, 455
find   458
finish   460, 478
fire   462
first   460
fifth month   464
five   438
flat   461
flat rock   431
flatten   453
float   475
flower   458
focus particle   438, 449, 471, 482
follow   473
food container   442
foot   431, 433
for   470
ford   440
forest   460
forget intentionally   477
forget unintentionally   477
fourth month   475
foxtail millet   432
fragrant   439
free time   438
frequently   466
frost   466
future   456

gallop   431
game animal   467
garden   455
garment   444, 445, 457
gate   438
gather   461, 473
gather (fruits, etc.)   474
get mixed   449
get untied   471
get used   453
get wet   456
girl   445, 448
give   432
give one's heart   480
give order (HON)   457
glorify   460
go   464, 480, 481
go against   469
go along   468

495

go around   449
go (HON)   436
goat's stomach   450
go away   436
go back and forth   442
goblet   473
go far away   448
good   480
go out   435
gossip   458
grab   472
grass   447
great   457
great lord   457
green   433
gromwell   451
group   451
grow   457
grow dark   447
grow old   468

hail   433
hair   442
hand   469, 471
hang   439
harbor   450, 472, 473
hard   441, 447
hare   478
hat   441
head   439, 441
headrest   448
heart   442, 443, 475
heaven   432
hem   468
hemp   433, 468, 478
hemp container   478
here   443, 469
hesitate   437, 458
hidden   438
hide   439, 440
high   469
hill   478
hit   474, 476
hold   449
hold between   459
hold inside [one's mouth]   461, 462
home   436, 437
hoof   474

horizontal   480
horizontally [stretched] mountains   480
horn   474
horse   451, 475
hot spring   481
house   436, 437, 478–479
how   434, 435
hundred   451
hunt   441
hurry   437
husband   465
hustle and bustle   464
hut   437

I   431, 433, 452, 476, 477
Ikapo (p.n.)   435
Ikoma (p.n.)   435
immediate   470
Inasa (p.n.)   436
increase   448
indeed   475
indefinite direct object prefix   478
indirect object prefix   435
ink   468
insert   455, 464
inside   453, 475, 476
interjection   434
interval   432, 447
invite   460, 464
Irima (p.n.)   437
Isiwi (p.n.)   437
island   466
its place   457

jewel   469
join   473
journey   469

kaya grass   441
know   467
Korea   440
Korean   440
koto   446
kudzu   447

ladder   459
lagoon   441
lament   452

INDEX

lamentable   435
land   446–447
lapwing   442
last night   445
late   457
leaf   458, 460
lean down   441
leave   456, 464, 470
leave behind   456
leek   450
leg   431
length   452
lick   453
lie   478
lie down   462, 481
life   436, 480
life time   480
lift up high in one's hands   464
like   434, 449, 451
lily   481
limit   439
listen   444
live   435, 468
liver   445
locative prefix   456
lodge   437
long   452
long for   445–446, 446–467
long sword   470
look   449
look for   451
look up   462
lord   444
love   449, 456
lovely   440
low   460
lowly   468
lucky arrow   464

maiden   459, 471
make   454, 474
make alive   435
make a strong promise   441
make crawl   459
make float   475
make noise   464
make someone cry   453
make someone know of one's love intentions
        459

make someone/something run into   459
make something approach   480
make something cross over   446
make something stand   470
makura-kotoba   470
male   477
male hairstyle   450
manage household affairs   453
mandarin orange   470
mansion   471
many   443, 451, 462, 464
maple   440
marsh   455
mat made from wild rice straw
        442
matter   444
measure of length   463
meat   467
medicine   447
meet   432
mesh   462
metal   439, 440
metal adorned gate   439
middle   453, 459
mirror   439
mist   441
mistress of the house   473
month   474
moon   474
more and more   438
morning   433
morning glory   433
mother   432, 456, 459
mountain   479
mountain ridge   478
mountain saddle   471
mouth   447
muddy   455
mulberry tree   469
multitude   475

nail   446
name   452
needle   459
neighbor   472
nest   468
new   455
night   481
night time   481

no   436, 452
noisy   465
nominal prefix 'thing-'   435
noⁿgan-ape-   455
not   465
not exist   452
now   435, 448
nursery (for plants)   467

oak   441, 453, 461
obsidian   431
offer (HUM)   448
offing   456
old   458, 462
old woman   471
one   441, 461
one-room house   451
onomatopoeia for squeezing the meat of
    sitaⁿdami   445
opposite side   451
ordinary   461
outside   480
overgrown   466

paddy   469
painful   437
paint   438
paper mulberry tree   438
paper or cloth offerings for deities   456
parent   458
part   477
pass   468
pass along   474
past tentative auxiliary   442
pasture fence   475
peak   450, 454, 478
pearl   469
pebble   465
pelt   440
perform divination   451
permanent epithet   472
permanent epithet to Mr. Nipita   467
person   461
pheasant   445
pickle   467
pick up   461
picture   477
pierce   455

pile up   441, 451
pillar   459
pillow   448
pine   448
pivot   447
place   456, 468, 472
plant   476
poem   476
point   464
pot   473
pray   436
prepare   480
present   448
protect   436, 451
protrusion   463
province   446–447
pull   460
pungent   441
purify oneself   436
push   457
push and shake   457
put   456, 458
put forth   459
put inside   437
put on the head   437

quotation verb   471

rain   432
rainbow   455
rapids   465
reach   437, 466, 473
real   448
reason   482
receding tide   475
receive   439
receive (HUM)   470
recite   472
red   432
red earth   466
red pigment   466
reed   433
reeds and grasses used to thatch roofs of
    house   442
reflection   439
regrettable   435, 478
rein   478
rely   480

INDEX

report   473
repugnant   466
resist   433
return   440
rice straw mat   470
rice wine   463
ride   455
rinse   468
rise   450, 470
river   440, 452, 479
river bed   440
road   450, 472
roaring   471
rock   431, 436, 437, 457, 468
rock(?)   437
rocks in the sea not connected to the shore   459
rocky shore   437, 457
roll   447
room   451
root   451, 454
rope   453, 474
rough   432
round   448
row   443
rub   451, 468
rudder   438
rumor   458
rustle softly   465

sad   440
safely   463, 464
sakura   441
salt   467
same   458
sandbank   461, 468
sandbar   468
sash   456, 480
sashimi   453
satisfy   431
say   437, 455
say (HUM)   449
scold   443, 456
sea   433, 475, 479
sea plain   475
search   475
seashore   458
seaweed   450, 477

sedge   468
see   449
seed   469
seedling   453
send   456, 479
send away   479
separate   459, 463
separated   458, 459, 460, 463, 477
serve   473
set   441, 464
seven   453
shadow   439
shape   441
shield   470
shine   471, 473
ship's bow   460
shoes   447
shoo   468
shop   479
shore   452, 458, 460, 478
shoulder   441
shrine   479
sickness   481
side   441, 449, 450, 458, 460
sigh   435
sing   457
sit   477
sita^{n}dami seashells   467
skin   458
sky   468
sleep   435, 450, 454, 481
sleep in one's clothes   448
sleeve   468
slippery   456
slope   463
small   464
small branch   466
snow   480, 481
so   466
soaked   473
soft   452, 455
sound   453, 454, 457, 472
space   447
spin   475
spotted   447
spouse   474
spread   464
spring   459

499

squeeze   459
stable   475
stalk   446
stallion   445
stand   470
stand in line   453
stand side by side   453
stay   472
step   462
still   453
stone   437
stop   470, 479
strange   434
stretch   459
stretch out   452
string   478
stroke   452
submerge   466
sudden   433, 455
suffer   454
summit   454
sun   460
sunset   434
superior   448
sure   448
surge   472
swell   472

tail   478
take   449, 472, 473
take along   477
take off (a bow-string)   460
talk   441, 446
talk with   444
taste   453
tell   455
temporary   441
that   438, 440, 465, 478
the place where *inaw* [are offered]   436
thick   466
thing   449, 451
think   434, 456
think about future   440
this   442, 443
this morning   442
thorny tree   475
thousand   472
thread   437

thus   438, 463
tide   467
tideland   441
tie   451, 474, 481
tiger   473
time   443, 461, 462, 466, 469, 471
today   442
tomorrow   433
top   438, 475
top branch   475
top of a plant   475
top of a tree   475
to receive (HUM)   469
touch   462
tough   432
trail   470, 471
trap   477
trash   444
travel   469
tray table   474
tread   462
treat with care   436
tree   442, 445
true   447
trust   470
turn   451
turn around   450
turn out to graze   458
turn red/yellow   451
two   462

untie   471
unusual   434
unworthy   466
use as a pillow   448

very   438
very extremely   437
vessel   460
vicinity   433
village   464
vine   441, 473, 474
visit   442
voice   438

waist   444
wait   448
walk   441

INDEX

want   461
warrior   435
wash   433
watch   454
water   449, 450
water leek   452
wave   453, 462
waver   434
way   468
we   476
wear   444, 458
weep   453
well noticeable   438
well worn   453
what   431, 453
wheat   451
when   438, 466
where   435
which   435
white   467
white bark strip hanging   481
who   469, 470
why   431, 434
wide   461

wife   436, 447, 449, 474
wild duck   438, 439, 443
wild goose   441
wild rice   443
willow   479
win   441
wind   442
wing   458
wisteria   462
with   450, 451
wither   441
woman   449
word   442, 444
worry about future   440
wrap   447, 474
writing brush   462

year   458, 472
yearn   466–467
yes   478
yet   435
yew   437
you   436, 452, 454
young   476